Between Chance an(

Interdisciplinary Perspectives
on Determinism

Edited by
Harald Atmanspacher and Robert Bishop

Imprint Academic

Published in the UK by Imprint Academic
PO Box 200, Exeter EX5 5YX, UK

Published in the USA by Imprint Academic
Philosophy Documentation Center
PO Box 7147, Charlottesville, VA 22906-7147, USA

ISBN 9 780907 845 218 (hbk.)
ISBN 9 781845 400 842 (pbk.)

A CIP catalogue record for this book is available from the
British Library and US Library of Congress

imprint-academic.com

Table of Contents

Preface

Harald Atmanspacher and Robert Bishop

Are choice and free will possible in a world governed by deterministic fundamental equations? What sense would determinism make if many events and processes in the world seem to be governed by chance? These and other questions emphasize the fact that chance and choice are two leading actors on stage whenever issues of determinism are under discussion.

The machine sculpture "Klamauk" (English: hubbub) by the Swiss artist Jean Tinguely (1925–1991), featured on the cover, looks like a perfect example of a deterministic process, but it also looks as if thrown together "by chance". This tension between determinism and chance has been of long-standing concern in the sciences and the humanities. And nowhere is this tension stronger than in debates about free will and our place in the world, where determinism seems bound to crowd freedom out of the picture, yet freedom in the absence of some ordered realm of causes seems inconceivable.

The desire to foster an interdisciplinary dialogue on determinism, chance and free will was the initial impetus leading to an international workshop on determinism taking place at Ringberg Castle near Lake Tegernsee, south of Munich, in June 2001. Representatives from mathematics, physics, cognitive and social science, and various branches of philosophy convened to discuss numerous aspects of determinism from their disciplinary perspectives. This volume is based on elaborated and refereed manuscripts of their lectures.

The contributions by Bishop and Nickel form an introduction to the topics discussed in the volume, focusing on aspects of determinism as they arise in mathematics, physics, psychology, and philosophy. These essays discuss characteristics for determinism in these fields as well as bring out the clash between the deterministic perspective of the natural sciences and the phenomenological perspective of lived experience. It is suggested that this clash may be eased through broadening our notions of causation and by realizing that the scientific and every day views are particular perspectives, among many possible ones, from which we may analyze or understand our world.

The first principle subdivision of the volume mainly is devoted to the relation between determinism and chance. Atmanspacher in his contribution distinguishes between determinism and determinability using a distinction between ontic and epistemic states in physical descriptions. Lombardi, using this same distinction, addresses Putnam's notion of internal realism in the context of physics, arguing that there is no single, pre-given ontology because the questions we ask, both theoretical and experimental, "cut into" reality in a way determining much of the chosen ontology. What is ontic and what is epistemic depends on the questions scientists ask.

Primas and Gustafson discuss results on embedding descriptions of stochastic processes into larger deterministic descriptions. One important feature of these results, according to Gustafson, is that any innovation process, i.e. process losing information as it proceeds forward in time, cannot be time-reversed. Primas refers to embedding theorems as providing a "hidden" determinism in physics and discusses this determinism in relation to the free actions of scientists. Both authors agree that the meaning of the embedding results for the reality of determinism is unclear.

In a related contribution, Misra shows how it is possible to move from a deterministic evolution to an irreversible probabilistic process via a mathematical transformation between the two types of descriptions. This approach shows most clearly that the distinction between determinism and chance for a wide class of systems can be conceived as a matter of description rather than an ontological issue.

Christidis, Kronz and McLaughlin, Dieks, and Berkovitz address chance and determinism from historical and philosophical viewpoints. Christidis interprets some of the fragments of Heraclitus as early precursors of guiding ideas in work by Prigogine and his colleagues. Kronz and McLaughlin discuss Peirce's evolutionary cosmology, where the universe starts out indeterministically and becomes increasingly deterministic by "habituation". Dieks raises questions regarding some implications of physical indeterminism for our ordinary language concepts such as novelty and openness of the future. Berkovitz's contribution examines the roles of determinism and indeterminism as assumptions in causal models using examples from economics.

This first subdivision ends with two papers discussing different aspects of control. Mahler and colleagues show that in the context of quantum mechanics the irreversibility connected with the increase of entropy is associated with a set of robust macro-level (thermodynamic) properties enabling various types of large-scale prediction and control of systems even as prediction and control of the micro-level (statistical) properties are progressively lost. Greenberger and Svozil discuss the consistency requirements for the prediction and control of events and apply them to a quantum mechanical model for time travel.

The second subdivision addresses determinism and free will. Dowe's contribution compares the folk notion of determinism with standard approaches to determinism based on science and discusses causation as a folk notion. Guignon sets out to dissolve the problem of reconciling free will with determinism by questioning the very framework within which the problem is formulated. He explores the realm of human action as a holistic, meaning-filled, embodied lifeworld, where we are always already engaging the world around us in practical ways.

Dorato defends a compatibilist view of free will, focusing on conceptual and pragmatic issues of the debate between compatibilists and incompatibilists. Kane defends an incompatibilist view of free will, invoking a novel indeterministic strategy, and responds to Dorato's discussion of his view in this volume. Martin and Sugarman, working within a broadly compatibilist framework, discuss a developmental account of agency. Richardson and Bishop, in the context of the social sciences, examine and call into question various assumptions shared by both compatibilist and incompatibilist accounts of free will.

Psychology takes center stage in the contributions by Gantt and Slife. Gantt discusses the problems of a reductive biologization in psychology and proposes phenomenological alternatives treating our lived experience as primary for understanding action, meaning, morality, etc. Slife questions the role that atomistic conceptions of time and information have played in psychological theories and proposes holistic alternatives that make better sense of how our view of the past, present and future shape our current actions and vice verse. In the final contribution in this subdivision, Abe and Kobayashi discuss Eastern views of determinism, and compare and reinterpret them from a scientific point of view.

Ringberg Castle is operated as a conference center of the Max Planck Society, whose hospitality is gratefully acknowledged. In particular we would like to thank Axel Hörmann and the staff of the center for their help in matters large and small ensuring the success of this workshop. The Institut für Grenzgebiete der Psychologie und Psychohygiene (IGPP) at Freiburg supported both the workshop and this volume financially. Keith Sutherland (Imprint Academic) provided competent advice for the smooth and fast publication of the volume. Finally we would like to thank Gundel Jaeger (IGPP) for a terrific job on conference pre-arangements and in preparing the manuscripts.

Deterministic and Indeterministic Descriptions

Robert C. Bishop

Abstract

In the practice of physics, a very general and precise description of a deterministic process in terms of group or semigroup operators can be given, characterized by three crucial properties: differential dynamics, unique evolution and value determinateness. In contrast quantum mechanics offers some models for indeterministic processes, but an analogous general description of indeterministic physical processes is lacking. It is clear that one of the elements of an indeterministic description is that it should be expressed in terms of semigroup operators, since indeterministic processes are time irreversible. What other elements are necessary and sufficient to qualify a description as indeterministic remain unclarified, however. In the practice of human sciences such as psychology, on the other hand, general forms of deterministic or indeterministic descriptions are not well developed. Some difficulties for developing general yet precise deterministic and indeterministic descriptions focusing specifically on psychology are explored.

1 Introduction

Determinism is often thought of as a metaphysical doctrine about our world. I am not going to address the truth or falsity, or even the applicability, of such a doctrine here, except with a few comments at the end. Rather, I want to focus on the general characteristics of deterministic and indeterministic descriptions. That is to say, I want to explore the properties that make particular theories or models about systems in our world deterministic or indeterministic. Although the properties making a description of a physical system deterministic can be identified rather easily, identifying the corresponding properties that make a description of a physical system indeterministic with precision is not so easy. And when we turn to the question of properties making descriptions in human sciences, such as psychology, deterministic or indeterministic, things become even murkier and more complicated.

2   Deterministic Descriptions in Physics

Let me begin with a distinction that is immediately relevant to physical descriptions, namely the ontic/epistemic distinction. This distinction is applied to states and properties of a physical system. Roughly, ontic states and properties refer to features of physical systems as they are "when nobody is looking," while epistemic states and properties refer to the features of physical systems accessible to empirical observation. Scheibe (1973) first introduced this distinction. It has been subsequently developed in various versions (Primas 1990, 1994; Atmanspacher 1994; d'Espagnat 1994; see also Atmanspacher in this volume). An important special case of ontic states and properties are those that are deterministic and describable in terms of points in an appropriate phase space. An important special case of epistemic states and properties are those that are describable in terms of probability distributions (or density operators) on some appropriate phase space.

A phase space is an abstract space of points where each point represents a possible state of the model. A simple example would be characterizing the possible states of a physical system in terms of its generalized momenta and positions.[1] A model can be studied in phase space by following its trajectory from an initial state (q_o, p_o) to some final state (q_f, p_f) (see Figure 1).

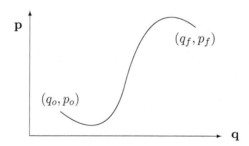

Figure 1: Path of the state of a physical system in phase space.

---

[1]Using generalized coordinates and momenta allow for systems to be characterized by variables other than linear momentum and position (e.g. angles and angular momentum in the case of a pendulum).

2.1   Laplacean Determinism

Clocks, cannon balls fired from cannons and the solar system are taken to be paradigm examples of deterministic systems in classical physics. In the practice of physics, we are able to give a very general and precise description of deterministic systems conceived of ontically. For definiteness I will focus on classical particle mechanics (CPM), which inspired Laplace's famous description of determinism (Laplace 1814/1951, p. 4). Suppose that a state of a system is characterized by the values of the positions and momenta of all the particles composing the system and that a physical state corresponds to a point in phase space through these values. We can then develop mathematical models for the evolution of these points in phase space and such models are taken to represent the physical systems of interest. Three properties have been identified playing a crucial role in such deterministic descriptions expressing Laplace's conception of determinism (Stone 1989; Kellert 1993; Bishop 1999, chap. 2):

(DD) Differential Dynamics: An algorithm relates a state of a system at any given time to a state at any other time and the algorithm is not probabilistic.

(UE) Unique Evolution: A given state is always followed (preceded) by the same history of state transitions.

(DD) Value Determinateness: Any state can be described with arbitrarily small (nonzero) error.

Differential dynamics is motivated by actual physical theories expressed in terms of mathematical equations. These equations, along with their initial and boundary conditions, are required to be nonprobabilistic. This requirement expresses the Laplacean belief that CPM contains no indeterministic elements like those present in some versions of quantum mechanics. Such equations describe the individual trajectories of ontic states in phase space.

Unique evolution is closely associated with DD. It expresses the Laplacean belief that CPM systems will repeat exactly the same trajectory if the same initial and boundary conditions are specified (cf. Nickel's formal characterization in his contribution in this volume). For example the equations of motion for a frictionless pendulum will produce the same solution for the motion as long as the same initial velocity and initial position are chosen. Roughly, the idea is that every time we return the mathematical model to the same initial state, it will undergo the same history of transitions from state to state. In other words the evolution of the model will be unique with respect to a particular specification of the initial and boundary conditions. Furthermore we can choose any state in the history of state transitions as the initial starting point and the model's history will remain unchanged.

Although a strong requirement, UE is important if physical determinism is to be a meaningful concept. Imagine a typical model m as a film. Unique evolution means that if we were to start the film over and over at the same frame (returning the model to the same initial state), then m would repeat every detail of its total history, and identical copies of the film would produce the same sequence of pictures. So no matter whether we always start *Jurassic Park* at the beginning frame, the middle frame or any other frame, it plays the same. No new frames are added to the movie nor is the sequence of the frames changed simply by starting it at an arbitrary frame.

By contrast, suppose that returning m to the same initial state produced a different sequence of state transitions on some of the runs. Consider a model m to be like a computer that generates a different sequence of pictures on some occasions when starting from the same initial picture. Imagine further that such a model has the property that simply by starting with any picture normally appearing in the sequence, it is sometimes the case that the chosen picture is not followed by the usual sequence of pictures or that some pictures often do not appear in the sequence or that new ones are added from time to time. Such a model would fail to have unique evolution.

Value determinateness is motivated by the Laplacean belief that there is nothing *in principle* in CPM preventing mathematical descriptions of arbitrary accuracy. For example the models of CPM all presuppose precise values for the constants and variables used in the equations of motion. This, again, is consistent with the description of ontic states having precise, definite values. Glymour (1971, pp. 744–745) takes value determinateness as one of the necessary criteria for determinism and cites Peirce and Reichenbach as examples of philosophers who have included this criterion in their analyses of determinism. Since CPM is often taken as the paradigm example of a deterministic theory, it is natural that value determinateness would come to be seen as part of the Laplacean vision for classical physics. It is only with the advent of quantum mechanics that questions were raised about the applicability of value determinateness to all of physics.[2]

The three properties of Laplacean determinism can easily be related to the types of group and semigroup operators used in various physical theories

---

[2]Historically a fourth property known as absolute predictability completed the picture of determinism as conceived by Laplace, but the relationship of predictability to determinism is more subtle than typically realized and the type of predictability implied by DD, UE and VD is also much weaker than often conceived (Bishop 1999, chap. 2).

(Bishop 1999, pp. 30–32; see also Nickel in this volume).[3] First, as the source for the equations of motion of CPM, such operators give a precise prescription for how to go from one state of the system to another (DD). Second, the phase space trajectory governed by these operators remains unique no matter what state in the trajectory's history is chosen as the initial state (UE). Third, the operators and the resulting equations of motion operate on determinate values as exhibited by the uniqueness and existence theorems for the differential equations of CPM (VD). Thus group and semigroup operators yield a precise, nonvacuous realization of the properties DD, UE and VD of deterministic descriptions.

3 Towards an Indeterministic Description in Physics

According to the ontic/epistemic distinction, indeterministic descriptions are typically associated with epistemic properties of physical systems; that is to say, properties accessible to observation (e.g. a system interacting with a measuring apparatus). The question naturally arises as to whether there can be an ontic description of a physical system that is fundamentally indeterministic.

Although the example of the computer that did not always display the same sequence of pictures even if we always started with the identical first picture looks on the surface to be a candidate indeterministic system, the paradigm examples for indeterministic physical systems are found in quantum mechanics (e.g. radioactive decay). So let me give a simple illustration of quantum mechanics. In our everyday world, stop lights operate with a predictable sequential pattern of green, followed by yellow followed by red. To get a sense for how different the quantum realm is, suppose quantum stop lights have two possible sequential patterns: either green, yellow, red, or green, red, yellow. Furthermore suppose we keep the standard meaning for the three colors: Green means go, yellow means caution, red means stop.

Suppose that observations show quantum stop lights have a probability of 50% for exhibiting the green-yellow-red pattern and of 50% for exhibiting the green-red-yellow pattern. Let me emphasize that the probability refers

---

[3]A group of operators differs from a semigroup of operators in that the former includes inverse elements lacking in the latter. This can be thought of in the following way: Group operators describe physical processes that can go forwards and backwards in time whereas semigroup operators describe processes going in one temporal direction.

to the patterns and not to the appearance of any individual color.[4] If the light is red when you approach the intersection, there is no problem. You simply stop and wait. If the light is green while you approach, it could turn red any moment. But if you were approaching a quantum stop light that was currently yellow, you would not know if the light was going to turn red or green next, because you would not know what pattern the light was exhibiting. You could observe the quantum stop light over a long period of time to determine probabilities for the two patterns. But you have no way of knowing *in advance* which pattern the light will exhibit as you come to the intersection, because the patterns at the level of observation are indeterministic; that is, we cannot say with certainty in which pattern we will find a quantum stop light on any given approach to an intersection.

We have observed that there is a 50% probability for each pattern to be exhibited by a quantum stop light. How are we to understand the nature of this probability? One possibility is that there is some additional factor, a hidden mechanism, such that once we discover and understand this mechanism, we would be able to predict the observed behavior of the quantum stop light with certainty (physicists call such an approach "hidden variable theory"). Or perhaps there is an interaction with the broader environment (the trees and buildings surrounding the intersection, say) that we have not taken into account in our observations and which explains how these probabilities arise (physicists call such an approach "decoherence"). In either one of these scenarios, we would interpret the observed indeterministic behavior of the stop light as an expression of our ignorance about the actual workings of the stop light. Under this interpretation indeterminism would not be a fundamental feature of the quantum stop light, but merely *epistemic* in nature due to our lack of knowledge about the system. Quantum stop lights would turn out to be deterministic from an ontic point of view.

The alternative possibility is that the indeterministic behavior of a quantum stop light is *ontic*, i.e. all the relevant factors do not fully determine which pattern the stop light is going to exhibit at any given moment.[5]

---

[4]For those who know some quantum mechanics, the patterns of the quantum stop lights are analogous to a two-state system. The green-yellow-red pattern would be an up state and the green-red-yellow pattern would be a down state. Approaching the intersection would be analogous to a measurement on the system.

[5]I have presented these possibilities for understanding the behavior of a quantum stop light in a simplified manner. The basic physical states must be described as a superposition of probability amplitudes, each probability corresponding to a particular outcome or pattern. On some construals of quantum mechanics, measurements do not require a superposition of probabilities to indeterministically collapse to one outcome. Then such

It would be helpful if physics had a general description of indeterministic systems available where the key properties making a system indeterministic could be identified as in the case of deterministic descriptions described in section 2. This is not the case, however. Nevertheless, one might begin developing the general features of such an indeterministic description by modifying the properties of a deterministic description (DD, UE and VD).

3.1 Value Determinateness

Suppose we begin by dropping VD. If one thinks that determinateness and determinism are closely related – as Glymour (1971) suggests – then dropping VD would guarantee indeterminism in a physical description. Although value determinateness applies to CPM, according to many construals of quantum mechanics physical variables do not have sharp or definite values. The technical results of interest are the Bell inequalities (Bell 1987) and the Kochen-Specker theorem (Kochen and Specker 1967): Given the formalism of quantum mechanics, the assumption of 1) locality (motivated by special relativity) and 2) definite physical values leads to contradictions.[6] In the face of problems raised by Bell for locality, and by Kochen and Specker for contextualism and locality, however, it is possible to revise determinism to allow for set- and interval-valued properties evolving along uniquely determined paths (Fine 1971; Teller 1979; Earman 1986, pp. 217–218).[7] Dropping VD, then, is not sufficient to guarantee an indeterministic description.

---

systems would behave deterministically. On other construals, there is an indeterministic collapse that would lead to indeterministic behavior in such systems. This implies that for chaotic systems, due to sensitive dependence, there may be cases where different interpretations or theories of quantum mechanics make a difference in the behavior of the chaotic macroscopic system, raising questions about whether such chaotic systems are deterministic or not (Bishop and Kronz 1999). Some implications of such questions for free will theories based on chaotic brain states amplifying quantum fluctuations (e.g. Kane 1996) are discussed by Bishop (2002a) and Kane (this volume).

[6]The locality requirement implies there is no backwards-in-time causation or violations of special relativity. The Kochen-Specker theorem requires contextualism as an additional assumption.

[7]If one is willing to consider *nonlocal* hidden-variable theories that do not violate special relativity (e.g. Bohm's quantum theory (1952a,b)), then value determinateness can be made consistent with quantum mechanics. The results of the local no hidden-variables theorems of Bell, and Kochen and Specker do not hold if the assumption of locality is dropped. Since the analysis of measurements is no more problematic for such interpretations of quantum mechanics than for local ones, these proposals represent viable alternatives for maintaining VD as a necessary property for a description of determinism even at the quantum level (depending on one's view of the measurement problem).

3.2 Differential Dynamics

Suppose we drop DD, thus allowing our equations to make explicit references to probability. Simply relaxing this restriction is not sufficient to render a model composed of such equations indeterministic, however. For example Schrödinger's equation in quantum mechanics describes the evolution of probability amplitudes, but this evolution is strictly deterministic: Given a wave function representing a superposition of probability amplitudes and the same initial and boundary conditions, the wave function will evolve the same way under repeated applications of Schrödinger's equation in analogy with a film. Actual terms in our model equations will have to be probabilistic, and/or the initial or boundary conditions will have to be probabilistic.

It turns out, nonetheless, that even requiring probabilistic terms and/or probabilistic initial and boundary conditions will not be sufficient to render a mathematical description indeterministic. For, as Gustafson and collaborators have demonstrated, many types of probabilistic descriptions of processes can be embedded within larger deterministic descriptions (Gustafson and Goodrich 1980, Antoniou and Gustafson 1993, Gustafson 1997; see also Gustafson's contribution in this volume). So we still face a fundamental question: What is the nature of the probabilities involved? Are they due to mere ignorance of underlying deterministic processes or are they irreducible to such processes? In other words we still need to know whether the probabilities are epistemic or ontic, but this is precisely the job we want our eventual criteria for indeterministic descriptions to do. It may be possible in particular instances to argue that a probability is irreducible to any deterministic processes as, for example, in the case of recent work by Prigogine and his Brussels-Austin colleagues (cf. Atmanspacher et al. 2001, p. 63–67; Bishop 2002b), but that is not the same as having some general properties characterizing indeterministic descriptions.

3.3 Unique Evolution

What about dropping UE? Kellert (1993, pp. 69–75) argues that UE can be separated from determinism because chaotic systems can amplify quantum fluctuations due to sensitive dependence (cf. Hobbs 1991, p. 157). Briefly, the reasoning runs as follows. Given two chaotic systems of CPM in nearly identical initial states (e.g. initial positions and velocities), they will evolve in radically different ways as the slight differences in initial conditions are amplified exponentially. There is no known lower limit to this sensitivity, thus, nothing prevents the possibility of chaotic macroscopic systems from being sensitive to quantum fluctuations. Quantum mechanics would then set a lower bound on how precisely the initial conditions can be specified. Hence UE must fail for chaotic CPM models.

However, these kinds of sensitivity arguments depend crucially on how quantum mechanics itself and measurements are interpreted as in the case of the quantum stop light (Bishop 1999, chap. 3; Bishop and Kronz 1999, pp. 134–138). Furthermore, although abstract sensitivity arguments do correctly lead to the conclusion that the smallest effects can be amplified, applying such arguments to concrete physical systems shows that the amplification process may be severely constrained. For example investigating the role of quantum effects in the process of friction in sliding surfaces indicates quantum effects can be amplified by chaos to produce a difference in macroscopic behavior only if the fluctuations are large enough to break molecular bonds and are amplified quickly enough (Bishop 1999, pp. 82–86).

As suggested by comparing the examples of a film that plays the same on each run with a computer that shows different pictures on each run, UE is significant for any conception of determinism. But would dropping UE yield indeterminism? To find out we need to see whether it is possible to drop UE and get indeterminism purely from an evolution equation. According to van Fraassen, we can build a set of "indeterministic counterparts" to the group and semigroup operators mentioned above. Let S be a subset of the phase space and b a positive number. Then (van Fraassen 1991, p. 51)

$$T_b(S) = \{x : \text{for some possible* trajectory } u, \text{ time } t, \text{ and some state } y \text{ in } S,$$
$$u(t) = y \text{ and } u(t+b) = x\};$$

$$T_b^\dagger(S) = \{y : \text{for some possible* trajectory } u, \text{ time } t, \text{ and some state } x \text{ in }$$
$$S, u(t) = y \text{ and } u(t+b) = x\},$$

where a trajectory $u(t)$ is possible* relative to $v(t)$ exactly when $u(t) = v(t)$ for all $t \leq t_1$. The trajectories $u(t)$ and $v(t)$ may disagree for all $t > t_1$ (Fig. 2). Obviously, $T_b T_b^\dagger(S)$ *does not* return to the original state in S. Furthermore these operators require a change in the notion of possibility from the standard one used in groups and semigroups. The operators T yield a phase space structure defining a set of possible* trajectories that can be continuations beyond time t_1. Both u and v are possible continuants, but no one is guaranteed to be *the* continuant. Thus unique evolution is lost with no explicit introduction of probability into any equations (DD can be fully preserved).

Another observation is that the operators T must form a semigroup of operators (so there are no inverse operators). Suppose that we start at some point $p(t_o)$ and apply T_b. This operation would be equivalent to tracing out

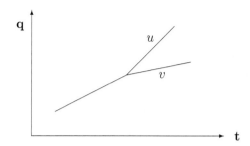

Figure 2: Two possible continuants u and v of a trajectory,
agreeing over part of their history, then diverging at some point in time.

a trajectory from the point $p(t_o)$ to the point $p(t_o + b)$. There is no guarantee
that applying T_{-b} to $p(t_o+b)$ would retrace the trajectory back to the original
point $p(t_o)$, because there are any number of possible continuants and no one
of them is guaranteed on any given application of an operator T_{-b} (in Figure
2, suppose that the application of T_b traces out the trajectory u ending at
$p(t_o+b)$, and that the application of T_{-b} traces out the inverse of v starting at
point $p(t_o + b)$). Furthermore the operators T obey the semigroup property
$T_b T_c = T_{b+c}$, though there is no guarantee that applying T_{b+c} to the same
point $p(t_o)$ will yield the same trajectory because there are many possible*
continuants.[8]

The structure defined by T on the phase space is clearly indeterministic.
It is too weak, however, to generate an adequately informative theory. The
theory generated by T tells us what possible continuants $u(t)$ has for times
greater than t_1, but it does not make any assignments for how probable any
of the possible continuants are. Suppose the theory generated by T tells us
that, given an initial state, a model of T will evolve through various indeterministic branching points (analogous to a computer that can produce a
different sequence of pictures on each run). Unless the evolution equation for
the model gives the probabilities for following the various branching points,
we have no more information from our theory than that it is indeterministic.
Strictly speaking, then, the loss of UE does not imply that the evolution
equation be explicitly probabilistic, but in order to have much *intelligible* to

---

[8]This feature is related to an argument by Reichenbach (1956, p. 211) that the assumption of time-reversibility and indeterminism yields a contradiction. Presumably for
indeterminism to be true, the evolution from $p(t_o)$ to $p(t_o + b)$ must be unreliable in
the sense that $p(t_o + b)$ can be any arbitrary point allowable on the phase space. Time-
reversibility, in contrast, requires reliable evolution between $p(t_o)$ and $p(t_o + b)$ in both
temporal directions.

say other than the model is indeterministic, an explicitly probabilistic pre-scription seems required, forcing us to drop DD in tandem with dropping UE in order to have a theory that is precise enough for calculation purposes.

One can object to the way I have used the term "indeterministic" in the previous paragraph. For example there are physical systems known as *Kolmogorov flows*, or K-flows, having the defining property that the current state plus the entire past history of state transitions is insufficient to fix or determine the next state transition from a statistical or coarse-grained perspective. Which is to say that if we were to divide the phase space into small squares of area α, no matter how small we make α, the trajectory will jump to the next state in such a way that we cannot determine with probability one (complete certainty) what that next state will be. We can, of course, recover a deterministic description for K-flows in the limit where α is zero and we focus on individual trajectories and states of the system. But from the coarse-grained perspective, K-flows behave just like the description of the theory T sketched in the preceding paragraph. This suggests that the nature of the probability in such descriptions is crucial to the question of indeterminism.

Another possible problem for the operators T is that the notion of pos-sible* is a philosopher's notion. It is not clear at all if or how we are to mathematize such a notion so that it becomes precise enough to use in an indeterministic description. One might hope that the lack of informativeness problem I just described can be overcome by an appropriate mathematical formulation of this notion of possibility. Unfortunately none seems to be available at the moment.

3.4 Taking Stock

Provisionally, the modified set of properties of an indeterministic description might take the following form:

(DD*) An algorithm relates a state of a system at any given time to a state at any other time (possibly) probabilistically.

(UE*) A given state may be followed (preceded) by the same history of state transitions.

(VD*) Any state may be described with determinate values.

(P*) Probabilities must be irreducible to the trajectories of individual states.

As indicated above, modifying UE in the fashion suggested appears to necessitate modifying DD and VD as well, though modifying either DD or VD alone does not imply that UE must be modified. Furthermore the semigroup T exhibits the properties DD*, UE* and VD*.

Yet things are still too vague in two respects. First the semigroup T, though suggestive, is not mathematically precise enough for calculations. Second the nature – ontic or epistemic – of the probability invoked in DD* remains unclarified. Property P* is an attempt to clarify a minimal requirement for indeterminism. The intuition is that the probabilities arising in indeterministic processes cannot be reduced to or redescribed in terms of the trajectories of individual states (e.g. Bishop 2002b). For example the conventional approach to describing physical systems within CPM relies on a representation of states (e.g. of particles) as points in an appropriate phase space (recall Figure 1). This means that the dynamics of a system are derived using particle trajectories as a fundamental explanatory element of its models (provided the states of the systems are parametrized by time). When there are too many states involved to make these types of calculations feasible (as in gases or liquids), coarse-grained averages are used to develop a statistical picture of how the system behaves rather than focusing on the behavior of individual states. Nevertheless the individual states remain ontically primary in these descriptions (recall the discussion of K-flows above).

In contrast the probabilities having property P* are such that the behavior of the system is no longer governed by the dynamics of individual states, but by the probability distributions (or density operators) themselves. Hence the probability distributions are the fundamental explanatory elements and so are to be conceived as ontic rather than merely epistemic. Though these intuitions suggest some possible directions for further research, much work remains to clarify this notion of probability.

In summary then, if we are willing, for the moment, to forgo full mathematical precision, the key property defining an indeterministic description has been identified as UE*. It implies that the identical initial state at t_o plus the evolution equations would be *insufficient* to specify the same state at a later time t_i, clearly rendering the description indeterministic (for technical examples in CPM, see Earman 1986, Bishop and Kronz 1999, Xia 1992). To say anything mathematically precise in terms of a condition distinguishing indeterministic from deterministic descriptions runs into an interpretive question regarding the nature of the probability involved.

The obvious move here is to examine the physical process being modeled as to whether it is indeterministic, hence, removing the ambiguity. However, this simply moves the interpretive question back one more step in the sense that the probabilistic process we observe (say in a quantum stop light) can be interpreted ontically or epistemically. Not surprisingly our observations underdetermine these possibilities. One could appeal to the embedding results I mentioned above: Under fairly general conditions, probabilistic descriptions can be transformed into deterministic descriptions by embedding them within a larger deterministic system. However, since these results are also at the level of our descriptions, they do not settle the issue of whether a physical process is deterministic or not. After all, simply transforming an indeterministic description mathematically into a deterministic one says nothing about the nature of the physical process we are investigating.[9] So it appears that we cannot read determinism out of our best physical theories or our observations in some unambiguous way.

Ultimately, wether we interpret a physical process as being deterministic or indeterministic derives from our metaphysical commitments regarding determinism. If we are metaphysical determinists, then naturally we will read the probability expressed in P* as ultimately a measure of our ignorance about the underlying determinism. If we do not make any metaphysical presuppositions regarding determinism, then we read conditions like P* with an empirical attitude towards our experiments and best theories. We do not have to understand them as implying metaphysical determinism.

Methodologically, agnosticism with respect to or denial of metaphysical determinism only means that we do not seek always in the past for the necessary and sufficient reasons for the occurrence of an event (e.g. looking for causes simultaneous to events or even pursuing kinds of formal causation analogous with the influence symmetry principles and conservation laws possess in physics). To be sure metaphysical determinism has provided a framework in which the ontologies underlying physics have been developed, but its experimental methodologies do not necessarily derive any support from metaphysical determinism.[10] However, eliminating those metaphysi-

---

[9]In his contribution in this volume, Primas refers to the possibility that the larger deterministic systems invoked in such embeddings are fictions.

[10]The development of the doctrine of divine freedom played a crucial role in the historical development of empirical science as a self-sustaining practice. For example, renewed theological emphasis on the contingent nature of creation – i.e. that it could have been otherwise than it is due to divine freedom – flowing out of the condemnation of Averroism in 1277, led to a growing emphasis on the importance of observation and the need for hypotheses and theories to match observed individual facts. The Aristotelian ideal that theories could start with self-evident first principles and proceed by deduction continued to exert strong influence on medieval thinkers, but its grip was slowly loosed. As questions shifted from "How must the world be?" to "What is *this* world like?", a shift suggested by divine freedom in creation, the approaches for answering questions in natural philosophy

cal commitments will have few, if any, substantial effects on the practice of
physics.

4 Deterministic and Indeterministic Descriptions in Psychology

In the practice of human sciences such as psychology, general forms of deterministic or indeterministic descriptions are not well developed. Determinism, however, plays a crucial role in most personality theories as well
as broader theoretical movements in psychology (Slife and Williams 1995,
Bishop 2002c). Furthermore determinism in psychology is described in the
language of efficient causation, patterned after the physical sciences. Though
various approaches within psychology differ in many theoretical aspects, one
thing most of them share in common – along with much of the rest of behavioral science – is a belief that the past is causally sufficient to explain present
and future behavior; that is to say, past events *determine* present and future behavior. For example taking a history of a patient – i.e. collecting the
unique experiences, important life events, parental interactions, etc. – is a
standard feature of virtually all therapeutic practice. Although therapists
will differ with respect to the emphasis placed on distant versus immediate
past events, they almost universally agree that past events are the keys to
understanding current behaviors.

4.1 Psychological Models of Determinism

I briefly want to explore two different versions of efficient causation and
determinism, one or the other of which shape many, if not most, theoretical
approaches in psychology at their core.

The first I will call the *physics model*. The idea here is that just as an
appropriate accounting of the relevant physical forces enables us to understand the dynamics of some physical process, an appropriate accounting of

---

had to undergo a corresponding shift. Over time the warrant for hypotheses and theories
shifted from a self-evident basis to extrinsic empirical evidence, but this shift did not happen immediately (McMullin 1965, pp. 108–113; Lindberg 1992, pp. 230–244). Theodoric
of Freiburg is one of the few medieval examples of a natural philosopher pursuing actual
experiments using flasks of water in his studies of refraction models in order to understand
rainbows (McMullin 1965, p. 121; Lindberg 1992, p. 253). The use of experiments to answer questions about the world gradually increased through the fourteenth and fifteenth
centuries (e.g. Marliani, Cusa, da Vinci), but it was through Galileo that experiment finally
took center stage in physics.

the relevant psychological and social forces involved enables us to understand the human behavior in question. For example both psychodynamics and behaviorism exemplify this approach. Human behaviors are explained in terms of the forces producing them (drives and so forth in psychodynamics; stimuli and reinforcement in behaviorism). In the case of psychodynamics, behavior is governed by depth psychological forces in combination with some external social forces. Take the example of a father who never expresses love or praise thereby causing his son to grow up with a set of perfectionist behavior patterns always trying to win the approval of potential father/authority figures. These early childhood dynamics set in motion an internal set of psychological forces operating at an unconscious level in the son that govern his social interactions with both peers and authority figures.

Instead of viewing people as creators of meanings and values, the physics model views them more like electrons responding to forces in a law-like way. For example, behaviorist theory reduces loving to "loving behaviors" which are brought about by environmental forces. So instead of loving being imbued with the meaningfulness, purposive character, and creativity we commonly believe it to have, we simply exhibit loving behaviors because ultimately these behaviors have been shaped or conditioned by brute environmental forces and contingencies. Like electrons, we respond to these external forces in law-like ways and engage in behaviors determined by these forces.

The second model might be called the *computer model*. Here the causal role is not played by forces as in the physics model, but by the rules and structures governing the input-processing-output scheme of the mind and by the nature of the information input into the system (Slife and Williams 1995, pp. 37–45). Consider a word processor. The hardware fixes the basic possibilities for processing while the software provides instructions for the particular types of processing the hardware will carry out. But the information I type (information input) is crucial to the response of the system. For example, if I misspell a word, the program may automatically correct it or place a red line under it to indicate a problem.

Cognitive psychology exemplifies this model with its reliance on the crucial role information input and processing play in explaining behavior. All human behaviors along with motives, intentions, desires, etc. are reduced to information input and the processing of the cognitive apparatus. Returning to the example of the approval-seeking son, the childhood interactions with his father can be viewed as "programming" or "software" providing instructions on how to process new information derived from his social interactions with peers and authority figures.

Instead of viewing people as creators of meanings and values, this model views them more like computers operating according to logical or rational information processing rules. All questions about behavior are reduced to questions about the structure of the cognitive system and the nature of the information input into that system. On the computer model analysis, loving is reduced to information input, representation and cognitive computation. The implication is that loving – indeed all our relationships with other people – is the result of processing information inputs along cost-benefit, Bayesian or other lines of analysis. Again this implies that loving does not have the same meaningfulness and creativity with which we commonly associate it, but, rather, is conditioned on information input and processing.[11]

Note that both these models are mechanistic rather than humanistic in thrust. There is a smaller, diverse, relatively marginal group of humanist, existentialist, or phenomenological thinkers in psychology, who explicitly reject such mechanistic approaches to understanding human agency. But they usually fail to take note of the fact that the realization of their nonmechanistic ideals actually depends upon some reliable connectedness among the events of human experience. Partly for that reason, these psychologists rarely develop any plausible alternative account of this connectedness, and so must still rely on, and are haunted by, the very sort of efficient causal deterministic viewpoint which they reject.

4.2   Deterministic Descriptions in Psychology

In a deterministic description of a physical system, we can give precise mathematical formulations of the conditions DD, UE and VD. By contrast, in describing a "psychological system" we have no mathematically precise way to formulate conditions. Standard mathematical tools are not immediately useful for psychological descriptions, in spite of the mechanistic flavor of the physics and computer models of behavior.[12] Nevertheless it is possible to formulate conceptual conditions for a deterministic psychological description.

Taking a cue from the crucial role UE plays in physical deterministic descriptions, let us start by giving the "story line" for the analogous property in the physics and computer models. In the physics model, given the

---

[11]Some of the philosophical and moral presuppositions and implications of these models are explored by Bishop (2002c); see also the contributions by Gantt, Guignon, Richardson and Bishop, and Slife in this volume for related discussions.

[12]Torretti (2000) has pointed out that the belief that "the really real can be adequately represented as a mathematical structure" represents a return to a Pythagorean prejudice rather than a conclusion derived from scientific practice. We must be careful not to fall prey to this prejudice when thinking about psychology.

identical psychological and social forces along with the identical biological-neurological system ("multiple runs" with "identical initial conditions"), a person would presumably repeat their same behaviors in terms of their life history. That is to say, if we insert the identical person into the identical world with the identical circumstances, they will live an identical life. In the computer model, given the identical cognitive processing apparatus and identical information input, a person would presumably repeat their same behaviors in terms of their life history as well.

Formulated in terms of life histories, it is clear that we have to worry about robustness. For example, are worlds physically identical in their totality required for generating identical life histories for an individual on "multiple runs"? How much physical difference in a given world can be tolerated before that introduces some relevant difference in the psychological/social forces (in the physics model) or the information input and processing (in the computer model) producing behavior changes with respect to a person's behavior in a given control or baseline world? Or suppose that two worlds are identical in every detail except that a girl, say, is born with red hair in one world and blond hair in another. What kinds of changes will result in the social forces or information inputs leading to differences in her behavior?

It is far from clear how to answer these robustness questions for entire life histories, so perhaps we should look at a weaker demand. After all, the requirement that psychological explanations of present behavior be found in the past does not necessarily require determinism in the sense of identical life histories. Robustness in psychological determinants – in a typical counseling situation say – can be understood along the lines of finding significant historical/relational events or patterns that serve as the cause for a person's behavior.

Recall the example of the son and his unaffirming father. The childhood interactions with the unaffirming father form the crucial events that serve to determine the son's behavior in all other circumstances. On the physics model, this is a set of psychological/social forces that are robust in the sense that changes in other circumstances or configurations of other psychological/social forces have little or no effect on dislodging the perfectionist behavior patterns and the drive for approval. Upon the son's leaving home (at age 18, say), if he faced an identical set of psychological/social forces, he could conceivably exhibit the identical life history of behaviors, though such a requirement is not necessary. All that is required for a deterministic psychological description is that the forces of his past interactions with his father be strong enough to dominate all other psychological/social forces in determining his subsequent behaviors.

I propose capturing this property of a psychological description with the following "principle":

(PD) Principle of Determination: Some fixed set of (at least partially) identifiable crucial factors in a person's past governs their response to present events.

For therapeutic practice, as well as other purposes, the determining factors should be at least partially identifiable if psychologists are going to be in the "helping" or "clarifying" business. As formulated, PD leaves open the possibility that, facing the identical circumstances, a person would behave identically or merely very similarly. I take it that similarity of response is a strong enough requirement to sufficiently clarify the sense in which the determining set of past factors governs responses (i.e. limiting the range of responses down to one or some small set of similar responses). So each time the son's quest for approval is denied, he gets angry, but perhaps there is some slight variation to what he does with the anger.

4.3   Indeterministic Descriptions in Psychology

Though PD is suggestive, it lacks the kind of clarity we can achieve with UE in physical theories. Things get more vague in thinking about what kind of property characterizes an indeterministic description in psychology. Again, following the lead of our physics discussion, I want to explore what the negation of PD might mean. One obvious candidate to poke is the requirement that the set of past factors be fixed. Although we can only loosely define the boundaries of this set, it should be such that the collection of factors composing it are by far the strongest determinants of a person's behavior. Now if this set is constantly expanding and contracting, or if the members of this set are constantly changing, then there would be no consistent factors that are determining or shaping a person's behavior. That would call into question the idea of trying to pattern a principle of determination after UE, as I have tried to do with PD. Suppose the set of determining factors is changing. This does not imply that a person's behaviors are not governed by *some* set of factors from the past. So this suggests an even weaker "principle":

(PD*) Principle of Determination*: Some (possibly fixed) set of (at least partially) identifiable crucial factors in a person's past governs their response to present events.

What would the negation of PD* mean? I take it that the crucial element in the principle is that of governance. The sense of the word "govern" carries with it the idea of limiting the range of something (e.g. the governor on a carburetor limiting the speed of a car). I have already suggested the weaker notion of similar responses as appropriate for deterministic descriptions in psychology, but this leads to the question of how much similarity is required to count before a response would be judged "dissimilar". Not surprisingly, we find ourselves in the middle of all those thorny free will questions (see, e.g., the contributions by Dorato, Guignon, Kane, Martin and Sugarman, Richardson and Bishop in this volume). Obviously, if we make the range of possible responses wide enough, the sense in which any past factors are "governing" responses to present events becomes vacuous. Likewise it becomes difficult to understand how the responses come about.

On the other hand, if we take some of the elements in the set of determining past factors to be ones which we contributed to that set and which were not fixed by some prior factors earlier in history, then the sense of "govern" in (PD*) sounds less and less like determinism and more and more like incompatibilist free will. That kind of free will is thought to be inconsistent with determinism in the sense that we are the originators at an earlier point of some of the values guiding our actions in the present. In this case, our past history is consistent with, but underdetermines, this origination (Kane 1996 and in this volume). Of course there are problems with incompatibilist (and compatibilist) accounts of free will (e.g. Dorato, and Richardson and Bishop in this volume). Perhaps, then, it should be no surprise that some thoughtful critics within psychology (e.g. Slife and Williams 1995; Richardson, Guignon and Fowers 1999) argue that psychology needs to look beyond familiar debates concerning whether or not we are entirely subject to efficient causal influences stemming from the past and consider the possibility that notions of final and formal causation might make better sense of how meanings and values guide our activities and projects in the human realm.[13]

4.4   Taking Stock

At this point, it seems that we have reached an impasse similar to the one encountered in trying to frame a satisfactory description of physical indeterminism. Here we might appeal to our first person experience and observations of others to help adjudicate the ambiguity in an indeterministic psychological description. After all, our everyday experience is that of agents acting

---

[13]Some appeal to formal causation seems inescapable. For example, both PD and PD* assume that current circumstances form a context in which past influences can come to expression. The context of present circumstances is a formal cause influencing or constraining responses.

in the world producing effects and influencing outcomes, overcoming obstacles, voluntarily cooperating with others, and so forth. However, it appears that in psychology, as well as in physics, whether we interpret these experiences as being deterministic or indeterministic is not inscribed on the events themselves, but derives from our independently arrived at metaphysical commitments regarding determinism. Indeed, many of the free will debates turn on exactly this point. If we are convinced metaphysical determinists, then the negation of a principle like PD* will certainly not appear to yield an unambiguous statement of indeterminism in psychology. If we do not make any metaphysical presuppositions regarding determinism, then, in light of our first person experience and natural inclination to think of ourselves as having free will, the negation of principles like PD* will not appear suggestive of any deterministic construals.

Practically speaking, endorsing, denying, or remaining agnostic toward metaphysical determinism will almost certainly impact the practice of psychology more significantly than that of physics. This is not only because much of the methodology in psychology, in the minds of its practitioners, seems directly tied to a metaphysically assumed determinism, but also because the assumption of determinism directly impacts our conception of ourselves and others as persons (Rychlak 1979; Slife and Williams 1995; Richardson, Guignon and Fowers 1999; Gantt, and Slife in this volume). Hence the appeal of developing theories and explanations in psychology that give a central place to forms of final and formal causation. Such accounts clarify how human action is not so much propelled from behind, as it were, by efficient causes, but shaped and guided in different situations by shared goals and meanings – frequently renegotiated or reinterpreted in the business of living. Thinkers who take this path endeavor to develop a new ontology of the human life-world in which we can make better sense of the circumstances and influences that shape us and the ways we modify them in turn (see Guignon, Gantt, Richardson and Bishop, and Slife in this volume).[14]

---

[14]As Gunton (1993, pp. 51–61) argues, the development of the doctrine of divine freedom in the context of understanding creation – described briefly in footnote 11 – also plays a role in the sundering of the relationship between universals and particulars, as well as the sundering of relationships between particulars, that had a deleterious effect on our modern conception of human beings. This modern conception views humans as constituted primarily by abstract properties rather than constituted by the particularity of embodiment and relationship to other beings and the world. A life-world ontology would de-emphasize the former conception and emphasize the latter.

5 Discussion

To summarize, we have DD, UE and VD yielding precise mathematical properties for characterizing a deterministic description in physics, and we have DD*, UE*, VD* giving a conceptual characterization of indeterministic descriptions in physics. The property P* is an attempt to further clarify the properties of such an indeterministic description. In psychology, however, we have a rather vague PD and PD* as candidates for properties characterizing deterministic descriptions along with the quagmire of trying to understand what the properties of an indeterministic description might be like.

It may be possible to bring more mathematical precision to the properties of an indeterministic description in physics, and to further clarify some aspects of as well as alternative formulations to PD and PD*. However, I believe we can draw a general lesson from our explorations here: It appears unavoidable that our attitude toward metaphysical determinism plays an important role in understanding both the meaning and possibility of deterministic and indeterministic descriptions in both disciplines.

Do we have any evidence in favor of metaphysical determinism? Our first person experience of agency in the world certainly does not immediately suggest metaphysical determinism. Indeed, the assumption of metaphysical determinism requires us to go to considerable lengths – controversial at best as to their success – to reinterpret our notions of agency, individuality, creativity, praiseworthiness, blameworthiness and the like in order to make sense of them in a deterministic world (e.g. Honderich 1988, 1993; Pereboom 1995, 2001; Bishop 2002c). Phenomenological hermeneutics, and some kinds of final and formal causation are more in concert with our lived experience (see the contributions by Gantt, Guignon, Richardson and Bishop, and Slife in this volume).

One could argue that our best theories are deterministic and that this is evidence in support of metaphysical determinism. But it seems to me that it remains quite ambiguous as to whether theories such as quantum mechanics should be read in terms of ignorance or ontological construals of probability (cf. section 3). Furthermore, our best scientific descriptions are abstractions representing our best attempts to describe a complex world given our intellectual limitations and our purposes (Bishop 2002c). Our theoretical understanding, therefore, is always partial, limited and inexact even in our best theories and models. At best, then, these considerations point toward agnosticism about metaphysical determinism, so far as physics is concerned. Given the harsh clash between metaphysical determinism and our first person experience – which seems virtually impossible to eradicate from our understanding of ourselves in everyday life (Gantt, Guignon, Kane, and Richardson and Bishop in this volume) – I would lean in the direction of denying metaphysical determinism.

One might take this conclusion – that metaphysical determinism is not strongly supported by our best theories and first person experience – to mean we are forced into an instrumental attitude toward theories; namely, viewing theories as simply calculation tools that make no reference to real entities in the world (cf. van Fraassen 1980). After all, scientific realism – viewing the terms in our theories as referring in some subtle or complex ways to objects in the world – is often taken to go hand in glove with determinism. However, although I cannot really defend the point in this essay, I would suggest that agnosticism toward or even denial of metaphysical determinism is entirely consistent with either a realist or an instrumentalist attitude toward such theories.

The cost of doing away with metaphysical determinism in physics seems relatively minor, as indicated in section 3.4 above. In contrast, the effect of dropping this assumption in psychology leads to highly significant changes in our very conception of ourselves and others as persons, and in how we relate to and influence one another in important life enterprises. It also would lead to significant changes in social science methodology. The difficulty and uncomfortableness of such a change may be the price we have to pay for a better understanding of the human predicament. A number of the presentations in this volume speak to this vexing and important question.

Appendix:
A Comment on Differential Dynamics

Kellert takes DD to be both a necessary and sufficient condition for a model to be deterministic, if neither the mathematical representation of the system (including initial and boundary conditions) nor the differential equations make explicit reference to probabilities. This is the most fundamental layer of determinism in Kellert's analysis and is also the most obscure. That is because of an ambiguity in the meaning of determinism as differential dynamics. On the one hand, differential dynamics as determinism is the thesis that future states of a model or system evolve from past states in a mathematically definable way if the dynamical model makes no reference to probability (Kellert 1993, p. 57):

> ... a dynamical system has two parts: a representation of all possible
> states of the system and a set of equations that describes how the state

of the system changes with time. When neither of these two parts involves chance explicitly, we have deterministic dynamical systems.

On this view (Kellert 1993, p. 56) "the way a system is at this moment determines, establishes, and specifies the way it will be at the next moment" by the equations describing the system. It is in this sense that unique evolution applies to models, systems and possibly, as some have thought, to our physical world.

On the other hand, differential dynamics also functions for Kellert (1993, p. 58) as a methodological tenet for scientific investigation:

> On the broadest scale, one could say that determinism as differential dynamics is just the tenet that we should keep looking for reasons for events in their pasts. The injunction is: use mathematical expressions (differential equations) to model the changes of physical systems; seek to understand or predict the future by relating it to the past with mathematical rules. Perhaps these rules will provide strictly unique implications and perhaps not, but keep trying to explain or predict until you cannot any more.

Methodologically, we seek to use "differential equations that make no explicit reference to chance – the equations must not include ... inherently stochastic elements" (Kellert 1993, p. 75). The import of this methodological point is to continue to use differential equations in our study of the world *without concern for whether UE holds*.

This methodological rule has its problems, however. First it is potentially misleading and uninformative. For example irreducible indeterminism in the initial conditions of chaotic systems due to quantum mechanics would be a case where the injunction will not produce models faithful to the dynamics of the physical system (Bishop and Kronz 1999). The methodological injunction would lead us astray in our attempt to model chaotic systems. The rule essentially tells us to use deterministic models (differential equations with no reference to chance) to capture the dynamics of chaotic systems when such systems may actually be indeterministic. Kellert's methodological construal of differential dynamics would leave us pursuing theories like T described in section 3.3 above in our attempts to model and understand physical systems – a rather uninformative and potentially misleading half-way house between deterministic and indeterministic theories.

Second there is a question as to what the methodological rule means. We could construe it as a strong injunction in the sense that we are to use differential equations with no reference to indeterminism in our investigations of nature and push such models as far as we possibly can. Such a construal rules out any indeterministic collapse interpretation of quantum mechanics and, therefore, would undercut Kellert's main argument that UE can be completely separated from DD because macroscopic chaotic systems could amplify quantum effects (section 3.3 above). On the other hand we could construe the rule as a weak injunction in the sense that we start with non-probabilistic mathematical models as a first approximation and add in probabilistic elements as soon as it becomes apparent they are needed. On this weak construal, indeterministic collapse interpretations of quantum mechanics are allowed, but such an injunction adds nothing new to the physicist's tool bag.

That last point leads to an additional question concerning the binding force of the methodological injunction to use nonstochastic differential equations for the practice of science. For example the models and practices used in statistical mechanics plainly ignore the injunction because of the large number of parameters that compose the systems under study. Furthermore since the introduction of statistical methods in the 1800s, physics has made tremendous progress in terms of models that enable us to better understand a number of fundamental processes as well as to build countless practical devices. And even in cases where systems have a small number of relevant parameters but extremely complicated behavior – like chaotic systems – physicists do not always follow the rule. Instead they adopt whatever approaches are most likely to yield results. The force of differential dynamics as a methodological rule is weak at best in the face of the physicist's pragmatism.

Acknowledgments

Useful conversations with Harald Atmanspacher, Fred Kronz, Michael Silberstein, and Frank Richardson are gratefully acknowledged.

References

Antoniou I. and Gustafson K. (1993): From probabilistic descriptions to deterministic dynamics. *Physica A* **197**, 153–166.

Atmanspacher H. (1994): Is the ontic/epistemic distinction sufficient to describe quantum systems exhaustively? In *Symposium on the Foundations of Modern Physics 1994*, ed. by K. Laurikainen, C. Montonen and K. Sunnarborg, Editions Frontières, Gif-sur-Yvette, pp. 15–32.

Atmanspacher H., Bishop R. and Amann A. (2001): Extrinsic and intrinsic irreversibility in probabilistic dynamical laws. In *Foundaitons of Probability and Physics*, ed. by A. Khrennikov, World Scientific, Singapore, pp. 50–70.

Bell J. (1987): *Speakable and Unspeakable in Quantum Mechanics*, Cambridge University Press, Cambridge.

Bishop R. (1999): *Chaotic Dynamics, Indeterminacy and Free Will*. Ph.D. Dissertation. University of Texas at Austin.

Bishop R. (2002a): Chaos, indeterminism and free will. In *The Oxford Handbook on Free Will*, ed. by R. Kane, Oxford University Press, Oxford, pp. 111–124.

Bishop R. (2002b): Brussels-Austin nonequilibrium statistical mechanics: large Poincaré systems and rigged Hilbert space. *Studies in History and Philosophy of Modern Physics*, in press.

Bishop R. (2002c): Crisis in the behavioral sciences. Forthcoming.

Bishop R. and Kronz F. (1999): Is chaos indeterministic? In *Language, Quantum, Music: Selected Contributed Papers of the Tenth International Congress of Logic, Methodology & Philosophy of Science*, ed. by M. Dalla Chiara, R. Guintini and F. Laudisa, Kluwer, London, 129–141.

Bohm D. (1952a): A suggested interpretation of the quantum theory in terms of 'hidden variables' I . *Physical Review* **85**, 166–179.

Bohm D. (1952b): A suggested interpretation of the quantum theory in terms of 'hidden variables' II . *Physical Review* **85**, 180–193.

D'Espagnat B. (1994): *Veiled Reality: An Analysis of Present-Day Quantum Mechanical Concepts*, Addison-Wesley, Reading MA.

Earman J. (1986): *A Primer on Determinism*, Reidel, Dordrecht.

Fine A. (1971): Probability in quantum mechanics and other statistical theories. In *Problems in the Foundations of Physics*, ed. by M. Bunge, Springer, New York.

Gunton C. (1993): *The One, the Three and the Many: God, Creation and the Culture of Modernity*, Cambridge University Press, Cambridge.

Gustafson K. (1997): *Lectures on Computational Fluid Dynamics, Mathematical Physics, and Linear Algebra*, World Scientific, Singapore.

Gustafson K. and Goodrich R. (1980): A Banach-Lamperti theorem and similarity transformations in statistical mechanics. *Colloquium of the Mathematical Society of Janos Bolyai* **35**, 567–579.

Kane R. (1996): *The Significance of Free Will*, Oxford University Press, Oxford.

Hobbs J. (1991): Chaos and indeterminism. *Canadian Journal of Philosophy* **21**, 141–164.

Honderich T. (1988): *A Theory of Determinism: The Mind, Neuroscience and Life-Hopes*, Clarendon Press, Oxford.

Honderich T. (1993): *How Free Are You? The Determinism Problem*, Oxford University Press, Oxford.

Kellert S. (1993): *In the Wake of Chaos*, University of Chicago Press, Chicago.

Laplace P. (1814/1951): *A Philosophical Essay on Probabilities*, Dover, New York.

Lindberg D. (1992): *The Beginnings of Western Science: The European Scientific Tradition in Philosophical, Religious, and Institutional Context, 600 B.C. to A.D. 1450*, University of Chicago Press, Chicago.

Kochen S. and Specker E. (1967): The problem of hidden variables in quantum mechanics. *Journal of Mathematics and Mechanics* **17**, 59–87.

McMullin E. (1965): Medieval and modern science: continuity or discontinuity? *International Philosophical Quarterly* **5**, 103–129.

Pereboom D. (1995): Determinism al dente. *Noûs* **29**, 21–45.

Pereboom D. (2000): *Living Without Free Will*, Cambridge University Press, Cambridge.

Primas H. (1990): Mathematical and philosophical questions in the theory of open and macroscopic quantum systems. In *Sixty-Two Years of Uncertainty*, ed. by A. Miller, Plenum, New York, pp. 233–257.

Primas H. (1994): Endo- and exotheories of matter. In *Inside Versus Outside*, ed. by H. Atmanspacher and G. Dalenoort, Springer, Berlin, pp. 163–193.

Reichenbach H. (1956): *The Direction of Time*, University of California Press, Berkeley.

Richardson F., Fowers B. and Guignon C. (1999): *Re-envisioning Psychology: Moral Dimensions of Theory and Practice*, Jossey-Bass, San Francisco.

Rychlak J. (1979): *Discovering Free Will and Personal Responsibility*, Oxford University Press, Oxford.

Scheibe E. (1973): *The Logical Analysis of Quantum Mechanics*, Pergamon Press, Oxford.

Slife B.D. and Williams R.N. (1995): *What's Behind the Research? Discovering Hidden Assumptions in the Behavioral Sciences*, SAGE Publications, Thousand Oaks.

Stone M A. (1989): Chaos, prediction and Laplacean determinism. *American Philosophical Quarterly* **26**, 123–131.

Teller P. (1979): Quantum mechanics and the nature of continuous physical magnitudes. *Journal of Philosophy* **76**, 345–361.

Torretti R. (2000): 'Scientific realism' and scientific practice. In *The Reality of the Unobservable: Observability, Unobservability and Their Impact on the Issue of Scientific Realism*, ed. by E. Agazzi and M. Pauri, Kluwer, Dordrecht.

van Fraassen B. (1980): *The Scientific Image*, Oxford University Press, Oxford.

van Fraassen B. (1991): *Quantum Mechanics: An Empiricists View*, Clarendon Press, Oxford.

Xia Z. (1992): The existence of noncollision singularities in Newtonian systems. *Annals of Mathematics* **135**, 411–468.

Perspectives on Scientific Determinism

Gregor Nickel

> After the decisive advance attained through Hume and Kant in the analysis of the causal problem, it is no longer possible to regard the causal relation as a simple connection between things, or to prove or disprove it in this sense.　　　　　Ernst Cassirer

1　Introduction

The task of any philosophical consideration of (scientific) determinism should follow two paths: First, freedom – probably in a richer sense than mere origination (see Gantt and Guignon in this volume) – has to be asserted, since discussing the problem should make *sense*. Second, the "(unreasonable) effectiveness" of modern natural science should become understandable. And scientific determinism is certainly fundamental for natural science. There seems to be a contradiction between these two paths. A transcendental approach, i.e. not exploring the properties of "things" directly, but rather exploring the "nature" of a (scientific) *observation* of things, is *one* possible strategy – starting with Kant – to deal with this problem. This includes a critique of scientific or instumental reason (see Richardson and Bishop in this volume) and avoids the pitfalls of a naive compatibilism or incompatibilism with respect to the issue of free will.

In this article, I will try to be aware of Cassirer's warning quoted above (Cassirer 1956, p. 20), which he issued in his great essay *Determinism and Indeterminism in Modern Physics* – still one of the best works on this problem. I will focus on the second path and analyze the formal structure of determinism in modern natural science, with only a brief look at interpretational issues. In the next section, I will recall some elements of Cassirer's position as background. In the third section, I will propose a mathematical structure representing a framework for scientific determinism. Finally, I will have a critical look at the position of Emil du Bois-Reymond, representing the perspective of (classical) natural science.[1]

---

[1] With respect to a more detailed discussion of some philosophical perspectives (e.g. of

2   Ernst Cassirer

According to Cassirer, four different levels of scientific propositions can be distinguished:

1. Results of measurement[2] (this value here and now),

2. Scientific laws (e.g. the law of falling bodies),

3. Scientific principles (e.g. the principle of least action),

4. The causal principle (determinism).[3]

From each level to the next there is a *transcendental* transition, that is, e.g., a scientific law is not only a simple collection of measurement results. Rather, its formation requires (and provides) new insight not available at the lower level. Each higher level expresses a principle of unification with respect to the lower one.

The "causal principle" – according to Cassirer – says nothing about the physical objects, let alone the "world". It is only a principle for "the formation of empirical concepts" (Cassirer 1956, p. 19). Thus, it is only a methodological, not an ontological principle. However, it is constitutive for natural science, since it "guarantees" the unlimited possibility of scientific objectification.[4]

It is important to notice that Cassirer's description of determinism as a methodological principle, and its distinction from an ontological one, stands *outside* natural science. It is not to be confused with the distinction between "ontic" and "epistemic" descriptions as descriptions *within* science (see At-

---

Plato, Leibniz, Hume, and Kant), the reader is referred to Nickel (2000).

[2]Of course, there are no "brute facts" (measurement results) independent of theories or principles. Nevertheless, measurement results are here considered as "primitive elements" of physical theory. Their formation is itself a highly involved problem. Already at this point, an overly naive adoption of everyday language in the discussion of scientific theory appears problematic – science is formulated as a symbolic language from the very beginning.

[3]Though important for natural philosophy and scientific discussion, we will not focus on the difference between determinism (bidirectional in time) and causality (forward directed in time). For Cassirer, and also for the scope of this article, only their common structure is considered. So it should not be confusing when both terms will appear almost synonymously.

[4]This also cuts the connection between the causal principle and predictability, which is stressed by Cassirer (see also Atmanspacher and Primas in this volume).

manspacher in this volume).[5] All I have to say about scientific determinism is epistemic insofar as it does not refer to things as they are, when they are not observed (a mathematical formulation is a perspective as well as any other formulation). On the other hand, there is also an ontic aspect insofar as I will not deal with questions of determinability.

Following Cassirer's perspective, determinism will not be understood as a property of "things" or of the "world", but, rather, as an *a priori* principle for the scientific observer's *perspective* on things (compare Lombardi in this volume). Hence, the observer's *freedom* to choose a perspective or – closer to the language of science – to choose a theoretical framework and an experimental setting is fundamental (cf. Guignon and Primas in this volume). It is part of the freedom of the observer to choose a scientific perspective. Within this perspective, then, there are strict conditions which must not be violated. On Cassirer's view, one of these conditions is the principle of determinism.[6]

However, it is hardly possible to describe the formal principle of determinism used by Cassirer concretely and to discuss it *within* the framework of science. Therefore, I will follow a less formal procedure to formulate and discuss scientific determinism. During this discussion, I will repeatedly focus on the status of the observer.

3   A Mathematical Structure for Scientific Determinism

Following Kant, natural science has to be understood in terms of mathematical formalism and scientific experiment (Kant 1965, B XIIIf):

> Reason, holding in one hand its principles, according to which alone concordant appearances can be admitted as equivalent to laws, and in the other hand the experiment which it has devised in conformity with these principles, must approach nature in order to be taught by it. It must not, however, do so in the character of a pupil who listens to

---

[5]However, the ontic-epistemic distinction could be considered as a model for the tension between ontological and epistemological aspects of theories or things (or even more general: of perspective-dependence and -independence).

[6]It is important to note that scientific determinism regarded as a regulative principle has at least two different functions. First, it qualifies the correct scientific laws and concepts. Second, however, a completely deterministic representation of any system (taking into account all possible influences, thus leading to a deterministic representation of the world) is never accessible, so determinism expresses a "limit concept". Since an ultimately deterministic theory cannot be obtained in finite time, determinism as a regulative principle "guarantees" that the development of natural science will not terminate.

everything that the teacher chooses to say, but of an appointed judge
who compels the witnesses to answer questions which he has himself
formulated.

In this section, I will concentrate on the principles of reason as they are
codified in mathematical terms and propose a mathematical structure, sufficiently concrete to be instructive and sufficiently abstract to cover a large
part of contemporary natural science. Thus, I will use the term (scientific)
determimism only for describing a concept of natural science. What this has
to do with determination in a philosophical sense remains open (compare
Guignon, or Abe and Kobayashi, in this volume).

However, scientific determinism can be used as a framework for the discussion of concepts such as *reversible* and *irreversible* motion, *autonomous* and
nonautonomous motion, and also for *stochastic* motion, both in scientific and
in natural philosophy contexts. Implicit assumptions could become explicit,
and the discussion could be clarified. In many *philosophical* discussions it is
rather unclear what scientific determinism means, or – even worse – concepts
such as nonautonomous motion and indeterministic motion are confused. On
the other hand, for a *scientist* the framework of scientific determinism is usually much too clear, and it is worthwhile to realize that its basic assumptions
are contingent and have to be justified. Needless to say, a representation of
motion (i.e. change) in a mathematical framework (i.e. the unchanged/-able
par excellence) is paradoxical enough.

Here and in the following, the term *motion* refers to any and all forms of
temporal change. This is much more general than a mere change of loca-
tion. As a mathematical framework for *scientific determinism*, the following
conditions will be used.[7]

1. The object of inquiry is the *motion* of a *system* in *time*. All three
   concepts are represented by mathematical structures (sets).

2. *Time* is represented by the additive group of real numbers $\mathbb{R}$ (for reversible motion) or the additive semigroup of positive or negative real
   numbers $\mathbb{R}_+$ or $\mathbb{R}_-$ (for irreversible motion). We thus use the structure

---

[7]It should be emphasized again that these conditions are not self-evident. They represent the *historically* developed framework (still) used in a large spectrum of the sciences.
Even in mathematics there are various concepts for modeling motion; we are concentrating
here on the case of (reversible) motion with continuous time and global existence, and
assume a particular time regularity. However, more complicated behavior can be discussed
in a similar setting.

of a one-dimensional, homogeneous, ordered continuum $\mathcal{T}$ consisting of single points.[8]

3. The *system* under consideration is characterized by a set $\mathcal{Z}$ – the *state space*[9] – of distinct states $z \in \mathcal{Z}$, whose temporal sequence is to be studied. The set of all possible states of the system is thus fixed from the outset. For example, the state space of a planetary system is established by the positions and velocities (or momenta) of all planets, or the state space of an eco-system is established by the number of individuals belonging to each relevant species. For a stochastic time evolution, the state space is a space $L^1(\Omega)$ of probability densities.[10]

4. The *motion* of the system is represented by the temporal sequence of states, thus by a function $\mathcal{T} \ni t \mapsto z(t) \in \mathcal{Z}$, which maps each instant $t \in \mathcal{T}$ to one and only one state $z(t) \in \mathcal{Z}$.

These conditions describe the motion of a system as a mapping from time $\mathcal{T}$ into the state space $\mathcal{Z}$.[11] Motion, thus, inherits basic properties of the presupposed structure of time. Up to now, only one motion of the system has been described; no alternatives are taken into account. An observer *outside* the system can (at least theoretically) have a view of this motion as a whole by considering the complete function $z(\cdot)$. At a particular instant in time,

---

[8]This identification is not so innocent as it might appear. While many criticisms of it could be cited here, one from Hume will suffice (Hume 1974, p. 424): "The absurdity of these bold determinations of the abstract sciences seems to become, if possible, still more palpable with regard to time ... An infinite number of real parts of time, passing in succession, and exhausted one after the other, appears so evident a contradiction, that no man, one should think, whose judgement is not corrupted, instead of being improved, by the sciences, would ever be able to admit of it" (cf. Slife in this volume). It is remarkable that time in this setting is given by the same set $\mathcal{T}$ for all systems, while the state space depends on the system under consideration and the observer's preferences.

[9]In scientific applications, the state space has at least an additional (topological) structure defining for every state a neighborhood of similar states (see Primas this volume). While time in this setting is essentially the same for all systems, the state space depends on the particular system considered (or the observer's preferences).

[10]We thus consider a common framework for ontic or epistemic descriptions. For a formulation of determinism, this distinction is less important than for the interpretation of the state concept (compare Atmanspacher and Misra in this volume). This is to say, the evolution of a probability distribution following statistical laws can be given by the same mathematical structure (group or semigroup) as the evolution of a pure state. The "ontic" status of both is then considered to be the same.

[11]To avoid problems of notation, the discussion is now restricted to reversible motion, thus considering time as represented by the entire real axis $\mathbb{R}$.

the system itself has no option to "choose" any value of this function other than the prescribed value at this time.

In this situation the following (trivial) equation holds:

$$z((t - s) + (s - r)) = z(t - r) \tag{1}$$

for all $t, s, r \in \mathcal{T}$. The consequence of such an abstract decomposition of motion due to a presupposed atomic structure of time into individual steps – from r to s and from s to t – becomes clear only if a set of *all possible motions* is taken into account. This change of perspective is of major importance. The (human) observer definitely steps back from the stage and describes the motion from *outside* as if he could *repeat* the course of the world arbitrarily often at any given time.[12] This perspective, including the possibility of preparing suitable initial states, is thus a necessary condition for experimentation and, therefore, constitutive for modern natural science.

5. For every instant $t_0 \in \mathcal{T}$ and every initial state $z_0 \in \mathcal{Z}$ there exists one and only one (necessarily determined) motion $z_{t_0, z_0} : \mathcal{T} \to \mathcal{Z}$ which at time t_0 yields the state z_0 ($z_{t_0, z_0}(t_0) = z_0$).

Varying the initial time $t_0 \in \mathcal{T}$ and the final time $t_1 \in \mathcal{T}$ we obtain a family of mappings $\Phi_{t_1, t_0} : \mathcal{Z} \to \mathcal{Z}$ for the system under consideration. Every function Φ_{t_1, t_0} maps an arbitrary initial state $z_0 \in \mathcal{Z}$ to the state $z_{t_0, z_0}(t_1)$, reached at time t_1 by the unique motion starting at time t_0 in state z_0. Formally, we can write

$$\Phi_{t_1, t_0}(z_0) := z_{t_0, z_0}(t_1).$$

Every state $z_1 = \Phi_{t_1, t_0}(z_0)$ can itself be regarded as another initial state. The motion determined by the pair (t_1, z_1) must coincide with the original motion, otherwise there were two different motions passing through (t_1, z_1), contradicting condition 5. In terms of the mappings, the following equation holds:

$$\Phi_{t_2, t_1}(z_1) = \Phi_{t_2, t_1}(\Phi_{t_1, t_0}(z_0)) = \Phi_{t_2, t_0}(z_0).$$

Thus, we have the following fundamental equation

$$\Phi_{t, s} \circ \Phi_{s, r} = \Phi_{t, r} \tag{2}$$

---

[12] The importance of this step has been explicitly pointed out by Mach. Following his argumentation there is no cause and effect (or determined motion) in nature, since there is only *one* nature. It is *our* definition of similar (or equal) initial conditions yielding similar (or equal) effects (or motion), which enables us to speak of causality (Cassirer 1956, p. 195). Compare also Bishop, this volume.

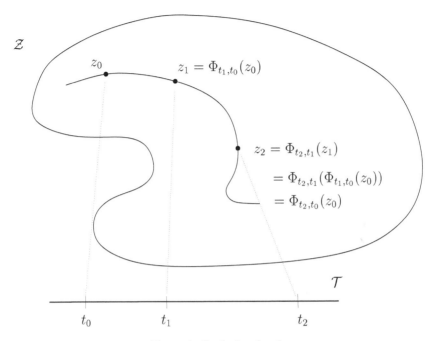

Figure 1: Evolution family

for all $t, s, r \in \mathcal{T}$. Moreover,

$$\Phi_{t,t} = Id \qquad (3)$$

with the identical mapping $Id : z \mapsto z$ (compare Fig. 1).

This entire construction can be called *deterministic* on the basis of the following characteristics: the *a priori* choice of the state space, the representation of time by the set of real numbers $\mathbb{R}$, and, finally, the necessary existence of a unique motion for every possible initial state (see condition 5). In mathematical terms, a deterministic motion is given by a state space $\mathcal{Z}$, time $\mathcal{T}$, and a family of mappings (called an evolution family or propagator) $\Phi_{t,s} : \mathcal{Z} \to \mathcal{Z}$, satisfying equations (2) and (3).[13]

---

[13] The discussion of the implications of decomposing a motion into individual steps goes back at least to Aristotle. In his lecture on nature, he sharply distinguishes between an *actual* interruption of movement (that of a *"mobile"*, i.e. a moving object along a line) and its mere *possibility*: "... whereas any point between the extremities may be made to function dually in the sense explained [as beginning and as end], it does not actually function unless the mobile actually divides the line by stopping and beginning to move again. Else there were one movement, not two, for it is just this that erects the 'point between' into a beginning and an end ..." (Aristotle 1963, p. 373). In a case of continuous

In special situations, it can be assumed additionally that the system is not subject to external influences in the course of time. Such systems are called *autonomous*. The momentary state of their motion depends solely on the initial state z_0 and the time *difference* t between initial and final time. The identity $\Phi_{t_1,t_o} = \Phi_{t_1+t,t_o+t}$ thus holds for any $t \in \mathcal{T}$, and a unique mapping

$$T_t : \mathcal{Z} \to \mathcal{Z}, \quad T_t := \Phi_{t,0} = \Phi_{t+t_o,t_o}$$

can be defined, which maps every initial state z_0 to the final state $z_1 = T_t(z_0)$, depending on the elapsed time difference t. The immediate consequences of equations (2) and (3) for the function T are

$$T_s T_t = T_{t+s}, \quad T_0 = Id. \tag{4}$$

A family of mappings satisfying equation (4) is called either a one-parameter group (for $t \in \mathbb{R}$ in the reversible case) or a one-parameter semigroup (for $t \in \mathbb{R}_+$ or $t \in \mathbb{R}_-$ in the irreversible case).[14] The structure of a one-parameter (semi)group is, therefore, a mathematical model of autonomous, deterministic motion.[15]

---

motion, there is no justification for locating the object in the intermediate position (during a given period of time). "But if anyone should say that it [the mobile A, G.N.] has 'arrived' at every potential division in succession and 'departed' from it, he will have to assert that as it moved it was continually coming to a stand. For it cannot 'have arrived' at a point [B, G.N.] (which implies that it is there) and 'have departed' from it (which implies that it is not there) at the same point in time. So there are two points of time concerned, with a period of time between them; and consequently A will be at rest at B ..." (Aristotle 1963, p. 375). From this quite consistent perspective, the deduction of a relation as given in (2) certainly is problematic. And regarding the measurement problem of quantum mechanics, Aristotle's view seems quite modern.

[14]Irreversiblity implies a conceptual problem for an outside observer, since the *relative* time direction of the system and the observer must then be addressed, thus also his own motion. For a detailed discussion of the arrow of time see Primas in this volume.

[15]The semigroup equation (4) was explicitly used rather late in the literature of mathematical physics. Hille (1965, pp. 55–66), one of the founders of modern semigroup theory, writes: "Like Monsieur Jourdain in Le Bourgeois Gentilhomme, who found to his great surprise that he had spoken prose all his life, mathematicians are becoming aware of the fact that they have used semi-groups extensively even if not always consciously. ... The concept was formulated as recently as 1904, and it is such a primitive notion that one may well be in doubt of its value and possible implications." One of the first scientists who used semigroups to formulate a mathematical concept of determinism was Hadamard in his lectures on differential equations (Hadamard 1952, p. 53). With reference to Huygens' treatment of light diffusion, Hadamard discusses Huygens' "principle" in the form of a syllogism, whose major premise implicitly contains the semigroup law: "(major premise). The action of phenomena produced at the instant $t = 0$ on the state of matter at the

Whether the initial state determines the total motion, depends mainly on the choice of the state space. (For example, in the trivial, single-element state space $\mathcal{Z}_{Parmenides} := \{z_1\}$ there is only the (deterministic) trivial motion). However, the state space for a sensible description of a system should be established by those properties relevant for the observer, and, in addition, a given state at a specific time should determine any further motion. This corresponds to Cassirer's statement (Cassirer 1956, p. 6):

> The answer that an epistemology of science gives to the problem of causality never stands alone but always depends on a certain assumption as to the nature of the object in science. These two are intimately connected and mutually determine each other.

These (scientific, not objective!) requirements necessitate a careful balancing. The proper state space is precisely that which, on the one hand, contains all relevant properties, and, on the other hand, guarantees a deterministic motion (cf. Primas in this volume).[16] The history of physics shows numerous examples of how a state space was chosen that contained the relevant properties, but later was altered – usually enlarged – with the goal of achieving a deterministic motion, or semigroup property.

4 Emil du Bois-Reymond's Perspective on Nature

In 1872, the biologist, physiologist, and philosopher du Bois-Reymond reanimated the famous demon of Laplace (which correctly should be called Leibniz's demon), the notion of an intelligence overseeing the entire universe in all its details, in his address *On the Limits of Our Knowledge of Nature*. Years before the rise of quantum mechanics, the classical physical paradigm was particularly clearly expressed by du Bois-Reymond. It is worthwhile to consider his position since it reflects many problems discussed in the present debate in great clarity.

First, du Bois-Reymond formulated scientific determinism in a fairly clear cut way, although enabling its interpretation as an ontological and as a

---

instant $t = t_0$ takes place by the mediation of every intermediate instant $t = t'$, i.e. (assuming $0 < t' < t_0$), in order to find out what takes place for $t = t_0$, we can deduce from the state at $t = 0$ the state at $t = t'$ and, from the latter, the required state at $t = t_0$." The premise is designated as a *"law of thought,"* or as a *"truism,"* which nevertheless has interesting consequences. For it corresponds (Hadamard 1952, p. 53) *"to the fact that the integration of partial differential equations defines certain groups of functional operations; and this for instance leads to quite remarkable identities ..."*

[16]For the case of hereditary mechanics the discussion about the proper state space and determinism is analyzed in Israel (1991).

methodological principle at the same time. Second, he discussed the problem of qualia and intentionality, emphasizing the tension between introspection and an outside scientific perspective. Third, he described the scientific perspective explicitly. Fourth, concerning the question of free will versus determinism, he tried to assert a consistent scientific world view, albeit with explicitly mentioned serious problems.

I do not agree with all his positions, but – in my opinion – du Bois-Reymond serves as a paradigm for the perspective of a natural scientist, both professionally and personally.

Within the framework of his scientific description of nature, he suggested a universal formula that would guarantee complete transparency (du Bois-Reymond 1912a, p. 443):[17]

> It is even conceivable that our scientific knowledge will reach a point which would allow the operation of the entire universe to be represented by One mathematical formula, by One immeasurable system of simultaneous differential equations, from which the position, the direction of motion, and the speed of every atom in the universe could be calculated at any time.

At the same time, however, du Bois-Reymond set up strict limits to knowledge. First, atomic matter, as presupposed by mechanics, is nothing more than a useful fiction; a "philosophical atom", conceived as existing beyond this pragmatic construction, is "on closer examination an absurdity" (du Bois-Reymond 1912a, p. 447). Second, not only consciousness, but even the simplest qualitative sensations, are irremediably out of reach for the natural scientist. Even complete and "astronomically exact" knowledge of all material systems, including the human brain, which is *in principle* attainable,[18]

---

[17] "... es läßt sich eine Stufe der Naturerkenntnis denken, auf welcher der ganze Weltvorgang durch Eine mathematische Formel vorgestellt würde, durch Ein unermeßliches System simultaner Differentialgleichungen, aus dem sich Ort, Bewegungsrichtung und Geschwindigkeit jedes Atoms im Weltall zu jeder Zeit ergäbe."

[18] It is remarkable that he does not mention the problem of the exact determinability of initial states and dynamical instabilities. This is in accordance with a long tradition at least from Leibniz on who already mentioned the "butterfly effect" in his small essay "On Destiny" (Leibniz 1951, pp. 571–572): "And often, such small things can cause very important changes. I used to say a fly can change the whole state, in case it should buzz around a great king's head while he is weighing important counsels of state ... . And even this effect of small things causes those who do not consider things correctly to imagine some things happen accidently and are not determined by destiny, for this distinction arises not in the facts but in our understanding." For Leibniz as for du Bois-Reymond the phenomenon of a sensitive dependence on initial conditions was no argument against a metaphysical determinism. One can ask why the opposite has become so popular nowadays.

so du Bois-Reymond, leaves the question of the nature of consciousness untouched, and natural scientists will always have to reply to this question with "ignorabimus". This claim is justified by the insurmountable gulf separating the quality-free descriptions of mechanics and the qualities of perception and intentionality (du Bois-Reymond 1912a, p. 457):[19]

> Astronomical knowledge of the brain ... reveals it to be nothing but matter in motion ... What conceivable connection is there between particular movements of particular atoms in my brain, on the one side, and, on the other, the facts which are primary, undefinable, indisputable for me: 'I feel pain, I feel pleasure; I taste something sweet, smell the scent of roses, hear the piping of the organ, see red' ... It is quite incomprehensible, and shall remain so for ever, that for a number of carbon, hydrogen, nitrogen, and oxygen atoms it is not a matter of complete indifference where they are and where they are going, where they were and where they went, where they will be and where they will be going ...

Du Bois-Reymond ascribes great importance to the "irreconcilable contradiction" between the "world-view established by mechanical physics" and the "freedom of the will". However, this contradiction is held to be logically subordinate to the problem of sensory qualities. Du Bois-Reymond's position in this matter is peculiarly vague. After having curtly brushed aside the various historical efforts[20] at grappling with the problem of free will as "most dark and self-inflicted aberrations", he formulates his "monistic view" as the result of a consequential application of the law of the conservation of energy (du Bois-Reymond 1912b, p. 82):[21]

---

[19] "Die astronomische Kenntnis des Gehirns, die höchste, die wir davon erlangen können, enthüllt uns darin nichts als bewegte Materie. Durch keine zu ersinnende Anordnung oder Bewegung materieller Teilchen aber läßt sich eine Brücke ins Reich des Bewußtseins schlagen. ... Die neben den materiellen Vorgängen im Gehirn einhergehenden geistigen Vorgänge entbehren also für unseren Verstand des zureichenden Grundes. Sie stehen außerhalb des Kausalgesetzes, und schon darum sind sie nicht zu verstehen, ... Es ist durchaus und für immer unbegreiflich, daß es einer Anzahl von Kohlenstoff-, Wassenstoff-, Stickstoff-, Sauerstoff-, usw. Atomen nicht sollte gleichgültig sein, wie sie liegen und sich bewegen, wie sie lagen und sich bewegten, wie sie liegen und sich bewegen werden."

[20] He refers, albeit negatively, to the efforts of contemporary French mathematicians to make room for free will within the framework of a theory of differential equations. According to these attempts, free will could be integrated into mechanical descriptions by taking into account bifurcations, which imply a breakdown of the uniqueness of the solutions of differential equations (see Israel 1991, and also Primas in this volume).

[21] "Die Erhaltung der Energie besagt, daß so wenig wie Materie, jemals Kraft entsteht oder vergeht. ... Die Hirnmolekeln können stets nur auf bestimmte Weise fallen, so sicher

> Conservation of energy means that force cannot be created or destroyed just as matter cannot ... The molecules of the brain can only fall in a particular way, as ineluctably as dice fall after leaving the tumbler ... Now if, as monism conceives it, our thoughts and inclinations, and this includes our acts of volition, are incomprehensible yet necessary side effects of the stirrings and fluctuations of our brain molecules, then it makes sense to say that there is no freedom of the will. For monism, the world is mechanistic, and in a mechanism there is no room for freedom of the will.

Yet eventually, du Bois-Reymond considerably qualifies his position in view of the exigencies of practical life. Even the "most resolute monist" could hardly maintain that each and every action is already predetermined by mechanical necessity. While it could be acceptable that unimportant actions are determined, this is hardly acceptable for meaningful (e.g. moral) decisions (cf. Guignon and Kane, this volume). With respect to a statistical determination, one could find acceptable that a statistically determined amount of letters have wrong addresses, but the assertion of a statistically determined amount of thieves in a society is scandalous.[22] For du Bois-Reymond, there is a fundamental and rationally undecidable alternative between strictly denying free will or asserting such free will at the expense of conceding an unsolvable "mystery". Thus, in du Bois-Reymond's account, the problem finds a new formulation rather than a solution.

---

wie Würfel, nachdem sie den Becher verließen. Wiche eine Molekel ohne zureichenden Grund aus ihrer Lage oder Bahn, so wäre das ein Wunder so groß als bräche der Jupiter aus seiner Ellipse und versetzte das Planetensystem in Aufruhr. Wenn nun, wie der Monismus es sich denkt, unsere Vorstellungen und Strebungen, also auch unsere Willensakte, zwar unbegreifliche, doch notwendige und eindeutige Begleiterscheinungen der Bewegungen und Umlagerungen unserer Hirnmolekeln sind, so leuchtet ein, daß es keine Willensfreiheit gibt; dem Monismus ist die Welt ein Mechanismus, und in einem Mechanismus ist kein Platz für Willensfreiheit."

[22] "... man gibt leicht zu, daß man nicht frei, sondern als Werkzeug verborgener Ursachen handelt, so lange die Handlung gleichgültig ist. Ob Caesar in Gedanken die rechte oder linke Caliga zuerst anlegt, bleibt sich gleich, ... ob er aber den Rubicon überschreitet oder nicht, davon hängt der Lauf der Weltgeschichte ab. ... Wenn Herr Stephan uns berichtet, daß auf hunderttausend Briefe Jahr aus Jahr ein so und so viel entfallen, welche ohne Adresse in den Kasten geworfen werden, denken wir uns nichts besonderes dabei. Aber daß nach Quetelet unter hunderttausend Einwohnern einer Stadt Jahr aus Jahr ein so und so viel Diebe, Mörder und Brandstifter sind, das empört unser sittliches Gefühl ..." (du Bois-Reymond 1912b, p. 86).

5   A Perspective on du Bois-Reymond's Position

Let me finally add some remarks on du Bois-Reymond's position, the perspective of a typical scientific observer. For him, objects are given by mechanical atoms within a state space $\mathbb{R}^{6N}$; the connection between atomism and his natural philosophy is remarkably close. Natural science and the mechanics of atoms are almost identical.[23] However, there is an ambiguity in du Bois-Reymond's atomism: On the one hand, the real world has to be analyzed in terms of the motion of atoms, but, on the other hand, he thinks of the atom merely as a "useful fiction". A similar ambiguity holds for his considerations on determinism and free will.

The origin of these ambiguities can be found in his perspective of an outside observer, detached from the phenomena (cf. Gantt and Guignon, this volume). A scientific observer looks at a system (including his own brain) and considers every detail without being involved. Du Bois-Reymond calls this an "Archimedean perspective" and describes it often with great pathos in his writings.[24] Although he admits the one-sidedness of the scientific perspective,[25] he defends it as unique and objective in contrast to other per-

---

[23] "Kant's Behauptung in der Vorrede zu den Metaphysischen Anfangsgründen der Naturwissenschaft, 'daß in jeder besonderen Naturlehre nur so viel eigentliche Wissenschaft angetroffen werden könne, als darin Mathematik anzutreffen sei' – ist also vielmehr noch dahin zu verschärfen, daß für Mathematik Mechanik der Atome zu setzen ist" (du Bois-Reymond 1912a, p. 442). In quantum mechancis, and also in continuum mechanics, the concept of objects is quite different, but it remains to be clarified whether this has substantial implications for the problem of determinism.

[24] "Aber man denke sich einen Augenblick den unendlichen Raum, und im unendlichen Raume verteilt Nebel chaotischer Materie, Sternhaufen, Sonnensysteme; man denke sich, als verschwindenden Punkt in dieser Unendlichkeit, unsere Sonne in unbekannte Himmelsräume stürzend, um sie her die Planeten ... Wir wollen diese der anthropozentrischen entgegengesetzte Art, die Vorgänge auf der Erde zu betrachten, die archimedische Perspektive nennen, weil wir dabei geistig einen Standpunkt außerhalb der Erde wählen ... Wie armselig und unbedeutend erscheinen so gesehen die irdischen Dinge! ... Wie gänzlich wahnsinnig ihr Beginnen, wenn eine Versammlung der ernstesten, gelehrtesten, tiefstdenkenden Männer ihrer Zeit über Wesensgleichheit oder Wesensähnlichkeit von Vater und Sohn zu Rate sitzen!" (du Bois-Reymond 1912a, p. 595f) This perspective includes an "introspection from the outside": "Es wäre grenzenlos interessant, wenn wir so mit geistigem Auge in uns hineinblickend die zu einem Rechenexempel gehörige Hirnmechanik sich abspielen sähen ..." (du Bois-Reymond 1912a, p. 457).

[25] "In diesem Sinne schein uns heute erlaubt, ja nützlich, das Weltproblem von verschiedenen Standpunkten aus anzugreifen, und demgemäß eine mechanische Welttheorie aufzustellen und in sich zu begründen, unbekümmert zunächst darum, wie Ethik, Rechtslehre und hergebrachte menschliche Vorstellungen damit fertig werden" (du Bois-Reymond 1912a, p. 531).

spectives. Any "introspection" is explicitly rejected as part of the scientific method (du Bois-Reymond 1912b, p. 85f).[26]

On the other hand, du Bois-Reymond does not disregard the dilemma of inner and outer perspectives, which is normally avoided by the "sleepwalking one-sided scientist or poet".[27] Perhaps this dilemma could be more properly appreciated if the scientific world view were understood as one particular perspective among many (cf. Guignon, this volume). In Kant's words (Kant 1965, A 125f):

> ... the order and regularity in the appearances, which we entitle nature, we ourselves introduce. We could never find them in appearances, had not we ourselves, or the nature of our mind, originally set them there. For this unity of nature has to be a necessary one, that is, has to be an a priori certain unity of the connection of appearances; and such synthetic unity could not be established a priori if there were not subjective grounds of such unity contained a priori in the original cognitive powers of our mind, and if these subjective conditions, inasmuch as they are the grounds of the possibility of knowing any object whatsoever in experience, were not at the same time objectively valid.

Kant (and later Cassirer) provide examples of a balanced conception, asserting freedom (as a fundament), but at the same time appreciating the plausibility and effectiveness of science and scientific determinism. However, the twofold meaning of the word "nature" in the preceding quote renews the problem. Kant's transcendental position was misinterpreted psychologically, and, more seriously, his dualistic balance – with a courteous distance to a possible unifying ground – was given up in German idealism (monism of spirit, where natural philosophy and natural science are almost disjoint)

---

[26]Every attempt to analyze the *subject* of experience and reason immediately collapses to an "objective" picture: "Wenn wir auf den Fluß unserer Gedanken achten, bemerken wir bald, wie unabhängig von unserem Wollen Einfälle kommen, Bilder aufleuchten und verlöschen. Sollten unsere vermeintlichen Willensakte in der Tat viel willkürlicher sein?"

[27]"Wer gleichsam schlafwandelnd durch das Leben geht, ... wer als Historiker, Jurist, Poet in einseitiger Beschaulichkeit mehr mit menschlichen Leidenschaften und Satzungen, oder wer naturforschend und -beherrschend eben so beschränkten Blickes nur mit Naturkräften und Gesetzen verkehrt: der vergißt jenes Dilemma, auf dessen Hörner gespießt unser Verstand gleich der Beute des Neuntöters schmachtet; wie wir die Doppelbilder vergessen, welche Schwindel erregend uns sonst überall verfolgen würden" (du Bois-Reymond 1912b, p. 87). In this context, Buber's diagnosis in *Ich und Du* (Buber 1983) is of interest. Mental impairments produced by a worldview based on doom ("Verhängnis") and arbitrariness ("Willkür"), as more or less unrelated aspects of determinism and chance, are contrasted with fate ("Schicksal") and freedom ("Freiheit"), being related in a meaningful way.

or materialism (monism of matter, where at most natural science is taken seriously).

The structure of Kant's argument could be revived by turning away from the *a priori* emphasis on both Euclidean time and space and Aristotelian logic. This would lead to a picture in which Kant's categories (including causality) are valid only in some local sense. A "transcendental pragmatic" or "transcendental phenomenological" account might try to understand the human observer (at least) as reasoning *and* acting (as Blondel (1893) pointed out). The determining force of logical reasoning is then only *one* important aspect/possibility for the constitution of human existence.[28]

Certainly, such approaches cannot immediately provide *definite* solutions (since *freedom* is crucial). But they could lead to a re-action of thinking to the contingent history of science and philosophy and to a renewal of the Kantian balance. Maybe they could even lead to a viewpoint integrating the position of du Bois-Reymond (1912b, p. 87):[29]

> The writings of the metaphysicians offer a long series of attempts at reconciling freedom of the will and moral law with a mechanical order of the universe. If anyone, Kant for example, had achieved this squaring of the circle, then this series would reach its end. Only inconquerable problems are in the habit of being so immortal.

References

Aristotle (1963): *Physics*, transl. by P.H. Wicksteed and F.M. Cornford, William Heinemann, Cambridge.

Blondel M. (1893): *L'Action. Essai d'une critique de la vie et d'une science de la pratique*, Alcan, Paris. See also his "L'illusion idèaliste", *Revue de mètaphysique et de morale* **6** (1898), 726–745, and his "La point de départ de la recherche philosophique", *Annales de philosophie chrétienne* **151** (1906), 337–360.

Buber M. (1983): *Ich und Du*, Lambert Schneider, Heidelberg.

---

[28] See also the arguments presented by Guignon in this volume. Perhaps, a transcendental version of Peirce's picture, as presented by Kronz and McLaughlin in this volume, might also be relevant.

[29] "Die Schriften der Metaphysiker bieten eine lange Reihe von Versuchen, Willensfreiheit und Sittengesetz mit mechanischer Weltordnung zu versöhnen. Wäre einem, etwa Kant, diese Quadratur wirklich gelungen, so hätte wohl die Reihe ein Ende. So unsterblich pflegen nur unbesiegbare Probleme zu sein."

Cassirer E. (1956): *Determinism and Indeterminism in Modern Physics*, Yale University Press, New Haven.

du Bois-Reymond E. (1912a): *Reden in zwei Bänden, Band 1*, Veit, Leipzig.

du Bois-Reymond E. (1912b): *Reden in zwei Bänden, Band 2*, Veit, Leipzig.

Hadamard J. (1952): *Lectures on Cauchy's Problem in Linear Partial Differential Equations*, Dover, New York.

Hille E. (1965): What is a semi–group? In *Studies in Real and Complex Analysis*, ed. by J. Hirschmann, *MAA Stud. Math.* **3**, 55–66.

Hume D. (1974): An enquiry concerning human understanding. In *The Empirists*, Anchor Book, Garden City, New York.

Israel G. (1991): Il determinismo e la teoria delle equazioni differenziali ordinarie. *Physis* **28**, 305–358.

Kant I. (1965): *Critique of Pure Reason*, transl. by N.K. Smith, St. Martin's Press, New York.

Leibniz G.W. (1951): *Selections*, ed. by P.P. Wiener, Charles Scribner's Sons, New York.

Nickel G. (2000): Determinism: Scenes from the interplay between metaphysics and mathematics. In *One-Parameter Semigroups for Linear Evolution Equations*, ed. by K. Engel and R. Nagel, Springer, Berlin, pp. 531–553.

Determinism Is Ontic, Determinability Is Epistemic

Harald Atmanspacher

Abstract

Philosophical discourse traditionally distinguishes between ontology and epistemology and generally enforces this distinction by keeping the two subject areas separated. However, the relationship between the two areas is of central importance to physics and philosophy of physics. For instance, many measurement-related problems force us to consider *both* our knowledge of the states and observables of a system (epistemic perspective) *and* its states and observables independent of such knowledge (ontic perspective). This applies to quantum systems in particular.

This contribution presents an example showing the importance of distinguishing between ontic and epistemic levels of description even for classical systems. Corresponding conceptions of ontic and epistemic states and their evolution are introduced and discussed with respect to aspects of stability and information flow. These aspects show why the ontic/epistemic distinction is particularly important for systems exhibiting deterministic chaos. Moreover, this distinction provides some understanding of the relationships between determinism, causation, predictability, randomness, and stochasticity.

1 Introduction

Can nature be observed and described as it is in itself independent of those who observe and describe – that is to say, nature as it is "when nobody looks"? This question has been debated throughout the history of philosophy with no clearly decided answer one way or the other. Each perspective has strengths and weaknesses, and each epoch has had its critics and proponents with repect to these perspectives. In contemporary terminology, the two perspectives can be distinguished as topics of ontology and epistemology. Ontological questions refer to the structure and behavior of a system as such, whereas epistemological questions refer to the knowledge of information gathering and using systems, such as human beings.

In philosophical discourse it is considered a serious fallacy to confuse these two areas. For instance, Fetzer and Almeder (1993) emphasize that "an ontic answer to an epistemic question (or vice versa) normally commits a category mistake". Nevertheless, such mistakes are frequently committed in many fields of research when addressing subjects where the distinction between ontological and epistemological arguments is important. Recently, the vast literature on consciousness-related topics has provided many examples of this kind of category confusion (cf., for instance, Searle's criticism of Churchland (Searle 1997, pp. 30/31) and of Dennett (Searle 1997, pp. 113/114)).

In physics, the rise of quantum theory with its interpretational problems was one of the first major challenges to the ontic/epistemic distinction. The discussions between Bohr and Einstein in the 1920s and 1930s is a famous historical example. Einstein's arguments were generally ontically motivated; that is to say, he emphasized a viewpoint independent of observers or measurements. By contrast, Bohr's emphasis was generally epistemically motivated, focusing on what we could know and infer from observed quantum phenomena. Since Bohr and Einstein never made their basic viewpoints explicit, it is not surprising that they talked past each other in a number of respects (see Howard 1997). Examples of approaches trying to avoid the confusions of the Bohr-Einstein discussions are Heisenberg's distinction of actuality and potentiality (Heisenberg 1958), Bohm's ideas on explicate and implicate orders (Bohm 1980), or d'Espagnat's scheme of an empirical, weakly objective reality and an objective (veiled) reality independent of observers and their minds (d'Espagnat 1995).[1]

A first attempt to draw an explicit distinction between ontic and epistemic descriptions for quantum systems was introduced by Scheibe (1973) who himself, however, put strong emphasis on the epistemic realm. Later, Primas developed this distinction in the formal framework of algebraic quantum theory (see Primas 1990). The basic structure of the ontic/epistemic distinction, which will be made more precise below, can be understood according to the following rough characterization (for more details, the reader is referred to Primas 1990, 1994):

> *Ontic states* describe all properties of a physical system exhaustively. ("Exhaustive" in this context means that an ontic state is "precisely the way it is", without any reference to epistemic

---

[1] Further terms fitting into the context of these distinctions are latency (Margenau 1949), propensity (Popper 1957), or disposition (Harré 1997). See also Jammer's discussion of these notions, including their criticism and additional references (Jammer 1974; pp. 448–453, 504–507).

knowledge or ignorance.) Ontic states are the referents of individual descriptions, the properties of the system are treated as *intrinsic properties*.[2] Their temporal evolution (dynamics) is reversible and follows *universal, deterministic laws*. As a rule, ontic states in this sense are empirically inaccessible. *Epistemic states* describe our (usually non-exhaustive) knowledge of the properties of a physical system, i.e. based on a finite partition of the relevant phase space. The referents of statistical descriptions are epistemic states, the properties of the system are treated as *contextual properties*. Their temporal evolution (dynamics) typically follows *phenomenological, irreversible laws*. Epistemic states are, at least in principle, empirically accessible.

The combination of the ontic/epistemic distinction with the formalism of algebraic quantum theory provides a framework that is both formally and conceptually satisfying. Although the formalism of algebraic quantum theory is often hard to handle for specific physical applications, it offers significant clarifications concerning the basic structure and the philosophical implications of quantum theory. For instance, the modern achievements of algebraic quantum theory make clear in what sense pioneer quantum mechanics (which von Neumann (1932) implicitly formulated epistemically) as well as classical and statistical mechanics can be considered as limiting cases of a more general theory. Compared to the framework of von Neumann's monograph (1932), important extensions are obtained by giving up the irreducibility of the algebra of observables (not admitting observables which commute with every observable in the same algebra) and the restriction to locally compact phase spaces (admitting only finitely many degrees of freedom). As a consequence, modern quantum physics is able to deal with open systems in addition to isolated ones; it can involve infinitely many degrees of freedom such as the modes of a radiation field; it can properly consider interactions with the environment of a system; superselection rules, classical observables, and phase transitions can be formulated which would be impossible in an irreducible algebra of observables; there are in general infinitely many representations inequivalent to the Fock representation; and non-automorphic, irreversible dynamical evolutions can be successfully incorporated and even derived.

---

[2]In a more technical terminology, one speaks of "observables" (mathematically represented by "operators") rather than properties of a system. Prima facie, the term "observable" has nothing to do with the actual observability of a corresponding property.

In addition to this remarkable progress, the mathematical rigor of algebraic quantum theory in combination with the ontic/epistemic distinction allows us to address quite a number of unresolved conceptual and interpretational problems of pioneer quantum mechanics from a new perspective. First, the distinction between different concepts of states as well as observables provides a much better understanding of many confusing issues in earlier conceptions, including alleged paradoxes such as those of Einstein, Podolsky, and Rosen (1935) or Schrödinger's cat (Schrödinger 1935). Second, a clearcut characterization of these concepts is a necessary precondition to explore new approaches, beyond von Neumann's projection postulate, toward the central problem that pervades all quantum theory from its very beginning: the measurement problem. Third, a number of much-discussed interpretations of quantum theory and their variants can be appreciated more properly if they are considered from the perspective of an algebraic formulation.

One of the most striking differences between the concepts of ontic and epistemic states is their difference concerning operational access, i.e. observability and measurability. At first sight it might appear pointless to keep a level of description which is not related to what can be operationalized empirically. However, a most appealing feature at this ontic level is the existence of first principles and universal laws that cannot be obtained at the epistemic level. Furthermore, it is possible to rigorously deduce (e.g. to "GNS-construct"; cf. Primas 1994, 1998) a proper epistemic description from an ontic description if enough details about the empirically given situation are known. These aspects show that the crucial point is not to decide whether ontic or epistemic levels of discussions are right or wrong in a mutually exclusive sense. There are always ontic and epistemic elements to be taken into account for a proper description of a system. This requires the definition of ontic and epistemic terms to be relativized with respect to some selected framework within a set of (hierarchical) descriptions (Atmanspacher and Kronz 1998; see also Lombardi in this volume). The problem is then to use the proper level of description for a given context, and to develop and explore well-defined relations between different levels.

These relations are not universally prescribed; they depend on contexts of various kinds. The concepts of reduction and emergence are of crucial significance here. In contrast to the majority of publications dealing with these topics, it is possible to precisely specify their meaning in mathematical terms. Contexts, or contingent conditions, can be formally incorporated as topologies in which particular asymptotic limits give rise to novel, emergent properties unavailable without those contexts (see Primas 1998 for more details). It should also be mentioned that the distinction between ontic and epistemic descriptions is *neither* identical with that of parts and wholes *nor* with that of micro- and macrostates as used in statistical mechanics or thermodynamics. The thermodynamic limit of an infinite number of degrees of freedom provides only one example of a contextual topology, others are the Born-Oppenheimer limit in molecular physics or the short-wavelength limit in geometrical optics. It is an interesting question whether other kinds of emergence, such as that of phenotypes from genotypes, of consciousness from brain tissue, or of semantics from syntax, can be related to this discussion.

These examples indicate that the usefulness or even inevitability of the ontic/epistemic distinction is not restricted to quantum systems. It plays a significant role in the description of classical systems as well. There is a special class of classical systems for which the distinction of ontic and epistemic descriptions is necessary if category mistakes and corresponding interpretational fallacies are to be avoided: systems exhibiting "deterministic chaos".

2   Ontic and Epistemic States of Classical Systems

Let us consider the representation of a system in a phase space Ω. The ontic state of such a system is represented by a point $x \in \Omega$, so that the phase space Ω is also a state space in this case.[3] The intrinsic properties of the system are represented by real-valued functions on Ω, such as the positions and momenta of point particles. In the algebraic formulation the intrinsic properties of the system are represented by elements of the commutative C*-algebra $C_0(\Omega)$ of all complex-valued continuous functions on the locally compact phase space Ω. Since there is a one-to-one correspondence between the points $x \in \Omega$ and the pure state functionals on $C_0(\Omega)$ (i.e., the extremal positive linear functionals on $C_0(\Omega)$), ontic states are represented by pure state functionals. The ontic valuation of any observable $B \in C_0(\Omega)$ is dispersion free, $\rho(B^2) = \rho(B)^2$. Classical point mechanics is an example. The pointwise representation of an ontic state in Ω illustrates that the finiteness of information, and therefore an information theoretical characterization, is not effective for ontic descriptions.

---

[3]The concept of a phase space is here understood in terms of a general mathematical structure, e.g. a manifold. Additional constraints, e.g. a symplectic structure of the manifold, lead to more specific types of phase space. It is useful to distinguish the concept of a phase space from that of a state space, since states are not necessarily represented by elements of a phase space.

For an epistemic description, such as in statistical mechanics, one defines a Kolmogorov space (Ω, Σ, ν), with a countably additive probability measure ν (a reference measure, typically the Lebesgue measure) on a σ-algebra Σ of Borel subsets A. Since epistemic descriptions refer to empirical purposes, Σ is required to be the Boolean algebra of experimentally decidable alternatives. Any measure μ which is absolutely continuous with reference to ν characterizes an epistemic (statistical) state. Note that such an epistemic state is an element of the Kolmogorov space (Ω, Σ, ν), not of the phase space Ω. It refers to our knowledge as to whether an ontic (individual) state x is more likely to be in some Borel subset A rather than in others. An ensemble (à la Gibbs) of ontic states is an example of a clearly statistical concept of an epistemic state. However, the corresponding probability distribution can also be viewed in an individual, ontic interpretation (in terms of a distribution "as a whole"), as in kinetic theory (à la Boltzmann) or in classical continuum mechanics.

Equivalently, epistemic states can be represented by Radon–Nikodým derivatives $d\mu/d\nu$, called probability densities or distributions. They are positive and normalized elements of the Banach space $L^1(\Omega, \Sigma, \nu)$. The dual of this Banach space is the W*-algebra $L^\infty(\Omega, \Sigma, \nu)$ of ν-essentially bounded Borel-measurable functions on Ω, the algebra of bounded observables. Insofar as the probability measure μ representing an epistemic state has finite support, it represents finite information about the ontic state. This finiteness can be due to the imprecision of measurements or due to the fact that any decimal expansion of real numbers has to be truncated somewhere for computational purposes. Such a representation of epistemic states (and their associated properties) generally requires a finite partition of Ω.

The temporal evolution of an ontic state $x \in \Omega$ as a function of time $t \in \mathbb{R}$ is a trajectory $t \mapsto x(t)$; the ontic state $x(t)$ determines the intrinsic properties that a system has at time t exhaustively. The temporal evolution of an epistemic state μ corresponds to the evolution of a bundle of trajectories $x(t)$ in Ω. The concept of an individual trajectory of an individual, ontic state is irrelevant within a purely epistemic description.

If the dynamics is reversible then $\mu(T^{-1}(A)) = \mu(T(A)) = \mu(A)$ for all $A \in \Sigma$, where $T : \Omega \to \Omega$ is an automorphism on the state space Ω. For a one-parameter group of such a μ-preserving invertible transformation, the evolution of a corresponding system is both forward and backward deterministic, if the parameter is chosen to be a (discrete or continuous) time t. In such a case, there is no preferred direction of time. Fundamental physical laws (e.g. in Newton's mechanics, Maxwell's electrodynamics, relativity theory) are time-reversal symmetric in this sense. Phenomenological theories such as thermodynamics operate with a distinguished direction of time. The fundamental time-reversal symmetry is broken, thus leading to an irreversible dynamics given by a one-parameter semigroup of non-invertible transformations.

2.1 Stability

In the theory of dynamical systems, the map $t \mapsto T_t = T(x, t)$ is often called a flow $\{T_t \mid t \in \mathbb{R}\}$ on the phase space Ω, where x is a phase point in Ω representing the ontic state of a system. This flow is said to be generated by a transformation F that can be discrete, e.g.

$$x(t+1) = F(x(t)), \tag{1}$$

or continuous in time t, e.g.

$$\frac{dx(t)}{dt} = \dot{x}(t) = F(x(t)). \tag{2}$$

Equation (2) represents a first-order, ordinary differential equation system as a very simple example which, however, is sufficient to illustrate the basic notions. The trajectory $\{x(t)\}$ characterizes the state of the system as a function of time t; its components represent its continuous observables $(x_1, ..., x_d)$. F is a matrix containing the generally nonlinear coupling among the observables, whose number defines the dimension d of the phase space Ω.

To characterize the flow $\{T_t\}$, i.e. the temporal evolution of $x(t)$ as the solution of (2), one has to study how $\{T_t\}$ behaves under the influence of small perturbations δx. Such a characterization specifies the stability of the system and can be obtained in terms of a linear stability analysis. Skipping over the details, a linear stability analysis yields local (in Ω) rates of amplification or damping of perturbations $\delta x(t)$ with respect to a reference state or a reference trajectory $\{x(t)\}$, respectively. From these local rates one can obtain a global dynamical invariant of $\{T_t\}$, essentially as a temporal average of the local rates. These global invariants are the so-called Lyapunov exponents:

$$\lambda_i = \lim_{t \to \infty} \frac{1}{t} \ln \left| \frac{\delta x_i(t)}{\delta x_i(0)} \right| \tag{3}$$

The sum of all (d) Lyapunov exponents allows an elegant and fundamental classification of dynamical systems.

- $\sum \lambda_i > 0$ characterizes systems which are unstable in a global sense, for instance random systems. Their phase volume spreads over the entire phase space as $t \to \infty$.

- $\sum \lambda_i = 0$ characterizes conservative (e.g. Hamiltonian) systems. Since the sum of their Lyapunov exponents is non-negative, they are stable, but not asymptotically stable. Their phase volume remains constant in time (Liouville's theorem). Conservative systems with at least on positive Lyapunov exponent are so-called K-flows.

- $\sum \lambda_i < 0$ characterizes dissipative systems. They have a shrinking phase volume and are asymptotically stable. It is intuitively suggestive (but not finally understood, see Ruelle 1981, Milnor 1985) that the flow $\{T_t\}$ of a dissipative system is asymptotically restricted to a finite subspace of the entire phase space. This subspace is called an attractor. If $\lambda_i < 0 \ \forall i$ this attractor is a fixed point. If there are k vanishing Lyapunov exponents and $(d-k)$ negative ones, then the attractor is a k-torus (limit cycle for $k = 1$). For systems with at least three degrees of freedom, $d \geq 3$, the condition of a negative sum of Lyapunov exponents can be satisfied by a combination of positive and negative ones. This situation defines a chaotic (strange) attractor in the sense of deterministic chaos.

2.2 Dynamical Entropy

The Lyapunov exponents can be related to the concept of a dynamical entropy, i.e., the entropy of a temporal evolution. The dynamical entropy according to Kolmogorov (1958) and Sinai (1959), briefly KS-entropy, has received particular attention among a number of alternative dynamical entropies (Wehrl 1991). The main reason for this popularity is that KS-entropy has turned out to be an extremely useful tool in the characterization of systems showing chaotic behavior in the sense of deterministic chaos. The original proposals by Kolmogorov and Sinai did not explicitly mention this scope of interest. Instead, they were concerned with the way in which an entropy can be ascribed to the automorphism $T : \Omega \to \Omega$. This can be done by considering a partition P in Ω with disjoint measurable sets A_i ($i = 1, ..., m$) and studying its temporal evolution $TP, T^2 P, ...$ If the entropy $H(P)$ of P is given by

$$H(P) = -\sum \mu(A_i) \ln \mu(A_i), \qquad (4)$$

then the dynamical KS-entropy h_T is defined as the supremum of $H(P,T)$ over all partitions P,

$$h_T = \sup_P H(P,T), \tag{5}$$

with

$$H(P,T) = \lim_{n \to \infty} \frac{1}{n} H(P \vee TP \vee ... \vee T^{n-1}P). \tag{6}$$

Remarks: (1) The latter limit is well-defined because H is subadditive, i.e., $H(P \vee P') \leq H(P) + H(P')$ for two partitions P, P'. (2) The partition providing the supremum of $H(P,T)$ is the so-called generating partition or, more specifically, the so-called K-partition (Cornfeld et al. 1982). The generating partition is constructively given by the dynamics of a system. (3) The KS-entropy is a relevant concept for commutative (Abelian) algebras of observables but cannot naively be taken over to non-commuting observables in the sense of conventional quantum theory. It can, however, acquire significant meaning for operator algebras in Koopman representations of classical systems. For non-commutative (non-Abelian) algebras of observables of conventional quantum systems, alternative concepts (mathematically generalizing the classical KS-entropy) have been introduced, e.g., by Connes, Narnhofer, and Thirring (1987), see also Hudetz (1988).

Under particular conditions the sum of all positive Lyapunov exponents can be identified as the KS-entropy h_T:

$$h_T = \sum_i \lambda_i^+ = \begin{cases} \sum \lambda_i & \text{if } \lambda_i > 0 \\ 0 & \text{otherwise} \end{cases} \tag{7}$$

More precisely, Ledrappier and Young (1985) have proven that $\sum \lambda_i^+ D_i = h_T$ where D_i is the partial information dimension $0 \leq D_i \leq 1$ if T is a C^2-diffeomorphism and μ an associated T-invariant ergodic measure. Moreover: if T is hyperbolic and μ is absolutely continuous with respect to the Lebesgue measure along the unstable manifolds of T, then μ is called a Sinai-Ruelle-Bowen (SRB) measure and $D_i = 1$ such that $\sum \lambda_i^+ = h_T$. This is the Pesin identity (Pesin 1977). While the conditions for the result of Ledrappier and Young are fairly general, the essential condition for Pesin's identity, i.e., that the natural measure is a SRB measure, is perhaps not always satisfied for practically relevant systems (cf. Tasaki et al. (1993) for a proposed extension of the SRB criterion). In any case we have the inequality $\sum \lambda_i^+ \geq h_T$.

Both conservative K-flows and dissipative chaotic attractors provide what has now become well-known as sensitive dependence of the evolution of a system on small perturbations in the initial conditions. This dependence is due to an intrinsic instability that is formally reflected by the existence of positive Lyapunov exponents. The KS-entropy of a system is an operationally accessible quantity (Grassberger and Procaccia 1983). A positive (finite) KS-entropy is a necessary and sufficient condition for chaos in conservative as well as in dissipative systems (with a finite number of degrees of freedom). Chaos in this sense covers the entire spectrum between totally unpredictable random processes, such as white noise ($h_T \to \infty$), and regular (e.g. periodic, etc.) processes with $h_T = 0$. See Sect. 4 for a more detailed discussion of this point.

> **Remark:** The characterization of a dynamical system by its KS-entropy is not necessarily complete. For instance, systems with the same KS-entropy may reach equilibrium with different rates. Although their spectral and statistical properties are indistinguishable as far as expectation values (e.g. suitable limits) are concerned, they are not isomorphic concerning the way in which these expectation values (limits) are approached. See Antoniou and Qiao (1996) for a specific demonstration of this difference with respect to the spectral decomposition of the tent map; and see Antoniou et al. (1999) for further subtleties. Another formal way to deal with problems like this is known as "large deviations statistics", a relatively new field of mathematical statistics which is applicable to the context of dynamical systems (Oono 1989).

From a historical point of view, it is interesting to note that chaotic behavior in the sense described above was for the first time explicitly mentioned in a paper by Koopman and von Neumann (1932): "... the states of motion corresponding to any set M in Ω become more and more spread out into an amorphous everywhere dense chaos. Periodic orbits, and such like, appear only as very special possibilities of negligible probability." Earlier, less specific indications of chaotic behavior are due to Maxwell and Poincaré (cf. Hunt and Yorke 1993). They will be taken up in the philosophical discussion of determinism, causation, and predictability in Sect. 3.

2.3   Information Flow

According to the generally accepted terminology, information theory deals with the transmission and reception of *knowledge* so that information is a purely epistemic concept. Insofar as information is only finitely accessible, it corresponds to limited, incomplete knowledge. Dynamical systems can be interpreted as information-processing systems (Shaw 1981) with the KS-entropy h_T as the information flow rate (Goldstein 1981). This can be demonstrated replacing the notion of a perturbation δx in Sect. 2.1 by the notion of a corresponding uncertainty (incomplete knowledge). In this way the stability analysis of a system is changed into an informational analysis. At the same time, the discussion is shifted from an ontic description (reference state as phase point) to an epistemic description (uncertainty as phase volume). An approximation of the resulting flow of Shannon information I is given by

$$I(t) = I(0) - h_T t. \tag{8}$$

It applies to conservative as well as dissipative systems. In information theoretical terms, the inverse of h_T estimates the time interval τ for which the behavior of the system can reasonably well be predicted from its deterministic equations.

> **Remarks:** (1) Here and in the remainder of this article, the concept of information is restricted to Shannon information, i.e., it is solely used in a syntactic sense, without any reference to semantics or pragmatics. (2) The partition due to uncertainties is in general different from the partition P introduced in Section 2.2. For instance, the generating partition is generically given by the dynamics of a system, whereas the concept of an uncertainty refers to an experimental resolution or other external conditions. (3) The linearity of the information flow is "spurious" in the sense that it is a mere consequence of the linearity of the stability analysis on which its derivation is based. It is well-known that any linear analysis is only locally valid, hence the KS-entropy h_T, interpreted as an information flow rate, represents a (moving) average of local information flow rates. (4) Strictly speaking, there is an additional contribution of the partial dimensions in the proportionality factor for t (Farmer 1982) (cf. the remark on Pesin's identity in Section 2). See Caves (1994) for a more detailed discussion of information flow in chaotic Hamiltonian systems.

The temporal decrease of $I(t)$ for $h_T > 0$ describes how fast an external observer loses information about the actual state of a system with time. It is tempting to interpret this as an increasing amount of information in the system itself, generated by its intrinsic instability due to positive Lyapunov exponents amplifying initial uncertainties exponentially (Atmanspacher and Scheingraber 1987). Since such an internal view goes beyond the regime of a purely epistemic scenario, this temptation must be resisted if one wishes to stay within the scheme provided by a clean ontic/epistemic distinction. The same argument holds if the notion of information is replaced by entropy (Elskens and Prigogine 1986). Weizsäcker's terminology uses *potential* information (Weizsäcker 1985, Zucker 1974), indicating exactly where the problem lies: the referent of this term becomes *actual* information if and only if it becomes epistemic. Atmanspacher (1989) discusses the interplay between these concepts, including the transition from infinite to finite information and some of its ramifications.

Another approach dealing with this problem area has been proposed by Zurek (1989) (see also Caves 1993). He defines "physical entropy" as the sum of missing information plus known randomness according to $S = H + C$, where H is the conventional statistical entropy (outside view) and C is the algorithmic randomness (à la Kolmogorov (1965) and Chaitin (1966), also called algorithmic information content or algorithmic complexity) of a data string produced by the system's evolution (inside view). The problem with the second term is that the corresponding states of the system must be "known" to some "information gathering and using system" (IGUS). Insofar as an IGUS is definitely epistemic if it is supposed to gather and use information (finitely), it cannot be relevant at the ontic, internal level. However, Zurek's favorite IGUS, a universal Turing machine (UTM), has infinite capabilities of storing and processing information. This can justify an ontic interpretation of C but cuts the connection to empirical access. A UTM in this sense is nothing other than Laplace's, Maxwell's, or someone else's demon. In the framework of a strict distinction of ontic and epistemic levels of description, Zurek's approach thus appears conceptually problematic.

There is by definition no way of gathering (or using) information about a reality referred to by an ontic description since it is exactly the act of information gathering that leads to an epistemic concept of realism differing from its ontic counterpart. Yet one may want to discuss how far insight into an ontic reality might be inferrable in an *indirect* manner. Rössler's conception of "endophysics" ("the study of demons"; Rössler 1987) seems to be inclined toward such a purpose. But eventually, endophysics according to Rössler is even more ambitious than addressing an ontic reality in the sense of quantum theory (for a corresponding discussion see Atmanspacher and Dalenoort 1994). Hence the question remains open whether the framework of an ontic/epistemic distinction provides a suitable embedding for approaches like Rössler's.

In another paper (Atmanspacher 1997) it has been argued in more detail why concepts such as information and complexity are unsuitable for ontic descriptions. This implies that approaches seeking to derive fundamental natural laws from information theoretical arguments (e.g. Stonier 1990 or Frieden 1998, but also Chalmers 1996 (pp. 276–319) in his double-aspect approach to treat the "hard problem" of consciousness) are ill-posed in principle and represent another wide-spread example of a category mistake resulting from a confusion of ontic and epistemic perspectives. Even the simplest, syntactical, information theoretical concepts always require a context and an associated contextual topology to be specified with respect to which information can be defined. A basic example is a (finite) phase space partition without which (finite) information about the state of a system cannot be defined. According to different contexts, different partitions can or must be used. For instance, the generating partition that provides the KS-entropy of a system (cf. Sec. 2.2) is inhomogeneous for any nonlinear system and depends on its particular dynamics.

> **Remark:** Searle has paraphrased the same objection with his dictum that syntax is not intrinsic to physics just as semantics is not intrinsic to syntax (Searle 1997, pp. 17, 109). To be precise, this objection presupposes a certain kind of (analytical) bottom-up argumentation in the sense that information can be decomposed into its syntactic, semantic, and pragmatic components. From a top-down point of view one could argue that the phenomenological ("Lebenswelt"-) significance of information derives from the irrelevance of such a decomposition. In such a perspective, every element of syntax is inseparably linked to aspects of meaning and use, and it does not make sense to consider each of them separately. Admitting this as a possible conception, however, does not tell us how it could possibly be related to the analytical perspective dealing with fundamental natural laws.

The value of approaches using syntactic information lies somewhere else. Instead of searching for the significance of these approaches in fundamental, ontic descriptions, information can be extremely useful as an epistemic concept mediating between different levels in a hierarchy of descriptions. Such a usage highlights information as a paradigm of a conceptual tool for intertheoretical purposes, i.e., for syntactic relations between different levels of description (see, e.g., Atmanspacher et al. 1991). This, however, does not allow us to dispense with the crucial requirement that each one of these levels needs to be contextually defined rather than being universally prescribed.

3 Determinism, Causation, and Predictability

3.1 Laplace, Maxwell, Poincaré

In his famous quotation on determinism in his "Essai philosophique sur les probabilités", Laplace (1812) addressed a distinctively ontic type of determinism:

> "We ought to regard the present state of the universe as the effect of its antecedent state and as the cause of the state that is to follow. An

intelligence knowing all the forces acting in nature at a given instant, as well as the momentary position of all things in the universe, would be able to comprehend in one single formula the motions of the largest bodies as well as the lightest atoms in the world, provided that its intellect were sufficiently powerful to subject all data to analysis; to it nothing would be uncertain, the future as well as the past would be present to its eyes."

The intelligence in question became known as Laplace's demon; its capabilities reach beyond the epistemic realm of empirical observation and knowledge. Moreover, Laplace presumes a direction of time when talking about cause and effect. Such a temporal order is absent in the last two lines of the quotation which refer to a type of determinism more general than causation.

More than half a century later, in 1873, Maxwell delivered an address at Cambridge University concerning the debate between determinism and free will in which he said (Campbell and Garnett 1882):

"It is a metaphysical doctrine that from the same antecedents follow the same consequences. No one can gainsay this. But it is not of much use in a world like this, in which the same antecedents never again concur, and nothing ever happens twice. ... The physical axiom which has a somewhat similar aspect is 'that from like antecedents follow like consequences'. But here we have passed ... from absolute accuracy to a more or less rough approximation. There are certain classes of phenomena ... in which a small error in the data only introduces a small error in the result. ... There are other classes of phenomena which are more complicated, and in which cases of instability may occur ..."

Maxwell clearly distinguishes ontic and epistemic descriptions as based on the notions of stability and uncertainty in this quote. His focus is on causation though – his argument is on antecedents and consequences in the sense of causes and effects. If they are understood as ontic states at earlier and later times, the statement "from like antecedents follow like consequences" characterizes a strong version of causation which is not applicable to chaotic systems. Weak causation, which is relevant for chaotic systems, does not contradict the "metaphysical" (ontological) statement that "from the same antecedents follow the same consequences". In the framework of strong causation small changes in the intial conditions for a process can only result in small changes after any amount of time. Weak causation includes the possibility that small changes in the initial conditions can be amplified as a function of time. Corresponding processes depend sensitively on initial conditions such that "same consequences" can only be obtained by "same antecedents".

Early in the last century, Maxwell's formulation was refined by Poincaré (1908):

> "If we knew exactly the laws of nature and the situation of the universe at the initial moment, we could predict exactly the situation of that same universe at a succeeding moment. But, even if it were the case that the natural laws had no longer any secret for us, we could still only know the initial situation approximately. If that enabled us to predict the succeeding situation with the same approximation, that is all we require, and we should say that the phenomenon had been predicted, that it is governed by laws. But it is not always so; it may happen that small differences in the initial conditions produce very great ones in the final phenomena. A small error in the former will produce an enormous error in the latter. Prediction becomes impossible ..."

Here, the issue of predictability is addressed explicitly. Its obviously epistemic meaning at the end of the quote appears to be somewhat confused with ontic arguments at its beginning. "If we knew exactly ..." alludes to Laplace's demon with its ontic realm of relevance, but it is immediately mixed up with causation ("initial conditions", "succeeding moment") and epistemic predictability ("we could predict"). Let us now look at these concepts and their role in chaotic behavior in a more systematic way.

3.2 Ontic Determinism and Epistemic Chaos

The recent creation of the term "deterministic chaos" expresses the tension between ontic (hidden) lawfulness and epistemic (apparent) irregularity in chaotic systems. Our description of the underlying laws of nature, e.g. by differential equations governing the dynamics of such systems, is no doubt deterministic, but their observable behavior is everything but determinable (in the sense of measurable, computable, or predictable) with arbitrary precision. Deterministic chaos is deterministic, yet not determinable. This distinction between determinism and determinability again refers to the distinction between ontic and epistemic descriptions. While determinism relates to inquiries into an independent ("when nobody looks"), ontic reality, determinability expresses an approach referring to our epistemic knowledge about that reality.

Although the original motivation for an ontic/epistemic distinction in physics came from quantum theory, the preceding sections have demonstrated that it is also important and useful in classical physics. Classical point mechanics provides an illustrative example of a "degeneracy" which confuses ontic and epistemic levels, whereas classical statistical mechanics is clearly epistemic. States in the sense of phase points $x \in \Omega$ and continuous trajectories $\{x(t)\}$ refer to an ontic description that can formally be expressed by an infinite refinement of Ω. Referring to empirically accessible states would require one to use phase volumes associated with finite knowledge. Corresponding concepts like probability measures μ, measurable subsets A, or partitions P are relevant in epistemic descriptions. Insofar as our knowledge about a state of a system and its properties is incomplete in principle, epistemic states rather than ontic states have to be used for a description of the empirically accessible world. In this spirit, the notion of a perturbation δx together with an ontic reference state may be understood to constitute a measurable subset $A \subset \Omega$, i.e. a phase volume $(\delta x)^d$. And, of course, such a volume can then be reasonably endowed with an interpretation in terms of a finite amount of information.

> **Remark:** As Bishop (1999) has pointed out in detail, recent work of the Brussels-Austin group of Prigogine and collaborators contains aspects in which they deal with epistemic terms in an ontic manner. This is most conspicuous in their treatment of distributions rather than points as their fundamental representation of the state of a system. Although this can easily lead to ontic/epistemic confusions, such a conception is not a priori wrong. It can acquire consistent meaning if distributions are considered as inseparable wholes, formalized by ontic set functions rather than epistemic probability distributions over ontic point functions (cf. relative onticity, Atmanspacher and Kronz 1998, Lombardi in this volume). Prigogine's apparently contradictory ideas of irreversibility as an ontic property and its epistemic emergence from reversibility (Petrosky and Prigogine 1997) may be reconcilable on such a basis.

The temporal evolution of an ontic state remains empirically unrecognizable as long as this ontic state belongs to the same epistemic state, i.e., as long as it stays in one and the same phase cell of a chosen or otherwise given partition. Refinements of partitions are possible, but they can never be infinite for all empirical purposes. If neighboring phase points keep their initial distance from each other constant during the evolution of the system, they will (as a rule) not change their status of indistinguishability with respect to a given partition. However, if this distance increases as a function of time, this is no longer so. Initially indistinguishable phase points may become distinguishable after a certain amount of time τ, since they may move into different phase cells. This is precisely the case for chaotic systems, for which τ can be estimated by h_T^{-1}. For $t < \tau$, one can speak of a specific type of temporal nonlocality (Misra and Prigogine 1983, Atmanspacher and Amann 1998).

This clearly constitutes a measurement problem, though conceptually different from that of quantum theory (Crutchfield 1994, Atmanspacher et al. 1995). As we know today, classical point mechanics gets along with its ontic/epistemic degeneracy only if chaotic processes are disregarded. Misusing a notion coined by Whittaker (1943), one might paraphrase the deterministic, yet non-determinable behavior of such systems as "cryptodeterminism". Using the terminology of causation, chaotic systems are weakly causative, whereas non-chaotic systems with $h_T = 0$ are strongly causative.

The basic ontic determinism of any deterministic system (including deterministic chaos) is referred to by a time-reversal symmetric (reversible) kinematical description of the evolution of its ontic state. If the time-reversal symmetry is broken, two types of evolution with temporal directions describable by two semigroups, are obtained. In general, one of them corresponds to the kind of forward causation which we observe and characterize with the statement "causes precede effects". The other one, corresponding to backward causation, is usually disregarded in science. It expresses the strange feature of effects temporally preceding causes as a form of *causa finalis* as opposed to *causa efficiens*. It is important to realize, however, that there are no a priori reasons to select one of the two temporal directions at the expense of the other. Such a selection has to be based on additional arguments; see, e.g., Primas (1992).

> **Remark:** *Causa efficiens* and *causa finalis* are only two among four causes as introduced by Aristotle. They can be used in correspondence with the two temporal directions obtained by breaking the time-reversal symmetry of a unitary group evolution. In this usage they refer to the same level of description. It may be speculated that the remaining two causes, *causa formalis* and *causa materialis*, can be interpreted according to interlevel relationships in the sense of "downward" and "upward" causation. In any case, such an interlevel causation must not be confused with "intralevel" causation as discussed here.

The introduction of a temporal direction is a decisive step, required to proceed from determinism in a most general sense to forward and/or backward causation. In the case of chaotic systems, the selection of forward causation is realized by focusing on positive Lyapunov exponents and, correspondingly, positive KS-entropy as in Sections 2.1 and 2.2. Weak causation (forward or backward) is compatible with Maxwell's "metaphysical" (ontological) statement that same causes are needed to provide same effects. Its variant, that like causes lead to like effects, reflects strong causation and stands in question when epistemic terms like predictability and retrodictability as specific types of determinability (in contrast to determinism) are addressed. Strong causation is incompatible with the behavior of chaotic systems where predictions with arbitrary accuracy are impossible. However, this does not imply anything against determinism in its basic sense (see Boyd 1972, Earman 1986, Stone 1989). An incorrect prediction does not falsify determinism just as a correct prediction does not verify determinism.

4 Determinism, Randomness, and Stochasticity

The concept of determinism is insufficiently represented if it is compared only with causality and predictability. Two other important areas with their own traditions are the determinism–freewill and determinism–randomness controversies. While the issue of free will and freedom in general definitely exceeds the scope of this contribution (see Honderich 1988, Kane 1996; see also Guignon, Honderich, Kane, Richardson and Bishop in this volume) some fragmentary remarks concerning the relationships between determinism, randomness, and stochasticity are of interest.

From the viewpoint of the theory of nonlinear dynamical systems as discussed in Sec. 2.1, randomness is often considered as the behavior of a system with $h_T \to \infty$, i.e. $\tau \to 0$. The classification sketched in Sec. 2.1 provides the tools to reconsider the traditional dichotomy of perfectly regular and perfectly "random" behavior ($h_T = 0$ and $h_T \to \infty$, respectively) as extreme cases of a continuum of chaotic behavior ($0 \leq h_T < \infty$). This reflects the idea of finite predictability horizons whose limiting values are $\tau \to \infty$ in perfectly regular processes and $\tau \to 0$ for perfectly "random" processes.

Random behavior is a key topic in the theory of stochastic processes, where the behavior of a system is described in terms of so-called random variables $\xi(x)$, i.e., real-valued Borel functions defined on Ω. In the framework of Kolmogorov's probability theory a statistical observable defines an equivalence class $[\xi(x)]$ of random variables on a Kolmogorov space (Ω, Σ, ν). A stochastic process, parametrized by time $t \in \mathbb{R}$, is then represented by a family of equivalence classes $\{[\xi(t|x)]\}$. The description of a system in terms of an individual trajectory corresponds to a point dynamics of an ontic state, whereas a description in terms of an equivalence class of trajectories and an associated probability measure corresponds to an ensemble dynamics of an epistemic state. For a compact overview containing more details, see Primas (1999).

In the theory of stochastic processes, the extreme cases mentioned above correspond to special types of transition matrices. For instance, singular stochastic processes are completely deterministic and allow a perfect prediction of the future from the past. The general case of limited predictability is covered by the notion of a regular stochastic process. This analogy notwithstanding, comprehensive accounts or textbooks dealing with explicit relationships between the theories of nonlinear systems and stochastic processes in general have only become available recently, see the books by Lasota and Mackey (1995) and Arnold (1998). The difference between deterministic and stochastic approaches is made especially clear in Arnold's discussion of conceptual differences between the "two cultures" (e.g. pp. 68ff).

A major point of discrepancy in this respect is that (in most standard treatises) stochastic processes are intrinsically understood as time-directed (semigroup evolution). By contrast, the ergodic theory of dynamical systems considers a time-reversal symmetric (group) dynamics, offering the possibility of symmetry breakings that lead to forward as well as backward deterministic processes. In earlier work, Arnold and Kliemann (1983) introduced the concept of Lyapunov exponents for linear stochastic systems (of arbitrary dimension) rather than low-dimensional chaos in nonlinear deterministic systems. More recently, the basis of these approaches, Oseledec's multiplicative ergodic theorem, has been generalized from formulations in Euclidean space to manifolds (cf. Arnold 1998).

The dichotomy of ontic and epistemic descriptions is also prominent in the theory of stochastic differential equations. For instance, Langevin type equations generally treat stochastic contributions in addition to a deterministic flow in terms of fluctuations around the trajectory of a point x in phase space. Such a picture clearly reflects an ontic approach. On the other hand, the evolution of epistemic states μ, i.e., densities, is typically described by Fokker-Planck type equations with drift terms and diffusion terms accounting for deterministic and non-deterministic (i.e., random or stochastic) contributions to the motion of μ in phase space. Although both types of formulations can be shown to be "equivalent" in a certain sense (see, e.g., Haken 1983 for an elementary discussion), this must not be misunderstood as a conceptual equivalence. Knowledge which would be available in an ontic description is missing in an epistemic description.

It is not surprising that deterministic processes such as fixed points or periodic cycles can be considered as special cases of more general formulations in terms of stochastic processes. What comes somewhat as a surprise is the converse, namely that stochastic processes can be understood in terms of deterministic processes. This has been accomplished by means of a mathematical theory of so-called natural extensions or dilations of stochastic processes (see Gustafson and Misra in this volume).

> **Remark:** Gustafson (1997) discusses three types of corresponding di-
> lation theories. Consider a flow T_t on subsets of a phase space Ω,
> and consider the space (Ω, Σ, ν) of probability densities μ defined over
> Ω. Then dilations according to Halmos, Sz. Nagy, Foias, Naimark and
> others dilate the densities μ, dilations according to Kolmogorov and
> Rokhlin dilate the flow T_t, and dilations according to Akcoglu, Suche-
> ston and others dilate the reference measure ν. For details on literature
> see also Gustafson and Rao (1997).

Their common feature is the extension of a (non-invertible, irreversible)
Markov semigroup evolution to a (reversible, invertible) unitary group evolution. Applying the dilation theory of exact systems to K-flows (Rokhlin
1961, cf. Lasota and Mackey 1995, e.g. Sec. 4.5), Antoniou and Gustafson
(1997) have recently achieved important progress with the proof of a theorem on the positivity-preservation of densities in unitary dilations (see also
Gustafson 1997, pp. 61–68). Roughly speaking, the significance of this theorem is that stochastic processes can generally be embedded deterministically.
Its meaning in particular physical contexts remains to be specified.

5 Summary

The distinction between ontic and epistemic descriptions of physical systems
has been primarily discussed for quantum systems so far. In this contribution, this distinction is demonstrated to be equally important for a special
class of classical systems, namely those denoted as K-flows or deterministic
chaos.

It turns out that stability aspects generically relate to ontic descriptions,
whereas information aspects relate to epistemic descriptions. The dynamical
entropy according to Kolmogorov and Sinai can be considered as a concept
mediating between the two kinds of description. A number of information
theoretical claims in the contemporary literature about chaos are shown to
be misleading due to their confusion of ontic and epistemic levels.

The concepts of determinism, causation, and predictability are distinguished and related to each other by their ontic and epistemic relevance,
respectively. Determinism in the basic sense addressed here is the most ontic of the three terms. It requires neither a direction of time nor makes
use of any epistemic state concept. Causation (forward or backward) needs
a direction of time. In its weak and strong versions, it can be related to
epistemic and ontic concepts, respectively. Predictability based on the past
(e.g. memory) and retrodictability based on the future (e.g. anticipation)
are specific types of determinability as opposed to determinism, referring to

epistemic states only and presupposing the breaking of a basic deterministic time-reversal symmetry.

Finally, it is well-known (and trivial) that deterministic systems can be embedded in the framework of stochastic systems. Less well known is the fact that the converse is also true: using the theory of natural extensions, stochastic processes can be embedded deterministically.

Acknowledgments

I am grateful to Robert Bishop, Karl Gustafson, and Hans Primas for suggestions how to improve an earlier version of this article.

References

Amann A. and Atmanspacher H. (1998): Fluctuations in the dynamics of single quantum systems. *Stud. Hist. Phil. Mod. Phys.* **29**, 151–182.

Antoniou I. and Qiao B. (1996): Spectral decomposition of the tent maps and the isomorphism of dynamical systems. *Phys. Lett. A* **215**, 280–290.

Antoniou I. and Gustafson K. (1997): From irreversible Markov semigroups to chaotic dynamics. *Physica A* **236**, 296–308.

Antoniou I., Sadovnichii V.A., and Shkarin S.A. (1999): New extended spectral decomposition of the Renyi map. *Phys. Lett. A* **258**, 237–243.

Arnold L. (1998): *Random Dynamical Systems*, Springer, Berlin.

Arnold L. and Kliemann W. (1983): Qualitative theory of stochastic systems. In *Probabilistic Analysis and Related Topics, Vol. 3*, ed. by A.T. Bharucha-Reid, Academic Press, New York, pp. 1–79.

Atmanspacher H. (1989): The aspect of information production in the process of observation. *Found. Phys.* **19**, 553–577.

Atmanspacher H., Krueger F.R., and Scheingraber, H. (1991): A modal propositional calculus fr quantum facts and dynamical theories. In *Parallelism, Learning, Evolution*, ed. by J.D. Becker, I. Eisele, and F.W. Mündemann (Springer, Berlin), pp. 304–314.

Atmanspacher H. (1997): Cartesian cut, Heisenberg cut, and the concept of complexity. *World Futures* **49**, 333–355.

Atmanspacher H. and Dalenoort G.J. (1994): Introduction. In *Inside Versus Outside*, ed. by H. Atmanspacher and G.J. Dalenoort (Springer, Berlin), pp. 1–12; in particular pp. 6–9.

Atmanspacher H. and Kronz F. (1998): Many realisms. *Acta Polytechnica Scandinavica* **Ma-91**, 31–43.

Atmanspacher H. and Scheingraber H. (1987): A fundamental link between system theory and statistical mechanics. *Found. Phys.* **17**, 939–963.

Atmanspacher H., Wiedenmann G., and Amann A. (1995): Descartes revisited – the endo/exo-distinction and its relevance for the study of complex systems. *Complexity* **1**(3), pp. 15–21.

Bishop R. (1999): Chaotic Dynamics, Indeterminacy, and Free Will. PhD thesis, University of Texas at Austin.

Bohm D. (1980): *Wholeness and the Implicate Order*. Routledge and Kegan Paul, London.

Boyd R. (1972): Determinism, laws and predictability in principle. *Philosophy of Science* **39**, 431–450.

Campbell L. and Garnett W. (1882): *The Life of James Clerk Maxwell*, Macmillan, London. Reprinted by Johnson Reprint, New York 1969, p. 440.

Caves C.M. (1993): Information and entropy. *Phys. Rev. A* **47**, 4010–4017.

Caves C. (1994): Information, entropy, and chaos. In *Physical Origins of Time Asymmetry*, ed. by J.J. Halliwell, J. Pérez-Mercader, and W.H. Zurek (Cambridge University Press, Cambridge), pp. 47–89.

Chaitin, G. (1966): On the length of programs for computing finite binary sequences. *J. ACM* **13**, 145–159.

Chalmers D. (1996): *The Conscious Mind*, Oxford University Press, Oxford.

Cornfeld I.P., Fomin S.V., and Sinai Ya.G. (1982): *Ergodic Theory* (Springer, Berlin), 250–252, 280–284.

Connes A., Narnhofer H., and Thirring W. (1987): Dynamical entropy of C^*-algebras and von Neumann algebras. *Commun. Math. Phys.* **112**, 691–719.

Crutchfield J.P. (1994): Observing complexity and the complexity of observation. In *Inside Versus Outside*, ed. by H. Atmanspacher and G.J. Dalenoort (Springer, Berlin), 235–272; in particular sec. 2.1.

d'Espagnat B. (1995): *Veiled Reality*. Addison-Wesley, Reading.

Earman J. (1986): *A Primer on Determinism*. Dordrecht, Reidel, Chap. II.

Einstein A., Podolsky B., and Rosen N. (1935): Can quantum-mechanical description of physical reality be considered complete? *Phys. Rev.* **47**, 777–780.

Elskens Y. and Prigogine I. (1986): From instability to irreversibility. *Proc. Natl. Acad. Sci. USA* **83**, 5756–5760.

Farmer D. (1982): Information dimension and the probabilistic structure of chaos. *Z. Naturforsch.* **37a**, 1304–1325.

Fetzer J.H. and Almeder R.F. (1993): *Glossary of Epistemology/Philosophy of Science* (Paragon House, New York), p. 100f.

Frieden B.R. (1998): *Physics from Fisher Information*, Cambridge University Press, Cambridge.

Goldstein S. (1981): Entropy increase in dynamical systems. *Israel J. Math.* **38**, 241–256.

Grassberger P. and Procaccia I. (1983): Estimation of the Kolmogorov entropy from a chaotic signal. *Phys. Rev. A* **28**, 2591–2593.

Gustafson K. (1997). *Lectures on Computational Fluid Dynamics, Mathematical Physics, and Linear Algebra.* World Scientific, Singapore, pp. 61–68.

Gustafson K.E. and Rao D.K.M. (1997). *Numerical Range.* Springer, Berlin, pp. 42–46.

Haken H. (1983): *Synergetics.* Springer, Berlin, Chap. 6.

Harré R. (1997): Is there a basic ontology for the physical sciences? *Dialectica* **51**, 17–34.

Heisenberg W. (1958): *Physics and Philosophy*, Harper and Row, New York.

Honderich T. (1988): *A Theory of Determinism*, Oxford University Press, Oxford.

Howard D. (1997): Space-time and separability: problems of identity and individuation in fundamental physics. In *Potentiality, Entanglement, and Passion-at-a-Distance*, ed. by R.S. Cohen, M. Horne, and J. Stachel (Kluwer, Dordrecht), pp. 113–141.

Hudetz T. (1988): Spacetime dynamical entropy of quantum systems. *Lett. Math. Phys.* **16**, 151–161.

Hunt B.R. and Yorke J.A. (1993): Maxwell on chaos. *Nonlinear Science Today* **3**(1), 1–4.

Jammer M. (1974): *The Philosophy of Quantum Mechanics*, Wiley, New York.

Kane R. (1996): *The Significance of Free Will*, Oxford University Press, Oxford.

Kolmogorov A.N. (1958): A new metric invariant of transitive systems and automorphisms of Lebesgue spaces. *Dokl. Akad. Nauk SSSR* **119**, 861–864.

Kolmogorov, A.N. (1965): Three approaches to the quantitative definition of complexity. *Problems in Inf. Transm.* **1**, 3–11.

Koopman B. and Neumann J. von (1932): Dynamical systems of continuous spectra. *Proc. Natl. Acad. Sci. USA* **18**, 255–263, here: p. 261.

Laplace P.S. de (1812): Preface to *A Philosophical Essay on Probabilities*, Dover, New York 1951. Quoted from E.Nagel: *The Structure of Science*, Harcourt, Brace, and World, New York 1961, p. 281–282.

Lasota A. and Mackey M.C. (1985): *Chaos, Fractals, and Noise*. Springer, Berlin.

Ledrappier F. and Young L.-S. (1985): The metric entropy of diffeomorphisms. Part I: Characterization of measures satisfying Pesin's entropy formula. Part II: Relations between entropy, exponents, and dimension. *Ann. Math.* **122**, 509–574.

Margenau H. (1949): Reality in quantum mechanics. *Phil. Science* **16**, 287–302, here: p. 297.

Milnor J. (1985): On the concept of attractor. *Commun. Math. Phys.* **99**, 177–195; correction and remark: *Commun. Math. Phys.* **102**, 517–519 (1985).

Misra B. and Prigogine I. (1983): Irreversibility and nonlocality. *Lett. Math. Phys.* **7**, 421–429.

Neumann, J. von (1932): *Mathematische Grundlagen der Quantenmechanik* (Springer, Berlin). English translation: *Mathematical Foundations of Quantum Mechanics* (Princeton University Press, Princeton 1955).

Oono Y. (1989): Large deviations and statistical physics. *Prog. Theor. Phys. Suppl.* **99**, 165–205.

Pesin Ya.B. (1977): Characteristic Lyapunov exponents and smooth ergodic theory. *Russian Math. Surveys* **32**, 55–114. Russian original: *Uspekhi Mat. Nauk* **32**, 55–112.

Petrosky T. and Prigogine I. (1997): The Liouville space extension of quantum mechanics. *Adv. Chem. Phys.* **XCIX**, 1–120, here p. 71.

Poincaré H. (1908): *Science et Méthode*, Flammarion, Paris 1908. Translated by F. Maitland: *Science and Method*, Dover, New York 1952, p. 68.

Popper K.R. (1957): The propensity interpretation of probability, and quantum mechanics. In *Observation and Interpretation in the Philosophy of Physics – With special reference to Quantum Mechanics*, ed. by S. Körner in collaboration with M.H.L. Pryce (Constable, London), pp. 65–70. Reprinted by Dover, New York 1962.

Primas H. (1990): Mathematical and philosophical questions in the theory of open and macroscopic quantum systems. In *Sixty-Two Years of Uncertainty*, ed. by A.I. Miller (Plenum, New York), pp. 233–257.

Primas H. (1992): Time-asymmetric phenomena in biology. Complementary exophysical descriptions arising from deterministic quantum endophysics. *Open Systems & Information Dynamics* **1**, 3–34.

Primas H. (1994): Endo- and exo-theories of matter. In *Inside Versus Outside. Endo- and Exo-Concepts of Observation and Knowledge in Physics, Philosophy, and Cognitive Science*, ed. by H. Atmanspacher and G.J. Dalenoort (Springer, Berlin), pp. 163–193.

Primas H. (1998): Emergence in exact natural sciences. *Acta Polytechnica Scandinavica* **Ma 91**, 83–98. See also Primas (1983), *Chemistry, Quantum Mechanics, and Reductionism* (Springer, Berlin), Chap. 6.

Primas H. (1999): Basic elements and problems of probability theory. *J. Sci. Explor.* **13**, 579–613.

Rössler O.E. (1987): Endophysics. In *Real Brains, Artificial Minds*, ed. by J.L. Casti and A. Karlqvist (North Holland, New York), 25–46.

Rokhlin V.A. (1961): Exact endomorphisms of a Lebesgue space. *Izv. Acad. Sci. USSR, Ser. Mat.* **25**, 499–530. English translation: *AMS Transl.* **39**, 1–36 (1964).

Ruelle D. (1981): Small random perturbations of dynamical systems and the definition of attractors. *Commun. Math. Phys.* **82**, 137–151.

Scheibe E. (1973): *The Logical Analysis of Quantum Mechanics* (Pergamon, Oxford), pp. 82–88.

Schrödinger E. (1935): Die gegenwärtige Situation in der Quantenmechanik. *Naturwiss.* **23**, 807–812, 823–828, 844–849.

Searle J.R. (1997): *The Mystery of Consciousness*, New York Review of Books, New York.

Shaw R. (1981): Strange attractors, chaotic behavior, and information flow. *Z. Naturforsch.* **36a**, 80–112.

Sinai Ya.G. (1959): On the concept of entropy of a dynamical system. *Dokl. Akad. Nauk SSSR* **124**, 768–771.

Stone M. (1989): Chaos, prediction, and Laplacian determinism. *Am. Phil. Quart.* **26**, 123–131.

Stonier T. (1990): *Information and the Internal Structure of the Universe.* Springer, London.

Tasaki S., Suchanecki Z., and Antoniou I. (1993): Ergodic properties of piecewise linear maps on fractal repellers. *Phys. Lett. A* **179**, 103–110.

Wehrl A. (1991): The many facets of entropy. *Rep. Math. Phys.* **30**, 119–129.

Weizsäcker C.F. von (1985): *Aufbau der Physik* (Hanser, München), Chap. 5

Whittaker E.T. (1943): Chance, freewill, and necessity in the scientific conception of the universe. *Proc. Phys. Soc. (London)* **55**, 459–471; here p. 461.

Zucker F.J. (1974): Information, Entropie, Komplementarität und Zeit. In *Offene Systeme I*, ed. by E. v. Weizsäcker, Klett, Stuttgart, pp. 35–81.

Zurek W.H. (1989): Algorithmic randomness and physical entropy. *Phys. Rev. A* **40**, 4731–4751.

Determinism, Internalism and Objectivity

Olimpia Lombardi

Abstract

One of the most long-standing debates in the history of philosophy results from the confrontation between realism and relativism. For the metaphysical realist there is only one "real" ontology, and this ontology is taken as the object of our objective knowledge. For the relativist, by contrast, objectivity is relative to the historical or cultural context. Putnam's internalism has been proposed as a middle way between these opposing views, and has wide repercussion for many areas of philosophy. According to internalism, ontology is framework-dependent, so "objective" does not mean independent of the subject, but, rather, resulting from applying our frameworks to a reality behind the world of our experience.

The internalist perspective was not originally proposed to face controversial questions in philosophy of science, such as the problem of the objectivity of scientific descriptions. Nevertheless, it will be argued that internalism provides the proper philosophical approach to deal with the problem of the compatibility between deterministic and indeterministic descriptions in highly unstable systems. When the framework-dependence of ontology is accepted, both descriptions become objective because each one of them cuts out its own entities from the same underlying reality. It will also be suggested that internalism can be applied to other traditional problems in the philosophy of physics – such as debates about irreversibility and locality – and to the classical mind-matter problem in the philosophy of mind. Finally, some remaining problems regarding the notion of an underlying reality and the conception of reduction will be discussed.

1   Chaos Theory

Even though the precise definition of chaos is still a matter of debate (cf. Batterman 1993, Smith 1998), most authors agree on some central points:

- Chaotic systems are described by nonlinear differential equations whose solutions always exist and are unique. This means that there is only one possible evolution of the system for each initial condition.

- Chaotic systems are highly sensitive to initial conditions; that is, their time evolutions diverge exponentially fast. This feature has an important physical consequence: It becomes impossible to predict the long-time behavior of chaotic systems because their initial conditions can only be fixed with finite accuracy and errors increase exponentially fast.

These concepts are usually formulated in the geometric language of phase space. Given a system, its phase space is a Euclidean space of dimension n, where each coordinate represents a mechanical variable of the system, each point of the phase space represents a micro-state, and the system's evolution is represented by a trajectory starting at the point representative of the initial conditions. The *micro*-description of chaotic systems is *deterministic*, meaning that, given the point representative of the initial conditions, there is only one trajectory that never intersects itself. However, one can define a macro-level resulting from a coarse-grained partition of the phase space, where each cell of non-zero volume represents a macro-state of the system and each possible macro-evolution is defined by a possible succession of macro-states. It can be proved that, at this macro-level, chaotic systems have the statistical properties of a K-system. In a K-system, the only macro-states that can be univocally predicted are those that have probability zero or one independent of the macro-history of the system. This means that the *macro*-description of chaotic systems is *indeterministic* because the past macro-evolution of the system does not fix its future macro-evolution. The Kolmogorov entropy K measuring the degree of the system's instability is the most important quantity for characterizing chaotic motion. For chaotic systems, K has a value larger than zero and is independent of the size of the coarse-grained partition (cf. Schuster 1984).

2   The Problem of Determinism

If in chaotic systems micro-descriptions are deterministic and coarse-grained macro-descriptions are indeterministic, the question as to how to interpret the statistical properties of the macro-level arises. There are disagreements about whether macro-evolutions in such highly unstable systems are objective or subjective.

Some commentators consider the objective description of chaotic systems to be given by the differential equations at the micro-level. For them, since the macro-description is reducible to an underlying deterministic evolution, its statistical properties are *subjective*, apparent, mere illusions only due to our observational limitations. In other words, if we knew the exact microscopic initial conditions of the system, we could predict its future micro-evolution completely and would not need statistical descriptions. This perspective expresses the traditional Laplacean vision, according to which reality is deterministic and probabilities only measure our ignorance about the objective description of the world.

In contrast, other authors consider the statistical properties of chaotic systems as *objective* because they result from the underlying micro-dynamics; that is, because deterministic micro-evolutions are not only compatible with, but actually entail macro-randomness. For example, Ford states that "for chaotic systems, Newtonian determinism may be only a theorist's unattainable dream" (Ford 1983, p. 43). Prigogine expresses the same idea when he announces the final death of Laplace's demon and claims that randomness has become a central element of classical dynamics (see, e.g., Wagensberg 1986). A powerful argument in favor of this interpretation is given by the fact that the K-entropy is independent of the size of the coarse-grained partition. In other words, the statistical properties of chaotic systems do not depend on the observational precision, provided the precision remains finite.

This shows that both interpretations have good arguments for being taken seriously. Maybe for this reason some people fluctuate between them even in the same paper. This is the case for Davies, who claims that chaos "frees" the universe and shows the "reality" of free will, but, at the same time, asserts that "deterministic chaos appears random because we are necessarily ignorant of the ultra-fine detail of just a few degrees of freedom" (Davies 1990, p. 51).

To summarize, the problem of determinism can be stated as follows: is macro-indeterminism subjective due to its reducibility to an underlying deterministic dynamics, or objective because it is generated by the micro-dynamics? In other words, are the probabilities of transitions between macro-states objective or subjective?

3 The Interpretation of Probability

Leaving aside the logical approach to probability and assuming that probability refers to facts, what does probability measure? Subjective probability measures the degree of knowledge about a fact, and is usually referred to as "probability due to ignorance". Its value is a function of the available information about the fact and changes when such information changes. Objective probability, in contrast, measures the degree of the objective possibility of a fact, where possibility is understood in its physical meaning. Both interpretations have their field of application, but we are interested in the relationships between each kind of probability and the determinism or indeterminism of the world. The traditional vision relates determinism to subjective probabilities and indeterminism to objective probabilities. For example, d'Espagnat (1985) assumes this position, linking subjective probabilities to an "apparent" indeterminism, due only to the ignorance of fine details. Popper adopts the same perspective (Popper 1992, p. 105):

> Today I can see why so many determinists, and even ex-determinists who believe in the deterministic character of classical physics, seriously believe in a subjectivist interpretation of probability: it is, in a way, the *only reasonable possibility* which they can accept; for objective physical probabilities are incompatible with determinism.

This traditional vision still has many adherents. For example, in a recent book Kosso distinguishes between the two kinds of probability in the following way (Kosso 1998, p. 114):

> Objective probability is a property of nature itself and applies to events that are genuinely not deterministic [...] Subjective probability is a property of our knowledge of nature and applies to cases where we lack information and so we are uncertain.

But this dichotomy between determinism with subjective probabilities on the one hand, and indeterminism with objective probabilities on the other, deserves closer attention.

Let us suppose that the dynamical description of a system assigns nontrivial transition probabilities to its states. If this description is considered as irreducible, opinions tend to converge towards an objectivist interpretation of probability. But the statistical description may be reducible to a deterministic dynamics in terms of micro-states, in such a way that probabilities vanish from the description. In this case, the traditional vision interprets reducible probabilities as probabilities whose objectivity is apparent only; they are actually subjective probabilities that measure the degree of our ignorance about the real and precise evolution of the system described in terms of micro-states. Therefore, the supposed indeterminism of the statistical descriptions is a mere illusion only due to our partial knowledge of the system.

The question is: why are reducible probabilities subjective? The traditional vision rests on the implicit assumption that *there is only one objective way of describing reality*. Then, every description which does not agree with the objective description is hopelessly subjective. But it is precisely this assumption which requires revision. Let us consider the case of one fair die throw. Whereas the mechanical micro-evolutions are deterministic, at the macro-level the probability of getting, for example, a six is $1/6$. This probability is not subject-dependent but generated by the objective underlying dynamics. The exact form of the dynamical micro-evolution and the proper coarse-graining are precisely the elements that induce the non-trivial probabilities of transition at the macro-level. So, if we are not tied to the traditional assumption about the uniqueness of the objective description of reality, it is hard to deny objectivity to the macro-behavior of the system.

However, those who defend the traditional vision might argue that, if we really knew the exact microscopic initial conditions of the dice, any probability would in reality be reduced to 0 or 1; in our case, the value of the probability of getting a six would go from being $1/6$ to 0 or 1. Then this probability may not be objective because its value changes with the available information about the system, and all non-trivial probabilities arise exclusively as a result of ignorance. But this argument ignores an essential point. The probability $1/6$ of getting a six in the die throw is not an absolute probability, but the conditional probability of getting a six given that the system was in the *initial macro-state E_0*, that is, the die in the dice-cup. The new probability 1 of getting a six is also a conditional probability but different from the first one; it is the probability of getting a six given that the system was in the *initial micro-state e_0*, that is, given the exact mechanical initial conditions. In other words, $1/6$ and 1 are not two values of the subjective probability $Pr(h)$ applied to a single fact, but the values of two conditional probabilities, $Pr(h/E_0)$ and $Pr(h/e_0)$, conditioned on *different initial states*. Then, it is not surprising that two different objective probabilities have different values. In short, $Pr(h/E_0)$ and $Pr(h/e_0)$ are two conditional probabilities, both objective, and each one of them defined at its own level of description. The reducibility of the first one is not an argument against its objectivity. Even though this is not the usual view, some commentators are beginning to admit that the reducibility of a probability does not imply its subjectivity. Clark, for example, explicitly claims (Clark 1987, p. 203): "That every probability is reducible ... in no way shows that those probability measures are not physically real, i.e. are not well-founded dynamically". Earman expresses the same opinion saying (Earman 1986, p. 151):

> The inference: 'objective' as applied to probabilities implies that the probabilities are irreducible, which in turn implies that determinism is false: goes wrong at the first step. $p = 1/2$ (say) for a coin can represent an objective tendency for the coin to land heads up. And the attribution of such an objective tendency is not undercut by the discovery that the outcome of any flip is uniquely determined by the prior micro-state of the system; indeed, if statistical mechanics is our guide, determinism can form part of the explanation of the tendency to land heads up $1/2$ of the time.

In conclusion, the definition of the states and evolution of a system is *relative* to a particular level of description, but this fact does not imply that they are subjective entities. Physics is full of relative concepts, whose objectivity is not questioned. If the traditional assumption about the uniqueness of the objective description of reality is rejected, the alternative between determinism with subjective probabilities and indeterminism with objective probabilities becomes untenable. Objective determinism and indeterminism at different descriptive levels may coexist consistently. The coffee I was drinking while writing these words was not a subjective entity because it can be alternatively described as water with solid particles in suspension, as an aggregate of molecules or as a collection of atoms; each description is relative to some level, but retains its objectivity at its level. Therefore, the point is not to look for the "True Theory", but to realize that different theories cut out their entities from reality in different but equally appropiate ways. It is precisely this vision which leads us to seriously consider internalism as the proper philosophical framework for understanding the problem of determinism in highly unstable systems.

4 Internalist Realism

Putnam begins his book *Reason, Truth and History* (Putnam 1981) by rejecting the objective-subjective dichotomy. From this starting point, he tries to find a middle way between metaphysical realism and radical relativism. Putnam usually calls his vision "internalism" or "internalist realism" as contrasted with externalism or metaphysical realism, also referred to as "the God's Eye perspective".

According to externalism, the objects of the world exist independently of our knowledge and theories, and constitute a fixed totality. Then, there is only one true and complete description of the world, whose truth consists in the correspondence between words and objects. By supposing that reference is a relationship between the words of the language and the external, independent ontology, externalism needs a non-human point of view – God's Eye – to fix the reference of the language and, with this, the truth-value of its sentences.

As Pérez Ransanz (1999) argues, the key to understanding the disagreements between externalism and internalism is the concept of *object*. For the internalist, objects do not exist independently of conceptual schemes because we cut up the world into objects when we introduce one or another descriptive scheme (Putnam 1981). In other words, objects depend on the conceptual schemes in a strong sense, which includes existence. This means that conceptual schemes are not mere intermediary elements between subjects and objects; rather, they play an essential role in the constitution of objects. Therefore, even though there is a reality independent of the subject – a noumenal reality if you will – ontology only arises from a conceptual scheme. Objects resulting from the synthesis between each conceptual scheme and the noumenal reality are the only objects. Objectivity does not mean independence from the subject, but results from our conceptual schemes applied to reality. This is an objectivity *for us*, but it is the only possible objectivity when we have given up the idea of God's point of view.

Now we can go back to the problem of determinism in highly unstable systems. The traditional view implicitly adopts an externalist perspective: if there is a single objective description of reality, then the microscopic description is the objective description and it represents the true ontology. Therefore, chaotic systems are deterministic and the statistical macro-description is a mere subjective appearance due only to our limited observational power. But many scientists are reluctant to accept this conclusion; their scientific work shows them that statistical properties may not be conceived as illusions because they are generated by the micro-dynamics of the system. Then, the indeterministic macro-evolutions are as objective as the underlying deterministic micro-evolutions. However, when the externalist insists on asking for the "true" description of these systems, scientists usually lack satisfactory answers; by not rejecting the externalist assumption, they tend to make category mistakes confusing ontological and epistemological arguments.

An internalist realism gives us a new philosophical framework to deal with this problem. From this point of view, the states and evolutions of a physical system are not description-independent; on the contrary, each theory constitutes a relative ontology when it cuts its own states and evolutions out of the same noumenal substratum. In chaotic systems, the micro-description defines an ontology with micro-states represented by phase points, and deterministic evolutions represented by trajectories in phase space; the macro-description defines an ontology with macro-states represented by cells of non-zero volume, and indeterministic macro-evolutions with their conditional transition probabilities between macro-states (cf. Atmanspacher, this volume). But since the privileged viewpoint of God's Eye does not exist, there is no single true ontology, and both descriptions are equally objective. In this way, the seeming contradiction of assigning determinism and indeterminism to the same system vanishes. When we talk about the same system, we are referring to the *same noumenal substratum*; but there is no contradiction in applying incompatible properties to different ontologies.

5   Perspectives

Assuming that different conceptual schemes define different ontologies leads to the thesis of *ontological pluralism*, a central feature of Putnam's internalism. This thesis has been used against scientific externalism, according to which physics converges to the true description of the real ontology. But internalism applied to the problem of determinism in highly unstable systems adds a new element to the argument. Different ontologies might coexist even in the context of a single paradigm. Despite the fact that these ontologies include different entities, their descriptions can be translated into each other. Therefore, from a consistent internalist point of view we must accept a new ontological picture: Our *phenomenal* world may be organized in many different ontological levels in such a way that the entities and regularities of one level are the result of the entities and regularities of another level. In this stratified reality, no level has ontological priority over the others. All descriptions have the same objective status. Reducibility does not entail non-objectivity.

This new ontological vision is not only useful for unraveling the problem of determinism and indeterminism in chaotic systems, but may be successfully applied to other controversial questions in the philosophy of physics. For example, in the traditional discussion about irreversibility, one of the central problems is explaining how objective macroscopic irreversibility may arise from an underlying reversible dynamics. In the context of quantum mechanics, the problem is about non-locality; that is, how the local, separable objects of our classical theories may emerge from the non-local, holistic ontology described by quantum theory. Both cases share a common feature with the case of unstable systems: at the macro-level there is a property whose objectivity we cannot deny; the problem is explaining such objectivity when the underlying micro-level does not possess this property. Even though determinism, reversibility and locality have their own technical peculiarities, the common feature they share suggests that internalism might be the proper philosophical approach for seeking solutions.

Crossing the frontiers of physical sciences, it is conceivable that the internalist perspective may also be applied to the traditional mind-matter problem in the philosophy of mind. Kim (1978) describes the relationship between mental properties and physical properties as *supervenience*, meaning that mental properties supervene on physical properties in the same way as macroscopic properties of physical objects supervene on their physical micro-structure: If two individuals have the same physical properties, then they have the same mental properties; hence, though the physical level determines the causal behavior of the subject, the mental properties have the same causal effects as the physical properties on which they supervene. An analogous perspective is adopted by Searle (1984) with his idea that consciousness (mind) emerges as a higher level property of the brain (matter) as liquidity emerges as a higher level property of water. Both authors extrapolate the emergence of properties from the physical realm to the psychological realm, tacitly assuming that the philosophical problem of emergence has a clear answer in physics. But our previous discussion shows us that, even in physics, it is not an obvious matter to decide about the objectivity of reducible descriptions and, consequently, about the ontological status of high level properties. It is possible to speculate that internalism may be a fruitful philosophical perspective for those who reject the metaphysical dualism of mind and matter but want to admit the objectivity of mental properties and processes.

An interesting alternative to the idea that mind emerges from matter is provided by a new ontological picture, according to which both mind and matter are emergent entities. This would mean that there is a very deep ontological level where mental and material properties do not exist: the mind-matter distinction arises as the result of a symmetry breaking in a higher ontological level. If quantum non-locality is strictly interpreted as holism, the features of the ontology defined by quantum theory support this new vision. But even in this case, internalism may serve as the proper philosophical basis. Here ontological pluralism is needed to support the objectivity not only of the mental level but also of the material world.

6 Some Remaining Problems

Speculations about the wide applicability of the internalist perspective should not obscure some remaining problems. Putnam's starting point is the attempt to find a middle way between externalism and relativism, but his main arguments are directed against the externalist realist. Rejecting relativism requires the explanation of why not just anything goes: Not all descriptions, but only those descriptions *that work* have the same objective status. At this point, Putnam's arguments are far from clear; he talks about some experiential inputs coming from reality, but it is difficult to understand what these inputs are.

That not any arbitrary description is proper is a matter of fact. But the main challenge is to explain *why* not just any description is correct. From the internalist viewpoint, when we pose questions to reality – the subject-independent, noumenal reality – it is forced to answer in the same language in which the question was formulated; but, even in this case, reality has the power of returning a negative answer. This is what makes internalism a realist doctrine and not a radical relativism. But, why does this happen? Does this fact tell us anything about noumenal reality?

Kant coined the term "noumena" to refer to a subject-independent reality. The noumenal world has no features or determinations; we can say nothing about the noumenal world other than that it exists. The very notion of noumena represents a kind of barrier to human thought (a "limitation of thought" in Putnam's terms) rather than a clear concept; thought tends to but never reaches the noumenal world. So it is tempting to conceive noumena as an absolutely amorphous realm; ontology only arises from the synthesis between our conceptual scheme and this amorphous reality. Yet, if this is the case, how can we explain that noumena resists some conceptualizations? Why does an amorphous realm not fit with particular descriptions? These questions lead us to ask whether noumena is really as amorphous as we first supposed. Perhaps the noumenal reality has a structure, an intrinsic organization, which explains its rejection of some descriptions. This does not mean that we can "discover" such a structure, because we only have access to reality through our conceptual schemes. The existence of a subject-independent though structured reality would still constitute a limitation toward which human thinking can move but at which can never fully arrive, because ontology always results from applying a conceptual scheme to this noumenal reality.

Another controversial point is the problem of reduction, usually related to the problem of emergence. From the traditional philosophical view (e.g. Nagel 1961), reduction is a logical relationship; the links between theories are mere analytical definitions or contingent conditions. This implies that the reduced theory adds no nomological content to the reducing theory. This view is perfectly consistent with the assumption of a single objective description of reality, which is, of course, the description given by the reducing theory. Therefore, emergent properties posed by the reduced theory are not really properties. In other words, emergent predicates have no ontological reference; they are only economical ways of saying what we could have said, in principle, without such predicates.

This traditional concept of analytical reduction is rejected by Primas (1998) when he argues that reduction is not a logical relationship. Discussing several concrete examples of reduction in the physical sciences, Primas shows the necessity of formulating with precision all the auxiliary conditions required for the reduced theory to be rigorously and completely deduced from the reducing theory. These auxiliary conditions are the context defining the validity domain of the reduced theory. Therefore, the specification of the context is at least as important for reduction as the laws of the reducing theory. Primas introduces the notion of *contextual ontologies* as the reference of context-dependent theories: Contextual objects and emergent properties are the elements of such higher level ontologies. Atmanspacher and Kronz (1998) discuss Primas' ideas as an example of their notion of *relative onticity* – an extension of Quine's ontological relativity – according to which the reduction relationship between two levels of description can be shifted to cover the entire hierarchy of complex systems. This means that a theory derived from a more basic one may become a reducing theory with respect to a higher level theory if the new context is properly specified. From this point of view, the many contextual ontologies with their corresponding emergent properties are hierarchically organized in growing levels of complexity.

These ideas are very appealing from the internalist perspective because they both point to the non-uniqueness of ontology and to the view that objects and properties are always relative to a theory or conceptual scheme. If we have given up the God's Eye point of view, there is no privileged perspective, and all descriptions have the same level of objectivity – all ontologies are equally real. Therefore, we cannot assume that fundamental theories describe reality as it is in itself – that is, the noumenal reality – since these theories are also conceptual schemes through which relative ontologies arise. On the other hand, emergent properties have the same ontological status as fundamental properties. This fact philosophically explains the causal efficiency of emergent properties such as temperature or chirality. But, how can we conceive reduction from the internalist viewpoint?

Primas is right when he rejects the traditional idea of analytical reduction, but this is not sufficient for explaining the objectivity of emergent properties. In order to formulate this philosophical explanation we must make a decision about the status of the auxiliary conditions necessary for the effective deduction of the reduced theory from the reducing theory. One alternative would be to suppose that they are purely conventional conditions which allow us to retain what we consider as relevant while disregarding elements considered as non-essential for our purposes. In other words, passing from a certain level of description to another one involves an abstraction; that is, we neglect some irrelevant aspects and *ontologize* contextual objects and properties as if they were actually existing. Then, the reduced theory refers to our partial knowledge of the ontology described by the reducing theory. Although useful, this partial knowledge only reflects some aspects of the basic ontology. But from this ignorance interpretation it is hard to argue that emergent properties have the same ontological status as fundamental properties, that they are "real" and not just a matter of description. It is difficult to reject the argument that they are nothing else than useful but dispensable descriptive tools.

I think that, in order to defend the objectivity of emergent properties, it is necessary to stress that the context is not a contingent and conventional element of reduction, but that it has a *nomological character*. This implies laying aside the traditional view, according to which the nomological content of science is concentrated at the so called "laws" of the theories, whereas contextual and auxiliary conditions represent the contingent aspects of each situation (cf. Wilson 1989, pp. 519–520). From my point of view, contextual conditions necessary for reduction do not play a role as passive as the traditional vision suggests, but, rather, they express an essential part of our scientific knowledge. This conception of reduction as *nomological reduction* implies rejecting not only the traditional analytical approach, but also every conventionalist view of reduction. The context is not a mere convenient tool to describe some aspects of a single ontology in response to our practical purposes. The context has a nomological content which refers to the *objective relationships* between different relative yet objective ontologies. This does not mean that we are describing the structure of the noumenal reality, because it is beyond any description. But this view allows us to live in a *stratified phenomenal reality*, hierarchically organized in multiple ontological levels, each one of them non-trivially depending on a more basic one. From this philosophical vision we can explain the emergence of novelty in the higher ontological levels of a diversified reality.

Of course, this short summary of some remaining problems for internalism does not solve every philosophical difficulty with this perspective. Questions remain open and there is still a lot of work to do. But I think that we must face these problems if we want to adopt an internalist realism consistent with present scientific knowledge.

References

Atmanspacher H. and Kronz F. (1998): Many realisms. *Acta Polytechnica Scandinavica* **91**, 31–43.

Batterman R. W. (1993): Defining chaos. *Philosophy of Science* **60**, 43–66.

Clark P. (1987): Determinism and probability in physics. *Proceedings of the Aristotelian Society* **61**, 185–210.

Davies P. (1990): Chaos frees the universe. *New Scientist* **128**, 48–51.

d'Espagnat B. (1985): *Une Incertaine Réalité*, Gauthier-Villars, Paris.

Earman J. (1986): *A Primer on Determinism*, Reidel, Dordrecht.

Ford J. (1983): How random is a coin toss? *Physics Today* **36**, 40–47.

Kim J. (1978): Supervenience and nomological incommensurables, *American Philosophical Quarterly* **15**, 149–156.

Kosso P. (1998): *Appearance and Reality*, Oxford University Press, Oxford.

Nagel E. (1961): *The Structure of Science*, Harcourt, Brace and World, New York.

Pérez Ransanz A.R. (1999): *Kuhn y el Cambio Científico*, Fondo de Cultura Economica, Mexico.

Popper K. (1992): *Quantum Theory and the Schism in Physics*, Routledge, London.

Primas H. (1998): Emergence in exact natural science. *Acta Polytechnica Scandinavica* **91**, 83–98.

Putnam H. (1981): *Reason, Truth and History*, Cambridge University Press, Cambridge.

Schuster H. G. (1984): *Deterministic Chaos*, VCH, Weinheim.

Searle J. (1984): *Minds, Brains and Science*, Harvard University Press, Cambridge.

Smith P. (1998): *Explaining Chaos*, Cambridge University Press, Cambridge.

Wagensberg J., ed. (1986): *Proceso al Azar*, Tusquets, Barcelona.

Wilson M. (1989): John Earman's 'A Primer on Determinism'. *Philosophy of Science* **56**, 502–532.

Hidden Determinism, Probability, and Time's Arrow

Hans Primas

Abstract

In present-day physics, fundamental dynamical laws are taken as time-translation invariant and time-reversal invariant one-parameter groups of automorphisms of the underlying mathematical structure. In this context-independent and empirically inaccessible description there is no past, present or future, hence no distinction between cause and effect.

To get the familiar description in terms of causes and effects, the time-reversal symmetry of the fundamental dynamics has to be broken. Thereby one gets *two* representations, one satisfying the generally accepted rules of retarded causality ("no effect can precede its cause"). The other one describes the strange rules of advanced causality. For *entangled* (but not necessarily interacting) quantum systems the arrow of time must have the same direction for all subsystems. But for classical systems, or for classical subsystems of quantum systems, this argument does not hold. As a consequence, classical systems allow the conceptual possibility of advanced causality in addition to retarded causality.

Every mathematically formulated dynamics of statistically reproducible events can be extended to a description in terms of a one-parameter group of automorphisms of an enlarged mathematical structure which describes a *fictitious hidden determinism*. Consequently, randomness in the sense of mathematical probability theory is only a weak generalization of determinism. The popular ideas that in quantum theory there are gaps in the causal chain which allow the accommodation of the freedom of human action are fantasies which have no basis in present-day quantum mechanics. Quantum events are governed by *strict* statistical laws.

Freedom of action is a constitutive necessity of all experimental science which requires a violation of the statistical predictions of physics. We conclude that the presently adopted first principles of theoretical physics can neither explain the autonomy of the psyche nor account for the freedom of action necessary for experimental science.

1   Determinism Does not Deal with Predictions

A large part of the difficulty with the "determinism versus indeterminism" debate lies in the failure to define the terms of discussion clearly. Many physicists and philosophers do not make the important distinction between determinism and the concept of predictability, and thereby commit a category mistake by claiming that determinism implies the possibility of prediction the future course of the universe.

For example, Born considers the distinction between determinism and predictability as hairsplitting and completely superfluous.[1] He maintains that classical point mechanics is not deterministic since there are unstable mechanical systems which are epistemically not predictable.

I think the following remarks by Earman (1986, p. 7f) are appropriate:

> The history of philosophy is littered with examples where ontology and epistemology have been stirred together into a confused and confusing brew. ... Producing an 'epistemological sense' of determinism is an abuse of language since we already have a perfectly adequate and more accurate term – prediction – and it also invites potentially misleading argumentation – e.g., in such-and-such a case prediction is not possible and, therefore, determinism fails.

That is, *determinism does not deal with predictions*. Nevertheless, ontic descriptions are often confused with epistemic ones.[2] In the philosophical literature there are many examples for such category mistakes. For example Carnap (1966, p. 192) says: "Causal relation means predictability". Likewise, Popper (1982, p. 36) maintains: "Scientific determinism is the doctrine that the state of any closed physical system at any future instant can be predicted". Physicists drop similar careless assertions; for example Brillouin (1964, p. 135): "The Poincaré discontinuities correspond to conditions where prediction is actually impossible and determinism cannot exist".

2   Terminology and Basic Concepts

In order to set the stage for my discussion, I introduce some definitions and notions I will use in the following.

---

[1]Compare for example Born (1955a,b, 1958). For a critique of Born's view compare von Laue (1955).

[2]For more details on the ontic/epistemic distinction compare the contribution by Atmanspacher in this volume.

Determinism: First of all, determinism will be taken to refer exclusively to *ontic descriptions*, and should not be confused with statements concerning our knowledge or beliefs. In particular, according to the definition adopted here, *determinism does not imply predictability*. Both, predictability and retrodictability have their proper place only in the framework of *epistemic descriptions*.

Causal relations: A process within which one event is a necessary condition for another event is described by a *causal relation*. The producing event is known as the *cause* and the event produced as its *effect*. *A causal relationship is an irreflexive, antisymmetric and transitive binary relation between two events.* That is:

- no event can be the cause of itself;
- if a is the cause of b, then b cannot be the cause of a;
- if a is the cause of b, and b the cause of c, then a is the cause of c.

Causal ordering: A causal nexus requires some universal order. A fundamental issue is the relation of causality to time. According to Hume (1793, part 3, p. 466) causal relations have three components: contiguity of time and place, temporal priority of the cause, and constant conjunction. For Hume "all inferences from experience ... are effects of custom, not of reasoning" (Hume 1748, section V, part 1), so that according to Hume's view the idea of cause and effect is not a matter of fact but a mental habit of association, that is, essentially subjectively fabricated. Hume's characterization implies that causal and temporal arrows are related *by definition*. Yet, this merging of the two very different ideas of causal order and temporal order is conceptually not sound. Moreover, it precludes many *logical* possibilities, like a backward causation, or a time-independent ordering of the causal nexus. [3]

Arrowless time in physics: If one wants to characterize causal ordering by temporal ordering, then one has first to introduce a *temporal direction*. Yet, the generally adopted first principles of physics do not distinguish the future from the past. First principles are characterized by high symmetries. A corresponding physical law is said to be fundamental if it is as independent as possible of any particular context. For example, we assume that the laws of nature are the same all the time and everywhere.

The assumption that there is neither a favored point of origin nor a preferred direction in time and space is a basic symmetry postulate required in all fundamental physical theories. Since a fundamental theorem by Noether (1918) implies a deep connection between symmetries and conservation laws,

---

[3] For a discussion of the many possible relations between the correlation and causation compare the contribution by Berkovitz in this volume.

the idea that fundamental laws should be characterized by high symmetries is not just an aesthetic concept.[4] For example, Noether's theorem requires that the time-translation symmetry implies and is implied by the conservation of energy. In fundamental physical theories the basic dynamical laws are not only taken as time-translation invariant but also as time-reversal invariant. In mathematical jargon we say that a fundamental dynamics is given by a *time-translation invariant* and *time-reversal invariant* one-parameter group of automorphisms of the underlying mathematical structure.

If we consider the time-reversal symmetry as primary, then there is no ordering so that we cannot use the concepts of cause and effect. In such a formulation of physics all reality is already pre-existent, and nothing new can come into existence. In order for time and causality to be genuinely active, some degree of freedom is necessary to provide a mechanism by which events "come into being". Without breaking the time-reversal symmetry nothing new can ever arise. Within special contexts a spontaneous breaking of this symmetry is possible, so that the direction of time has to be considered as *contextual*.

3   Breaking the Time-Reversal Symmetry

Every experiment requires nonanticipative measuring instruments, hence a distinction between past and future. In engineering physics the direction of causation is always assumed to go from past to future. That is, to derive experimental physics from first principles, the time-reversal symmetry of the fundamental laws has to be broken. The anisotropy of time is a *precondition* for any theory of irreversible processes.

The phenomenon of symmetry breaking is well understood in modern physical theories. It is not an ad hoc postulate, but follows from the first principles of theoretical physics. Nevertheless, an important problem remains. The time-reversal symmetry is represented by a group of order two. If the time-reversal symmetry is broken one gets *two* representations, one satisfying the generally accepted rules of retarded causality (forward causation) and the other one the strange rules of advanced causality (backward causation).

That is, if it is possible at all to derive the principle of retarded causality ("no effect can precede its cause"), then the very same methods allow the

---

[4]Noether's theorem says that if the action integral of a dynamical system is invariant with respect to a n-parameter continuous group of symmetry transformation, then the equations of motion have n linearly independent conservation laws.

derivation of processes governed by advanced causality. The decision which of the two possibilities is appropriate can therefore not be derived from the first principles of physics. *So the conceptual problem is not the breaking of the time-reversal symmetry, but the proper selection of one or the other one-sided realization.*

4 Arrow of Time

Mechanical and electrical input–output systems are non-anticipative. In other words, they are characterized by the fact that any present output values do not depend on future input values. The success of such traditional phenomenological physical descriptions suggests that in epistemic descriptions the time-reversal symmetry is always broken. Also, conscious perception and cognition seem to presuppose the usual forward direction of time, implying a memory of the past, but no anticipation of the future. The one-way property of time which we experience in our everyday life, and which we find in phenomenological physical laws, has been called "time's arrow" by Eddington (1928, p. 68).

In spite of these empirical facts, advanced causality is a conceptual possibility which is not ruled out by any fundamental physical law. So even at an ontic level we have to distinguish between the following *two* possibilities:

- *Forward determinism*, that is the thesis that, given the past of a physical system, there is a *unique future* (retarded realization).

- *Backward determinism*, that is the thesis that, given the future of a physical system, there is a *unique past* (advanced realization).

The nature and origin of a temporal asymmetry in the physical world is a perplexing problem for a theoretician. What is the *origin* of the arrow of time? Why do most (perhaps all) observable processes show the *same* arrow of time? What is puzzling about this temporal asymmetry is the *universality* of the direction of the arrow of time. The usual choice of retarded causality cannot be explained by a statistical mechanical formulation of the "second law" without an a priori postulate imposing an asymmetric evolution toward increasing time.

Backward causation is usually disregarded in science, but – as indicated above – should not be excluded rashly. From the viewpoint of physical first principles there are no reasons to select one of the two temporal directions. The question of whether epistemic descriptions in terms of backward causality are rewarding or not should not be decided by some a priori argument. It seems to be more reasonable not to hold any prejudices, but first to work out the theory in full mathematical detail and then discuss the consequences.[5]

5 Indeterminism

The phrase "indeterminism" hides a number of different concepts and implications. It can refer to limits of knowledge, inherent or practical unpredictability, unpredictable mechanistic or non-mechanistic causation, uncaused action, or even lawlessness.

First we have to emphasize that *noncausation has to be distinguished from indeterminism*. On the other hand, there are ontically deterministic systems which produce epistemically irreducible random outcomes. In addition, *the existence of strict statistical laws for certain random events suggests that there must be some causation*. If a system produces epistemically irreducible random outcomes which fulfill the statistical laws of Kolmogorov's probability theory (Kolmogoroff 1933), then we speak of *statistical causation*. It may be tempting to exclude indeterministic events which are not ruled by the laws of mathematical probability or any kind of statistical laws. But this would be premature without further arguments. The concept of *noncausation* will be used to refer to such events.

6 Statistical Causality

A broken time-reversal symmetry gives rise to two *epistemic* causal relations: *prediction* and *retrodiction*. Forward causality is logically independent from backward causality. Ontic determinism implies neither epistemic predictability nor epistemic retrodictability.

The usual causal explanations have predictive power and refer to a world to be acted on. Predictions require a *memory of the past*, they refer to probabilistic inferences of the future behavior of a system from empirically estimated past states. In a statistical description, predictive processes are entropy-increasing. Retrodictive explanations require a Carrollian *"memory of the future"*, they refer to probabilistic inferences of the past behavior of a system. In a statistical description retrodictive processes are entropy-decreasing; for details cf. Watanabe (1968, 1969, 1970, 1975, 1986).

Forward causal and backward causal descriptions have the same logical status a priori. Progress in science depends on the discovery of causal con-

---

[5]Compare also the contribution by Dowe in this volume.

nections between events, regardless of whether this nexus is backward or forward. In spite of the fact that memories usually store past events only, *we have to acknowledge that advanced causations are not forbidden by the first principles of physics.*

A theme recurring again and again is the obsession that the second law of thermodynamics is related with the arrow of time, and that it precludes the existence of entropy-decreasing systems. However, a system showing a globally entropy-increasing behavior can nevertheless possess open subsystems with locally retrodictive and entropy-decreasing behavior. There are many everyday physical examples for entropy-decreasing systems. A successful retrodictive teleological description of entropy-decreasing *living systems* is just as legitimate as the predictive description of an entropy-increasing system.

7   Why Can There Be Laws of Chance?

Mathematical probability theory refers to events or processes whose outcomes are *individually random*, but are governed by *strict statistical laws*. This theory has a rich mathematical structure so we have to ask *under which conditions* the usual "laws of chance" are valid. Long ago, von Smoluchowsky (1918) pointed out that the concept of probability can be defined, and the laws of probability can be derived from the theory of strictly deterministic but nonrobust classical dynamical systems. So it may be tempting to presume that chance events satisfying the axioms of classical mathematical probability theory always result from the deterministic behavior of an underlying physical system. Such a claim cannot be demonstrated though. What can be proven is the weaker statement that every probabilistic system which fulfills the axioms of classical mathematical probability theory can be embedded into a fictitious larger deterministic description.

To understand this claim we recall that the logic of classical probability theory is given by a (usually nonatomic) Boolean σ-algebra. Mathematical probability is defined as a σ-additive norm on a Boolean σ-algebra. A theorem by Loomis and Sikorski implies that every probabilistic system has a (nonunique) extension to an *atomic* Boolean algebra, such that every probability can be represented as a mean over two-valued states. *It follows that random variables fulfill the laws of chance if and only if it is possible to find a larger Boolean system such that every expectation value is the mean of a (possibly hidden) variable with respect to a two-valued state of the enlarged system.* Such deterministic embeddings are usually not constructive and nothing substantial can be said about a possible ontic interpretation of hidden variables of the enlarged deterministic system. The important point is that *the strict statistical regularities are due to the mere possibility of a deterministic mathematical description.*

Mathematical details on probability and hidden determinism

Mathematical probabilistic theory[6] can be described in terms of a probability algebra $(\mathcal{B}, p)$ where the probability p is a strictly positive σ-additive normed measure on the elements of a Boolean σ-algebra $\mathcal{B}$ of events. According to the fundamental Loomis–Sikorski representation theorem every Boolean σ-algebra $\mathcal{B}$ is isomorphic to a σ-algebra Ω/Δ, where Ω is some point set and Δ is a σ-ideal Σ, $\mathcal{B} \sim \Omega/\Delta$ (Loomis 1947, cf. also Sikorski 1969, p. 117). Every statistical state can be represented by a probability p on $\mathcal{B}$, or equivalently, by the restriction of a probability measure μ on the measurable space (Ω, Σ) to the Boolean algebra Ω/Δ. Equivalently, a statistical state can be represented by the restriction of a probability measure μ on the measurable space (Ω, Σ) to the Boolean algebra Ω/Δ. In this representation the nonnegative number $\mu(\mathcal{B})$ is the probability of the event $\mathcal{B} \in \Sigma$ in this statistical state.

The power set $\Pi(\Omega)$ of all subsets of the set Ω is a complete and atomic Boolean algebra which can be considered as an extension of the Boolean σ-algebra $\mathcal{B}$ of events. Every element $\omega \in \Omega$ defines a dispersion-free individual state χ_ω by

$$\chi_\omega(\mathcal{B}) = \left\{ \begin{array}{ll} 1 & \omega \in \mathcal{B} \\ 0 & \omega \notin \mathcal{B} \end{array} \right. , \quad \mathcal{B} \in \Pi(\Omega) \quad .$$

The classical system characterized by the Boolean algebra $\Pi(\Omega)$ is one of the many possible hidden-variable extension of the probability algebra $(\mathcal{B}, p)$, or equivalently, of the Kolmogorov probability space (Ω, Σ, μ). Every probability measure ν on (Ω, Σ) is a mean over a family $\{\chi_\omega \,|\, \omega \in \Omega\}$ of two-valued states of the extended system with the Boolean algebra $\Pi(\Omega)$ (Kamber 1964, §7; 1965, §14):

$$\nu(\mathcal{B}) = \int_\mathcal{B} \chi_\omega \, \nu(d\omega) \quad , \quad \mathcal{B} \in \Sigma \quad .$$

Usually the sample space Ω is uncountable so that an atom $\omega \in \Omega$ cannot represent an experimental proposition. In spite of the fact that the points of an uncountable phase space have no epistemic relevance whatsoever, the introduction of such "hidden variables" is a convenient

---

[6]For an outline of the "point-free" approach to probability, compare Halmos (1944), Kolmogoroff (1948), Łoś (1955), Kappos (1969).

mathematical tool. *This result implies that random variables fulfill the laws of chance if and only if they can formally be reduced to hidden two-valued variables.*

Since the requirement $\Omega/\Delta \sim \mathcal{B}$ does not determine the set Ω uniquely, any interpretation of individual points of the Kolmogorov probability space (Ω, Σ, μ) can be misleading and should be avoided.

The possibility of a fictitious deterministic embedding of the statistical laws of mathematical probability theory explains the possibility of a *frequency interpretation* of probabilistic physics. Similarly, the modern consistent formulations of *subjective* probabilities postulate that a rational man acts as if he had a deterministic model compatible with his preknowledge.[7] Accordingly, these theories also presuppose a hidden Boolean determinism as an underpinning for a coherent rational behavior.

Conclusion: A probabilistic system fulfills the axioms of classical mathematical probability theory if and only if it can be embedded into a larger deterministic system. The question whether physical theories are deterministic or merely probabilistic in the sense of mathematical probability theory is empirically undecidable.

8 Are There Statistically Irreproducible Events?

From a logical point of view one can neither exclude the occurrence of unique irreproducible events nor the existence of chance events for which the traditional "laws of chance" do not apply. Empirically this question is not decidable. Within the framework of the usual frequency interpretation of probability one encounters the well-known difficulty of "small probabilities". Already in 1866 Venn tried to define a probability explicitly in terms of relative frequencies of the occurrence of events "in the long run". He added that "the run must be supposed to be very long, in fact never to stop." Yet, without additional assumptions nothing can be inferred about the value of the limiting frequency of a finite segment, no matter how long it may be. Supplementary decision rules that allow to decide which probability statements we should accept are notoriously difficult to formulate. Even Kolmogorov (1933, p. 4, postulate B) had to adopt the working rule by Cournot (1843): *If the probability of an event is sufficiently small, one should act in a way as if this event will not occur at a solitary realization.*

---

[7]Compare for example Savage (1954, 1962), Good (1965), Jeffrey (1965), de Finetti (1972, 1974, 1975). For a convenient collection of the most important papers on the modern subjective interpretation, compare Kyburg and Smokler (1964).

Yet, the theory gives no criterion for deciding what is "sufficiently small". As emphasized by Pauli (1954, p. 114), no frequency interpretation can avoid a subjective factor:[8]

> In [its] purely mathematical form, Bernoulli's theorem is thus not as yet susceptible to empirical test. For this purpose it is necessary somewhere or other to include a rule for the attitude in practice of the human observer, or in particular the scientist, which takes account of the subjective factor as well, namely that the realisation, even on a single occasion, of a very unlikely event is regarded from a certain point on as impossible in practice. Theoretically it must be conceded that there is still a chance, different from zero, of error; but in practice actual decisions are arrived at in this way, in particular also decisions about the empirical correctness of the statistical assertions of the theories of physics or natural science. At this point one finally reaches the limits which are set in principle to the possibility of carrying out the original programme of the rational objectivation of the unique subjective expectation.

Pauli made the inspiring proposal to characterize unique events by the absence of any type of statistical regularity:[9]

> The synchronicity phenomena considered by [Jung] elude being captured by *"laws"* of nature, since they are not reproducible, that is to say, they are unique and *blurred* by the statistics of large numbers. In physics, on the other hand, 'acausalities' are *captured* just by statistical laws (of large numbers).

9   Hadamard's Principle of Scientific Determinism

For a mathematical formulation the traditional philosophical doctrine that each event is the necessary and unique consequence of prior events has to be sharpened by introducing the concept of the *state* of a physical system. What changes in a *dynamical system* is called the *state* of the system.

In modern system theory a state of a nonanticipative input-output system is represented by a kind of memory. It represents "the minimal amount of information about the past history of the system which suffices to predict the

---

[8]English translation quoted according to Pauli (1994), p. 45.

[9]Letter of June 3, 1952, by Pauli to Fierz, translated from von Meyenn (1996), p. 634. German original: "Die von [Jung] betrachteten Synchronizitätsphänomene ... entziehen sich der Einfangung in Natur-*'Gesetze'*, da sie nicht-reproduzierbar, d.h. einmalig, sind und durch die Statistik grosser Zahlen *verwischt* werden. In der Physik dagegen sind die 'Akausalitäten' gerade durch statistische Gesetze (grosse Zahlen) *erfassbar*."

effect of the past upon the future" (Kalman 1963, p. 154; see also Kalman, Falb, and Arbib 1969, section 1.1). Intuitively a system-theoretical state can be considered as a kind of memory, representing the relevant history of the system. Under very general conditions there exists a state space realization for every nonanticipative input-output system. The most compact description is given by the so-called *Nerode state* at time t, defined as the equivalence class of all histories for $t < 0$ of the system which give rise to the same output for all conceivable future.[10] No particular ontic or epistemic interpretation is implied by this definition.

A well-posed nonanticipative dynamical system requires a rule for determining the Nerode state at a given future time from a given present state. *Hadamard's principle of scientific determinism* requests that in a well-posed forward-deterministic dynamical system every initial state determines all future states uniquely (Hadamard 1923; cf. also Hille and Phillips (1957), sect. 23.6). Hadamard's principle of scientific determinism is not a natural law but a regulative principle which leads to an appropriate choice of the state space. If Hadamard's principle is not fulfilled then it can often be enforced by choosing a larger state space.

Example: Hadamard's principle in classical point mechanics

Newton's second law $m\ddot{\boldsymbol{q}}_t = \boldsymbol{F}(\boldsymbol{q}_t, t)$, $\boldsymbol{q}_t \in \mathbb{R}^3$, for a point particle of mass m under the influence of a force $\boldsymbol{F}$ does not fulfill Hadamard's principle for the configuration space $\mathbb{R}^3$. All the information about the past is given by the specification of the position and the velocity of every point particle at a particular time. The Lagrangian formulation considers the position $\boldsymbol{q}$ and the velocity $\boldsymbol{v} := \dot{\boldsymbol{q}}$ as *independent* variables. This move allows us to rewrite Newton's second law in a system-theoretic form as a system of two *first order* differential equations, $\dot{\boldsymbol{q}}_t = \boldsymbol{v}_t$, $m\dot{\boldsymbol{v}}_t = \boldsymbol{F}(\boldsymbol{q}_t, t)$, $\boldsymbol{q}_t \in \mathbb{R}^3$, $\boldsymbol{v}_t \in \mathbb{R}^3$. This Lagrangian formulation fulfills Hadamard's principle in the state space $\mathbb{R}^6$. The pair $\{\boldsymbol{q}_0, \boldsymbol{v}_0\} \in \mathbb{R}^6$ represents the Nerode state specifying the initial conditions necessary for the unique determination of the solution of the equations of motion for $t > 0$.

Since a stochastic process is nothing else but a family of random variables (Doob 1953, p. 46), every stochastic process can be dilated to a family of two-valued variables. Moreover, under appropriate continuity conditions, *every stochastic process can be dilated to a Hadamard-deterministic process.*

---

[10]For the first time this idea was clearly expressed by Nerode (1958) in the context of automata theory. Compare also Kalman, Falb, and Arbib (1969), chapters 1.3 , 6.3, and 7.2.

Nevertheless, without further assumptions no ontological implication can be attributed to such a dilation.

Mathematical models for deterministic motions

The mathematical description of any kind of motion uses an uninterpreted concept of time. In fundamental descriptions time is represented by the additive *group* $\{t \mid t \in \mathbb{R}\}$ of real numbers. Our ability to distinguish between *before* and *after* requires that time intervals are *oriented*. If the time interval $t_2 - t_1$ between two instants is positive, the time t_2 is said to be *later* than t_1. The physically fundamental equations of motion are not only invariant under translations $t \to t' = t + \tau$, $\tau \in \mathbb{R}$, but also under the time-reversal transformation, an involution which exchanges the time parameter t by $-t$.[11] If the time-reversal symmetry is broken, time is represented either by the additive semigroup $\{t \mid t \geq 0\}$, or by the additive semigroup $\{t \mid t \leq 0\}$.

In a mathematical description of a dynamical system a *Nerode state* at time t is represented by an element $\boldsymbol{x}_t$ of some topological space, called the *state space* $\mathfrak{X}$. A *motion* of the system is represented by a function $t \mapsto \boldsymbol{x}_t \in \mathfrak{X}$ which maps each instant t on exactly one element $\boldsymbol{x}_t$ of the state space.

For a Hadamard-deterministic system the motion $t \mapsto \boldsymbol{x}_t$ of a system-theoretical state element $\boldsymbol{x}_t$ is ruled by a family $\{\varphi_{r,s} \mid 0 \leq s \leq r\}$ of continuous *state transition maps* $\varphi_{s,t}$, fulfilling

$$\varphi_{r,s} \circ \varphi_{s,t} = \varphi_{r,t} \quad , \quad \varphi_{t,t} = \text{identity} \quad , \quad 0 \leq t \leq s \leq r \quad .$$

The dynamics of a Hadamard-deterministic system is then given by the functional relation $\boldsymbol{x}_s = \varphi_{s,t}\{\boldsymbol{x}_t\}$ with $s \geq t$.

A dynamical system is called *autonomous* if it is not subject to time-varying external influences. In this case the state transition map $\varphi_{s,t}$ depends only on the difference $s - t$ so that the time evolution is *time-translation invariant* and given by the *one-parameter semigroup* $\{\varphi_t \mid t \geq 0\}$ with $\varphi_t = \varphi_{0,t}$ and $\varphi_s \circ \varphi_t = \varphi_{s+t}$. The semigroup of time-translation invariant state transition maps φ_t is called a *semiflow*. Under very general conditions, a non-autonomous dynamical system can be embedded into a larger autonomous dynamical system.[12]

---

[11]An involution is an operation whose square is the identity. The involution associated with time reversal does not only change the direction of time but also associated quantities like the velocity, the momentum, the angular momentum, the electrical current and the magnetic field. In elementary particle physics, the invariant involution PCT is associated with time reversal T ($T^2 = 1$) also involves the space reflection P ($P^2 = 1$) and the charge conjugation C ($C^2 = 1$) (PCT-theorem).

[12]Compare Howland (1974); Reed and Simon (1975), section X.12; Nickel (1996); Engel and Nagel (2000); section VI.9. Compare also the contribution by Nickel in this volume.

An autononous dynamical system is said to be *reversible* if for each $t \geq 0$ the inverse state transition map φ_t^{-1} exists. If the family of state transition maps φ_t forms a one-parameter group, $\varphi_s \circ \varphi_t = \varphi_{s+t}$, $s, t \in \mathbb{R}$, then $\{\varphi_t \,|\, t \in \mathbb{R}\}$ is called a *flow*. For every initial state element x_0 the state element x_t at a later instant t is given by $x_t = \varphi_t \{x_0\}$. For a reversible time-translation invariant dynamical system the inverse φ_t^{-1} is given by φ_{-t}, so that the trajectory $s \mapsto \varphi_{-s} \{x_s\}$, $0 \leq s \leq t$, arrives back at x_0 after the time t, $x_0 = \varphi_{-t} \{x_t\}$. Since the dynamics can be uniquely reversed, we speak of a *time-reversal invariant dynamics*. Note that a time-reversal invariant dynamics entails the possibility of a *process reversal*, not the reversal of the direction of time.

10 Experimental Science Requires Freedom of Action

The premise that we often have a choice about what we are going to do is called the *free-will thesis* (van Inwagen 1983, p. 222). Some philosophers claim the laws of physics and the freedom of will are of different type and operate at a different level so that one can without contradiction subscribe to both determinism and free will. An example for such a "compatibilist viewpoint" is the suggestion that we should abandon the view that the laws of nature act like inviolable prescriptions, and that we should adopt a descriptive view of natural laws so that the problem of free will does not even arise. This descriptive view claims that, whatever happens in the world, there are true descriptions of those events, and that, whatever you do, there is a true description of what you have done. Other philosophers and scientists opt for another variant, claiming that all behavior is determined, and that "free will" is a "meaningless concept", or an "illusion".

At present the problem of how free will relates to physics seems to be intractable since no known physical theory deals with consciousness or free will. Fortunately, the topic at issue here is a much simpler one. It is neither our experience of personal freedom, nor the question whether the idea of freedom could be an illusion, nor whether we are responsible for our actions. The topic here is *that the framework of experimental science requires a freedom of action in the material world as a constitutive presupposition.* In this way "freedom" refers to actions in a material domain which are not governed by deterministic first principles of physics.

To get a clearer idea of what is essential in this argument we recall that the most consequential accomplishment by Newton was his insight that the *laws of nature* have to be separated from *initial conditions*. The initial conditions are not accounted for by first principles of physics, they are assumed to be "given". In experimental physics it is always taken for granted that the experimenter has the freedom to choose these initial conditions, and to repeat his experiment at any particular instant. To deny this freedom of action is to deny the possibility of experimental science.

In other words, we assume that the physical system under investigation is governed by strictly deterministic or probabilistic laws. On the other hand, we also have to assume that the experimentalist stands out of these natural laws. The traditional assumption of theoretical physics that the basic deterministic laws are universally and globally valid for all matter thus entails a pragmatic contradiction between theory and practice. *A globally deterministic physics is impossible.*

11   Quantum Randomness

It is often claimed that according to quantum mechanics "the basic constituents of matter behave in a fundamentally random way" (cf., e.g., Barrett 1999, p. 1), or that quantum mechanics allows "uncaused" events (Margenau 1957, p. 724). Such statements are misleading since all quantum events are governed by *strict statistical laws*. Probability is an essential element in every complete epistemic description of quantum events. From an epistemic viewpoint, individual quantum events are in general irreducibly random. But this epistemic quantum randomness does neither imply ontic randomness nor that determinism has been refuted by quantum theory. As the following example illustrates, *a link between randomness and determinism, analogous to that discussed in Section 7, holds for quantum physics as well.*

Example: deterministic embedding for quantum measurements

In spite of the fact that no experiment can ever realize a measurement of the first kind, it is worthwhile to discuss this customary idealization in the framework of quantum theory. We consider the simple example of a first-kind measurement of the observable σ_3,

$$\sigma_3 = |\alpha\rangle\langle\alpha| - |\beta\rangle\langle\beta| \ , \quad \alpha, \beta \in \mathbb{C}^2 \ , \quad \langle\alpha|\alpha\rangle = \langle\beta|\beta\rangle = 1 \ , \quad \langle\alpha|\beta\rangle = 0 \ ,$$

of a two-level quantum object system. We assume that the initial state is pure. It can either be described by a normalized state vector $\Psi_{\text{initial}} = c_1\,\alpha + c_2\,\beta \in \mathbb{C}^2$, or by the density operator $D_{\text{initial}} = |\Psi_{\text{initial}}\rangle\langle\Psi_{\text{initial}}|$.

The result of any measurement is irreversibly recorded by a *Boolean* device. Therefore a full statistical description of a first-kind measurement process has to include the object system, the measuring apparatus, and the classical recording device. In the framework of algebraic quantum mechanics such a full description is possible. Here we discuss only the resulting statistical state transition map $D_{\text{initial}} \rightarrow D_{\text{final}}$ connecting the initial state with the final state of the object system.

For a first-kind measurement of σ_3 the final density operator of the object system is given by

$$D_{\text{final}} = |c_1|^2 \, |\alpha\rangle\langle\alpha| + |c_2|^2 \, |\beta\rangle\langle\beta| = \tfrac{1}{2}\sigma_3 + \tfrac{1}{2}\text{Tr}\{D_{\text{initial}} \, \sigma_3\} \, \sigma_3 \quad .$$

Since in quantum mechanics the set of statistical state functionals is not a simplex, the final density operator D_{final} allows infinitely many distinct convex decompositions into pure states. Therefore the linear map $D_{\text{initial}} \rightarrow D_{\text{final}}$ *does not imply* that the final state is a classical mixture of pure states described by the density operators $|\alpha\rangle\langle\alpha|$ and $|\beta\rangle\langle\beta|$. Nevertheless, the probabilities $|c_1|^2$ and $|c_2|^2$ are the correct *conditional* probabilities for a measurement of the first kind. The condition is that the classical measuring instrument has factually and irreversibly registered one of the eigenvalues of the observable σ_3. In other words, the density operator D_{final} is the *conditional expectation* of D_{initial}, conditioned by the commutative W*-algebra generated by the observable σ_3.

The simplest dynamical description of the state transition map $D_{\text{initial}} \rightarrow D_{\text{final}}$ is given by the linear dynamical semigroup

$$\dot{D}(t) = \frac{\omega}{2i} \, [\sigma_3, D(t)] - \frac{\kappa}{4} \, [\sigma_3, [\sigma_3, D(t)]] \quad ,$$

with $D_{\text{initial}} = D(0)$, $D_{\text{final}} = D(\infty)$. The constant $\omega \in \mathbb{R}$ is an angular frequency describing the Hamiltonian dynamics, and $\kappa > 0$ is a relaxation frequency describing the dissipative interaction with the environment. For an arbitrary initial density matrix $D(0)$ we get the asymptotic density matrix $D(\infty)$,

$$D(\infty) := \lim_{t \to \infty} D(t) = \tfrac{1}{2}\sigma_3 + \tfrac{1}{2}\text{Tr}\{D(0) \, \sigma_3\} \, \sigma_3 \quad .$$

The statistical map $D_{\text{initial}} \rightarrow D_{\text{final}}$ can be generated in many different ways by an individual Hadamard deterministic motion. Consider for example a solution $t \mapsto \Phi(t)$ of the following nonlinear stochastic Schrödinger equation in the sense of Stratonovich

$$i \, d\Phi(t) = \tfrac{1}{2} \, \omega \, \sigma_3 \, \Phi(t) \, dt + i\kappa \, \langle\Phi(t) \,|\, \sigma_3 \, \Phi(t)\rangle \Big\{ \sigma_3 - \langle\Phi(t) \,|\, \sigma_3 \, \Phi(t)\rangle \Big\} \, \Phi(t)$$
$$+ \, i\sqrt{\kappa/2} \, \Big\{ \sigma_3 - \langle\Phi(t) \,|\, \sigma_3 \, \Phi(t)\rangle \Big\} \, \Phi(t) \circ dw(t) \, , \quad \Phi(0) = \Psi_{\text{initial}}.$$

Then the mean density operator $D_\Phi(t) = \mathcal{E}\{|\Phi(t)\rangle\langle\Phi(t)|\}$ satisfies the same dynamical semigroup as the density operator $D(t)$. Moreover, an individual trajectory $t \mapsto \Phi(t)$ describes the individual behavior of the object system within the hypothetical extended description. For an arbitrary initial state vector Ψ_{initial} one gets asymptotically (Gisin 1984)

$$\Psi_{\text{initial}} \xrightarrow{t \to \infty} \begin{cases} \alpha & \text{with probability } |\langle \alpha | \Psi_{\text{initial}} \rangle|^2 \\ \beta & \text{with probability } |\langle \beta | \Psi_{\text{initial}} \rangle|^2 \end{cases},$$

where α and β are the normalized eigenvectors of σ_3.

The white noise process $t \mapsto dw(t)/dt$ is a generalized stationary Gaussian process. It is well known that the trajectories of every continuous Gaussian processes can be generated by a linear Hamiltonian system (cf., e.g., Picci 1988). A physically realistic stochastic differential equation is never driven by white noise processes but by some variant of band-limited smooth noise processes . A theorem by Wong and Zakai (1965a,b) implies that the white-noise limit of a stochastic differential equation with an essentially band-limited noise process is the solution of the corresponding stochastic differential equations in the sense of Stratonovich. Therefore the stochastic Stratonovich equation mentioned above has a Hadamard deterministic dilation to a Hamiltonian equation of motion for the deterministic trajectories of the stochastic process $t \mapsto \Phi(t)$.

Of course, the sketched construction of a deterministic representation of a quantum measurement process is quite ad hoc and implies nothing about an ontic interpretation. The salient point is to show that the strict statistical regularities of a quantum measuring process can be understood in terms of a hidden determinism. Note that the various theorems which show that in quantum theory it is impossible to introduce hidden variables only say that it is impossible to embed quantum theory into a deterministic *Boolean* theory.

The context-independent laws of an ontic description of quantum mechanics are strictly deterministic but refer to a *non-Boolean* logical structure. The epistemically irreducible probabilistic structure of quantum theory is due to the fact that every communication in terms of an unequivocal language requires a Boolean domain of discourse. The nonpredictable outcome of a quantum experiment is related to the projection of the non-Boolean lattice of the deterministic ontic description to the Boolean algebra of the epistemic description of a particular experiment. The associated epistemic quantum-theoretical probabilities cannot be attributed to the object system; they are *conditional* probabilities for state transitions induced by the interaction of the object system with a classical measuring apparatus. The epistemic probabilities depend on the experimental arrangement, but for a fixed context they are objective since the underlying ontic structure is deterministic.

12 Quantum Mechanics Cannot Explain Free Will

Since the Hadamard determinism of classical mechanics and the freedom of action collide, some physicists and many philosophers find delight in the belief that the so-called "uncertainty principle" of quantum mechanics can solve the problem of freedom.[13] For instance, the neurophysiologist Eccles argued that in addition to the material world there is a nonmaterial and nonsubstantial mental world. He speculated that our mind acts on the brain at the quantum level by momentarily increasing the probability of exocytosis in selected cortical areas and thereby controlling "quantum jumps", turning them into voluntary excitations of the neurons that account for body motion (Beck and Eccles 1992, Eccles 1994).

The main idea of all such fantasies seems to be that in quantum theory there are gaps in the causal chain which allow the accommodation of free will and corresponding action. Yet, quantum events are governed by the strict mathematical laws of Kolmogorov's probability theory which lead to the empirically reproducible statistical rules of statistical physics. Consequently, *quantum randomness is just a weak generalization of determinism.*[14] Human actions are, however, in general not reproducible, hence not subject to the mathematical laws of probability theory.[15] *Freedom of action requires a violation of the statistical predictions of quantum theory. Hence present-day quantum theory is neither in a position to explain the autonomy of the psyche nor the existence of free will.*

---

[13]Compare for example Jordan (1932, 1934), Jordan (1956, p. 114ff), Margenau (1957), Rohs (1996, pp. 232–239).

[14]Similarly, Pauli has stressed that "quantum mechanics is a very weak generalization of the old causality". In a letter to Fierz of November 26, 1949, Pauli writes: "Ich habe keinen Zweifel, daß die quantenmechanische 'statistische Korrespondenz' viel näher auf der Seite des alten Determinismus liegt als auf der Seite des Synchronizitätsphänomens. Vom letzteren aus betrachtet muß die Quantenmechanik als eine *sehr schwache* Verallgemeinerung der alten Kausalität gelten. Und doch scheint mir die Quantenmechanik auch jenen Wegweiser nach der anderen Richtung zu haben, wo von willkürlicher Reproduzierbarkeit keine Rede mehr sein kann. Die Quantenmechanik scheint mir eine Art *Mittelstellung* einzunehmen." Quoted from von Meyenn (1993, p. 710).

[15]Curiously, Weaver (1948, p. 33) claims "that individual human decisions, like the individual events of physics, are not ruled by causality; while the statistical behavior of a man, like the statistics of a physical ensemble, is ruled by causality." It may be that *some* human actions are ruled by statistical laws, but certainly there are also singular non-recurring human actions.

13   Why Does Time's Arrow Always Point in the Same Direction?

The presupposed possibility of breaking the time-reversal symmetry and defining the arrow of time locally is not yet sufficient to understand the seemingly global character of the direction of time. Why should the arrow of time in two noninteracting physical systems point to the same direction? Classical causality is local and cannot explain the *universality* of the direction of the arrow of time. In quantum physics the omnipresence of Einstein–Podolsky–Rosen correlations even between noninteracting subsystems implies a global character of the time-reversal operation in quantum systems. In an entangled system it is impossible to define a *local* time-reversal operation for one subsystem only. Consequently the arrow of time of *entangled* (but not necessarily interacting) quantum systems must have the same direction. *Quantum causality is holistic and requires the same direction of the arrow of time even for non-interacting entangled subsystems.*

Representing time-reversal symmetry in quantum mechanics

In the C*-algebraic description of arbitrary physical systems a symmetry is represented by a *Jordan automorphism* of the underlying C*-algebra $\mathfrak{A}$. A Jordan automorphism is a linear *-preserving bijection which respects the symmetrized product (cf., e.g., Emch 1972, p. 152),

$$\alpha(A^*) = \alpha(A)^* \ , \quad \alpha(AB+BA) = \alpha(A)\alpha(B)+\alpha(B)\alpha(A) \ , \quad A, B \in \mathfrak{A} \ .$$

A C*-automorphism α is a Jordan-automorphism which preserves the order of the ordinary product, $\alpha(AB) = \alpha(A)\alpha(B)$. An anti-automorphism α, which reverses the order of the terms in the ordinary product, $\alpha(AB) = \alpha(B)\alpha(A)$, is also a Jordan *-isomorphism. Every Jordan automorphism of a C*-algebra is the sum of a C*-automorphism and a C*-anti-automorphism (Kadison 1951, theorem 10).

In the irreducible representation of quantum mechanics on a Hilbert space $\mathcal{H}$, the time reversal is represented by an anti-unitary operator on the algebra $\mathfrak{B}(\mathcal{H})$ (Wigner 1932, see also Wigner 1959, chap. 26), so that it implements a C*-anti-automophism on the algebra $\mathfrak{B}(\mathcal{H})$. More generally, for an arbitrary physical system, the time reversal is represented by an involutary anti-automorphism τ of the underlying C*-algebra $\mathfrak{A}$,

$$\tau(A^*) = \tau(A)^* \ , \quad \tau(AB) = \tau(B)\tau(A) \ , \quad \tau\{\tau(A)\} = A \ , \quad A, B \in \mathfrak{A} \ .$$

The time-reversal map τ is positive, but for quantum systems (where

$\mathfrak{A}$ is noncommutative) the map τ is *not completely positive.*[16] That is, if $(\mathfrak{A}_1, \tau_1)$ and $(\mathfrak{A}_2, \tau_2)$ describe two noninteracting quantum systems, then the *local* map $\tau_1 \otimes \mathbf{1}_2$ and the *local* map $\mathbf{1}_1 \otimes \tau_2$ on the minimal C*-tensor product $\mathfrak{A}_1 \otimes \mathfrak{A}_2$ are not positive, hence they are not time-reversal maps. The time-reversal map for the composite quantum system is given by the *global* positive map

$$(\tau_1 \otimes \mathbf{1}_2)(\mathbf{1}_1 \otimes \tau_2) \; = \; \tau_1 \otimes \tau_2 \quad .$$

This fact implies that even when the two quantum systems do *not interact* in any way, the time-reversal for the first quantum system is *not given by* $\tau_1 \otimes \mathbf{1}_2$. *The map* $\tau_1 \otimes \mathbf{1}_2$ *represents the time-reversal operator for the first subsystem if and only if the two systems are not entangled with Einstein–Podolsky–Rosen correlations.* This is the case for every state of the combined system if and only if at least one of the subsystems is classical (in the sense that either $\mathfrak{A}_1$ or $\mathfrak{A}_2$ is commutative).[17] In an entangled system with broken time-reversal symmetry the direction of the arrow of time has to point to the same direction for all (even noninteracting) subsystems. This requirement of *global consistency* distinguishes quantum causality from classical causality.

14 Hadamard Determinism Cannot Be Globally Valid

Complex systems can sometimes establish truly novel emergent properties, new properties that the component parts do not have. Often the doctrine of determinism is opposed by the principle of emergence. Yet, if the underlying physical system is deterministic in the sense of Hadamard, then all consistent higher-level theories can be extended to deterministic systems in the sense of Hadamard.

From the point of view adopted here freedom refers to actions in the material world which are not determined by the presently adopted first principles of physics. Such a view violates the usually assumed universal validity of the first principles of physics. Yet, such a violation is not surprising. The postulate that the underlying fundamental time evolution should be an *automorphism* is a queer assumption indeed. An automorphism is by definition *a map which does not change any physically relevant feature.* From a physical

---

[16]A linear map $\tau : \mathfrak{A} \to \mathfrak{A}$ is said to be *completely positive* if the linear map $\tau \otimes \mathbf{1}_n :$ $\mathfrak{A} \otimes \mathfrak{B}(\mathbb{C}^n) \to \mathfrak{A} \otimes \mathfrak{B}(\mathbb{C}^n)$ is positive for all $n \geq 1$, where $B(\mathbb{C}^n)$ is the C*-algebra of all complex $n \times n$-matrices and $\mathbf{1}_n$ is the identity transformation of $B(\mathbb{C}^n)$ onto itself.

[17]This is a consequence of theorem 4.14 in Takesaki (1979, p. 211).

point of view the dynamics of interacting systems cannot simply be postulated to be automorphic, but has to be *derived* from first principles. Yet, a mathematically consistent theory of interactions does not yet exist.

Remarks on deriving the dynamics from first principles

Nowadays it is generally accepted that *all known interactions of matter are due to gauge fields*. The dynamics of so-called *bare elementary systems* is known to be automorphic. Here, a bare elementary system is defined as an indecomposable representation of a kinematical group (like the Galilei or Lorentz group), disregarding interactions intermediated by gauge fields. Such elementary systems are are called *bare* since they only characterize the transformation properties under the actions of the kinematical group. Yet, elementary systems with non-zero mass or non-zero electrical charge are inevitably coupled to the gravitational or electromagnetic gauge fields. Due to this interaction, a bare elementary system acquires a complicated structure. This process is referred to as *dressing*. The derivation of the dynamics of a dressed system from the group-theoretically known automorphic dynamics of the bare elementary systems and the bare gauge fields in a mathematically rigorous way involves many difficulties. In particular our understanding of radiation effects and the infinities of self-interactions is far from satisfactory. It is an open question whether the resulting dynamic is automorphic. In spite of the fact that present-day quantum field theory is quite successful, it has only the status of a phenomenological theory.

Notwithstanding the problematic character of automorphic time evolutions, mounting evidence shows that for practically all concrete applications the time evolution of any open subsystem of the material world can be described by the restriction of an automorphic dynamics of a larger system consisting of the object system and its environment. So we have to ask why a hypothetical universal automorphic dynamics leads to contradictions. A possible answer derives from the remark that not everything that is locally true is necessarily true globally. So it may be worthwhile to contemplate about theories which *only locally, but not globally* correspond to contemporary theories. At present we have no idea how to achieve such a goal. Besides, it is questionable whether a solution of this problem could contribute to an understanding of the problem of freedom of action in the material world.

It is disquieting that *we have no idea where precisely in the material domain the presently adopted first principles of physics do not apply*. Presumably new physical principles will need to be discovered. Since in physics time is used in a rather ad hoc manner, one could think about a more physical concept of time, say as *time operator* which represents time as a dynamical observable.[18] But it is very much an open question what form a physical theory including the freedom of action will take.

Acknowledgements

I am grateful to Harald Atmanspacher for helpful comments on an earlier version of this contribution.

References

Barrett J.A. (1999): *The Quantum Mechanics of Minds and Worlds*, Oxford University Press, New York.

Beck F. and Eccles J.C. (1992): Quantum aspects of brain activity and the role of consciousness. *Proceedings of the National Academy of Sciences of the United States of America* **89**, 11357–11361.

Born M. (1955a): Ist die klassische Mechanik wirklich deterministisch?. *Physikalische Blätter* **11**, 49–54.

Born M. (1955b): Continuity, determinism and reality. *Danske Vidensk-abernes Selskab Mathematisk Fysiske Meddelelser* **30**(2), 1–26.

Born M. (1958): Vorausagbarkeit in der klassischen Physik. *Zeitschrift für Physik* **153**, 372–388.

Brillouin L. (1964): *Scientific Uncertainty, and Information*, Academic Press, New York.

Carnap R. (1966): *Philosophical Foundations of Physics: An Introduction to the Philosophy of Science*, ed. by M. Gardner, Basic Books, New York.

Cournot A.A. (1843): *Exposition de la théorie des chances et des probabilitiés*, Paris.

Doob J.L. (1953): *Stochastic Processes*, Wiley, New York.

Earman J. (1986): *A Primer on Determinism*. Reidel, Dordrecht.

Eccles J.C. (1994): *How the Self Controls Its Brain*, Springer, Berlin.

Eddington A.S. (1928): *The Nature of the Physical World*, Cambridge University Press, Cambridge.

Emch G.G. (1972): *Algebraic Methods in Statistical Mechanics and Quantum Field Theory*, Wiley, New York.

---

[18]Compare for example the ideas discussed by Misra (1995).

Engel K.-J. and Nagel R. (2000): *One-Parameter Semigroups for Linear Evolution Equations*, Springer, New York.

Finetti B. de (1972): *Probability, Induction and Statistics. The Art of Guessing*, Wiley, London.

Finetti B. de (1974): *Theory of Probability. A Critical Introductory Treatment, Volume 1*, Wiley, London.

Finetti B. de (1975): *Theory of Probability. A Critical Introductory Treatment, Volume 2*, Wiley, London.

Gisin N. (1984): Quantum measurements and stochastic processes. *Physical Review Letters* **52**, 1657–1660.

Good I.J. (1965): *The Estimation of Probabilities. An Essay on Modern Bayesian Methods*, MIT Press, Cambridge, Massachusetts.

Hadamard J. (1923): *Lectures on Cauchy's Problem in Linear Partial Differential Equations*, Yale University Press, New Haven.

Halmos P.R. (1944): The foundations of probability. *American Mathematical Monthly* **51**, 493–510.

Hille E. and Phillips R.S. (1957): *Functional Analysis and Semi-groups*, American Mathematical Society, Providence, Rhode Island.

Howland J.S. (1974): Stationary scattering theory for time-dependent Hamiltonians. *Mathematische Annalen* **207**, 315–335.

Hume D. (1748): *An Enquiry Concerning Human Understanding*, London.

Hume D. (1793): *A Treatise of Human Nature. Book 1*, London.

Inwagen P. van (1983): *An Essay on Free Will*, Clarendon Press, Oxford.

Jeffrey R.C. (1965): *The Logic of Decision*, McGraw-Hill, New York.

Jordan P. (1932): Die Quantenphysik und die Grundprobleme der Biologie und Psychologie. *Naturwissenschaften* **20**, 815–821.

Jordan P. (1934): Quantenphysikalische Bemerkungen zur Biologie und Psychologie. *Erkenntnis* **4**, 215–252.

Jordan P. (1956): *Der gescheiterte Aufstand. Betrachtungen zur Gegenwart*, Klostermann, Frankfurt.

Kadison R.V. (1951): Isometries of operator algebras. *Annals of Mathematics* **54**, 325–338.

Kalman R.E. (1963): Mathematical description of linear dynamical systems. *SIAM Journal on Control* **1**, 152–192.

Kalman R.E., Falb P.L., and Arbib M.A. (1969): *Topics in Mathematical System Theory*, McGraw-Hill, New York.

Kamber F. (1964): Die Struktur des Aussagenkalküls in einer physikalischen Theorie. *Nachrichten der Akademie der Wissenschaften, Göttingen. Mathematisch Physikalische Klasse* **10**, 103–124.

Kamber F. (1965): Zweiwertige Wahrscheinlichkeitsfunktionen auf orthokomplementären Verbänden. *Mathematische Annalen* **158**, 158–196.

Kappos D.A. (1969): *Probability Algebras and Stochastic Spaces*, Academic Press, New York.

Kolmogoroff A.N. (1933): *Grundbegriffe der Wahrscheinlichkeitsrechnung*, Springer, Berlin.

Kolmogoroff A.N. (1948): Algèbres de Boole métriques complètes. *Annales de la Societe Polonaise de Mathematique* **20**, 21–30.

Kyburg H.E. and Smokler H.E. (1964): *Studies in Subjective Probability*, Wiley, New York.

von Laue M. (1955): Ist die klassische Physik wirklich deterministisch? *Physikalische Blätter* **11**, 269–270.

Loomis L.H. (1947): On the representation of σ-complete Boolean algebras. *Bulletin of the American Mathematical Society* **53**, 757–760.

Loś J. (1955): On the axiomatic treatment of probability. *Colloquium Mathematicum (Wroclaw)* **3**, 125–137.

Margenau H. (1957): Quantum mechanics, free will, and determinism. *Journal of Philosophy* **54**, 714–725.

Meyenn K. von (1993): *Wolfgang Pauli. Wissenschaftlicher Briefwechsel, Band III: 1940–1949*, Springer, Berlin.

Meyenn K. von (1996): *Wolfgang Pauli. Wissenschaftlicher Briefwechsel, Band IV, Teil I: 1950–1952*, Springer, Berlin.

Misra B. (1995): From time operator to chronons. *Foundations of Physics* **25**, 1087–1104.

Nerode A. (1958): Linear automaton transformations. *Proceedings of the American Mathematical Society* **9**, 541–544.

Nickel G. (1996): On evolution semigroups and nonautonomous Cauchy problems. *Dissertation Summaries in Mathematics* **1**, 195–202.

Noether E. (1918): Invariante Variationsprobleme. *Nachrichten von der Gesellschaft der Wissenschaften, Göttingen. Mathematisch Physikalische Klasse* **1918**, 235–257.

Pauli W. (1954): Wahrscheinlichkeit und Physik. *Dialectica* **8**, 112–124.

Pauli W. (1994): *Writings on Physics and Philosophy*, ed. by C.P. Enz and K. von Meyenn, Springer, Berlin.

Picci G. (1988): Hamiltonian representation of stationary processes. In *Operator Theory: Advances and Applications*, ed. by I. Gohberg, J.W. Helton, and L. Rodman, Birkhäuser, Basel, pp.193–215.

Popper K. (1982): *The Open Universe: An Argument for Indeterminism*, Hutchinson, London.

Reed M. and Simon B. (1975): *Methods of Modern Mathematical Physics. II: Fourier Analysis, Self-Adjointness*, Academic Press, New York.

Rohs P. (1996): *Feld, Zeit, Ich. Entwurf einer feldtheoretischen Transzendentalphilosophie*, Klostermann, Frankfurt.

Savage L.J. (1954): *The Foundations of Statistics*, Wiley, New York.

Savage L.J. (1962): *The Foundations of Statistical Inference. A Discussion*, Methuen, London.

Sikorski R. (1969): *Boolean Algebras*. Springer, Berlin.

Smoluchowsky M. von (1918): Über den Begriff des Zufalls und den Ursprung der Wahrscheinlichkeitsgesetze in der Physik. *Naturwissenschaften* **6**, 253–263.

Takesaki M. (1979): *Theory of Operator Algebras I*, Springer, New York.

Watanabe S. (1968): "Teleological" explanations in biophysics. *Supplement of the Progresss of Theoretical Physics*, Extra Number, 495–497.

Watanabe S. (1969): *Knowing and Guessing. A Quantitative Study of Inference and Information*, Wiley, New York.

Watanabe S. (1970): Creative time. *Studium Generale* **23**, 1057–1087.

Watanabe S. (1975): Norbert Wiener and cybernetical concept of time. *IEEE Transactions on Systems, Man, and Cybernetics* **SMC-5**, 372–375.

Watanabe S. (1986): Separation of an acausal subsystem from a causal total system. In *Proceedings of the 2nd International Symposium. Foundations of Quantum Mechanics in the Light of New Technology*, ed. by M. Namiki, Physical Society of Japan, pp. 276–281.

Weaver W. (1948): Statistical freedom of the will. *Reviews of Modern Physics* **20**, 31–34.

Wigner E.P. (1932): Über die Operation der Zeitumkehr in der Quanten-mechanik. *Nachrichten von der Gesellschaft der Wissenschaften, Göttingen. Mathematisch Physikalische Klasse* **31**, 546–559.

Wigner E.P. (1959): *Group Theory*, Academic Press, New York.

Wong E. and Zakai M. (1965a): On the convergence of ordinary integrals to stochastic integrals. *Annals of Mathematical Statististics* **36**, 1560–1564.

Wong E. and Zakai M. (1965b): On the relation between ordinary and stochastic differential equations. *International Journal of Engineering Science* **3**, 213-229.

Time-Space Dilations and Stochastic-Deterministic Dynamics

Karl Gustafson

Abstract

First I will review and interpret our recent results on the embedding of stochastic processes into larger deterministic dynamics. Second, I will argue that one must know not only the past but also the future in order to describe the present. Third, I will question the notion of time as a Cartesian independent variable. Fourth, I will take the liberty of a personal digression on determinism.

Dedicated to my Aunt Leona Troxell Dodds, who had no doubts at all about *determinism*. Though Aunt Leona had no children of her own, she is still partially with us (I manage her affairs). She was an incredibly loving and giving person, who almost singlehandly through superhuman effort elected Winthrop Rockefeller Governor of Arkansas. The daughter of a reverend, and a bible-toting Baptist, Aunt Leona always told me, especially when things were not going so well: "The Lord has a purpose for everything. Everything will work out the way it was supposed to. There is a reason for all things which happen to us, good and bad." For Aunt Leona, everything was deterministic.

1   Introduction

I could easily use the rest of my life to write this paper. Instead, I only have a few weeks. A second salient fact affecting the writing of this paper: the Workshop on Determinism for which it is intended has been constituted not only from a wide variety of scientists but also from philosophers, psychologists, and others. Therefore I do not want to be overly mathematical here. Thirdly, it is probable that I will not be physically present at the Workshop due to another commitment. Accordingly the paper should stand on its own.

I have thought about these boundary conditions and what I want to say and I have made some decisions. First, to meet the time constraint, I will take full advantage of the *past*. That is to say, I will frequently refer during the exposition to published papers (mine and others) or even to my private notes. Many technical details will be skipped here. So the paper will be a commentary, attempting to deliver some comprehension, with no attempt at completeness. I hope in this way that I may communicate in the *present* (this paper) with nonspecialists. Where I am right or wrong or where my opinions provoke argument, outrage, delight, these things will take care of themselves in the *future*.

I will leave to others systematic discussions, dissections, deliberations, definitions, etc., of the concept(s) of determinism. In other words, I will not look at the "core questions" the Workshop organizers proposed. Those 7 "core questions" have mostly to do with the various definitions of determinism. As the reader of this paper will surmise, over time I have become more and more suspicious of anyone who purports to know "final answers". That is not to say that definitions are unimportant. Indeed, one of the secrets of success in pure mathematics is to concentrate on the definitions. Suffice it to say here, I will happily leave attempted written taxonomies of *determinism* to the dictionaries and encyclopedias of all written languages, and the cultural and historical contexts from which those dictionaries and encyclopedias all evolved, and to those other authors here who wish to give their own taxonomies. At the moment it seems to me that the English word "determinism" has many, rather than few, uses. However, I will indirectly address some of those uses as they occur naturally within the context of my contribution. Also I will interject historical commentary or other relevant commentary as I like.

The flow of the paper will be governed by the four goals stated in the Abstract. First, in reviewing our results which provide for the dilation of a stochastic description to a deterministic description, I will of necessity have to refer to some mathematics. The dilation machinery is very advanced, relatively recent, and very technical mathematics which even many thoroughgoing functional analysts have not learned. But I will try to provide an understandable overview here. Also I will try to augment, rather than repeat, what has already been said elsewhere. This task constitutes Sections 2, 3, and 4. My second goal is to present the postulate that the present makes no sense unless you acknowledge the past and anticipate a future. This premise is meant to be provocative and speculative but unavoidable. Here I will use some mathematical frameworks to support that contention but such mathematics will be standard. This task constitutes Sections 5 and 6. My third goal, that of questioning the notion of time as a Cartesian independent variable when in a stochastic setting, occurred to me recently in my research on the very important stochastic partial differential equations used worldwide in real time to control financial portfolios. My discussion here will be principally within that context, although, naturally, I believe that issue to be of wider importance. I present this issue in Section 7.

I chose the title of this paper, Time-Space Dilations and Stochastic-Deterministic Dynamics, to imply both a precision and a vagueness for what I am presenting here. It is the tone which I would like to contribute to the whole Workshop. The Greek *stochastikos* means "guessing in aiming" which presumes an interval of *time* during which some *deterministic dynamics* is proceeding or is to be estimated within a *spatial* context. Although one could suppose that the five words I have italicized here are presumably well defined, hence precise, hence enabling of some precise discussion, I doubt this. Moreover I believe that all of those concepts are inextricably intermingled when they occur in reality. For that reason I do take the liberty of a personal digression on determinism in Sections 8 and 9. That is my fourth and last goal here. Section 8 is a critique dealing with the question of whether we create reality or simply discover it. Section 9 is more important because beyond stating a few of my current opinions, I also went to some effort in the second draft of this paper to incorporate important and in some cases not so well known opinions stated by some of the great physical scientists.

2 Dilations of Stochastic Descriptions to Deterministic Dynamics

These 'dilation' equations arose, as far as I was concerned, in a 1979 visit by my friend and colleague Baidyanath Misra to Boulder (who has his own contribution in this volume). Misra, Prigogine and Courbage (1979) had developed a theory from which deterministic measure preserving dynamical systems $(\Omega, \mathcal{B}, \mu, S_t)$, whose evolution in state space was described by a unitary evolution group according to $(U_t\rho)(\omega) = \rho(S_{-t}\omega)$, could be shown to be 'equivalent' via a positivity-preserving similarity transformation Λ, to a stochastic Markov process. Here Ω is a given phase space (read: the underlying physical space), $\mathcal{B}$ is the event σ-algebra (read: the possible physical configurations), μ is the probability measure (read: $\mu(\Omega) = 1$), and S_t is the measure-preserving dynamics (read: the changing of events) in the phase space. The corresponding state space (read: the probability densities ρ) is the function space $\mathcal{L}^2(\Omega, \mathcal{B}, \mu)$. The change of representation operator Λ mapping $\mathcal{L}^2(\Omega, \mathcal{B}, \mu)$ into itself has a long history, but in particular it was to satisfy the following properties:

(a) Λ is positivity-preserving, i.e., $\rho \geq 0 \Rightarrow \Lambda\rho \geq 0$,

(b) $\int_\Omega \rho d\mu = \int \Lambda \rho d\mu$,

(c) $\Lambda 1 = 1$,

(d) Λ is one-to-one with densely defined inverse Λ^{-1},

(e) $\Lambda U_t \Lambda^{-1} = W_t^*$ is a contraction semigroup satisfying the conditions:

    (i) W_t is positivity preserving,

    (ii) $W_t 1 = 1$,

    (iii) $W_t^* 1 = 1$,

    (iv) $\|W_t^*(\rho - 1)\| \to 0$ strictly monotonically as $t \to \infty$ for all nonnegative states $\rho \not\equiv 1$ with $\int_\Omega \rho d\mu = 1$.

I do not want to go into all technical and physical aspects underlying these assumptions; suffice it to say, they are natural in the classical statistical mechanics of state probability distributions which eventually tend to an equilibrium distribution (read: the state $\rho \equiv 1$), and they are applied reasonably elsewhere as well.

We were asked by Misra whether the transformed evolution $\Lambda U_t \Lambda^{-1}$ could ever be deterministic (read: possess an underlying measure-preserving phase space set and point dynamics S_t). We showed (Gustafson and Goodrich 1980, Goodrich, Gustafson and Misra 1980, Gustafson, Goodrich and Misra 1981), that the key to this issue was that Λ^{-1} could not also be positivity preserving (read: Λ^{-1} could not also preserve probabilities) if W_t^* was to be stochastic and not deterministic. After this, we also answered a long-standing question in functional analysis (Gustafson and Goodrich 1980), about exactly which isometries on a Hilbert space of states come from measure-preserving underlying point transformations. Banach and Lamperti had shown for $\mathcal{L}^p(\Omega, \mathcal{B}, \mu)$, $0 < p < \infty$, $p \neq 2$, that all linear isometries possessed underlying point transformations. We showed for $p = 2$ that such "deterministic" isometries had to be (if and only if) positivity preserving. The other isometries on Hilbert spaces, and Hilbert spaces have a lot of them, we regard as nondeterministic.[1] Our result later became known as the Koopman Converse: Let U_t be a strongly continuous one parameter group of operators on $\mathcal{L}^2(\Omega, \mathcal{B}, \mu)$ such that $U_t(1) = 1$ and U_t is positivity preserving. Then there is an underlying measure-preserving point dynamical group S_t such that $U_t \rho(w) = \rho(S_t w)$. Koopman (1931) had shown much earlier that given

---

[1]For applications to physics, see, e.g., Goldstein, Misra, Courbage (1981).

an underlying deterministic measure-preserving phase space dynamics S_t, it generated a unitary state space dynamics U_t via the same relationship as just written.

Following these findings, for example with the condition that the change of representation Λ^{-1} should not preserve probabilities so that the transformed evolution $M_t = \Lambda U_t \Lambda^{-1}$ is not deterministic, I asked (Gustafson and Goodrich 1980, Section 7) more generally: when can one dilate an arbitrary Markov stochastic semigroup M_t into a "larger" unitary group evolution U_t which itself possesses an underlying point dynamics. The idea was to use the recently developed pure operator theory mathematical dilation theories. I will discuss such dilation theories in more detail in the next section. In a series of papers (Gustafson and Goodrich 1985, Goodrich, Gustafson and Misra 1986, Antoniou and Gustafson 1993, Antoniou and Gustafson 1997, Antoniou, Gustafson and Suchanecki 1998), we showed that all measure preserving stationary stochastic Markov processes M_t possess such deterministic dilations and that, moreover, those dilations are Kolmogorov dynamical systems. For more details on those results I refer the reader to those papers, although I will discuss them a bit more in Section 4. See also Gustafson (1997a, Chapter II).

3 Mathematical Dilation Theories

I have described the mathematical dilation theories in a limited way in two books (Gustafson 1997a, Gustafson and Rao 1997). There I presented three dilation theories. Here I will try to elaborate the essentials of those theories and complement my earlier discussions. Also I will add a discussion of a fourth dilation theory which I had overlooked in those books.

The dilation theory apparently started with Naimark (1943), where a semispectral measure is represented as the compression of a spectral measure on a larger Hilbert space. Another way to say this is as follows. Let $(\Omega, \mathcal{B}, \mu)$ be a finite measure space where μ is operator valued, i.e., μ maps the Borel sets in $\mathcal{B}$ into the non-negative selfadjoint operators on a Hilbert space $\mathcal{H}$. The countable additivity of μ is to be in the weak operator topology and $\mu(\Omega) = I$, the identity operator. Then there is a larger Hilbert space $\mathcal{K}$ containing $\mathcal{H}$ as a proper subspace and there is a spectral measure E on $\mathcal{B}$ such that

$$\mu(\Sigma)P = PE(\Sigma)P$$

for all Borel sets Σ in $\mathcal{B}$. Here P is the orthogonal projection of $\mathcal{K}$ onto $\mathcal{H}$. In other words, Naimark (1943) was working in the theory of operator valued projection valued measures, and he was seeking a spectral theory for nonnormal operators A somehow resembling that for selfadjoint ($A = A^*$), normal ($A^*A = AA^*$), and in particular, unitary operators ($U^*U = UU^* = I$), to be obtained by 'dilating' A to a larger space where its dilation $\widetilde{A}$ possessed a spectral theory.

Quickly Julia (1944) considered operators themselves, rather than working with them through measures, and showed that every linear contraction operator ($\|A\| \leq 1$, A a bounded operator on a Hilbert space $\mathcal{H}$) can be represented as a compression of an isometry ($\|\widetilde{A}x\| = \|x\|$) for all x on a larger Hilbert space $\mathcal{K}$ in which $\mathcal{H}$ is a subspace. For A to be a compression of $\widetilde{A}$ means exactly

$$AP = P\widetilde{A}P$$

where P is the orthogonal projection of $\mathcal{K}$ onto $\mathcal{H}$. Again the goal was to dilate an arbitrary (e.g., nonnormal) operator A to a larger operator $\widetilde{A}$ possessing a spectral decomposition, in the hopes of thereby gaining more information about A. Isometries $\widetilde{A}$ satisfy $\widetilde{A}^*\widetilde{A} = I$ and, when they are onto $\mathcal{K}$, they are unitary operators. Unitary operators of course have a full spectral theory.

Julia's dilation is particularly interesting because it is a small dilation and uses only A and A^*. The unitary dilation of A is

$$\widetilde{A} = \left[\begin{array}{cc} A & (I - AA^*)^{1/2} \\ (I - A^*A)^{1/2} & -A^* \end{array} \right]$$

on $\mathcal{K} = \mathcal{H} \oplus \mathcal{H}$. As another example, any finite matrix A has a normal dilation $\widetilde{A} = \left[\begin{array}{cc} A & A^* \\ A^* & A \end{array} \right]$. In the early 1950's there were a number of dilation results, e.g. by Sz. Nagy (1953) and others. See Gustafson (1997a) and Gustafson and Rao (1997) and citations therein for more detail.

However, in our work related to physics described in the previous section, where we want to dilate a (stochastic) Markov semigroup M_t to a (deterministic) unitary group U_t on a larger space, there was another feature which was quite important to us: positivity preservation. In other words, we want dilations carrying at least some probabilistic properties related to those of the physical semigroup M_t with which we started into the dilated framework. I will further discuss this issue in the next section. Suffice it to say, we turned to a second and a third dilation theory which better, although not completely, met our needs. I want to now briefly summarize what I shall regard as four mathematical dilation theories.

The first dilation theory, called the Sz. Nagy dilation theory for short in abuse of all other contributors to it, is the one described above. To make a long story short, even in the elaborations (power dilation theory) of this theory, the dilations do not generally carry any meaningful positivity preservation property to the dilations on the larger space. For example, even if A is positivity preserving, there is no guarantee that the square root operators in the Julia dilation $\tilde{A}$ will also be positivity preserving. Moreover, in the larger dilation Hilbert spaces $\mathcal{K}$ that one encounters in that theory (sometimes $\mathcal{K}$ must contain an infinite number of copies of $\mathcal{H}$ ...), it is generally not clear what should correspond to an equilibrium probability distribution.

Therefore we considered next what I call the Rokhlin (1964) dilation theory. In this theory, one is concerned with what are called exact dynamical systems, e.g. systems corresponding to particular measure preserving phase space dynamics, which one can dilate to a larger deterministic dynamics within the class of Kolmogorov systems. Kolmogorov systems are very similar, see, e.g., Antoniou and Gustafson (1999), to regular stationary stochastic processes (see Doob 1953), and these stochastic processes are built upon filters of increasingly rich σ-algebras $\mathcal{B}_t$. Thus one can carry positivity preservation into the dilation through these measure-theoretic lattice properties.

The third dilation theory I call the Akcoglu (1975) dilation theory, abusing all other contributors. It has the advantage over the Rokhlin methods of not being restricted only to Markov semigroups which are implementable by exact endomorphisms corresponding to exact dynamical systems. Therefore we were able to obtain deterministic dilations for more general semigroups M_t using this dilation theory. These Akcoglu methods were only known for a discrete time parameter and we had to extend them to continuous time.

There is a fourth dilation theory which I have not described elsewhere, except for some mention in our most recent paper (Antoniou, Gustafson and Suchanecki 1998). It is reputed to be the "most general" but I will show in the next section that such a claim depends on your needs.[2] This fourth dilation theory is a theory of dilations of quantum stochastic processes. In mathematical terms we could express this 'dilation theory' as one of dilations of completely positive operators on C^* and W^* algebras. The quantum stochastic calculus within which this dilation theory is set is described by Parthasarathy (1992); see also citations [58–61] of Antoniou, Gustafson and Suchanecki (1998).

Two important papers related to this fourth dilation theory, which I

---

[2]Amazingly, I should have known of this theory in 1980 for it was presented at a conference I organized and co-chaired (see Hudson, Ion and Parthasarathy 1981)! However, I did not attend that particular talk.

have not cited elsewhere, are Stinespring (1955) and Lindblad (1975). In
the first of them, Naimark's (1943) dilation approach is generalized from
Boolean algebras and measures to operator algebras and linear operator-
valued functions μ. In particular it is shown that if $\mathcal{A}$ is a C^* algebra with
unit and μ is a linear function from $\mathcal{A}$ to $B(\mathcal{H})$ where $\mathcal{H}$ is some Hilbert space
and $B(\mathcal{H})$ denotes all bounded operators on $\mathcal{H}$, then μ has a $*$-representation
satisfying

$$\mu(A) = V^*\rho(A)V$$

where V is a bounded linear operator: $\mathcal{H} \to \mathcal{H}'$, $\mathcal{H}'$ another Hilbert space,
if and only if μ is completely positive. I will discuss what this means in
the next section. The second paper Lindblad (1975) extended the Naimark–
Stinespring theory to the quantum stochastic setting.

4 Physical Interpretations of Dilations

My own interest in using mathematical dilation theory, as I described in
Section 2, was one of *mathematical physics*, which I define to be rigorous
mathematical theory applied to nonrigorous physical models. As I stated
in an early paper (Gustafson, Goodrich and Misra 1981), "results of this
type establish a principle often used intuitively in chemistry that a forward
moving (e.g. Markov) process that loses information cannot be reversed."
That paper is a good one if you want genuine background for our initial
motivations.

So the physical picture was that of classical statistical mechanics, where
one chooses to work with the statistical distribution functions $\rho_t(\omega)$ rather
than the underlying physical dynamics ω_t. Mathematically this then becomes
a setting of operators on $\mathcal{L}^p(\Omega, \mathcal{B}, \mu)$ state spaces. A good source for the flavor
of this setting and its applications is the book by Lasota and Mackey (1985).
There are two important comments about physical interpretation to be made
immediately.

First, you will find that all of the mathematical theory of such stochastic
analysis assumes a finite measure μ. To make this a probability theory, one
normalizes the measure to $\mu(\Omega) = 1$. If you look at mathematical ergodic
theory, integration theory, and like literature, you will always find this assumption. The fact that conditional expectations are positive projections,
which is used throughout ergodic theory, depends upon it. I do not like
this limitation, but no one else seems to mind. I elaborated this point in
Antoniou and Gustafson (1999).

The second comment concerns our interest in positivity preservation.

Isometries on $\mathcal{L}^p(\Omega, \mathcal{B}, \mu)$ spaces for $p \neq 2$ always have underlying point maps. This statement extends generally to many Banach spaces (see Stroescu 1973). But for $p = 2$, i.e. the Hilbert space case, it is only the positivity preserving unitary evolutions U_t which possess an underlying measure preserving dynamics. Because we want to select only physical evolutions, i.e., those which do not violate probability preservation, we prefer the Hilbert space setting for our dilations. This gives us a rich class of physically relevant processes.

I emphasize this choice of $\mathcal{L}^2$ viewpoint in Gustafson (1997a, Remark 1.2.4, page 62). One could alternatively work in $\mathcal{L}^1$ state spaces. These are really the most natural for pure probability theory. Or one could work in $\mathcal{L}^\infty$ state spaces. In some sense one is always working there because many of the technical arguments in all four dilation theories depend essentially on working first with the dense set of characteristic functions of all subsets of the event algebra $\mathcal{B}$. We specifically discussed these choices in Gustafson and Goodrich (1980, Section 6). The $\mathcal{L}^1$ context, actually $\mathcal{L}^1 \cap \mathcal{L}^2$ if you are careful, requires that U be multiplicative: $U(fg) = U(f)U(g)$. This is the viewpoint of group representations (Mackey 1963): group representations can be viewed themselves as a kind of dilation theory. The $\mathcal{L}^\infty$, von Neumann algebra context, requires that U intertwines multiplications. It is that latter context which is generalized to quantum stochastic processes, the fourth dilation theory I discussed above. The third dilation theory, which I called the Akcoglu theory, holds in $\mathcal{L}^p$ spaces, but it is basically the $\mathcal{L}^1$ approach. The second, Rokhlin dilations of exact systems, is firmly rooted in the Kolmogrov school's dynamical system theory. It emphasizes the underlying dynamical maps themselves rather than the states. The first, Sz. Nagy dilation theory, was motivated as it developed, not at all by considerations from physics or probability. It became pure operator theory. The hope was that by dilating nonnormal operators to normal operators on larger spaces, one could find a spectral theory for all operators. You should read the encyclopedic Dunford and Schwartz (1973) to see this dream in action, and its end. I would also like to bring to your attention pages 2054–2063 of Dunford and Schwartz (1973), where they discuss determinism, especially as related to well-posed problems, in a historical perspective.

Here is the problem with just using Sz. Nagy dilations: they do not take into account function positivity. Stated another way, the lattice structures of $\mathcal{L}^p$ spaces are ignored because the dilation theory is pure operator theoretic. What I call the Akcoglu dilations have nice positivity preserving properties in their dilations. Kern, Nagel and Palm (1977) showed in some generality that the positive dilations then usually preserve the ergodic, mixing, and irreducibility of the original Markov semigroup.

Ojima (1997) in his commentary on our theory, raised some interesting points about the $\mathcal{L}^1, \mathcal{L}^2, \mathcal{L}^\infty$ choice, once that choice is put into the quantum (e.g. operator algebra) setting. He points out that then the meanings of the positivity of the maps W_t, W_t^*, Λ of the irreversibility theories must be carefully reexamined. One may regard these concerns as falling within the context of the fourth dilation theory, which I may portray as the extension of the $\mathcal{L}^\infty$ theory to a C^* and W^* algebra setting. Ojima's specialty is quantum field theory and, therefore, naturally gravitates to the operator algebra or, if you prefer, the second quantization perspective. As I mentioned above, the result of Stinespring (1955) is that the correct, or at least a natural and to some extent necessary, positivity in that context is complete positivity.

Complete positivity (I do not give the rather technical definition here, see Parthasarathy (1992)) is quite a strong assumption. I may decribe it as saying (e.g. for a matrix A) that not only A but also all of its principle submatrices must be positive semidefinite in the quadratic form sense (see Gustafson and Rao 1997). Note that one generally cannot relate pointwise positivity preservation ($f \geq 0 \Rightarrow Af \geq 0$) with quadratic form positivity ($\langle Af, f \rangle \geq 0$ for all f). The latter guarantees the positivity of all of A's eigenvalues, $\lambda_i \geq 0$, hence A's trace $\text{Tr}(A) = \sum_{i=1}^{n} \lambda_i \geq 0$. These are spectral positivity properties more natural to the fourth dilation theory. We were more interested in function positivity properties, i.e., preservation of probabilities under state space mappings.

Kummerer (1985) points out another physical interpretation of the $\mathcal{L}^\infty$ approach: that a stationary Markov process, when generated from a given Markov kernel, may be viewed as a dilation itself. He also shows that in the fourth dilation theory, the resulting dilation can fail to be Markov, but that when the dilation is Markov, then a closer relation between the dilation and the original dynamical system may be discerned.

Lindblad (1975) discusses the physical interpretation of the fourth, operator algebra complete positivity dilation theory. He shows that the relative entropy functional of a finite quantum system is nonincreasing under a completlely positive map of the states into themselves. In that setting the states are the density operators, i.e., selfadjoint positive definite (quadratic form sense) operators whose eigenvalues are all nonnegative and sum to one. But it is then true that the complete positivity of the fourth (second quantization) dilation theory and the classical positivity preservation that we want are in agreement in goal: probabilities are mapped to probabilities.

A popular motivation for the fourth dilation theory was the perspective of open quantum mechanical systems as motivated by the need for a rigorous treatment of non-equilibrium quantum statistical mechanics. This approach is nicely presented by Davies (1976). Some of the physical ideas are coupling the external world to the earlier pure quantum theory by use of reservoirs (e.g. for decay products), measuring instruments modelled as operations between C^* algebras, and so on. Parts of this theory I like and parts I do not like. What I do not like was that as I watched that development I saw it move farther and farther away from physics.

One of the important physical results of our investigations was that all of the Markov processes that we were able to dilate were shown to arise necessarily as projections of Kolmogorov dynamical systems. The latter have positive entropy production and, according to Kolmogorov, are the prototypes of chaos. Thus all such Markov processes, usually thought of as having stochasticity as their main property, can be viewed as projections of a larger chaotic and ergodic dynamical system. This is a pleasing picture because the more chaotic an underlying dynamics, the more regular an overlying stochastic state space dynamics should be.

I could go on. Let me instead close this section by reiterating my comment in Gustafson (1997a, Remark 1.2.14, p. 68), that I would prefer to have dilations which take into account the specific physics of the originating semigroup M_t and its underlying physical dynamics. I do not mean just positivity (e.g. probabilities) preservation. I would like the same thing as is desired in cancer research: to know the causal link. I am referring to problems such as the early strong statistical correlations of tobacco smoking to cancer and yet in contrast the frustratingly long and difficult attempt to demonstrate a precise causal link. I cannot resist telling you that shortly after we published Antoniou and Gustafson (1993), we received a request from the R.J. Reynolds Tobacco Company, Reynolds (1993), for a reprint of our paper.

5 Time and Space

I have indicated some of my feelings about Time in Gustafson (1999b), in my review of Atmanspacher and Ruhnau (1997). Of course that book contains much, much more, and from its articles' citations you will find much, much more. Please note here that I chose to use the word "feelings" above because "I feel" is one of the weakest statements one can make. "I feel" is much weaker than "I think" which is much weaker than "I believe". Suffice it to say, I believe that no one understands the true physical nature of Time.

Time and space is a huge subject, so what am I after in this section? I just want to establish a few perspectives whose tone may carry into the following sections of this paper. To that end let us recall the generally accepted notion of time as an ordering of events along a world-line. This conceptualization of the meaning of time is pretty general and includes the classical physics of Newtonian time, special relativity time, and general relativity time. In Newtonian time it does not depend on a frame of reference, in special and general relativity it does. But in all such classical theories of physics we do presume the notion that a physical trajectory can be ordered in time and, hence, has a world-line. Let me call this sense of time *deterministic time.*

By the way, I am not going to go into the variety of perceptions of space here. I take it to be three-dimensional Euclidean space even though I am sure that is wrong and that on the atomic scale we have no idea of what the space between an electron and the nucleus really means, and even if the Higgs boson is ever found I doubt if it will lead to any final answers about space-time. Also I do not want to go into esoteric theories of multiple times, etc., that one finds in the relativity literature, and the like, beyond what is necessary to my discussion.

The most common use of deterministic time is clock time. Let me observe that clock time is historically solar system time, i.e. years, days, minutes, seconds, based upon local heavenly body revolution or rotation rates. In other words, clock time is based upon perceived (solar system) periodicities. We know now that those periodicities are not exact. They contain irregularities, minor perturbations occur intermittently, to say nothing of gradual everpresent losses due to interbody friction and extra-solar system tug and pulls that we do not understand at all. But we may say that clock time ushered in the notion that a standard time scale should be defined in terms of some universally accepted periodic motion.

This notion that Time should be based upon some universal periodic motion persisted even after it was decided to use atomic clocks. I refer you to Kleppner (2001) for an entertaining recent account of the latest improvements in atomic time and spatial meter measurement. As Kleppner repeatedly points out, all improved theoretical definitions of space and time, upon becoming accepted scientific standards, are quickly rendered obsolete as experimental increases in precision replace them.

The account of Kleppner (2001) points out in particular that in the 1970's it was found that the frequency of an atomic clock could be correlated to the frequency of a laser with high precision. This gave a more accurate measure of the speed of light: laser frequency multiplied by laser wavelength. Since it is assumed that space and time are uniquely and universally connected by

c, the speed of light, you can allow any two of x, s, c (a meter of length, a second of time, the speed of light) to be independent variables. Since atomic rotation rates or laser emission frequencies seem more universal, the length unit x has become a dependent variable, derivable from the other two. For example, $\lambda = c/f$ gives the laser wavelength in terms of c and f (frequency, which we take to correspond to the unit of time). This is an atomic scale version of the good old classical $d = vt$, distance is velocity multiplied by time.

My point in going into this brief account of how we set perspectives and standards for what clock time should be, besides the fact that I find it interesting and indisputably real physics (i.e., it is experimentally based) is to raise the issue: when is time really an independent variable? I will come back to this question in Section 7 in a stochastic setting. In the discussion above, the speed of light c was the overwhelming winner as to the most fundamental 'variable', especially because it was a constant (the big assumption). For example, the most recent experiments have shown that the speed of light is frequency independent to a precision of 10^{-21}. Thus the choice comes down to: What can we measure more accurately in the laboratory, clock time or spatial meter. Clock time has won out so far. The latest atomic clocks can measure time to one part in 10^{18}. So space becomes the dependent variable and speed of light and time are the independent variables.

A second common way in which we use deterministic time in everyday life is as a coordinate against which we plot something. Granted, this use of Time is less reflected upon by the common man than by scientists, census takers, or the time to the next paycheck. And this second use of Time usually thinks of the t coordinate as clock time in terms of whatever time scale one is plotting against. In Section 7 I will bring out an important situation where I think this second use of Time is erroneous. The point is that one should not confuse the use of t as independent clock-time variable with its use as a dynamical plotting label.

In the next Section 6, I will even question the common view of a deterministic time world-line. This discussion needs more development, but it is the best I can do for now.

Remark: In writing the second (final) draft of this paper, I was able to add some interesting thoughts of some of the great scientists which I will attempt to relate to the perspectives I have put forth in this paper. These will be found in Section 9.

6   Knowing the Present

If time were discrete, then past, present, and future would be disconnected, even if related. More likely, time could be a connected set of discrete increments. These increments need not be equally weighted, they could each depend upon many other variables, one could posit something like Cantor's singular continuous step function as a time scale, and so on. Personally I would conjecture time to be something more stochastic, more like a disconnected set of event-determined world-line increments. I will return to this point of view later in the paper.

But even then, you see, we have pictured all of this within a frame of a continuous underlying one-dimensional coordinate 'time' axis upon which we superimpose our time scale, be it continuous, discrete, or stochastic. So let us stick with this usual continuous time for the moment. Also let us forget the fact that time and space are related relativistically from the standard point of view presented in the previous section. The point to be made here is different. It is the assertion that one must know not only the past but also the future in order to describe the present. I will try to support this assertion though several examples.

The first example is the dilation theory I discussed in Section 3. As shown there, any $n \times n$ matrix A may be dilated to a $2n \times 2n$ normal matrix $\widetilde{A} = \begin{bmatrix} A & A^* \\ A^* & A \end{bmatrix}$. What does this mean if we are discussing semigroup evolutions M_t, $t \geq 0$, where for simplicity I take $t = 0$ to be the present? The adjoint semigroup M_t^* may then be viewed as running into the past. If we dilate M_t to $\widetilde{M_t} = \begin{bmatrix} M_t & M_t^* \\ M_t^* & M_t \end{bmatrix}$ we see that the dilated normal semigroup evolution links the past with the future. Since the infinitesimal generators of semigroups, i.e., the underlying dynamics, are defined by the derivative $L = s-\lim_{t \to 0^+} (M_t - I)/t$, we also see that we have tacitly accepted that we must anticipate the future to know the dynamics of the present. Thus the future, past and present are linked in any semigroup, group, or dilation theory, and, moreover, in whatever might be the underlying physical dynamics.

The unitary Julia dilation $\widetilde{M_t} = \begin{bmatrix} M_t & (I - M_t M_t^*)^{1/2} \\ (I - M_t^* M_t)^{1/2} & -M_t^* \end{bmatrix}$ has the same properties. However, it contains an interesting additional feature: the presence of a square root. Square root operators are the key to much mystery in physics. I cannot develop this thesis fully here, but let me assert that they are the key to getting from the Schrödinger equations to the Dirac equations of quantum mechanics. They occur crucially in several parts of quantum probability. And, somehow, I believe that they often underlly the choice of time direction in any phase-dependent physics. In any case let me just make a couple of comments. First, you chose the positive selfadjoint square root $(I - M_t M_t^*)^{1/2}$ when you wrote that down. Why did you do that? Second, as I mentioned in Section 3, it is not clear when square roots of positivity preserving operators are themselves positivity preserving. So a dilation can change the meaning of the present because it can change the meanings of past and future.

As a next example let me just consider the spectral representation $H = \int \lambda dE_\lambda$ for a selfadjoint or Hermitian operator H. For the interesting case of continuous spectrum $-\infty < \lambda < \infty$, one needs to make a choice of how the jumps dE_λ may occur in all theoretical treatments. The usual convention is the French *cadlag*: continuous from the right, limit from the left. Doing that, you have continuously connected the future, if λ be time (e.g. frequency), to the present. The past, e.g., the jump, has been presumed to be of lesser interest. If you do it the other way, you have chosen to favor the past.

I may take this second example to the third. Consider a signal $f(t)$, $-\infty < t < \infty$, and its Fourier transform $\hat{f}(\lambda) = \int_{-\infty}^{\infty} e^{-2\pi i \lambda t} f(t) dt$. First note the obvious fact that to know the transform, you must know f for all time. So you cannot know all of the signal's frequencies if you are only given the signal up to the present.

Next the uncertainty relation between f and $\hat{f}$ is

$$\left[\int_{-\infty}^{\infty} (t - t_0)^2 |f(t)|^2 dt \right]^{1/2} \left[\int_{-\infty}^{\infty} (\lambda - \lambda_0)^2 |\hat{f}(\lambda)|^2 d\lambda \right]^{1/2} \gtreqless \frac{\|f\|}{4\pi}$$

where $\|f\| = \int_{-\infty}^{\infty} |f(t)|^2 dt$ is the $\mathcal{L}^2$ norm of the signal $f(t)$. The uncertainty principle connects the allowable time spread around an instant t_0 to the allowable frequency spread around a given frequency λ_0. This principle states that if the signal be confined to a very short time interval, then its Fourier Transform cannot be confined to a small frequency interval. In other words, if you want to put a lot of energy into a signal very quickly, you must use a large number of (e.g. high) frequencies. For a signal $f \in \mathcal{L}^1(-\infty, \infty) \cap \mathcal{L}^2(-\infty, \infty)$, its energy density at time t_0 and fequency λ_0 is given by

$$H(t_0, \lambda_0, f) = 2 \int_{-\infty}^{\infty} f(t_0 + t) \overline{f(t_0 - t)} e^{-4\pi i \lambda_0 t} dt$$

e.g. see Wigner (1932). This means in particular that if we take $t_0 = 0$ to be the present, to know the energy density $H(0, \lambda, f) = \int_{-\infty}^{\infty} f(t) \overline{f(-t)} dt$ at any frequency λ, we must know both the past and future of the signal. You may say that you do not care, but then you cannot hear my voice because each sound I utter is a time and frequency dependent energy density.

As I said I cannot fully develop this thesis about what it takes to know the present here, so I shall close with one more example. I take this from Reichenbach (1944). Reichenbach is concerned, as many of us also have been, with the underlying role of the complex number field as it enters the wave function solution $\psi(t)$ of the Schrödinger wave mechanics partial differential equation. In quantum mechanics one uses the real quantity $|\psi(t)|^2$ to represent the (in principle, physically observable) statistics, so what is the meaning of the complex valued wave function itself? Fixing a moment in time t, we may look at the wave function $\psi(q)$ as it is spread over three-dimensional physical space q and we may assert that the probability of observing the wave function at q is $|\psi(q)|^2$. Similarly we may assert that the probability of observing the wave function with momentum p is $|\sigma(p)|^2$, where $\sigma(p)$ is the eigencoefficient of ψ from ψ's eigenexpansion representation in energy space. I remark that, thus, $\sigma(p)$ is a probability density very much like the energy density $H(t_0, p, \psi)$ in the example above. But I want to go beyond that example here, beyond just the uncertainty principle. Continuing, in the early days it was hoped that if you knew both of the probability distributions $dq = |\psi(q)|^2$ and $dp = |\sigma(p)|^2$, perhaps you could know the whole wave function ψ. Remember that I am concerned in this section with what it takes to know the present, so let me take $t = 0$ to remind you that we would like to know the quantum mechanical wave function now, i.e. we would like to know $\psi(0)$.

But this turned out not to be the case (see Reichenbach 1944). Several investigators showed that one must know more than dq and dp. In particular it was shown that if you included some time dependence $\psi(q, t)$ as knowable for the wave function ψ, then $\psi(q, t_0)$ could be determined. Specifically, $\psi(q, 0)$ could be determined up to a phase factor if you knew both $dq|_{t=0}$ and its time derivative $\frac{\partial}{\partial t} dq \, |_{t=0}$. The proof of this latter fact uses the Schrödinger equation itself, which after all does connect the shape of the wave function ψ in configuration space to one time derivative. But notice carefully now, that in positing that you know the time derivative $\frac{\partial}{\partial t} dq \, |_{t=0}$ you have posited that you know the probability distribution dq for at least a small future time interval – or a past one, or both.

7 Financial Option Theory

Here I want to question the notion of time as an independent Cartesian variable when used in some stochastic settings. I have already recalled the intrinsic interdependence of time and space in the relativistic settings of Section 5. The point to be made here is different. Essentially I am going to argue that some important assumptions made in financial risk theory are suspect. I was led to this thought in Gustafson (2002), where more details on the ramifications for financial risk theory may be found. If I am right, the management of large (\$ trillions) investment portfolios is partly based upon myth.

This myth appears in the derivation of the so-called Black–Scholes equations which are widely used in the finance industry, most notably by the large hedge funds. I do not try to present that theory here; it has taken me about seven years now of part-time teaching and study. Suffice it to say, the level of the mathematics used there should not be underestimated. There is a large body of literature (one widely cited source which I can recommend is Duffie 1996). I managed to get a short treatment of the basic Black–Scholes partial differential equation into Gustafson (1999a), so I will start from there, and assume the reader may also start from there.

Briefly, from Markovian market assumptions and the use of the Ito stochastic calculus, one can derive the famous Black–Scholes partial differential equation

$$\frac{dV}{dt} + \frac{\sigma^2 S^2}{2}\frac{\partial^2 V}{\partial S^2} + rS\frac{\partial V}{\partial S} - rV = 0.$$

Here $V = V(S,t)$ is the estimated price of a call or put option. An option is a right to buy (call) or sell (put) at a precise time (the expiry date) and precise price (the exercise price) in the future. The asset price S and the time t are regarded as independent variables. The coefficients σ (volatility) and r (risk-free interest rate, e.g., U.S. treasury rate) are regarded as known or knowable.

By a change of variable the Black–Scholes PDE can be converted to the heat equation $u_\tau - u_{xx} = 0$. The solution to the latter is available as the integral of the heat kernel, i.e.,

$$u(x,\tau) = \int_{=\infty}^{\infty} \frac{e^{-(x-y)^2/4\tau}}{\sqrt{4\pi\tau}} u(y,0)dy.$$

The Black–Scholes final condition (the exercise price) has been converted to the initial value $u(y,0)$ by the change of variables and, hence, is known. Because the heat kernel is a Gaussian, after reversing steps back to the original financial variables the whole option pricing business is reduced to a use of standard probability tables for the normal distribution.

Black–Scholes theory is known to be imperfect, and many papers and books have dealt with its imperfections. I do not want to go into those here. But because the Black–Scholes PDE is linear with volatility and interest rate coefficients known or estimatible in real time from market monitoring, and because the resulting (famous) Black–Scholes formula coming from the Green's function solution representation above needs only the standard normal probability tables to implement, that formula is widely used to price options.

The usual hedge argument needed to derive the Black–Scholes PDE in order to make the option price $V(S,t)$ riskless is given in Gustafson (1999a). Briefly, suppose you ask, how much more of this option you should buy? The augmented value $d(V+\delta S)$ is calculated from the Ito calculus and is set equal to what you would get in a risk-free bank account $r(V+\delta S)dt$. After you eliminate the stochastic terms you end up with the Black–Scholes PDE. This kind of hedge argument can be shown to hold more generally and is widely employed in more general forms in portfolio management. However, it can be seen that all such methods assume the existence of a self-financing strategy $Y_t = a_t S_t + b_t B_t$ for portfolio balancing, e.g. between stocks S_t and bonds B_t.

My concerns came from an analysis of more exotic Asian options (where you can cash in before the expiry date), but I may express it here as follows. Everyone knows that stock price S and time t are not independent in financial markets. But Black–Scholes theory works because it is derived from an assumption that stock price changes ΔS are random. Indeed, shocking as that was after the first market studies in the 1930's revealed that fact, numerous further studies have borne it out. This ansatz is implemented in the Black–Scholes partial differential equations in the form of lognormal statistics. That is all fine, but is stochastic independence, e.g. of causally arriving price change increments, the same as Cartesian independence, e.g. of algebraically and functionally complete independent variables S and t?

I have investigated the ramifications of this question for the Black–Scholes theory in Gustafson (2002). In particular, I was led to raise this issue from recent applications of numerical methods from computational fluid dynamics in Black–Scholes pricing. These methods allow you to rapidly compute Black–Scholes option prices simultaneously for a large number of asset prices, expiry dates, and the other market parameters. Portfoios are often updated several times a second. These CFD methods, and the other pricing methods in use, all presume a Cartesian grid of S and t.

But to my mind, stochastic time-independence is more akin to the second, labeling, use of time I discussed in Section 5. Of course I am familiar with the theory of stochastic processes, the notion that each little time interval is an "innovation instant", that each new increment of a stochastic process may be regarded as a new "totally independent innovation", that such processes have "orthogonal" or "uncorrelated" increments, that the essence of the Ito stochastic calculus is that it is rigorously kept non-anticipatory in virtually every one of its properties. Yet this is not the same as independent variables S and t in Descartes' sense, which you are properly entitled to draw geometrically as perpendicular axes.

I have investigated this distinction between stochastic and Cartesian independence and its possible implications for Black–Scholes pricing theory at some length elsewhere (see Gustafson 2002). Here I may mention two things. First, it seems that the very notion of hedging (instantaneously) is a myth. Second, it is possible that the potential errors caused by using Cartesian-based hedging models may be rendered insignificant by the rapidity of updated repricing.

8   Changeux and Connes, and Chaitin

An interesting recent dialogue related to determinism may be found in Changeux and Connes (1995). Changeux is a neurobiologist, Connes is a mathematician, and both are well known.[3] The Changeux–Connes debate can be portrayed as focusing on a precise question: Do we create mathematics (Changeux's position), or do we discover mathematics (Connes' position)? To Changeux's credit, he keeps probing. To Connes' credit, he sticks to his guns on the given reality of mathematics. I leave it to you to read the debate.

I would like here to view this question as a gedanken experiment about determinism. If we create mathematics, then if we have free will, mathematics cannot be deterministic, for you and I may create different outcomes. Furthermore, I could then in principle create mathematical and also physical

---

[3]I was recently led to this book by chance when reading Gardner (2001), which I recommend. Gardner (2001) is concerned that science (e.g. biology, physics) is displacing philosophy (e.g. religion, ethics) too rapidly in how we try to understand human consciousness. I do not want to wander off into many potentially endless discussions that could ensue from the issues that Gardner raises. Such issues seem to me to at base to often come down to some version of the nature versus nurture debate. I will however comment that generally I believe that all such discussions are inconclusive, that the "truth" of any of our conclusions is usually just some language-limited approximation of some small part of much larger "truths" that we will never fully see.

theories which are to be as I like, either deterministic or nondeterministic. On the other side, if we only discover mathematics, then we have "no free will" about that. But what we discover could well be either deterministic or nondeterministic, depending on what "God" had intended us to find. Also, of course, each of us has nonidentical minds, so what we discover is nonidentical.

I wanted to ground my further reactions to the Changeux–Connes debate in some expert literature. The most well known pertinent treatise is Kuhn (1962). There, already on page 2, Kuhn carefully states "the historian ... must determine by what man and at what point in time each contemporary scientific fact, law, and theory was *discovered or invented*." On page 3 we find again "inventions and discoveries". Although later, I assume for efficiency, Kuhn often just uses the word "discovery", he is careful not to exclude invention. For example, on page 52, we find: "We must now ask how changes of this sort can come about, considering first discoveries, or novelties of fact, and then inventions, or novelties of theory. That distinction between discovery and invention or between fact or theory will, however, immediately prove to be exceedingly artificial. Its artificiality is an important clue to several of this essay's main theses." For further grounding, I checked Kuhn (2000) for his thoughts a number of years later. Right there, on page 15, we find: "The discovery (in cases like these invention may be a better word) of Newton's second law of motion ...". So Kuhn is still being careful to *not* choose irrevocably between discovery and creation in science.

I now want to use the Changeux–Connes book to demonstrate an axiom: that virtually every one of our arguments in any discussion is prejudiced. If at this point you insist on a mathematical model for my statement, go ahead and now view each sentence as I write it here as a conditional expectation of a stochastic process representing the current state of my thinking based upon an ever-changing irregular nonstationary non-Boolean filter of events fleeting through my mind, partially induced by underlying dynamics in both my conscious and unconscious phase spaces to say nothing of the environment around me. There is nothing wrong with modelling so long as it is useful and one remembers that it is only a model, and not full reality. And the examples of prejudice that I now select from Changeux and Connes (1995) are not criticisms – I like the book.

When they get to "Thinking Machines" (Chapter 6), it is clear to me that both are out of their element. I have been in and out of computing for 40 years (see, e.g., Gustafson 1999c). I can assure you that it does not suffice to reduce a discussion of computing to Gödel's Theorem and the Turing model. One needs a lot of real experience if you are to intelligently discuss computing machines and all of their different architectures and what they have done and what they might be able to do. However, I did like Connes' detour in this chapter into an analogy between the S-matrix in physics and functionalism in psychology, both being "black box" approaches. It is too bad that one of the two debaters did not state in the dialogue that a significant part of the burgeoning field of neural network computing is based upon exactly such a black box approach. Instead we are taken off to S-matrix theory and then to string theory. But the S-matrix theory was on Connes' mind, also string theory and the standard model. It was also surprising that as a neurobiologist Changeux apparently, nonetheless, is not up to date on recent developments in sixth generation computing, such as all of the developments in neural networks. So he prejudices his comments upon pleasure versus displeasure, a more psychological context. In sum, neither of the debaters can escape their limited experience base and so their opinions and conclusions are automatically prejudiced.

Another example from the same passages is Connes' fixation on the need for an "evaluation function". This is classic Bourbaki, an intuition honed on too much training about linear functionals and dual measures. Of course my own thinking is also frequently prejudiced by seeking some familiar tool, sometimes from functional analysis, with which I can bridge to a new situation. We are all like Changeux and Connes.

Here I must recount an anecdote, a true one. In June of 2000 I was Professeur Invité at the Université de Bordeaux, invited there by the computational fluid dynamics group. By chance there occurred at the same time there an international meeting (one of the IWOTA series) on operator theory (e.g. functional analysis). By chance at a restaurant I met a colleague, Professor Zemanek (Warsaw), whom I had not seen in twenty years. With him as we walked back to his hotel was a younger colleague from Morroco. This fellow made the statement, I have heard it many times, that a pure mathematician is better because he can always do any applied mathematics if and when he chooses. I asked him a few "computing and applied" questions, but he just sidestepped them, murmuring the usual mantra. Then I presented him with the names of several famous "pure" mathematicians (e.g. Ralph Phillips comes now to my mind) who were formerly engineers, and I asked him to tell me some engineers who had been previously pure mathematicians. We were on a narrow sidewalk and at that moment my fine young fellow walked right into a lightpole. He bounced against a nearby wall and I was genuinely concerned about him, but he straightened up and we continued on our way.

Overall of course due to my own experience-based prejudices, I agreed much more with Connes than with Changeux. My point is: how can we hope to achieve complete synchronicity of understanding exactly what determinism is, if our minds are always different and always in flux?

One feature that I liked about Changeux and Connes is that they took what I call the "engineering" approach. Focus on a specific problem and try to solve it in a practical way. It was refreshing for me, a good pure mathematician who squanders a lot of time also on applied, computational, and interdisciplinary mathematics and science, to see a brilliant pure mathematician like Connes, reaching out. It does not matter that their discussion was at times naive, confused, and that they, in the words of Gardner (2001), "were sufficiently dismissive of each other that they resembled two French tankers passing each other at midnight."

In this paper I know I am being at times naive, confused, and because of the overly mathematical portions of this paper, I may "pass the philosophers and some others in the night". But I believe in the "engineering approach": ask a concrete question and try to find a solution in a practical way. I have done a fair amount of interdisciplinary work jointly with engineers and I can tell you that it is a rewarding way to sharpen your thinking.

To conclude this section, I now want to reverse my prejudices and go to the Gödel and Turing world, which I disparaged above as being far too limited. Specifically, I want to discuss the interesting work of Chaitin (1999), who goes beyond Gödel and Turing. From within this very pure, limited work of theoretical computational and algorithmic complexity, one can argue in a seemingly absolute way that nothing is deterministic.

As is well-known, Gödel's results show that there are always some mathematical theorems that you will not be able to prove. Turing's results show that there are mathematical things which you will never be able to compute. More precisely, there are no instructions which you can program into a computer to enable it to decide in advance whether the given program will finish its task and then stop. You must just wait and see. Chaitin went beyond Turing and looked at all possible programs that you could give to the computer and asked about the probability that a single program chosen at random would stop. It turned out that this probability, called omega, has a very interesting property: it is uncomputable. There will be no instruction set which can tell you how to compute omega. The best you can say is that omega consists of an unending string of independent binary bits which are randomly 0's or 1's.

Just as Gödel's results startled the world into realizing the limits of mathematical axiomization of science, and Turing's results forced the world to realize the limits of what you could expect to compute in a finite time,

Chaitin's results are a strong argument for randomness at the very foundations of mathematics. Chaitin (1999) concludes that mathematics itself is at best quasi-empirical, much more intuitive than many would like to admit, and that much of the mathematics we hold so dear is really true for no particular reason other than the accident of its discovery and usefulness to us. To me, these developments are a strong argument for indeterminism, certainly in mathematics, and also in nature.

9   Digression on Determinism

I have purposely, as I have said earlier in this paper, avoided defining *determinism*, leaving the several senses of that word to the dictionaries and to the efforts of others. However, to be fair, let us now trace back through what I have written to this point to see which facets of determinism I have actually addressed.

In the dedication to my Aunt Leona in the Abstract, determinism meant *predestination.* I am now compelled to consult my Webster's (1971, p. 616) and that is the sense 1c: *theological determinism.* In the Introduction I noted that it seemed to me that "determinism" has many, rather than few, uses. Thus I am now a little surprised at how few senses of determinism Webster's lists (take a look yourself). Our dilations in Section 2 were predicated upon a presumably desired determinism which meant the existence of a "concrete physical dynamics" in the phase space, rather than just a knowledge of some probabilities in the state space. Note carefully that a number of physicists will equate unitary evolutions with reversibility with determinism, but we also insist on both probability preservation in state space or its equivalent, a physical dynamics in phase space. Let me call that *dynamical determinism.* The closest to this that Webster's has is 1b: cosmological determinism, that everything in nature takes place according to natural laws. Of course it is possible that all "natural laws" that God gave us are only probabilistic. Would that be cosmological determinism? What is Webster's (1971) 1a: all acts of the will result from causes which determine them in such a way that we cannot act in any other way?[4] This is close to the debate of Changeux and Connes (1995) which I discussed in Section 8: 1a would imply that we only can discover mathematics, rather than create it. Webster's calls 1a *ethical determinism*, which is not quite the same as saying that creating mathematics rather than discovering it is unethical! By the way, have I created this article, or only discovered it?

---

[4]Compare the contributions by Guignon and Kane in this volume.

Now leaving the constraints of determinism according to Webster's (1971), Sections 5, 6, and 7 focused on Time. Let me make the assertion now that any discussion of determinism has a prerequisite notion: Time. To reinforce this point, any notion of indeterminism requires the possibility of randomness or stochasticity and in any case requires a prerequisite notion of uncertainty. Any notion of uncertainty means uncertainty about the outcome of some event. But any outcome of any event implies an action which must take place in Time. Therefore I conclude that any good understanding of determinism must be written within the context of Time.

Disclaimer: to any written words one may always find argument. This sad fact which I came to many, many moons ago has already been realized by many, many others, Wittgenstein, Peirce, anyone who has sought to write about deeper meanings of words, e.g. meanings of meanings, and the like. The meaning of life will never be captured with words. Words are a very crude system; think of them as a cultural computing machine, allowing us to store thoughts and then communicate or compute upon those thoughts. But when you commit even a single thought to writing on some tablet, as I am doing at this very moment, you realize that you have at best recorded that thought in only an incomplete, time dependent, approximate, way. The feelings you had when the thought flashed across your mind, the emotional response that led you to cross the room and reach for the tablet: they have been lost. Thousands of neuronal synapses and the bright sun streaming into the window and the blue skies of winter and the feeling of well being do not enter the codification. So the meaning of life will never be captured with words. The same can be said about physical laws and mathematical formulae – and determinism.

Then there are the variables of content and context. For example, you are far up in the deep blue sky and you look down at the top of a great white cloud-top full of turbulence. There you see disorder. What I claim is that even if your glance downward took no time (it does take time, of course, because it is an event to glance down ...), even such a turbulent-top-of-cloud snapshot is not deterministic. Each feature, major and minute, seems fixed. If your eye could have infinite precision, perhaps you would see all of the features that exist. But your eye or the camera has finite precision, and the details you cannot see are there nonetheless. Bergson, James, and others knew this. They also knew that if you could see everything, all frequencies, hear all sounds, you would go mad. Let us ignore this point here. If you somehow could use a microscope to see a single cloud droplet penetrating down to the quantum level of an H_2O atom, the position of the electron is fixed only up to the uncertainty of its momentum. So whether something is deterministic depends on both content (e.g. the scale) of the situation and the context in which that content may be viewed. And that context may change instantaneously with time.

I think one could go on and on with a discussion like this. Perhaps that is why my initial intuition as to what I wanted to say in this paper was: do not let such a frame dictate your thoughts. Go at more concrete examples which appeal to me and will be more meaningful to others.

If pressed at this moment to choose between determinism and indeterminism of the world, I would probably prefer a world which is governed by a deterministic Nature for which all of our description is inexact, hence indeterministic. I would even protest against such a forced choice because I find anathema the idea of such "one bit" binary value systems so prevalent in human society.

Moreover if further pressed, I would probably back off from the nice idea of a deterministic Nature. Even if our quantum mechanics picture would yield to a finer level of dynamics which is really a "certainty" picture down to the motion of each electron and each quark and each gluon and each interaction field, my intuition gives me disquiet about what Time then really consists of in the micro-micro-micros below any level where we claim to know it.

To continue this section, let me quickly comment that there are many aspects of determinism which I did not discuss here but which could have been brought to bear upon the topics I did go into. First, I did not go into issues of epistemological versus ontological models and confusions that may result when they are improperly mixed. See Atmanspacher and Kronz (1998), Bishop (2002), Primas (1981) for wide ranging investigations of these and related issues. Second, I did not go into Time operators (Antoniou and Gustafson 2000), Gustafson 1997a,b, Atmanspacher and Amann 1998; see also Misra in this volume). I am sure I have also not touched many other important facets of determinism.

Remark: As I mentioned at the end of Sections 1 and 5, when converting the first draft of this paper into its second and final draft, I found that I had a little extra time to bring in some thoughts of some great scientists, as they might relate to this paper. So I conclude this section thusly. These are just a random collection of such thoughts which I note and nothing definitive is intended. You may make of them what you like. Notice, however, that the views that I have selected are the mature views of these scientists later in their lives.

It is well-known that Einstein never liked the indeterministic properties of the quantum theory. He claimed that "I have thought a hundred times as much about the quantum problems as I have about general relativity theory." But the quote about this that I like the best is Einstein (1967): "I can, if the worst comes to the worst, still realize that God may have created a world in which there are no natural laws. In short, a chaos. But that there should be statistical laws with definite solutions, i.e., laws that compel God to throw dice in each individual case, I find highly disagreeble."

Although I know it is an unfair comparison, I think my Aunt Leona would thoroughly agree with Einstein's statement.

Heisenberg, of course, was a defender of the indeterministic properties of the quantum theory, which he helped develop. In Heisenberg (1955) I found an interesting exposé of his beliefs. He states the problem clearly:

> However, all the opponents of the Copenhagen interpretation do agree on one point. It would, in their view, be desirable to return to the reality concept of classical physics or, more generally expressed, to the ontology of materialism; that is, to the idea of an objective real world, whose smallest parts exist objectively in the same way as stones and trees, independently of whether or not we observe them. We shall explain once more ... that this is impossible ...

Heisenberg then does his best to dispose of each of the opponents of the Copenhagen interpretation. He concludes:

> The Copenhagen interpretation is indeed based upon the existence of processes which can be simply described in terms of space and time, i.e. in terms of classical concepts, and which thus compose our 'reality' in the proper sense. If we attempt to penetrate behind this reality into the details of atomic events, the contours of this 'objectively real' world dissolve – not in the mist of a new and yet unclear idea of reality, but in the transparent clarity of a mathematics whose laws govern the possible and not the actual. ... At this point we realize the simple fact that natural science is not Nature itself but a part of the relation between Man and Nature, and therefore is dependent on Man.

I would like to assert that my reservation expressed earlier (Gustafson 1999b) and above about the inherent limitations of anything we can express in words or formulas, is consistent with Heisenberg's words. Please note, however, that his words are also a limited filter and certainly reflect his prejudices. They are also an incomplete codification of a richer underlying reality. Probably we will never know any final truths. And our life-long conditioned intuitions may in some cases be closer to final truths than any attempted rendering of those intuitions into words and mathematical symbols.

Dirac, also one of the great pioneers of the quantum theory, was quite intuitive. Rigor was not his goal. Later in his life he wrote a small book on quantum field theory (Dirac 1966). At the end he gives a physical interpretation of his view of quantum field theory as he has developed it in this book. To oversimiplify, Dirac gives up incoming fields and so he has no S-matrix. Everything is emission. Then I find interesting his statement:

> You will note that there is less determinism in the present theory than there is in the usual theory involving the Schrödinger wave function. The reason for this is that the quantity $K|O_t\rangle$, which gives all that is observable at one particular time, does not fix what is observable at a later time, because of the latent terms in K-latent terms in K which you could provide with any coefficients you like and they will not contribute anything observable at time t, but they will still influence observable things at another time.

I submit that there is a strong analogy between Dirac's thinking and the mathematical framework of regular stationary stochastic processes which I alluded to when describing the Rokhlin–Kolmogorov dynamical systems theory in Section 3. I do not want to misinterpret Dirac's thoughts, but recall that the regular stochastic process theory can be built upon increasingly rich σ-algebra event filters in phase space (see Gustafson and Goodrich 1985, or Antoniou and Gustafson 1999). In that causal (I am not sure how much causality Dirac wanted to presume in his theory) stochastic process framework, one need not have the Markov property, so that new information "may come in from the future or the past," the idea I presented in Section 6.

As is well known, in 1931 Dirac postulated that empty space was not empty, but that it was really a sea of electrons of negative energies. In 1932, Anderson found these anti-particles experimentally and we now call the antielectron of Dirac the positron. In 1949 Feynman created his path-integral theory for quantum electrodynamics. In this theory there are some paths in which the electron is moving backward in time. To quote Feynman (1985), "this phenomenon is general. Every particle in Nature has an amplitude to move backwards in time, and therefore has an anti-particle." I would like to assert that this sea of acausal vacuum interactions, albeit however short-lived they are due to quick particle-antiparticle annihilations, is an instance in the microworld of my thesis of Section 6, where both past and future are needed to determine the present.

Causality is a topic collateral to determinism, and like determinism, I did not want here to get into a taxonomy of it. However, when the renowned mathematician Segal (1976) departed his usual domain of functional analysis and went off into cosmology, he found that he had to deal with causality. Because he wants to remain in a framework of smooth continuous variables, he concludes that "the 'future' may be represented by an essentially arbitrary

nontrivial closed convex cone in the underlying linear (space-time) manifold."
To develop a nonlinear theory, he then "suggests as a starting point for
causality considerations ... a structure consisting in the assignment to each
point of a closed convex cone in the tangent space at the point." Segal here is
adapting the classical notion of a domain of influence of a hyperbolic partial
differential equation (see Gustafson 1999a), to his more general conformal
space-time framework

What I found interesting in Segal (1976), however, was the cost of demanding all the smoothness of space-time. To dispense with this concern
early in his treatment, he states:

> All this is not to say that it would not be interesting or possible to
> have a treatment of causally structured spaces which did not depend
> on the local smoothness of the space. ... But until one has a better
> understanding of causality matters in the more accessible context of
> smooth manifolds, it might well be mathematically foolhardy as well
> as physically irrelevant to attempt to obtain results for such general
> spaces comparable to what might be expected to be available in the
> smooth manifold case.

I realize now that the issue I raised in Section 5, that Time need not be
a geometric variable, and the instance of that proposed in Section 7, where
Time is stochastic, take me into the 'foolhardy' world Segal certainly did
not want to deal with. I would also like to conjecture that Feynman's 'backward in time' particle probability amplitudes could possibly be reformulated
with time, rather than state, as the stochastic creature. My idea here could
be stated in an ergodic way: that we should be more concerned with the
percentages of time (which becomes the stochastic variable) that a particle spends in each of its Feynman paths, rather than with its mixed state
amplitudes.

To move to a more classical context, I found the recent article by Rohrlich
(2000) interesting. Rohrlich, of course, knows classical electron dynamics
about as well as anyone, there is his famous book with Jauch, and he has been
a strong defender of conventional quantum mechanics as well. However, in
the cited paper he deals with classical time, whether it be Newtonian, special
relativity, or general relativity, and he focuses in particular on the effect of
any classical object's self-field. His point is to argue that the self-force caused
by the self-field "spoils the time reversal invariance of the equation of motion
in all cases."

Rohrlich's view is consistent with my idea put forth in Section 6. To
paraphrase my thesis here, let me oversimplify it: you have to know past
or future to know present. Looking more closely at Rohrlich (2000) we

find "the self-field causes a self-interaction that modifies the equations of motion in such a way that they are no longer time reversal invariant. In all modificatioins a choice is available whether retarded or advanced self-interactions should be used. Causality makes us opt for the retarded case." I would assert that the view I put forth in Gustafson (1997a,b) is much more extensive and general than that. There I point out how often the arrow of time is set by a binary choice, sometimes unwittingly by scientists in their various theories. Rohrlich's opting for the retarded case is just one such binary choice.

10   Final Thoughts

I want to close this paper by leaving you with two thoughts, one from 900 years ago, and one from yesterday.

The first is well known. I imagine that most of you have already heard the words of Khayyam (1101). I would assert that how you know them, how you remember them, how you say them, your mental and emotional reaction to them as you read them, is not exactly the same as mine ...

> Ah, but my Computations, People say,
> Reduc'd the Year to better reckoning? –Nay,
> 'Twas only striking from the Calendar
> Unborn To-morrow, and dead Yesterday.

What does that poetry mean to *you*?

The second thought is a true story which I hope you enjoy. I have lived in Colorado most of my life, with much time spent enjoying the mountains. Boulder sits exactly where the great plains meets the mountains which begin at the city limits. Yesterday (Wednesday, April 4, 2001) my friend Kathy called me and wanted me to take a break from my immersion in this paper, to take a hike at 5 pm after work. We had another obligation in town at 7 pm, so it had to be a short hike. We met at the Chautauqua ranger station parking lot. At first we took the Royal Arch trail. But time was too short so we branched onto the 2nd Flatiron trail. Quickly we left its steepness to descend and branch onto the Baird trail. This brought us to the Bluebell Shelter house. I suggested we then go along the Mesa trail awhile. An outhouse presented itself, so we stopped a few minutes to use it. After a few minutes on the Mesa trail we came to the junction with the McClintoch trail, which descends back toward Chautauqua. I suggested it was time to be getting back so we took the McClintoch trail. About 5 minutes down, at about 6 pm, we came upon a young woman about 20 meters below us who was standing very still, facing us, eyes wide, pointing to her right, to our left, finger on her lips. I whispered to Kathy "some tourist has seen a deer ..." as we glanced to our left. Seeing nothing, we looked again at the woman, who, motionless, said silently with her lips "mountain lion". Immediately our adrenalin flared, we moved down a couple of steps, and only about 10 meters to our left was a full sized, mature, calm, lion, looking directly at us. In 50 years I have seen everything in Colorado, from moose, badger, martin, bear, bobcat, beaver, mountain sheep, goat, you name it, but never a lion. And here was this formidable individual, eyes matched to ours. Their eyes are truly hypnotic. It was sitting upright, dog fashion, fully alert, staring at us. 10 meters is not a great distance.

I said "we should move on, slowly" and we did. The young woman climbed up past us at the same time. The lion never moved. A great event.

Now I ask you, was that a random event? Or a deterministic one? And do not tell me that the expected value of my seeing a mountain lion at some time in my life was all that we may discuss. And do not forget all the trail change decisions we made before we happened upon the lion.

References

Akcoglu M. (1975): Positive contractions on L_1-spaces. *Math. Zeitschr.* **143**, 1–13.

Antoniou I. and Gustafson K. (1993): From probabilistic description to deterministic dynamics. *Physica A* **197**, 153–166.

Antoniou I. and Gustafson K. (1997): From irreversible Markov semigroups to chaotic dynamics. *Physica A* **236**, 296–308.

Antoniou I. and Gustafson K. (1999): Wavelets and stochastic processes. *Mathematics and Computers in Simulation* **49**, 81–104.

Antoniou I. and Gustafson K. (2000): The time operator of wavelets. *Chaos, Solitons and Fractals* **11**, 443–452.

Antoniou I., Gustafson K., and Suchanecki Z. (1998): On the inverse problem of statistical physics: from irreversible semigroups to chaotic dynamics. *Physica A* **252**, 345–361.

Atmanspacher H. and Amann A. (1998): Positive-operator-valued measures and projection-valued measures of noncommutative time operators. *Intern. J. Theor. Phys.* **37**, 629–650.

Atmanspacher H. and Kronz F. (1998): Many realisms. *Acta Polytechnica Scandinavica* **Ma 91**, 31–43 (1998).

Atmanspacher H. and Ruhnau E. (1997): *Time, Temporality, Now*, Springer, Berlin.

Bishop R. (2002): Brussels–Austin nonequilibrium statistical mechanics: large Poincaré systems and rigged Hilbert space. *Stud. Hist. Phil. Mod. Phys.*, in press.

Chaitin G. (1999): *The Unknowable*, Springer, Singapore.

Changeux J.P. and Connes A. (1995): *Conversations on Mind, Matter, Mathematics*, Princeton University Press, Princeton.

Davies E.B. (1976): *Quantum Theory of Open Systems*, Academic Press, London.

Dirac P. (1966): *Lectures on Quantum Field Theory*, Academic Press, New York.

Doob J. (1953): *Stochastic Processes*, Wiley, New York.

Duffie D. (1996): *Dynamic Asset Pricing Theory*, Princeton University Press, Princeton.

Dunford N. and Schwartz J.T. (1973): *Linear operators III*, Wiley, New York.

Einstein A. (1967): Comment to James Franck. In *Einstein: A Centennary Volume*, ed. by A.P. French, Harvard University Press, Cambridge, 1979. I traced this quote back to C.P. Snow (1967): *Variety of Men*, MacMillan, London, p. 83. Unfortunately Snow also did not cite the exact date of Einstein's comment to Franck.

Feynman R. (1985): *QED – The Strange Theory of Light and Matter*, Princeton University Press, Princeton.

Gardner H. (2001): The philosophy-science continuum. *The Chronicle of Higher Education*, Vol. XLVII, No. 26 (March 9), B7–B10.

Goldstein S., Misra B., and Courbage M. (1981): On intrinsic randomness of dynamical systems. *J. Stat. Phys.* **25**, 111–126.

Goodrich K., Gustafson K., and Misra B. (1980): On converse to Koopman's lemma. *Physica A* **102**, 379–388.

Goodrich K., Gustafson K., and Misra B. (1986): On K-flows and irreversibility. *J. Stat. Phys.* **43**, 317–320.

Gustafson K. (1997a): *Lectures on Computational Fluid Dynamics, Mathematical Physics, and Linear Algebra*, World-Scientific, Singapore.

Gustafson K. (1997b): Operator spectral states. *Computers Math. Applic.* **34**, 467–508

Gustafson K. (1999a): *Partial Differential Equations and Hilbert Space Methods*, Dover, New York.

Gustafson K. (1999b): Review of *Time, Temporality, Now*, ed. by H. Atmanspacher and E. Ruhnau, Springer, Berlin, 1997. *J. Scient. Expl.* **13**, 695–703; cf. *J. Scient. Expl.* **14** (2000), 139, for the bibliography which was inadvertently omitted in **13**.

Gustafson K. (1999c): Parallel computing forty years ago. *Mathematics and Computers in Simulation* **51**, 47–62.

Gustafson K. (2002): On the nature of the hedge. To appear.

Gustafson K. and Goodrich K. (1980): A Banach–Lamperti theorem and similarity transformations in statistical mechanics. *Coll. Math. Soc. Janos Bolyai* **35**, 567–579.

Gustafson K. and Goodrich K. (1985): Kolmogorov systems and Haar systems. *Coll. Math. Soc. Janos Bolyai* **49**, 401–416.

Gustafson K., Goodrich K., and Misra B. (1981): Irreversibility and stochasticity of chemical processes. In *Quantum Mechanics in Mathematics, Chemistry, and Physics*, ed. by K. Gustafson and W. Reinhardt, Plenum, New York, pp. 203–210.

Gustafson K. and Rao D. (1997): *Numerical Range*, Springer, Berlin.

Heisenberg W. (1955): The development of the interpretation of the quantum theory. In *Niels Bohr and the Development of Physics*, ed. by W. Pauli, Pergamon Press, London, pp. 12–29.

Hudson R., Ion P., and Parthasarathy K. (1981): The Feynman–Kac formula for Boson Wiener processes. In *Quantum Mechanics in Mathematics, Chemistry, and Physics*, ed. by K. Gustafson and W. Reinhardt, Plenum, New York, pp. 479–498.

Julia G. (1944): Sur les projections des systèmes orthonormaux de l'espace hilbertien. *C. R Acad. Sci. Paris* **218**, 892–895; see also: Les projections des systèmes orthonormaux de l'espace hilbertien et les opérateur bornés. *C. R Acad. Sci. Paris* **219**, 8–11; Sur la représentation analytique des opérateur bornés de l'espace hilbertien. *C. R Acad. Sci. Paris* **219**, 225–227.

Kern M., Nagel R., and Palm G. (1977): Dilations of positive operators; construction and ergodic theory. *Math. Zeitschr..* **156**, 265–277.

Khayyam O. (1101): *The Rubaiyat*, Peter Pauper Press, Mt. Vernon, N.Y.

Kleppner D. (2001): On the matter of the meter. *Physics Today*, March, 11–12.

Koopman B. O. (1931): Hamiltonian systems and transformations in Hilbert spaces. *Proc. Nat. Acad. Sci. USA*, **17**, 315–318.

Kuhn T. (1962): *The Structure of Scientific Revolutions*, University of Chicago Press, Chicago.

Kuhn T. (2000): *The Road Since Structure*, University of Chicago Press, Chicago.

Kümmerer B. (1985): Markov dilations on W^*-algebras. *J. Functional Analysis* **63**, 139–177.

Lasota A. and Mackey M. (1985): *Probabilistic Properties of Deterministic Systems*, Cambridge University Press, Cambridge.

Lindblad G. (1975): Completely positive maps and entropy inequalities. *Comm. Math. Phys.* **40**, 147–151.

Mackey G. (1963): *The Foundations of Quantum Mechanics*, Benjamin, Reading, MA.

Misra B., Prigogine I., and Courbage M. (1979): From deterministic dynamics to probabilistic descriptions. *Physica A* **98**, 1–26.

Naimark M. (1943): Positive definite operator valued functions on a commutative group. *Izvestiya Acad. Sci. USSR* **7**, 237–244.

Ojima I. (1997): Brief comments on Part II, Chapter 1, Probabilistic and Deterministic Description. In K. Gustafson, *Lectures on Computational Fluid Dynamics, Mathematical Physics, and Linear Algebra*, World Scientific, Singapore, pp. 167–168.

Parthasarathy K. (1992): *An Introduction to Quantum Stochastic Calculus*, Birkhäuser, Basel.

Primas H. (1981): *Chemistry, Quantum Mechanics and Reductionism*, Springer, Berlin.

Reichenbach H. (1944): *Philosophical Foundations of Quantum Mechanics*, University of California Press, Berkeley.

Reynolds, R.J. Tobacco Co. (1993): Postcard request for reprint of I. Antoniou and K. Gustafson, From probabilistic description to deterministic dynamics, *Physica A* **197** (1993). Winston-Salem, N.C.

Rohrlich F. (2000): Causality and the arrow of classical time. *Stud. Hist. Phil. Mod. Phys.* **31**, 1–13.

Rokhlin V. (1964): On the fundamental ideas of measure theory. *Am. Math. Soc. Transl.* **39**, 1–36.

Segal I. (1976): *Mathematical Cosmology and Extragalactic Astronomy*, Academic Press, New York.

Stinespring W. F. (1955): Positive functions on C^*-algebras. *Proc. Amer. Math. Soc.* **6**, 211–216.

Stroescu E. (1973): Isometric dilations of contractions on Banach spaces. *Pac. J. Math.* **47**, 257–262.

Sz. Nagy B. (1953): Sur les contractions de l'espace de Hilbert. *Acta Sci. Math.* **15**, 87–92.

Webster N. (1971): *Third New International Dictionary*, Merriam Publishers, Springfield, MA.

Wigner E. (1932): On the quantum correction for thermodynamic equilibrium. *Phys. Rev.* **45**, 749–759.

Transitions from Deterministic Evolution to Irreversible Probabilistic Processes and the Quantum Measurement Problem

Baidyanath Misra

1 Introduction

The tension between determinism on the one hand and the role of chance and freewill on the other has been felt very early in the history of human thought. I am not a scholar of ancient thought, but I will begin by mentioning some examples of this tension.

Gosala was an older contemporary of Buddha in the 6th century B.C. Gosala is little known now. But he must have had a large following in his time, for Buddha felt the need to oppose his world view. Gosala held a completely deterministic world view. He preached that just as a ball of woolen string unrolls itself when thrown, each segment of the string coming one after the other in a determined way, so does the world process unfold in a determined manner. Therefore, all man can do is to live with equanimity and patience. The only bright spot in this world picture was that every being was destined to reach the state of perfection during the predetermined process of cosmic evolution. Buddha, in contrast, believed that man can reach perfection by human effort. This presupposes efficacy of purposeful action and freewill. Buddha therefore provided a theory of "dependent causation" which to his mind ensured efficacy of human action rather than committing him to a completely deterministic world view.

This tension is felt in the Vedic literature as well. The *Shewtashwatara Upanishad* begins with the question: What is the ultimate principle? Is it *niyati* (necessity, determinism) or *yadriccha* (chance)? The term *Yadriccha* is generally translated as chance. But its root meaning is related to freewill. Anyway, the *Upanishad* does not resolve the issue but sees the "self nature of God" (*devatma shakti*) as the governing principle of the world process. This seems akin to Spinoza's solution of the tension between a strictly deterministic world view and the posssibility of ethical action.

The same tension was felt in Greek thought as well. The atomists held that the atoms follow deterministic paths. The Epicureans, who believed that even souls are composed of atoms, could not accept the idea of absolutely no freewill. To allow for deviations from an otherwise determined state of affairs they introduced the concept of a special motion of atoms called "Swerve" which was assumed to take place occasionally.

The mentioned tension will be discussed in this volume at great depth and from a modern perspective by philosophers and cognitive scientists. Here I shall address the question of possible connections between deterministic dynamical evolution and probabilistic processes. This may contribute to the debate between determinism and freewill insofar as strict determinism, on the face of it, does not allow any role for freewill whereas probabilistic laws leave room for it.

Since Newton and until the advent of quantum theory it was unquestionably believed that only deterministic descriptions provide a complete and objective picture of the physical world. Quantum mechanics has placed probability at the fundamental level of description of physical systems. Nevertheless, there is continuing uneasiness as to how probabilistic descriptions can be regarded as complete and objective – hence the continuing interest in hidden variables in quantum mechanics.

Underlying this uneasiness with regard to probability is the generally held belief that probabilistic descriptions can be obtained from deterministic dynamics only as a result of some form of coarse graining and approximation. The appearance of probability is thus seen to be the consequence of ignorance of a more fundamental and complete description of the physical world.

In this essay I shall review work done in the past two, three decades, which developed a totally different possibility of obtaining probabilistic (Markov) processes from deterministic dynamical evolution. It shows that probabilistic processes can arise from deterministic dynamical evolution through an invertible similarity transformation. This puts the role of probability in the physical description of the world in a new perspective. The appearance of probability is no longer tied to the introduction of "ignorance" through coarse graining. Instead, probability arises because of dynamical conditions expressed by a suitable form of instability of dynamical motion. This approach also addresses the question of time asymmetry of the physical world.

Finally, I shall briefly discuss the problem of the quantum measurement process. I shall indicate how the incorporation of irreversibility in the framework of quantum dynamics will possibly lead toward a solution of the, so far, intractable quantum measurement problem.

2 Deterministic Dynamics and Probabilistic Markov Processes

To formulate the problem of the existence of an invertible similarity transformation leading from deterministic dynamical evolution to probabilistic Markov processes let us briefly recall the conflicting and common points between the two. Classical dynamics views the the temporal evolution of a system in terms of a deterministic motion of phase points, describing initial conditions, along deterministic phase space trajectories. A classical dynamical system is thus described by its phase space Γ (or more precisely a constant energy surface of Γ) and a group S_t (t is the time parameter) of one-to-one transformations of Γ onto itself. A phase point $\omega \in \Gamma$ moves in time t to the unique point $S_t\omega = \omega_t$. According to the Liouville theorem there is an invariant measure μ with respect to S_t, $\mu(S_t\Delta) = \mu(\Delta)$, for any (measurable) subset Δ of Γ. For convenience we shall assume the Liouville measure to be normalized, $\mu(\Gamma) = 1$.

Koopman (1931) formulated the theory of dynamical motion in terms of the evolution of (Gibbs) density functions on phase space. Under the dynamical evolution, the density function ρ on the phase space Γ evolves in time t to ρ_t given by $\rho_t(\omega) = \rho(S_{-t}\omega)$. Because of the invariance of the Liouville measure μ, the evolution $\rho \rightarrow \rho_t$ is given by a unitary group U_t in $L^2_\mu : (U_t\rho)(\omega) \equiv \rho(S_{-t}\omega)$.

A unitary group U_t as defined above is said to be induced by the transformation group S_t. There are, of course, unitary groups in L^2_μ which are not induced by groups S_t of point transformations of the phase space Γ. But more recently it has been shown (Goodrich et al. 1980) that every unitary group U_t in L^2_μ that takes density functions to density functions, i.e. preserves the positivity of functions and maps the unit function 1 to itself, is induced by a group of point transformations of the phase space. There is thus a one-to-one correspondence between the trajectory evolution of phase points and the unitary evolution of density functions. This emphasizes that the formulation of dynamical evolution in terms of a unitary evolution of probability distributions on the phase space (called the Liouville formulation) does not by itself take us away from a deterministic evolution of phase points.

But it is not without important gain. As we shall shortly see, it puts the theory of dynamical evolution and that of probabilistic Markov processes in the same mathematical framework. This will help to formulate the problem of the transition from deterministic evolution to probabilistic processes. The Liouville formulation also avoids the well-known Poincaré type recurrence for (non-singular) distribution functions, except in the case of simple dynamical systems. The reason for this is that the "Poincaré recurrence time" depends irregularly on phase points. This fact is important for the relation between time reversible dynamical evolution and entropy increasing irreversible evolution.

A probabilistic (Markov) process is specified by the transition probabilities $P(t, \omega, \Delta)$ that the system starting from an initial state $\omega \in \Gamma$ will reach the subset Δ of Γ in time t. The transition probabilities $P(t, \omega, \Delta)$ satisfy all the usual properties of transition probabilities. In particular, for every fixed t and ω $P(t, \omega, \Delta)$ defines a probability measure on the subsets Δ of Γ. In addition, the transition probabilities for a Markov process satisfy the well-known Chapman-Kolmogorov condition (Yosida 1965). This condition expresses the absence of "memory effects" in the evolution described by the Markov process. Finally, the invariance of the measure μ on Γ under the process is expressed by the condition $\int P(t, \omega, \Delta) d\mu(\omega) = \mu(\Delta)$ for all $t \geq 0$ and (measurable) subsets Δ of Γ.

One can now formulate the relation between Markov processes and contraction semigroups in L_μ^2. Consider the operator W_t defined by $(W_t f)(\omega) = \int f(\omega') P(t, \omega, \delta\omega')$, $f \in L_\mu^2$. Then the usual properties of transition probabilities $P(t, \omega, \Delta)$ and the Chapman-Kolmogorov condition imply:

    (i) W_t preserves the positivity of functions.
    (ii) $W_t \cdot 1 = 1$.
    (iii) W_t forms a semigroup; $W_t W_s = W_{t+s}$ for $t, s \geq 0$.

The evolution of the distribution function $\rho \to \rho_t$ under the Markov process is now described by the adjoint semigroup W_t^* which also preserves positivity, $\rho \to \rho_t \equiv W_t^* \rho$. The invariance of the measure μ for the process implies:

    (iv) $W_t^* \cdot 1 = 1$.

Every Markov process with invariant measure is thus associated with a semigroup of operators on L_μ^2 satisfying conditions (i)–(iv). Conversely, every contraction semigroup W_t in L_μ^2 satisfying conditions (i)–(iv) defines a Markov process with transition probabilities $P(t, \omega, \Delta) = (W_t \phi_\Delta)(\omega)$, where ϕ_Δ is the characteristic or indicator function of the set Δ (Dynkin 1965). There is thus a one-to-one correspondence between Markov processes and contraction semigroups with the stated properties. We shall be interested in a special class of Markov processes whose associated semigroups W_t satisfy the additional condition that the L_μ^2 norm $||W_t^* \rho - 1||$ decreases monotonically to 0 as $t \to \infty$. For such processes the usual expression for negative entropy $\int_\Gamma \rho_t \log \rho_t \, d\mu$, with $\rho_t = W_t^* \rho$, decreases monotonically as t increases for all distributions $\rho \neq 1$. Thus such processes describe entropy increasing irreversible evolution.

The problem now is how the semigroup W_t of a Markov process described above arises from a Liouville type unitary evolution U_t of a dynamical system. The usual approach is to resort to a coarse graining projection operator on the Liouville evolution followed by approximation schemes such as the $\lambda^2 t$ limit, the Boltzmann-Grad limit, etc. (cf. Spohn 1980). In these frameworks, the origin of probabilistic and irreversible evolution is seen in "ignorance" and approximations of an underlying deterministic evolution. As mentioned before, we review here an entirely different possibility existing for dynamical systems exhibiting a suitable form of instability of motion.

3 Instability of Motion and the Transition from Deterministic Dynamical Evolution to Probabilistic Processes

We now seek an operator Λ which provides a transition from the deterministic evolution of a system to a probabilistic process. More specifically, we seek a (bounded) operator Λ on $L^2_\mu(\Gamma)$ satisfying the following conditions:

(a) Λ preserves the positivity of functions;

(b) $\int_\Gamma \Lambda \rho \, d\mu = \int_\Gamma \rho \, d\mu$;

(c) the group U_t of deterministic evolution satisfies the intertwining relation $\Lambda U_t = W_t^* \Lambda$ for $t \geq 0$ with the semigroup W_t^* of an entropy increasing Markov process.

Conditions (a) and (b) express the requirement that Λ maps (Gibbs) distribution functions to distribution functions. Condition (c) expresses the requirement that the transformation Λ provides the desired transition from the deterministic evolution to an entropy increasing Markov process. This can be represented diagrammatically:

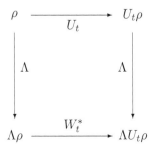

It should be emphasized that such a transition from a deterministic dynamical evolution to a Markov process is not possible for every dynamical system. As will become clear later, the existence and construction of Λ with the required properties are closely linked to the presence of a suitable form of instability (or sensitive dependence on initial conditions) of the dynamical motion.

I shall now summarize the main results of this approach to the transition from deterministic evolution to probabilistic processes. More precise details and proofs can be found in Misra (1978), Misra et al. (1979a,b), Goldstein et al. (1981), Prigogine (1980), Misra and Prigogine (1980, 1983), Misra (1995).

Let us see, in a preliminary way, why a transition to a probabilistic description of temporal evolution is natural for sufficiently unstable dynamical systems. Because of the limited accuracy of any determination of an initial condition, it can only be determined to lie in an open region of the phase space. This region can be made arbitrarily small, but it can never be reduced to a single phase point. This limitation is of no consequence for stable dynamical evolution, for which one can arrive at the concept of deterministic motion along a phase space trajectory as the idealized limit of the motion of smaller and smaller phase space regions.

However, if the dynamical system is sufficiently unstable, each open region of its phase space (no matter how small) contains phase points which move along (exponentially) diverging trajectories under the dynamical motion. In this situation the concept of a phase space trajectory cannot be reasonably maintained as the idealized limit of the motion of smaller and smaller phase space regions. Instability of motion thus points to a fundamental limitation of the concept of deterministic motion along phase space trajectories. The contemplated Λ transformation takes into account this limitation and leads to a probabilistic description of the temporal evolution of unstable dynamical systems.

A possible way to construct the desired Λ transformation is through the so-called (internal) time operator of the dynamical system (Misra 1978, Misra et al. 1979a). To define this concept, let us denote by $P_{-\infty}$ the projection onto the subspace of constant functions on the phase space Γ, and let $\mathbf{H}$ denote the subspace in L^2_μ that is orthogonal to the subspace of constant functions. Then a self-adjoint operator T in $\mathbf{H}$ is said to be a time operator for the unitary group U_t of the dynamical evolution if it satisfies two conditions:

(a) $U_t^* T U_t = T + t\mathbb{1}$ (the infinitesimal form of this relation is the familiar canonical commutation relation $[T, L] = i\mathbb{1}$ between the generator L (Liouville operator) of the dynamical group U_t and the operator T).

(b) The projections $P_\lambda \equiv E_\lambda + P_{-\infty}$ associated with T preserve the positivity of functions. Here the projections E_λ are the spectral projections of the operator T: $(f, Tg) = \int \lambda \, d(f, E_\lambda g)$ for functions f, g in the domain of T. The projections P_λ associated with T satisfy the conditions $P_\lambda > P_\mu$ if $\lambda > \mu$, $\lim_{\lambda \to -\infty} P_\lambda = P_{-\infty}$ and $\lim_{\lambda \to \infty} P_\lambda = 1$. Moreover, P_λ satisfies the imprimitivity condition $U_t P_\lambda U_t^* = P_{\lambda+t}$. This condition is equivalent with condition (a) on T.

Condition (b) is usually omitted in the definition of the time operator. In fact, when a time operator is introduced in a different context (e.g., for purely non-deterministic stationary stochastic processes (Gustafson and Misra 1976)), a condition corresponding to (b) is not required. Condition (b) is, however, essential if Λ with the required properties is to be constructed in terms of T. Therefore, here we shall mean by a time operator an operator T satisfying both (a) and (b).

Such a time operator is not expected to exist for every dynamical system. In fact, its existence expresses a strong form of instability of dynamical motion. If a time operator T exists, one can interpret the quantity $\langle T \rangle_\rho \equiv (\bar{\rho}, T\bar{\rho})/(\bar{\rho}, \bar{\rho})$ (with $\bar{\rho} = \rho - 1$) as the (average) "age" of the distribution function ρ. The condition (a) on T then expresses the desirable requirement that in the course of the dynamical evolution $\rho \to \rho_t = U_t \rho$ the "age" of ρ_t advances in step with the increase of the external time parameter t: $\langle T \rangle_{\rho_t} = \langle T \rangle_\rho + t$.

If a dynamical system admits a time operator T then a transformation Λ leading from the deterministic evolution U_t to an entropy increasing Markov process W_t^* can be constructed as an operator function of T. More explicitly, Λ will be given by $\Lambda = \int h(\lambda) \, dE_\lambda + P_{-\infty}$ (where E_λ are the spectral projections of T) for suitable choices of the function $h(\lambda)$.

There are two cases to be considered. First, the operator Λ is required to have a densely defined inverse Λ^{-1}. In this case the resulting semigroup W_t^* is similar or non-unitarily equivalent to U_t: $W_t^* = \Lambda U_t \Lambda^{-1}$ (for $t \geq 0$). Such an invertible Λ is obtained if $h(\lambda)$ satisfies the following conditions:

(i) $h(\lambda)$ is a monotonically decreasing function of λ with $\lim_{\lambda \to -\infty} h(\lambda) = 1$ and $\lim_{\lambda \to \infty} h(\lambda) = 0$;

(ii) $h(\lambda + s)/h(\lambda) \equiv h_s(\lambda)$ is a monotonically decreasing function of λ for every $s > 0$.

It should be emphasized that, although operators $\Lambda U_t \Lambda^{-1}$ define also a semigroup for $t < 0$, it can be shown that they will not preserve the positivity of functions and hence will not map (Gibbs) distribution functions to distribution functions. Therefore the operators $\Lambda U_t \Lambda^{-1}$ do not describe any physical evolution for $t < 0$. The Λ transformation thus breaks the time reversal symmetry of the dynamical evolution U_t and leads to an entropy increasing Markov process for the "forward" direction of time ($t \geq 0$) alone. We shall come back to this issue at the end of this section.

The other possibility for Λ is to be a projection operator. This is the case if $h(\lambda) = 1$ for $\lambda \in (-\infty, 0]$ and $h(\lambda) = 0$ for $\lambda > 0$. For this choice of $h(\lambda)$, Λ turns out to be the projection P_o of the time operator T. The resulting semigroup W_t^* of entropy increasing Markov processes is given by $W_t^* = P_o U_t P_o$ for $t \geq 0$. It is the imprimitivity condition satisfied by P_λ associated with T (and the fact $P_\lambda > P_\mu$ if $\lambda > \mu$) that assures the semigroup property for the operators $P_o U_t P_o$ for $t \geq 0$.

Since a transformation Λ with the desired properties can be constructed in terms of a time operator of particular dynamical systems, it is necessary to determine the class of dynamical systems for which a time operator exists. For this purpose we recall the definition of an important class of unstable dynamical systems, the Kolmogorov flows or K-flows for short (Arnold and Avez 1968, Cornfeld et al. 1982).

A dynamical system (Γ, S_t, μ) is called a K-flow if there exists a distinguished partition ζ_o of the phase space Γ into (an uncountable number of) disjoint cells such that:

The partition ζ_t is finer than ζ_s if $t > s$, where ζ_t denotes the partition into which the partition ζ_o evolves under $S_t : \zeta_t \equiv S_t \zeta_o$.

The least fine partition $\bigvee_{t=-\infty}^{\infty} \zeta_t$ which is finer than each ζ_t ($-\infty < t < \infty$) is identical with the partition of the phase space into individual phase points.

The (finest) partition $\bigwedge_{t=-\infty}^{\infty} \zeta_t$ that is less fine than each ζ_t is the trivial partition consisting of a cell of full measure 1.

Such a partition ζ_o is called a K-partition. Because of the reversibility of dynamical motion a K-flow admits, along with a K-partition, an anti-K-partition which becomes progressively less fine under the dynamical motion as t increases. The existence of K-partitions and anti-K-partitions expresses the high degree of instability of K-flows.

Returning to the question about the existence of a time operator, it can be shown that a dynamical system admits a time operator if and only if it is a K-flow (Misra 1978, Misra and Prigogine 1983). In fact, if the system is a K-flow, a time operator can be constructed in terms of the projections $P(\zeta_\lambda)$

of conditional expectations with respect to the partitions $\zeta_\lambda \equiv S_\lambda \zeta_o$ (where ζ_o is the K-partition). By definition, $P(\zeta_\lambda)$ is the projection operator onto the subspace of all (square integrable) functions measurable with respect to the σ-algebra formed only by subsets Δ that are unions of complete cells of the partition ζ_λ. In physical terms, $P(\zeta_\lambda)$ is the projection of "coarse graining" with respect to the partition ζ_λ. The projections $P(\zeta_\lambda)$ preserve the positivity of functions. Since $\zeta_\lambda \equiv S_\lambda \zeta_o$, it follows that

$$P(\zeta_\lambda) > P(\zeta_\mu) \text{ if } \lambda > \mu,$$
$$\lim_{\lambda \to -\infty} P(\zeta_\lambda) = P_{-\infty},$$
$$\lim_{\lambda \to \infty} P(\zeta_\lambda) = 1,$$
$$U_t P(\zeta_\lambda) U_t^* = P(\zeta_{\lambda+t}).$$

These properties of $P(\zeta_\lambda)$ ensure that the operator T given by $T = \int \lambda \, dE_\lambda$ (where $E_\lambda \equiv P(\zeta_\lambda) - P_{-\infty}$) is a time operator for the K-flow. Conversely, if a dynamical system admits a time operator T with associated projections $P_\lambda \equiv E_\lambda + P_{-\infty}$ (E_λ being the spectral projections of T), condition (b) on P_λ implies that each projection P_λ is the projection of conditional expectation with respect to a partition ζ_λ (Bahadur 1955). The properties of the projections P_λ mentioned above then imply that the partition ζ_o with respect to which P_o is the projection of conditional expectation is a K-partition.

   These considerations then lead to the following results. If the dynamical system is a K-flow then there exists an invertible transformation Λ such that $W_t^* = \Lambda U_t \Lambda^{-1}$ is the semigroup of an entropy increasing Markov process for $t \geq 0$ (Misra et al. 1979a, Goldstein et al. 1981). It is unknown if the condition that a dynamical system be a K-flow is also necessary for the existence of such a Λ. But it is known that for such a Λ to exist it is necessary that the dynamical system must at least be mixing (Misra 1978, Misra et al. 1979a). For the existence of a projection P_o such that $P_o U_t P_o = W_t^*$ (for $t \geq 0$) is the semigroup of an entropy increasing Markov process it is both necessary and sufficient that the dynamical system is a K-flow (Misra and Prigogine 1980, 1983; Goodrich et al. 1986).

   We have thus seen that in the presence of a suitable instability of motion (as in K-flows) it is possible to construct an invertible transformation Λ which leads from the deterministic dynamical evolution to a probabilistic (Markov) process. As said before, the Λ transformation breaks the time reversal symmetry of U_t as it leads from the dynamical evolution group U_t to an entropy increasing irreversible semigroup W_t^* (for $t \geq 0$). The existence of a Λ transformation expresses at the dynamical level the irreversibility implied by the second law of thermodynamics. However, it does not account for the existence of a *common* "arrow of time" in the physical world.

In fact, the time reversibility of a dynamical evolution U_t implies that, if a similarity transformation Λ exists such that $\Lambda U_t \Lambda^{-1} \equiv W_t^*$ is an entropy increasing semigroup for $t \geq 0$, then there exists also a necessarily different transformation Λ_- for which $\Lambda_- U_t \Lambda_-^{-1} \equiv W_t^{*-}$ is an entropy increasing semigroup for $t < 0$. The approach to time symmetry breaking through the Λ transformation thus provides two different semigroups, one for the "forward" direction ($t \geq 0$) and the other for the "backward" direction ($t < 0$) of time. It may be mentioned that this is also the situation in a somewhat different, though related, approach to the problem of irreversibility (Antoniou and Prigogine 1993). The question about a common "arrow of time" is the question as to why *all* physical systems "choose" the semigroup for the same direction of time. An answer will probably involve cosmological considerations. (See also the contribution by Primas in this volume.)

4   The Quantum Measurement Problem

In order to see what constitutes the quantum measurement problem let us consider the measurement of spin σ_3 along a given direction (called the z-direction) of a spin $1/2$ quantum system. There are two eigenstates ψ_+ and ψ_- corresponding to the spin of the system in the z-direction being definitely "up" or "down", respectively, in these states. For measurement, the quantum system is coupled to an apparatus. Let Φ_o be the state of the apparatus at the commencement of measurement such that the state of the combined system is initially $\psi_+ \otimes \Phi_o$ or $\psi_- \otimes \Phi_o$. For a mesurement of σ_3 to occur the interaction between apparatus and the spin system should be chosen such that under the dynamical evolution of the combined system the initial states should make the transitions:

$$\psi_+ \otimes \Phi_o \to \psi_+ \otimes \Phi_+ \equiv \eta_+$$
$$\psi_- \otimes \Phi_o \to \psi_- \otimes \Phi_- \equiv \eta_-$$

Here, Φ_+ and Φ_- are states of the apparatus corresponding to "pointer positions" indicating the spin of the system being "up" or "down", respectively, along the z-direction. If the initial state of the spin system is not aligned in the z-direction but along a different direction, such a state is represented by a coherent superposition $\alpha\psi_+ + \beta\psi_-$ (with $|\alpha|^2 + |\beta|^2 = 1$).

According to the linearity of quantum evolution, the initial state of the {system & apparatus}, $(\alpha\psi_+ + \beta\psi_-) \otimes \Phi_o$, will then make the transition:

$$(\alpha\psi_+ + \beta\psi_-) \otimes \Phi_o \to \alpha\eta_+ + \beta\eta_- \equiv \eta$$

However, if the initial state of the system is $\alpha\psi_+ + \beta\psi_-$, in (a series of identical) measurements of σ_3 the apparatus pointer acquires definite positions showing σ_3 to be either "up" or "down" with relative frequencies $|\alpha|^2$ and $|\beta|^2$, respectively. Accordingly, the state of the {system & apparatus} after measurement is the incoherent mixture

$$|\alpha|^2|\eta_+\rangle\langle\eta_+|\beta|^2|\eta_-\rangle\langle\eta_-| \equiv \rho,$$

and not the coherent superposition $\alpha\eta_+ + \beta\eta_-$ to which quantum dynamical evolution leads. The question of how to account for the replacement of $\alpha\eta_+ + \beta\eta_-$ by the incoherent mixture ρ, which is expected to result from the measurement process, is the problem of measurement in quantum theory. The replacement of $\alpha\eta_+ + \beta\eta_-$ by the incoherent mixture ρ is commonly referred to as the "reduction of the state vector".

The coherent superposition $\alpha\eta_+ + \beta\eta_-$ is distinguishable from the mixture ρ by the presence of interference terms like $\alpha^*\beta\langle\eta_+, A\eta_-\rangle$ in the expectation values of observables A in the state $\alpha\eta_+ + \beta\eta_-$. Therefore, a solution to the measurement problem will emerge if $\langle\eta_+, A\eta_-\rangle = 0$ for all physical observables A. In this case the apparently coherent superposition $\alpha\eta_+ + \beta\eta_-$ resulting from dynamical evolution is indistinguishable from the mixture ρ resulting from measurement.

States whose (apparently) coherent superpositions are always equivalent to corresponding (incoherent) mixtures occur naturally in the (C*-algebraic) theory of quantum systems with infinitely many degrees of freedom. They are so-called *disjoint states*. To explain the concept of disjoint states let us, very briefly, recall some concepts of the algebraic formulation of quantum theory. No attempt will be made to give precise definitions and explanations of these concepts. For this the reader may consult Dixmier (1977, 1981), Haag (1992), or Segal (1947).

In the algebraic formulation of quantum theory the observables of a physical system are represented by the (self-adjoint) elements of a C*- algebra M. The states of the system are represented by positive linear functionals ω on M. Given two states ω_1 and ω_2, the state $\omega = \lambda_1\omega_1 + \lambda_2\omega_2$ is a (incoherent) mixture of the states ω_1 and ω_2 for $\lambda_1, \lambda_2 \geq 0$ and $\lambda_1 + \lambda_2 = 1$. To define (coherent) superpositions of ω_1 and ω_2 we have to go to a (suitable) representation of the algebra M as an operator algebra in a Hilbert space. By a representation Π of M one means a mapping $A \to \Pi(A)$ of M to an algebra $\Pi(M)$ of operators in a Hilbert space H_Π such that the mapping $A \to \Pi(A)$ preserves the algebraic structure of M. Every vector ψ in H_Π of a representation Π defines a state ω_ψ on M given by $\omega_\psi(A) = \langle\psi, \Pi(A)\psi\rangle$, $A \in M$. Such states ω_ψ associated with vectors ψ of H_Π of a representation

Π are called vector states of the representation Π. In general, the algebra M has many inequivalent representations.

If two states ω_1 and ω_2 of M are both vector states for some representation Π of M corresponding to (orthogonal) vectors ψ_1 and ψ_2 of H_Π, one can consider the state $\omega\psi$ of M corresponding to the vector $\psi = \alpha\psi_1 + \beta\psi_2$ ($|\alpha|^2 + |\beta|^2 = 1$) as a superposition of ω_1 and ω_2. However, it is possible that $\omega\psi$ is identical with the corresponding (incoherent) mixture $|\alpha|^2\omega_1 + |\beta|^2\omega_2$. The possibility of forming *coherent* superpositions of states ω_1 and ω_2 (different from the corresponding mixtures) exists if and only if there exists a representation Π of M for which both ω_1 and ω_2 are vector states (corresponding to vectors ψ_1 and ψ_2 in H_Π) such that $\langle\psi_1, \Pi(A)\psi_2\rangle \neq 0$ for some $A \in M$.

In this case, the states ψ_1 and ψ_2 are said to be coherent. If they are *not* coherent, they are *disjoint states*. More explicitly, two states ψ_1 and ψ_2 are disjoint if and only if for *every* representation Π of M for which ψ_1 and ψ_2 are vector states corresponding to ψ_1 and ψ_2 in H_Π, $\langle\psi_1, \Pi(A)\psi_2\rangle = 0$ for *all* $A \in M$ (Haag 1992). Disjoint states exist for the algebra of physical observables of systems with infinitely many degrees of freedom. Apparent superpositions of such states are always indistinguishable from corresponding mixtures. In physical terms, disjoint states are separated by *superselection rules* (Wick et al. 1952).

In the algebraic approach, the Heisenberg evolution of observables is given by a group α_t of automorphisms of the C*-algebra of the physical system. The evolution of observables given by α_t induces an evolution of states ω of M: $\omega \to \omega_t$, where $\omega_t(A) = \omega(\alpha_t(A))$ for $A \in M$.

An important step toward a solution of the measurement problem was achieved by Hepp (1972) on the basis of the existence of disjoint states for systems with infinitely many degrees of freedom. Hepp showed in several models of measurements of spin σ_3 (with the apparatus being an infinite system) that initially *coherent* states ω_1 and ω_2 (corresponding to the states $\psi_+ \otimes \Phi_o$ and $\psi_- \otimes \Phi_o$) of the {system & apparatus} approach *disjoint states* ω_∞^1 and ω_∞^2 in the limit $t \to \infty$ under the automorphism group α_t of dynamical evolution. An initial coherent superposition of ω_1 and ω_2 (corresponding to the state $(\alpha\psi_+ + \beta\psi_-) \otimes \Phi_o$) will therefore, in the limit $t \to \infty$, approach the incoherent mixture $|\alpha|^2\omega_\infty^1 + |\beta|^2\omega_\infty^2$ as required in the measurement process.

Nevertheless, an important argument by Bell (1975) indicated a limitation of Hepp's solution. Bell showed that although an initial coherent superposition of states ω_1 and ω_2 approach an incoherent mixture of ω_∞^1 and ω_∞^2 as $t \to \infty$, the time evolved state of the initial superposition at *any* finite time can be brought back to the initial coherent superposition by a perturbation allowed in Hepp's approach. In other words, the measurement can be undone at any finite time, no matter how large.

Bell's argument points to the need of recognizing the measurement process as an irreversible dynamical process. In fact, as Hepp (1972) himself remarked, "the solution of the problem of measurement is closely connected with the yet unknown correct description of irreversibility in quantum mechanics". An attempt in this direction has been made by Misra et al. (1979b) and Lockhart and Misra (1986). It is argued there that to incorporate the irreversible behavior of appropriate quantum dynamical systems (in particular measurement apparatuses) one needs to restrict the physical observables of the system to a proper subalgebra M_o of the initial algebra M of the dynamical system such that $M_t \subset M_s$ for $t < s$, where $M_t \equiv \alpha_t M_o$ is the algebra to which M_o evolves under the dynamical automorphism group α_t. Let E_o be a suitable projection of conditional expectation of M to M_o. Then one can show that $E_o \alpha_t E_o \equiv W_t$ is an irreversible and contractive semigroup of the evolution of observables for $t \geq 0$.

It should be emphasized that such an algebra does not exist for every dynamical group α_t. General conditions on the dynamical systems permitting the existence of a subalgebra M_o and a corresponding projection E_o of conditional expectation are not yet known. However, in a model of measurement of spin σ_3 (with the apparatus being an infinite system) the existence of a subalgebra M_o and corresponding projection E_o is proven. Under the evolution of states induced from $W_t \equiv E_o \alpha_t E_o$ ($t \geq 0$) the initially coherent states ω_1 and ω_2 of the {system & apparatus} approach disjoint states as $t \to \infty$. But the approach to disjoint states now proceeds irreversibly and progressively with time, and Bell's argument concerning the "reversibility of measurement" does not apply.

It should also be emphasized that in the approach to quantum measurement described by Hepp (1972), Misra et al. (1979b), and Lockhart and Misra (1986), the "reduction of the state vector" is obtained *exactly* under the evolution of the {system & apparatus} considered as a *closed* quantum system. In contrast, in another approach to the measurement problem the "reduction of the state vector" is obtained through so-called environment-induced "decoherence". However, interference effects will be observed if suitable observables of the combined system {"environment" & system & apparatus} are measured. In fact, d'Espagnat (1995) exhibited such an observable in a model of measurement with "decoherence". I shall not argue the point any further here; but it seems to me that "environment-induced decoherence" does not lead to a fundamental solution of the measurement problem. Such a solution requires a deeper understanding of the occurence of *disjoint states* separated by *superselection rules* and an incorporation of irreversibility in the theory of an appropriate class of quantum systems. It is not claimed that the approach by Misra et al. (1979b) and Lockhart and Misra (1986) briefly outlined here provides a final solution of these problems. But it is a promising first step in this direction.

Acknowledgments

I am thankful to Prof. I. Antoniou, Dr. H. Atmanspacher and Prof. H. Primas for many stimulating discussions.

References

Antoniou I. and Prigogine I. (1993): Intrinsic irreversibility and integrability of dynamics. *Physica A* **192**, 443–464.

Arnold V.I. and Avez A. (1968): *Ergodic Problems of Classical Mechanics.* Benjamin, New York.

Bahadur R.R. (1955): Measurable subspaces and subalgebras. *Proc. Am. Math. Soc.* **6**, 565–570.

Bell J.S. (1975): On wave packet reduction in the Coleman-Hepp model. *Helv. Phys. Acta* **48**, 93–98.

Cornfeld I.P., Fomin S.V., and Sinai Ya.G. (1982): *Ergodic Theory.* Springer, Berlin.

d'Espagnat B. (1995): *Veiled Reality.* Addison-Wesley, Reading.

Dixmier J. (1977): *C*-Algebras.* North-Holland, Amsterdam.

Dixmier J. (1981): *Von Neumann Algebras.* North-Holland, Amsterdam.

Dynkin E.B. (1965): *Markov Processes.* Springer, Berlin.

Goldstein S., Misra B., and Courbage M. (1981): On intrinsic randomness of dynamical systems. *J. Stat. Phys.* **25**, 111–126.

Goodrich K., Gustafson K., and Misra B. (1980): On a converse of Koopman's lemma. *Physica A* **102**, 379–388.

Goodrich K., Gustafson K., and Misra B. (1986): On K-flows and irreversibility. *J. Stat. Phys.* **43**, 317–320.

Gustafson K. and Misra B. (1976). Canonical commutation relations of quantum mechanics and stochastic regularity. *Lett. Math. Phys.* **1**, 275–280.

Haag R. (1992). *Local Quantum Physics.* Springer, Berlin.

Hepp K. (1972): Quantum theory of measurement and macroscopic observables. *Helv. Phys. Acta* **45**, 237–248.

Koopman B. (1931): Hamiltonian systems and transformations in Hilbert space. *Proc. Natl. Acad. Sci. USA* **17**, 315–318.

Lockhart C.M. and Misra B. (1986): Irreversibility and measurement in quantum mechanics. *Physica A* **136**, 47–76.

Misra B. (1978): Nonequilibrium entropy, Lyapounov variables, and ergodic properties of classical systems. *Proc. Ntl. Acad. Sci. USA* **75**, 1627–1631.

Misra B. (1995): From time operator to chronons. *Found. Phys.* **25**, 1087–1104.

Misra B., Prigogine I., and Courbage M. (1979a): From deterministic dynamics to probabilistic descriptions. *Physica A* **98**, 1–26.

Misra B., Prigogine I., and Courbage M. (1979b): Lyapounov variable, entropy and measurement in quantum mechanics. *Proc. Ntl. Acad. Sci. USA* **76**, 4768–4772.

Misra B. and Prigogine I. (1980): Foundation of kinetic theory. *Progr. Theor. Phys. (Suppl.)* **69**, 101–110.

Misra B. and Prigogine I. (1983): Time, probability, and dynamics. In *Long-Time Prediction in Dynamics*, ed. by C. Horton jr., L. Reichl, and V. Szebehely, Wiley, New York, pp. 21–43.

Prigogine I. (1980): *From Being to Becoming.* Freeman, San Francisco.

Segal I. (1947): Postulates for general quantum mechanics. *Ann. Math.* **48**, 930–948.

Spohn H. (1980): Kinetic equations from Hamiltonian dynamics: Markovian limits. *Rev. Mod. Phys.* **52**, 569–615.

Wick G.C., Wightman A.S., and Wigner E.P. (1952): The intrinsic parity of elementary particles. *Phys. Rev.* **88**, 101–105.

Yosida K. (1965): *Functional Analysis.* Springer, Berlin.

Probabilistic Causality and Irreversibility: Heraclitus and Prigogine

Theodoros Christidis

Abstract

In this paper I examine some of Heraclitus' ideas comprised in several fragments from his unpreserved book *On Nature*, which seem to be very close to ideas expressed by Prigogine in the last fifty years and summarized in his book *The End of Certainty*. It is a fact that nature does not completely disclose herself, but rather likes to hide. The epistemological problem, thus, can only be solved on the basis of those hidden elements of which nature gives us some indications. And, as all things (and processes) are steered through all, the only possibility of solving the epistemological problem is to describe natural systems by operators acting on the evolution of probability with time (Prigogine's answer) rather than by deterministic equations. I also touch on the cosmological considerations of Heraclitus as well as on his thesis on the problem of time, with a brief reference to Prigogine's ideas.

1   Introduction

What is the most remarkable feature of the relationship between the mathematical theories of physics and the actual situations to which they are purportedly applicable? "Roughly stated, it is this: on the one hand, physical states of affairs agree only *approximately* with the mathematical theories that physics brings to bear on them, so that such theories can furnish, at best, only an *idealized* representation of physical reality; on the other hand, mature physical theories include a precise quantitative estimate of their respective degree of approximation (or imprecision)" (Torretti 1990). This trend, namely the construction of mathematical theories to represent physical reality based on idealizations, is often characterized as the *Platonic orientation*, which is a complementary version of the Phythagorean orientation, the former with an emphasis on combining mathematical description with idealizations, and the latter supposing that the universe is ruled by simple mathematical relations giving rise to order and harmony. The Platonic trend has been followed by almost all scientists since the times of Galileo and Newton and with so much devotion that some leading scientists believed that they could force their theories *on nature*. This produced a number of paradoxes, which contemporary science has to solve. I will mention two of them.

The first is the *incompatibility paradox* (as I call it), which emerged as follows: during the first thirty years of the 20th century, two great theories in physics have been postulated, relativity theory and quantum theory. These theories have proved successful in two different domains or worlds: the world of stars and galaxies, and the world of atoms and elementary particles. But the world in which we live is one, a consistent whole. The problem is that these two great theories, the best we now possess, are mutually incompatible.

Although some physicists continue to work using the one or the other theory according to the needs of their research, one can ask if the universe really is so strange as to be divided at its fundamental level, thus requiring two incompatible theories. This constitutes a *fundamental paradox*, not only because of our conviction (inherited from the Presocratics) that nature is unified, but also because nature herself imposes the need to explore this unity: there are instances, such as black holes and the Big Bang epoch, in which we are forced to use both general relativity and quantum theory because in both cases we have incredibly massive objects in tiny space dimensions. Yet, any effort to make calculations by merging the equations of the two theories leads to infinities. This shows that both theories are not complete, in the sense that each one of them cannot contain the description of the whole set of physical processes.

Plato constructed the *world of Ideas* inspired by Socrates' teaching that ethical concepts, such as beauty, justice, or goodness, should be considered as *ideals* which could be grasped through a laborious philosophical effort. Plato's world of Ideas comprised the totality of entities, which should be the object of *episteme*, because the latter ought to deal with entities that are immutable, changeless, and eternal.[1] He, thus, suggests that in order

---

[1] His motives, among others, were: his opposition to the Sophists' relativistic position, and his belief "that only by some cognitive access to such entities (the Forms) could human minds form the notion of properties that attach to things as a matter of objective fact, and not simply relatively to the point of view of some observer or thinker" (White 1995, p. 394). This was Socrates' credo that the concepts are absolute, not relative, but difficult to define. Plato raised this dichotomy between the relative and the absolute concepts to a dichotomy in the body of beings, the one part including the visible beings (the sensible world) and the other the invisible beings (the world of Ideas, or Forms; cf. Phaedo 79a). The visible beings are continually changing, they constitute the world of becoming, of which we cannot have knowledge, only a 'true belief'. "In refusing the term

to attain a knowledge qualified by a *principle of objectivity*, which means a knowledge not dependent on the view of any observer (in the language of physics, not dependent on any reference frame), we must make abstractions and idealizations in order to approach the cognition of Forms. Having followed this route, we will have acquired the appropriate notions for the description of the world of appearances. Almost all physical theories have been formulated according to this scheme. Idealizations and use of the language of mathematics are their main characteristics. Among the criteria used by the proponents of these theories are simplicity and beauty. For example, Newton's and Einstein's theories are rightfully considered as two of the greatest scientific achievements in the history of science; yet we must admit that both scientists had persistent prejudices and made bad choices: Newton about the nature of space and time, and Einstein about determinism and irreversibility.[2]

Thus far I have referred to one of the current paradoxes in physics, the *incompatibility paradox*. Now some physicists are trying to solve this paradox working on *string theories* along the Platonic line of thought: idealizations plus mathematics.[3] Yet there is another paradox, the *time paradox*, which

---

knowledge to propositions of ordinary experience and of the observational sciences, Plato is downgrading quite deliberately those truth-seeking and truth-grounding procedures which cannot be assimilated to deductive reasoning and cannot yield formal certainty; and this has enormous implications – theoretical, and also practical ones" (cf. Vlastos 1995, p. 163).

[2]Both of them also used criteria like simplicity and beauty, and based their theories on some premises which included *idealizations*: Newton's first law of inertia is an idealization; and Einstein's fundamental imaginative representation of a freely falling man, which led him to postulate his *principle of equivalence*, also had a sort of idealization (the gravitational field was considered *homogeneous*).

[3]Some forty years ago, physicists and mathematicians pursued the goal of constructing a unified theory, dubbed the *Theory of Everything*, which hopefully would resolve this paradox. In 1970 Nambu, Nielsen and Susskind showed that "if one modeled elementary particles as little, vibrating, one-dimensional strings, their nuclear interactions could be described exactly by Euler's function" (Greene 1999, pp. 136-137), as Veneziano had already suggested in 1968. In 1974 Schwarz and Scherk, "after studying the puzzling messenger-like patterns of string vibration, realized that their properties matched perfectly those of the hypothesized messenger particle of the gravitational force – the graviton. They extended the goal of string theory: String theory, they proclaimed, is not just a theory of the strong force; it is a quantum theory that includes gravity as well" (Greene 1999, p. 138). In 1984 Green and Schwarz "in a landmark paper culminating more than a dozen years of intense research, established that the subtle quantum conflict afflicting string theory could be resolved". The first 'Superstring Revolution' began and "more than a thousand research papers on string theory were written. These works showed conclusively that numerous features of the standard model *emerge naturally and simply from the grand structure of string theory*. These developments convinced many physicists that string theory was well

was first elaborated in the second half of the 19th century by Boltzmann, and has served as one decisive motivation for a new and alternative reformulation of physics in the course of the 20th century by Prigogine and his collaborators. This paradox consists in the following: on the one hand, we have the basic laws of physics, which are time reversible in the sense that they do not make any distinction between past and future, and, on the other, there is tremendous evidence (in physics, chemistry, geology, cosmology, biology, and the human sciences) that past and future play different roles. Prigogine (1997, p. 2) asks: "How can the arrow of time emerge from what physics describes as a time-symmetrical world?" The fact that the entropy of a closed system increases until the system reaches equilibrium, and the entropy attains its maximum value, is pointing to the idea of the arrow of time and irreversibility (Prigogine 1997, p. 18):[4]

---

on its way to fulfilling its promise of being the ultimate unified theory" (Greene 1999, pp. 138-139). But string theory was limited to finding approximate solutions to approximate equations. New methods with the power to go beyond such approximations were required. Then, in 1995 Witten in a famous lecture at the Strings 1995 Conference (at the University of South California) announced a plan for taking the next step, thereby igniting the Second Superstring Revolution, which is now in a phase of fruitful development.

I consider superstring theory as a *provisionally metaphysical theory*. It is metaphysical in the sense that the final elementary constituents of matter it introduces, the strings, are entities which live in tiny dimensions (of the order of the Planck's length, 10^{-33} cm) and in spaces of ten or more dimensions. These tiny elementary entities are beyond any realistic human attempt to reach the energies needed to see them. And it is provisionally metaphysical in the sense that "physicists *have not as yet been able* to make predictions with the precision necessary to confront experimental data". Although Witten has declared that "string theory has already made a dramatic and experimentally confirmed prediction ('String theory has the remarkable property of predicting gravity')", this is in fact a "postdiction", and "there are many (physicists) who find this postdiction of gravity unconvincing experimental confirmation of string theory. Most physicists would be far happier with one of two things: a bona fide prediction from string theory that experimentalists could confirm, or a postdiction of some property of the world (like the mass of the electron or the existence of three families of particles) for which there is currently no explanation" (Greene 1999, pp. 210-211). With our current technological possibilities it is impossible to see strings directly. So, the test of string theory would only be possible in an indirect manner: "we will have to determine physical implications of the theory that can be observed on length scales that are far larger than the size of a string itself" (Greene 1999, p. 215). Thus the qualification of the 'metaphysical' as 'provisional' has to do with our optimistic expectation for a new prediction or a 'genuine postdiction' as described above. In the same sense, Democritus' atomic theory was metaphysical, as the atoms were meant to be the truly elementary particles, the constituents of matter that cannot be cut up or divided up. (Unfortunately, only a few fragments from his work have been saved, so we do not know how he had reached the notion of atoms starting from pondering the entities of everyday experience).

[4]Boltzmann, although he "was convinced that in order to understand nature we have

Nature involves both time-reversible and time-irreversible processes, but it is fair to say that irreversible processes are the rule and reversible processes the exception. Reversible processes correspond to idealizations: We have to ignore friction to make the pendulum move reversibly. Such idealizations are problematic, because there is no absolute void in nature. Time reversible processes are described by equations of motion, which are invariant with respect to time inversion, as is the case in Newton's equation in classical mechanics or Schrödinger's equation in quantum mechanics. For irreversible processes, however, we need a description that breaks time symmetry.

The collapse of determinism is closely related to the time paradox in Prigogine's approach, and the two of them constitute the two pillars on which his approach is based. According to two recent developments, the spectacular growth of non-equilibrium physics and the dynamics of unstable systems and chaos, the certainty about the prediction of the future, even in principle, has fallen down. "Once instability is included, the meaning of the laws of nature (even of classical mechanics) changes radically, for they now express *possibilities or probabilities*" (Prigogine 1997, p. 4).

It is worth noting that Prigogine starts the first chapter of his most recent book *The End of Certainty* by referring to the Presocratics: "Is the universe ruled by deterministic laws? What is the nature of time? These questions were formulated by the Presocratics at the very start of Western rationality." And on the next page he says: "For Heraclitus, as understood by Popper, 'truth lies in having grasped the essential *becoming* of nature, i.e., having represented it as implicitly infinite, as a *process in itself*.'" This is the only phrase in which Prigogine refers to Heraclitus. And a few lines below, he makes a comment on Plato's point of view on the determinism-indeterminism dilemma: "Plato linked truth with being, that is, with unchanging reality beyond becoming. Yet, he was conscious of the paradoxical character of this position, because it would debase both life and thought. In *The Sophist*, he concluded that we need both being and becoming."

I will argue that, despite the fact that Prigogine is referring only once to Heraclitus, he is an adherent of the *theory of nature* the Ephesian had formulated around 500 years BC. Thus, my intention is to open the dialogue between the philosopher and the scientist.

---

to include evolutionary features (following Darwin's theory), and that irreversibility, as defined by the second law of thermodynamics, was a decisive step in this direction", tried unsuccessfully to interpret this law in the framework of classical dynamics because of his adherence to the strength of the latter. "The fact that this attempt would end in failure now seems self-evident" (cf. Prigogine 1997, p. 21).

2 A Dialogue between Heraclitus and Prigogine

Before presenting the fragments from Heraclitus' lost book *On Nature* relevant to the epistemological issue, I want to make some general comments.
First, philosophical discourse began with the Presocratics, who started to
use rational arguments in the place of mythological descriptions. Thus, it
is natural that they had to start from the beginning by introducing new
concepts and inaugurating the new language of philosophy. Second, due to
this lack of established conceptual framework, Heraclitus (just as the other
Presocratics) has introduced a few new concepts, but in order to express his
theory, he mainly has used *metaphors*. This, of course, is a drawback, but
his mastery has turned it to advantage as we shall see. Third, Heraclitus
seems to put every word and every sentence to exhaustive tests in order to
choose the more appropriate ones.[5] Thus, it is very tempting to interpret his
fragments in a biased manner, as his pronouncements are obscure, sometimes
cryptic or ambiguous.

Nevertheless, I will try to keep in my mind Heisenberg's warning (Heisenberg 1962, p. 73–75, italics added):

> After this comparison of the modern views in atomic physics with Greek
> philosophy we have to add a *warning*, that *this comparison should not
> be misunderstood*. It may seem at first sight that the Greek philoso-
> phers *have by some kind of ingenious intuition come to the same or
> very similar conclusions as we have in modern times* only after sev-
> eral centuries of hard labor with experiments and mathematics. This
> interpretation of our comparison would, however, be a complete misun-
> derstanding. There is an enormous difference between modern science
> and Greek philosophy, and that is just the empiristic attitude of mod-
> ern science. ... Therefore, modern science has from its beginning stood
> upon a much more modest, but at the same time much firmer, basis
> than ancient philosophy ... *All the same, some statements of ancient*

---

[5]Figuratively speaking, I could say, he makes them pass through successive 'distillations'
in order to filter them and to take out their deepest essence. For that reason we must be
very careful when we deal with his sayings, and scrutinize every word and image he uses.
Especially when a physicist tries to analyze his fragments, he is tempted to find direct
correspondences between his ideas and those that have been developed, or are developing
in physics during the last decades. There is great difficulty in deciphering the 'real' meaning
of his sayings, because the fragments from his work have reached us from citations of ancient
writers of dissimilar origin and of various degrees of reliability. Thus, if I succumb to the
temptation of interpreting some fragments with hindsight, it is not exclusively my fault,
but also the fault of those who have contributed to the destruction of almost all of the
books of Presocratic philosophers (remember that the library of Alexandria was burned
twice).

philosophy are rather near to those of modern science. This simply shows how far *one can get* by combining the ordinary experience of nature that we have without doing experiments with the untiring effort to get some logical order into this experience to understand it *from general principles.*

I now proceed to examine some of Heraclitus' fragments, which I consider relevant to the discussion of my subject. I first come to the cosmological principle of the beginning of the world. I quote again Heisenberg (1962, p. 63, italics added):

> That there should be a material cause for all things was a natural starting point since the world consists of matter. But when one carried the idea of fundamental *unity* to the extreme, one came to that infinite and eternal undifferentiated Being which, whether material or not, cannot in itself explain the infinite variety of things. This leads to the *antithesis of Being and Becoming*, and finally to the solution of Heraclitus, that *the change itself is the fundamental principle*; the 'imperishable change, that *innovates the world*', as the poets have called it. But change in itself is not a material cause, and therefore is represented in the philosophy of Heraclitus by the fire as the basic element, which is both matter and a moving force. We may remark at this point that modern physics is in some way extremely near to the doctrines of Heraclitus. *If we replace the word 'fire' by the word 'energy', we can almost repeat his statements word for word from our modern point of view".*

I quote now the relevant fragments of Heraclitus:

> Fragment 30: This world, the same for all, neither god nor man has made, but it ever was, and is, and will be: *fire everliving, kindling in measures, and in measures going out.*
> In fragments 31a and 31b Heraclitus points out that the known elements (sea-water, and earth) are but *tropai*, that is transformations, of fire, which obey a law of conservation, as stated in
> Fragment 90: All things are an equal exchange *(antamivi)* for fire, and fire for all things, as goods for gold and gold for goods.

Thus, the total amount of fire in the world is kept constant. But where does this fire comes from? Here we probably have the first encounter of Heraclitus' thought with Prigogine's. One could support the view that fr. 30 alludes to the idea of successive universes, as in this fragment it is said that this world is *ever-living* fire, thus it is born when fire is kindling, and it goes out of existence when the fire is going out (the participle *ever-living* gives a metaphorical account of this process: life is eternal, because it is a succession of births and deaths). Heraclitus was undoubtedly influenced by the Milesians, and especially by Anaximander, who very likely spoke of many worlds born out of his *apeiron*. There is also a passage in Aristotle (*De Caelo* 279 b 14), where it is said that Heraclitus and Empedocles made the world fluctuate between its present condition and destruction. If this is true, then, in Heraclitus' case, the many worlds are meant to be created successively, according to fr. 30. However, Kirk disagrees with this interpretation of fr. 30 (Kirk and Raven 1960).[6] Thus, for Heraclitus, time is not identified with the life of this world, in which we live, but it is eternal.[7]

------

[6] "Cosmos itself, which sprang from primary fire, is bound to return to it again by a double process which, however protracted its duration, operates in fixed periods, and will constantly repeat its operation Thus he (Heraclitus) reached a point of departure when nothing but fire existed To him, a ball of fire marks the starting point and the goal of each cosmic period" (Gomperz 1901).

[7] I also want to make another point here concerning the affinity between Anaximander and Heraclitus. I refer to the concept of strife, which the latter identifies with justice. This must be stressed, because it could be considered as another point of *affinity of views*, since Heraclitus never mentions the Milesian when he cites some philosophers or poets of the past with whom he disagrees (e.g. Pythagoras). There are many similarities as well as differences in the theories of the two philosophers. Let me stress one striking similarity of views not only between Anaximander and Heraclitus, but also among many other philosophers (e.g. Democritus). Anaximander was the first to use an abstract concept, that of the *apeiron*, the boundless, as the arche (principle). But the point I want to make is best described by Guthrie as follows: "With Anaximander physical theory takes a momentous step, to a notion from which it has retreated many times before its reappearance in very different form in the modern world: the notion of the *non-perceptible*. 'The physical view of the world', writes the physicist von Weizsäcker, 'has always had a tendency towards the non-perceptible. This stems immediately from the endeavor of physics to achieve a unified world-view. We do not accept appearances in their many-colored fullness, but we want to explain them, that is, we want to reduce one fact to another. In this process what is perceptible is often explained by what is not perceptible' ... Anaximander had also a more specific reason for adopting it, and this introduces a fundamental feature of Greek thought with a long and influential history, namely the notion of the primary opposites" (Guthrie 1962, p. 78). Furthermore, let us see what Anaximander, according to Simplicius (Phys. 24.13), says in relation to justice: "And into those things from which existing things take their rise, they pass away once more, *according to just necessity* ($\kappa\alpha\tau\alpha$ τo $\chi\rho\varepsilon\omega\nu$); for they render *justice* and reparation to one another for their injustice *according to the ordering of time*." I see here both a similarity and a difference with Heraclitus' use of justice. The similarity is that the strife between the opposites leads to the removal of the injustice and the re-establishment of justice. The difference is in that Heraclitus links justice with strife in such a way as to give also rise to states (we would say) far from equilibrium, as in the case of kykeon. And, as for the problem of the infinity of time, this view is more explicitly expressed in Anaximander than in Heraclitus work. "In dealing with Anaximander I had occasion to remark that the drawing of distinctions between different meanings of the same word belongs to a fairly advanced stage of thought (in my view the same is valid for Heraclitus, too). When he spoke of the *arche* of all things as the *apeiron* – the Unlimited, or Infinite – he meant by this not only that there was an indefinitely

Prigogine supports the same idea when he says (Prigogine 1997, p. 166):

> We consider the big bang an irreversible process *par excellence*. We suggest that there would have been an irreversible phase transition from a preuniverse that we call the *quantum vacuum*. ... We argue that irreversible processes associated with dynamical processes have probably played a decisive role in the birth of our universe. From our perspective *time is eternal*. We have an age, our civilization has an age, our universe has an age, but time itself has neither a beginning nor an end.

Another common point in both Heraclitus and Prigogine is the concept of *change*, which for the former is a *fundamental principle*. A universal law, which Heraclitus calls logos, rules change. This law is common for all the processes in nature. Change at every level obeys this law. I see two kinds of change in Heraclitus' theory. The first is a kind of cyclic change. "If a thing X changes to Y, and then back to X, then it must have been the same all the time" (Guthrie 1962, p. 452). This kind of change is related to the transformation of fire into the fundamental elements (fragments 31a, 31b, and 90) and vice versa. Thus, in essence, the fundamental 'stuff' has always been the same, that is *fire-energy*. Let us listen to the relevant fragment 50: "Listening not to me but to logos, it is wise to agree that *all things are one*."

I call this *the ontological component* of *logos*. This ontological aspect of change expresses *the unity of nature*. But there is also, in Heraclitus' theory of nature, a second aspect of change, or a second component of *logos*, the *dynamical one*. This is linked to the constructive role of *logos*. As Guthrie (1962, p. 448) points out: "For Pythagoras the best state was one in which opposite qualities were so blended by a law of proportion, that their oppositions were neutralized and they produced, for example, euphony in music, health in the body, cosmos – order and beauty – in the universe as a whole ... Heraclitus rejects all these value judgements."

I will now deal with three fragments, whose meaning is very close to contemporary ideas. I begin with fr. 125, cited by Theophrastus (*De Vertigine* 9): "For the things which by nature undergo this movement, at other times even hold together because of it, but if it fails, then as Heraclitus says *even the barley-drink disintegrates if it is not moved*" (Kirk 1962). Here, if we trust Theophrastus, his introductory phrase has the meaning that the motion sometimes leads to new 'coherent structures', i.e. *things are held together*

---

large amount of it but also that (*in contrast to the cosmos which was formed within it*) it had no beginning in time ... Nothing which has a beginning and end is either everlasting or *apeiron* ..." (Guthrie 1962, p. 337). I would add that the same argument holds for Heraclitus' *ever-living fire*.

because of motion. To support this view, Theophrastus adduces Heraclitus' phrase referring to kykeon, which has exactly the same meaning: in order to have the structure known as *kykeon*[8] (the barley-posset), one has to maintain the mixture with motion, otherwise it disintegrates. There are two states in the posset. If it is not stirred (not moving), then it disintegrates and ends up in a state of stable equilibrium, with its solid ingredients at the bottom of the cup. But if it is stirred, a new 'non-equilibrium structure' appears (cf. Prigogine 1980), which is maintained as long as motion persists.

This idea is also expressed in fr. 84a: *'changing it rests'.* That is, while something changes, it subsequently rests, giving rise to a new order.[9] Thus, this fragment could be read as follows: change, as a principle, rules the processes by which new kinds of order can be established.[10] But change is a principle *imposed* by *nature itself*, because for a thing to remain in the same state and to obey the same restrictions is weariness, as fr. 84b says: *"It is weariness to toil and be ruled by the same".* This fragment, cited also by Plotinus (*Enneades* IV, 8, 1) immediately after fr. 84a, complements and also clarifies the sense of the latter.[11] [12]

---

[8]Kykeon is made of ground barley, grated cheese and wine; sometimes honey is added.

[9]It is usual for Heraclitus to describe more general situations using metaphors by adapting illustrations from concrete natural processes (as, e.g., kykeon, or the image of a river), or from the life of people. Change, as I said, is a fundamental and universal principle. Commenting on fr. 125, Kirk says: "If change between opposites ceased, then the opposites themselves would cease to be connected with each other; the only unity between them, and so the only unity subsisting in the world, would be destroyed. There would be no such thing as $\kappa o\sigma\mu o\varsigma$ (order), just as there would be no such thing as kykeon if its ingredients existed in isolation from each other. The fragment is of greater importance than it first appears: it is the only direct quotation that asserts, even though only in an image, the consequences of an interruption in the reciprocity of opposites" (Kirk 1962, p. 256).

[10]Kirk attributes to the participle *changing* either a temporal or a causal meaning; he reads it as "it rests while, or by, changing".

[11]The saying *"changing it rests"* seems, according to Kirk, rather paradoxical, because "our experience causes us normally to associate *rest* with *absence of change, with stability rather than the reverse* ... [In the present case] Heraclitus is trying to account for change in terms of, but not in accordance with, men's own feelings; no sort of rational explanation is given and we are left little the wiser" (Kirk 1962, p. 252-253). Here, it is worth noting that Plotinus, who cites the two phrases, makes the following comment on them: "[Heraclitus] seems to conjecture (these ideas), though neglecting to make the argument clear for us, as though we should perhaps seek in ourselves, as he also sought and found" (Kirk 1962, p. 250, Kirk's translation). Recall that Heraclitus is well known as *the obscure philosopher.* I am saying all this, because I consider the case of his profound thoughts as revealing that he came too close to general principles which are valid in contemporary science, as Heisenberg has pointed out.

[12]The two sayings are generalizations of natural processes, as conceived by Heraclitus,

I proceed now to fr. 41, which I consider as the most significant statement of Heraclitus concerning the functioning of nature: *"Wisdom is one thing, to be skilled in true judgement, how all things are governed through all (other things)"*. But how is it that all things are governed through all? The only valuable answer is: *through their mutual interactions, which should be mutually consistent*. Here, Heraclitus does use one metaphor, as the verb govern ($\kappa\upsilon\beta\varepsilon\rho\nu\omega$, hence cybernetics) refers to the captain of a boat, but he makes a generalization, as the action of this verb is reflected by everything through everything. Thus, this statement, that everything in the universe interacts with all the other entities in it, could be seen as a *principle of self-consistency of the Universe*.

Hippolytus saved several fragments from Heraclitus' book. I now give his citation of fr. 64 and 65 (the words in italics are Heraclitus'): *"Thunderbolt steers all things*, that is directs; by 'thunderbolt' he means the eternal fire; he says also that this fire is sagacious and cause of the management of the universe. He calls it *deprivation and satiety*; deprivation is the world ordering, according to him, and the consumption by fire ['ecpyrosis'] is satiety." We have here three words expressing new and difficult to understand concepts: *thunderbolt, deprivation*, and *satiety*. I restrict myself in stressing the comments of Hippolytus (who perhaps had acquaintance with Heraclitus' book). 'Thunderbolt' is the eternal fire, but, from what follows, it seems that it concerns a kind of 'force' causing order in the world. The process in which order is produced is characterized by Heraclitus as *deprivation*; that is fire (or energy) is consumed to produce things (which are composed of the elements and their combinations); these products represent *order*, while the converse process leads to pure fire and is called *satiety*. As Heraclitus often places opposing concepts side by side, it is reasonable to infer that this second process results in *disorder*.

Let us now see the cause of change in the world. According to fr. 80 *"one must know that war is common and justice is strife, and that all things are happening by strife and necessity"*. We see again the metaphoric use of terms like *war, strife*, and *dike* (justice). War as well as strife (which

---

and described in terms of metaphors "derived from human experience, and applied to external events" (Kirk 1962, p. 252). Thus, the second saying, *"it is weariness to toil for and be ruled by the same"*, is less paradoxical than the other, "just as it is wearisome for a servant to continue toiling for the same master without change of scene or occupation, so (it may be inferred) it is wearisome for matter of any kind to remain indefinitely in the same relationship with its surroundings ... As they stand, then, the sayings of frs. 84a and 84b are of wide application, and in view of other comparable generalizations they may be taken to describe the behavior of things in general" (Kirk 1962, p. 253–254).

is used synonymously) are crucial concepts in Heraclitus' theory of nature. The ruling force of becoming in nature is the war between opposites. War is common (to all processes) and nothing could be done without war-strife, thus strife is 'the right way', the normal and just way things are becoming.[13] Thus, all things are becoming (or happening) by strife ($\varepsilon\rho\iota\zeta$) and necessity ($\chi\rho\varepsilon\omega\nu$). It must be stressed that the word $\chi\rho\varepsilon\omega\nu$ is equivalent to $\alpha\nu\alpha\gamma\kappa\eta$, but, as Kirk points out, "even $\alpha\nu\alpha\gamma\kappa\eta$ in Presocratic contexts often means much less than 'absolute necessity' (our modern term is determinism), and is used to account for regular events which could not be *rationally* explained: particularly, perhaps, for the origin and continuation of physical change and motion" (Vlastos 1993, p. 241). *Strife*, on the other hand, is *justice*, a notion that refers to Anaximander, whom Heraclitus never mentions. And we must keep in mind that Anaximander sees the whole process accomplished *according to the ordering of time*. Is there any echo of this role of time in Heraclitus? My answer is *yes*, but I will come to this in a moment. I first want to make some comments on the famous river statement.

There are three basic quotations referring to this famous illustration of the concept of change:

> Fragment 12: *Upon those who step into the same rivers, different and again different waters flow* (Cleanthes, see Arius Didymus).
> Fragment 91a: *One cannot step twice into the same river* (Plutarch).
> Fragment 49a: [Heraclitus the obscure says...] *Into the same rivers we step and do not step, we are and we are not* (Heraclitus Homericus).

There is no general agreement as to which of them is the genuine saying of Heraclitus.[14] It is very probable (I omit the relevant arguments) that Plato's and Aristotle's versions are closer to what Heraclitus said. The third fragment, 49a, has a slightly different meaning, but it is essentially in the spirit of Heraclitus (Kirk 1962, p. xiii). I come now to the question what Heraclitus meant by the river statement. The Platonic view, with which Aristotle agrees, is that everything moves and nothing stays still. Aristotle adds the idea that "the perpetual change 'escapes our perception'."[15]

---

[13]Kirk comments: "War or strife must symbolize the interaction between opposites; for all change, as Heraclitus and many of his contemporaries seem to have believed, could be resolved into change between opposites: the unity which Heraclitus detected in particular pairs of opposites extended to the whole sum of things" (cf. Vlastos 1993, p. 241).

[14]Plutarch has given three versions, one of which is 91a (*de E* 18, 392 B), the second is very similar, both of them following the Platonic and the Aristotelian versions, but Plutarch's third version is a combination of the first and the second: *Into the same rivers you could not step twice, as different waters flow* (successively – the verb is $\varepsilon\pi\rho\rho\varepsilon\iota$).

[15]Kirk disagrees with this interpretation: "According to this interpretation everything

Furthermore, in Plutarch (*de E* 18) we read (italics are Heraclitus original words): "... for it is impossible to step twice into the same river according to Heraclitus, or to lay hands twice on mortal substances in a fixed condition; but by swiftness and speed of its change *it disperses* and *again gathers*, or rather not 'again' or 'afterwards', but at the same time *it comes together and flows away, and approaches and departs* ..." These verb pairs literally give the picture of a river whose waters are in continuous and disordered motion.[16]

The only fragment in which Heraclitus refers to time is fr. 52: "*Aeon is a child at play, playing draughts; the kingship is a child's.*" Aeon, according to Kirk, "is most likely to refer to human life ... It is unlikely to mean 'time' absolutely ...". This is a view supported by many scholars.[17] Other contemporary scholars give to aeon the meaning of *time* (Diels translates it as *die Zeit*). If the fragment belongs to the 'anthropocentric' ones, as Kirk

---

is constantly changing by an invisible and as it were molecular addition and subtraction of fire, water and earth. This is *perhaps* contrary to what Heraclitus tell us in the fragments. ... Of course, [the idea of the river-statement] is an image, but it must have been an image designed to throw light on some particular belief. Plato took that belief to be that all things are constantly changing. He went beyond Heraclitus in making the river-analogy into a metaphor, not a simile; but this apprehension of the underlying idea is unlikely to have been completely at fault. The mistake he made was one of emphasis; what Heraclitus meant to illustrate in the river-statement was the coincidence between *stability* (of the whole river) and *change* (of the waters flowing past a fixed point), rather than continuity of change ... Not that this fragment is merely another specific instance of the coincidence of opposites, in this case of 'the same' and 'other' ..." (Kirk 1962, p. 377). Kirk concludes by stating his basic thesis on this fragment: "Fr. 12, then, appears to be an instance of identity of a kind persisting through change. Yet, not all change preserves such an identity, and here a special quality of rivers is relevant: only because the waters flow *regularly* (but see 49b, Plutarch) and replace each other by balanced amounts is the identity preserved. This, of course, is precisely the principle of $\mu\varepsilon\tau\rho o\nu$, which was detected in the cosmological fragments." As a matter of fact, Kirk wants to point out that Heraclitus is engaged in proving that *cosmos, order* and *stability* are the final goal of all physical properties. By doing so, he is telling us half of the truth. It is true that, in view of the version (3) above (i.e. fr. 49a, cited by Heraclitus Homericus), we are inclined to agree that both instances occur: in the same rivers *we step and do not step*, an idea fitting perfectly with Heraclitus' fundamental line of thought. But Kirk is wrong when he concludes that Heraclitus is for order and stability. In this, I agree with Guthrie, whom I mentioned earlier (who contrasts Heraclitus to Pythagorean ideals).

[16]The dispersion and gathering property is typical of chaotic motion. For example, Kolmogorov systems with positive entropy production are characterized by expanding and contracting motions, corresponding to dispersion and gathering (cf. Cornfeld et al. 1982.)

[17]These scholars support their views based on the meaning that *aeon* has: in Homer's *Ilias* [E 685, and Π 453] it means life, in Pindar the duration of life from the birth till the death. For Euripides *aeon* is the child of time (Diggle 1984, pp. 899–900).

believes, then it must have a rather simple meaning. And yet, the meaning of the whole fragment is especially obscure, because we do not know the context to which these few words belong. If we accept the view that aeon is the duration of human life, the meaning of the fragment could be extended as follows: the child-time is the 'king' who rules the time of the life of people according to the *rules* of the 'game of life' in which the element of *chance* is also involved. The rules of the game are the laws that govern the lives of living beings. Thus, in a subset of the set of the entities of the world, that is in people's lives, the child-time plays the role I have described.

Would it be, then, unlikely that Heraclitus *did* mean that the same picture still holds for the whole set of entities in the world, that is for all physical beings and processes? In support of this view I will refer to another fragment in which he brings the laws of beings under the more general and common law that governs the world, the *logos*: "Those men who speak with right-mindedness must hold fast to what is shared by all, as a city holds to its law, and even more firmly; *for all human laws are nourished by the divine one*; it prevails as it will and suffices and is more than enough" (fr. 114). But the divine law, in Heraclitus' thought, is the *logos*. Thus, we see that in this fragment Heraclitus subordinates human laws to the universal law, to *logos*. The analogy is obvious.

Nevertheless, I deem it worthwhile to scrutinize every word in this fragment, and see it as a metaphorical representation of a more general truth referring to what is mainly at stake in Heraclitus' theory of nature. Even if Heraclitus refers to human, or moral, or political affairs, we must keep in mind that he is mostly interested in nature, cosmos, the universe and the processes taking place in it. Let me now ask the relevant questions which I will try to answer.

1. Why is time-aeon figuratively represented as a child?

2. Why does time-child play pessoi (draughts)? That is, what is the meaning of this image, in which the child is playing, and especially is playing draughts?

3. Why does the kingship belong to that child?

To answer the first question, we must catch the thread of Heraclitus' thought: A child is 'innocent' in the sense that he does not judge according to adults' criteria of what is good or bad. In this context, we can compare the difference between a child and adults with the distinction made in fr. 102 between god and men: "To god all things are beautiful and good and just, but men have supposed some things to be unjust, others just". God, or deity, in Heraclitus' sayings is tantamount to nature or, rather, to the ruling power in it, as more explicitly expressed in fr. 67: "God is day/night, winter/summer, war/peace, satiety/hunger ['all the opposites', Hippolytus comments, 'this is the meaning'] and undergoes alteration in the way that fire, when it is mixed with spices, is named according to the scent of each of them". That is, nature comprises all the opposites and reveals herself in them without any preference. Now, the thread we are searching for is this: The child-time is like god, who does not have the 'moral' criteria of men for whom some things are unjust, others just; thus the child-time can play an analogous role.

As for the second question, my sense is that again the choice of play, and the kind of play, are significant for deciphering the meaning of the fragment: any play, and especially draughts, combines *rules and chance*.[18] And the meaning in this fragment, in my view, is about the play, i.e. about how the world works, how the physical processes are developed and lead to the result of the becoming of this world; and this cosmic play has its rules, the laws of nature, but chance also intervenes in the physical processes.

As for the third question, in the light of the preceding, I think Heraclitus' idea is likely to have originated from what was the practice in this kind of play.[19] Yet at the same time, Heraclitus, who undoubtedly knew Anaximander's work, probably had in mind the latter's saying that "[the things come into existence or pass away] according to necessity; for they render justice and reparation to one another for their injustices *according to the ordering of time.*" This enabled Heraclitus to postulate, in my opinion, one of the deepest ideas in a very condensed sentence (using a metaphor, as he usually did). It is true, as a matter of fact, that the word *chance* is not mentioned in the text, but it could be inferred, if my reasoning is right.

Is there, in some other fragment, any explicit reference to the idea of *chance* (in relation to the world)? I can cite one, and make one comment. Fr. 124 says: *"The fairest order in the world is a heap of random sweepings"*.[20] I restrict myself to saying that Theophrastus (Metaphysics 7a) saves the fragment in the following context, which is quite revealing for the im-

---

[18] Draughts was a game with cylindrical pawns, which the players moved on a plate according to some rules and to the numbers obtained by throwing the dice.

[19] The tradition says that the winning child-player became the 'king' and gave the orders to the others (cf. Plato, Theaet. 146 a).

[20] This fragment, although referring to the cosmos, is not located in the so-called cosmic fragments of Heraclitus, which Kirk has studied.

portance Heraclitus ascribed to the role of chance in physical processes.[21] The introductory text of Theophrastus is this: "And that again would seem absurd, that, if on the one hand the whole heaven and each of the parts are all in order and according to measure [λογωι], and [having] their forms, and forces and periodic movements, yet, on the other, in [the matter of] principles nothing like that [happens to be], but [i.e. on the contrary], as Heraclitus says, *the fairest order in the world is a heap of random sweepings*". It is true that this fragment has embarassed many scholars, who tried to get rid of the fact (as I understand it) that Heraclitus involved chance in his theory of nature. But Theophrastus, as I said, points very eloquently to this fact.

In summary, I would say that Heraclitus supported a *theory of nature*, in which there is a general and common law, *logos*, which imposes measure on physical processes, but war, the strife between the opposites, is a ruling factor through which an infinite variety of changes occur in such a way as to give *chance* the possibility to intervene in them, and *time* to play the role of a king in the cosmic play.

I will now list some fragments and thoughts of Heraclitus and the corresponding ideas of Prigogine as a kind of dialogue between them.

Heraclitus	Prigogine
Nature loves to hide. Non-perceptible [or hidden] harmony is better than the perceptible [the obvious] one. The Lord whose oracle is in Delphi neither declares nor conceals, but gives signs.	Once instability is included, the meaning of the laws of nature changes, for they now express possibilities or probabilities. The only possibility of solving the epistemological problem is to describe natural systems by operators acting on the evolution probability with time rather than by deterministic equations.
The river metaphor.	Irreversibility, the arrow of time.
Listening not to me but to logos... [reality is observer-independent].	Once it is shown that instability breaks time symmetry, the observer is no longer essential.

---

[21]One may consider that it is very probable that the book of the Ephesian comprised many other references to similar topics, which were omitted because they were quite obscure and incomprehensible to his contemporaries as well as to the doxographers, who had read his book.

Cosmos is ever-living fire.

Time has no beginning, and probably no end.

All human laws are nourished by the divine law [that is: logos, the universal law].

Considering ourselves as distinct from the natural world would imply a dualism that is difficult for the modern mind to accept.

Time is a child at play, playing draughts; the kingship is a child's [laws *and* chance].

Chance, or probability, is no longer a convenient way of accepting ignorance, but rather part of a new, extended rationality. What now is emerging is an intermediate description that lies somewhere between the two alienating images of a deterministic world (which leaves no place for novelty) and an arbitrary world of pure chance.

Wisdom is one thing, to be skilled in true judgement how all things are steered through all [all things in the universe are in mutual and unceasing interaction].

The role of persistent (non-transient) interactions in irreversibility.

Kykeon disintegrates unless it is stirred. Changing it rests. It is weariness to toil and ruled by the same. Thunderbolt steers all things. Deprivation (the becoming of beings, order) and satiety (probably disorder).

Dissipative structures emerging far from equilibrium. A nonequilibrium system may evolve spontaneously to a state of increased complexity. The origin of the variety in nature we observe around us. Matter acquires new properties when far from equilibrium in that fluctuations and instabilities are now the norm. Matter becomes more active.

Heraclitus' epistemology

Prigogine's epistemology

Preference of evidence of the senses; fr. 55: "Whatever comes from sight, hearing, learning from experience, this I prefer." [we collect events, and we trust them].

"We need not only laws, but also events that bring an element of radical novelty to the description of nature" (Prigogine 1997, p. 5).

But, this is not enough; fr. 107: "Eyes and ears are bad witnesses for men if their souls are barbarous" [if they do not understand the language of nature].

With rational thinking and intuition we can: (i) have access to the hidden harmony, and (ii) try to understand nature by means of what she *really* reveals, and by listening to her 'utterances', the signs she gives to us. And not behave like the many, who strongly dissent from *what they meet with every day* and act and speak like men asleep (fr. 72–73).

"Distance from equilibrium becomes an essential parameter in describing nature much like temperature in equilibrium thermodynamics" (Prigogine 1997, p. 68).

"We owe to the ancient Greeks two ideals: (i) the *intelligibility of nature*, or in Whitehead's words "the attempt to frame a coherent, logical, necessary system of general ideas, in terms of which every element of our experience can be interpreted." (ii) "the idea of democracy based on the assumption of human freedom, creativity, and responsibility" (Prigogine 1997, p. 17). Irreversibility, instability, chaos, complexity are nature's 'utterances', on which we must base our efforts to describe her.

The wise man 'omo-logei', that is, agrees that the world is rational, governed by a universal law, the *logos*, which is ratio, interaction, rule of the becoming, and a unifying principle.

Einstein's dream of a unified theory that would include all interactions remains alive today. Nonetheless, such a theory would have to take into account the time-oriented character of the universe as associated with its birth and subsequent evolution. In other words, unification is not enough. We need a more dialectical view of nature.

3   Conclusions

In this paper I have tried to show that Prigogine has followed a line of thought which is in resonance with the spirit of Heraclitus. The key principles of Heraclitus' theory of nature are echoed in novel approaches in contemporary science. By contrast, Plato's line of investigation aspires to stability and invariance, a viewpoint more or less followed by most physicists and mathematicians up to now.

I consider Heraclitus' route more pragmatic, and more difficult to follow. Heraclitus investigated nature by first looking at the phenomena as manifested through the senses. But he did not believe that this route was sufficient and efficient in order to understand nature. He trusted mostly the eyes, but he stressed the point that "eyes and ears are bad witnesses for men if their souls are barbarous" (that is, uncultured, uneducated, unreasonable, so that they cannot understand the language of nature). For him, as in the case of Anaximander, one can approach closer to the knowledge of how ature functions by exploring, with the aid of rational thinking and intuition, the non-perceptible, that which is cast deep within perceptible beings. He said: "Nature loves to hide", that is the real nature of beings is cast, not explicitly exposed to us. But we should not be disappointed, because nature, personified as the god Apollo, gives us some signs: "The lord whose oracle is in Delphi neither declares nor conceals, but gives signs".

Thus the procedure is like this: We collect facts by means of the senses. However, because *nature likes to hide*, we appeal to rational thinking and intuition, by means of which we make the (metaphysical) assumption that there must be a hidden *harmony*, which is better than the manifest one.[22] Because nature gives us only some signs, we are forced to restrict our efforts to understanding and describing physical processes relying only on the elements of reality she discloses. nature 'speaks' like the deity through Pythia; the oracles are short sentences, which do not express certainty. On the contrary, the answers of Pythia are ambiguous, uncertain, and indeterminate. They contain elements from which one can infer the *probable* solution of the problem raised in the question to Pythia.[23]

Such signs, among others, are irreversibility and the ensuing arrow of time, instability and chaos, signs that have been revealed during the last hundred years or so. Many scientists, Prigogine among them, have understood their meaning for humanity's endeavor to understand and describe nature, and have devoted their scientific activity to develop a sound theory comprising all, or at least some, of these signs. This line of investigation is more difficult, because it is addressed to something new, which seemed to many unbelievable, almost unexpected. But, as Heraclitus said: "He who does not expect the unexpected, he will not find it, for it is trackless and un-

---

[22]Fragment 54 says: "the hidden harmony is better than the apparent" (Hippolytus, Refutatio, IX, 9, 5).

[23]I would like to mention here a well known oracle of Pythia. Someone posed the following question: "If I go to war, shall I come back [alive]"? Pythia' s answer was like this: "You shall go You shall come back not You shall die in war". Obviously the answer is ambiguous.

explored" (fr. 18). And in order to find it, one must work hard, and yet one will find only a piece of knowledge, like those who search for gold (obviously identified to knowledge): "Those who search for gold dig up much earth and find little" (fr. 22). Prigogine and his coworkers, during the last fifty years, have been searching to find this precious metal; they have found some, because they are working hard on the right subsoil, in the right direction. Let Apollo guide them until the end.

Now, the Platonic line of investigation, as I said earlier, is based on two pillars: Idealizations and the use of mathematics, which are becoming more and more abstract and sophisticated. The latter, of course, is valid for the other route chosen by Prigogine: Mathematics is the language of science; it is the only means for describing physical processes at the most general, and thus universal, level. Plato supported the idea of describing mathematically ideal situations, with the features of stability, order, and beauty. These features led, many outstanding scientists, Newton and Einstein among others, to commit themselves to ideas that were far from the apparent behavior of nature. I only recall two famous sayings of Einstein: "God does not play dice", and "Time is an illusion".

The Platonic route was and is still working – and, I would say, *fortunately*, for two reasons: The first is related to the question: Why did Newton's philosophical commitment to *absolute nature of space and time*, while it was a bad philosophy, lead to the postulation of his physics that triumphed and became the basis of science for the next two centuries? If Leibniz's *relational philosophical view of the nature of space and time* was better (and we now know that *it is*), why then could he not invent a better physics to go along with it? The answer to this question will give the first reason, to which I have previously referred: "Newton's view of space and time was initially more successful than Leibniz's, because it is much easier to construct a description of motion based on an absolute notion of space and time than on a relational notion" (Smolin 1997, pp. 223–224).[24] The conclusion is that, for the state

---

[24]The problem is that any relational description is necessarily complicated, because to tell where something is relationally one must bring the rest of the universe into the picture. Any relational theory of motion must treat the universe as a complex system involving many particles. This is hard to do. By contrast, an absolute theory of motion can be constructed one particle at a time, as the motion of each individual particle is described with respect to the fixed structure of absolute space and time. The laws that any one particle obeys are not affected by what the others are doing. By thus paying a certain price, an absolute theory of space and time allows us to realize the idea that a fundamental theory of physics should be simple. ... Newton understood this well, and was willing to pay the price, because he saw that none of his contemporaries had been able to construct a useful theory of motion based on relational ideas. Einstein also understood this, and has been quoted

of knowledge in Newton's times, it was impossible to follow the alternative route of Leibniz.

The second reason why continuing to work according to Plato's line is worthwhile is that it has proved productive and, combined with some further features, will hopefully merge with the route of Heraclitus. I will refer to an example: String theory has followed an agitated course, with ups and downs, and actually we are at the beginning of the 'second superstring revolution'. It is said that, in order to be able to choose between the five string theories, a new principle is needed. The fact is that irreversibility and the arrow of time impose a new principle, or a postulate, such as that offered by Prigogine: "All laws of physics must be compatible with the existence of the arrow of time." String theories satisfy the postulate that *the laws of physics referred to different levels of reality must be consistent, with no contradictions.* Perhaps the next step would be to incorporate Prigogine's postulate in string theories in order to advance further.

I have at length discussed some central issues of Heraclitus' theory to reach the conclusion that among the two alternatives, Heraclitus' and Plato's, the former is more realistic, disclosing *events* that bring an element of radical novelty to the description of nature. I will now summarize why I believe that Prigogine's and his coworkers' endeavor to obtain a realistic description of nature is the right direction. First, this approach suggests solutions to paradoxes that have been revealed during the last decades of the 19th and the first half of the 20th century, and answers new questions raised by the study of instability, chaos, and limited predictability, namely: (a) the incompatibility between thermodynamics and Newtonian dynamics; (b) the time paradox; (c) the quantum paradox. Second, this approach gives a definite solution to the problem of determinism: Not only quantum processes, but almost the whole of physical processes, including those of classical dynamics, need to be described *probabilistically* (see the contributions by Gustafson and Misra in this volume). In these cases there is no more certainty, one cannot use deterministic equations to describe orbits of classical objects. Determinism is abolished. The only way to have a realistic approach to the description of physical processes is to adopt *probabilistic causality.* As Prigogine (1997, pp. 4–6) points out:

> Classical science emphasized order and stability; now, in contrast, we see fluctuations, instability, multiple choices, and limited predictability at all levels of observation. In the classical view – and here we

---

by John Archibald Wheeler as praising Newton's 'courage and judgment' for going ahead to construct a workable theory against the better philosophy" (Smolin 1997, pp. 223–224).

include quantum mechanics and relativity – laws of nature express certitudes. When appropriate initial conditions are given, we can predict with certainty the future, or 'retrodict' the past. Once instability is included, this is no longer the case, and the meaning of the laws of nature changes radically, for they now express possibilities or probabilities. ... The role of the observer was a necessary concept in the introduction of irreversibility, or the flow of time, into quantum theory. But once it is shown that instability breaks time symmetry, the observer is no longer essential. In solving the time paradox, we also solve the quantum paradox, and obtain a new, realistic formulation of quantum theory. ... We are now able to include probabilities in the formulation of the basic laws of physics. Once this is done, Newtonian determinism fails; the future is no longer determined by the present, and the symmetry between past and future is broken. This confronts us with the most difficult questions of all: What are the roots of time? Did time start with the 'big bang'? Or does time preexist our universe? ... Although our universe has an age, the medium that produced our universe has none. Time has no beginning, and probably no end.

References

Cornfeld I., Fomin S., and Sinai Y. (1982): *Ergodic Theory*, Springer, Berlin.

Diggle J. (1984): Euripides Heracleidai. In *Euripides' Fabulae*, Clarendon, Oxford.

Gomperz T. (1901): *The Greek Thinkers, a History of Ancient Philosophy, Vol. I*, John Murray, London, pp. 64–65).

Greene B. (1999): *The Elegant Universe, Superstrings, Hidden Dimensions, and the Quest for the Ultimate Theory*, Vintage Random House, London.

Guthrie W.K.C. (1962): *A History of Greek Philosophy: The Earlier Presocratics and the Pythagoreans, Vol. I*, Cambridge University Press, Cambridge.

Heisenberg W. (1962): *Physics and Philosophy*, Harper Torchbook, New York.

Kirk G.S. and Raven J.E. (1960): *The Presocratic Philosophers*, Cambridge University Press, Cambridge, p. 202.

Kirk G.S. (1962): *Heraclitus, The Cosmic Fragments*, Cambridge University Press, Cambridge.

Prigogine I. (1980): *From Being to Becoming*, Freeman, New York.

Prigogine I. (1997): *The End of Certainty – Time, Chaos, and the New Laws of Nature*, Free Press, New York.

Smolin L. (1997): *The Life of the Cosmos*, Oxford University Press, Oxford.

Torretti R. (1990): *Creative Understanding: Philosophical Reflections on Physics*, The University of Chicago Press, Chicago, p. 137.

Vlastos G. (1993): *The Presocratics, Vol. I*, ed. by D.W. Graham, Princeton University Press, Princeton.

Vlastos G. (1995): *Studies in Greek Philosophy, Vol. II: Socrates, Plato, and Their Tradition*, ed. by D.W. Graham, Princeton University Press, Princeton.

White N.P. (1995): Plato's metaphysics. In *A Companion to Metaphysics*, ed. by J. Kim and E. Sosa, Blackwell, Oxford, pp. 393–397.

The Complementary Roles of Chance and Lawlike Elements in Peirce's Evolutionary Cosmology

Frederick M. Kronz and Amy L. McLaughlin

1 Introduction

Charles Sanders Peirce was trained and worked primarily as a scientist. His contributions within science are varied and extensive. Among his major scientific advancements are the following: reformation of stellar magnitude scales with the aid of instrumental photometry, discovery of an error in European gravitational measurements due to flexure of the pendulum stand and subsequent invention of a superior pendulum, determination of the length of the standard meter in terms of light wavelengths, development of a new form of map projection (a quincuncial map) using elliptical functions, and collaboration in the development of hydroelectric power.

While Peirce's work as a scientist is of substantial note, his first love was philosophy, and it is likely that it is for his contributions to philosophy that he will be best remembered. Logic and scientific method were primary among his philosophical interests, and it was in such interests that he was compelled to gain experience in scientific investigation. The practice of science served as a means to an end, and that end was to develop a systematic philosophy.

Within philosophy, Peirce is best known for founding pragmatism, the most significant movement in American philosophy. Over the last two decades, there has been a resurgence of interest in pragmatism. Its impact is widespread, influencing developments in all areas of philosophy. Among Peirce's most acclaimed philosophical achievements are the following: the Pragmatic Maxim,[1] the logic of relations, the theory of signs (semiotics), and a theory

---

[1]Peirce characterizes the Pragmatic Maxim as follows: "Consider what effects, which might conceivably have practical bearings, we conceive the object of our conception to have. Then, our conception of these effects is the whole of our conception of the object" (CP 5.402: "How to Make our Ideas Clear"). Here and in what follows, CP refers to Peirce (1931–1935, 1958).

of abduction (inference to the best explanation). He also studied broader issues in aesthetics, ethics, epistemology and metaphysics.

Peirce's metaphysics has been historically under appreciated. This is unfortunate because a close examination of his metaphysical writings reveals numerous of Peirce's insights and clever arguments which otherwise would be missed. Part of the reason for its neglect is no doubt tied to the rise and eventual hegemony of the positivist movement in twentieth century philosophy. Since positivism seems to be a natural offshoot from the Pragmatic Maxim with its strongly operationalistic overtones, it was easy to ignore Peirce's metaphysical writings. Though Peirce was a pragmatist (an advocate of the Pragmatic Maxim), he did not therefore think that metaphysics was to be neglected or shunned. Indeed, he thought that the metaphysics he defended obeys the Pragmatic Maxim, and that it has substantial and empirically testable consequences for science. This essay focuses on central features of Peirce's evolutionary cosmology, the core of his metaphysics.

2 Tychism and Evolutionary Cosmology

Peirce's metaphysical system was developed in reaction to necessitarianism (which he also refers to as mechanism). He characterizes that position as follows (CP 6.37: "The Doctrine of Necessity Examined"):

> The proposition in question is that the state of things existing at any time, together with certain immutable laws, completely determine the state of things at every other time (for a limitation to *future* time is indefensible). Thus, given the state of the universe in the original nebula, and given the laws of mechanics, a sufficiently powerful mind could deduce from these data the precise form of every curlicue of every letter I am now writing.

The above is closely related to what is often referred to as Laplacean (or strict) Determinism (see, e.g., Bishop in this volume), though his statement is somewhat broader than that of Laplace. There are a number of figures in the history of philosophy that Peirce regards as necessitarians. Among them are Democritus, Newton, Leibniz, Hume, Laplace, Spencer, and Carus.

The metaphysics that Peirce developed in reaction to necessitarianism first appears in his writings in the late 1870s. It is convenient to distinguish three periods during which Peirce developed the metaphysical views characterized below. The crucial period, from the standpoint of publications, is the *Monist* period; Peirce published several articles in *The Monist* in the early 1890s. Five of these are referred to repeatedly in what follows, and they are among the best known of Peirce's published writings. There are also two earlier works that are seminal to his *Monist* publications, and two later elaborations that shed additional light on the themes of the *Monist* pieces. The nine writings alluded to above are the following:

The Pre-*Monist* period:
"A Guess at the Riddle" (1877–1878): This is the outline of a book that was never published, containing many ideas of the *Monist* series.
"Design and Chance" (1884): This was presented to the Metaphysical Club in Cambridge, but it was never published.

The *Monist* period (five papers published in *The Monist*):[2]
"The Architecture of Theories" (1891),
"The Doctrine of Necessity Examined" (1892),
"The Law of Mind" (1892),
"Man's Glassy Essence" (1892),
"A Reply to the Necessitarians; Rejoinder to Dr. Carus" (1893).

The Post-*Monist* period:
"Habit" (1898): This is a version of Lecture 7 of Peirce's Cambridge lecture series.
"Uniformity" (1902): This was published in Baldwin's dictionary.

In these writings there are two key metaphysical doctrines that constitute the core of Peirce's metaphysical system: tychism and an evolutionary cosmology.

Peirce held that there is a non-negligible, irreducible, indeterministic element involved in all physical, biological, psychological, and sociological processes. He refers to this indeterministic element as "chance" and to the corresponding thesis as "tychism":[3] Tychism was inspired by the ancient philosophers, Epicurus and Lucretius, and by some French philosophers who were

---

[2]This list is a bit nonstandard. Usually the set of Peirce's articles referred to as "the *Monist* series" includes his "Evolutionary Love" and not his reply to Carus. Both were published in *The Monist* in 1893.

[3]He does so in CP 6.102 ("The Law of Mind"): "In an article published in *The Monist* for January, 1891, I endeavored to show what ideas ought to form the warp of a system of philosophy, and particularly emphasized that of absolute chance. In the number of April, 1892, I argued further in favor of that way of thinking, which it will be convenient to christen tychism (from {tyché}, chance)."

contemporaries of Peirce.[4] In "Design and Chance", Peirce writes (Houser and Kloesel 1992):

> I suppose that on excessively rare sporadic occasions a law of nature is violated in some infinitesimal degree; that may be called *absolute chance*; but ordinary chance is merely relative to the causes that are taken into account.

This passage makes it clear that Peirce's notion is not merely an epistemic one, which typically reduces to some form of ignorance about some of the causal elements; but, rather, it is an ontic notion.[5] The existence of chance in an ontically robust sense entails that there are no strict laws of nature (CP 1.407: "A Guess at the Riddle"):

> We are brought, then, to this: conformity to law exists only within a limited range of events and even there is not perfect, for an element of pure spontaneity or lawless originality mingles, or at least must be supposed to mingle, with law everywhere. Moreover, conformity with law is a fact requiring to be explained; and since law in general cannot be explained by any law in particular, the explanation must consist in showing how law is developed out of pure chance, irregularity, and indeterminacy.

This passage is of particular note because it reveals an interesting and important theme that Peirce develops in other places, the idea that laws of nature can be and, indeed, must be explained. This theme is at least part of what motivates Peirce to adopt tychism, and it is explored in more detail later.

Complementing tychism is Peirce's evolutionary cosmology according to which all existents (except, perhaps, God) are subject to evolutionary changes that crucially involve chance. This includes natural processes, laws of nature, and the natures of rational agents. This thesis was inspired by the evolutionary theories of Darwin, Lamarck, and Spencer; but it is much broader than any of those theories. He refers to the broader evolutionary thesis as "evolutionary cosmology" (CP 6.102: "The Law of Mind"):

---

[4]In CP 6.511 ("Answers to Questions concerning My Belief in God"), Peirce refers to Renouvier, Charles (1854–1864): Essais de critique générale (appendice IX), *Les Principes de la Nature* (Paris), to Fouillée, Alfred (1872): *La Liberté et le déterminisme* (Ladrange, Paris), and to Delboeuf, Joseph (1882): Déterminisme et liberté, Revue Philosophique **13**, pp. 453–480, 608–638; **14**, pp. 156–189. In *The Nation*, p. 208 (1899), Peirce alludes to Boutroux, Emile (1874): *De la contingence des lois de la nature* (G. Baillière, Paris).

[5]Atmanspacher (this volume) discusses a basic distinction between ontic and epistemic states of a system. Bishop (this volume) discusses the possibility of ontic indeterministic states which would correspond somewhat to what Peirce has in mind here.

> [T]ychism must give birth to an evolutionary cosmology, in which all the regularities of nature and of mind are regarded as products of growth, and to a Schelling-fashioned idealism which holds matter to be mere specialized and partially deadened mind.

Two points in this passage are particularly significant. One is Peirce's advocacy of a sort of idealism. This aspect of Peirce's system is explored more fully below. The second point is that Peirce sees his evolutionary cosmology as a direct consequence of his brand of tychism, which involves the idea that the universe was born from pure chaos. He writes (CP 6.33: "The Architecture of Theories"):[6]

> Like some of the most ancient and some of the most recent speculations it [an appropriate metaphysics, given the current state of knowledge] would be a Cosmogonic Philosophy. It would suppose that in the beginning – infinitely remote – there was a chaos of unpersonalized feeling, which being without connection or regularity would properly be without existence. This feeling, sporting here and there in pure arbitrariness, would have started the germ of a generalizing tendency. Its other sportings would be evanescent, but this would have a growing virtue. Thus, the tendency to habit would be started; and from this, with the other principles of evolution, all the regularities of the universe would be evolved. At any time, however, an element of pure chance survives and will remain until the world becomes an absolutely perfect, rational, and symmetrical system, in which mind is at last crystallized in the infinitely distant future.

The picture is of an evolution from pure chaos, that Peirce argued would naturally and immediately begin the formation of habits, to an eventually perfectly lawful universe.

3 The Arguments for Tychism and Evolutionary Cosmology

Peirce supports the key elements of his new metaphysical system by introducing at least five distinct sorts of considerations. In what follows, we

---

[6]Peirce summarizes what is expressed here rather concisely as follows (CP 1.409–1.410: "A Guess at the Riddle"): "[T]hree elements are active in the world: first, chance; second, law; and third, habit-taking. ... We must show that there is some method of deducing the characters of the laws which could result in this way by the action of habit-taking on purely fortuitous occurrences, and a method of ascertaining whether such characters belong to the actual laws of nature".

consider his arguments from axiomatics, from complexity, from probability, from explanation, and from evolution.

3.1 From Axiomatics

Peirce claimed that metaphysics is in large part underwritten by mathematics, particularly geometry. He followed the developments of non-Euclidean geometry, and was influenced by the works of Gauss, Lobachevski, Bolyai, Riemann, Cayley, Klein, and Clifford. For instance (CP 1.401: "A Guess at the Riddle"):

> The unconditional surrender ... by the mathematicians of our time of the absolute exactitude of the axioms of geometry cannot prove an insignificant event for the history of philosophy. Gauss, the greatest of geometers, declares that "there is no reason to think that the sum of the three angles of a triangle is exactly equal to two right angles". It is true, experience shows that the deviation ... [is] excessively small ... but experience never can show any truth to be exact, nor so much as give the least reason to think it to be so, unless it be supported by some other considerations.

For Peirce, these new developments in geometry, which are based upon the rejection of particular axioms, suggested that new sorts of metaphysics must emerge as well (CP 1.402: "A Guess at the Riddle"):

> The absolute exactitude of the geometrical axioms is exploded; and the corresponding belief in the metaphysical axioms, considering the dependence of metaphysics on geometry, must surely follow it to the tomb of extinct creeds. The first to go must be the proposition that every event in the universe is precisely determined by causes according to inviolable law.

Peirce offers two arguments in favor of giving up the axiom of strict determinism. There are two possibilities for the claim that everything everywhere is strictly, causally determined by law – either this statement was somehow derived through observation, or it is innate. If it were derived through observation, though, it cannot be supposed to be absolute and exact. Peirce states: "We ... have no more reason to think that the error of the ordinary statement is precisely zero, than any one of an infinity of values in that neighborhood. The odds are infinity to one that it is not zero" (CP 1.402: "A Guess at the Riddle"). If one claims that the axiom is innate, then it must have been accepted by everyone at all times. But this is clearly not so. In fact, Peirce notes (CP 1.403: "A Guess at the Riddle") that strict causal determination as an axiom is historically altogether a modern notion, a loose inference from the discoveries of science. ... To the ancients ... the strange thing would have been to have said that there was no chance. So we are under no inward necessity of believing in perfect causality if we do not find any facts to bear it out.

Of course, the ancients that Peirce had in mind here are Epicurus and Lucretius. He also included Aristotle among the list of ancients who advocate absolute chance, but it is likely that Peirce misunderstood Aristotle's notion of chance.[7] The main thrust of his point, though, is that we are under no obligation to accept necessitarianism, as it does not (nor could it) follow directly from observation nor is it innate.

3.2 From Complexity

Having established that necessitarianism is not a foregone conclusion, Peirce argues further against the position by claiming that it contradicts particular observations. First, he argues that necessitarianism requires that the amount of complexity in the universe is constant – that is to say, it is fixed at the beginning and thereafter remains the same. The necessitarians hold that laws do not introduce complexity or diversity. Rather, laws preserve the amount of diversity that was introduced in the initial state of the universe. Peirce characterizes the necessitarians' argument for why the amount of diversity is preserved as follows (CP 6.56: "The Doctrine of Necessity Examined"):[8]

> The instantaneous state of a system of particles is defined by six times as many numbers as there are particles, three for the coordinates of each particle's position, and three more for the components of its velocity. This number of numbers, which expresses the amount of diversity in the system, remains the same at all times.

But Peirce cannot accept that conclusion on the grounds that it conflicts with the observation that a ubiquitous feature of the universe is its continually increasing complexity (CP 6.58: "The Doctrine of Necessity Examined"):

> Question any science which deals with the course of time. Consider the life of an individual animal or plant, or of a mind. Glance at the history of states, of institutions, of language, of ideas. Examine the successions

---

[7] For a discussion of this point, see Huang 1993.

[8] It appears that Peirce is faithfully representing the necessitarians' argument though that argument is rather naive insofar as it defines complexity solely in terms of the number of degrees of freedom (coordinate and velocity components).

> of forms shown by paleontology, the history of the globe as set forth
> in geology, of what the astronomer is able to make out concerning
> the changes of stellar systems. Everywhere the main fact is growth
> and increasing complexity. ... From these broad and ubiquitous facts
> we may fairly infer, by the most unexceptionable logic, that there is
> probably in nature some agency by which the complexity and diversity
> of things can be increased; and that consequently the rule of mechanical
> necessity meets in some way with interference.

What is required, then, is an explanation of this observation. Peirce provides
such an explanation, and bases it on the existence of absolute chance (CP
6.59: "The Doctrine of Necessity Examined"):

> By thus admitting pure spontaneity or life as a character of the universe,
> acting always and everywhere though restrained within narrow bounds
> by law, producing infinitesimal departures from law continually, and
> great ones with infinite infrequency, I account for all the variety and
> diversity of the universe, in the only sense in which the really *sui generis*
> and new can be said to be accounted for. The ordinary view has to
> admit the inexhaustible multitudinous variety of the world, has to admit
> that its mechanical law cannot account for this in the least, that variety
> can spring only from spontaneity, and yet denies without any evidence
> or reason the existence of this spontaneity, or else shoves it back to the
> beginning of time and supposes it dead ever since.

Since laws preclude any increase in variety, necessitarianism entails that all
extant variety existed in the original configuration of the universe and has
not increased since. Peirce concludes from this that since variety is on the
increase, it is so through the continual action of absolute chance or true
spontaneity. Note that Peirce does not claim that chance operating by itself is
sufficient to generate complexity. The suggestion in the passage above is that
chance and laws operate together to do so. But, this needs elucidation since
chance gives rise to law in Peirce's evolutionary cosmology. This point was
alluded to above, and is developed more fully below. Laws arise out of chance
occurrences within Peirce's evolutionary cosmology due to the possibility for
things to develop habits. Next we examine how it might be possible for
the operation of chance together with habit formation to give rise to lawlike
regularities, as well as diversity.

3.3 From Probability

Peirce uses a clever example to show how it is possible for diversity, and for
regularities, to arise from an initial homogeneous state of complete chaos.

The originators of diversity in Peirce's example, as in his metaphysical system, are chance occurrences and the development of propensities to form habits. In "Design and Chance", he writes (Houser and Kloesel 1992):

> A million players sit down to play a fair game ... suppose that the dice used by the players become worn down in the course of time. Chance changes everything & chance will change that. And we will suppose that they are worn down in such a way that every time a man wins, he has a slightly better chance of winning on subsequent trials. This will make little difference in the first million bets, but its ultimate effect would be to separate the players into two classes those who had gained and those who had lost with few or none who had neither gained nor lost and these classes would separate themselves more and more, faster and faster.

> If on the other hand the wearing down of the dice were to have the opposite effect and were to tend to make him lose who had heretofore gained and vice versa, the tendency would be to prevent the separation of rich and poor. But chance will act in various ways. At one time it will have one effect at another time another.
> If these effects were to be alternated after billions of trials, the effect would be to make numbers of distinct classes of players.

> ... as everything is subject to change everything will change after a time by chance, and among these changeable circumstances will be the effects of changes on the probability of further change. And from this it follows that chance must act to move things in the long run from a state of homogeneity to a state of heterogeneity.

This simple example illustrates how diversity can arise out of chance occurrences. The example is highly contrived; nevertheless, it does provide a plausible explication of the genesis of diversity in terms of Peirce's views. It also does so in connection with his views concerning the genesis of laws. Note that the dice acquire habits, and that these habits give rise to regularities. Thus, chance in conjunction with the tendency to form habits explains how diversity arises; it also serves to explain how it is that laws arise. Laws, in Peirce's view, are nothing more than habits that have become rigidly fixed.

3.4   From Explanation

For Peirce, chance is explanatorily basic while laws are derivative. The necessitarians' claim that laws are primary and are, therefore, inexplicable is erroneous, on Peirce's view. In his own words (CP 6.12: "The Architecture of Theories"):

> To suppose universal laws of nature capable of being apprehended by the mind and yet having no reason for their special forms, but standing inexplicable and irrational, is hardly a justifiable position. Uniformities are precisely the sort of facts that need to be accounted for. That a pitched coin should sometimes turn up heads and sometimes tails calls for no particular explanation; but if it shows heads every time, we wish to know how this result has been brought about. Law is par excellence the thing that wants a reason.

Peirce draws on our intuitions that random occurrences do not require explanation in making his case that regularities do. Necessitarianism takes regularities in the form of laws to be brute facts, and regards random occurrences as due merely to unknown causes, meaning that they are ultimately explicable in terms of laws. On the other hand, necessitarianism requires all actual randomness (in so far as any exists) to be associated only with the initial state of the universe. Any arbitrariness that exists, including the degree of complexity and the amount of diversity in the universe, cannot then be explained (CP 6.60–6.63: "The Doctrine of Necessity Examined"):

> When I ask the necessitarian how he would explain the diversity and irregularity of the universe, he replies to me out of the treasury of his wisdom that irregularity is something which from the nature of things we must not seek to explain. Abashed at this, I seek to cover my confusion by asking how he would explain the uniformity and regularity of the universe, whereupon he tells me that the laws of nature are immutable and ultimate facts, and no account is to be given of them. ... My view, on the contrary, hypothetizes nothing at all, unless it be hypothesis to say that all specification came about in some sense, and is not to be accepted as unaccountable. To undertake to account for anything by saying baldly that it is due to chance would, indeed, be futile. But this I do not do. I make use of chance chiefly to make room for a principle of generalization, or tendency to form habits, which I hold has produced all regularities. The mechanical philosopher leaves the whole specification of the world utterly unaccounted for ... I attribute it altogether to chance, it is true, but to chance in the form of a spontaneity which is to some degree regular.

Peirce's system is explanatorily more satisfying, since it does not maintain that regularities are inexplicable, brute fact. Regularities are to be explained as arising out of chance; specifically, these are born from the tendency for chance occurrences to develop habits. Further, the diversity of the universe is explained under Peirce's system, rather than accepted as a built-in and inexplicable feature. To follow is a more complete list of explanatory virtues Peirce claims for his system, in contrast to the necessitarian's position (CP 6.64: "The Doctrine of Necessity Examined"):

> [T]he necessitarian may say there are, at any rate, no observed phenomena which the hypothesis of chance could aid in explaining. In reply, I point first to the phenomenon of growth and developing complexity, which appears to be universal, and which, though it may possibly be an affair of mechanism perhaps, certainly presents all the appearance of increasing diversification. Then, there is variety itself, beyond comparison the most obtrusive character of the universe: no mechanism can account for this. Then, there is the very fact the necessitarian most insists upon, the regularity of the universe which for him serves only to block the road of inquiry. Then, there are the regular relationships between the laws of nature – similarities and comparative characters, which appeal to our intelligence as its cousins, and call upon us for a reason. Finally, there is consciousness, feeling, a patent fact enough, but a very inconvenient one to the mechanical philosopher.

Each of the foregoing phenomena defies appropriate explanation from the position of necessitarianism, but Peirce claims they are perfectly well accounted for by his alternative. Among these phenomena is consciousness, the consideration of which is presented in a later section. We have already seen glimpses of the explanatory role chance plays with respect to laws. Next we examine more fully how it is that laws arise in Peirce's system.

3.5 From Evolution

We have seen why Peirce requires explanation of the laws of nature as well as the seeds of how such explanation will proceed. In Peirce's example of the game of dice, he indirectly indicates his view that there is a generalizing tendency of things to develop habits. Regarding this tendency he states (CP 8.317: Letter to Christine Ladd–Franklin, 1891):

> The tendency to form habits or tendency to generalize, is something which grows by its own action, by the habit of taking habits itself growing. Its first germs arose from pure chance. There were slight tendencies to obey rules that had been followed, and these tendencies were rules which were more and more obeyed by their own action. There were also slight tendencies to do otherwise than previously, and these

destroyed themselves. To be sure, they would sometimes be strength-
ened by the opposite tendency, but the stronger they became the more
they would tend to destroy themselves.

For some chance events, their occurrence makes more likely future occurrences of events of this type. This tendency increases with such occurrences.
Other events' occurrences make future occurrences of events of that type less
likely. This negative tendency will quickly increase as well. The result in the
long run is growing regularities, and the tapering off of events unlikely to
result in regularities. Eventually the regularities will be firmly entrenched
enough to attain the status of laws. In the meantime, the universe remains
to some degree indeterministic while evolving in some sense. In CP 6.91
("Variety and Uniformity"), he says:

> [We hold] that uniformities are never absolutely exact, so that the va-
> riety of the universe is forever increasing. At the same time we hold
> that even these departures from law are subject to a certain law of
> probability, and that in the present state of the universe they are far
> too small to be detected by our observations. We adopt this hypothesis
> as the only possible escape from making the laws of nature monstrous
> arbitrary elements. We wish to make the laws themselves subject to
> law. For that purpose that law of laws must be a law capable of de-
> veloping itself. Now the only conceivable law of which that is true is
> an evolutionary law. We therefore suppose that all law is the result of
> evolution, and to suppose this is to suppose it to be imperfect.

Chance by itself does not produce the laws of nature. It is joined by a
tendency of things to form habits. Peirce characterizes this tendency as an
evolutionary law. Not only is this law involved in the evolution of all other
laws, it governs its own evolution as well. He holds (CP 6.101: "Variety and
Uniformity")

> that all laws are results of evolution; that underlying all other laws
> is the only tendency which can grow by its own virtue, the tendency
> of all things to take habits. ... In so far as evolution follows a law,
> the law of habit, instead of being a movement from homogeneity to
> heterogeneity, is growth from difformity to uniformity. But the chance
> divergences from law are perpetually acting to increase the variety of
> the world, and are checked by a sort of natural selection and otherwise
> (for the writer does not think the selective principle sufficient), so that
> the general result may be described as "organized heterogeneity" ...

The resulting state of organized heterogeneity allows for the regular operation of laws, as well as for slight deviations from these laws. The action
of chance is significant not only as the primary agency in the universe that

serves to explain how laws, complexity and diversity arise; it also provides ample room for mental phenomena. Peirce maintains that there is an intimate relationship between absolute chance, the primary category in his metaphysics, and mind.

4 Tychism and the Mental

Peirce argues that necessitarianism (mechanical causation) is explanatorily deficient with regards to increasing complexity and the origin of laws; these arguments were considered above. It was noted in passing that Peirce sees other explanatory problems for necessitarianism with regards to mental phenomena – including consciousness, mind, and free will – that are completely avoided within his cosmological framework.

As previously noted, Peirce explicitly characterizes his position as idealism. Two factors motivate his idealism. First, he wants consciousness and mind (these are separate notions for Peirce – this point is discussed below) to play active roles in his system, unlike the necessitarians, who relegate them to a secondary position at best (epiphenomenalism). Tychism makes possible these roles for consciousness and mind. Second, Peirce also wants to avoid the mind-body interaction problem of the dualists.[9] For him (CP 6.61: "The Doctrine of Necessity Examined"),

> [t]his is the way, then, that necessitarianism has to make up its accounts. It enters consciousness under the head of sundries, as a forgotten trifle; its scheme of the universe would be more satisfactory if this little fact could be dropped out of sight. On the other hand, by supposing the rigid exactitude of causation to yield, I care not how little ... we gain room to insert mind into our scheme, and to put it into the place where it is needed, into the position which, as the sole self-intelligible thing, it is entitled to occupy, that of the fountain of existence; and in so doing we resolve the problem of the connection of soul and body.

Thus, Peirce avoids the interaction problem by adopting the view that all matter is a form of mind; this is what he means when he says above that mind is the fountain of existence. But, this still leaves open the questions as to

---

[9]Peirce does not, as far as we know, discuss the viability of a non-necessitarian materialism. This is certainly an alternative, given the considerations introduced up to this point. Presumably, he thought that it would be much easier to explain how matter can arise out of mind rather than the reverse. But, such a materialist could give a quasi-Peircean account of how mind arises out of matter: mind is just matter that has the right sort of unstable equilibrium that makes possible the ability to readily take on and to lay aside habits.

the nature of mind and consciousness, and their relations to the fundamental categories of chance and habit formation in Peirce's system.

4.1 Consciousness and Mind

On Peirce's view, there is no room in necessitarianism for consciousness, except perhaps as an epiphenomenon (CP 6.613: "A Reply to the Necessitarians"):

> Mechanical causation, if absolute, leaves nothing for consciousness to do in the world of matter; and if the world of mind is merely a transcript of that of matter, there is nothing for consciousness to do even in the mental realm. The account of matters would be better if it could be left out of account. ... But consciousness ... is not to be ... reinstated without tychism; nor can the work be accomplished by assigning to the mind an occult power ...

What is required to escape this unsatisfying situation is the existence of absolute chance (tychism). According to Peirce, there is an intimate relationship between chance or spontaneity and consciousness. Consciousness, at root, is pure feeling. Peirce characterizes the relationship between chance and feeling as follows (CP 6.265: "Man's Glassy Essence"):

> Wherever chance-spontaneity is found, therein the same proportion feeling exists. In fact, chance is but the outward aspect of that which within itself is feeling. I long ago showed that real existence, or thing-ness, consists in regularities. So, that primeval chaos in which there was no regularity was mere nothing, from a physical aspect. Yet it was not a blank zero; for there was an intensity of consciousness there, in comparison with which all that we ever feel is but as the struggling of a molecule or two to throw off a little of the force of law to an endless and innumerable diversity of chance utterly unlimited.

As with the explanation of laws, chance alone is insufficient to adequately account for the existence of broadly varying degrees of consciousness or of quality of mind.[10] Peirce explains these, at least in part, by appeal to the propensity to form habits. In the case of explaining the latter, unlike the account of laws, Peirce also includes in his account the ability to break habits, which he explains in terms of states of unstable equilibrium. Peirce takes protoplasm to be exemplary of conscious beings more generally. To follow is some of what he says about this case (CP 6.264: "Man's Glassy Essence"):

---

[10]Mind and consciousness are distinct notions for Peirce. Consciousness is typically identified by Peirce with feeling, and mind with that which feels. Peirce follows Hartmann in claiming that there can be unconscious mind (CP 7.364: "Psychognosy").

If, then, we suppose that matter never does obey its ideal laws with absolute precision, but that there are almost insensible fortuitous departures from regularity, these will produce, in general, equally minute effects. But protoplasm is in an excessively unstable condition; and it is the characteristic of unstable equilibrium that near that point excessively minute causes may produce startlingly large effects. Here then, the usual departures from regularity will be followed by others that are very great; and the large fortuitous departures from law so produced will tend still further to break up the laws, supposing that these are of the nature of habits. Now, this breaking up of habit and renewed fortuitous spontaneity will ... be accompanied by an intensification of feeling. The nerve-protoplasm is, without doubt, in the most unstable condition of any kind of matter; and consequently there the resulting feeling is the most manifest.

Although Peirce says here that protoplasm is a kind of matter, he is an idealist. The question arises, then, as to how matter emerges within his scheme. He elaborates his position as follows (CP 6.101: "Variety and Uniformity"):

[W]e must, under this theory, regard matter as mind whose habits have become fixed so as to lose the powers of forming them and losing them, while mind is to be regarded as a chemical genus of extreme complexity and instability. It has acquired in a remarkable degree a habit of taking and laying aside habits. The fundamental divergences from law must here be most extraordinarily high, although probably very far indeed from attaining any directly observable magnitude. But their effect is to cause the laws of mind to be themselves of so fluid a character as to simulate divergences from law. All this, according to the writer, constitutes a hypothesis capable of being tested by experiment.

This passage nicely illustrates that Peirce saw his metaphysics – in this case his idealism – as leading to new and interesting scientific hypotheses, as required by his pragmatic maxim (characterized above in the introduction).

In Peirce's idealism, there is a broad spectrum of minds from stable (law-abiding) matter, which is "effete mind" (CP 6.25: "The Architecture of Theories"), to those that have nervous systems, which he suggests have the highest quality of mind (CP 6.613: "A Reply to the Necessitarians"):

Supposing matter to be but mind under the slavery of inveterate habit, the law of mind still applies to it. According to that law, consciousness subsides as habit becomes established, and is excited again at the breaking up of habit. But the highest quality of mind involves a great readiness to take habits, and a great readiness to lose them; and this implies a degree of feeling neither very intense nor very feeble.

This passage serves to show that consciousness and mind are distinct notions. The highest measure of consciousness is in the initial state where feeling is most intense. By contrast, the highest quality of mind has a middling degree of feeling that makes it possible to readily take on and lay aside habits. In the two passages cited immediately prior to the one under discussion, he connects the ability to readily take on and lay aside habits with the existence of states of unstable equilibrium, which involves a high degree of complexity and instability. In fact, Peirce regards unstable equilibrium as a necessary condition for mind: "Uncertain tendencies, unstable states of equilibrium are conditions *sine qua non* for the manifestation of Mind" (CP 7.381: "Psychognosy"). These considerations taken together suggest the following diagram.

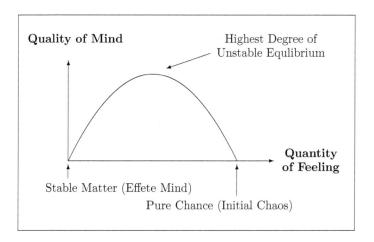

The highest quality of mind has the greatest degree of unstable equilibrium, which serves to explain how it is possible for such minds to readily take on and give up habits. It also plays a role in Peirce's views on free will.

4.2   Free Will

Accounting for free will is yet another advantage Peirce claims for his system over the necessitarians. Of the opposing position, he states (CP 6.61: "The Doctrine of Necessity Examined"):

> Our notion that we decide what we are going to do, if, as the necessitarian says, it has been calculable since the earliest times, is reduced to

illusion. Indeed, consciousness in general thus becomes a mere illusory aspect of a material system. ... Its feeling is but an inward aspect, a phantom.

Allowing for spontaneity, as Peirce's tychism does, certainly leaves the door open for freedom. Peirce has at least one very interesting and important passage where he expresses some of his own views on free will. He claims that it is not really the will that is free, rather it is the choice which long precedes the will that is free (CP 8.311: Peirce's correspondence with James, 1897):

> There are some things in your *Dilemma of Determinism* that I cannot assent to. I cannot admit the *will* is free in any appreciable measure, for reasons that may be found in my "Man's Glassy Essence". Namely, chance can only amount to much in a state of things closely approximating to unstable equilibrium. Now in the act of willing there is no such state of things. The freedom lies in the *choice* which long antecedes the will. There a state of nearly unstable equilibrium is found. But this makes a great difference in your doctrine.

Peirce takes a willing to be a concerted effort that requires a high degree of stability, meaning (presumably) the existence of a robust set of habits. Peirce noticed, as many others after him have, that freedom to act as one chooses requires not only some degree of indeterminacy, but also some degree of regularity. Without regularity of some sort, willing to act in a particular way would be futile, as it would be extremely unlikely to produce the desired result. Willing requires regularity in order to be effective. The choice that precedes such an effort requires a state of unstable equilibrium, which is related more to the ability to readily take on or to lay aside habits (cf. Kane in this volume).

5 Summary

Peirce advocates the view that chance and evolution are equally fundamental and integrally related. One aspect of this view is tychism, the doctrine that absolute chance is an active factor in the universe; another aspect is his evolutionary cosmology, the doctrine that laws evolve due to chance and the tendency of things to take habits. The doctrine of tychism does not originate with Peirce, but Peirce's tychistic cosmology is much further developed than those of his predecessors or contemporaries. His doctrine of evolution is a generalized application of evolutionary theory from the biological realm to the entire universe. Peirce's monism is a form of idealism that is radically different from the idealism of Berkeley (or any other form of idealism, for that matter). Peirce's monism is a serious attempt to unify the realms of the physical and mental – it is a monism that authenticates both inner and outer experience. Key aspects of Peirce's view are summarized and contrasted with those of the necessitarians in the following table.

Necessitarianism	Peirce's Tychism
Laws (of nature) are the only active factors in the universe; they completely determine all changes in the universe at all times.	Chance, approximate laws, and propensities to form habits operate severally to bring about all changes in the universe in varying proportions at different times.
Laws are eternal, immutable, inviolable, precise, and universal.	Laws arise and evolve due to chance; they are violable, approximate, and not universal.
Laws form the basis for all explanation and require no explanation.	Chance forms the basis for all explanation and requires no explanation.
Arbitrariness exists only at the "origin" of the universe.	Arbitrariness may exist anywhere at any time.
Chance is no more than law-governed factors that cannot now be calculated or predicted (epistemic).	Chance is an objective reality that is operative in the universe (ontic).
Chance is gradually eliminated as our knowledge and understanding of laws are refined.	Chance wanes as laws become more exact, and is only completely eliminated in the infinite future.
Consciousness is an artifact only; it does not affect the physical world, yet mysteriously arises from it.	Consciousness is intimately tied to chance by way of feeling; matter is mind deeply ingrained with habit.
There is no freedom of the will and no free choices; apparent freedom is merely an illusion.	Freedom lies in the choice which long antecedes the will.

References

Peirce C.S. (1931–1935): *The Collected Papers of Charles Sanders Peirce, Vols. 1–6*, ed. by C. Hartshorne and P. Weiss, Harvard University Press, Cambridge, MA.

Peirce C.S. (1958): *The Collected Papers of Charles Sanders Peirce, Vols. 7–8*, ed. by A.W. Burks, Harvard University Press, Cambridge, MA.

Houser N. and Kloesel C., eds. (1992): *The Essential Peirce, Vol. 1*, Indiana University Press, pp. 215–224.

Huang, P.H. (1993); Aristotle and Peirce on chance. In *Charles S. Peirce and the Philosophy of Science*, ed. by E.C. Moore, University of Alabama Press, Tuscaloosa, pp. 262–276.

Does Chance Make a Difference? The Philosophical Significance of Indeterminism

Dennis Dieks

Abstract

It is sometimes claimed that simply introducing indeterminism into physics leads to a fundamentally new view of the physical world with respect to such notions as novelty, becoming, and openness of the future. While deterministic theories imply a view according to which everything is fixed from the beginning and nothing novel can ever arise, indeterminism is intimately linked to novelty and originality – or so it is said. This conception is often accompanied by the idea that the acceptance of indeterminism entails an essentially time-asymmetrical and dynamical picture of the physical world, in which the future harbors unrealized possibilities, one of which unfolds itself in the present, whereas the past is fixed.

I will assess such claims critically and show that the concepts of indeterminism, chance and probability by themselves do not necessarily lead to new perspectives with regard to such notions as originality, the flow of time, openness of the future, and time-symmetry. Any expectation that such new perspectives would automatically arise is largely based on a conflation of concepts from ordinary language with technical concepts from fundamental physics. Although there may be some connection between our ordinary language and technical concepts, these connections are much more subtle than often realized.

1 Introduction

If physical determinism is true, the future cannot be different from what it actually is, given the past. In fact, according to the kind of determinism found in fundamental physical theories, the whole history of the universe is already contained in the state the universe has at one instant; for example the state at its very beginning. Intuitively speaking, it seems appropriate to say that nothing essentially new can ever arise in such a universe. In other words, determinism does not provide room for novelty or originality, at least as the latter are ordinarily (everyday sense) understood. A similar intuition is that since in a deterministic universe states of affairs cannot be different from what they actually are, determinism leads to a lack of freedom or even to compulsion.

By contrast, in an indeterministic world the whole history of the universe is not contained in or determined by the state of the universe at one instant. It seems plausible that in such a world there *is* room for spontaneity and originality. Furthermore, in a chancy universe there appears to be a fundamental difference between the past and the future, because only the past is fixed whereas the future contains unrealized possibilities of which one becomes real in a process of becoming associated with the flow of time. Finally, because things could have been different from what they actually are, it seems that freedom can be accommodated within indeterminism and that this provides new opportunities for the analysis of free will (e.g. Jantsch 1980, Prigogine 1980, 1997, Davies 1989, Kane 1996).[1] Such ideas about the philosophical significance of physical indeterminism are plausible enough at first blush. But do they stand up to detailed critical scrutiny?

Analyses of the wider philosophical significance of the determinism-indeterminism distinction have a long history. For example, within the Epicurean atomistic philosophy of nature handed down to us by Lucretius (1951), material bodies of completely new forms could come into being as a result of the sometimes erratic motion of the atoms (the indeterministic "swerve" postulated by the Atomists). If the atoms moved only deterministically, falling down in uniform motion along straight lines as the Atomists considered typical of determinism, there would be no collisions that could lead to complicated structures. Within the framework of the Epicurean atomistic world picture we thus obtain a justification of the notion that indeterminism is needed for novelty in a particular sense: Without the indeterministic swerves we could never have anything but individual atoms moving in straight lines. Novelty or originality is here given meaning in terms of complexity. As is already clear from this example, much will depend on the meaning attached to such notions as "novelty", "originality", "fixedness", "becoming", etc. This observation is reinforced when we look at the history of discussions about the relevance of physical determinism for the freedom of the will. In the course of these debates it has become abundantly clear that the meaning given to concepts like "freedom", "compulsion", and "natural law" is crucial

---

[1]Similar ideas have been put forward in discussions of the relation between science and religion (e.g. Peacocke 1990, Kirschenmann 2001, chap. 7).

(e.g. Dorato and Kane in this volume). According to a regularity interpretation of laws for example, scientific theories – be they deterministic or indeterministic – have nothing to do with compulsion. And if a voluntarist interpretation is given to the notion of human freedom, then there is no conflict between freedom and determinism. These observations constitute the core of the compatibilist position in the free will debate (e.g. Dorato in this volume). If, on the other hand, freedom of the will is given meaning in terms of "origination", in the sense of uncaused beginnings of causal chains, and if the notion of causality involved is interpreted as a physical notion, a conflict with physical determinism evidently does arise (e.g. Kane in this volume).

In the spirit of the above examples, it is the purpose of the present essay to continue critical discussion of the relevance of the determinism-indeterminism distinction as it occurs in modern physics for broader philosophical issues. Is it true, in classical and quantum mechanics, that the concepts of indeterminism employed there open up possibilities for novelty and originality that determinism is unable to offer? Does the introduction of chance lead to a dynamic picture of the universe, characterized by genuine becoming and an open future, whereas the truth of determinism would entail that we live in a static, "block universe"? The above examples make it clear that in order to be able to answer such questions we should be explicit about the meaning of the terms involved. First of all, we have to explain the meaning that will be attached to the terms "determinism" and "indeterminism".

My concern is the significance of the distinction between determinism and indeterminism as it actually occurs within the conceptual framework of fundamental theoretical physics. I will therefore consider physical systems, whose state can be represented mathematically by a point in phase space (in the case of classical physics) or a vector in Hilbert space (in quantum theory). I will not consider explicitly the more general quantum states represented by density matrices (doing so would not change any results). The temporal evolution is the solution of an evolution equation and is represented by a *trajectory* in phase space or Hilbert space. In classical mechanics this evolution equation is a differential equation connecting the accelerations in the system to the forces that operate; for a one-particle system it is $F=ma$, with F the force, m the particle's mass and a the particle's acceleration. In quantum mechanics the evolution equation is the Schrödinger equation, which is a differential equation expressing a relation between the time derivative of the state vector $|\psi>$ and the forces (or potentials) that are present.

An essential question for discussion is whether or not the evolution equation completely determines the trajectory in phase space. That is, given the state of the system at some instant t_0 together with boundary conditions, is there only one trajectory possible, only one solution of the evolution equation? If this is indeed the case then the evolution is deterministic. So in the case of deterministic evolution we find that there is only one state of the system at any future or past instant that is compatible with the state at t_0.[2] Put differently, in the case of deterministic evolution there is one unique future and past of the system, given the state at t_0 and the boundary conditions. As a consequence, systems that possess the same state and are in identical conditions at one instant will have the same state always.

The above characterization refers to features of the theoretical description of physical systems. It therefore appears to deal with determinism as a property of theories (an "epistemic" sense of determinism) rather than with determinism as a possible ontological property of the world. However, there is a close relation between these two senses of determinism: Physical systems (or worlds) that are completely and correctly described by a deterministic theory (for which this theory is true) can be said to be deterministic themselves, on the level of ontology.[3]

All fundamental physical theories that have been proposed and generally accepted to date exhibit deterministic time evolution in the sense of the above definition. For example, if in classical mechanics all forces, at all instants, plus the state at an initial moment are given, the system's state can follow only one trajectory through phase space. One often considers closed systems, in which all forces are internal, i.e. due to the particles in the system themselves. For such systems it is sufficient to give the initial state of the particle system in order to completely determine the future and past state evolution – no separate specification of forces is needed.[4] In quantum mechanics, too, the state is subject to deterministic evolution, this time in Hilbert space (unitary evolution given by Schrödinger's equation).

---

[2]This concept of determinism can be broken up into two further concepts: determinism with respect to the future and determinism with respect to the past. We will not need the latter concepts, because they do not play a basic role in fundamental physics.

[3]This is very similar to the definition given by Earman (1986). Earman phrases his definition in terms of possible worlds, which are required to be the same at all times given that they have the same state at some instant. If a "possible world" is taken to be a world that is governed by the same laws as the actual world, my definition results. It should be noted that Earman views his definition as being ontological (p. 14).

[4]A number of caveats are to be considered here. For example, in classical mechanics one typically studies the motion of idealized particles without spatial dimensions, so-called point particles. If two such particles collide, the interaction potential may become singular, and it becomes unclear whether the evolution is deterministic. We will not consider this and similar situations where the conditions under which the differential equations have unique solutions are not fulfilled (for discussion, see Earman 1986).

It should be noted that the latter statement is about how the *state vector in Hilbert space* evolves, as long as the Schrödinger equation applies. It is not immediately evident what this implies for the evolution of the physical properties of the system: We should be careful to distinguish between the mathematical representation of the system, as an element of Hilbert space, and the system itself, which surely is not a vector in an abstract space. In classical mechanics we did not need to be that cautious, because in classical mechanics the phase point (the mathematical representation of the system) is in one-to-one correspondence with the physical properties of the system. For example, in the simple case of a particle without internal degrees of freedom, the coordinates of the phase point are the particle's position and momentum, respectively. So in classical mechanics the deterministic evolution of the state corresponds to a deterministic evolution of physical characteristics of the system. In other words, if two similar classical systems (completely described by classical mechanics), with the same forces etc., have the same physical properties at one instant, they have the same properties at all times. Because of this fact we may call the evolution of such classical systems themselves deterministic. (Classical systems are systems of which classical mechanics is true; of course, it is another question whether such systems actually exist.)

In quantum mechanics the situation is fundamentally different. The interpretation usually given to the state vector $|\psi>$ is that it determines a *probability distribution of outcomes of measurements.* So the relation between the theoretical state on the one hand, and physical states of affairs on the other, is more complicated than in classical physics. A problematic aspect of the standard interpretation of the state vector is that it refers to the outcomes of *measurements* on the system rather than to physical characteristics of the physical system itself. This is a central issue in the controversial field of the interpretation of quantum mechanics, which, however, is not the main concern here. The essential point for the theme of determinism versus indeterminism is the non-controversial observation that the relation between the quantum state and physical reality, as we ordinarily describe it in terms of the presence or absence of physical characteristics, is probabilistic and not one-to-one. Given one state vector, representing the combination of object and measuring device, in general many physical outcomes, in which the device exhibits different measurement results, are possible. Knowledge of the state vector only enables one to assign probabilities to these various outcomes. This characteristic of quantum theory, namely that the theory operates with a state that obeys a deterministic evolution itself but corresponds to a probability distribution over physical possibilities, is typical of probabilistic theories in modern physics.

Indeterministic theories conflict with determinism as defined above; in other words, these theories do not fix the physical properties of a system for all times once its physical properties at one instant, plus boundary conditions, have been given. So according to indeterministic theories, physical systems having the same history up to a particular point in time, and finding themselves in identical circumstances, may nevertheless exhibit different behaviors in the future. To keep contact with present-day fundamental indeterministic physics (i.e. quantum theory) I will assume that such indeterministic theories operate with probabilities, in the manner explained above. That is, I will focus on theories in which the theoretical state corresponds to a probability distribution and obeys some dynamical equation defined by the theory. The probabilities are probabilities of the actual properties of the individual system, or of occurrent events (e.g. actual experimental outcomes). According to this definition, quantum mechanics is indeterministic, even though the temporal evolution of the theoretical state (the state vector in Hilbert space) is deterministic; by contrast, the fundamental theories of classical physics are deterministic.[5]

Before proceeding with the question of what the implications of physical (in)determinism are for the status of such notions as novelty, openness of the future, and time-asymmetry, an additional remark about quantum mechanics is in order. In the above sketch of the general structure of the theory I have only mentioned the time evolution governed by the Schrödinger equation. However, it is not uncontroversial whether Schrödinger evolution is the only time evolution that plays a role in quantum mechanics. In traditional accounts of the theory a role is often allotted to the so-called "collapse of the wave function" as an additional element of the dynamics. The idea is that as soon as a measurement has been performed, and one of the various possibilities of the outcome has been realized, the theoretical state should be updated in order to reflect the outcome that has become actual. Postulating a new state that assigns the probability 1 to the actual outcome fulfils this purpose (von Neumann 1932, p. 112, Dirac 1947, p. 36, Messiah 1969, p. 198). Put differently, according to this approach the state "collapses" to a new one when a measurement result becomes definite. If these collapses are accepted as an independent evolution process (as first proposed by von Neumann 1932), the temporal evolution of the state vector becomes indeterministic and time-asymmetric. However, there are reasons for doubting whether collapses should be regarded as part of the fundamental evolution process. First, as will be discussed later in this paper, there is no cogent con-

---

[5]See, however, footnote 4.

ceptual reason for assigning probability 1 to an event once it has occurred. This seems to undercut the motivation introducing collapses. Second, there are viable interpretations of measurement processes that require no such collapse, which are consistent with experiments and which have become more dominant among practicing physicists in recent years (e.g. Bub 1997).

I will adopt the point of view that there are no collapses in quantum mechanics in most parts of this paper, although quantum theories will always be considered as indeterministic in the sense defined above. Because my main interest is in the *conceptual* consequences of the introduction of indeterminism and probabilities, this is sufficient for my purposes. Moreover, as will be indicated, many of the conclusions remain valid even if collapses are taken seriously. Note as well that I am not arguing for or against actual indeterminism in physics; rather, I am arguing that the mere presence or absence of indeterminism in physics does not necessarily have the conceptual consequences for our ordinary language concepts that some have thought.

2 Novelty, Originality and Spontaneity

According to determinism the history of the world is fixed; but indeterminism supposedly removes the chains and provides room for novelty. In order to work out this intuition and make analysis possible, a specific meaning needs to be attached to novelty. We now face a difficulty, which will return again and again: As with most terms occurring in natural language, the meaning of novelty is to some extent vague. The way it should be applied to the behavior of physical systems is not clear a priori, and we should, therefore, stipulate explicitly how to connect this and other ordinary language concepts to physics. We already encountered one proposal, namely to define "novelty" and "originality" in terms of complexity, as implicit in Lucretius' *De Rerum Natura*. In the framework of Lucretius' philosophy this led to an immediate link with indeterminism, because complexity could only arise as a result of the indeterministic swerves sometimes undergone by the atoms. Can a similar move be made within the framework of modern physics?

For this idea to succeed, it would be necessary to show that determinism excludes (or at least makes improbable) particular states, namely states of high complexity, that become accessible (or more probable) if indeterministic elements are added to the theory. It seems obvious, however, that such a link between indeterminism and complexity cannot exist in general. If determinism is abandoned, this by itself implies nothing about new regions of phase space that become accessible or more probable. Take classical mechanics, the stock example of a deterministic theory. The properties of physical systems are fully specified by points in phase space, and their time evolution by trajectories in that space. If a property like ergodicity or mixing applies (as it is assumed in standard applications in statistical mechanics), all regions of phase space are accessible. Now suppose that some stochastic element is introduced in the time evolution. It is immediately clear that no new physical structures become available by this transition from determinism to indeterminism. The phase space remains the same as it was in ordinary classical mechanics, and no new regions of it become available, because the phase space already was completely accessible. In this example nothing new (in the sense of new structures) is achieved by adding indeterminism. It follows that there is no *logical* connection between indeterminism and novelty in the sense of new structures becoming possible in the sense of equating novelty with the more technical notion of complexity in classical physics.

This, of course, is only one counterexample, but it is sufficient to demonstrate that, in the context of complexity, there is no general conceptual link between novelty and indeterminism. There might be important cases in which indeterminism *is* responsible for the coming into being of novel structures. It is hard to imagine what such examples should be like, however. And given that the indeterministic schemes used by physicists within non-quantum physics (Markov chains, probabilistic treatments of chaotic systems, and so forth) can be embedded within larger deterministic schemes (see Gustafson and Misra in this volume), it is not clear that adding indeterminism adds anything new that cannot already be obtained from fundamental deterministic theories (cf. Primas, this volume, for another point of view).

Quantum theory does not make this different because there exists a deterministic alternative to quantum mechanics (the Bohm theory), which uses a classical configuration space and deterministic trajectories, and which is empirically equivalent to ordinary quantum mechanics so far as we know. So any novelty (in the complexity sense) due to quantum mechanics can be reproduced by a deterministic scheme. Admittedly, this holds only as long as we deal with structures on the level of *observational* phenomena – the *ontology* of the Bohm theory, it may be argued, is completely different from that of ordinary quantum mechanics. However, the observational level is generally unproblematic in the context of quantum theory; the theory's ontology, especially regarding what it says about situations in which no measurements take place, is controversial and unclear.

It is sometimes suggested that a link between indeterminism and novelty or originality becomes manifest in the context of classical *chaotic* systems. The characteristic feature of such systems is that minute differences in initial conditions blow up exponentially during temporal evolution, so that completely different situations quickly develop from initial conditions that were virtually identical. Although chaotic systems are thus defined in terms of phase points and trajectories, and the degree to which these trajectories diverge from each other in the course of their deterministic temporal evolution (an analysis in terms of Lyapunov exponents), it can sometimes be expedient to switch over to a description in terms of probabilities. This is particularly so if concrete predictions have to be made. Indeed, because of extreme sensitivity to initial conditions it will generally not be possible to predict exact trajectories – there will always be some uncertainty in our knowledge of the initial conditions. Another complication that might arise is that of trajectories becoming uncomputable (in the technical mathematical sense); i.e. that they cannot be approximated systematically by means of power series expansions. In this case "coarse graining" and recourse to a treatment by means of probability distributions may also be helpful.

However, from this description it is already clear that the introduction of probabilities does not lead to new possible structures for the chaotic systems. The probability distributions are defined over the same phase space that was already used in the deterministic treatment. Probabilities always are probabilities of *something;* and in this case they are probabilities of phase points being occupied and trajectories being followed. No new possibilities arise. As in the case of statistical mechanics, the probabilistic description is introduced via considerations about the deterministic underpinnings of that description; so how could new levels of complexity ever result by simply switching descriptions?

Let us therefore look at another initially plausible way of connecting indeterminism to the notions of novelty and originality. In classical, deterministic, Hamiltonian systems, whose trajectories in phase space are restricted to a finite volume in that phase space, *Poincaré recurrences* will occur. That means that in the course of its evolution the state of the system will come back arbitrarily close to the initial state (unless the initial state is very exceptional). More precisely, take any small phase space region around the initial phase point; Poincaré's recurrence theorem then says that the system's state will return to this region, no matter how small it is. (Still more precise: The measure of phase points in any small region that will not come back to that region is zero.) So, e.g., in a closed system with a finite energy and only a finite amount of space at its disposal (a hermetically closed room, for example), the atoms and molecules will at some future instant come arbitrarily close to their initial positions and velocities. This situation will then be indistinguishable from the starting situation; and this holds even if the system contained dissipative subsystems as components (e.g. a device, in the hermetically closed room, of which the moving parts come to rest after a while because of friction). Of course, after one repetition of the initial situation Poincaré's theorem can be applied again, so that we can infer that a new recurrence will take place; and then another one, and so forth. So any situation will repeat itself infinitely often. This certainly is a result that seems to imply that not much novelty can be found in the type of deterministic evolution that is typical of classical closed systems confined to a finite spatial volume having a bounded energy (the typical example in which the accessible phase space volume is finite) – they are caught in an eternal Sisyphean cycle. If indeterminism could break this cycle, surely that would be a feat that could be associated with the presence of an element of novelty. Conversely, if it turned out that Poincaré recurrences are to be expected in indeterministic theories, too, that would extend the earlier conclusion that there is no direct relation between indeterminism and novelty.

The prospects for indeterminism to achieve something here seem dim from the outset. The crucial ingredients in the derivation of Poincaré's theorem are the premises that the available phase space volume is finite and that the evolution is measure-preserving. Loosely speaking, there is in that case not enough phase space available to the system to stay away from its starting point forever (I will make this more precise in a moment). How could the mere introduction of an element of randomness in the evolution change this characteristic of the situation?

Poincaré's theorem can be proved in a simple way (Uhlenbeck and Ford 1963). It depends on Liouville's theorem, which states that in classical mechanics volumes in phase space are preserved under the equations of motion. Now, let A be an arbitrarily small region in phase space surrounding our system's initial state. Let B be a subset of A, consisting of the phase points in A that leave A and do not return to A. Define a time interval τ such that after this interval has lapsed, B has evolved into B_1, with $A \cap B_1 = \emptyset$. After another time interval τ, B_1 has developed into B_2, after yet another interval τ into B_3, and so on. The sets B_1, B_2, B_3, ..., B_n are all disjoint, as follows from the definition of τ. By virtue of Liouville's theorem, they all have the same phase space volume as B. The total phase space volume occupied by the union of B_1, B_2, ..., B_n is, therefore, given by n times the volume of B. Since there is no upper bound on the time during which B evolves, the total volume of the sets B_1, B_2, ..., B_n will grow without limit, unless the phase space volume of B is zero. Since the total available phase volume is finite by assumption, almost all points in A must be recurrent. This is Poincaré's theorem.

This outline of the proof makes it clear that Poincaré recurrences will occur in any dynamical system that is deterministic and measure preserving (i.e. in which phase volumes remain constant during the motion) and is confined to a finite phase volume.[6] Now consider the analogous situation in quantum mechanics. A quantum system confined to a finite energy range and a finite spatial volume (like a particle in a box) is represented by a unit-length state vector in a finite-dimensional Hilbert space. During the unitary Schrödinger evolution the tip of this vector moves across the surface of the unit sphere in Hilbert space. This motion on the surface of the sphere is measure preserving, because unitary motion preserves the angle between any two vectors. Any area on the sphere will therefore keep its exact form during the evolution. Since the total area of the surface of the sphere is finite the state vector will return arbitrarily close to its initial position, unless the initial state is very exceptional. Moreover, this will happen infinitely often. Although the state spaces are different, the situation is analogous to classical physics. In particular, it should be noted that the states available to the quantum system (corresponding to the points on the surface of the sphere) form a continuum, just like the points inside the finite volume in classical phase space. So the fact that the Hilbert space is finite-dimensional does not mean that the system can only reach a finite number of states. The initial state will be approximated with arbitrary accuracy in spite of the uncountable infinity of accessible states.

The argument no longer goes through if the Hilbert space has an infinite number of dimensions.[7] In this case there is no finite unit sphere along the surface of which the state vector moves, and as a consequence there will in general be no recurrences. This is analogous to what happens in classical deterministic systems if the available phase space volume is infinite. Poincaré's theorem, then, does not apply and there is in general no reason to expect that the system will return close to its initial state. Think, for instance, of a particle in rectilinear motion in infinite three-dimensional space. There is no

---

[6]Poincaré's theorem does not guarantee that each individual point will return to its initial position at the same time, meaning that the initial distribution of points may never recur although each individual point recurs. This is particularly relevant for mixing systems and K-flows. However, I am interested here in the behavior of an individual system, which is represented by the evolution of an individual phase point.

[7]In quantum theory the assumption of finite dimensionality may involve more idealization than the analogous assumption of a finite phase space volume in classical physics. For example, a particle in a box has a nonzero probability of escaping, via tunneling, if the potential representing the wall is finite. In this case an infinite dimensional Hilbert space may be needed. Instability of a particle may also require a treatment by means of an infinite dimensional Hilbert space.

reason, however, to associate such processes with novelty or originality (this would only lead to an equivocation, a point to which I will return below). If one nevertheless desires to do so, the point remains that in this respect there is no difference between deterministic classical mechanics and indeterministic quantum mechanics.

One might object that only unitary Schrödinger evolution has been considered. If a system interacts with its environment, however, the evolution of its state (its density matrix) is not unitary. This does not matter for the argument, though, because the unitary evolution would still apply to the larger whole consisting of the system and the environment with which it interacts. The same remark can be made in the context of classical theory: If there is an interaction with the environment the evolution of the system itself need not be measure preserving, and the premises of Poincaré's theorem will not be satisfied. Obvious examples are furnished by dissipative systems, which loose energy to their environment and, therefore, cool down, or come to rest through friction, in a seemingly irreversible process. But in this case, too, the original argument will hold for the larger system comprising the dissipative system plus its environment. As long as there is *some* finite total system obeying the fundamental classical equations and, therefore, having a measure preserving evolution, Poincaré's recurrences will occur in it. As a consequence, also the component system will return arbitrarily close to its earlier states. Again, the argument does not go through if the available phase space volume or the dimensionality of the Hilbert space is infinite. There need not be any recurrences in such cases. But this observation covers both deterministic and indeterministic cases and so does not show any particular relevance of indeterminism for the absence of recurrences.

Another doubt that may arise in the context of quantum mechanics is that I did not explicitly mention the collapse of the wave function. Suppose that we take the position that collapses are real physical processes; in that case the time evolution of the quantum state becomes indeterministic. Would that not make things different? Not necessarily. If collapses are added to the case in which the state vector moves unitarily across the surface of the unit sphere, the unitary evolution is interrupted from time to time and the state will change discontinuously to one of the eigenvectors of the observable being measured. Between these collapses the state will evolve unitarily again. The probability with which a collapse to a particular eigenvector takes place is given by the square of the length of the component of the state in the direction of that eigenvector. After a collapse and a (possibly brief) period of unitary evolution, all eigenvectors will in general have a probability greater than zero of being the next state to which a collapse will take place. Thus a Markov process with a finite state space is obtained in which all states can be reached from each other – all transition probabilities are greater than zero. It is a well-known result of probability theory that in such a case all states are recurrent and persistent (Feller 1970, chapters XIII, XV). That is, each of the system's states will recur infinitely often, given the qualifications mentioned earlier.

The situation can be made more complicated, for instance by considering destructive measurements. In this case it seems *prima facie* clear that the initial state will not be restored. But if the total system consisting of object system and measuring device, or an even larger system containing these systems, is subject to unitary evolution, as it is commonly assumed, Poincaré's theorem will hold again for this total system. In general, the situation is analogous to the one encountered within the deterministic framework of classical physics. The introduction of indeterminism does not add anything new to the situation.

I conclude that there is no particular logical or conceptual connection between the presence or absence of novelty on the one hand and the validity of determinism or indeterminism on the other. Of course, one could attempt to avoid this conclusion by *defining* novelty or originality, in the context of physics, to mean that an indeterministic theory applies. However, rephrasing the definition of indeterminism adding the labels "novel" or "original" seems an uninteresting maneuver, because it does not add anything to what we already knew about indeterminism before. Moreover, the meaning of novelty would then be made different from its ordinary meaning. That indeterminism leads to novelty would in this way not be a result that gives new insight into the significance of indeterminism. Instead it would become an analytic statement, true by fiat, leading to no interesting insights.

I have not yet commented on the relationship between (in)determinism and *spontaneity*. The reason is that here, more so than in the case of novelty, it is clear that we are dealing with a notion coming from a completely different context than physical determinism and indeterminism. Spontaneity is a concept from the sphere of human actions and intentions. This makes it very unclear how we should even begin establishing a connection with physical indeterminism. Here, too, it would be possible to *define* the presence of an element of spontaneity through the applicability of an indeterministic theory. But again, as in the case considered above, this would not lead to anything interesting. Moreover, also as in the case of novelty, such a redefinition would be more narrowly technical than the ordinary meaning attached to the term. As will be argued in the remainder of this essay, one might well ask whether more sophisticated attempts at forging a connection between (in)determinism and notions like novelty, originality, freedom, and so on, do not fall prey to the same objection. Indeed, unlike the technical physical terms, these latter notions derive from direct human experience and contain a substantial amount of vagueness. There certainly is a danger of confusion if we associate them too closely with the technical concepts.

3   Becoming, the Flow of Time, and the Block Universe

The second intuition to be addressed is that indeterminism avoids a "block universe" in which everything is fixed. By doing so, it is sometimes claimed, indeterminism creates "genuine becoming", and an ontological status of the future (namely, that it is "open") that is different from the past (which is "fixed"). As in the earlier discussion, much depends on the meaning attributed to the concepts involved; in this case the concepts "block universe", "becoming" and "openness", contain the same kind of vagueness as "novelty" and "spontaneity".

The term "block universe" seems to originate with James, in his essay *The Dilemma of Determinism* (James 1979, pp. 114–140). At the beginning of this essay James discusses the meaning of determinism, saying that determinism implies that the present state of the universe is compatible with only one totality. This is essentially the same definition I gave earlier. James (1979, p. 118) then summarizes the deterministic doctrine by stating that according to determinism "the whole is in each and every part, and welds it with the rest into an absolute unity, an iron block ...". This can be regarded as a poetic way of re-expressing what determinism is, and the picture of an iron block is a metaphor in this paraphrase of the definition. The block concept would not merit separate discussion if it only played this role of referring to the definition of determinism. However, later on in the same essay James discusses the role of time, and says (James 1979, p. 139; this is the place where the term block universe appears explicitly for the first time):

> A mind to whom all time is simultaneously present must see all things under the form of actuality ... And is not the notion of eternity being given at a stroke to omniscience only just another way of whacking upon us the block-universe, and of denying that possibilities exist?

Here James passes from the notion of a block universe in the sense of a universe viewed *sub specie aeternitatis*, "given at one stroke", as a whole, to a block in his earlier sense, namely a metaphor for determinism. Intuitively this may seem harmless, because if the totality of the universe's actual history is present before one's eyes, it may seem clear that there can be no "open possibilities" left and that, therefore, determinism reigns. But it is exactly this kind of maneuver, in which the vagueness of ordinary language concepts blurs technical distinctions, that is opposed in this paper. So I will start with the notion of a block universe in the sense of "universe given as a whole", and see what it entails for the validity of physical (in)determinism.

One way of giving content to the notion of a block universe as a whole is by means of a four-dimensional space-time representation in which the complete history of the universe is depicted. The view that this four-dimensional representation of the totality of space-time entails a "static" and "rigid" character of the universe is frequently put forward in the context of discussions of relativity theory (e.g. McCall 1994, p. 2; although it is perhaps fair to say that most authors silently presuppose something more than mere four-dimensional representability – see below). The idea is that past, present and future coexist in one undivided and unchanging whole. Of course, we will not be able to actually draw this space-time diagram in all its details, because we do not know all events; but the argument is about the existence in principle of such a representation rather than about our knowledge of it. Our presence here and now has a place in the diagram, as has Aristotles' peripatetic teaching in the Lyceum. Future events are part of the picture in the same way. Of course, all events are represented as they actually are. So if a sea battle, taking place tomorrow, is represented in the space-time diagram, it is necessary that a sea battle will actually take place tomorrow. This is just as necessary as that Aristotle walked around in his Lyceum, given that this past event is represented in the space-time diagram. So, one could argue, both future and past events happen *necessarily* if a block universe representation exists. Indeed, the events cannot be different from how they are represented in the diagram. Both future and past are fixed. Because everything happens necessarily, "determinism" reigns.

But this "determinism" is different from the notion defined in section 1. Indeed, for the existence of the block universe space-time diagram it does not matter whether physical theories are deterministic or indeterministic as defined in section 1: Both determinism and indeterminism *presuppose* the existence of this kind of block universe in so far as they assume the existence of definite state descriptions admitting four-dimensional representations.

However, most authors who employ the notion of a block universe intend something stronger. Not only is the concept meant to refer to a four-dimensional representation of the universe, but it also stipulates that this representation is complete, in the following sense. In the space-time block diagram, there is no privileged now-point on the time axis, let alone a moving now-point. Corresponding to this, it is assumed also that in the real (block) universe there is no "now", no "flow of time" and no "becoming" (e.g. Grünbaum 1973, Kroes 1985, Price 1996). These notions of "now", "flow" and "becoming" come from the doctrine that time is dynamical, i.e. that we cannot completely characterize time by specifying temporal *relations* between events. If time is dynamical, in addition to the specification of temporal relations, something should be said about the "now", a privileged point on the time axis, which is continually shifting its position (as in the A-series of McTaggart 1908). According to the dynamic view, the flow of the now makes events definite by making them present and then past. By contrast, the block universe is one static whole, and its temporal structure is fully represented by the time-relations between all events contained in it.

Whatever the pros and cons of the static and dynamic views of time, it should be clear that the question of which one of these two doctrines corresponds to the truth is independent of the question of the validity of physical determinism or indeterminism. According to the definitions in section 1, physical determinism and indeterminism are about *relations* between states of the universe at different times. Therefore, these notions do not depend in any way on whether or not there is a moving now. Both physical determinism and indeterminism are compatible with tenseless descriptions, which do not refer to the Past, Present and Future in an absolute way. In other words, both determinism and indeterminism can be combined with a static view of time (McTaggart's B-series), in which there is no flow of time and no "becoming". (I follow the usual terminology here, although this involves a misnomer: Of course, there is becoming in the block universe in the sense that objects may have different properties at different times, and, thus, may display change.) On the other hand, if there does exist a flow of time in reality, this is also compatible with both determinism and indeterminism. A "now", as a preferred point on the time axis, has in this case to be specified by means outside of the reach of present physical theory (because these theories by themselves only provide tenseless, relational descriptions). Such a specification of the shifting now, if it exists, can be added to histories conforming to both deterministic theories and indeterministic theories. Indeed, the relations between states at different instants are not affected by the mere introduction of a shifting now-point on the time axis.

I conclude that whether or not a "block universe" picture can adequately represent our universe has no relevance for the distinction between physical determinism and indeterminism. Furthermore, the question of whether a flow of time exists, and "becoming" in the sense of an objective shift in the boundary between Future and Past, is independent of the question of whether physical determinism or indeterminism apply to the universe's history. Conversely, physical indeterminism, being about the non-uniqueness of the *relation* between states at different instants of time, has no implications for whether time is static or dynamic.

4 Is the Notion of Chance Time-Asymmetric?

Within the conceptual framework of the deterministic laws of fundamental classical physics *prediction* and *retrodiction* have an equal status. That is, given data pertaining to one instant, it is possible to make calculations in both time directions, and both the past and the future (relative to the chosen instant) are subject to determinism. It is true that prediction or retrodiction may not always be possible in practice, as in the case of chaos. But in that case there are still existence theorems saying that only one unique past behavior, and one unique future behavior, is compatible with the initial data and the laws.

In fact, something stronger than this is true. The fundamental physical laws are *time-symmetric*, which means that if one considers a process whose evolution conforms to the dynamical laws, and reverses all velocities, the resulting process, which goes back from the final state of the first process to the original state, will again be in conformity with the dynamical laws. But my first concern here is not this type of time-symmetry and its consequences. Rather, I am interested in the more fundamental issue of time-symmetry *in the very concepts* of determinism and indeterminism.

As just pointed out, determinism can hold in both time directions; this is not at all surprising. The question I want to address is whether indeterministic theories must break this symmetry between past and present, and I will argue that this is not the case. This may be surprising, because intuition says that future events may have probabilities between 0 and 1, because they are still open, but that past events, events that already occurred, are fixed and determined, and therefore have probability 1. This intuition, and related ones, have been expressed by many authors (e.g. Bondi 1952, Eddington 1953, p. 51, Reichenbach 1953, pp. 154–157 and 1956, pp. 211–224). More recently, Lewis (1986) formulated the same thought this way: "The past is not chancy, but fixed". If this intuition turned out to correspond to an incontrovertible truth, there would be an inherent time-asymmetry in the very concept of indeterminism.

This asymmetry would perhaps correspond to a difference in ontological status of past and future. In the previous section I criticized the idea that indeterminism legitimizes the doctrine of the flow of time and, thereby, an ontological distinction between past and future (compare with Grünbaum 1973, chapter 10). But it may be thought that a tenseless variation on the same theme is viable: Given any instant of time, probability considerations can only apply to the future (with respect to the given instant), and not to the past (relative to the same instant).

Before discussing the status of probabilistic reasoning in the two time directions, I want to draw attention to the fact that in spite of the fundamental equivalence of past and future with regard to the applicability of deterministic theories, there still is a *pragmatic* difference in that case. We often *know* facts about the past, but possess no similar direct information about the future. So in practice we will hardly ever use scientific laws to retrodict what happened: Almost all applications of science relate to what will happen in the future. The background of this pragmatic asymmetry is related to the pervasive time-asymmetry in physical processes occurring around us. In particular, events very often leave traces in the future time direction. By looking at these traces we can get information about what happened, without making detailed physical calculations. For instance, if a bomb explodes it is to be expected that it will shatter windows in the wider surroundings of the explosion. Arriving at the scene later and seeing the broken glass everywhere, we infer that an explosion took place. But similar traces, now, of events that have yet to happen do not occur (or are at least very rare). So we cannot predict and retrodict with equal ease.

The explanation that is accepted by the vast majority of physicists is that this asymmetry is closely related to thermodynamic asymmetries and does not have a law-like character. That is, although the laws do not single out one direction of time over the other, the initial conditions are such that the processes that actually occur exhibit a pattern that is asymmetric in time. Ultimately, this asymmetry is, thus, a consequence of the universe's initial conditions. Because there is no law, at least in present-day physics, that governs these initial conditions, the asymmetry is considered to be fact-like rather than law-like. There is a minority point of view according to which the explanation should not be sought in initial and boundary conditions but should, rather, be based on a time-asymmetrical element in the laws themselves; and there exist also speculations about cosmological laws governing the universe's initial conditions. But these alternative points of view need not detain us here. The main question here is whether there is a time-asymmetry inherent in the very *concept* of chance, such that the introduction of chance automatically leads to a distinction between a still open and chancy future and a fixed past. If it turns out that the conceptual framework that is dominant in present-day physics does not recognize such an asymmetry, it follows *a fortiori* that there cannot be a time-asymmetry in the technical conception of chance.

Let me very briefly sum up the main features of the standard account (e.g. Stamp 1999). The first ingredient is that the initial condition of the universe (immediately after the "big bang") was characterized by a very homogeneous distribution of matter. It was therefore a state of very low entropy (the presence of gravitation is very relevant here; under the influence of gravitation matter tends to aggregate, and a homogeneous matter distribution, therefore, corresponds to a state far out of equilibrium, or – put differently – a state that exhibits a high degree of order). The second ingredient is that small systems (so-called "branch systems") frequently branch off of the total system; that is, they remain (quasi-) isolated for some time and then become part of the whole again. The branching off occurs in states of low entropy of the small systems, and the initial conditions are such that the entropy grows during the time they are isolated (on statistical grounds this is the overwhelmingly most probable evolution anyway, as first pointed out by Boltzmann). Reichenbach (1956) was the first to exploit the explanatory resources of this scenario in a systematic way (after suggestions by Schrödinger), and Grünbaum (1973) developed them further – see also Sklar (1993).

To see the significance of the branch systems hypothesis consider what would happen, according to a time-symmetrical deterministic theory, in a *closed* system. During most of the time the system would be near equilibrium, but occasionally substantial fluctuations would occur. The bigger the fluctuations, the rarer they would be. To be concrete, think of a glass of water that is isolated from its environment. Most of the time the water would be near thermal equilibrium, but sometimes there would be deviations from the equilibrium state. So, sometimes cubes of ice would come into being, while the water would warm up at other places. After such a spontaneous process of ice formation the ice cube would melt and the system would approach thermal equilibrium again. The whole evolution would be time-symmetric, with the formation of ice cubes occurring as frequently in the history of the system as the melting of them. It goes without saying that such time-symmetrical behavior is not what we experience. The explanation, according to the branch system hypothesis, is that the world around us does not consist of isolated closed systems. Rather, glasses of water in which an ice cube is floating will have branched off from a bigger system, and will have started their life in this low entropy state. Most probably, the ice will have come from a refrigerator and will have been put into the water not too long ago. This assumption justifies the inference that we ordinarily make, namely that the situation briefly before we first observed the ice was characterized by an even bigger ice cube, or, in other words, by a state even further out of equilibrium. If the glass with water were a closed system we would not be justified in drawing this conclusion. In that case the most probable thing would be that briefly before our observation of the cube there was less ice, and that we were facing a very rare phenomenon, namely a fluctuation of which this cube most probably was the most extreme manifestation. We would have to expect a smaller ice cube both before and after the observation – as first explained by Ehrenfest and Ehrenfest (1959). This example shows how the explanation of thermodynamic asymmetry, by means of the branch system hypothesis, also serves to explain the asymmetry in the occurrence of traces. The ice cube is a trace of a bigger ice cube that existed before. In a branch system the ice cube will melt, and the system will merge with its environment before enough time has passed to make a fluctuation possible during which a new ice cube can be formed. So, states that are far from equilibrium are signs that a state that was even farther out of equilibrium obtained before. In other words, according to the branch hypothesis traces occur in only one time direction (more accurately, the hypothesis says that the overwhelming majority of branch systems will show this time-asymmetric behavior).

The above example illustrates that the asymmetry in our knowledge, namely that we know much more about the past than about the future, need not be due to a time-asymmetry in physical laws or a time-asymmetry inherent in the concepts employed in the formulation of those laws. Rather, it can be attributed to contingent facts, namely the initial or boundary conditions characterizing our universe. Let me stress that it is not my purpose here to argue for this standard analysis of irreversibility. The reason that I explain it is, rather, that it seems evident that it constitutes a *consistent* approach to the problem of time-asymmetry; and its conceptual possibility casts light on the relations between the various concepts employed. In particular, if a similar account can be given within the context of indeterministic theories, this will constitute a proof that the notions of chance and probability by themselves do not necessarily imply anything about time-asymmetry.[8]

Indeterministic theories in physics work with probability distributions over possible physical situations. Only one of the possibilities will be actually

---

[8]Of course the mathematical concept of probability itself implies nothing about time-asymmetry. What is in question is how the concept of probability is deployed in an indeterministic theory.

realized. Should we say that the probability of that actualized possibility is 1 *after* (but not before) its realization? There is certainly no compelling reason to do so based only on the *meaning* of indeterminism, chance and probability. This point is independent of considerations about whether or not quantum theory is the correct physical theory.

Suppose for the sake of illustration that a fair die will be cast. Each face has a probability of $1/6$ of coming up. Suppose further that if (and only if) "six" comes up, I will be given a certain sum of money. It follows that the probability of my getting the money is $1/6$. Now the die is actually cast and the result happens to be "six". Will the probability of this result suddenly "collapse" to 1, and will the probability of my getting the money also become 1? There is no need to assume such sudden changes in probability. One can leave all probabilities the same as they were, including the *conditional* probability with value 1 of my getting the money if six results, and correctly recover all predictions. The actual outcome (six), together with the mentioned conditional probability, is sufficient for the conclusion that I will in fact obtain the money. So there is no need, from the point of view of the conceptual structure of probability theory, for chances and probabilities to be treated as subject to a dynamics according to which they are changing all the time. Probabilities can consistently be viewed as tenseless and depending on time *differences*, rather than on the time it is "now".

The point does not change, and in fact is nicely illustrated in the only fundamental indeterministic physical theory that we actually possess, quantum theory. On a plausible and empirically adequate version of this theory deterministic Schrödinger evolution always applies to the state vector, and there are no collapses. The theory is still indeterministic, of course, because the state vector determines only probabilities of physical states of affairs. The essential point is that in no-collapse quantum mechanics the evolution of the total state vector is not affected by which one of the possibilities is realized. In other words, the theory tells us that the realized state of affairs, immediately after its becoming real, has the same probability as it had immediately before – this probability will in general be smaller than 1, in spite of the fact that the event in question has become actual. That the probability is smaller than 1 indicates that the outcome could have been different from what it actually is (see Dieks (1998) for a more extensive discussion of this for the case of modal interpretations of quantum mechanics). This insensitivity of the probabilities to what actually happens is a direct consequence of the unitary evolution. In the absence of collapses, the quantum state will remain a superposition of different branches. The state will contain all possibilities, regardless of which one has become real.

The important aspect is that according to no-collapse quantum mechanics the past is obviously as chancy as the future. For all instants of time, whether they are in the past or in the future, the deterministic Schrödinger equation determines a state, which yields a probability distribution over possible physical situations. At any instant, be it in the past or in the future, only one possibility will be realized; but this does not make a difference for the probabilities assigned by the state vector.

It is essential for the viability of this no-collapse approach that it does not deny the fact that there actually *is* an asymmetry between past and future, namely that, at any instant, we have epistemic access to what happened in the past but do not know what the future will bring. This difference must certainly be accommodated within the conceptual framework I am explaining. This can in fact easily be done by making use of the asymmetry in the occurrence of traces discussed before. Just as there was no contradiction between the time-symmetry in the concept of determinism and the time-asymmetry in our actual application of deterministic theories, the fundamental time-symmetry of the concept of indeterminism does not exclude that there exists a *pragmatic* asymmetry in our use of indeterministic theories. As before, this asymmetry is due to an asymmetry in our *knowledge*: We often possess traces of the past, but do not have traces of the future.

This asymmetry can be expressed by the asymmetry of *conditional* probability distributions, in the following way. According to the no-collapse scheme, there are many possibilities for the present situation and also many possibilities for the past and future. All these possibilities have probabilities that are smaller than one. We can also ask, however, for the probabilities of future and past developments, *given* a particular state of the world now. This is a *conditional* probability. It is completely consistent to assume that such conditional probabilities of past events are close to 1, whereas the unconditional probabilities of these same events are much smaller. Consider, for the sake of illustration, a probability distribution over many possible courses of history, each one of which is nearly deterministic. In this case each possible past has a low probability, but given the situation now, it is almost certain what the past was. This is expressed by a conditional probability that is only slightly smaller than 1.

The asymmetry in our knowledge corresponds to an asymmetry in conditional probabilities, which in turn is due to the asymmetry in the availability of traces. Present conditions include the presence of traces that are reliably correlated to past events, so that the conditional probabilities of past events can become close to 1. There are fewer similar traces giving information about the future. As in the case of determinism, we can interpret the resulting asymmetry as contingent and not related to an inherent asymmetry in the very concepts of probability or chance.

Summing up, the analysis I am explaining is similar to the standard account set forth in the context of deterministic theories. The same grounds that make it understandable that there are thermodynamic time-asymmetries explain that events leave traces in the future time-direction and not in the past. These grounds do not bear on any inherent time-asymmetry in the concept of chance, but have to do with contingent, fact-like, circumstances. Because of the asymmetry in traces, there is a time-asymmetry in knowledge: Knowledge of the past can often be achieved by looking at reliable traces the past has left, whereas knowledge of the future is often much less certain. The fact that we possess knowledge of a past event does not imply, however, that the probability or chance of that event is 1. It is consistent to posit, and in fact this is the theoretical treatment offered by several interpretations of quantum mechanics, that the event in question has a probability smaller than 1. If there is a reliable correlation between the event and traces present now, the *conditional probability* that the event happened, given our information about the traces, is close to 1. This is consistent since we ourselves, as knowing and recording systems, are parts of the probabilistic structure. So our own actual situation, including the traces and our knowledge of them, also has a probability smaller than 1. This indicates that we *could* have observed something different. Probability theory has of course no problem in reconciling the statement that two situations both possess a low probability (viz., our actual conditions, including particular traces now on the one hand and correlated past events on the other) with the statement that the conditional probability of one situation, given the other, is almost 1.

According to this analysis, our measure of belief in past or future events (our credence) is not directly given by the chance or probability assigned to these events on the basis of the physical state. Certainly our knowledge of an event is compatible with a physical probability of that event being much less than 1: The certainty in our knowledge can be expressed by means of a conditional probability, or equivalently by the existence of a perfect correlation between the event and our present data. Such a perfect correlation can obviously exist between two events whose individual probabilities are smaller than 1. (This is to be contrasted with how Lewis (1986) uses his Principal Principle.)

So I conclude that the concepts of probability and chance do not contain an inherent time-asymmetry in no-collapse accounts of quantum mechanics. The case is different if collapses are introduced into the quantum mechanical evolution. The idea here is that immediately after an outcome has become actual, the theoretical state should be modified in order to give probability 1 to the actually realized outcome. My argument above shows that from the *conceptual* point of view there is no need to take such a step. Nevertheless it is sometimes argued that state vector collapse corresponds to an actual physical change in a quantum system and, in turn, must be reflected in a change of the probability assignments. Even so it remains true that the past is subject to probabilistic considerations. Given the present actual state of the world, which in this case is equivalent to the (collapsed) state, the past can in general only be retrodicted probabilistically. This is because in this case the time evolution of the state vector is no longer deterministic.

The conclusion I draw is that the transition to an indeterministic scheme does not by itself lead to a difference between past and future. Neither does quantum theory automatically lead to such a difference though this depends to some degree on the interpretation of the theory. Of course, one could insist on the intuition that the past is fixed and the future is open and *ordain* that this should be reflected in the physical description, by assigning past events probability 1. Something similar can be done in the context of deterministic theories, for instance by decreeing that past events should be suffixed by an "F" (for "fixed"), and future events by an "O". As I have demonstrated, however, such moves are superfluous: The differences in question can be accommodated in a natural way by relating them to the temporal asymmetry in our knowledge.

5   Concluding Remarks

The quantum revolution in physics, with its introduction of indeterminism at the fundamental level of physical theory, has from its inception aroused philosophical interest. For some, part of this interest has been due to the suggestion that indeterminism is intimately linked with novelty, creativity, becoming, the flow of time, and a fundamental asymmetry between past and future. These features seemed to imply a drastically new analysis of our place as humans within the physical world picture. It was thought that whereas a deterministic physical universe could only harbor robot-like creatures, indeterminism would make it possible to think of ourselves as creative beings, making our own decisions and dynamically shaping our own futures.

I have argued, however, that the supposed conceptual links between physical indeterminism on the one hand and novelty, originality, becoming, time-asymmetry, etc. on the other hand, are not nearly as clear as untutored intuition might lead us to believe. This parallels a point often defended in the context of the free-will debate, namely that there is no direct and clear conceptual connection between physical indeterminism, and randomness, on the one hand and the notion of freedom on the other. In that case, too, the idea that there is such a connection has an initial intuitive plausibility: Randomness seems to break the "compulsion" of the causal bond. But a more detailed analysis reveals that human freedom and physical indeterminism have no obvious logical relation (e.g. Dorato in this volume). Actually, the expectation that there would be such a clear and direct connection is not so plausible on second thought, given that the concepts of freedom and indeterminism stem from completely separate universes of discourse. We know how tantalizingly difficult questions about the mind-body relation are; questions about the relation between concepts like human freedom and concepts from fundamental physics should be at least as difficult to answer.

"Free will", "novelty", "originality", and also "becoming" and the "flow of time", are notions that play an indispensable role in the way we speak about our experiences and ourselves. These notions derive their meanings from the positions they occupy within the network of concepts we employ in our daily language, or a refined version of it. It turns out to be difficult to find more or less exact counterparts of these notions within the very different conceptual framework of fundamental physics. Indeed, statements that make perfect sense in ordinary language are sometimes transformed into outright contradictions if they are uncritically translated into physical statements. For instance, an important tradition within the free will debate seeks to explicate free will by proposing that a free decision originates a causal chain, is still *under the control* of the agent (as in agent causation theories; see Kane 1996, and Dorato and Kane in this volume). If the terms used here should be interpreted as referring to physical concepts, we would be asked to consider a situation in which there is an uncaused beginning of a chain of events, a beginning that, nevertheless, is under the causal influence of something else. That would be contradictory. However, in ordinary language there is no contradiction, and there may be many ways of making sense of the statement. One may think, e.g., of a causal chain of events that would not have come into existence without a human decision, whereas this human decision is the result of particular deliberations internal to the agent; etc. Another example in which an unjustified extrapolation of meaning may play a role is Kane's (this volume) use of the notion of indeterminism. Kane first equates physical indeterminism with the occurrence of "noise", and then relates this to an everyday sense of the word, namely an "obstacle" to be overcome (in this case by exertion of the will). Whether this can be justified deserves further analysis.

In conclusion, I submit that it is a mistake to look for direct physical counterparts of such concepts as freedom, novelty, creativity, spontaneity, and so on. A project that certainly is worthwhile is to investigate the role such notions play within their own universe of discourse (such analyses are attempted, from different perspectives, in several contributions to this volume). By thus looking at relations with other concepts within the same "language game", their various meanings can be clarified. An important question arising after such investigations concerns the physical conditions that have to be fulfilled in order to make the existence possible of creatures possessing these forms of freedom, responsibility and creativity. The physics of systems with the complexity of biological organisms is a field full of open questions, and one cannot be very confident about the features physical descriptions of such systems possess. As far as present-day insights go, however, it seems that the distinction between determinism and indeterminism in fundamental submicroscopic physics does not play a direct role on the level of physical complexity characteristic of biological systems. From a physical point of view it, therefore, appears that whether or not the world is fundamentally indeterministic is not vitally important for discussions about human originality, spontaneity and freedom.

References

Bondi H. (1952): Relativity and indeterminacy. *Nature* **169**, 660.

Bub J. (1997): *Interpreting the Quantum World*, Cambridge University Press, Cambridge.

Davies P. (1989): *The Cosmic Blueprint*, Unwin, London.

Dieks D. (1998): Locality and Lorentz-covariance in the modal interpretation of quantum mechanics. In *The Modal Interpretation of Quantum Mechanics*, ed. by D. Dieks and P.E. Vermaas, Kluwer, Dordrecht, pp. 49–67.

Dirac P.A.M. (1947): *The Principles of Quantum Mechanics*, 3rd edition, Clarendon Press, Oxford.

Earman J. (1986): *A Primer on Determinism*, Reidel, Dordrecht.

Eddington A.S. (1953): *Space, Time, and Gravitation*, Cambridge University Press, Cambridge.

Ehrenfest P. and Ehrenfest T. (1959): *The Conceptual Foundations of the Statistical Approach in Mechanics*, Cornell University Press, Ithaca. First published as "Begriffliche Grundlagen der statistischen Auffassung in der

Mechanik", Art. 32 in: *Enzyclopädie der mathematischen Wissenschaften, Vol. IV*, 1912.

Feller W. (1970): *An Introduction to Probability Theory and its Applications*, Wiley, New York.

Grünbaum A. (1973): *Philosophical Problems of Space and Time*, 2nd edition, Reidel, Dordrecht.

James W. (1979): *The Will to Believe*, Harvard University Press, Cambridge MA.

Jantsch E. (1980): *The Self-Organizing Universe: Scientific and Human Implications of the Emerging Paradigm of Evolution*, Pergamon, Oxford.

Kane R. (1996): *The Significance of Free Will*, Oxford University Press, Oxford.

Kirschenmann P.P. (2001): *Science, Nature and Ethics*, Eburon, Delft.

Kroes P. (1985): *Time: Its Structure and Role in Physical Theories*, Reidel, Dordrecht.

Lewis D. (1986): *Philosophical Papers, Vol. II*, Oxford University Press, Oxford.

Lucretius (1951): *On the Nature of the Universe*, Penguin Books, Harmondsworth.

McCall S. (1994): *A Model of the Universe*, Clarendon, Oxford.

McTaggart J.M.E. (1908): The unreality of time *Mind* **18**, 457–474.

Messiah A. (1969): *Quantum Mechanics*, North Holland, Amsterdam.

Peacocke A. (1990): *Theology for a Scientific Age: Being and Becoming – Natural and Divine*, Blackwell, Oxford.

Price H. (1996): *Time's Arrow and Archimedes' Point*, Oxford University Press, Oxford.

Prigogine I. (1980): *From Being to Becoming*, Freeman, San Francisco.

Prigogine I. (1997): *The End of Certainty, Time, Chaos, and the New Laws of Nature*, Free Press, New York.

Reichenbach H. (1953): Les fondaments logiques de la méchanique des quanta. *Annales de l'Institut Henri Poincaré* **13**, 109–158. English translation in *Hans Reichenbach, Selected Writings 1909–1953, Volume 2*, ed. by M. Reichenbach and R.S. Cohen, Reidel, Dordrecht, 1978, pp. 237–278.

Reichenbach H. (1956): *The Direction of Time*, University of California Press, Berkeley.

Sklar L. (1993): *Physics and Chance*, Cambridge University Press, Cambridge.

Stamp P. (1995): Time, decoherence, and 'reversible' measurements. In *Time's Arrows Today*, ed. by S.F. Savitt, Cambridge University Press, Cambridge, pp. 107–154.

Uhlenbeck G.E. and Ford G.W. (1963): *Lectures in Statistical Mechanics*, American Mathematical Society, Providence.

von Neumann J. (1955): *Mathematical Foundations of Quantum Mechanics*, Princeton University Press, Princeton. First published as *Mathematische Grundlagen der Quantenmechanik*, Springer, Berlin, 1932.

On Causal Inference
in Determinism and Indeterminism

Joseph Berkovitz

1 The Background

The inference from statistical data to causal hypotheses is of great importance in both the natural and social sciences. On the basis of such causal inferences, it is claimed, for example, that the statistical correlation between smoking and contracting cancer is due to the fact that smoking causes cancer: Other things being equal, smoking raises the chance of contracting various types of cancer. Furthermore, we are surrounded by statistical data that, if properly analyzed, can significantly enrich our knowledge of the causal relations between various factors. Consider the Bureau of Statistics. It accumulates an enormous amount of statistical data about various quantities. If we could decipher the causal relations among these quantities, statistical data would be invaluable for policy-making in governmental and public organizations and provide very efficient means for policy monitoring.

Causal inference is a very tricky business, however. First, there are different conceptions of causation in the market, and moreover there is ongoing controversy over the exact specification of each of these conceptions. Second, the nature of the relations between statistical correlations and causation is complex and controversial. Like 'causation', the term 'correlation' can have various specifications, and the relation between causation and correlation varies according to their exact meanings. Third, even when the terms 'causation' and 'correlation' are specified, the relation between them is typically intricate. First, not every correlation calls for causal explanation; e.g. both accidental correlation and correlation between non-distinct events or quantities do not call for causal explanation (sections 5–7). Second, even when a correlation calls for causal explanation, there are different possible explanations. It is commonly held that correlations between events (quantities) could only be due to a causal connection between them or a common cause. Yet, it seems that under determinism a correlation could also exist between causally independent events (quantities) that share no common cause (henceforth, 'causally unrelated events (quantities)'; see section 6).

These problems among others may (partially) explain the reluctance of many statisticians to deal with causal inference. Yet, a close analysis of many statistical inferences demonstrates that they frequently rely on implicit or explicit causal assumptions and, thus, in effect, are causal inferences.

In recent years, there has been a growing literature on causal inference, and significant progress has been achieved. But there is still ongoing controversy over many central issues. In this paper, I will focus on the question of how background assumptions of determinism and indeterminism affect the metaphysical, epistemological and empirical status of some central principles of causal inference.

While in the philosophical literature the focus is on theories of event causation, where causes and effects are events,[1] in the literature on causal inference the main focus is on random-variable causation, where both causes and effects are quantities that are represented by values of random variables. In my considerations below, I will discuss both event and random-variable causation. Yet, for the sake of simplicity, convenience and uniformity with the literature the discussion in some sections will concentrate on event causation whereas in others on random-variable causation. In any case, as event causation can be thought off as a special type of random-variable causation, where variables have only two values ('Yes' and 'No') corresponding to the occurrence and the non-occurrence of the event, the translation of the discussion from one type of causation to the other will typically be straightforward.

Theories of causation are divided into two general categories. Theories of singular causation, where causation denotes a relation or a connection among singular events or singular quantities; and theories of generic causation, where causation denotes a generalization of cases of singular causation, causal laws or a certain relation between event types or quantity types.[2] In the literature on causal inference the focus is on generic causation, and the

---

[1] The exact nature of events and of the causal relations among them varies from one theory to another, however. Among the most the prevalent theories of causation are probabilistic theories (Reichenbach 1956; Good 1961, 1962; Suppes 1970; Skyrms 1980; Cartwright 1983; Salmon 1984; Eells 1991), counterfactual theories (Lewis 1986; Menzies 1989, 1995), manipulation theories (Collingwood 1940; Gasking 1955; von Wright 1971; Menzies and Price 1993; Hausman and Woodward 1999), and process theories (Russell 1948; Reichenbach 1956; Salmon 1984; Dowe 1992).

[2] The relation between singular causation and generic causation is a matter of controversy that is beyond the scope of my discussion here. Here and henceforth, I will think about generic causation as a generalization of cases of singular causation.

attempt is to analyze inferences from statistical data to hypotheses about generic causation between quantity or events types.

2 Causal Inference, Determinism and Indeterminism

In social science and in various theories in natural science, it is frequently assumed that causation is deterministic. An effect (an event or a quantity) is determined by its causes (other events or other quantities). Accordingly, the probability of an effect given the totality of its causes is 1, and probabilities of effects other than 0 and 1 are attributed to ignorance about some of their causes.

The background assumption of determinism is common in the so-called 'linear causal models', which are very prevalent in social sciences. In these models, the value of an 'endogenous' variable is assumed to be determined by the value of its 'exogenous' variables, representing its presumed 'direct' causes, and the value of the 'error' term representing the influence of its unknown causes. That is, letting the random-variables X_i denote the exogenous variables, the random-variable U denote the error term and Y denote the endogenous variable, we have:[3]

$$Y = a_1 X_1 + a_2 X_2 + \cdots + a_n X_n + U \qquad (1)$$

Is this assumption of determinism justified? Does not modern physics challenge it? Following the success of quantum mechanics, it is frequently assumed that the world is genuinely indeterministic. This assumption may seem to cast doubt on the background assumption of determinism in social as well as in various natural sciences. It is noteworthy, however, that according to some quantum theories, such as Bohm's theory and 'many-worlds' interpretations, the world is fundamentally deterministic; and the probabilistic features of quantum phenomena are explained as a reflection of our ignorance about the precise states of physical systems. Also, the relations among

---

[3] In what follows, X, Y, Z, X_i and Y_i will denote random variables. $\mathbf{X}$, $\mathbf{Y}$ and $\mathbf{V}$ will denote sets of variables. $\mathbf{C_X}$ will denote a set of causes of X, $\mathbf{CC_{XY}}$ will denote a set of common causes of X and Y, and $Parents(X)$ will denote the set of the 'parental' causes of X in a set of variables $\mathbf{V}$, i.e. the causes of X in $\mathbf{V}$ that cause X 'directly'. (For more about 'parental' causes, see section 7.) A, B and D will denote the occurrence of the corresponding events, $\neg A$ will denote the absence of A. $\mathbf{C_A}$ will denote a set of A's causes and $\mathbf{CC_{AB}}$ will denote a set of common causes of A and B. x, y, v and w will denote real numbers that represent values of variables, and $\mathbf{x}, \mathbf{y}, \mathbf{v}$ and $\mathbf{w}$ will denote sets of real numbers that represent the values of sets of variables.

microscopic and macroscopic phenomena on the one hand, and physical and chemical, biological and especially social phenomena on the other hand are far from clear. Thus, the inference from indeterministic behavior at particular layers of the physical realm to indeterministic behavior at the social realm or other layers of the physical realm is unwarranted.[4]

In any case, my aim in this paper is not to discuss the status of the assumption of either determinism or indeterminism in various theories in current science. Rather my main focus will be on the implications of the assumptions of determinism and indeterminism for the status of particular central principles of causal inference.

3   The Common-Cause Principle

In what follows, I shall concentrate on one of the most celebrated and disputed principles of causal inference, the so-called 'principle of the common cause' (PCC), which was proposed by Reichenbach (1956, chapter 19) and has been developed by various authors. A typical formulation of PCC is the following:

PCC: For any non-accidental correlation between two distinct events (quantities), which are not causally connected to each other, there exists a common cause that screens off their correlation and thus renders them probabilistically independent of each other.

Correlation between two events A and B is typically characterized as some type of probabilistic dependence: A is correlated with B just in case the probability of $A(B)$ depends on $B(A)$, i.e.

$$P(A|B) \neq P(A) \qquad \text{and} \qquad P(B|A) \neq P(A), \tag{2}$$

which implies that the joint probability of A and B does not factorize:

$$P(A\&B) \neq P(A) \cdot P(B). \tag{3}$$

A common cause CC is said to screen off A from B just in case

$$P(A|B\&CC) = P(A|CC), \tag{4}$$

which implies that CC renders A and B probabilistically independent of each other:

$$P(A\&B|CC) = P(A|CC) \cdot P(B|CC). \tag{5}$$

---

[4]That is not to argue, of course, that the common assumption of determinism is warranted.

PCC can be motivated by two ideas, which can be expressed by two principles of causal inference: the Cause-Correlation Link (CCL) and Screening Off.

CCL: Any non-accidental correlation between two distinct events (quantities) is due to either (i) a causal connection between them, or (ii) a common cause, or (iii) both.

Screening Off: The common cause of any two distinct events (quantities), which are not causally connected to each other, screens off any non-accidental correlation between them, i.e. (4) obtains.

CCL and Screening Off relate causation to correlation. CCL postulates that any non-accidental correlation between distinct events (quantities) must have one of the causal explanations (i)–(iii) mentioned in CCL. And Screening Off imposes a substantial constraint on the nature of common causes: It states that common causes screen off any non-accidental correlation between their distinct effects which are not causally connected to each other.

PCC is central to causal thinking. It has been proposed as a metaphysical and epistemological principle as well as an empirical hypothesis. As a metaphysical principle, PCC postulates particular relations between causation, correlation, probability and events (quantities) and thus partly characterizes the nature of causation. As an epistemological principle, PCC has been widely used in causal inferences, causal modeling and causal explanations. And as an empirical hypothesis, PCC makes substantial claims about the world: If it were true, it would have significant empirical consequences.

Though CCL, PCC and Screening Off are widely accepted and prevalent in causal inferences, they are controversial and have been subjected to numerous challenges (e.g. sects. 5–7; Fine 1980; van Fraassen 1980, 1982; Sober 1988a,b, 2001; Cartwright 1989, 2000; Arntzenius 1993, 1999; Uffink 1999).

It is frequently argued that it is more difficult to motivate PCC and Screening Off under indeterminism. Moreover, a common view is that PCC is either false, unwarranted, or inapplicable in the quantum realm. But, there are those who challenge PCC and especially CCL also under determinism.

4   Some Remarks on Methodology

In many discussions of the prospects of PCC, CCL and Screening Off, the terms 'causation', 'correlation', 'event' and 'probability' are left largely unspecified. On the other hand, it is a common practice, especially in the literature on causal inference in social science, to take these terms as primitives and to impose on them formal constraints that are inspired by intuition and abstraction from practices of causal inference. The idea is to provide a set of axioms that use these terms without defining (or characterizing them), and to investigate the necessary consequences of these axioms and their relevance for familiar problem-cases and methods of causal inference (e.g. Spirtes et al. 1993, 2000).

Although these types of exercises are valuable, I am skeptical about their foundations. First, the plausibility and prospects of PCC, CCL and Screening Off as well as other related principles depend on the exact meaning of the terms 'causation', 'common cause', 'correlation', 'event', 'distinct events' and 'probability'. For PCC, CCL and Screening Off are not really principles but rather principle schemas. The terms above can have various specifications, and different specifications of these terms in effect yield different principles with different metaphysical, epistemological and empirical status (Berkovitz 2000a). Thus, it is the study of various notions of causation, correlation, probability and events that should inform us about the types of constraints we should reasonably impose on the relations among them.

Second, the axiomatic approach is also problematic from the epistemic viewpoint. The reliability of causal inferences depends crucially on the available causal knowledge, and it is doubtful that the required knowledge can be obtained if the terms 'causation', 'correlation' and 'event' are not sufficiently specified. My view then is that the way to progress in our understanding of PCC, CCL and Screening Off and their significance for causal inference is to investigate the metaphysical, epistemological and empirical status of various specifications of the PCC, CCL and Screening Off principle-schemas.[5] And my main aim in this paper is to point out the significance of the background assumptions of determinism and indeterminism for such investigation.

To establish the context for this discussion, I will first consider Reichenbach's influential specification of PCC.

5 Reichenbach's Specification of the Common-Cause Principle

Originally, Reichenbach (1956, p. 157) introduced PCC in this form: "If an improbable coincidence has occurred, there must exist a common cause."

By 'coincidences' Reichenbach meant the simultaneous occurrences of events (quantities), and (inspired by relativity theory) he presupposed that such events could not cause each other (1956, p. 40). So interpreted, PCC

---

[5]For want of space, I will discuss only partial specifications of these principle-schemas, i.e. specifications of some of the terms in these principles.

postulates that any improbable coincidences between events that are causally independent of each other must be due to a common cause.

Coincidence, for Reichenbach, was just one type of correlation. A different type of correlation is a positive statistical dependence: A and B are positively correlated just in case $P(A\&B) > P(A) \cdot P(B)$. For Reichenbach, these types of correlation were related: A positive (statistical) correlation appears when a coincidence is repeated a large number of times at a frequency higher than would be expected if the coincidences were a result of pure chance. Reichenbach did not say what he meant by 'improbable coincidence' or 'a frequency of coincidences higher than that expected by pure chance', and he did not explain in what sense positive statistical dependence expresses such frequency of coincidences. Yet, he explicitly ruled out the need to provide a causal explanation of correlations that are due to sheer chance, i.e. those correlations that are 'atypical' or 'unrepresentative'. For example, consider the series of 'heads' produced by two causally independent series of coin-tosses. In the long run, the relative frequency of 'heads' in one series should almost certainly be independent of the relative frequency of 'heads' in the other. Indeed, there is a minute chance that these types of events will be correlated (so that their frequencies will be dependent on each other) due to sheer accident. But such correlation does not require a causal explanation, as it does not reflect any underlying causal structure.

Reichenbach did not say explicitly what notion of event he had in mind. Yet, not any notion of event will do. A too liberal notion of event would expose PCC to many challenges (e.g. Arntzenius 1993). In particular, if correlations between events are to have causal explanations, the events in question have to be distinct from each other. For as Hume taught us, ('efficient') causation holds only between distinct events (quantities), and accordingly causal explanation is required only for correlation between such events (quantities).

In light of the above considerations, we may reformulate Reichenbach's principle as follows:

R-PCC: Any representative correlation between two distinct events (quantities), neither of which causes the other, must be due to a common cause.

R-PCC is quite vague. Reichenbach (1956, p. 159) offered the following (partial) specification (for further discussion, see Salmon 1984). He characterized correlation as positive statistical dependence: A is correlated with B just in case

$$P(A\&B) > P(A) \cdot P(B), \tag{R1}$$

where probabilities are 'representative' (relative) frequencies. According to

Reichenbach, for any such correlation between (distinct) events A and B, which are not causally connected to each other, there is a common cause CC that satisfies the following conditions:

$$P(A\&B|CC) = P(A|CC) \cdot P(B|CC); \qquad (R2)$$

$$P(A\&B|\neg CC) = P(A|\neg CC) \cdot P(B|\neg CC); \qquad (R3)$$

$$P(A|CC) > P(A|\neg CC); \qquad (R4)$$

$$P(B|CC) > P(B|\neg CC), \qquad (R5)$$

where, again, probabilities are representative (relative) frequencies, and $\neg CC$ denotes the absence of CC. In the general case, $\neg CC$ will not refer to one type of alternative cause to CC but rather to a set of different possible common causes (or in the case of random-variable causation, a set of different possible values of the common-cause variable).

As mentioned in section 3, one may interpret Reichenbach's specification of R-PCC as motivated by two principles: CCL and Screening Off. CCL implies that a correlation between distinct, causally independent events must be due to a common cause, and Screening Off motivates (R2) and (in special cases) (R3). (R4) and (R5) can be interpreted as a (partial) characterization of the notion of probabilistic cause. And the fact that (R2)-(R5) imply (R1) may be interpreted as a common-cause explanation of correlation between distinct events that are causally independent of each other (for more about this, see below).

(R1)–(R5) resolve much of the vagueness of the R-PCC schema. Yet, as we shall see below, the resultant principle is controversial. (R2)–(R5) impose substantial constraints on the nature of common causes. (R2) expresses the idea that common causes screen off the correlation between their effects that are causally independent of each other: If A and B are probabilistically dependent but causally independent of each other, their common causes screen off the correlation between them – $P(A|B\&CC) = P(A|CC)$ and $P(B|A\&CC) = P(B|CC)$ – and accordingly (R2) follows. And (R3) expresses the idea that $\neg CC$ should also screen off the correlation between A and B.

Screening Off, in turn, is commonly motivated by the view that probabilistic dependence among effects is the result of more basic probabilistic independence. The idea is that, although A and B are probabilistically dependent, their dependence is a result of mixing populations, each of which is causally 'homogeneous' and in each of which A and B are probabilistically independent.[6] Indeed, as Reichenbach demonstrated, this idea is reflected in the fact that, granted the assumption that causes raise the probability of their effects (i.e. granted (R4) and (R5)), (R2) and (R3) jointly imply (R1).

(R2) is not always warranted, however, even if we assume that any probabilistic dependence arises from probabilistic independencies. In general, common causes are only partial causes of their effects. Effects A and B typically have partial, separate causes, C_A and C_B, and a correlation between such causes would influence the correlation between A and B.

Agreed, assuming CCL, any correlation between C_A and C_B must be due to a causal connection between them or a common cause. If so, any correlation between C_A and C_B must be due to one of the common causes of A and B. For if the correlation between C_A and C_B is due to a common cause, such a cause will also be a common cause of A and B; and if the correlation between C_A and C_B is due to a direct causal connection between them, then either C_A or C_B will be a common cause of A and B.

Yet, as we shall see in section 6.1, there is no *a priori* reason to believe that CCL always holds, and if CCL failed, (R2) may fail even if probabilistic dependence always arises from probabilistic independence.

Here is an example. Let A and B be two correlated distinct events that are causally independent of each other. Let CC_{AB} be the set of all the common (partial) causes of A and B, C_A be a separate (partial) cause of A and C_B be a separate (partial) cause of B (see Fig. 1).[7] Suppose that C_A and CC_{AB} screen off A from B and C_B and CC_{AB} screen off B from A, i.e. suppose that $P(A|C_A\&CC_{AB}\&B) = P(A|C_A\&CC_{AB})$ and $P(B|C_B\&CC_{AB}\&A) = P(B|C_B\&CC_{AB})$, where (as before) probabilities are interpreted as representative (relative) frequencies. Suppose also that $P(A|CC_{AB}\&C_A) = 1$, $P(A|CC_{AB}\&\neg C_A) = 0$, $P(B|CC_{AB}\&C_B) = 1$, $P(B|CC_{AB}\&\neg C_B) = 0$ and $P(C_A) = P(C_B) = P(C_A\&C_B) = 1/2$. Finally, suppose that C_A and C_B are probabilistically independent of CC_{AB}, i.e. $P(C_A\&CC_{AB}) = P(C_A) \cdot P(CC_{AB})$ and $P(C_B\&CC_{AB}) = P(C_B) \cdot P(CC_{AB})$. Then we have $1/2 = P(A\&B|CC_{AB}) \neq P(A|CC_{AB}) \cdot P(B|CC_{AB}) = 1/4$, and $P(A|B\&CC_{AB}) \neq P(A|CC_{AB})$, and $P(B|CC_{AB}\&A) \neq P(B|CC_{AB})$. Therefore, CC_{AB} fails to screen off the correlation between A and B, although it is fundamentally a screener off: Given the (partial) separate causes of A and B, the (partial)

---

[6]Roughly speaking, a population is causally homogenous if all its 'units' share the same causal structure. For more about causally homogenous populations and their relevance for causal inference, see section 6.1.2.

[7]The discussion here is bound to be schematic, as the notion of 'cause' has not been specified yet. In section 7, I will consider the prospects of Screening Off for various notions of causation.

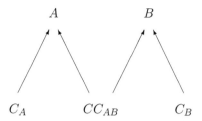

Figure 1: Screening off correlations between A and B
by the set CC_{AB} of all their common (partial) causes.

common causes CC_{AB} of A and B screen off the correlation between A and B.

So we have either to restrict the scope of (R2)'s applicability to cases where CCL holds or revise it as follows: If A and B are distinct, causally independent events, their common and separate causes screen them off from each other, i.e.

$$P(A|CC_{AB}\&C_A\&B) \; = \; P(A|CC_{AB}\&C_A) \qquad (6)$$
$$P(B|CC_{AB}\&C_B\&A) \; = \; P(B|CC_{AB}\&C_B)$$

The idea here is that common causes screen off correlations that are due to common causes and separate causes screen off correlations that are due to separate causes, and accordingly the common and separate causes of an event screen it off from any other event that is causally independent of it. Following this line of reasoning, it is not difficult to show that $CC_{AB}\&C_A$ screen off A from $B\&C_B$ and $CC_{AB}\&C_B$ screen off B from $A\&C_A$. Accordingly, we have the following modified version of (R2): If A and B are causally independent of each other, then:

$$P(A\&B|CC_{AB}\&C_A\&C_B) = P(A|CC_{AB}\&C_A) \cdot P(B|CC_{AB}\&C_B) \qquad (7)$$

While (R2) requires some qualification, (R3) is even more problematic. The absence of a common cause cannot always be thought of as a proper cause; for, in general, $\neg CC$ is overly disjunctive, lacking the unity required for an event to be qualified as a cause. For example, the consumption of three glasses of wine (CC) can (in some circumstances) be a common cause of headache (A) and fatigue (B). But the non-consumption of three glasses of wine $(\neg CC)$ can be the cause of neither headache nor its absence (similarly for fatigue). For $\neg CC$ is overly disjunctive in nature: It is a disjunction of any consumption other than exactly three glasses of wine. And non-consumption of wine has very different causal influence on headache and fatigue than consumption of e.g. 14 glasses of wine.[8] But if the absence of a common cause cannot always qualify as an alternative common cause, why should we assume that common causes satisfy (R3)?[9]

(R3) is better thought of as a special case with only one alternative cause to CC. We could generalize this special case as follows.

PCC*: For any representative correlation between distinct events A and B, neither of which causes the other, there exists a set of possible common causes (or a set of possible values of the common-cause variable), CC_1, CC_2, ..., CC_n, each of which screens off the correlation between A and B.[10]

Similarly to (R2) and (R3), (R4) and (R5) also impose constraints on the nature of common causes. And again these constraints are disputable; for as a stock of various examples demonstrates, probabilistic dependence *per se* is not necessary for causal dependence. First, there are the cases of over-determination and pre-emption, where one event causes another yet fails to change its probability. Second, (recalling Simpson's paradox) mixing causally homogenous populations might hinder the probabilistic dependence of an effect on its cause. Consider, for instance, a case in which C and D are two partial causes of A. Suppose that C is a contributing cause of A when D is present and counteracting otherwise. Suppose further that (in the relevant circumstances) $P(A|C\&D) = 0.7$, $P(A|\neg C\&D) = 0.3$, $P(A|C\&\neg D) = 0.3$,

---

[8] It is noteworthy that even if each of the terms in a disjunction constituting $\neg CC$ screens off the correlation between CC's effects, A and B, $\neg CC$ will generally fail to screen off the correlation between A and B.

[9] Another challenge that has been leveled against (R2) and (R3) is that even when some $CC(\neg CC)$ in the past of A and B succeeds in screening off their correlation, additional factors may well succeed in restoring it, or even in bringing about an opposite correlation (Uffink 1999). This is a special case of the so-called 'Simpson's paradox': A distribution with any type of correlation (positive, negative or zero) can be decomposed into a distribution with any other types of correlation (Cartwright 1983, p. 24; Uffink 1999). In reply to this challenge, it may be suggested that a warranted application of (R2) and (R3) should be restricted to cases where all the relevant causal factors are taken into account, so that screening off cannot be reversed. While this strategy improves the prospects of PCC as a metaphysical principle, it makes its application very demanding; we are hardly ever in a position to have the required causal knowledge for a warranted application of the resulting principle.

[10] Probably unaware of Reichenbach's principle, Bell (1987, chapters 4 and 7) based his celebrated theorem for the impossibility of 'local' quantum theories on PCC* (as applied to random-variable causation where CC_1, CC_2, ..., CC_n denote different possible values of the common-cause variable).

$P(A|\neg C\&\neg D) = 0.7$ and $P(D) = 0.5$. Then, as is easily shown, (R4) fails: $P(A|C) = P(A|\neg C)$.

The question of whether qualified relations of probabilistic dependence may constitute a necessary condition for causation (as Reichenbach seemed to assume) requires further investigation. But, in any case, as the above example demonstrates, the prospects of (R4) and (R5) would be better in causally homogeneous populations.

To sum up: Although very influential, Reichenbach's specification of the PCC-schema is disputable. In what follows in this paper, I will discuss various specifications of CCL and Screening Off principles. Since these principle schemas can motivate the PCC-schema, this discussion will in effect provide a consideration of alternative specifications of the PCC-schema. I will pay a special attention to the significance of the background assumptions of determinism and indeterminism for the metaphysical, epistemological and empirical status of CCL- and Screening Off-principle schemas for various specifications of the terms 'causation', 'correlation', 'common cause' and 'distinct events'.

6   The Cause-Correlation Link (CCL)

6.1   Determinism

Under determinism it seems possible, at least in principle, to have a correlation between causally unrelated events or quantities (i.e. causally independent events or quantities that share no common cause). The idea is that a correlation between events (quantities) in causally unrelated, deterministic processes (i.e. causally independent, deterministic processes that share no common cause) could in principle be due to the particular initial conditions and evolution of these processes.

Here are some examples. Imagine two roulettes that are based on 'random' generators, which are deterministic devices simulated by computer programs. (Although the generators are deterministic machines, due to the complexity of their programs the roulettes behave in a completely random fashion.) Suppose that the programs of both roulettes are identical, and that the two roulettes are causally unrelated to each other. Suppose also that the programs start at the same time. Then, although the frequency of 'Seven Red' in each of the roulettes is, say, 0.02, there will be a strict correlation between obtaining 'Seven Red' from one roulette and obtaining 'Seven Red' from the other.

Similarly, imagine two clocks that have the same deterministic mechanism, start from similar initial conditions and operate in very similar environments. Suppose that the relative frequency of days in which each of the clocks runs at least 2 minutes ahead is $1/2$. Suppose further that the clocks are causally unrelated to each other. Then, it would be plausible to expect that the event types 'Clock 1 being at least 2 minutes ahead on day i' and 'Clock 2 being at least 2 minutes ahead on day i' will be correlated.

Finally, consider the following example associated with the social sciences. Both Israel and Argentina suffered a period of high inflation in the 1980s. Suppose that during this period the economic processes that determined the rate of monthly inflation in the two economies were causally unrelated. Suppose further that these processes were deterministic and very similar in their (relevant) initial conditions and evolution. Then, it would be plausible to expect that the rates of monthly inflation in these economies would be correlated with each other.[11]

Agreed, all these examples are imaginary, and one may raise doubts as to their bearing on the prospects of CCL. According to our experience, it seems unlikely that two computer programs would be the same and would start at the same time, or that clocks would have just the same mechanisms and operate in very similar environments without any common cause. Similarly, it seems unlikely that the economic processes in Argentina and Israel in the 1980s were causally independent of each other and shared no common cause, not even a remote one.

Moreover, the prospects of conclusive empirical investigations concerning the existence of correlations between causally unrelated events or quantities seem dim. For example, analyses of statistical data about the Argentinean and Israeli economies and their implications for causality would very likely be inconclusive and highly theory-dependent. And anyway, assuming for the sake of the argument that the relevant economic processes in Argentina and Israel in the 1980s were causally unrelated, correlations between events in such causally unrelated processes, if they existed at all, would presumably be imperfect and short-lived and, thus, very difficult to vindicate.

Yet, in some scientific theories there are examples of correlations between events in causally unrelated, deterministic processes (Earman 1986, pp. 467–469, Earman 1995, chapter 5; Arntzenius 1999). Furthermore, even when events in causally independent, deterministic processes have some common causes, such causes might be so remote in time and space that they could hardly explain correlations between these events.

---

[11] For other examples of correlation between events in causally unrelated, deterministic processes see Sober (2001).

In any case, the question of the possibility of correlation between events in causally unrelated processes, and accordingly the question of the status of CCL, cannot be discounted on *a priori* grounds. In the rest of this section, I will consider three attempts to address this question.[12]

6.1.1   Strategy 1: Specify Correlation in Causal Terms

Recall (section 5) that Reichenbach (1956, pp. 157–158) maintained that only a particular type of correlation between causally independent, distinct events (quantities) calls for a common-cause explanation. That is, recall that he held that only coincidences between causally independent events, A and B, that are more frequent than expected by pure chance call for a common-cause explanation, and he said that such coincidences can be expressed in the form $P(A\&B) > P(A) \cdot P(B)$. It is not clear in what sense a positive statistical correlation between A and B represents a frequency of coincidences that is higher than that expected by pure chance; for the question arises as to what determines the expected frequency of coincidences. I suggest that a natural way to characterize this frequency is in causal terms. The general idea is that a frequency of coincidences between causally independent events A and B is expected (henceforth, 'expected correlation') if it is produced by A's and B's separated causes, and the frequency of coincidences between these causes is produced by their separate causes and so forth. Such correlation does not call for any further causal explanation. Any non-chancy (i.e. representative) frequency of coincidences that exceeds the expected frequency (henceforth, 'unexpected correlation') would call for a common-cause explanation.

Let us make this idea a bit more precise. Let $P1$ and $P2$ be the causal processes that lead to A and B, respectively. Let A's separate causes be A's causes that belong to $P1$ but not to $P2$, and let B's separate causes be B's causes that belong to $P2$ but not to $P1$. Let a set of A's separate causes be a 'complete' set of A's separate causes just in case the probability of A given this set of causes is independent of any other separate cause of A. Let C_{A1} denote any complete set of A's separate causes, and (for any $i > 1$) let C_{Ai} denote any complete set of C_{Ai-1}'s separate causes, i.e. a complete set of C_{Ai-1}'s causes that belong to $P1$ but not to $P2$. Similarly, let C_{B1} denote a complete set of B's separate causes, i.e. any complete set of B's causes that belong to $P2$ but not to $P1$, and (for any $i > 1$) let C_{Bi} denote a complete set of C_{Bi-1}'s separate causes, i.e. any complete set of C_{Bi}'s causes that

---

[12]For a discussion of some other attempts, see Berkovitz (2000a) and Sober (2001).

belong to $P2$ but not to $P1$.[13] Then we can define expected and unexpected correlation as follows:

Expected correlation: A correlation between causally independent event types A and B is *expected* just in case for any $C_{A1}, C_{B1}, C_{Ai-1}, C_{Bi-1}, C_{Ai}$ and C_{Bi}:

(i) $P(A\&B) \neq P(A) \cdot P(B)$

(ii) $P(A\&B|C_{A1}\&C_{B1}) = P(A|C_{A1}) \cdot P(B|C_{B1})$ (8)

(iii) $P(C_{Ai-1}\&C_{Bi-1}|C_{Ai}\&C_{Bi}) = P(C_{Ai-1}|C_{Ai}) \cdot P(C_{Bi-1}|C_{Bi}) \ \forall i > 1$

Unexpected correlation: A correlation between causally independent event types A and B is *unexpected* just in case for some $C_{A1}, C_{B1}, C_{Ai-1}, C_{Bi-1}, C_{Ai}$ and C_{Bi}:[14]

(i) $P(A\&B) \neq P(A) \cdot P(B)$

(ii) $P(A\&B|C_{A1}\&C_{B1}) \neq P(A|C_{A1}) \cdot P(B|C_{B1})$ or   (9)

      $\exists i > 1 : P(C_{Ai-1}\&C_{Bi-1}|C_{Ai}\&C_{Bi}) \neq P(C_{Ai-1}|C_{Ai}) \cdot P(C_{Bi-1}|C_{Bi})$

where $P(\ )$ denote representative (relative) long-run frequencies.

Granted this definition of unexpected correlation, we may formulate the following principle schema (which resembles the unspecified R-PCC schema):

CCL*: For any unexpected correlation between causally independent, distinct events (quantities) there must be a common cause.

Consider, for instance, Reichenbach's (1956, p. 156) example of several actors in a play who fell ill, showing symptoms of food poisoning. Suppose that the illness of the actors resulted from a dinner they had together in a restaurant after their evening show. Assuming that the process that caused the illness of each of the actors is causally unrelated to the processes that caused the illness of the other actors, the correlation between these events would be unexpected. Thus, since (by assumption) the illness of each of the actors did not influence the illness of the others, CCL* entails that there must be a common-cause explanation for the correlation between the actors' illness.

---

[13]Note that, in general, A will have more than one complete set of separate causes. But this will not matter for the definitions below.

[14]Note that the failure of the first inequality in (9ii) *per se* does not imply that the correlation between A and B is expected; for this inequality might fail because earlier effects of a common cause screen off the correlation between its later effects. A correlation between A and B is unexpected, if at least one of the inequalities in (9ii) holds.

On this specification of correlation, CCL* is a metaphysical principle-schema that postulates particular relations between causation and correlation. But CCL* could similarly be characterized as an epistemic principle. Let a correlation between A and B be unexpected just in case the joint probability of A and B given any complete sets of their presumed separate causes does not factorize, or the joint probability of these set of causes given any complete sets of their presumed separate causes does not factorize, and so forth. On this alternative specification of unexpected correlation, CCL* is an epistemic principle that governs inferences from statistical data and causal hypotheses to causal hypotheses.

The above specifications of the terms 'unexpected' and 'expected' correlation are incomplete; they require a specification of the term 'separate cause'. Yet, they illustrate how a characterization of 'correlation' in causal terms may provide ways to address the challenge of correlation between deterministic, causally unrelated processes.

A number of objections may be leveled against these specifications of the term 'correlation'. First, if (8) and (9) specify 'correlation', the application of CCL* becomes very demanding. Any warranted application of this principle would require causal knowledge that is frequently unavailable. That is, it may be argued that while this specification could motivate CCL* as a metaphysical principle, the epistemic value of the resulting principle is limited. On the other hand, if correlation is defined in terms of causal hypotheses, the application of CCL* will be warranted only given informed hypotheses about the relevant presumed causes, and such hypotheses require knowledge that is ordinarily unavailable.

Second, it may be argued that if (8) and (9) specify 'correlation', CCL* becomes trivial. Third, philosophers of empiricist leaning may regard this specification unattractive, as it renders correlation less observable and moreover it runs counter to the view that causation should be reduced to observable or occurrent facts, an idea frequently attributed to Reichenbach and some of his followers.

I believe that as many recent discussions demonstrate, the prospects of reducing causation to observed or occurrent facts are dim.[15] Similarly, I think that the prospects of specifying 'correlation' in terms of observed or occurrent facts are also dim. For recall that in CCL* (and CCL) only 'representative' correlations require causal explanation; a correlation that is due to pure chance requires no such explanation. But it is difficult to see how

---

[15]For some examples of the persistent problems that reductive analyses of causation encounter, see Lewis (1986, chapters 21 and 23), Cartwright (1989), and Menzies (1995).

the notion of representative correlation can be cashed out merely in terms of observed or occurrent facts. In any case, it is noteworthy that on the specification above, CCL* and thus PCC are not trivial principles. By postulating particular relations between causation and correlation, these principles impose non-trivial constraints on the nature of causation and the origin of correlation. In particular, CCL* dictates that unexpected correlation between events (quantities) in causally independent processes must be due to a common cause. Indeed, as we shall see in section 6.2, some authors challenge this version of CCL*. It is also noteworthy that occasionally we are in a position to draft informed hypotheses about whether a specific correlation is, or is not unexpected, and accordingly have reasonable grounds for believing the existence (or the non-existence) of unknown common causes.

6.1.2 Strategy 2: Limit CCL's Application to Causally Homogeneous Populations

Spirtes, Glymour and Scheines (in effect) hold that CCL applies only to (SGS-) causally homogeneous populations, i.e. populations in which all the units share the same causal structure and have the same probability distribution over the quantities (events) included in that structure (1993, pp. 57-65; 2000, p. 37).[16] And they claim that under determinism representative correlations between causally unrelated quantities (events) are always due to a mixing of SGS-causally homogeneous populations.[17] Thus, they maintain that such correlations are only apparent counterexamples for CCL.

Recall our imaginary example of correlation between the monthly inflation rates in the Argentinean and the Israeli economies in the 1980s. Suppose, as before, that during this period the (relevant parts of the) two economies were causally unrelated, and the processes that influenced the monthly inflation rates in both economies were deterministic. Then, according to Spirtes et al., any correlation between the monthly inflation rates in Argentina and in Israel in the 1980s would be due to a mixture of different SGS-causally homogeneous populations, each corresponding to the different causal structure these economies had in different months in the 1980s.

I will argue below that Spirtes et al.'s claim that under determinism any correlation between causally unrelated quantities (events) is due to mixtures

---

[16]Spirtes et al. do not talk explicitly about CCL, but from their discussion of the so-called 'Causal Markov' condition (see section 7.1) it is clear that they endorse this principle.

[17]For a similar claim, see Meek and Glymour (1994, p. 1006).

of SGS-causally homogeneous populations, is disputable.[18] But before turning to this argument, two remarks about the relation between causation and probabilities are in place. (i) In the literature on causal inference, many presuppose that causal structures can be inferred from probabilistic relations. This presupposition is controversial, however. As various examples demonstrate, probabilistic dependence is not always a reliable indication of causal dependence, and probabilistic independence is not always a reliable indication of causal independence. By contrast, inferences from causal structures to probabilistic relations are more warranted, at least if probabilities are interpreted as long-run 'representative' frequencies. Let us then suppose that the same types of causal structures give rise to the same probabilistic relations.[19] (ii) Here and henceforth, by no change in the relevant causal structures of an economy in the 1980s I will mean that the causes of the monthly inflation rate remains the same, that the probabilistic relations between the monthly inflation rate and its causes remain the same and that the probability distribution over the (values of the) variables that cause inflation remains the same.

With this background in mind, let us consider whether the strategy of restricting CCL to SGS-causally homogenous populations can meet the above challenge for CCL. Let us suppose that the relevant causal structure of the Argentinean and the Israeli economies remained unchanged in the 1980s. Then the population consisted of the relevant causal structures of these economies in different months in the 1980s is SGS-causally homogenous. For each month in the 1980s, let X (Y) be a variable representing 'the inflation rate in a month in Argentina (Israel)'. Let $\mathbf{CX}$ $(\mathbf{CY})$ denote a set of variables representing a 'complete' set of X's $(Y$'s) causes; where a set of X's causes is 'complete' just in case the probability distribution of X given this set is independent of any other cause of X. Let $\mathbf{CX} = \mathbf{x}$ $(\mathbf{CY} = \mathbf{y})$ be the proposition that the value of the variables $\mathbf{CX}$ $(\mathbf{CY})$ is $\mathbf{x}$ $(\mathbf{y})$. Then, as is not difficult to show, the joint probability distribution of X and Y, given any complete sets of X's and Y's complete causes, factorizes under determinism. In particular, for any $\mathbf{CX}$ and $\mathbf{CY}$ and for any values $\mathbf{x}$ and $\mathbf{y}$ we have:

$$P(X > 2\% \,\&\, Y > 2\%|\mathbf{CX} = \mathbf{x} \,\&\, \mathbf{CY} = \mathbf{y})$$
$$= P(X > 2\%|\mathbf{CX} = \mathbf{x}) \cdot P(Y > 2\%|\mathbf{CY} = \mathbf{y}) \qquad (10)$$

---

[18]For other objections to Spirtes et al.'s view, see Berkovitz (2000a, chapter 3.1), Cartwright (2000, p. 24), Hoover (forthcoming, chapter 7) and Sober (2001).

[19]It is noteworthy that in their theory of causal inference Spirtes et al. make much stronger assumptions about the relations between probabilities and causation.

where $P(\ )$ is the probability distribution of $X, \mathbf{CX}, Y$ and $\mathbf{CY}$, i.e. the probability distribution of the monthly inflation rate and its causes in both Israel and Argentina, and $X > 2\%$ $(Y > 2\%)$ is the proposition that the monthly inflation rate in Argentina (Israel) is higher than 2%. By the probability calculus, we also have:

$$P(X > 2\%) = \sum_x P(X > 2\% | \mathbf{CX} = \mathbf{x}) \cdot P(\mathbf{CX} = \mathbf{x}) \tag{11.1}$$

$$P(Y > 2\%) = \sum_y P(Y > 2\% | \mathbf{CY} = \mathbf{y}) \cdot P(\mathbf{CY} = \mathbf{y}) \tag{11.2}$$

$$P(X > 2\% \,\&\, Y > 2\%) = \sum_{x,y} P(X > 2\% \,\&\, Y > 2\% | \mathbf{CX} = \mathbf{x} \,\&\, \mathbf{CY} = \mathbf{y})$$
$$\cdot P(\mathbf{CX} = \mathbf{x} \,\&\, \mathbf{CY} = \mathbf{y}) \tag{11.3}$$

Equation (11.1) basically expresses the idea that the probability of $X > 2\%$ is a weighted average of the conditional probabilities of $X > 2\%$ given the different possible values contained in a complete set of its causes; and similarly, *mutatis mutandis*, for (11.2) and (11.3).

Now, suppose that the economic processes that influence the monthly inflation rates in Argentina and in Israel in the 1980s were causally unrelated to each other. Then, according to CCL, $X > 2\% \,\&\, Y > 2\%$ could not be correlated with each other. On the other hand, (10) and (11) jointly imply that $X > 2\%$ and $Y > 2\%$ may be correlated with each other, i.e.:

$$P(X > 2\% \,\&\, Y > 2\%) \neq P(X > 2\%) \cdot P(Y > 2\%) \tag{12}$$

if (for some $\mathbf{x}$ and $\mathbf{y}$) $\mathbf{CX} = \mathbf{x}$ and $\mathbf{CY} = \mathbf{y}$ are correlated with each other:

$$P(\mathbf{CX} = \mathbf{x} \,\&\, \mathbf{CY} = \mathbf{y}) \neq P(\mathbf{CX} = \mathbf{x}) \cdot P(\mathbf{CY} = \mathbf{y}) \tag{13}$$

So if we specify 'correlation' as statistical dependence and 'causation' (or more precisely, a 'complete' set of causes) along certain types of probabilistic theory of causation, a correlation between causally unrelated variables may obtain in SGS-causally homogenous populations. (The question of whether a correlation between causally unrelated quantities may obtain in SGS-causally homogenous populations according to other specifications of the terms 'correlation' and 'causation' require a further conceptual investigation that is beyond the scope of this paper.)

In response, it may be argued that although the prospects of a correlation between causally unrelated quantities could not be discounted *a priori*, as a matter of fact they never happen. In fact, Spirtes et al. (2000, pp. 32-38) seem to hold a similar view, namely that CCL is overwhelmingly supported by deterministic systems that can be put through repetitive processes and whose fundamental propensities can be tested.

It is difficult to evaluate this view. The analysis of observations is generally very complicated, inconclusive and theory/model-dependent, and the assumption that a certain population is SGS-causally homogenous could always be challenged on the ground that there are some hidden causal factors. One can always argue that an apparent failure of CCL is not genuine, i.e. that the population in question is not really SGS-causally homogenous.

6.1.3   Strategy 3: Weaken the Notion of Common Cause

A third way to try to meet the above challenge for CCL is to specify the term 'common cause' so that under determinism, correlations between causally independent quantities (events) always have common causes. For example, if we let conjunctions of distant separate causes qualify as common causes, under determinism correlation between causally independent quantities (events) will always share a common cause – the conjunction of their separate causes.

It may be objected that such a specification of the term 'common cause' trivializes CCL. Being so liberal about common causes, a common-cause explanation would be available even when processes do not really have any common origin. It is noteworthy, however, that while such specification would significantly weaken CCL and run counter to its intended interpretation, it would not render this principle trivially true under indeterminism.

Alternatively, one may suggest that the imaginary examples in section 6.1 are not really counterexamples to CCL since in all of them correlations do have some primordial common cause, such as the 'big bang' event. It is not clear that this strategy can always work, however. First, there is no *a priori* reason to think that such causes will always exist. For example, although influential theories (such as the Big-Bang theory) postulate that such common origin exists, these theories are not uncontroversial; and other theories might postulate correlations between causally unrelated events (Earman 1987, 1995, chapter 5; Arntzenius 1999). Second, as mentioned in section 6.1, it is not obvious that remote common causes could always explain the type of correlation discussed in section 6.1. For example, assuming for the moment that the Big-Bang theory is true, can remote events such as the 'big bang' explain correlations between quantities such as the monthly inflation rates in the Argentinean and the Israeli economies?

6.2 Indeterminism

Building on the discussion of section 6.1, it is not difficult to show that correlations between causally unrelated events could in principle exist also in indeterministic processes. Assuming indeterminism, let us consider, for example, a case, where C_{1A} and C_{2A} jointly constitute a complete set of A's causes, and C_{1B} and C_{2B} jointly constitute a complete set of B's causes. Suppose that A and B are causally unrelated, and accordingly the causal processes leading to C_{1A} and C_{2A} are causally unrelated to the causal processes leading to C_{1B} and C_{2B}. Suppose further that the processes leading to C_{2A} and C_{2B} are both deterministic, and suppose that due to the initial conditions and evolution of these processes C_{2A} and C_{2B} are correlated, i.e. $P(C_{2A}\&C_{2B}) \neq P(C_{2A}) \cdot P(C_{2B})$. Then (granted particular values for the probability of A given C_{1A} and C_{2A} and the probability of B given C_{1B} and C_{2B}), A and B will be correlated with each other, i.e. $P(A\&B) \neq P(A) \cdot P(B)$.

Although A and B are indeterministic effects, the correlation between them is due to a correlation between C_{1A} and C_{1B}, i.e. due to a correlation between events in causally unrelated, deterministic processes. Could a similar correlation hold between events in indeterministic processes?

It is difficult to answer this question in full generality. Yet, as the paradigmatic cases of indeterminism are given by quantum theories, we may concentrate on the more specific question of whether these theories provide examples of a correlation between causally unrelated events (quantities).

The characteristic cases of correlation between events in indeterministic processes in the quantum realm occur in correlation experiments, such as the famous Einstein-Podolsky-Rosen/Bohm (EPR/B) experiment. In the EPR/B experiment, pairs of particles are emitted from a source and fly off in opposite directions: 'left' and 'right'. When the particles are far apart, each of them encounters a measurement apparatus that can be set to measure various physical quantities, e.g. spins in different directions. According to the 'orthodox' interpretation of quantum mechanics and a number of other theories, the probability of spin 'up' in, say, the z-direction on a measurement in the left or the right wing is $1/2$. Yet, the joint probability of spin 'up' in the z-direction in both the left and the right wings is 0. Is this correlation compatible with CCL?

The exact nature of the causal relations in the EPR/B experiment is a controversial matter that depends on the metaphysics of causation and delicate questions about the interpretation of quantum and relativity theories (e.g. Readhead 1987; Cushing and McMullin 1989; Butterfield 1992c;

Maudlin 1994; Berkovitz 1998a,b, 2000b, and references therein). Some authors maintain that the measurement outcomes in the EPR/B experiment are causally dependent on each other, whereas others hold that they are not. Anyway, the consensus has it that the correlations between measurement outcomes in this experiment have a common cause - the emission event or the state of the particle pair before the measurements. Accordingly, it is commonly held that these correlations do not undermine CCL even if the distant outcomes do not cause each other. Yet, some authors argue that according to quantum field theory correlations between events in other quantum phenomena, such as correlations between vacuum excitations, are due to neither a causal connection between them nor a common cause (Redhead 1994).

7   Screening Off

In the previous section, I considered the prospects of the CCL-principle schema under determinism and indeterminism for various specifications of the term 'correlation' and 'common cause'. In section 7.1, I will consider the prospects of the Screening Off principle schema under determinism and indeterminism for various specifications of the term 'causation'.

Recall (section 5) that Screening Off can be formulated as follows. If A and B are distinct, causally independent events (quantities), their common and separate causes screen them off from each other. That is, letting C_A denote A's separate causes, C_B denote B's separate causes and CC_i denote a set of all the possible common causes of A and B:

$$P(A|B\&CC_i\&C_A) = P(A|CC_i\&C_A)$$
$$P(B|A\&CC_i\&C_B) = P(B|CC_i\&C_B)$$

In the next section, I will consider how screening off could be motivated by another central principle of causal inference, the so-called 'Causal Markov' (CM) condition. Then, in sections 7.2–7.4, I will consider the metaphysical, epistemological and empirical status of CM and Screening Off for various specifications of the terms 'causation' and 'distinct events' under determinism and indeterminism.

7.1   Motivating Screening Off: The Causal Markov Condition

The exact relation between causation and correlation has long occupied the literature on causal inference. Yet, the so-called 'Causal Markov' (CM) condition has been widely used as a general constraint on the relation between causation and correlation. A number of authors suggested that CM could motivate the Screening Off condition in (6) or a similar condition (e.g. Kiiveri and Speed 1982; Spirtes et al. 1993, 2000; Glymour 1997; Pearl 2000). Roughly speaking, CM asserts that the 'immediate' or 'direct' causes of an event or a quantity screen it off from any other event or quantity which is not among its effects.

Though intuitively clear, it is not easy to make the notions of 'immediate' or 'direct' causes precise outside the context of causal models, where considered causal structures are represented by causal graphs (see, for example, Fig. 2). Accordingly, CM is typically characterized and discussed in the context of such models. Here is an example of a prevalent characterization of CM in this context (Spirtes et al. 2000, p. 29ff).[20]

Causal Markov (CM): Let G be a causal graph, which models the causal relations among a set of variables $\mathbf{V}$ in a population of units all sharing the same causal relations. Let X and Y be two distinct variables in $\mathbf{V}$, and let x and y denote respectively particular values of X and Y. Let $P()$ denote a representative frequency distribution over the variables in $\mathbf{V}$. Let *Parents*(X) denote the set of all the 'direct' causes of X in G, i.e. all the variables in G that have an effect on X that is not mediated by effects on other variables in G.[21] Let also $\mathbf{v}$ be any particular value of (the variables in) *Parents*(X). Then, for any values x and y of X and Y, respectively, and for any value $\mathbf{v}$ of *Parents*(X), if Y does not cause X, *Parents*(X) screens off X from Y:[22]

$$P(X = x | Parents(X) = \mathbf{v} \,\&\, Y = y) = P(X = x | Parents(X) = \mathbf{v}) \quad (14)$$

Before turning to discuss the relation between CM and Screening Off, a remark about the scope of the application of CM is in order. As pointed out by various authors, the application of CM is warranted only in certain types of causal graphs (models). Spirtes et al. (1993, p. 45, 2000, p. 22) suggest that CM is warranted in the context of models satisfying a particular degree of 'causal completeness', given by the following condition:

Causal Sufficiency (CS): A set of variables (events) $\mathbf{V}$ is causally sufficient (CS) for a population just in case in the population any common cause of

---

[20]I will discuss CM in a model-independent context at the end of this section.

[21]For example, T and U are the direct causes of X in G, whereas C is an indirect cause of X in G.

[22]Spirtes et al. and other authors present CM as a condition. But CM may also be thought of as a principle of causal inference.

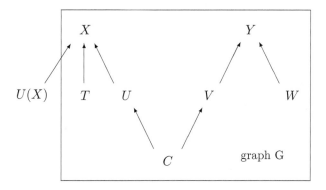

Figure 2: Graph G within the frame represents causal relations among
a set of variables. Causes not represented in the model are depicted by $U(X)$.

two or more variables (events) in **V** is also in V, or has the same value for
all the units in the population.[23]

CM embodies the idea that the probability of a quantity X is determined
by its causes and that the influence of X's earlier causes on its probability
must be mediated by its later causes. Thus, if Y is not among X's effects,
then whatever the sources of correlation between X and Y are, the influence
of these sources on the probability of X must be due to their influence on
X's later causes. Accordingly, X's later causes render Y probabilistically
irrelevant for (the value of) X. Now, in CS it is presupposed that if Y is
not among X's effects, then the source of correlation between X and Y can
only be causation from Y to X or a common cause. This presupposition is
commonly based on CCL. But, as we have seen in section 6, if correlation is
defined simply as statistical correlation (e.g. X and Y are correlated just in
case $P(X = x \& Y = y) \neq P(X = x) \cdot P(Y = y)$), CCL could be challenged.
For under determinism causally unrelated quantities X and Y could (in principle) be correlated due to a correlation between their separate causes. This
may suggest that CM be only warranted in the context of models satisfyig a
stronger degree of 'causal completeness', given by the following condition:

---

[23]As Cartwright (2000, p. 21) remarks, under Spirtes et al.'s (partial) specification of
the term 'common cause', CS becomes epistemologically very demanding. According to
Spirtes et al. CC is a common cause of X and Y just in case it is a direct cause of X and
Y, and CC is a direct cause of X just in case CC together with X's other causes jointly
fix X's value. But variables in causal graphs are seldom sufficient to fix the value of an
effect. Thus, in the discussion below I will not follow SGS-specification.

Causal Sufficiency* (CS*): A set of variables (events) **V** is *causally suffi-cient* (CS*) for a population just in case in the population any common cause of two or more variables (events) in **V** is also in **V**, or has the same value for all the units in the population, and all the correlated separated parental causes of variables (events) in **V** are also in **V**.

With this background in mind, I now turn to argue that Screening Off (or, more exactly, (16) below) follows from CM in CS*-models. The reasoning is as follows. Let X and Y be two distinct variables in a graph G, and let *Parents*(X) and *Parents*(Y) be respectively the parents of X and Y in G. Let *Ancestors*(X) and *Ancestors*(Y) be the sets that result from substituting all the variables in *Parents*(X) and *Parents*(Y) that are effects of the same common causes by their parents in G. (Granted CS* (or CS), *Ancestors*(X) and *Ancestors*(Y) must be in G.) Let x and y be respectively any particular values of X and Y, and let **v** and **w** be respectively any particular values of the variables in *Ancestors*(X) and *Ancestors*(Y). Then, it follows from CM and CS* that for any Y that is not among X's effects:

$$P(X = x | Ancestors(X) = \mathbf{v}\,\&\,Y = y) = P(X = x | Ancestors(X) = \mathbf{v})$$
$$(15)$$

Repeat the same operation on *Ancestors*(X) and *Ancestors*(Y), i.e. sub-stitute all the variables in *Ancestors*(X) and *Ancestors*(Y) that are effects of the same common causes by their parents represented in G, until *Ancestors*(X) and *Ancestors*(Y) include all the 'direct' common causes of the variables X and Y, i.e. the set of all the common causes in G that do not cause any other common causes in G. Let us call the resulting sets of variables *Ancestors**(X) and *Ancestors**(Y). Let *DirectCC*(X, Y) be the set of the 'di-rect' common causes of X and Y, i.e. all the common causes of X and Y in *Ancestors**(X) and *Ancestors**(Y), and let $\mathbf{C_X}$ be the subset of all X's sep-arate causes in *Ancestors**(X). Then, for any variable Y that is not among X's effects, for any values x and y of X and Y respectively, for any value **c** of *DirectCC*(X, Y), and for any value **v** of $\mathbf{C_X}$, if X does not cause Y, then:

$$P(X = x | DirectCC(X, Y) = \mathbf{c}\,\&\,\mathbf{C_X} = \mathbf{v}\,\&\,Y = y)$$
$$= P(X = x | DirectCC(X, Y) = \mathbf{c}\,\&\,\mathbf{C_X} = \mathbf{v}) \qquad (16)$$

The general idea here is that granted CS*, the 'direct' and 'indirect' causes in *Ancestors**(X) include all the sources or the influences of the sources of the correlation between X and Y. Accordingly, the causes in *Ancestors**(X) screen off X from Y. So in the context of CS*-models, CM implies Screening Off. Similarly, as is not difficult to show, CM and CCL jointly imply Screening Off in CS-models. Yet, CS* and even (the weaker condition) CS are very demanding conditions. We seldom have the knowledge required for constructing CS*- or (even) CS-models.[24] Thus, even if we presuppose CM, Screening Off would be unwarranted in many circumstances.

So far I have considered the relation between CM and Screening Off in the context of causal models. Can we similarly motivate CM as a metaphysical principle? The main obstacle in motivating such principle is that in a model-independent context it is difficult to make precise the notion of 'parental cause'. Yet, there are substitutes, at least in certain accounts of causation. For example, let a set of X's causes be a 'complete' set of X's causes just in case the probability of X given such a set of causes is independent of any other cause of X.[25] Substituting any complete set of X's causes for X's parents, the translation of the above model-dependent version of CM into a metaphysical principle is straightforward.

7.2 The Prospects of CM and Screening Off under Determinism

7.2.1 Manipulation Accounts of Causation

A number of philosophers advocated a manipulation account of causation (Collingwood 1940; Gasking 1955; von Wright 1971; Menzies and Price 1993; Hausman and Woodward 1999). The manipulation account is inspired by one of causation's main connotations, the means-ends connotation. According to this account, causes are means to bringing about their effects, and manipulating a cause is a way to manipulate its effects. Actually, it is not always possible to manipulate causes, but supporters of the manipulation account commonly appeal to modal notions of manipulation (for more about this, see below).

In the literature on causal inference, CM, CCL, Screening Off and PCC are frequently associated with some type of manipulation account of causation (e.g. Spirtes et al. 1993, 2000; Glymour 1997, p. 224; Pearl 2000). Yet, there are hardly any rigorous discussions of how manipulation accounts of causation can motivate CM and Screening Off. A notable exception is Hausman and Woodward (1999, sections 7, 8 and 10), who argue that there is a very intimate relation between CM and manipulation.

---

[24] Assuming SGS-characterization of 'common cause', CS becomes even more demanding.

[25] Recall (footnote 13) that, in general, an effect will have more than one complete set of causes. But this will not matter to our consideration, as any such set will do.

Hausman and Woodward define the relation between causation and manipulation in terms of a special type of interventions, i.e. interventions that set the values of variables in causal graphs.

H&W-intervention: An intervention I that sets the value of a variable X in a causal graph G that includes a set of variables **V** "is (roughly) ... a direct cause of X ... that bears no causal relation to other variables under consideration except for those arising from directly causing X ... I is not an effect of any variable in **V**, I does not cause any variable in **V** by a path that does not go through X" (Hausman and Woodward 1999, p. 535).[26]

Granted this notion of intervention, Hausman and Woodward formulate the basic principle relating causation and manipulation as follows (Hausman and Woodward 1999, p. 553):

Mod*: Let *Set-X* be a H&W-intervention to set X and *Set-X* $= x$ be a H&W-intervention to set X to the value x. Then, for all distinct variables X and Y in a graph G, for any values x and y of X and Y, respectively, and for any *Set-X* $= x$, if X does not cause Y, *Set-X* $= x$ and $Y = y$ are probabilistically independent of each other:

$$P(Y = y \,\&\, \text{Set-}X = x) = P(Y = y) \cdot P(\text{Set-}X = x); \qquad (17)$$

where, as before, probabilities are interpreted as representative frequencies.[27]

Hausman and Woodward (pp. 553–554) argue that granted the following premises (i)–(v), CM obtains just in case Mod* does: (i) CS (Causal Sufficiency); (ii) CCL (Cause-Correlation Link); (iii) Model incompleteness: Some of the causes of variables in the causal graph G are unrepresented in G; (iv) The represented and unrepresented direct causes of X are the only sources of variations in X's value; (v) A H&W-intervention to set X, *Set-X*, can be treated as a random variable.

The basic structure of Hausman and Woodward's argument is as follows. Granted (iii), X has unrepresented causes. Let $U(X)$ be a set of X's unrepresented causes. By definition, the variables in $U(X)$ are direct causes of X and, granted CS, the variables in $U(X)$ bear no causal relation to any variable in **V**, except for X and X's effects. Thus, the variables in $U(X)$

---

[26]This is only a rough characterization; it requires some qualification (Hausman and Woodward 1999, section 4). But the precise characterization of H&W-intervention will not be important for our consideration below.

[27]Hausman and Woodward (1999, pp. 542–543 and 553) say that the inspiration for Mod* comes from the idea that causal connections are invariant, that interventions can be treated as independent random variables, and that CCL obtains.

satisfy the definition of H&W-intervention with respect to X, and given CCL these variables are probabilistically independent of any variables in $\mathbf{V}$, except for X and X's effects. Now, by (iv), given any value of $Parents(X)$ the only source of variation in X is $U(X)$. Thus, any variable Y in $\mathbf{V}$ distinct from X can covary with X conditional on $Parents(X)$ just in case it covaries (unconditionally) with $U(X)$. In short, granted (i)–(v), for any value x of a variable X, for any value y of a (distinct) variable Y that is not among X's effects, for any Set-X, and for any value $\mathbf{v}$ of $Parents(X)$:

$$P(Y = y \,\&\, Set\text{-}X = x) \;\;=\;\; P(Y = y) \cdot P(Set\text{-}X = x)$$

$$\text{just in case} \tag{18}$$

$$P(X = x | Parents(X) = \mathbf{v} \,\&\, Y = y) \;\;=\;\; P(X = x | Parents(X) = \mathbf{v})$$

or, in other words, CM holds just in case Mod* holds.

Two objections may be raised against the argument above. First, the notion of intervention does not really play any role in Hausman and Woodward's argument for CM. For the statistical independence between $U(X), Y$ and $Parents(X)$ basically follows from CCL and CS, and granted this independence CM follows from Hausman and Woodward's assumption that $Parents(X)$ and $U(X)$ are the only sources of variation in X.[28]

Second, it is doubtful that Mod* could constitute a general characterization of the relation between manipulation and causation. As Hausman and Woodward (1999, p. 552) themselves maintain, it is sometimes actually impossible to intervene in the way specified by H&W-intervention. Thus, intervention and accordingly the relation between causation and manipulation have to be defined in modal terms, e.g. as follows.

Mod**: Let X and Y be distinct variables; let x and y be respectively particular values of X and Y. Let Set-$X = x$ be the proposition that the variable X is set to a particular value x by H&W-intervention. Then, for any X that does not cause Y, for any x and y, if Set-$X = x$ were to occur, the probability of Y having a value y would not have changed.

But Mod** does not imply Mod*. In Mod*, the probability of Y having a value y is independent of H&W-interventions to set X to x, whereas in Mod** the probability of Y having a value y is counterfactually independent of such interventions. And as counterfactual probabilities do not imply the corresponding conditional probabilities, counterfactual independence does not imply probabilistic independence (Butterfield 1992b,c; Mellor 1995;

---

[28]For a similar criticism of Hausman and Woodward's reasoning, see Cartwright (2000, p. 101).

Berkovitz 2002). Thus, even if Mod* played an important role in motivating CM, as Hausman and Woodward maintain, CM would not be warranted in the context of the H&W-manipulation account of causation.[29]

7.2.2 Probabilistic Causation

A more promising way to motivate CM and accordingly Screening Off is to appeal to accounts that relate causation and probabilities more intimately, i.e. accounts in which the objective probabilities of an effect (an event or a value of a quantity) are determined by its causes. The exact interpretation of probability and the metaphysical nature of the relation between probability and causation may vary.[30] But, in any such probabilistic account of causation, CM and Screening Off can be motivated as metaphysical principles under determinism. For example, let a set of events be a 'complete' set of A's causes just in case this set determines A's probability, such that given this set the probability of A will be independent of any other cause of A. Then, under determinism, the probability of A given any complete set of its causes will be 1, and accordingly CM, and thus Screening Off, will follow immediately by the probability calculus: Any complete set of A's causes will screen off A from any other event.

CM can similarly be motivated in the context of causal models that are sufficiently complete, i.e. models in which the probability of events given their parental causes is 1. But things are different in the context of causal models that are not sufficiently complete. Here, CM is unwarranted as a principle of causal inference. For as I will argue below the assumption that complete sets of A's causes determine A's probability does not imply the validity of CM as a principle of causal inference in incomplete causal models. The reasoning is as follows. Let G be a causal graph that models the relations among a set of events $\mathbf{V}$, and let A and B be any two (distinct) events represented in G. Let $Parents(A)$ be the direct causes of A in G (i.e. all the events in G that have an effect on A that is not mediated by effects on other variables in G), and let $U(A)$ be the unrepresented causes of A (i.e. the causes of A that are not represented in the model). $Parents(A)$ and $U(A)$ jointly screen off A from B; for the probability of A given $Parents(A)$ and $U(A)$ is 1. But, this does not imply that $Parents(A)$ screen off A from B even if we assume CCL and CS. That under determinism $Parents(A)$ and $U(A)$

---

[29] For other criticisms of Hausman and Woodward's characterization of intervention, see Cartwright (2000, chapter 4).

[30] For example, it may be assumed that the probability of an effect supervenes on its recent causes or that the probability of an effect is a property of its recent causes.

determine the probability of A to be 1 does not imply that if B causes A by causing $Parents(A)$ it cannot extract a non-Markovian influence on A's probability, so that the probability of A given $Parents(A)$ will depend on B. For the fact that, under determinism, complete sets of causes of A screen off A from any other event has nothing to do with the question of whether the world is, or is not, Markovian. In any theory in which particular sets of causes of A determine its probability to be 1, the probability of A given its causes will be independent of any other event. So CM is not generally warranted as an epistemic principle governing causal inference in CS-models.

7.2.3 Counterfactual Accounts

A common view has it that causation is closely related to counterfactuals. According to a prevalent version of the counterfactual account (henceforth, the 'first account'), an event B is causally dependent on a distinct event A just in case the actual probability of B with A is higher that the probability that B would have had, had A not occurred.[31] According to a different account (henceforth, the 'second account'), B is causally dependent on A just in case the probability that B would have had, had A not occurred, is not the same as its actual probability. Can we motivate CM as a metaphysical principle in the context of such counterfactual accounts?

Recall that CM postulates that some set of the 'direct' causes of A screen it off from any other event that is not among its effects. In the context of counterfactual accounts, we may define 'direct causation' to be causal dependence: E.g., in the first account, B is a direct cause of A just in case the probability that A would have had without B is lower than it actually is; and 'indirect' causation may be defined as the ancestral relation of direct causal relation: B is an indirect cause of A just in case B causes A via two or more direct causal connections. Now, according to the first counterfactual account, if A does not cause B, then had A not occurred the probability of B would not have been higher than it actually is. And according to the second counterfactual account, if A does not cause B, then if A had not occurred the probability of B would have been the same as it actually is. Either way, under determinism (and indeterminism) it does not follow that if A does not cause B, the 'direct' causes of A screen it off from B (i.e. that the probability of A given its direct causes is independent of B).[32]

---

[31] See Lewis (1986, chapters 17, 19, 21 and 23), Menzies (1989, 1996).

[32] Two remarks: (1) That is not to argue, of course, that CM cannot be motivated in the context of any counterfactual accounts. (2) For the kind of assumptions and the compli-

7.3   The Prospects of Screening Off under Indeterminism

As we have seen in section 7.2, under determinism CM and Screening Off can easily be motivated as metaphysical principles in certain probabilistic accounts of causation. The idea is that under determinism the probability of an event A, given any complete set of its causes, is 1. Thus, it follows immediately that any such set of A's causes screens off A from any other event. Things are very different under indeterminism. Here, the probability of A given any set of its causes is strictly between 0 and 1. Accordingly, the possibility that the probability of A, given complete sets of its causes, will depend on other events cannot be excluded *a priori*.

There have been various arguments for and against the validity of CM and Screening Off under indeterminism. Here are four examples. First, Cartwright (1989, chapter 6) and Chang and Cartwright (1993, section II) argue that a weaker version of Screening Off can be motivated in process accounts of causation, where the influence of causes on their effects are mediated by particular types of continuous processes. That is, they argue that the recent causes of events that are causally independent of each other screen them off from each other in accounts of causation that satisfy the following conditions. (i) Contiguity: The influence of a cause on the probability of its effects propagates continuously in space and time. (ii) General Causal Markov (GCM): The stages of causal processes have no memory; complete information on temporally intermediate stages makes earlier stages causally irrelevant. (iii) CCL (Cause-Correlation Link).

In their argument, Chang and Cartwright consider correlations between distant (space-like separated) events, and they assume that, granted the special theory of relativity (henceforth, STR), such events are causally independent of each other and, moreover, each of these events can be influenced only by events that occur in their backward light cone. The argument is basically the following. Let A and B be two space-like separated events. Then, granted CCL and the assumption that A and B are causally independent of each other, A and B must be correlated due to a common cause CC. By Contiguity, any influence of CC on A and B must propagate continuously. By STR, (iv) there must be stages $S(A)$ and $S(B)$ which lead to A and B, respectively, such that $S(A)$ is causally irrelevant to B and $S(B)$ is causally irrelevant to A. By CM, (v) $S(A)$ renders any earlier stages in the process leading to A causally irrelevant to A and $S(B)$ renders any earlier stages in the process leading to B causally irrelevant to B. Thus, argue Chang and

⎯⎯⎯⎯⎯⎯⎯⎯⎯⎯⎯⎯⎯⎯⎯⎯⎯⎯

cations involved in deriving probabilistic independence from counterfactual probabilistic independence, see Butterfield (1992a, 1994).

Cartwright, the stages $S(A)$ and $S(B)$ screen off any correlation between A and B.

Chang and Cartwright must have implicitly made an additional assumption about the relation between causation and probability; for (iv) and (v) do not imply that $S(A)$ and $S(B)$ render B irrelevant to the probability of A. Healey (1992) suggests that Chang and Cartwright implicitly assumed that the processes leading to A and B are separable, where a process leading to A which occurs in a space-time region R is separable just in case there is no difference in the process without any difference in the qualitative, intrinsic properties in the region R.[33]

Second, as I argued elsewhere (Berkovitz 1995, sections 2–5), CM and accordingly Screening Off obtain in Humphreys' (1989) theory of invariant causation, where a cause raises the chance of its effects invariantly in all the relevant physically possible circumstances. That is, I argued that in this theory the 'direct' causes of an event (quantity) screens it off from any events (quantities) that are not among its effects; here B is a 'direct' cause of A just in case A and B are distinct events and B raises the chance of A in all the relevant physically possible circumstances.

The application of the resulting CM and Screening Off principles is very demanding, however. Invariant causes are generally very complicated. In addition to what intuitively might be called 'the cause' of A, an invariant cause of A must also include the presence of all the nomological conditions that are necessary for the existence of A and the absence of any condition that jointly with the 'the cause' of A would have lowered A's chance. But, the knowledge of such invariant causes is often beyond our reach.

Third, CM and Screening Off also hold in Cartwright's (1989, chapters 3 and 6) theory of causation. Cartwright holds that cause and effect are connected to each other by 'operation' events: Causes operate to produce their effects.[34] In Berkovitz (1995, sections 6–10) I argued that if we define

---

[33]Intuitively, a property of a thing (an object or a space-time region) is *intrinsic* just in case the thing has this property in and of itself, independently of the existence or the state of other objects or things; and a property is *qualitative* (as opposed to individual) if does not depend on the existence of any particular object.

[34]Some may find Cartwright's theory attractive since it enables a richer classification of causal situations. For example, suppose that B and C are two potential contributing indeterministic causes of A. Suppose that B, C and A actually occur. According to Cartwright's theory, this situation is compatible with four different causal scenarios: (i) B, and not C, operated to produce A; (ii) C, and not B, operated to produce A; (iii) B and C both operated to produce A, i.e. B and C over-determined A; and (iv) B and C did not operate to produce A: A occurred spontaneously. Others, especially Humeans, would probably find the metaphysics of 'operations events' that bridge between causes and their

the direct causal past of an event A to include the start of the operation of A's causes to produce A, the direct causal past of A screens off A from any other event which is causally independent of it. Accordingly, CM and Screening Off hold in Cartwright's theory.[35]

Fourth, recall (section 7.2.1) that Hausman and Woodward (1999) argue that manipulation accounts of causation could motivate CM because of the intimate relation between intervention and causation. According to Hausman and Woodward's manipulation account of causation, effects of common causes are distinct events (quantities) only if they result from distinct mechanisms, i.e. if the mechanisms by which the common cause causes one effect is distinct from the mechanisms by which the common cause causes the others; where two mechanisms are distinct just in case it is possible to intervene in each of them without thus disrupting the other. On this account, it follows that the mechanisms of a common cause to produce distinct effects must be independent of each other. But, argue Hausman and Woodward, if the mechanisms of common causes to produce their effects are independent of each other, CM can be motivated by the H&W-manipulation account also under indeterminism.

Hausman and Woodward's argument relies on the presupposition that under indeterminism the general relation between intervention and causation is defined in terms of conditional probabilities: If X and Y are random variables, and Y does not cause X, then the probability distribution of X is independent of any H&W-intervention to set the value of Y. But, as we have seen in section 7.2.1, this cannot constitute a general characterization of the relation between intervention and causation. Intervention and the relation between intervention and causation have to be characterized in modal terms: E.g., if Y does not cause X, then, if we H&W-intervened to set the value of Y, the probability distribution of X would not change. But if the relation between intervention and causation is so characterized, the failure of Screening Off is compatible with a common cause's having a distinct causal mechanism for each of its distinct effects. The reasoning is as follows (for simplicity's sake, I will focus on event causation). Let A and B be causally

---

effects too extravagant.

[35]Two remarks: (1) If operation events had no structure, i.e. if they could not be divided into distinct stages, the start of the operation of causes to produce their effects would not be events and CM and Screening Off would not hold in Cartwright's theory. But if operation events had no structure, Cartwright's theory would probably seem metaphysically extravagant even to those who are sympathetic to the general idea that causes operate to produce their effects. (2) In both Cartwright's and Humphrey's theories, CM and Screening Off also obtain under determinism.

independent events that are distinct, common effects of a common cause CC. That the mechanisms by which CC produces A and B are distinct implies that it is possible in principle to intervene in the mechanism by which CC produces A without thus disrupting the mechanism by which CC produces B. This does not imply, however, that these mechanisms do not actually operate in tandem to produce A and B, so that the operation of CC to produce A is probabilistically dependent on its operation to produce B. But, if the operations of CC to produce A and B are correlated, CC or any of its effects might fail to screen off A from B. Thus, under indeterminism, CM and Screening Off cannot be motivated as metaphysical principles in the H&W-manipulation account of causation.

To sum up: The question of whether CM and Screening Off can be motivated as metaphysical principles on *a priori* grounds is rather complicated; it requires conceptual investigation into the relation between 'causation,' 'correlation' and 'distinct events' for various specifications of these terms. I have argued that these principles can be motivated on *a priori* grounds (i.e. on the basis of a conceptual investigation of the relation between the notions of causation, correlation and events) in some accounts of causation and not in others. But even if various specifications of the CM and Screening Off-schemas could not be motivated on *a priori* grounds, it may be argued that some of the resulting CM and Screening Off principles hold as a matter of contingent fact. The natural place to evaluate the prospects of such a claim is in what seems to be the most obvious indeterministic phenomena in our world, i.e. quantum phenomena.

7.4   The Prospects of Screening Off in the Quantum Realm

Recall (section 6.2) that the characteristic cases of correlation between events in indeterministic processes in the quantum realm[36] occur in correlation experiments, such as the EPR/B experiment. It is commonly agreed that the common cause of the measurement outcomes in the EPR/B experiment, i.e. the pair's state at the emission (or before both measurements occur), fails to screen off the correlation between its effects, i.e. the joint measurement outcomes. Yet, there is an ongoing controversy as to whether the Screening Off principle fails in this experiment.

First, there are those who believe that although the common cause of the measurement outcomes in the EPR/B experiment fails to screen off these outcomes from each other, this failure does not imply the violation of Screening

---

[36]In this section, I will focus on the quantum realm as depicted by indeterministic quantum theories.

Off. The correlation between the measurement outcomes would imply the violation of CM and Screening Off only if these outcomes were causally independent of each other (for recall that a common cause of events that are not causally independent of each other is not expected to screen off its effects). But, it is argued, in the EPR/B experiment the measurement outcomes are not causally independent of each other according to various accounts of causation (i.e. various specifications of the terms 'causation' and 'events').[37]

Second, some hold that the correlations between the distant measurement outcomes in the EPR/B experiment do not violate CM and Screening Off, as these outcomes are not really distinct (e.g. Skyrms 1984, who attributes this view to Lewis; Hausman and Woodward 1999). Recall that Screening Off states that the common (and separate) causes of distinct events that are causally independent of each other screen them off from each other. This principle does not imply, however, that common (and separate) causes screen off correlations between their *non-distinct* effects.

As Butterfield (1992b, section 5) pointed out, the outcomes in the EPR/B experiment are distinct events according to Lewis's (1986, chapters 21 and 23) account of events and causation. But that is not to say that the measurement outcomes in this experiment are distinct events on any account. Indeed, Hausman and Woodward (1999) argue that according to their manipulation account (see sections 7.2.1 and 7.3) these outcomes are non-distinct events. Recall (section 7.3) that according to their account, events are distinct (henceforth, H&W-distinct) only if they result from distinct mechanisms, i.e. if the mechanism by which the common cause causes one effect is distinct from the mechanisms by which the common cause causes the others. (Recall that two mechanisms are H&W-distinct just in case it is possible to intervene in each of them without disrupting the other.) Now, according to the orthodox interpretation of quantum mechanics and a number of other theories, the common cause in the EPR/B experiment is the non-separable state of the particle pair at emission time (or before the measurements).[38]

Hausman and Woodward argue that due to this non-separability, the mechanisms by which the common cause produces its effects are H&W-non-distinct. For an intervention in the mechanism by which the common cause produces the outcome in the left wing requires an interaction that changes the state of the left-wing particle. But such an interaction would immedi-

---

[37] For discussions of these types of reasoning see Butterfield (1989, 1992a, 1994) and Berkovitz (1995, 1998a,b, 2000b), and references therein.

[38] Here and henceforth by the non-separability of the pair's state, I mean that this state is not factorizable into the separate states of the left and the right particles.

ately change the state of the right-wing particle and, accordingly, disturb the mechanism by which the common cause produces the outcome in the right wing. Thus, since in Hausman and Woodward's account a common cause's having H&W-distinct mechanisms is a necessary condition for its effects to be distinct events, the failure of the pair's state to screen off the correlation between the measurement outcomes in the EPR/B experiment does not imply the violation of Screening Off.

The inference from non-separability of mechanisms to non-separablility of their effects and accordingly the inference from the non-distinctness of a common cause's mechanisms to the non-distinctness of its effects are disputable: Why can distinct effects not originate from a single mechanism? Furthermore, the reproduction of the EPR/B correlations requires the actual impossibility to manipulate each of the common-cause's mechanisms without thus disrupting the other. But recalling (sections 7.2.1 and 7.3) that the general relation between causation and intervention is to be characterized in modal terms, such actual impossibility does not imply that the distant measurement-outcomes are non-distinct. To demonstrate that the measurement outcomes in this experiment are H&W-non-distinct events, one has to show that it is impossible in principle (i.e. by law) to manipulate one of the common cause's mechanisms without thus disturbing the other.

On the usual understanding of quantum mechanics, it is impossible in principle to manipulate the mechanism by which the common cause produces the left measurement outcome without thus disrupting the mechanism by which the common cause produces the right measurement outcome. But that is not to say that non-separability holds in any other quantum theory.

Third, there are those who argue that the failure of the pair's state in the EPR/B experiment to screen off the correlation between the measurement outcomes is due to the failure of Screening Off (e.g. Fine 1981; Hellman 1982; van Fraassen 1982; Cartwright 1989, chapter 6; Teller 1989; Redhead 1989; Chang and Cartwright 1993). Hellman (1982) suggests that the correlations between the outcomes in the EPR/B experiment are due to conservation laws; as a consequence of these laws, the state of the particle pair at the source generates a functional relation between the measurement outcomes. Like other conservation laws, these laws are supposed to function over large distances without requiring any non-local influences. As a result, the chance of an outcome in the left wing does not depend causally on the outcome in the right wing (and vice versa). The probabilistic dependence between them is "merely statistical"; it corresponds to some kind of selection procedure, not to non-local influence (Hellman 1982, p. 477). Thus, it is concluded that Screening Off is unwarranted in the quantum realm.

Like Hellman, Cartwright (1989) and Chang and Cartwright (1993) also argue that Screening Off is unwarranted for quantum phenomena. For although they maintain that Screening Off can be motivated by particular process accounts of causation (cf. section 7.3), they argue that such accounts are inapplicable in quantum phenomena. In process accounts of causation, causal processes are contiguous – causes and effects are connected continuously in space and time. But, Cartwright and Chang argue that this is an unreasonable assumption in the quantum realm. Healey (1992) suggests that the non-separability of processes rather than their contiguity is responsible for the failure of Screening Off in the quantum realm. In particular, Screening Off fails in EPR/B experiments because of the non-separability of the processes leading to measurement outcomes in the distant wings.

The above different views about the prospects of Screening Off in the quantum realm may seem incompatible with each other. Yet, if CM and Screening Off are not principles but rather principle-schemas, these views need not be incompatible with each other. For they seem to appeal to different specifications of the CM and Screening Off schemas and/or different theoretical accounts of the EPR/B experiment.

8   Conclusions

In this paper, I considered the prospects of four major principles of causal inference: CCL (the cause-correlation link), CM (the Causal Markov principle), Screening Off and PCC (the principle of the common cause), with a special focus on the relevance of determinism and indeterminism for these prospects. The methodology of my investigation was inspired by the idea that CCL, CM, Screening Off and PCC are not really principles but rather principle schemas that require specification (Berkovitz 2000a). That is, the terms 'correlation,' 'causation,' 'cause,' 'distinct events' and 'probability' in the CCL-, CM-, Screening Off- and PCC-schemas require a specification; and for different specifications of these terms we have different principles.

I have argued that under determinism CCL, CM, Screening Off and PCC can be motivated as metaphysical principles by certain accounts of causation, correlation or events. However, the resulting principles are either controversial or very demanding in that their warranted application would require a type of causal knowledge that is frequently beyond our reach. CCL, CM, Screening Off and PCC can also be motivated under indeterminism by some accounts of causation and events, but the resulting principles seem even more controversial and/or demanding.

In general, there is a trade off between the metaphysical and the epistemological status of these principles. Versions of CCL, CM, Screening Off and PCC that are epistemologically less demanding tend to be metaphysically more disputable.

Finally, the empirical status of these principles depends on their specification and the nature of the world. Given that the analysis of the relevant data is non-straightforward, controversial and theory/model-dependent, the prospects of a conclusive empirical evaluation of the empirical status of these principles for various specifications of the terms 'causation,' 'correlation,' 'event' and 'probability' seem dim.

Acknowledgments

For discussions of and comments on earlier drafts of this paper, I thank the audiences at the International Interdisciplinary Determinism Workshop and in particular Robert Bishop and Carol Voeller. Special thanks are due to the editors Harald Atmanspacher and Robert Bishop.

References

Arntzenius F. (1993): The common cause principle. *PSA 1992, Vol. 2*, Philosophy of Science Association, East Lansing, pp. 227–237.

Arntzenius F. (1999): Reichenbach's common cause principle. In *Stanford Encyclopedia of Philosophy* (Spring 2000 edition), ed. by E.N. Zalta, http://plato.stanford.edu/archives/spr2000/entries/physics-Rpcc/.

Bell J. S. (1987): *Speakable and Unspeakable in Quantum Mechanics*, Cambridge University Press, Cambridge.

Berkovitz J. (1995): What econometrics cannot teach quantum mechanics. *Studies in History and Philosophy of Modern Physics* **26**, 163–200.

Berkovitz J. (1998a): Aspects of quantum non-locality I: Superluminal signaling, action-at-a-distance, non-separability and holism. *Studies in History and Philosophy of Modern Physics* **29**, 183–222.

Berkovitz J. (1998b): Aspects of quantum non-locality II: superluminal causation and relativity. *Studies in History and Philosophy of Modern Physics* **29**, 509–545.

Berkovitz J. (2000a): The many principles of the common cause. *Reports on Philosophy* **20**, 51–83.

Berkovitz J. (2000b): The nature of causality in quantum phenomena. *Theoria* **37**, 87–122.

Berkovitz J. (2002): On causal loops in the quantum realm. In *Modality, Probability and Bell's Theorem*, ed. by J.N. Butterfield and T. Placek, Kluwer, Dordrecht (forthcoming).

Butterfield J.N. (1989): A space-time approach to the Bell inequality. In *Philosophical Consequences of Quantum Theories: Reflections on Bell's Theorem*, University of Notre Dame Press, Notre Dame, pp. 114–144.

Butterfield J.N. (1992a): Bell's theorem: What it takes. *British Journal for the Philosophy of Science* **42**, 41–83.

Butterfield J.N. (1992b): David Lewis meets John Bell. *Philosophy of Science* **59**, 26–43.

Butterfield J.N. (1992c): Probabilities and conditionals: Distinction by example. *Proceedings of the Aristotelian Society* **92**, 251–272.

Butterfield J.N. (1994): Outcome dependence and stochastic Einstein nonlocality. In *Logic and Philosophy of Science in Uppsala*, ed. by D. Prawitz and D. Westerst, Kluwer, Dordrecht, pp. 385–424.

Cartwright C. (1983): *How the Laws of Physics Lie*, Clarendon Press, Oxford.

Cartwright C. (1989): *Nature's Capacities and Their Measurements*, Clarendon Press, Oxford.

Cartwright C. (2000): Measuring Causes: Invariance, Modularity and the Causal Markov Condition DP MEAS 10/00, *CPNSS Discussion Paper Series Measurement in Physics and Economics, LSE*.

Chang H. and Cartwright N. (1993): Causality and realism in the EPR experiment. *Erkenntnis* **38**, 169–190.

Collingwood R.G. (1940): *An Essay on Metaphysics*, Clarendon Press, Oxford.

Cushing J. and McMullin E., eds. (1989): *Philosophical Consequences of Quantum Theories: Reflections on Bell's Theorem*, University of Notre Dame Press, Notre Dame.

Dowe P. (1992): Wesley Salmon's process theory of causality and the conserved quantity theory. *Philosophy of Science* **59**, 195–216.

Earman J. (1986): Locality, nonlocality, and action at a distance: A skeptical review of some philosophical dogmas. In *Theoretical Physics in 100 Years*

Since Kelvin's Baltimore Lectures, ed. by P. Achinstein and R. Kargon, MIT Press, Cambridge Mass., pp. 449–490.

Earman J. (1995): *Bangs, Crunches, Whimpers and Shrieks*, Oxford University Press, Oxford.

Eells E. (1991): *Probabilistic Causality*, Cambridge University Press, Cambridge.

Fine A. (1981): Correlation and physical locality. In *PSA 1980, Vol. 2*, ed. by P. Asquith and R. Giere, Philosophy of Science Association, East Lansing, pp. 535–562.

Gasking D. (1955): Causation and recipes. *Mind* **64**, 479–487.

Glymour C. (1997): A view of recent work on the foundations of causal inference. In *Causality in Crisis? Statistical Methods and the Search for Causal Knowledge in Social Sciences*, ed. by V.R. McKim and S.P. Turner, University of Notre Dame Press, Notre Dame, pp. 201–248.

Glymour C. and Meek C. (1994): Conditioning and intervening. *British Journal for the Philosophy of Science* **45**, 1001-1021.

Good I.G. (1961): Causal calculus I. *British Journal for the Philosophy of Science* **11**, 305–318.

Good I.G. (1962): A causal calculus II. *British Journal for the Philosophy of Science* **12**, 43–51.

Hausman D. and Woodward J. (1999): Independence, invariance and the causal Markov condition. *British Journal for the Philosophy of Science* **50**, 521–583.

Healey R. (1992): Chasing quantum causes: how wild is the goose? *Philosophical Topics* **20**, 181–205.

Hellman G. (1982): Stochastic Einstein-locality. *Synthese* **53**, 461-504.

Hoover K. (forthcoming): *Causality in Macroeconomics*, Cambridge University Press, Cambridge.

Humphreys P. (1989): *The Chances of Explanation*, Princeton University Press, Princeton.

Kiiveri H. and Speed T. (1982): Structural analysis of multivariate: a review. In *Sociological Methodology*, ed. by S. Leinhardt, Jossey-Bass, San Francisco.

Lewis D. (1986): *Philosophical Papers, Vol. 2*, Oxford University Press, Oxford.

Meek C. and Glymour C. (1994): Conditioning and Intervening. *Brit. J. Phil. Science* **45**, 1001–1021.

Mellor D.H. (1995): *The Facts of Causation*, Routledge, London.

Menzies P. (1989): Probabilistic causation and causal process: A critique of Lewis. *Philosophy of Science* **59**, 642–663.

Menzies P. (1996): Probabilistic causation and the pre-emption problem. *Mind* **105**, 85–117.

Menzies P. and Price H. (1993): Causation and secondary quality. *British Journal for the Philosophy of Science* **44**, 187–203.

Pearl J. (2000): *Causality*, Cambridge University Press, Cambridge.

Redhead M.L.G. (1987): *Incompleteness, Nonlocality and Realism*, Oxford University Press, Oxford.

Redhead M.L.G. (1989): Nonfactorizability, stochastic causality, and passion-at-a-distance. In *Philosophical Consequences of Quantum Theories: Reflections on Bell's Theorem*, University of Notre Dame Press, Notre Dame, pp. 145–153.

Redhead M.L.G. (1994): The vacuum in relativistic quantum field theory. *PSA 1994, Vol. 2*, Philosophy of Science Association, East Lansing, pp. 77–87.

Reichenbach H. (1956): *The Direction of Time*, University of California Press, Berkeley.

Russell B. (1948): *Human Knowledge*, Simon and Schuster, New York.

Salmon W. C. (1984): *Scientific Explanation and the Causal Structure of the World*, Princeton University Press, Princeton.

Skyrms B. (1984): EPR: Lessons for metaphysics. *Midwest Studies in Philosophy* **9**, 245–255.

Sober E. (1988a): The principle of the common cause. In *Probability and Causality*, ed. by J.H. Fetzer, Reidel, Dordrecht, pp. 211–228.

Sober E. (1988b): *Reconstructing the Past: Parsimony, Evolution and Inference*, MIT Press, Cambridge, Mass.

Sober E. (2001): Venetian sea levels, British bread prices, and the principle of the common cause. *British Journal for the Philosophical of Science* **52**, 1–16.

Spirtes P., Glymour C., and Scheines R. (1993): *Causation, Prediction, and Search*, Springer, New York.

Spirtes P., Glymour C., and Scheines R. (2000): *Causation, Prediction, and Search* (2nd edition with additional material by D. Heckerman, C. Meek, G.F. Cooper and T. Richardson), MIT Press, Cambridge Mass.

Spohn W. (1991): On Reichenbach's principle of the common cause. In *Logic, Language and the Structure of Scientific Theories: Proceeding of the Carnap-Reichenbach Centennial*, ed. by W.C. Salmon and G. Wolters, University of Pittsburgh Press, Pittsburgh.

Suppes P. (1970): *A Probabilistic Theory of Causation*, North-Holland, Amsterdam.

Teller P. (1989): Relativity, relational holism and quantum mechanics. In *Philosophical Consequences of Quantum Theories: Reflections on Bell's Theorem*, University of Notre Dame Press, Notre Dame, pp. 208–223.

Uffink J. (1999): The principle of the common cause faces the Bernstein Paradox. *PSA 1998*, Philosophy of Science Association, East Lansing, pp. S512–S525.

van Fraassen B.C. (1980): *The Scientific Image*, Oxford University Press, Oxford.

van Fraassen B.C. (1982): The charybdis of realism. *Synthese* **52**, 25–38, page reference to reprint in *Philosophical Consequences of Quantum Theories: Reflections on Bell's Theorem*, University of Notre Dame Press, Notre Dame, pp. 97–113.

von Wright G.H. (1971): On the logic and epistemology of causal relation. In *Causation*, ed. by E. Sosa and M. Tooley, Oxford University Press, Oxford 1987, pp. 105–124.

Yule G.U. (1903): Notes on theory of association of attributes in statistics. *Biometrica* **2**, 121–134.

Fundamental Limits of Control: A Quantum Approach to the Second Law

Günter Mahler, Jochen Gemmer, and Alexander Otte

Abstract

The second law postulates the existence of a state function, called entropy, which for closed systems cannot decrease. It thus defines some sort of irreversibility (direction of evolution). While this rather universal behavior can be associated with the loss of micro-control, it also gives rise to robust and universal thermodynamic equilibrium properties (macro-control). Based on quantum mechanics we intend to clarify the interrelation between these two levels of description.

1 Introduction

The second law (Schlögl 1988) is arguably one of the most fundamental and far reaching laws of physics; nevertheless, its origin remains puzzling. In particular, the reconciliation of the postulated irreversibility with the notorious reversibility of all fundamental physical laws has been a serious challenge of statistical physics over decades. Boltzmann's as well as Gibbs' ensemble approach claim to account for that problem, but have to acknowledge some additional assumptions, which do not follow from the underlying microscopic laws.

Therefore, researchers like L. D. Landau, E. Schrödinger, J. von Neumann (von Neumann 1930), W. Pauli, and G. Lindblad, to name but a few, suggested quantum mechanics as a possible remedy.

Isolated systems are a (sometimes convenient) fiction. In a quantum approach the interaction of any system considered with its environment will necessarily lead to some "entanglement", which implies that local properties tend to become ill-defined, even if the state of the total system is completely specified ("pure"). It is remarkable that this entanglement is responsible for largely different phenomena: it may be considered as the main resource for quantum information processing (Nielsen and Chuang 2000), a prerequisite for quantum measurements, the source of decoherence (quenching of local quantum features; Zeh 1996), but also, as will be discussed below, as the origin of irreversible tendencies towards maximum entropy states (Gemmer et al. 2001).

The intended quantum approach to the second law can be interpreted at least in two different ways: (i) as an attempt to prove the quantum origin of the second law, and (ii) as an attempt to see signatures of the equilibrium behavior emerge as quantum systems approach some appropriately defined thermodynamic limit. Both lines of arguments support each other: The quantum foundation of the second law becomes more plausible, if signatures of this law can be found already in small quantum systems, where deterministic and non-deterministic types of evolutions may coexist.

2 Hilbert Space Statistics

For N classical point particles the phase space dimension is $d = 6N$ and thus proportional to the number $3N$ of independent coordinates, the so-called "mechanical degrees of freedom". Now, what the phase space is for classical states, Hilbert space is for wave functions. However, its dimension has little if anything to do with those classical degrees of freedom. This should be kept in mind, when we start referring to thermodynamic limits (see below).

Any pure state $|\Psi\rangle$, a vector in a Hilbert space of finite dimension n, can be represented by a set of complete, orthogonal states $|j\rangle$, $j = 1, 2, ...n$, as $|\Psi\rangle = \sum \psi_j |j\rangle$, where ψ_j denotes the complex amplitude of the state with respect to the representation $|j\rangle$.

Now, let $f = f(|\Psi\rangle) = f(\psi_j)$ be some function on the state vector space. Then we may define its Hilbert space average $\langle\langle f \rangle\rangle$ and distribution $D(f')$, respectively, as

$$\langle\langle f \rangle\rangle = \int w(\psi_j) f(\psi_j) d\psi_j \tag{1}$$

$$D(f') = \int \delta(f(\psi_j) - f') w(\psi_j) d\psi_j \tag{2}$$

where $w(\psi_j)$ denotes the unique uniform distribution in pure state space (Skyora 1974; Zyczkowski and Sommers 2000), and f' some arbitrary but fixed value. This $w(\psi_j)$ is invariant under any unitary transformation, i.e., loosely speaking, the distribution does not depend on how we look at the state space.

We now turn to a quantum system defined on a space with dimension n partitioned into the quantum system proper g (Hilbert space dimension n_g)

and some environment c (dimension n_c) such that $n = n_g n_c$ (Mahler and Weberuss 1998). (The total Hilbert space is thus a so-called tensor product of the two subspaces.) In the next paragraph g will stand for "gas" and c for "container". We assume that this total closed system is always in a pure state $|\Psi_{g,c}\rangle$:

$$|\Psi_{g,c}\rangle = \sum_{j,k} \psi_{j,k}^{g,c} |j\rangle \otimes |k\rangle \tag{3}$$

Here, state $|j\rangle$ refers to subsystem g and $|k\rangle$ to subsystem c, while $\otimes$ denotes the tensor-product. If we cannot find a representation in which $|\Psi\rangle$ can be written as a simple product of one wavefunction for g times one wavefunction for c, this $|\Psi\rangle$ is called "entangled".

This entanglement may be seen as a consequence of the superposition principle generalized to composite quantum systems. It implies that the subsystem states are non-pure and can thus be specified only by their respective density operators, e.g. for subsystem g:

$$\hat{\rho}_g = \text{Tr}_c\{|\Psi_{g,c}\rangle\langle\Psi_{g,c}|\} \tag{4}$$

Here Tr_c means "trace over subsystem c". A convenient purity measure is given by:

$$P_g = \text{Tr}_g\{\hat{\rho}_g^2\} \tag{5}$$

$P_g = 1$, its maximum value, for a pure state; it approaches its minimum value $1/n_g$ for a complete "mixture". In such a completely mixed state all observables $\hat{A}$ are "undefined" in the sense that under a measurement any allowed eigenvalue of $\hat{A}$ would be found with the same probability (no a priori information).

P_g represents a function f on the pure states $|\Psi\rangle$ in the sense of Eq. (1). Its Hilbert space average $\langle\langle P_g\rangle\rangle$ can be shown to be given by (Lubkin 1978, Zyczkowski and Sommers 2000):

$$\langle\langle P_g\rangle\rangle = \frac{n_g + n_c}{n_g n_c + 1} = \langle\langle P_c\rangle\rangle \tag{6}$$

The distribution $D(P_g)$ is shown in Fig. 1 for $n_g = 2$ and $n_c = 2, 4, 8$. We see that $D(P_g)$ approaches a peak at the minimum value $P_g = 1/n_g$ as we increase n_c.

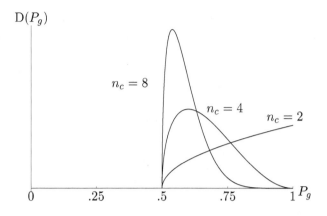

Figure 1: Purity distribution $D(P_g)$ for $n_g = 2$.

As the non-pure character of subsystem g derives here exclusively from entanglement, we may also use the quantity $S_g^{(2)} = 1 - P_g$ as an entanglement measure, where $S^{(q)}$ denotes the so-called Tsallis entropy (Tsallis 1988):

$$S^{(q)} \quad = \quad \frac{1}{1-q}(\text{Tr}\{\hat{\rho}^q\} - 1) \tag{7}$$

The measure $S_g^{(2)}$ is often more convenient than the von Neumann entropy S_g of subsystem g,

$$S_g \quad = \quad -\text{Tr}_g\{\hat{\rho}(g)\ln\hat{\rho}(g)\}\ , \tag{8}$$

which is identical with the Tsallis entropy for $q \to 1$. On the other hand, only the latter seems to have the correct thermodynamic limit; under equilibrium conditions, S_g is expected to be directly related to the classical entropy of thermodynamics. The behavior of $\langle\langle S_g \rangle\rangle$ is plotted in Fig. 2 for $n_g = 2$ and $n_c \geq 2$. We see that for $n_c \gg n_g$ this average rapidly approaches its maximum value (associated with a minimum value for P_g). Typical states $|\Psi\rangle$ are highly entangled, which thus implies "undefined" properties of g (as well as of c).

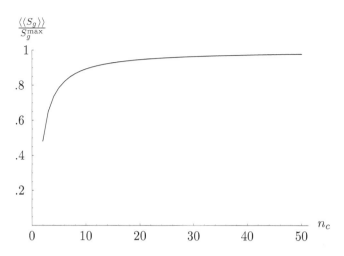

Figure 2: Average entropy $\frac{\langle\langle S_g\rangle\rangle}{S_g^{\max}}$ of subsystem g $(n_g = 2)$, depending on the dimension n_c of the environment.

3   Microcanonical and Canonical Constraints

So far we have been concerned with the quantum mechanical state space only. Now we include some aspects of the actual physical system defined by its Hamilton operator $\hat{H}$.

Realistic descriptions of quantum systems can never be complete. Here we will take the view that we have incomplete knowledge of the initial state and of the total system Hamiltonian. Our results will therefore still contain statistical aspects, as before, but now under some additional constraints. These typically derive from constants of motion (invariants), by which initial conditions enter as characteristic parameters, as will be shown below.

We again restrict ourselves to a bi-partite system, consisting of the system proper g ("gas") and the environment c ("container"). Let us first consider the so-called "microcanonical constraints". Classically, these imply fixed energy and fixed volume for g. In the quantum domain more caution has to be exercised, as boundary conditions are necessarily physical, not just mathematical constraints.

The fixed volume condition amounts to introducing an appropriate external potential which enters the corresponding Hamilton model:

$$\hat{H}(g_j, c_k) = \hat{H}_0(g_j) + \hat{H}_0(c_k) + \hat{W}_0(g_j, c_k) \tag{9}$$

Here, g_j and c_k denote dynamical variables like momenta, spatial coordinates etc., $\hat{H}_0(g_j)$ and $\hat{H}_0(c_k)$ describe the "free gas" and the "free container", respectively. Introducing a quasiclassical mean potential $\hat{V}_c(g_j)$, we rearrange Eq. (9) in terms of

$$\hat{H}(g_j) = \hat{H}_0 + \hat{V}_c(g_j) , \tag{10}$$

describing the gas in a box, and

$$\hat{W}(g_j, c_k) = \hat{W}_0(g_j, c_k) - \hat{V}_c(g_j) \tag{11}$$

which can typically be treated as a small perturbation. This perturbation is due to the fact that the container is, in fact, a dynamical many particle system rather than a static box.

We interpret the fixed energy condition to mean that there is no energy exchange between the gas g and its container c, which constrains the type of interaction $\hat{W}$. Let the total pure state at time t be given by (cf. Eq. (3)):

$$|\Psi_{g,c}(t)\rangle = \sum_{A,r;B,s} \psi^{g,c}_{A,r;B,s}(t)|A, r\rangle \otimes |B, s\rangle. \tag{12}$$

Here we have used a double-index notation, in which $A(B)$ specifies the energy eigenvalue of $g(c)$, and $r = 1, 2, ...N^g_A$, $s = 1, 2, ...N^c_B$ allow for degeneracies (different states for the same energy A, B). Then the microcanonical constraint implies that the energy distribution

$$w_{A,B} = \sum_{r,s} |\psi^{g,c}_{A,r;B,s}(t)|^2 = const. \tag{13}$$

is a constant of motion. If the initial state at time $t = 0$ is taken to be a product state (as we will do here), then $w_{A,B} = w^g_A(0)w^c_B(0)$.

We reconsider the Hilbert space average of P_g, but now under the constraints of Eq. (13), representing the additional information (control) we have. For complete degeneracy ($A = B = 1$), we recover the result of Eq. (6) with n_g replaced by N^g_1 and n_c by N^c_1. For non-degenerate states the Hilbert space average of P_g is found to be (Gemmer and Mahler 2001):

$$\langle\langle P_g\rangle\rangle = \sum_A (w^g_A(0))^2 + \sum_B (w^c_B(0))^2 - \sum_{A,B} (w^g_A(0))^2 (w^c_B(0))^2 \tag{14}$$

If the accessible state space of at least one of the subsystems was just one unique state, P_g would be identically 1, the corresponding entropy S_g zero. On the other hand, if the number of occupied states of subsystem c was large compared with that of g, which, in turn, should be large compared to 1, $\langle\langle P_g \rangle\rangle$ is approximately independent of the environment c, and close to its minimum value consistent with Eq. (13). We tentatively associate the (quantum) thermodynamic limit with these conditions.

To allow for energy exchange, we now turn to the so-called canonical constraints. For this purpose we replace the invariants of Eq. (13) by the much weaker constraint

$$w(E) = \sum_{\substack{A,B \\ E^A + E^B = E}} w_{A,B} = const. \tag{15}$$

The most probable $w_{A,B}$ can then be shown to be:

$$w_{A,B} = \frac{N_A^g N_B^c w(E)}{\sum_{A,B} N_A^g N_B^c} \tag{16}$$

Finally, if $w(E)$ is sufficiently peaked, the marginal w_A will approach:

$$w_A \sim \exp\left(-E_A \beta\right) \tag{17}$$

This is the well-known Boltzmann factor, if we identify β with $1/k_B T$, the inverse temperature. Also, in this case $\langle\langle P_g \rangle\rangle$ is close to its minimum value consistent with the boundary conditions of Eq. (16), if the thermodynamic limit is satisfied. Condition (16) can then, in turn, be interpreted as the usual fixed average energy condition on subsystem g.

But if the average of some function f is close to its minimum (maximum), the corresponding distribution $D(f)$ must be sharply peaked at the minimum (maximum). This means that almost all pure states are characterized by the minimum purity P_g or the maximum entropy S_g. It also means that it is the average S_g, and no longer the detailed initial conditions leading to this average, which specifies the state. S_g becomes a state function.

4 Approach to Equilibrium

Why should a (quantum) system approach a universal equilibrium state with maximum entropy? One should first note that, microscopically, the equilibrium state is not one single state, but rather a "typical state". Which typical state this is, is as irrelevant as whether *all* typical states will be visited or not.

While quantum trajectories do not exist in phase space (as these would violate the uncertainty relations), paths are well-defined in Hilbert space.

Any such path is generated by the corresponding total Hamiltonian $\hat{H}$ for a specific initial state $|\Psi(0)\rangle$. The evolution of the total system is completely deterministic, the entropy of the total state therefore always remains zero.

We first observe that the path velocity, v_{eff}, is constant and given by (Gemmer et al. 2001):

$$v_{\text{eff}}^2 \;=\; \frac{1}{\hbar^2}\langle\Psi_{g,c}(0)|\hat{H}^2|\Psi_{g,c}(0)\rangle \;=\; const. \tag{18}$$

As a consequence, the time average of any function f, denoted by $\overline{f}$, always equals the (geometric) path average. This holds, in particular, for the purity P_g and the entropy S_g.

Incomplete knowledge does not allow us to uniquely specify the path under consideration. Instead, we will have to refer to "typical paths", which are located in "typical areas" of the Hilbert space, possibly constrained by additional invariants.

As noted, typical areas of Hilbert space are characterized by minimum purity P_g. Then, because of Eq. (18), almost all paths should be located in those areas of minimum purity. Even paths that start from $P_g = 1$ (and zero entropy), will typically be found in states with minimum P_g, if the path has become long enough, i.e. if we have waited long enough. (Ergodicity in the sense that the trajectory should come close to *any state* within the nominally accessible state space is not needed though!) Of course, we cannot say how long this waiting time has to be; we cannot even exclude that the waiting time might go to infinity for special conditions.

Note that minimum purity implies maximum entropy S_g; further note that our incomplete knowledge does in no way enter the "objective" measure of local information loss expressed by S_g. Finally, in this thermodynamic limit the entropies of subsystems making up system g become additive as the entanglement *between* these subsystems tends to disappear. Such an additivity property would not hold for the corresponding purities!

While maximum entropy means maximum loss of micro-control, the tendency towards equilibrium opens up new classes of robust and universal behavior, which can be predicted from very limited knowledge. It is remarkable that these stable macro-features begin to emerge already far from the thermodynamic limit proper, as will be discussed below.

5 Signatures of Equilibrium Far from the Thermodynamic Limit

We look for a situation in which dynamical corrections $\hat{W}$ to an effective potential $\hat{V}_c(g)$ are responsible for the build-up of entanglement in some most elementary way, while the total system is still far away from the thermodynamic limit. We intend to show that, nevertheless, even irreversible behavior may result in a predictable way.

The two-particle problem is completely separable. Therefore, the simpliest non-separable candidate could be the closed three-particle system, which, due to its only nine classical degrees of freedom, is clearly far from the classical thermodynamic limit. We cast this model into a form to describe one electron, system g, bound via Coulomb forces to two protons (system c), the mutual nuclear interaction of which is modeled as an isotropic infinitely high potential well. We refrain from reducing this "He-Ion"–problem to a separable two-particle problem consisting of a doubly charged point nucleus and the point-like electron, as is typically done. The coupling to the electromagnetic field giving rise to another strong decay mechanism will not be included here.

Our model can be written in the form of Eqs. (9,10,11) with (Gemmer and Mahler 2001)

$$\hat{V}_c(\vec{R}_g) = -\frac{2\alpha\hbar c}{|\vec{R}_g|} \tag{19}$$

$$\hat{W}(\vec{R}_g, \vec{R}_c) = -\alpha\hbar c\left(\frac{1}{|\vec{R}_g - \vec{R}_c/2|} + \frac{1}{|\vec{R}_g + \vec{R}_c/2|} - \frac{2}{|\vec{R}_g|}\right) \tag{20}$$

where $\vec{R}_g$ denotes the distance vector between the center of the nucleus and the electron, $\vec{R}_c$ the difference vector between the two protons, α the fine-structure constant, and c the velocity of light.

The effect of $\hat{W}$ can be treated in first-order perturbation theory. We restrict ourselves to states with vanishing orbital momentum for both subsystems, noting that the first-order perturbation does not connect states with different angular momentum. Both relevant subsystem state spaces are then, effectively, non-degenerate and completely characterized by their respective energy indices A, B. The resulting shifts $E^1_{A,B}$ of the unperturbed energies $E^0_{A,B} = E^0_A + E^0_B$ are:

$$E^1_{A,B} = \frac{\alpha\hbar c r_0^2}{(6a_B A)^3(A!)^2}\left(\frac{1}{3} - \frac{1}{2\pi^2 B^2}\right) \tag{21}$$

Here, $r_0 = 10^{-15}$m is the radius of an α-particle, a_B is the Bohr radius. For $A, B \approx 1$ these shifts are on the order of 10^{-10} eV, which is negligibly small compared to the unperturbed energies, $E_{A,B}$. Nevertheless, these corrections may suffice to cause significant deviations of P_g from 1.

For initial states with the nucleus c residing in a simple pure state (energy eigenstate), no entanglement can develop (cf. Sect. 4). This is the typical situation in the laboratory. From a formal point of view, however, typical initial states may be a product of highly superimposed states of both subsystems, which must be expected to develop entanglement.

Presently, we restrict ourselves to the following three model initial states:

$$|\Psi_{g,c}(0)\rangle = 1/2\,(|1\rangle + |2\rangle) \otimes (|1\rangle + |2\rangle) \tag{22}$$

$$|\Psi_{g,c}(0)\rangle = 1/2\,(|1\rangle + |2\rangle) \otimes (|14\rangle + |15\rangle) \tag{23}$$

$$|\Psi_{g,c}(0)\rangle = 1/10\,(\sum_{A=1}^{10} |A\rangle) \otimes (\sum_{B=1}^{10} |B\rangle) \tag{24}$$

$|A\rangle, |B\rangle$ are the unperturbed energy eigenstates of g, c, respectively. For the first two cases we find oscillatory behavior with a period on the 10^{-5}s and 10^{19}s time scale, respectively. For the last case with the microcanonical constraints (due to the different energy scales, there is virtually no energy exchange possible between g and c)

$$w_A^g(0) = w_B^c(0) = 0.1 \quad \text{for} \quad A, B = 1, 2, ...10 \tag{25}$$

we find on a time scale of one second a relaxation to $\overline{P_g} = 0.19$, which is in perfect agreement with the Hilbert space average $\langle\langle P_g \rangle\rangle$ according to Eq. (14)! This means that for predicting $\overline{P_g}$ we do not have to solve the complete Schrödinger-equation (cf. Jensen and Shankar 1985).

For all the above initial states the quantum thermodynamic limit is not reached yet. This could easily be changed, if we increased the state space occupied by the two subsystems. However, as indicated before, such an initial state can hardly be realized experimentally, as the microcanonical constraints like (25) would require extremely broad invariant energy distributions. This leads us to suspect that in cases, where the classical thermodynamic limit does not hold, also the quantum thermodynamic limit will typically not be accessible.

6   Breakdown of the Second Law?

The second law is often associated with the impossibility of a perpetuum mobile of the second kind (Schlögl 1998). Classical attempts to overcome this constraint have never been successful. But this does not imply that the second law should be unconditionally true. We may ask with Ball (1999): "...in what manner does the second law break down in going from irreversible macroscopic systems to reversible microscopic ones?"

A quantum version of the perpetuum mobile may be introduced in the form of a quantum computer program: If the state $|\Psi_g(0)\rangle$ of the gas was completely known and a sufficiently ingenious machinery was at hand to implement unitary transformations as desired, one should be able to transform $|\Psi_g(0)\rangle$ into a state with the same energy, but a large collective momentum. Based on this state, one could then extract mechanical work beyond the limits of the second law. The extent, to which neither $|\Psi_g(0)\rangle$ nor the machinery (interaction without entanglement) is available, clearly limits any such attempt. But there should be a continuum of intermediate cases.

Entanglement is an important ingredient in the first steps of quantum measurements; it correlates the quantum object with some degrees of freedom of the measurement apparatus. After complete measurement we have gained complete information, and the object is (in the ideal case) in a pure state (i.e. entanglement has been destroyed). This picture seems to contradict our present equilibrium model, in which entanglement (i) generically cannot decrease and (ii) implies loss rather than gain of control.

Taking free will as a fact without which experimental science was not consistently possible (see Primas, this volume), we have to admit that microscopic (unentangled) states of some (usually small) part of the universe can be prepared in the laboratory. That this is possible, though in an unpredictable way, may be called the "measurement problem".

Besides measurement, there appear to be two further options, by which one might hope to suppress the typical states and the typical paths discussed in the preceding section. One could think of some active control to keep the system far from equilibrium (compare machines like the heat pump). Alternatively, one might try to select specific (classes of) paths in Hilbert space with the help of a passive design of the system under consideration (additional invariants). All these options are under scrutiny in the quest for large-scale quantum computation (Nielsen and Chuang 2000).

7   Summary and Conclusions

The relationship between deterministic and indeterministic descriptions is one of the central themes of this volume. It has long since been realized that reduced descriptions tend to render an originally deterministic evolution indeterministic (for a recent discussion see Landsberg 2000). However, even though limited control abounds in any realistic account of physical scenarios, it is often not clear how to justify such a reduction (e.g. "coarse-graining") without invoking ambiguous subjective notions.

Of course, we cannot hope to solve the set of coupled equations of motion of some 10^{20} particles within a box, and even if we could, we would be unable to measure the initial state necessary to select the pertinent solution. This is a convincing argument to resort to statistical methods; it is much less convincing as a foundation of thermodynamics as a universal theory for macroscopic equilibrium systems.

In the present investigation we have restricted ourselves to quantum systems in finite-dimensional state spaces; we thus dispense with interesting mathematical properties (like inequivalent representations, stability issues and inherent irreversibility) emerging in the infinite-dimensional limit only (cf. Misra, this volume). We expect, though, that any important and fundamental physical effect should become visible long before this limit is reached (cf. Sect. 5).

We have made use of the fact that partitioning a closed quantum system generically leads to non-pure states of its parts. This already works for a partition into just two subsystems, here taken to be a gas g and a container c. As a result, a local entropy $S_g > 0$ appears that is defined at any instant of time, even if the total system always resides in a pure state $|\Psi\rangle$. In general, we will neither know $|\Psi\rangle$ nor the exact Hamiltonian controlling its evolution. But while this limited knowledge does not *enter* S_g, it suffices to *infer* the *typical* value of S_g!

We have introduced a quantum version of the thermodynamic limit (referring to Hilbert space), in addition to its conventional classical definition (referring to phase space). These need not coincide; it seems, though, that far away from the classical thermodynamic limit also the quantum thermodynamic limit cannot be reached.

Signatures of statistical equilibrium behavior can be found in quantum systems far from the thermodynamic limit. In this case, of course, the full set of thermodynamic rules does not apply yet. For instance, the entropy may not be sharp, may be fluctuating in time, may depend on the environment, may not be additive etc. (These results should be distinguished from true non-equilibrium behavior.)

In the quantum thermodynamic limit the distribution of S_g becomes strongly peaked at its maximum value, subject to the appropriate boundary conditions, in agreement with the second law of thermodynamics. S_g becomes a state function.

Our results are in accordance with the popular statement that the "universe as a whole" evolves deterministically, while parts may appear to be random. (If one likes, one might relate these two levels of description to "ontic" and "epistemic" frameworks, see Atmanspacher in this volume.) Randomness or indeterminism, though, hold only on the microscopic level of description. On the macro-level it is just the second law which gives rise to new deterministic rules governing almost dispersion-free "classical" parameters. Such classical parameters, in turn, are a prerequisite for performing quantum measurements to begin with.

Acknowledgements

One of us (A.O.) thanks the Deutsche Forschungsgemeinschaft for financial support.

References

Ball P. (1999): Transitions still to be made. *Nature* **402**, Suppl., C73-C76.

Gemmer J., Otte A. and Mahler G. (2001): Quantum approach to a derivation of the second law of thermodynamics. *Phys. Rev. Lett.* **68**, 1927-1930.

Gemmer J. and Mahler G. (2001): Failure of effective potential approach: Nucleus-electron entanglement in the He$^+$-ion. Submitted.

Jensen R.V. and Shankar R. (1985): *Phys. Rev. Lett.* **54**, 1879-1882.

Landsberg P.T. (2000): *Seeking Ultimates*, Institute of Physics, Bristol.

Lubkin E. (1978): Entropy of an n-system from its correlation with a k-reservoir. *Math. Phys.* **19**, 1028-1031.

Mahler G. and Weberuss V.A. (1998): *Quantum Networks*, Springer, Berlin.

von Neumann J. (1930): Beweis des Ergodensatzes und des H-Theorems in der neuen Mechanik. *Zeitschr. f. Physik* **57**, 30-70.

Nielsen M.A. and Chuang I.L. (2000): *Quantum Computation and Quantum Information*, Cambridge University Press, Cambridge.

Schlögl F. (1998): *Probability and Heat*, Vieweg, Braunschweig.

Skyora S. (1974): Quantum theory an the Bayesian inference problems. *J. Stat. Phys.* **11**, 17-27.

Tsallis C. (1988): Possible generalization of Boltzmann-Gibbs statistics. *J. Stat. Phys.* **52**, 479-487.

Zeh H.D. (1996): The program of decoherence: ideas and concepts. In: *Decoherence and the Appearance of a Classical World in Quantum Theory*, ed. by D. Giulini et al., Springer, Berlin, pp. 5-34.

Zyczkowski K. and Sommers H.J. (2000): Induced measures in the space of mixed quantum states. *LANL preprint* quant-ph/0012101.

A Quantum Mechanical Look at Time Travel and Free Will

Daniel Greenberger and Karl Svozil

Abstract

Consequences of the basic and most evident consistency requirement – that measured events cannot happen and not happen at the same time – are reviewed. Particular emphasis is given to event forecast and event control. As a consequence, particular, very general bounds on the forecast and control of events within the known laws of physics result. These bounds are of a global, statistical nature and need not affect singular events or groups of events. We also present a quantum mechanical model of time travel and discuss chronology protection schemes. Such models impose restrictions upon particular capacities of event control.

1 Classical Part

1.1 Principle of Self-Consistency

An irreducible, atomic physical phenomenon manifests itself as a click of some detector. Either there is a click or there is no click. This yes-no scheme is experimental physics in a nutshell (at least according to a theoretician). From this kind of elementary observation, all of our physical evidence is accumulated.

Such irreversibly observed events (whatever the relevance or meaning of those terms is (Wigner 1961, Wheeler 1983, Greenberger and YaSin 1989, Herzog et al. 1995)) are subject to the primary condition of *consistency* or *self-consistency: Any particular irreversibly observed event either happens or does not happen, but it cannot both happen and not happen.*

Indeed, so trivial seems the requirement of consistency that Hilbert polemicized against "another author" with the following words (Hilbert 1926), "... for me, the opinion that the [physical] facts and events themselves can be contradictory is a good example of thoughtlessness."

Just as in mathematics, inconsistency, i.e. the coexistence of truth and falsity of propositions, is a fatal property of any physical theory. Nevertheless, in a particular very precise sense, quantum mechanics incorporates inconsistencies in a very subtle way, which assures overall consistency. For instance, a particle wave function or quantum state is said to "pass" a double slit through both slits at once, which is classically impossible. (Such considerations may, however, be considered as mere trickery, quantum talk devoid of any operational meaning.) Yet, neither particle wave functions nor quantum states can be directly associated with any sort of irreversible observed event of physical reality. We shall come back to a particular quantum case in the second part of this investigation.

And just as in mathematics and in formal logic, it can be argued that overly strong capacities of intrinsic event forecast and intrinsic event control render the system overall inconsistent. This fact may indeed be considered as one decisive feature in finite deterministic ("algorithmic") models (Svozil 1993). It manifests itself already in the early stages of Cantorian set theory: any claim that it is possible to enumerate the real numbers leads, via the diagonalization method, to an outright contradiction. The only consistent alternative is the acceptance that no such capacity of enumeration exists. Gödel's incompleteness theorem (Gödel 1931) states that any formal system rich enough to include arithmetic and elementary logic could not be both consistent and complete. Turing's theorem on the recursive unsolvability of the halting problem (Turing 1936/1937), as well as Chaitin's Ω numbers (Chaitin 1992) are formalizations of related limitations in formal logics, computer science and mathematics.

In what follows we will proceed along very similar lines. We will first argue that any capacity of total forecast or event control – even in a totally deterministic environment – contradicts the (idealistic) idea that decisions between alternatives are possible; or, stated differently, that there is free will. Then we shall proceed with possibilities of forecast and event control which are consistent with both free will and the known laws of physics.

Evidently, some form of forecast and event control is possible – indeed, this is one of the main achievements of contemporary natural science, and we make everyday use of it, e.g. by switching on the light. These capacities of forecast and event control are characterized by a high degree of reproducibility, which does not depend on single events.

We will concentrate on very general bounds for these capacities, which follow from the requirement of consistency and do not depend on any particular physical model. They are valid for all conceivable forms of physical theories – classical, quantum and forthcoming alike.

1.2 Strong Forecasting

Let us first consider forecasting the future. Even if physical phenomena occur deterministically and can be accounted for ("computed") on a higher level of abstraction, from within the system such a complete description may not be of much practical, operational use (Toffoli 1978, Svozil 1996).

Indeed, suppose that free will exists. Suppose further that an agent could predict *all* future events, without exceptions. We shall call this the *strong form of forecasting*. In this case, the agent could freely decide to act in such a way as to invalidate any prediction. Hence, in order to avoid inconsistencies and paradoxes, either free will has to be abandoned, or it has to be accepted that complete prediction is impossible.[1]

Another possibility would be to consider strong forms of forecasting which are, however, not utilized to alter the system. Effectively, this results in the abandonment of free will, amounting to an extrinsic, detached viewpoint. After all, what is knowledge and what is it good for if it cannot be applied and utilized?

Recent advances in the foundations of quantum (information) theory have shown that, due to complementarity and the impossibility to clone generic states, single events may have important meanings to some observers, although they make no sense at all to other observers. One example for this is quantum cryptography. Many of these events are stochastic and are postulated to satisfy all conceivable statistical laws (correlations are nonclassical, though). In such frameworks, high degrees of reproducibility cannot be guaranteed, although single events may carry valuable information, which can even be distilled and purified.

1.3 Strong Event Control

A very similar argument holds for event control and the production of "miracles" (Frank 1932). Suppose that free will exists. Suppose further that an agent could entirely control the future. We will call this the *strong form of event control*. Then this agent could freely decide to invalidate the laws of physics. In order to avoid a paradox, either free will or some physical laws would have to be abandoned, or it has to be accepted that complete event control is impossible.

---

[1] This argument is of an ancient type (Anderson 1970). As has already been mentioned, it has been formalized recently in set theory, formal logic and recursive function theory, where it is called the "diagonalization method."

1.4   Weak Forecasting and Event Control

Already from what has been said, it is reasonable to assume that *forecast and event control should be possible only if these capacities cannot be associated with any paradox or contradiction.*

Thus the requirement for consistency of the phenomena seems to impose rather stringent conditions on forecasting and event control. Similar ideas have already been discussed in the context of time paradoxes in relativity theory (cf. Friedman et al. 1990 and Nahin 1998, p. 272: "the only solutions to the laws of physics that can occur locally ... are those which are globally self-consistent").

There is, however, a possibility that the forecast and control of future events *is* conceivable for *singular* events within the statistical bounds. Such occurrences may be "singular miracles" which are well accounted for within the known laws of physics. They will be called *weak forms of forecasting and event control.* In order to obey overall consistency, such a framework should not be extendible to any forms of strong forecast or event control, because, as has been argued before, this could either violate global consistency criteria or would make necessary a revision of the known laws of physics.

The relevant laws of statistics (e.g. all recursively enumerable laws) impose rather lax constraints, especially on finite sequences, and do not exclude local, singular, improbable events. For example, a binary sequence such as 11111111111111111111111111111111 is just as probable as the sequences 11100101110101000111000011010101 and 01010101010101010101010101010101, and its occurrence in a test is equally likely, although the "meaning" an observer could ascribe to it is rather different. These sequences may be embedded in and be part of much longer stochastic sequences. If short finite regular (or "meaningful") sequences are embedded into long irregular ("meaningless") ones, those sequences become statistically indistinguishable for all practical purposes from the previous sequences. Of course, the "meaning" of any such sequence may vary with different observers. Some of them may be able to decipher a sequence, others may not be able to do so.

It may seem evident that by definition any finite regularity in an otherwise stochastic environment should exclude the type of high reproducibility characteristic of the natural sciences. On the contrary: single "meaningful" events, which are hardly reproducible, might indicate a new category of phenomena dual to the usual "lawful" and highly predictable ones.[2]

---

[2]In this context compare the contribution by Primas (particularly sections 6–8) in this volume.

Just as it is perfectly all right to consider the statement "This statement is true" to be true, it may be perfectly reasonable to speculate that some events are forecasted and controlled within the domain of statistical laws. But in order to be within the statistical laws, any such method *need not be guaranteed* to work at all times.

To put it pointedly: it may be perfectly reasonable to become rich, say, by singular forecasts of the stock market, future values or the outcomes of horse races, but such an ability must necessarily be irreproducible, secretive, and not extendible; at least to such an extent that no guarantee for an overall strategy and regularity can be derived from it.

The associated weak forms of forecasting and event control are thus beyond any global statistical significance. Their importance and meaning seems to lie mainly on a "subjective" level of singular events. This comes close to what Jung imagined as the principle of "synchronicity" (Jung 1952), and is dual to the more reproducible forms one is usually accustomed to.

1.5 Against the Odds

Let us review a couple of experiments which suggest themselves in the context of weak forecast and event control. They are all based on the observation whether or not an agent is capable of correctly forecasting or controlling future events such as, say, the tossing of a fair coin.

In the first run of such an experiment, no consequence is derived from the agent's capacities despite the mere recording of the data. The second run of the experiment is like the first run, but the *meaning* of the forecasts or controlled events is different. The events are taken as outcomes, e.g., of gambling against other individuals (i) with or (ii) without similar capacities, or against (iii) an anonymous "mechanical" agent such as a casino or a stock exchange. (As a variant of this experiment, the partners or adversaries of the agent are informed about the agent's intentions.)

In the third run of the experiment, the experimenter attempts to counteract the agent's capacities. Let us assume the experimenter has total control over the event. If the agent predicts or attempts to bring about a particular future event, the experimenter causes the event not to happen and so on.

It might be interesting to record just how much the agent's capacities are changed by the setup. An expectation might be defined from a dichotomic observable

$$e(A, i) = \begin{cases} +1 & \text{correct guess} \\ -1 & \text{incorrect guess} \end{cases}$$

where A stands for agent A and i stands for the ith experiment. An expectation function can then be defined as usual by the average over N experiments; i.e.

$$E(A) = \frac{1}{N} \sum_{i=1}^{N} e(A, i).$$

From the first to the second type of experiment it should become more and more unlikely that the agent operates correctly, since his performance is leveled against other agents with more or less the same capacities. The third type of experiment should produce a total anticorrelation. Formally, this should result in a decrease of E when compared to the first round of experiment.

Another, rather subtle deviation from probabilistic laws may be observed if *correlated* events are considered. Just as in the case of quantum entanglement, it may happen that individual components of correlated systems behave totally at random and exhibit more disorder than the system as a whole (Nielsen and Kempe 2001).

If once again one assumes two dichotomic observables $e(A, i)$ and $e(B, i)$ of a correlated subsystem, then the correlation function

$$C(A, B) = \frac{1}{N} \sum_{i=1}^{N} e(A, i) \; e(B, i)$$

and the associated probabilities may give rise to violations of the Boole-Bell inequalities – Boole's *conditions of possible (classical) experience* (Boole 1862, Hailperin 1976, Pitowsky 1989, 1994) – and may even exceed (Krenn and Svozil 1998) the Tsirelson bounds (Cirel'son 1980, Tsirel'son 1987, Cirel'son 1993) for *conditions of possible (quantum) experience*. There, the agent should concentrate on influencing the *coincidences* of the event rather than the single individual events. In such a case, the *individual* observables may behave perfectly random, while the associated *correlations* might be nonclassical and even stronger-than-quantum, and might give rise to highly nonlocal phenomena. As long as the individual events cannot be controlled, this does not need to violate Einstein causality. (But, even then, consistent scenarios remain (Svozil 2000)).

In summary, it can be stated that, although total forecasting and event control are incompatible with free will, more subtle forms of these capacities remain conceivable even beyond the present laws of physics; at least as long as their effects upon the "fabric of phenomena" are consistent. These capacities are characterized by singular events and not by statistically reproducible patterns, which are often encountered under the known laws of physics. Whether or not such capacities exist remains an open question. Nevertheless, despite the elusiveness of the phenomenology involved, it does not appear unreasonable that the hypothesis could be operationalized, tested and even put to use in particular contexts.

2   Quantum Part

2.1   Quantum Information

By coherent superposition, quantum theory manages to implement two classically inconsistent bits of information by one quantum bit. For example, consider the states $|+\rangle$ and $|-\rangle$ associated with the proposition that the spin of an electron in a particular direction is "up" or "down," respectively. The coherent superposition of these two states $(|+\rangle + |-\rangle)/\sqrt{2}$ is a 50:50 mixture of these two classically distinct possibilities and at the same time is a perfect quantum state.

Based upon this feature, we speculate that we may be able to solve some tasks which are classically intractable or even inconsistent by superposing quantum states in a self-consistent manner. In particular, we could speculate that diagonalization tasks using *not*-gates may become feasable, although the capacities of agents within such semi-closed time loops may be limited by requirements of (self-)consistency, which translate into bounds due to unitary quantum time evolution. These quantum consistency requirements, however, may be less restrictive than in the classical case (Svozil 1995a,b).

2.2   Mach-Zehnder Interferometer with Feedback Loop

In what follows we shall consider a Mach-Zehnder interferometer as drawn in Fig. 1 with two input and two output ports (Greenberger et al. 1993). The novel feature of this device is a feedback loop from the future of one output port into the past of an input port. Thereby we leave open the question of such a feedback loop into the past and how it can (if ever) be realized. Indeed, if one dislikes the idea of backwards-in-time communication, one may think of this feedback loop as a channel which, by synchronizing the beams, acts as if a beam from the future enters the input port, while this beam actually was emitted in the past from the output port.

If one merely introduced feedback as in classical electrical engineering, this would defy unitarity, as two input channels would be going into one forward channel, which could not be uniquely reversed. So one needs a feedback coupling that resembles a beam-splitter, as in Fig. 1. The operator

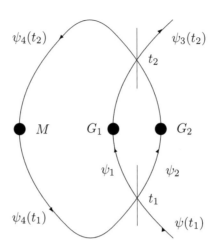

Figure 1: Mach-Zehnder device with backwards-in-time output $\psi_4(t_2)$
which passes M and serves as input $\psi_4(t_1)$.

M generates the effects of the feedback in time. These "beam-splitters" are figurative. Their role is to couple the two incoming channels to two outgoing channels. The operator G_1 represents the ordinary time development in the absence of time feedback. The operator G_2 represents an alternate possible time evolution that can take place and compete with G_1 because there is feedback. We want to find .... in the presence of the feedback in time that is generated by the operator M. At the beam splitters, the forward amplitude is α, while the reflected amplitude is $i\beta$. The beam splitters are shown in Fig. 2. They perform the unitary transformation:

$$\begin{aligned} |a\rangle &= \alpha|d\rangle + i\beta|c\rangle \\ |b\rangle &= \alpha|c\rangle + i\beta|d\rangle \end{aligned} \tag{1}$$

Here we assume for simplicity that α and β are real. We can invert this to obtain:

$$\begin{aligned} |d\rangle &= \alpha|a\rangle - i\beta|b\rangle \\ |c\rangle &= \alpha|b\rangle - i\beta|a\rangle \end{aligned} \tag{2}$$

The overall governing equations can be read from Fig. 2. At time t_2 the second beam-splitter determines $\psi_3(t_2)$ and $\psi_4(t_2)$. We have

$$\psi_3(t_2) \equiv \psi_3' = \alpha\psi_1(t_2) - i\beta\psi_2(t_2) = \alpha\psi_1' - i\beta\psi_2', \tag{3}$$

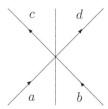

Figure 2: Reflection and transmission through a mirror
with reflection coefficient β and transmission coefficient α.

where the prime indicates the time t_2 in the argument, and no prime indicates
the time t_1. The wave functions ψ_1 and ψ_2 are determined at time t_2 by

$$\psi_1(t_2) \equiv \psi_1' = G_1\psi_1(t_1) = G_1\psi_1, \tag{4}$$
$$\psi_2(t_2) \equiv \psi_2' = G_2\psi_2(t_1) = G_2\psi_2, \tag{5}$$

so that from eq. (3),

$$\psi_3' = \alpha G_1\psi_1 - i\beta G_2\psi_2, \tag{6}$$

and equivalently:

$$\psi_4' = \alpha G_2\psi_2 - i\beta G_1\psi_1 \tag{7}$$

The propagator M is what produces the feedback in time, propagating from
t_2 back to t_1, so that $\psi_4(t_1) = M\psi_4(t_2)$, or

$$\psi_4 = M\psi_4'. \tag{8}$$

At the beamsplitter at t_1, we have:

$$\psi_1 = \alpha\psi - i\beta\psi_4, \tag{9}$$
$$\psi_2 = \alpha\psi_4 - i\beta\psi. \tag{10}$$

2.3 The Solution

First, we want to eliminate the ψ_4 in eqs. (9) and (10), to get equations for
ψ_1 and ψ_2. Then from eq. (6) we can obtain ψ_3'. From eqs. (7) and (8), we
have:

$$\psi_4 = M\psi_4' = \alpha MG_2\psi_2 - i\beta MG_1\psi_1 \tag{11}$$

We plug this into eqs. (9) and (10),

$$\psi_1 = \alpha\psi - i\beta(\alpha MG_2\psi_2 - i\beta MG_1\psi_1), \tag{12}$$
$$\psi_2 = \alpha(\alpha MG_2\psi_2 - i\beta MG_1\psi_1) - i\beta\psi, \tag{13}$$

and rewrite these as:

$$\psi_1 = (1 + \beta^2 MG_1)^{-1}(-i\alpha\beta MG_2)\psi_2 + \alpha(1 + \beta^2 MG_1)^{-1}\psi, \quad (14)$$
$$\psi_2 = (1 - \alpha^2 MG_2)^{-1}(-i\alpha\beta MG_1)\psi_1 - i\beta(1 - \alpha^2 MG_2)^{-1}\psi. \quad (15)$$

These two simultaneous equations must be solved to find ψ_1 and ψ_2 as functions of ψ. To solve for ψ_1, substitute eq. (15) into (14) such that

$$\psi_1 = (1 + \beta^2 MG_1)^{-1}(-i\alpha\beta MG_2)[(1 - \alpha^2 MG_2)^{-1}(-i\alpha\beta MG_1)\psi_1$$
$$-i\beta(1 - \alpha^2 MG_2)^{-1}\psi] + \alpha(1 + \beta^2 MG_1)^{-1}\psi \quad (16)$$

or:

$$[1 + \alpha^2\beta^2(1 + \beta^2 MG_1)^{-1}(MG_2)(1 - \alpha^2 MG_2)^{-1}(MG_1)]\psi_1$$
$$= (1 + \beta^2 MG_1)^{-1}[-\alpha\beta^2 MG_2(1 - \alpha^2 MG_2)^{-1} + \alpha]\psi \quad (17)$$

If we rewrite this as

$$[X]\psi_1 = (Y)^{-1}[Z]\psi, \quad (18)$$

we can simplify the equation as:

$$\begin{aligned} XY &= 1 + \beta^2 MG_1 + \alpha^2\beta^2 MG_2(1 - \alpha^2 MG_2)^{-1}MG_1 \\ &= 1 + \beta^2[1 + (1 - \alpha^2 MG_2)^{-1}\alpha^2 MG_2]MG_1 \\ &= 1 + \beta^2(1 - \alpha^2 MG_2)^{-1}MG_1, \quad (19) \end{aligned}$$

and

$$\begin{aligned} Z &= \alpha(1 - \alpha^2 MG_2)^{-1}(1 - \alpha^2 MG_2 - \beta^2 MG_2) \\ &= \alpha(1 - \alpha^2 MG_2)^{-1}(1 - MG_2). \quad (20) \end{aligned}$$

Thus,

$$\psi_1 = \alpha[1 + \beta^2(1 - \alpha^2 MG_2)^{-1}MG_1]^{-1}(1 - \alpha^2 MG_2)^{-1}(1 - MG_2)\psi. \quad (21)$$

Then, using the identity $A^{-1}B^{-1} = (BA)^{-1}$, we finally obtain

$$\psi_1 = \alpha(1 - \alpha^2 MG_2 + \beta^2 MG_1)^{-1}(1 - MG_2)\psi. \quad (22)$$

We can solve for ψ_2 similarly, by substituting eq. (14) into (15):

$$\psi_2 = -i\beta(1 - \alpha^2 MG_2 + \beta^2 MG_1)^{-1}(1 + MG_1)\psi. \quad (23)$$

Notice that in the denominator terms in eqs. (22) and (23), α and β have reversed the role of the operators they apply to. We can finally use eq. (6) to solve for $\psi_3' = \psi_3(t_2)$:

$$\psi_3(t_2) = [\alpha^2 G_1 D(1 - MG_2) - \beta^2 G_2 D(1 + MG_1)]\psi(t_1), \quad (24)$$

where $D = (1 + \beta^2 MG_1 - \alpha^2 MG_2)^{-1}$.

2.4   Important Special Cases

(i) For commuting M, G_1 and G_2, $D = \beta^2(1 + MG_1) + \alpha^2(1 - MG_2)$, and

$$\psi_3' = \frac{\alpha^2 G_1 - \beta^2 G_2 - MG_1 G_2}{1 + \beta^2 MG_1 - \alpha^2 MG_2}\psi(t_1). \tag{25}$$

(ii) For $\alpha = 1$, $\beta = 0$, there is no feedback. Here

$$\psi_3' = G_1(1 - MG_2)^{-1}(1 - MG_2)\psi = G_1\psi. \tag{26}$$

(iii) For $\beta = 1$, $\alpha = 0$, there is only feedback. Here

$$\psi_3' = -G_2(1 + MG_1)^{-1}(1 + MG_1)\psi = -G_2\psi. \tag{27}$$

(iv) $G_1 = G_2 \equiv G$:

$$\psi_3' = G[1 + (\beta^2 - \alpha^2)MG]^{-1}(\alpha^2 - \beta^2 - MG)\psi. \tag{28}$$

(iv') If also $\alpha^2 = \beta^2 = \frac{1}{2}$, then

$$\psi_3' = -GMG\psi. \tag{29}$$

(v) If $\beta \ll 1$, which is expected to be the usual case, then the solution only depends on $\beta^2 = \gamma$. Also, $\alpha^2 = 1 - \beta^2 = 1 - \gamma$. Then, to lowest order in γ, the denominator D in eq. (24) becomes

$$\begin{aligned} D &= [1 + \gamma MG_1 - (1 - \gamma)MG_2]^{-1} \\ &= (1 - MG_2)^{-1} - \gamma(1 - MG_2)^{-1}(MG_1 + MG_2)(1 - MG_2)^{-1} \end{aligned} \tag{30}$$

so that

$$\begin{aligned} \psi_3' &= \{(1 - \gamma)G_1[1 - \gamma(1 - MG_2)^{-1}(MG_1 + MG_2)]\}\psi \\ &\quad - \{\gamma G_2(1 - MG_2)^{-1}(1 + MG_1)\}\psi \\ &= [G_1 - \gamma(G_1 + G_2)(1 - MG_2)(1 + MG_1)]\psi. \end{aligned} \tag{31}$$

(vi) The case that corresponds to the classical paradox that an agent shoots his father before he has met the agent's mother, so that the agent can never be born, has an interesting quantum-mechanical resolution. This is the case $G_1 = 0$, where there is a perfect absorber in the beam so that the system would never get to evolve to time t_2. But quantum mechanically, there is another path along G_2, at which the agent does not shoot his father, that has a probability β without feedback. The solution in this case is

$$\psi_3' = -\beta^2 G_2(1 - \alpha^2 MG_2)^{-1}\psi. \tag{32}$$

We assume for simplicity that G_2 is the standard time evolution operator

$$G_2 = e^{-iE(t_2-t_1)/\hbar}, \tag{33}$$

and M is the simplest backwards-in-time evolution operator

$$M = e^{-iE(t_1-t_2)/\hbar+i\varphi}, \tag{34}$$

where we have also allowed for an extra phase shift. Then

$$\begin{aligned}
\psi_3' &= -\beta e^{-iE(t_2-t_1)/\hbar}[1-\alpha^2 e^{i\varphi}]^{-1}\psi, \\
|\psi_3'|^2 &= \frac{\beta^4}{(1-\alpha^2 e^{i\varphi})(1-\alpha^2 e^{-i\varphi})}|\psi|^2 \\
&= \frac{1}{1+4(\alpha^2/\beta^2)\sin^2(\varphi/2)}|\psi|^2.
\end{aligned} \tag{35}$$

Note that for $\varphi = 0$, $\psi_3' = -e^{-iE\Delta t/\hbar}\psi$ for *any* value of β. This means that no matter how small the probability that the agent ever reached here in the first place, the fact that he *is* here ($\alpha \neq 1$) guarantees that, even though he is certain to have shot his father if he had met him ($G_1 = 0$), the agent will not have met him! The agent will have taken the other path with 100% certainty.

How can we understand this result? In our model, with $\varphi = 0$, we have $G_1 = 0$, and $MG_2 = 1$. Also, we will assume that $\beta \ll 1$, even though this is not necessary. The various amplitudes are

$$\begin{aligned}
|\psi_1| = 0, \quad |\psi_2/\psi| = 1/\beta, \\
|\psi_4/\psi| = \alpha/\beta, \quad |\psi_3'/\psi| = 1.
\end{aligned} \tag{36}$$

So we see that the two paths of the beam-splitter at t_1 leading to the path ψ_1 cancel out. But of the beam ψ, α passes through, while of the beam ψ_4, only β leaks through. So the beam ψ_4 must have a very large amplitude, which it does, as we can see from eqs. (36). In fact, it has a much larger amplitude than the original beam. Similarly, in order that $|\psi_3'| = |\psi|$, ψ_2 must have a very large amplitude. Thus we see that there is a large current flowing around the system, between ψ_2 and ψ_4. But does this not violate unitarity? The answer is that if they were both running forward in time, it would. But one of these currents is running forward in time, while the other runs backward in time, and so they do not in this case violate unitarity. This is how our solution is possible.

So, according to our quantum model, if one could travel into the past, one would only see those alternatives consistent with the world one left. In other words, while one could see the past, one could not change it. No matter how unlikely the events are that could have led to one's present circumstances, once they have actually occurred, they cannot be changed. One's trip would set up resonances that are consistent with the future that has already unfolded.

This also has consequences for the paradoxes of free will. It shows that it is perfectly logical to assume that one has many choices and that one is free to take any one of them. Until a choice is taken, the future is not determined. However, once a choice is taken, it was inevitable. It could not have been otherwise. So, looking backwards, the world is deterministic. However, looking forwards, the future is probabilistic.

The model also has consequences concerning a many worlds interpretation of quantum theory. The world may appear to keep splitting so far as the future is concerned, however once a measurement is made, only those histories consistent with that measurement are possible. In other words, with time travel, other alternative worlds do not exist, as once a measurement has been made, they would be impossible to reach from the original one.

Another interesting point comes from examining eq. (35). For small angles φ we see that

$$|\psi'_3|^2 = \frac{1}{1 + 4\frac{\alpha^2}{\beta^4}\sin^2(\varphi/2)}|\psi|^2 \rightarrow \frac{1}{1 + \frac{\alpha^2\varphi^2}{\beta^4}}|\psi|^2, \tag{37}$$

so that the above result is strongly resonant, with a Lorentzian shape, and a width $\Delta\varphi \approx \beta^2$, since $\alpha \approx 1$. Thus less "deterministic" and fuzzier time-travelling might be possible.

(vii) Sustained case: if we require the input and output state to be identical, i.e. $\psi_3(t_2) = \psi(t_1)$, then we obtain a sustainment condition (for commuting M, G_1, G_2) of

$$1 = G_1(\alpha^2 - \beta^2 M) + G_2(\alpha^2 M - \beta^2) - MG_1G_2. \tag{38}$$

Another case is $G_1 = G_2 = 1$, a phase shift in $M = e^{i\varphi}$, and $\alpha = \beta = 1/\sqrt{2}$, for which we obtain $|\psi'_3| = |\psi|$. For $\beta = \sqrt{1 - \alpha^2} = 1/4$,

$$|\psi'_3| = \frac{112 - 113\cos\varphi - 15i\sin\varphi}{54|1 - 7e^{i\varphi}/8|^2}|\psi|. \tag{39}$$

We summarize by stating that the structure of a quantum time travel through a Mach-Zehnder device is rich and unexpectedly elaborate. This suggests totally new szenarios for the possibility of free will and the capacities available to an agent acting in such a time loop.

References

Anderson A.R. (1970): Paul's epistle to Titus. In *The Paradox of the Liar*, ed. by R.L. Martin, Yale University Press, New Haven. The Bible contains a passage which refers to Epimenides, a Crete living in the capital city of Cnossus: "One of themselves, a prophet of their own, said, 'Cretans are always liars, evil beasts, lazy gluttons'.", St. Paul, Epistle to Titus I (12–13).

Boole G. (1862): On the theory of probabilities. *Philosophical Transactions of the Royal Society of London* **152**, 225–252.

Chaitin G.J. (1992): *Information-Theoretic Incompleteness*, World Scientific, Singapore.

Cirel'son B.S. (1980): Quantum generalizations of Bell's inequality. *Letters in Mathematical Physics* **4**, 93–100.

Tsirel'son B.S. (= Cirel'son) (1987): Quantum analogues of the Bell inequalities. The case of two spatially separated domains. *Journal of Soviet Mathematics* **36**(4), ...–....

Csirel'son B.S. (1993): Some results and problems on quantum Bell-type inequalities. *Hadronic Journal Supplement* **8**, 329–345.

Davis M. (1965): *The Undecidable*, Raven Press, New York.

Feferman S., Dawson J.W., Kleene S.C., Moore G.H., Solovay R.M., and van Heijenoort J., eds. (1986): *Kurt Gödel, Collected Works. Publications 1929-1936. Volume I*, Oxford University Press, Oxford.

Frank P. (1932): *Das Kausalgesetz und seine Grenzen*, Springer, Vienna.

Friedman J., Morris M.-S., Novikov I.-D., Echeverria F., Klinkhammer G., Thorne K.S., and Yurtsever U. (1990): Cauchy problem in spacetimes with closed timelike curves. *Physical Review D* **42**, 1915–1930.

Gödel K. (1931): Über formal unentscheidbare Sätze der Principia Mathematica und verwandter Systeme. *Monatshefte für Mathematik und Physik* **38**, 173–198. English translation in Feferman et al. (1986) and in Davis (1965).

Greenberger D.B. and YaSin A. (1989): "Haunted" measurements in quantum theory. *Foundation of Physics* **19**, 679–704.

Greenberger D.B., Horne M., and Zeilinger A. (1993): Multiparticle interferometry and the superposition principle. *Physics Today* **46**, 22–29.

Hailperin T. (1976): *Boole's Logic and Probability*, North-Holland, Amsterdam.

Herzog T.J., Kwiat P.G., Weinfurter H., and Zeilinger A. (1995): Complementarity and the quantum eraser. *Physical Review Letters* **75**, 3034–3037.

Hilbert D. (1926): Über das Unendliche. *Mathematische Annalen* **95**, 161–190.

Jung C.G. (1952): Synchronizität als ein Prinzip akausaler Zusammenhänge. In *Naturerklärung und Psyche*, ed. by C.G. Jung and W. Pauli, Rascher, Zürich.

Krenn G. and Svozil K. (1998): Stronger-than-quantum correlations. *Foundations of Physics* **28**, 971–984.

Nahin P.J. (1998): *Time Travel*, second edition, Springer, New York.

Nielsen M.A. and Kempe J. (2001): Separable states are more disordered globally than locally. *Physical Review Letters* **86**, 5184–5187.

Pitowsky I. (1989): *Quantum Probability – Quantum Logic*, Springer, Berlin.

Pitowsky I. (1994): George Boole's 'conditions of possible experience' and the quantum puzzle. *Brit. J. Phil. Sci.* **45**, 95–125.

Svozil K. (1993): *Randomness & Undecidability in Physics*, World Scientific, Singapore.

Svozil K. (1995a): On the computational power of physical systems, undecidability, the consistency of phenomena and the practical uses of paradoxa. In *Fundamental Problems in Quantum Theory: A Conference Held in Honor of Professor John A. Wheeler. Annals of the New York Academy of Sciences* **755**, ed. by D. M. Greenberger and A. Zeilinger, Academy of Sciences, New York, pp. 834–841.

Svozil K. (1995b): Consistent use of paradoxes in deriving contraints on the dynamics of physical systems and of no-go-theorems. *Foundations of Physics Letters* **8**, 523–535.

Svozil K. (1996): Undecidability everywhere? In *Boundaries and Barriers. On the Limits to Scientific Knowledge*, Addison-Wesley, Reading, pp. 215–237.

Svozil K. (2000): Relativizing relativity. *Foundations of Physics* **30**, 1001–1016.

Toffoli T. (1978): The role of the observer in uniform systems. In *Applied General Systems Research*, ed. by G. Klir, Plenum Press, New York, pp. ...–....

Turing A.M. (1936/1937): On computable numbers, with an application to the Entscheidungsproblem. *Proceedings of the London Mathematical Society, Series 2,* **42** and **43**, 230–265 and 544–546. Reprinted in Davis (1965).

Wheeler J.A. and Zurek W.H., eds. (1983): *Quantum Theory and Measurement,* Princeton University Press, Princeton.

Wheeler J.A. (1983): Law without law. In *Quantum Theory and Measurement,* ed. by J.A. Wheeler and W.H. Zurek, Princeton University Press, Princeton, pp. 182–213.

Wigner E.P. (1961): Remarks on the mind-body question. In *The Scientist Speculates,* ed. by I.J. Good Basic Books, New York, pp. 284–302. Reprinted in Wheeler and Zurek (1983) pp. 168–181.

What is Determinism?

Phil Dowe

Abstract

Many people worry about determinism in connection to free will. For them, whether or not my decision to go drinking tonight is determined – for example by factors such as my genes or upbringing – is important to whether or not that decision is free. In this paper I address this 'folk' notion of determinism which raises problems for some in relation to free will. I leave aside the question what is free will and whether it is compatible with determinism. My methodology in examining this concept will be to consider various hypothetical situations, and invite the reader to agree that the folk worriers would or would not feel the worry in those circumstances. (Although I think such questions are scientific questions, requiring sociological research, I offer the following as speculation in the absence of such evidence.) I will use these results as evidence for or against various analyses of determinism. I begin with an outline of a 'standard' approach to this question. Whether this indeed is standard is not of concern – even if it is a strawperson it will still be instructive.

1 The Standard Approach

According to the standard approach we should look to science to establish whether the world is indeed deterministic. But before we do this, we must establish what we mean by determinism. This in itself is a philosophical controversy. In order to fix a rough idea consider a box of gas molecules or a box of billiard balls in space or whatever. This box represents a deterministic system just if the state of the system, which specifies for example all the positions and momenta of the molecules, fixes the state at all later times. Or, we could say, all later times and all previous times. The relevant sense of 'fixes', of course, needs explaining.

With this rough picture in place, goes the standard approach, we can turn to the alternative theories. There are four. The first is the causal theory, captured by the maxim 'every event has a cause', or perhaps 'every event has a sufficient cause'. So according to this theory, folk worriers are concerned if my decision to go drinking tonight is caused by factors such as my genes or upbringing.

There are a number of standard objections to the causal theory. One is that it requires an account of causation, which is problematic. As Earman puts it, "it explains a vague concept – determinism – in terms of a truly obscure one – causation" (Earman 1986, p. 5). Another objection sometimes raised at this point is that causation is asymmetric with respect to time – causes occur before their effects – whereas determinism is a symmetric notion, as we saw with the case of the box of gas molecules.

A second theory of determinism is Popper's predictability theory. A system is deterministic if and only if all its states are predicable by the right kind of being with knowledge of the present state and the laws of nature. For Popper the "right kind of being", which he sometimes calls the superscientist, is itself part of the universe, with a large but finite capacity for knowledge. The usual objection to this view is that it confuses epistemology with ontology – predictability being an epistemic notion and determinism being an ontological matter (cf. Atmanspacher in this volume), as illustrated by the fact that it makes deterministic chaotic systems indeterministic.

A third theory is the mathematical function theory of Russell. On this account the universe is deterministic just if there exists a functional relation relating variables at a given time to variables at all other times. Russell writes (Russell 1913, p. 18):

> A system is said to be 'deterministic' when, given certain data $e_1, e_2, ..., e_n$ at times $t_1, t_2, ..., t_n$, respectively, concerning this system, if E_t is the state of the system at any time t, there is a functional relation of the form $E_t = f(e_1, t_1, e_2, t_2, ..., e_n, t_n, t)$. The system will be 'deterministic throughout the given period' if t, in the above formula, may be any time within that period, though outside that period the formula may be no longer true. If the universe as a whole is such a system, determinism is true of the universe; if not, not.

A problem with this account, that Russell himself notes, is that it holds, trivially, of any possible world. Any possible set of data admits of a function, however complex, of the above form. But determinism is contingent – it is possible that the world is deterministic and it is possible that world is not.

The fourth account utilizes the notion of physical necessity. In the modal-nomic theory of Earman a physically possible world W is deterministic just if for any other physically possible world W', if W and W' agree at any time then they agree at all times (Earman 1986, p. 13). The difficulty facing this view is to give an account of laws. For an empiricist like Earman, this means providing an account of the distinction between accidental and nomological regularities. Nevertheless, an account like this would be the front runner for the appropriate theory of determinism.

Having answered the question what is determinism, so the standard picture goes, we can now turn to science to settle whether the world is relevantly deterministic.

2   The Asymmetry of Determinism

However, I would argue that the standard picture has already changed the topic. A slide has occurred in the above reasoning. We began asking about the concept of determinism as it appears as the object of people's concerns in relation to free will, and we ended up with an answer more appropriate as an account of what is determinism as it appears in science. The two concepts may not be the same, and indeed I will argue that they are different with respect to a key notion of symmetry/asymmetry in time. Folk determinism is asymmetric whereas scientific concepts based on functions, laws, or predictability are all probably symmetric in time, given our current understanding of scientific laws. It is therefore evidence for this slide that the causal theory was, in the standard picture, taken to be defective on account of its asymmetry. I will now give three arguments for the conclusion that the folk concept of determinism is asymmetric.

(1) The first argument concerns retrodiction, i.e. prediction of past events. Retrodiction of our actions or decisions does not concern us in the way that determinism does. Suppose I am told that given that I have a hangover, in the circumstances, someone can predict with 100% certainty that I decided to go for a drink last night. This does not raise any concerns in relation to my free will in deciding to go for a drink. It just means that my choice was predicted by its effects, not that my choice was determined.

It follows, firstly, that retrodiction is not a case of determinism, and that, since retrodiction is prediction, that determinism is not predictability. Secondly, the problem is the asymmetry of determinism. Prediction is symmetric with respect to time, since the notion of predictability is based on laws of nature which we take to be symmetric in time. But our example illustrates that although we do not worry about our actions or decisions being predicted in the past, the same does not apply from the future. Hence we have reason to think that the folk notion of determinism is asymmetric with respect to time.

(2) The second argument concerns necessary causes. This argument is related to the first, but here I focus on the modal-nomic theory rather than

predictability. The point is that the mere fact that my choice or action leads to something that could not have come about any other way in the circumstances does not mean that my free will has been violated. Suppose my father sends me money for an air-ticket to Spain. I am poor, such that there is no way in the circumstances that I could have gone to Spain apart from my father's generosity. I decide to go. His sending the money is a necessary (but not sufficient) cause of my going to Spain. Then there will be no physically possible world in which I go to Spain identical to our world at the time of my going to Spain, in which I am not sent money by my father. It follows from the appropriate refinement of the modal-nomic theory that my father's sending the money is determined. But no folk worrier would thereby be concerned about my father's free will in sending me the money or his choice to do so, I claim.

Therefore the modal-nomic theory of determinism is false. Again, the problem is asymmetry. The laws behind the modal-nomic theory are symmetric in time, the folk notion of determinism is not. An objection here might go as follows. The only way the child's life could be saved was if I dove into the river, which I did, saving the child. I say, I felt compelled, I had to do it, I had no choice. Given this, we might conclude that cases where my action or decision is a necessary cause of an outcome do in and of themselves raise exactly the kind of worry that folk have in connection with free will, and that my previous argument is wrong.

However, I think this objection fails. The compulsion here is not from the future. Rather it arises from my own past mental states, anticipating the future. Seeing that there was no other way the child could be saved and not wanting that to happen, I was compelled by my own past thoughts, desires and character to do what I did. Whether this is free will or not I leave aside, but it is not a worry that arises on account of the mere fact that my action is a necessary cause.

(3) The third argument concerns overdetermination. I have argued that certain cases where future events physically necessitate, or allow 100% reliable prediction of, earlier decisions or actions are not cases of determinism in the folk sense. However, it is conceivable that there is such a case. Suppose I take seriously the claim that my decision to go drinking tonight is caused by the action of a voodoo doctor next Sunday. (More discussion will be given below about the significance of such a possibility for my thesis of the asymmetry of determinism.) Suppose I am also told that that same decision is caused by my genes and upbringing. Then I have a prima facie worry about overdetermination. How can something be determined by a future event and by a past event? It would be doubly determined.

But that is always so in normal deterministic contexts on the scientific approaches to determinism. I am referring now to cases where we do not have the worry about the future determining my choice. Predictability, mathematical functions, and modal-nomic accounts all entail that in deterministic contexts an action is overdetermined, yet we do not feel the same prima facie worry about overdetermination. Again, the problem lies in the fact that these are symmetric while the folk notion of determinism is asymmetric with respect to time.

I conclude from this discussion that we need a notion of determinism which is asymmetric in time. The causal account is the only account among those listed above that has this feature. Our world is such that causes generally if not always precede their effects, although it is conceivable that they do not. Thus, on the causal theory of determinism, our world is such that the past generally if not always determines my actions or decisions if anything does, although it is conceivable that something future might. The asymmetry of determinism evident in the folk notion derives from the asymmetry of causation.

I, therefore, consider the notion of causation in more detail. First, however, a possible reply on behalf of the scientific theories of determinism. Could we define folk determinism as the future oriented aspect of the scientific notion of determinism? For example, let determinism occur when there is physical necessitation of an event by past factors.

This would indeed secure a notion of determinism which is asymmetric in time. However, it is too strong, because it makes it analytic that my actions are only determined by past factors. This rules out a priori even the conceptual possibility of being determined by the future. But it seems conceivable that there are cases like the voodoo doctor, and in such a case worries about determinism would arise. Thus forcing the asymmetry 'by hand' is too strong a result.

The kind of asymmetry we seek is what we get with causation – mostly causes precede their effects, although it is conceptually possible and perhaps occasionally actual that some backward causation occurs (Dowe 2000, Chap. 8).

3   The Contingency of Determinism

Another requirement of a satisfactory theory of determinism is contingency. As we have already noted, our theory must make it possible that the world is deterministic and possible that it is not, and it was an objection to Russell's functional theory that it makes determinism a necessary feature of all possible worlds. There are different ways to secure determinism's contingency, on a causal theory. One, the simplest, is that (local) determinism is the case where my decision or action is caused by particular factors, and indeterminism is the case where it is uncaused. Globally, a deterministic world is one where every event has a cause, and indeterminism is where some events have no cause. Thus we would need to look to science to determine whether the world is such that every event has a cause, and in particular whether my actions or decisions always have causes.

A second way that the contingency of determinism could be secured on the causal theory is if causation comes in degrees. Then we could define the deterministic case as that where the causes of my action/decision are jointly a sufficient cause, and indeterminism as the case where the causes do not amount to a sufficient cause. Globally, a deterministic world is one where every event has a sufficient cause, and indeterminism is where some events have no cause or just an insufficient cause. Then we would need to look to science to determine whether the world is such that my actions or decisions always have sufficient causes.

A third possibility, to my knowledge not previously noticed, is where the determinism/indeterminism divide is drawn somewhere short of sufficiency, and perhaps is vague and/or context dependent. Again, this requires that causation comes in degrees. Then we could define the deterministic case as that where the causes of my action/decision jointly cause to a certain degree, say 70%, and indeterminism as the case where the causes jointly cause to less than degree 70%. Then we would need to look to science to determine whether the world is such that my actions or decisions always have causes of that strength. But what degree of causal efficacy should in fact define the determinism/indeterminism divide? I take it that on this proposal we simply survey folk to see which cases raise worries in connection with free will. This will almost certainly be vague and may even turn out to be context dependent. It is also possible that the worry itself comes in degrees.

This indicates how we should determine which of these three ways of securing the contingency of determinism is correct. Suppose we have a case where my decision to go for a drink tonight is determined to degree 95% by my genes and environmental factors in my past. Does this case raise the folk worry about determinism in connection to free will? I suggest that it does raise the same kind of worry as the 100% case, and if there is a difference it is just a matter of degree.

Now the first option – that indeterminism is where there is no cause at all – if it allows causation by degrees, will understand this as a case of causation but not determinism. Or if it does not allow causation by degrees, it will understand this as a case neither of causation nor determinism. Either way it gets the wrong result – since the case does raise the appropriate folk worry in connection to free will. The second option – the most common amongst contemporary philosophers – also gets the wrong result, since it takes the 95% case to be a case of indeterministic causation.

I conclude that the third option is the appropriate way to secure the contingency of determinism. This means that to get a satisfactory causal theory of determinism, we need a notion of causation which admits causation by degree. Further, we would require the relation between deterministic and indeterministic causation to be transparent.

4 Theories of Causation

We now turn to the question what is causation. We have already seen the objection that the causal theory replaces a vague concept with an obscure one, so to defend the causal theory we have the obligation to spell out a concept of causation in such a way that meets this objection. Further, we have a number of desiderata which would have to be met by a concept of causation adequate for a causal theory of determinism. We need to get the right kind of asymmetry in time and the right kind of contingency. In this section I will survey a few theories to see if they meet our criteria.

(1) Regularity Theory. This is the most famous account of causation, the conventional reading of Hume, known as the regularity theory of causation. According to this account there are two essential conditions for singular causation. Occurring event c is the cause of occurring event e just if (a) there is a relation of priority – c occurs before e; and (b) there is a relation of sufficiency – in fact all cases of C-type events are followed by E-type events.

There is nothing obscure about any of the elements in this theory, so it meets Earman's objection. But there are two problems with Hume's account as an account of causation which can underpin the causal theory of determinism. The first problem is priority, the second sufficiency. Priority gives the wrong kind of temporal asymmetry of determinism, since it makes it analytic that my action/decision is not determined by future factors. I have argued that this is too strong a solution. Sufficiency gives the wrong kind of contingency, since because it does not allow indeterministic causation it entails that indeterminism must be the case where there is no cause. For instance, it entails that the 95% case is not a case of causation, thus not a case of determinism. As argued above, this is not the folk notion of determinism.

(2) Process Theory. According to Salmon and myself, causation is a matter of the network of causal processes and interactions (Salmon 1998, Dowe 2000). A causal process is the worldline of an object which (on Salmon's version) transmits a conserved quantity – such as momentum or mass-energy – and a causal interaction is an intersection between causal processes involving an exchange of a conserved quantity. The distinction between a cause and an effect is given by the fork theory – the direction of a causal process is determined by any open conjunctive fork which it partly constitutes (Dowe 2000, Chap. 8).

The notion of a conjunctive fork is due originally to Reichenbach. Simplifying for the sake of exposition, a conjunctive fork may be defined as a set of three events A, B and C such that (see Salmon 1984, pp. 159–160):

$$P(A \cdot B) \quad > \quad P(A)P(B) \tag{1}$$
$$P(A \cdot B | C) \quad = \quad P(A|C)P(B|C) \tag{2}$$

Equation (1) expresses a statistical correlation between two events, namely, that they are not independent. Equation (2) expresses a 'screening-off' relation, where a third event C is found that when accounted for, renders A and B independent (cf. the contribution by Berkovitz, this volume). Together, such a set of events form a conjunctive fork. Reichenbach defined a 'closed fork', as a fork with screening-off events in the past and in the future. A fork not screened off in both directions Reichenbach calls an open fork. This account gives the right kind of temporal asymmetry. Conceptually, open forks can be open either to the future or the past. However, as a matter of fact here are no, or very few, conjunctive forks open to the past. Correlations in fact are never screened off by a future event, except where they are also screened off by a past event.

But the process theory scores poorly on another score. It provides no account of how causation comes in degrees, and hence no satisfactory account of the contingency of determinism. It could, without any elaboration, allow a definition of indeterminism as the absence of causation, but as we have seen this gives the wrong account of determinism's contingency.

(3) Counterfactual Theory. According to the counterfactual theory of Lewis (1986), occurring event c causes occurring event e if either there is a relation of counterfactual dependence such that were c not to occur, e would not occur; or there is a relation of probabilistic dependence, such that if the chance of e were c to occur is p, and the chance of e were c not to occur is q, where $p \gg q$.

This is usually taken to give a relation for determinism – counterfactual dependence – and a relation for causation under indeterminism – probabilistic dependence (although Lewis himself notes that counterfactual dependence works for some cases of indeterminism).

There are two problems with this account. First, it makes the relation between deterministic and indeterministic causation obscure. Counterfactual dependence is indeed one kind of "deterministic limit" – hopefully it will be equivalent to the case where q is zero, i.e. the chance of the effect were the cause not to occur is zero. But it is easy to see that this is the wrong limit for the folk notion of determinism. We want determinism to be where p – the chance of e were c to occur – to be 1 or at least to meet the appropriate standards. But counterfactual dependence is independent of the value of p.

To use a previous example for a different purpose, suppose my father sends me money for an air ticket to go to Spain, without which I could not go. Suppose I cannot decide, so I roll a die intending to go only if I roll 6. I roll 6 and decide to go to Spain. My father's sending me the money is a necessary but insufficient cause of my going to Spain. There is a relation of counterfactual dependence, and also a relation of probabilistic dependence since $q = 0$ and $p < 1/6$. Thus we have, on Lewis' account, a case of causation where the deterministic limit holds (counterfactual dependence and $q = 0$). But it is the wrong limit for the folk notion of determinism, since no worry arises that my father coerces me or in some way violates my free will. The appropriate deterministic limit would be where $p = 1$ or meets high enough standards.

A second problem with Lewis' account stems from his account of counterfactual chance. According to Lewis chance – i.e. objective single case chance – is time and world dependent such that the chance of A at time t obtains in virtue of the history of the world up to t. This entails that the chance of actual past events is always 1 and that the chance of non-actual past events is always 0. But this makes it analytic on the probabilistic dependence account that causes precede their effects, and thus that my actions/decisions are never determined by future factors. This is also at odds with the sophisticated semantics for counterfactuals that Lewis provides in terms of his notorious "similarity" measure across worlds, which allows for the possibility of backward causation on the counterfactual dependence account. We need a similarly sophisticated account of chance which secures the same kind of asymmetry – Lewis notes the problem, but unfortunately gives us no clues about how to solve it.

5   A Suggestion: Causal Chances

I propose that we start with a symmetric notion of chance. Take, for example, the account in Mellor (1995). The chance of B contingent on A – written $\mathrm{ch}_A(B)$ – is also contingent on the local circumstances S of A, and has as its truthmakers the local instantiations of laws. Since to the best of our knowledge the laws of nature are time symmetric, this means chance is time symmetric. Events will have chances contingent on future events in their local circumstances. Thus there will be no temporal asymmetry of chances.

Second, we can define causal chances as the chances which causes in their circumstances give their effects, $\mathrm{ch}_c(e)$ in S. Thus some, but not all, chances will be causal chances. For example, consider the chances that effects give their causes. Such chances exist and (in my view) need to be equal to 1, but will not be causal chances on the above definition. Thus, since there is an asymmetry of causation, there will be a temporal asymmetry of causal chances. They will in fact usually if not always point towards the future, although it is conceptually possible that they do not.

We can define determinism/indeterminism as follows. Event E (e.g. my decision or action) is determined if the chance that E's causes give E is one, or of the appropriate standard. E is not determined if it has no cause or if the chance that E's causes give E is not of the appropriate standard.

This, however, still requires an account of causation. But now we may appeal to the process theory, since it gives the appropriate temporal asymmetry of causation, and it would not need to tell us about the degree of causation since our concept of chance does that.

Then we have the result that E is determined if the chance that E's causes give E is of the appropriate standard, where E's causes are related to E by a set of causal processes and interactions partly constituting various forks. The contingency of the fork asymmetry secures the appropriate temporal asymmetry, while the definition of determinism in terms of causal chances secures the right kind of contingency for determinism.

References

Dowe P. (2000): *Physical Causation*, Cambridge University Press, New York.

Earman J. (1986): *A Primer on Determinism*, Reidel, Dordrecht.

Lewis D. (1986): *Philosophical Papers, Vol. II*, Oxford University Press, New York.

Mellor D. (1995): *The Facts of Causation*, Routledge, London.

Russell B. (1913): On the Notion of 'Cause'. *Proceedings of the Aristotelian Society* **13**, 1–26.

Salmon W. (1984): *Scientific Explanation and the Causal Structure of the World*, Princeton University Press, Princeton.

Salmon W. (1998): *Causality and Explanation*, Oxford University Press, New York.

Ontological Presuppositions
of the Determinism–Free Will Debate

Charles Guignon

1

The current philosophical debate about free will must look extremely bizarre to nonphilosophers. The question of free will is generally posed by presenting one or two jejune and thinly described examples of supposed free agency. We are told, for example, to consider what is involved in lifting one's arm, or to imagine a case where a Mr. Green shoots and kills a Ms. Peacock. Our natural inclination in such cases is to assume that the action has been performed through the agent's free will. The debate then shifts to reviewing facts about neurological processes or to examining counterexamples to the claim that the action is the result of free will. In this stage of the argument, we are asked to imagine cases where strange interventions have occurred in the agent's central nervous system, or where brainwashing has turned the agent into a sort of zombie. These suppositions and scenarios have a certain charm to them, and the whole line of reasoning might be said to have some relevance for rather specialized questions in forensics. But as providing insight into our actual, day-to-day experience of agency, the whole business seems far too arcane and byzantine to have any real interest.

A number of philosophers in the phenomenological and hermeneutic traditions – I am thinking of such figures as Heidegger, Merleau-Ponty, Wittgenstein, Taylor and Dreyfus – have tried to diagnose this feeling of a disconnect between mainstream philosophical investigations and actual life. What these phenomenologists have in common is a shared belief that mainstream philosophy, quite unknowingly, tends to operate with a set of uncritical ontological assumptions about our human condition, assumptions that load the dice in advance in favor of the conclusions that follow. In their modern form, these assumptions are drawn from the worldview formulated by modern science – the view Dennett calls the "default setting" of contemporary philosophy.[1]

---

[1] Dennett (1993, p. 214) speaks of "the conservative default ontology" of contemporary

What hermeneutic phenomenologists suggest is not that science is wrong, but rather that the view of reality we get from science, for all its great advantages, gives us a distorted view of things when it is applied to our everyday, pretheoretical lives. On this view, if we can get clear about the nature of our everyday lives, we will also see that what we initially took to be free will is not really what we want when we speak of valuing freedom. In what follows, I want to show how this phenomenological diagnosis might transform the contours of the free will versus determinism debate.

2

As few phenomenologists have addressed the free will issue in the terms in which it is currently discussed, we should begin by looking at how the issue is currently conceived. I think the best way to understand what philosophers have in mind when they speak of free will is found in Kane's notion of ultimate responsibility, his condition UR (Kane 1996, p. 35: see also Kane's contribution in this volume). The core idea behind UR is the idea of *origination*. To say that an agent is responsible for specific events or states is to say that the ultimate *source* or *origin* of those events or states lies in the agent and not in something other than the agent. This notion of ultimate responsibility captures the idea of *being in control* that is central to the notion of free will. It is the idea that, no matter what causal factors may be operating on me, the decisive and determining impetus for my decision and the action that follows from it comes from my own freely made choice. William Ernest Henley captured this notion of control in the lines that Timothy McVeigh chose for his last words: "I am the master of my fate; I am the captain of my soul."

The idea that individuals are in many cases ultimately responsible for their choices underlies our feeling that we can hold them morally responsible for their actions. Pereboom (2001, p. 4) emphasizes this notion of moral responsibility in his construal of the concept of ultimate responsibility:

> If an agent is morally responsible for her deciding to perform an action, then the production of this decision must be something over which the agent has control, and an agent is not morally responsible for the decision if it is produced by a source over which she has no control.

---

reductionist naturalism, according to which "patterns are patterns of prior elements, even if you don't know what those elements are (yet)." Alternatively, in *The Intentional Stance* (Dennett 1987, p. 5) he says that "the objective, third-person world of physical sciences" he adopts "is the orthodox choice today in the English-speaking world."

Though the notion of ultimate responsibility is clearly a necessary condition for free agency, it might not be regarded as a sufficient condition. For freedom in the sense that implies moral responsibility also seems to presuppose that the agent could have done otherwise, that is to say, that there were alternate possibilities open to the agent so that he or she could have done otherwise. Thus, it seems that a full account of free will should include the ideas of both ultimate responsibility and alternative possibilities.

The philosophical problem of free will arises when we take into consideration the principle of efficient causality, a principle that seems indubitable to many philosophers. According to this principle, every event has a cause, and the fully specified cause of any event determines that the event occurs in just the way it does. The physical determinism that most impresses philosophers holds that, for any event that occurs at a given time, that event is rendered inevitable by the state of the universe at some prior time together with the laws of physics. Since human actions are events, they must be caused by antecedent events, and those causal events are themselves caused by earlier events, and so on. It follows that any action can be seen as the effect of a causal chain stretching back through the history of the universe to a time before the agent came into being. And if this is the case, it seems to follow that every action is caused by events that are outside the control of the agent. In other words, contrary to our natural assumptions, there is no free will, and hence there is no moral responsibility.

So far as I have been able to see, most philosophers who deal with the problem of free will accept the truth of determinism, but contend that even if determinism is true, humans have something very much like moral responsibility. The principle of universal determination seems so central to our rationality that most philosophers cling to it even though it seems to imply manifest absurdities. For example, it seems to imply that Shakespeare's *Hamlet* has the exact form it has because of causal factors operating on Shakespeare over which he had no control, with the result that it is a mistake to praise Shakespeare for this play. Again, it seems to imply that cultivation or *Bildung*, the very process by which we try to expand and enrich a young person's ability to make intelligent choices, is in fact no different in kind from brainwashing, and that its ultimate effect is to undercut a person's ability to make free choices. When we turn away from the kinds of artificial or jejune examples that make up the philosopher's stock in trade and look at actual life, determinism seems wildly implausible, a view one would expect from madcap science fiction writers rather than from sane people.

Given such counterintuitive results, it might be worthwhile to critically assess the conception of determinism that generates such conclusions. What is the source of the seeming self-evidence of determinism? I would like to suggest that it results from the appeal of a particular model of explanation that has come to dominate so much of our thought today. This is the view, expressed in Fischer's succinct formulation, that "all events can in principle be fully explained by previous events and the laws of nature" (Fischer 1994, p. 6). In this formulation, explanation is taken as, by definition, a matter of identifying efficient causes that bring about specific effects in law-like ways. The exemplary form of such explanations is found in cases where scientists are able to objectively specify causes and effects under controlled, replicable conditions, and then formulate generalizations about the correlation between cause and effect.

Though the idea that explanation involves identifying efficient causes has come to seem self-evident to us today, it is important to see that it has not always been so. The notion of cause, a translation of the Greek word *aitia*, could be understood in four different ways in the premodern, Aristotelian framework that dominated Western thought prior to the rise of modern science. As Rychlak (1979, 2000) aptly points out, it was the great success of mechanistic explanations in seventeenth- and eighteenth-century sciences that led to the rejection of teleological explanation as a possible way of making sense of things. On the new view of explanation that arose at the time, the only way to make something intelligible is to show how it is necessitated by antecedent causes.

The new Galilean and Newtonian conception of science brought with it a set of ontological assumptions that have dominated our thought ever since. Reality is no longer regarded as a meaningful cosmic order; rather, it is seen as a "universe", that is, as a vast aggregate of causally interacting material substances in a space-time coordinate system.[2] The result is an objectifying ontology that treats as real only the objectively specifiable properties of things, where "objectively specifiable" means "in a way not subject to interpretive dispute," ideally, those properties that are quantifiable. Humans occupy an oddly ambiguous position in this conception of the natural order. On the one hand, they are regarded as organisms in a natural environment, products of evolutionary forces, constantly affected by causal factors in the surrounding world. On the other hand, they are seen as knowing subjects who are capable of grasping the external world and transforming it for their own purposes. Given either account, a human is regarded as an object that is distinct from, yet in constant causal interchange with, the array of non-

---

[2]This is not to say that Galileo and Newton held such a view of the cosmos, but that their followers developed the conception in this direction.

human and human objects surrounding it in the world. As Richardson and Bishop point out in this volume, the modern conception of human existence is inextricably tied to a particular moral ideal. In contemporary life, we see our worth as humans as depending on our ability to be autonomous centers of experience and will who can step back from the world and view it objectively as a source of raw materials on hand for our use. From this standpoint, our sense of dignity hangs on our degree of efficacy in manipulating that world for our own purposes (see also Taylor 1985, 1995).

The upshot of the rise of modern science has been a cluster of basic assumptions that color our understanding of ourselves and our world. We understand ourselves in terms of the subject/object dichotomy, according to which we are entities who are set over against, though interacting with, the surrounding material world. We assume that reality, at its most basic level, consists of material substances in causal interactions. We believe that even if all phenomena are not reducible to the physical level, the physical constrains what can count as an explanation in any area. We think that the kind of explanation found in classical physics is the paradigm for explanation in any area of inquiry. And, consequently, we assume that making things intelligible is a matter of showing how those things are caused to be, where the relevant causes are seen as law-governed efficient causes.

In appraising the objectifying ontology we inherit from natural science, phenomenologists generally suggest that, though this model may be quite useful in undertaking inquiry in particular regions of our lives, there is no reason to uncritically assume that it will be applicable in all areas of our lives. In different ways, Heidegger, Merleau-Ponty and the later Wittgenstein try to lead us to see that the objectifying model of modern science is derivative from and parasitic on a more "primordial" understanding of ourselves and our world, a way of experiencing and grasping things that cannot be adequately captured in the terms dictated by the objectifying model. The aim of phenomenology is not to *solve* the problem of free will – indeed, given the framework in which the problem is poised, phenomenologists would say that there can be no solution which would accord with common sense. Instead, the aim is to dissolve the problem by challenging the very framework in terms of which the problem is formulated. It is to that challenge I now turn.

3

Hermeneutic phenomenologists have often called attention to the centrality of representationalism in our culture. Representationalism is the view that, at a basic level, we are subjects who are forming representations of the world in our minds and then interacting with the world on the basis of those representations. There are two possible "directions of fit" representations can have (Anscombe 1957). We may want our representations to fit the world (e.g., in forming beliefs about things), or we may want the world to fit our representations (e.g., in having desires about how things should be). Representations therefore seem to play a critical role in making sense of both knowing and action. With respect to questions about our knowledge of the world, representationalism assumes that we encounter the world only indirectly, through the mediation of our representations. With respect to making sense of action, it means that human agency must be understood in terms of beliefs and desires in the mind of the agent causing bodily movements in order to realize desired states of affairs. In both cases, a sharp distinction is made between the representations formed within the mental receptacle on the one hand, and the "external world" on the other.

Hermeneutic writers have tried to undercut the subject/object model built into representationalism by characterizing our most basic mode of comportment toward the world in everyday life as being-in-the-world, as *In-der-Welt-sein* or *être-au-monde*. These terms are supposed to capture our ways of being absorbed in familiar practical activities before we begin theorizing and reflection. The claim here is that the forms of explicit intending and goal-setting that come to the fore when we step back and theorize about action are in fact rather specialized modes of comportment toward the world. On the phenomenological view, forming intentions and making decisions to act are ways of relating to things that are first made possible by a prior *background* of skillful coping or absorbed involvement which cannot itself be grasped in terms of the traditional representationalist model. It follows, then, that our entire ability to frame representations, as well as the representations we frame, are made possible by our prior ability to cope with things in a variety of ways – by our ability as embodied agents to find our way around in our surroundings, to get into the flow of shared situation, to be attuned to others, and so on (Taylor, forthcoming, p. 2). This shared background of pre-understanding or know-how provides the basis on which any higher-level, explicit forms of awareness and cognition can appear.

The meaning-filled and holistic nature of being-in-the-world becomes apparent in the descriptions phenomenologists offer of our everyday contexts of agency. Heidegger tries to characterize what he calls a *situation* in the life of a person, where a situation is understood as a whole bound together by a meaning. For example, teaching my daughter to drive counts as a situation in this sense, even though it unfolded over several days. When Heidegger says, "every situation is an 'event' *(Ereignis)* and not a 'process' *(Vorgang)*" (Heidegger 1987, p. 206) he means that a situation cannot be thought of as a set of items and causally related occurrences located in a geographical space. On the contrary, life-situations present themselves to us as totalities bound together by significance relations; they are contexts of meaning manifesting and expressing concerns that make us who we are.

As an example of a situation, Heidegger asks us to consider the event of climbing a hill to see the sunrise. As I wind my way through the woods to the foot of the hill, my mind is totally absorbed with things I have to do later in the day. But even though my mind is "a million miles away", different features of the terrain are present for me in distinctive ways, as obstacles, supports, openings, rough spots, and so on. I encounter features of the environment from the perspective of my concerns as soliciting responses and affording certain ways of moving. These affordances are defined by this concrete worldly context in which I currently find myself, not by representations and intentions flitting before my mind's eye (Dreyfus, unpublished manuscript, p. 5). Heidegger suggests that, when caught up in the flow of walking through familiar terrain, the self or "I" is not present as a *thing* distinct from the situation; instead, the self is out of sight: "it swims together [with everything else] in the situation" (Heidegger 1987, p. 206).

Everyday situations have a fluid and dynamic character. The meaning of the situation can shift suddenly and unexpectedly. Suppose I hear a rather large animal crashing through the underbrush below and I recall that a mountain lion has been spotted in these parts. Now things stand out for me differently: the surroundings "take on a new valence, the environment is traversed with new lines of force, in which the vectors of possible attack have an important place" (Taylor, forthcoming, p. 4). Then perhaps I see the neighbor's dog appear from behind a bush, and the entire mood of the environmental context shifts from one of alert tension to amused relief. The surrounding thickets regain their familiar, homey look.

The phenomenological description of an everyday situation shows how familiar contexts of action have a smooth, flowing quality in which embodied skills fold neatly into practical settings. In such contexts, agency takes the form of complying with the solicitations and affordances of a specific situation. There is no clear role to be played by the idea of intentions causally correlated with bodily movements. When intentions do come into play – for example, when I stop halfway up the hill and try to decide whether I have time for the entire roundtrip – they are embedded in and make sense in terms of the wider, tacit sense of the context that defines my skillful coping. At such moments of explicit deliberation, the all-pervasive background of embodied understanding recedes into darkness. But phenomenological description shows that this background is crucial to the sense of things that makes this particular bit of deliberation possible.

The question now arises of how we should think of this holistic and dynamic context of being-in-the-world. Those who accept the claim that science is the default setting of modern thought will hold that the entire complex of relations and interactions described by the phenomenologist should be understood as a matter of central nervous systems causally interacting with clouds of particles according to the laws of nature. On this view, the fact that the worldhood of a familiar lifeworld presents itself to us as a meaningful context for agency is a mere side-effect or epiphenomenon, the result of imposing subjective coloring onto things. We are told that what is *really* going on in such cases is that particles are bunching together and colliding in law-governed ways. All the rest is a sort of illusion.

The phenomenologists' reply to this line of argument, which cannot be developed in detail here, has three parts. First, the phenomenologist calls attention to the fact that the default setting of modernity, the scientific image, is just that – a setting, an image, one perspective among others, one of the ways humans try to cope – and not a privileged and inescapable truth about the way things are. But then there is no reason to assume that the scientific description of the situation is the only correct account of what shows up for us in the world. Second, phenomenologists argue that our everyday being-in-the-world cannot be made intelligible solely in terms of the objectifying ontology we inherit from modern science. Here, the claim is that actual life-situations and events (in Heidegger's sense of this term) have a holistic and dynamic structure that can never be adequately captured in the atomistic and mechanistic terms presupposed by the scientific outlook. And, finally, phenomenologists argue that science itself – the dominant view of reality and intelligibility of modernity – is in fact a way of seeing things that is derived from, and always depends on, the richer and fuller background sense of things that constitutes being-in-the-world.[3]

What is the relevance of this account of being-in-the-world to the free will/determinism debate? What I want to suggest is that the standard way of formulating the free will issue – that is, deploying thought-experiments involving rather artificial cases of agency abstracted from all the contexts in which action makes sense – tends to conceal the background conditions that

[3]Heidegger's conception of a background is similar to Polanyi's notion of the "tacit knowledge" that scientists pick up in being initiated into the practices of a community (see Polanyi (1967), also Kuhn (1970, pp. 191–198), and Dreyfus (1992)).

make agency possible, and so gives us a distorted view of human agency. Seen from the phenomenologist's standpoint, actions are embedded in and make sense only in relation to the wider context of an unfolding life-story, a story that is inseparably bound up with a meaningful life-world. A life-story, understood in this way, cannot be adequately made intelligible in terms of a set of causal connections between discrete intentions and bodily movements. When agency is seen as meaningful expression in a context of significance, the idea that what is *really* happening is a matter of causal interactions among electrochemical discharges in the brain and movements in a space-time coordinate system begins to look like an unwarranted assumption. In Heidegger's vocabulary, instances where detached subjects form intentions and then act on them are seen as cases of a *breakdown*, a radical changeover in one's way of being that occurs when the otherwise smooth flow of everyday practical activity is no longer functioning and explicit deliberation and intending come to the fore.

4

So far I have tried to establish three claims. First, I suggested that the free will versus determinism problem appears to be a pressing problem only because it uncritically assumes the conception of reality dictated by what I have described as the perspective of modern science. Second, I argued that this scientific outlook is motivated by, and makes sense only in relation to, a particular conception of what is involved in making things intelligible – the model of explanation we derive primarily from seventeenth- and eighteenth-century mechanics and astronomy. And, third, I have tried to show that this conception of making things intelligible is totally inappropriate in trying to make sense of the human lifeworld. The upshot of these claims is that the free will debate, in its standard form, has very little relevance to making real-life situations intelligible. It is like a cog in a machine that turns when nothing else is turning, irrelevant to our real interests in trying to grasp human agency.

I now want to turn to the question of how we *can* make everyday agency intelligible, drawing especially on Heidegger's characterization of human existence as "being-there" or *Dasein*. In trying to make sense of our being as agents, Heidegger rejects the traditional assumption that humans must be thought of as things or objects in some sense, and instead proposes that we think of the human as an *event* or *happening* – as an ongoing life-course unfolding "from birth to death" (Heidegger 1962, §72). We can see the mo-

tivation for this conception of a human being as an event if we consider
what is involved in individuating an action. As is well known, actions can
be correctly described in a number of different ways. Raising my hand at a
meeting can be correctly described as indicating my desire to speak, moving air molecules, flexing my deltoids, irritating my colleagues, shifting my
center of gravity, and so on. Which description is most accurate depends on
the place of the action in the context of the institutional setting in which it
occurs and its place in the unfolding story of overall projects of an agent in a
shared lifeworld. In a classroom, then, it would be correct to say that raising
my hand is signaling my desire to speak because (1) raising one's hand is
how one gains recognition in a classroom setting, and (2) it is part of my
life-story that I have something to say about the topic at hand.

There is a common assumption in mainstream philosophy that in any
given case of agency it is possible to identify a *basic action* for which different
descriptions provide possible modes of identification. But, as MacIntyre has
argued, there are no basic actions or brute movements that can be identified
independent of the ongoing stories of which they are a part. In his words
(MacIntyre 1981, pp. 197 and 199),

> [I]n successfully identifying and understanding what someone ... is do-
> ing we always move towards placing a particular episode in the context
> of a set of narrative histories, histories both of the individual concerned
> and of the settings in which they act and suffer. ... An action is a
> moment in a possible or actual history or in a number of such histories.

Even the description "raising his hand" is true of me in this context
only if I am in on the forms of life involved in participating in academic
settings, and so am in a position to have something to say. It follows that
"the characterization of actions allegedly prior to any narrative form being
imposed upon them will always turn out to be the presentation of what
are plainly the disjointed parts of some possible narrative" (MacIntyre 1981,
p. 200). In other words, an event can count as a human action only if it has
a place in some narrative or set of narratives.

Heidegger's conception of life as a happening *(Geschehen)* with the form
of a story *(Geschichte)* is motivated by this idea that agency is intelligible
only as embedded in a unified, ongoing narrative. To capture this narrativity
of life, Heidegger describes human existence as having two basic dimensions
corresponding to the past and future of the unfolding story-line of a person's
life. First, *Dasein* is always *thrown* into a world, situated in the midst of
public situations, already committed to certain courses of action depending
on the choices it has made. This dimension of a person's life-story Heidegger

calls *facticity*, where this term refers not to a set of brute facts that can be objectively specified, but rather to the meaningful prior commitments and involvements in terms of which an agent grasps what is at stake in a situation. On this view, facticity has a particular weightiness in our lives – it has to be taken into account in taking a stand in a given situation. Yet our facticity is also fluid and open-ended, subject to changing interpretations as the course of events unfolds and takes on different meanings.

The second dimension of human existence is called *futurity*, and it refers to the way we are always projected forward into an open range of possibilities in undertaking projects in our everyday lives. In Heidegger's view, the stands we take at any time always carry consequences for the future, and, as a result, our actions at any moment embody commitments with respect to what is yet to come. When I promise my daughter I will take her to the zoo, I am making a commitment not only to take her to the zoo, but to being a father (and a human being) of a particular sort. The idea that we exist as projections into the future is what Heidegger is referring to when he says that *Dasein*, human existence, is "always already ahead of itself", coming toward *(zukommend)* its future *(Zukunft)* in all its actions (Heidegger 1962, §§41 and 65). To say that human existence is essentially futural in its being is to say that humans always stand outward into an open leeway *(Spielraum)* of possibilities, and so are always already pressing forward into those possibilities at any moment. Whether we are aware of it or not, we are choosing our identity in what we do by seizing on particular possibilities while letting others slide. The open range of possibilities standing before us is a fundamental part of what we are as agents – it is not just a set of abstract options on hand for us to play with.

Facticity and projection make possible the experience of past and future for humans. Heidegger holds that, in human lived time, the future has a particular priority. It is only because we are projected into the future, underway in realizing possibilities, that we can experience the events of the past as assets or liabilities for achieving things in the present. Lived time is characterized by future-directedness because of this priority of our purposive involvements.[4]

As we have already seen, the life-story that constitutes the being of any human is inseparably bound up with a meaningful life-world. We are being-in-the-world to the extent that our agency is enmeshed in concrete worldly

---

[4]In *Being and Time*, §§78–82, Heidegger argues that both the everyday experience of time and the conception of time in physics are derived from the deeper existential sense of time built into human existence as such. See Blattner (1999).

situations and involved with others in realizing shared projects and goals. I can be a father of a particular type in my cultural context only because the norms and conventions for realizing that sort of possibility have been laid out in advance in the historical formation of my culture. In Heidegger's vocabulary, this means that I always exist as the They or the one *(das Man)* – as a placeholder or participant in an irreducibly public space of shared goods and attuned undertakings. And this means that my being is characterized by historicity *(Geschichtlichkeit)* in a dual sense: my own life has a story-shaped structure, and it has the shape of a story only because it is embedded in and indebted to the stories that make up a shared cultural history.

Given the conception of human existence as a life-story enmeshed in the wider context of a cultural history, we can come to see human actions as flowing out of and dependent upon the ongoing story that makes up an agent's facticity. For example, my choice of the sorbet dessert on a particular occasion makes sense only in terms of a longer story having to do with dissatisfaction with my chronic indulgence in fatty desserts, an evolving pattern of more healthy approaches to things, a concern with dignity as interpreted by my culture, a vague sense of the situation as an inappropriate setting for displays of gluttony, and so forth. But how all these factors count in influencing my choice depends on the meaning they have in this particular situation, a meaning which itself can be understood only in the light of the entire "being-in-the-world" of the situation. When actions are seen in the context of an overarching life-story, the idea that they must be explained in terms of some peculiar mental event – an exertion of will or decision correlated with some event in the brain – becomes less plausible.

The contextualization of agency in a life-story shows why the lived human past is not marked by the kind of fixity that physical processes are assumed to have. What has come before in my life – the very *being* of the human past – is constantly subject to reinterpretation in terms of the possible self-understandings that shape my current ways of pressing forward into the future at any time. And, as we have seen, these projections into the future are themselves always shaped and defined by the background of facticity that sets me on my course at any moment. The past is therefore constantly subject to change, depending on the shifting meanings the situation can have. By the same token, the description of what a person is *currently doing* at any given moment is also subject to interpretative dispute, since the characterization of an action depends on interpretations of the meaning of the situation that change with changes in a person's projections. If the identification of both past and present events depends on defeasible meanings attributed to the situation, however, then there are no brute "facts of the matter", no objectively specifiable givens, that could serve as the basis for describing actions in the causal terms required by the natural sciences. In other words, if we accept the conception of human action Heidegger proposes, it seems that the kinds of causal connection philosophers regard as undermining free will cannot be identified.

Heidegger's conception of human action brings to light two fundamental features of human agency that seem to make a thoroughgoing determinism untenable.[5] First, humans have the ability to reflect on what has come before, redefining the past by endowing it with a different meaning. Since there are no facts about the past independent of these meanings, there is no way to specify the causal antecedent of an action in a way that satisfies the requirement of generality of causal statements. And, second, humans are beings who can envision a range of possibilities as defined by the cultural context in which they act, and so always make choices against a backdrop of alternative ways of acting. This "standing out into a range of possibilities" is not something that can be grasped by physicalist causal statements.

On the view of action we get from Heidegger, the underlying physical make up of the world should be seen as a constraint on our actions, not as the cause of what we do. In trying to make our actions intelligible, we need an account of how our choices and interpretations make the physical world behave in the way it does, not an account of how the physical world determines our choices and interpretations. This conclusion, as I see it, follows from a fairly obvious point about the nature of explanation. An explanation should be suited to what it is supposed to explain. Just as it would be pointless to try to explain the computational functions of a computer in terms of the physical properties of a particular machine, so it would be pointless to try to explain my going to the store in terms of the workings of an internal combustion engine. At the level of explanation suitable to making action intelligible, determinism simply has no role to play.

5

At the outset of this chapter I suggested that developing a fuller and more realistic understanding of human agency might lead us to a more meaningful conception of free will than is usually presupposed in the free will debate. In trying to clarify the current philosophical problem of free will, I started with Kane's notion of ultimate responsibility. The UR conception supposes that, although a variety of factors may be influencing an agent in forming

---

[5]Compare Bruner's summary (1990, pp. 109-110) of a position developed by Gergen.

decisions and acting, the ultimate origination – the determining efficient cause – is something that lies in the agent's own spontaneity, to use the Kantian term. It is the view that my action is free only if, as it were, the buck stops here.

Underlying the conception of free will as ultimate authority is the assumption that external influences count as negatives when it comes to ascribing free will. Kane calls our attention to a particularly insidious case of external control, a case of "behind-the-scenes manipulation", where a group of people manipulate the wills of others while making them think that they have made up their own minds and are acting "of their own free wills." In cases where there is what Kane calls covert nonconstraining control (CNC), agents do what they want to do, but what they *want* is controlled by others through a process of behavior control and manipulation. As an example, Kane considers the scenario of Skinner's *Walden Two*, where social engineers preprogram people to always want what is best for the functioning of the community as a whole (Kane 1996, pp. 64-65).

Now it is hard to disagree with Kane's claim that the form of control imagined in *Walden Two* undermines free will. But it is not clear to me how we should draw the line between this sort of control and the benign forms of control we use in child-rearing and education. My worry is that philosophers who debate the free will question have a tendency, rooted in Enlightenment ideals, to suppose that authority is always the opposite of freedom, and that true free will exists only when authority has been cast aside in the name of individual responsibility, rational deliberation and personal liberty. Gadamer has argued, however, that it is a mistake to assume that authority is always the enemy of freedom and reason. For authority "can also be a source of truth" (Gadamer 1975, p. 247). We respect our teachers and parent and spiritual counselors not because we see them as arbitrary forces to whom we must submit, but rather because we recognize them as bearers and carriers of deep traditions of reason and moral wisdom that have withstood the test of time and are binding on us because they define the people we are. The process of growing up into a tradition, becoming "attuned" to the forms of life of a community, is not something that robs us of our capacity for free choice. On the contrary, such *Bildung* is an enabling condition: it first gives us the ability to make any meaningful choices at all.

When we fully grasp the conception of being-in-the-world formulated by hermeneutic phenomenology, we can see that freedom is not achieved by somehow distancing ourselves from or overcoming the influence of the "public" or the "herd." Instead, meaningful freedom is achieved only through enculturation, that is, by becoming more and more deeply enmeshed in the forms of life and shared patterns of response of a historical culture. Seen in this light, ultimate responsibility, understood as what Richardson and Bishop in their chapter call "situated freedom",[6] presupposes a solid grounding in the background of understanding that defines one's communal context. Only through initiation into this background can we develop the ability to recognize what is at issue in facing a situation, to intelligently weigh alternative courses of action, and to use *phronesis* in thinking about the application of general ideals to concrete action. Only through *Bildung* can we develop the firm character and virtues we need to be able to make clear-sighted, meaningful choices in difficult situations. Our enculturation into the shared goals of our community is also the condition for formulating overarching goals and directions for one's life, goals and ideals that then make it possible to restrain and govern one's desires and appetites in particular circumstances. And it is through modeling our own lives on the exemplary lives of authority figures that we learn what it is to be wholehearted in our fundamental commitments, and to be courageous and steadfast in following our ideals.

Certainly all of this cultural formation can go terribly wrong – one has only to think of the rise of Nazism to see how the experience of belongingness and indebtedness to a public world can lead to horrifying results. But the fact that authority and tradition can go wrong does not entail that there is a standpoint outside all tradition and authority – a standpoint of freedom regarded as pure radical choice – which offers a finer sort of autonomy and responsibility than that found in our everyday thrownness into the midst of things. For, as Taylor has argued, the Sartrean conception of radical choice – the notion of being able to just leap in any direction, without being influenced by any factors whatsoever – is not so much a description of ultimate responsibility as it is of a person who is enslaved to every passing whim and caprice, totally unable to make any choice at all (Taylor 1985, especially pp. 27-35; see also Richardson et al. 1999, Chapter 5).

How, then, should we think of genuine freedom? I believe that Heidegger's rich and complex account of authentic existence can give us a clue to what genuine freedom might be. On the Heideggerian view, being free means living in such a way that one's life is focused and cohesive, guided by overarching commitments drawn from the historical culture in which one lives. Here, freedom is experienced not as a vertiginous leap that leaves behind all influences, but as being able to do what one clearly ought to do in challenging situations. It is the kind of freedom exemplified by Luther's words before the Diet of Worms: *"Hier stehe ich; ich kann nicht anders"*. It is the freedom

---

[6]The term comes from Taylor's *Hegel and Modern Society* (1979).

envisioned in the well-known words: "The only real freedom is knowing what you have to do and being able to do it."[7]

References

Adler M.J. (1958): *The Idea of Freedom. A Dialectical Examination of the Conceptions of Freedom, Vol. I*, Doubleday, Garden City.

Anscombe E. (1957): *Intention*, Blackwell, Oxford.

Blattner W.D. (1999): *Heidegger's Temporal Idealism*, Cambridge University Press, Cambridge.

Bruner J. (1990): *Acts of Meaning*, Harvard University Press, Cambridge, MA.

Dennett D. (1987): *The Intentional Stance*, MIT Press, Cambridge, MA.

Dennett D. (1993): Back from the drawing board. In *Dennett and His Critics*, ed. by B. Dahldom, MIT Press, Cambridge MA.

Dreyfus H.L. (1992): *What Computers Still Cant Do: A Critique of Artificial Intelligence*, MIT Press, Cambridge, MA.

Dreyfus H.L. (unpublished manuscript): Intelligence Without Representation, http://www.hfac.uh.edu/cogsci/dreyfus.html.

Fischer J.M. (1994): *The Metaphysics of Free Will*, Blackwell, Oxford.

Gadamer H.-G. (1975): *Truth and Method*, transl. by J. Weinsheimer, Seabury Press, New York.

Heidegger M. (1962): *Being and Time*, transl. by J. Macquarrie and E. Robinson, Harper and Row, New York.

Heidegger M. (1987): *Zur Bestimmung der Philosophie, Gesamtausgabe 56/57*, Klostermann, Frankfurt.

---

[7]Adler (1958) distinguishes between freedom conceived as a natural capacity for "self-determination" – freedom seen as "free decision" or *liberum arbitrium*, where unpredictability, causal initiative and creativity are the key notions – and freedom conceived as an acquired capacity for self-perfection, according to which one is free only if one has developed a certain character or state of will. As an example of this second conception, Adler (1958, p. 253) cites Cicero, who says that he alone is free "who follows the things that are right, who delights in his duty, who has a well-considered path of life before him, who does not obey the laws because of fear but follows and respects them because he adjudges them to be most conducive to his health" (*Paradoxica Stoicorum* V, 34-35). Using Adler's classification, I might say that, in my view, freedom as self-perfection is prior to, and more basic than, freedom as self-determination. My thanks to Ted Honderich for calling attention to Adler's distinctions.

Kane R. (1996): *The Significance of Free Will*, Oxford University Press, Oxford.

Kuhn T. (1970): *The Structure of Scientific Revolutions*, 2nd ed., University of Chicago Press, Chicago.

MacIntyre A. (1981): *After Virtue*, University of Notre Dame Press, Notre Dame.

Pereboom D. (2001): *Living Without Free Will*, Cambridge University Press, Cambridge.

Polanyi M. (1967): *Personal Knowledge*, Anchor, Garden City.

Richardson F.C., Fowers B.J., and Guignon C.B. (1999): *Re-envisioning Psychology: Moral Dimensions of Theory and Practice*, Jossey-Bass, San Francisco.

Rychlak J.F. (1979): *Discovering Free Will and Personal Agency*, Oxford University Press, Oxford.

Rychlak J.F. (2000): A psychotherapist's lessons from the philosophy of science, *American Psychologist* **55**, October 2000.

Taylor C. (1979): *Hegel and Modern Society*, Cambridge University Press, Cambridge.

Taylor C. (1985): Legitimation crisis? In *Philosophy and the Human Sciences, Philosophical Papers, Vol. 2*, Cambridge University Press, Cambridge.

Taylor C. (1985): What is human agency? In *Human Agency and Language, Philosophical Papers, Vol. 1*, Cambridge University Press, Cambridge.

Taylor C. (1995): Overcoming epistemology. In *Philosophical Arguments*, Harvard University Press, Cambridge MA.

Taylor C. (forthcoming): Rorty and philosophy. In *Contemporary Philosophy in Focus: Richard Rorty*, ed. by C. Guignon and D. Hiley, Cambridge University Press, Cambridge.

Determinism, Chance, and Freedom

Mauro Dorato

Abstract

After a brief but necessary characterization of the notion of determinism, I will discuss and critically evaluate four views on the relationship between determinism and free will by taking into account
both (1) what matters most to us in terms of a free will worth-wanting
and (2) which capacities can be legitimately attributed to human beings without contradicting what we currently know from natural science. The main point of the paper is to argue that the libertarian
faces a dilemma: On the one hand, the possibility of "doing otherwise"
– a necessary condition of free will according to the libertarian – requires indeterminism or chance, but any kind of indeterminism has the
undesirable consequence of separating our actions from our character
and our past. On the other hand, if our character has to be fully expressed by our actions, determinism becomes necessary and we seem
to be metaphysically unfree. I will conclude by showing that the dispute between compatibilists and libertarians possesses an important
but hitherto very neglected *pragmatic component* as well, dependent
on two different ethical attitudes about a meaningful life. The first,
recommended by compatibilists, focuses on the joy or serenity entailed
by regarding ourselves as being part of a necessary natural order; the
second stresses the importance of being able to influence our character
and the world according to autonomous desires and intentions.

1 What Is Determinism?

From the role of fate in the archaic myths to the theological problem of
predestination, from the a *priori* arguments against free will discussed by
Aristotle *vis à vis* the principle of bivalence to the early modern conception of nature regarded as ruled by inescapable mechanistic laws, the problem of the relationship between determinism and free will has accompanied
the whole history of western thought. Considering its complexity, and the
fact that it relates to many other philosophical puzzles – among which are
causation, time, laws, the body-mind relationship, and moral and juridical

responsibility – it should be obvious why any conceivable solution depends on basic metaphysical options, having to do with the way in which one sees the place of human beings in the universe. Schematically, it is possible to distinguish four different positions on the relationship between determinism and freedom, which I will refer to as *dissolutionism, hard determinism, libertarianism and compatibilism.* Such conceptions basically agree on how to understand determinism, but part ways when trying to elucidate the meaning of *freedom or free will* and its relationship to determinism.

I will refer to determinism as a scientific-philosophical doctrine according to which the state of a physical system at one instant of time t (whatever that means) univocally fixes any other temporal states of that system, past or future. If the universe may be regarded as such a system, then universal determinism holds. In this case, the future does not contain any contingent events, namely events which may or may not happen, and what will occur will occur necessarily. In other words, there are no different future possibilities all compatible with the same present state of the world: no event could happen in a different way. It follows that *if* our actions fall within the domain of such a universal form of determinism, any choice of ours could have not been different, and in any circumstance of our life we could have not acted differently from the way we actually chose to act. In a word, we could have not done otherwise (unless, of course, we had different desires or beliefs, something that implies, however, a counterfactual change in our past).

Three remarks are worth mentioning before embarking on our project. The first is that determinism as defined above makes no reference to epistemic notions such as *predictability, calculability,* and so on. Though controversial, this is a point that in the following I will simply take for granted (see Earman 1986). The second remark is a simple *caveat* to the effect that the four philosophical positions mentioned above make a significant distinction between *determinism* and *fatalism,* as the latter notion implies that what will occur is completely independent of our decisions to act or abstain from acting. While the fatalist maintains that our actions are useless or superfluous (say, I will get healthy independently of my decisions to take or not to take medication), determinists are not bound to deny that future events are, *at least* in part, brought about and produced by our actions. As evidence for this claim, to affirm that a present action A (deterministically) causes a future event B means, among other things, that had A (counterfactually) not been performed, the actual future would have been different, as B would not have occurred.

The third remark consists in pointing out that the philosophical debate on the relationship between determinism and free will typically does *not* revolve around trying to establish whether the actual world in which we live and act is deterministic and our actions fall within its scope. Such an important question, we are told, is either left to "scientists", or is regarded as one which cannot be answered on the basis of what we know about the universe and ourselves today. Determinism is rather presented as a thesis which is *true of a physically (and, therefore, logically) possible world*, in which each event is necessarily caused by a preceding even and in which, as James (1956, p. 150) put it, "the future has no ambiguous possibilities hidden in its womb: the part that we call present is compatible with just one fixed totality". Also in this paper, the question of the relationship between determinism and free will can be posed by presupposing such a possible world, without asking whether this possible world coincides with the *actual* world.

In a word, the task of the philosopher writing on the determinism–free will debate, in my view, consists in an evaluation of the conceptual consequences of determinism realized by presupposing a possible world in which it rules universally.

2 Four Doctrines on the Relationship Between Determinism and Free Will

Let us start with *dissolutionism*, a thesis defending free will by blunting the threat of determinism. The dissolutionist strategy consists in declaring that the issue of the compatibility of determinism and free will is really a *pseudo-question*. While admitting that the macroscopic natural world may be ruled by universal determinism, the dissolutionist argues that, *if* it were meaningless to claim that actions have *causes, then* determinism (or indeterminism) would not apply.

The defense of this conditional has a Wittgensteinian flavour and a two-stage structure. First, it is stressed that merely referring to the concept of freedom implies the adoption of an *evaluative* attitude toward an action or its doer, and, therefore, an attitude which is conceptually independent and autonomous from the *descriptive* approach typical of the natural sciences and of their deterministic (indeterministic) theories (see Ryle 1949). Once the talk of causes is eliminated, the threat of determinism to our freedom is thereby eliminated, too, since it would be meaningless to claim that our actions are determined by antecedent causes. The linguistic games in which the notion of *cause* is relevant are completely independent of those involving the notion of *action* (Anscombe 1959, Kenny 1963). To put it simply, the dissolution of the problem of the relationship between determinism and free will calls into play a linguistic analysis of the respective conceptual domains, from which the conclusion emerges that they are *incommensurable.*

The remaining three positions distinguish themselves from dissolutionism because they grant that human actions may be subject, in principle, to causal explanations. This means that they claim that it is perfectly meaningful and conceptually appropriate to ask what is the cause of any action, but part ways both in virtue of the different conceptions of freedom they advocate, and their approach to an explanation of human actions. In particular, according to hard incompatibilist determinism, our actions require deterministic explanations which exclude free will *tout court.* The "hard" determinist claims in fact that all actions are causally determined, and that their causes can be traced back to events preceding our birth that are, therefore, beyond our control. In other words, our impression of freely choosing different alternatives is a mere *illusion,* and can be explained by our ignorance of the *causes* (biological, psychological or social or a combination of these) univocally determining the choice.

To use a brilliant simile due to Spinoza – who, however, was a compatibilist – people believing that they are free are similar to a hypothetical sentient stone which, in "free fall" under its weight, is convinced that it can choose the place, velocity and time of its fall, deciding somewhat its trajectory. For the hard determinist, all our actions are determined in such a way that any form of freedom or autonomy is impossible, a position that in the Enlightenment was defended by authors like d'Holbach and in our century by various scientists and philosophers, like the psychologist Skinner and the Cambridge philosopher Broad.

Libertarianism shares with hard determinism the claim that determinism is incompatible with free will, but differs from the former position by arguing that at least some of our choices and actions escape universal determinism. In particular, a human being is free not only in the sense that she can do what she wants to do – a kind of freedom which is only *negative,* because it is synonymous with the absence of obstacles to the realization of an action, and is, therefore, *compatible with determinism.* An agent is also free because either (i) *she could do otherwise,* that is, her past and present are compatible with *undetermined,* alternative possible futures, or (ii) her conscious choice autonomously originates a new causal chain, a sense of freedom not unlike that advocated by Kant (see also Honderich 1993). These two brands of libertarianism differ on how they interpret causation and selfhood: The first, especially in Kane's version (see Kane 1996), claims that the irreducibly probabilistic causation that takes place in particular human choices belongs to naturalistic, "normal" forms, in principle explainable by science, while the second brand invokes "exceptional" forms of causation, occurring only within the self.

It is important to keep in mind that for libertarians not all intentional actions require a violation of determinism. For the successful performance of what could be called "semi-automatic actions" – like turning the light on or turning the steering wheel, usually *reliably* resulting in the desired effects – there must be a *deterministic* link between our desires and the actions they motivate. According to libertarians, it is only *before some choices* are made that the right sort of causation – either natural but indeterministic or just typical of the agent – comes into play. In the first hypothesis, some libertarians suggest that the choice itself is the joint product of our effort to decide between two conflicting desires and some indeterministic processes in the brain elicited by the conflict. In the second hypothesis, the causal process leading to the choice emerges from natural causation, in such a way as to maintain a sort of autonomy from the latter. In Kantian language, this sort of *agent causation* would be a "causation of freedom", existing side by side with, and beyond, natural-deterministic or indeterministic causation, and amounting to an unconditioned power to *originate* events. To the extent that the outcome of our actions can be thought of as if they are devoid of preceding natural causes, they are a direct product of the "Self".[1]

The defenders of *compatibilism* claim, like hard determinists, that our actions are determined, in the sense that they are no exception to the way other natural events are caused when they are caused deterministically. However, such a determination is absolutely compatible with our freedom, regarded as the *power to do what we want*. Hobbes, Spinoza, Voltaire, Hume, Schopenhauer, Russell, Schlick and Grünbaum among others, have defended this position, which is popular among those philosophers tending toward naturalism or materialism, and which regard human beings as subject, as much as the other animals, to *laws of nature*. Here is a well-known defense of such a position in Voltaire's *Philosophical Dictionary*:

> *A* And what does then your freedom reduce to, if not to the power to do what your will wants with absolute necessity?
>
> *B* You are embarrassing me: freedom reduces then to the power to do what I want to do?
>
> *A* Think about it, and see whether it can be conceived in any other way.
>
> *B* But in this case, my dog is as free as I am, as he necessarily has the will to run when he sees a hare, and the power to run if he

---

[1] For a well-known, contemporary version of this theory, see Chisholm (1982).

> has no pain in the legs. I would not have anything more than my
> dog then: you are reducing me to the condition of the brutes!
>
> A Here you are well afflicted by discovering to be as free as your
> dog! But don't you look like him in thousands of things? Don't
> you share with him hunger, thirst, sleep, the five senses? Would
> you want to smell with something different from your nose?

As it is evident from this quotation, the philosophical difference between compatibilists and libertarians boils down to a conceptual disagreement as to what must be understood for freedom. According to compatibilists, as for Voltaire, whose opinion in the dialogue is clearly voiced by *A, our freedom consists in the absence of obstacles* to the realization of our will, although our will is regarded, as any other natural (macroscopic) mechanism, determined by preceding causes. According to libertarians, freedom requires as its necessary condition the so-called *Principle of Alternative Possibilities*, which in turns requires either the correct amount of natural indeterminism, or a power immanent to the self giving origin to a completely new causal chain, whose first member is completely independent of previous events (absolute origination). As we will see, it is difficult to imagine how such a power could ever be described in scientific terms, as it is difficult to locate such a power within an evolutionary context which regards, antidualistically, the human brain as the exclusive "cause" of our mental capacities.

3   Why Dissolutionism Must Be Dissolved

Under careful examination, it seems plausible to claim that dissolutionism can be defended only if we are ready to modify the reasons usually invoked to defend it. In other words, it can be perhaps correct to claim that the problem of the relationship between determinism and free will is not genuine, but this cannot be argued on the basis of the two reasons given above.[2]

Starting with the first of these two reasons, we can certainly admit that we often use the term "free" to appreciate, evaluate or morally judge a particular action – as one says, of an agent, that she did *x freely*, without any constraints or threats. However, the problem whether that action is a consequence of

---

[2]Though this line of argument will not be explored here, one could try to claim that all our actions cannot be described in physical language and that the notion of determinism is simply inapplicable outside of physical theories (e.g. Guignon, this volume). To block this way out, defenders of the other positions would have to argue that for the meaningfulness of the problem, the mere *logical possibility* of a completely deterministic world suffices, a world, that is, in which there are very complex laws capable of uniquely fixing the future given the present state.

a choice caused by an alleged "autonomous self", as the libertarian wants, or instead can be explained on the basis of wishes, intentions and beliefs of the agent regarded as ordinary causes, as the compatibilist requires, *does not seem meaningless at all.*

Note that to claim that the linguistic game in which we speak of a "free action" or a "free agent" is essentially evaluative and non-descriptive does not imply at all that it be incommensurable with an attempt to causally explain the action itself, *describing it* as an effect of preceding causes. For instance, when we invoke a childhood trauma or a particular kind of education undergone in childhood as *factors contributing* to making choices of particular partners rather than others, are we not regarding such factors as *causally relevant* in the explanation? This explanation does not rule out the possibility that we can *evaluate* the action in question as being completely free, as partially free, or as completely compulsive, for various considerations touching upon the kind of causal explanation that seems most appropriate in the circumstance.

There are two interesting remarks that can be drawn from this simple example. The first is a confirmation of the view that our evaluations always refer to facts, even though they can be considered as logically independent of them, in agreement with the conceptual separation between facts and values sanctioned by Hume's principle: "No ought from is". The second remark is more relevant to our problem: If the kind of description we are willing to give in circumstances in which we are explaining an action constitutes, among other presupposed norms, the *justification* of the moral evaluation of an action, the descriptive and the normative component of the word "free" cannot be regarded as incommensurable.

In other words, not only would logical independence not entail incommensurability of the relevant "linguistic games" (if we really want to stick to this way of speaking), but the example above shows that talking of "causes of actions" is not at all meaningless. On the contrary, it is a necessary presupposition of a description of the psychological development of the human being that has the ambition of being inter-subjectively valid and empirically testable. It is important to be clear about the import of the preceding sentence: I am not trying to defend an analysis of ordinary language as *the* method of philosophy. Rather, to the extent that such an analysis is considered to be the milestone of philosophy, a view that I do not endorse, one should admit *the existence of a well-entrenched use of particular expressions.* This fact indicates that human actions can be, and *de facto* are, subsumed under causal explicative schemata.

The latter remark also partially meets the second objection against the meaningfulness of causal explanations of actions. Following Davidson, I regard as plausible the view that reasons for actions are particular kinds of causes: Our intentional desires and our beliefs about how to satisfy them, can be regarded as *causal factors* explaining the action, in the sense of being sufficient conditions for it. The *reason* why I get closer to the refrigerator (my action) is my belief that it contains a bottle of ice water, together with my desire (intention) to drink, caused by a chemical state we call thirst.

The claim that this simple explanatory schema – regarding intentions and beliefs as causes of our behavior – can also be applied in much more complicated circumstances, like the choice of a partner or a course of study, is very complex and cannot be fully articulated in this essay. Here, it will suffice to consider a simple argument that has hitherto been partially neglected, but that should convince us of the view that reasons must be particular sort of causes: Presupposing a motivational state (a reason) that is also cause of the behavior is indispensable in order to explain how it is that we can move our limbs to act. From this viewpoint, any desire, while indicating the aim of the action, must also be regarded as its partial cause, or *conditio sine qua non*. If a reason were, as the dissolutionist argues, a mere *ens abstractum* and, therefore, causally inert in the sense that it cannot be coded in a brain state as a disposition to act, how could it cause us to move? Therefore, the dissolutionist faces the following dilemma: *Either the reason to act does not cause the action* and then it could not explain or justify it – given that the action would mysteriously occur in coincidence with its neurophysiologically non-describable, abstract motive – or it does explain it, and, therefore, it must cause it. There cannot be any gap between the reasons for our actions and their causes, otherwise we would have to adopt strong forms of body-mind occasionalism as mysterious as those invoked by early modern philosophers like Malebranche and Guelincx.

Clearly, a desire by itself does not suffice for causal explanation: Without a well-defined set of specific beliefs on the most rational way to obtain our goals, we would not act as we do. On the instrumentalist conception of rationality adopted here, the belief that by doing x we can get y essentially means that the former is a means or a cause of the latter, its effect. If, furthermore, we consider that any explanation referring to aims or goals (a teleological explanation) must refer to *evolutionary* factors, that is, to causal factors (see Salmon 1990), there is no reason to defend the distinction between reasons and causes, at least if we do not want to lengthen the list of the "Wittgensteinian red books" (cf. Davidson 1984) so widespread in the sixties.

4 How to Avoid Terminological Disputes on the True Meaning of Freedom

It will be recalled that hard determinism and libertarianism oppose compatibilism because they hold that determinism is incompatible with "what we intuitively mean by freedom", or with "a freedom which is worth wanting", because it rescues our moral responsibility. Given that the latter expression ("a freedom worth wanting") introduces in the discussion an important *evaluative* and, therefore, potentially subjective aspect to be dealt with in the last section of the paper (namely which sort of freedom do we value most?), it is to the former issue that we now devote our attention: Which notion of freedom is referred to by the deceptively simple expression "intuitive notion of freedom"?

It is very important to stress that there are *at least three different intuitive notions of freedom discussed in the literature*, and deciding which among these really captures the essential character of "what we mean or should mean by freedom" (what we could term freedom with a capital f) is very difficult if not impossible, considering the vagueness of our conceptual and linguistic intuitions. The three notions in question are (1) freedom meant as an absence of obstacles to the realization of our desire; (2) freedom meant as a power or capacity to bring about a new causal chain; and (3) freedom meant as the power of doing otherwise in the very same circumstances.

The philosophical debate between hard determinists and libertarians on one side and compatibilists on the other, can, therefore, be explained with the following hypothesis. While the latter claim that freedom essentially coincides with the unconstrained power to do what we want – let us call it, with a somewhat inelegant but useful notation, freedom$_1$ – and that such a notion is *sufficient* to guarantee whatever is important to us from a moral point of view, the former deny this very thesis. Libertarians, in particular, defend the idea that it is only the possibility of originating a new causal chain in an unconditioned way (freedom$_2$), or the power to do otherwise in the same circumstance (freedom$_3$), that would guarantee our *moral responsibility*. Consequently, libertarians are bound to believe that human beings are effectively and actually endowed with one or both of these capacities, a belief attacked by compatibilists.

At this point, a methodological remarks seems appropriate. If one is convinced, as I am, that there is no internal faculty (the mind's eye) capable of discriminating with absolute precision and certainty the essential properties of complex concepts like that of freedom, one should avoid reconstructing the debate between hard determinists, compatibilists and libertarians as one revolving around the question: *Which, among the three senses of freedom presented above, is the essential or the right one?* It is instead plausible to suppose that there are no essential features characterizing our notion of freedom, and that the attempt to individuate it would transform the philosophical debate into a purely terminological dispute on the meaning of the word "free" and on how it is used in ordinary language.

Rather, after having distinguished the three notions above, it seems a much more promising line of inquiry to try to accomplish the following three tasks: (i) to recognize that *each of these notions* has an important role to play in the philosophical dispute; (ii) to study their conceptual relationship; (iii) to ask which of the capacities and power presupposed by each of them is actually possessed by human beings. This latter problem has an important *a posteriori, empirical* component, as it depends on how we can describe our biological and social nature, and in particular on how we want to construe, philosophically, the relationship between mind and body. Examined from this vantage point, the debate between libertarians, hard determinists and compatibilists has no terminological connotation regarding the alleged essence of the notion of freedom, and this looks like a decisive advantage.

5   The Three Conceptions of Freedom and Their Metaphysical Presuppositions

Passing now to examine the logical relationship among the three notions of freedom, let us start from what could be called the "minimal conception" of freedom (freedom$_1$) regarded as an absence of obstacles to the realization of our desires, and regarded by compatibilists as necessary and sufficient for our free will, and by libertarians and hard determinists as merely *necessary*. As the previous quotation from Voltaire has made clear, on the basis of this notion of freedom one acts freely if one acts on the basis of a desire or a consciously formulated intention without physical impediments (the person is not tied up, is not gagged, etc.)[3] or psychological constraints (the person is neither threatened nor blackmailed, neither hypnotized nor doped)[4], although desires and intentions are determined *ab initio* to be what they are

---

[3]There is an important trace of this conception of freedom in ordinary language, as when we say that the street or the sky is "free" meaning that it is not *blocked* or *obstructed* by cars or clouds.

[4]Acting under the influence of a drug may controversially be regarded as acting under a hindering force in such a way as to let the compatibilist exclude it from the kind of actions that would be considered as free.

because they are part of a causal chain dating back to events that occurred well before our birth.

By adopting this conception, and by presupposing the universal validity and scope of determinism, we accept that in every circumstance we cannot do *otherwise* from what we have chosen to do. In order for us to be "capable" of doing otherwise, in fact, we would have to have desires and intentions that *differ* from those that we actually have – since it is these desires and beliefs that cause us to act. Such a difference, however, presupposes in turn that we have a past that is different from the one we have in fact lived, and we must, therefore, suppose a history of the universe that differs slightly from the actual history. If determinism holds, we "could" do otherwise only in *possible worlds* differing from the actual one in their initial or boundary conditions (holding fixed the laws of nature).

Here it is of utmost importance to clarify a source of misunderstanding about the correct import of the doctrine of universal determinism. The problem lies in the ambiguity of "capable" and "could" as addressed above. There are in fact two possible readings of "capable" and "could". One of them is given by interpreting "capable" as meaning "having the ability to do something" and the other by physical or metaphysical *possibility*. Obviously what is at stake in the dispute between compatibilist and libertarians is the second sense of "could" in "she could not have done otherwise". Suppose it is determined from time immemorial that at 10:30 a.m. today I pinch my left hand rather than scratching it, despite an intense itch ("a compensation action"). In the first sense of "could", it is obvious that *if* I am not handicapped, I *do have* the capacity of scratching my hand if I want to at any time in my life, and, therefore, that "I could have done otherwise in this very circumstance". This means that I have learned the corresponding ability, I know how to scratch and I have not lost the ability of scratching my hand at 10:30 a.m. today. But if determinism is true, notes the libertarian, there is another sense of "could" that is not available to me at 10:30, and this sense is given by physical possibility. As a consequence of the very meaning of a deterministic evolution of a physical system, any action different from the actual one is metaphysically or physically impossible. I take it that the libertarian is correct in pointing this out, and that the compatibilist should not try to defend her position by resorting to complex but misleading discussions involving other possible senses of "could". Therefore, it follows that, from the viewpoint of a coherent compatibilist determinism, both freedom meant as the capacity of originating a new causal chain *absolutely or partially independent from the past* (freedom$_2$) and meant as the possibility of doing otherwise in the same circumstance (freedom$_3$), are regarded as impossible.

The former (freedom$_2$), regarded in its absolute sense, would imply the existence of events, such as those originating some of our actions, that are *either* literally without causes, and, therefore, unexplainable, *or* caused by a mysterious Self, and therefore metaphysically independent on any natural or social event, a postulation that Fichte correctly regarded as justifiable only *via* an act of *faith*.[5] The latter (freedom$_3$) presupposes some sort of indeterminism by definition, since if given the very same circumstances in which I have to act, and supposing the same beliefs, inclinations and desires, I could do otherwise, in the sense that there is a non-epistemic, future probability that I do x and that I do y, it is obvious that the causes of my action are not sufficient to determine it, and are, therefore, only *probabilistic causes*. Let us note in passing that according to some philosophers of causation, probabilistic causes can only be *epistemic*, meaning that the probability attached to them depend really on our *ignorance* of the complete field determining the effects. There are also philosophers defending the view that probabilistic causes are *ontic*, meaning that they cannot *be reduced* to our ignorance. The libertarian should embrace the latter option, and for the sake of argument I will assume from now onward that this move is legitimate.

Taking for granted that all the different positions in the debate agree that freedom$_1$ is compatible with determinism, let us remark that while the dispute separating compatibilists from libertarians has both a *conceptual* and an *empirical* component, the debate between hard determinists and compatibilists is exclusively of a conceptual nature, as they both agree that determinism holds sway.

Historically, compatibilists have defended (and logically can defend) their position by following three different paths. (1) They have argued that their favorite conception of freedom, freedom$_1$, coincides with or fully expresses *Freedom*, the essential core of what we mean or should mean by freedom. (2) Alternatively, they have argued that freedom$_1$ is the only kind of freedom that we presumably possess, given the neurological and psychological constraints of our nature, a nature that excludes the other two forms of freedom. (3) Finally, they have argued on a purely conceptual level that determinism suffices to rescue moral responsibility and our worth as moral agents.

On the basis of what has been said above, compatibilists should prefer the third option (cf. section 8), thereby rejecting any sort of essentialism concerning an allegedly infallible conceptual intuition, which is the first way above (1). As for (2), this is currently a hotly debated empirical question.

---

[5] A mid-way position between absolute origination and complete chance in originating a new action is introduced below. Here I refer merely to *absolute* origination.

However, factual arguments can and should be used against the conception of freedom requiring *complete* autonomy from the past, since it is implausible to suppose that we may ever have sufficient empirical evidence to infer that human beings are capable of giving *absolute* origination to a new causal chain (freedom$_2$). In order to motivate this claim, I will first consider the conceptual relationship between freedom$_2$ and freedom$_3$. We have already established that freedom meant as the possibility to do otherwise in the same circumstances (freedom$_3$) necessarily presupposes some form of indeterminism, as it requires that the same set of events, mental or physical as they may be, occurring in the same individual in the present, be compatible at the same time with *two* or more distinct future courses of actions, and not just with one necessary course, as determinism enjoins. The "Principle of Alternative Possibilities" (AP) that is made possible by *ontic, non-epistemic indeterminism* is regarded by many libertarians as necessary both for our responsibility and for freedom: "The agent is presented with alternative possibilities (that is, she can do otherwise) with respect to A in the sense that at time t, the agent can (has the power or the ability to) do A and can (has the power or the ability to) do otherwise" (Kane 1996, p. 33).

It takes only a little reflection to notice that freedom meant as the power to initiate a new causal chain (freedom$_2$) is not automatically guaranteed by freedom$_3$, in the sense that the sort of indeterminism required by the latter is not sufficient to generate the kind of complete autonomy from any sort of natural and social influence implied by freedom$_2$. A system evolving in an indeterministic fashion (included human decisional processes as construed by libertarians) can in fact have probabilistic causes – granted that these are not the fruit of our ignorance and are rigorously definable – which, however, do not guarantee at all the *complete* causal independence requested by freedom$_3$ as here presented. However, to the effect that some genuine indeterminacies might affect some of our choices, the possibility of doing otherwise could ground *some amount of origination*, where the "some" reflects the kind of partial conditioning of the choice by prior causes advocated by some libertarians. In other words, while AP is not sufficient for *absolute* origination (freedom$_2$), it might suffice for *partial* origination, *to the extent that the libertarian can show that partially determined choices are still the agent's choice, or the product of her effort* (cf. section 6).

While freedom$_3$ is not sufficient for freedom$_2$, it is somewhat more complicated to establish whether the converse implication holds, given that it is necessary to spell out in a clear way the notion of agency presupposed by freedom$_2$. With this end in mind we discuss three possible interpretations of the kind of causal link presupposed by freedom as origination.

The *first* is given by the hypothesis that an unconditioned event of the kind generated by an "originating Self" be indistinguishable from completely indeterministic events, given that the latter also are devoid of antecedent causes. On such a hypothesis, the event desired by the agent initiating a new causal chain must be devoid of any previous causal influence, in such a way that freedom$_2$ requires the sort of indeterminism associated with freedom$_3$ as its *necessary* condition. On the basis of the *second* interpretation, one supposes that freedom$_2$ requires, as it is often maintained, a special causal relation, a causation *sui generis*, such that the Self (capitalized, of course) that produces the choice is determined by some sort of transcendent cause residing within it and to be regarded as *causa sui*. In this hypothesis, freedom$_2$ would not presuppose the indeterminism of freedom$_3$, but only a (deterministic?) causation typical of the agent, and active only within human beings. The third possible reading of freedom$_2$ weakens the requirement of absolute independence from the past of the originating action: In case the self's capacity of determining its choices were only partial, the dependence on the past of the action would also be partial, and freedom$_2$, *regarded in this non absolute sense*, would *suffice* for AP and for freedom$_3$.

Considering its exercise as indistinguishable from a completely indeterministic event, the first reading of the power of origination makes a mockery of the original intention of the libertarian. If an absolutely unconditioned choice C is one which just "occurs" or "happens" to the agent and as such has no cause whatsoever, certainly we should conclude that it is not the *agent's* choice: If nothing can cause C, the agent cannot cause it either.

As to the *second* reading of the power of origination, consider that the notion of an event e that is *causa sui* is highly doubtful, even independently of purely conceptual issues,[6] because its existence would conflict with the principle of the conservation of energy. In fact, where does e gets its energy from, if it is not caused by any other previous event and yet it is not purely chancy? This difficulty alone should direct us toward the third interpretation. As an additional reason to prefer such an interpretation, think how difficult it would be to reconcile the idea of a self that is completely independent of any causal influence (natural or social) with all we know about the psychology of children and about the influence of parents on their offspring, or about the relationship between our mood and neurochemistry.

If a completely unconditioned self creates many more difficulties than solves due to its providing us with the illusory freedom of self-creation, why should we not suppose that the self originating a new causal chain is not

---

[6]One might object that the meaning of "cause" excludes the notion of being *causa sui*.

completely independent – causally speaking – from the brain and the environment? In this sense, such a partially determined self could be, at least in part, *self-determined*, as the will of an agent depends only on itself. Once again, this solution, in taking a mid-way position between the extremes of complete indeterminism (typical of events lacking a cause) and of an absolute self-creation of the self, can make sense only in an indeterministic context. If our will, in fact, were completely determined by natural and social causes preceding our choices, there would be no room left for a partial determination of a choice *via* an emergent causal chain. In other words: Since any reasonable interpretation of freedom$_2$ presupposes some form of indeterminism and, therefore, freedom$_3$ and the correlated AP, we must evaluate whether any form of indeterminism, from pure chance to probabilistic causation or dispositions, is sufficient to rescue the important intuition that we are at least in part responsible for the kind of persons we have become.

The conclusion that I will defend in the final part of the paper is that freedom$_1$ should be regarded as *sufficient* for grounding the sense of our moral responsibility for what we have become, since, if we were free$_2$, our sense of being moral agents would be diminished by the intervention of indeterministic processes, no matter how small such an intervention is. Considering the evaluative and emotional aspect of the debate, however, and *giving due weight to our current ignorance about the empirical aspect of the debate* (we do not know whether the causes of our action are deterministic or indeterministic), there is no reason why the many libertarians that are still unsatisfied by the minimal conception of freedom should not embrace a pragmatic solution to the problem of free will. While lacking decisive empirical evidence about the causes of our behavior, *they should act as if they had freedom$_2$*. Whoever feels at home in a deterministic universe, should instead gratefully accept the restrictions of freedom$_1$ as an intellectual instrument to avoid unnecessary anxiety and fear about the future and obsessive regrets about wrongful actions committed in the past.

6 Why Indeterminism Is Neither Sufficient Nor Necessary for Moral Responsibility

In order to understand why AP has difficulties grounding the concept of moral responsibility, let us focus on *two conditions* that libertarians often conceive as jointly *necessary* for a *morally responsible action*. The first is that the will of the agent be a decisive factor in the causal process leading to a choice or to an action; the second is that the agent could have done otherwise according to AP.[7] I will now try to argue that endorsing the two principles above has consequences that, if not in outright conflict with each other – something that would render any theory of moral responsibility requiring them both contradictory – are such as to weaken to an undesirable degree our sense of having rationally *chosen* the kind of persons we have become.

With this aim in mind, it will be useful at this point to briefly summarize Kane's brilliant attempt to reconcile the principle of choice with some amount of indeterminism, in such a way as to rescue us from the tyranny of a completely determining past. I should say at the outset that I wholeheartedly agree with Kane's thoroughly *naturalistic* approach to agent causation; moreover, I think that that he has successfully shown that many traditional "conceptual equations" linking indeterminism with lack of choice need more reflection or are even mistaken. Nevertheless, to the extent that I have understood it correctly, I think that his attack to compatibilism is affected by some serious problems, involving the kind of *control* we have on the outcome of our probabilistically-caused action, its *faithfulness* to our past values and character, and its *justifiability* and, therefore, to that extent, its rationality. This will lead me to conclude that compatibilism and freedom₁ is the only option we have left.

In a nutshell, Kane argues that there are some choices in the story of our lives that are *self-forming*, in the sense that they truly *shape* our character while being *partially indeterministic*, and, therefore, obey AP. According to Kane, the existence of self-forming actions of this sort is *sufficient* to claim that we are *ultimately responsible* for the kind of persons we have become and even to claim that we "create" or "originate" ourselves, *at least to some degree.* While Kane partially agrees with Frankfurt and Dennett that it is not necessary to suppose that AP applies *to each and every choice of our life,* he argues with the typical libertarian incompatibilist that at least in some of the critical moments of our past our actions must have obeyed AP in order to ground our being responsible for our character. Whenever self-forming actions took place, there must have been at least two conflicting desires to do two opposite actions: Kane's *empirical* hypothesis here is that it is our being undecided about what to do, and our consequent effort to come to a

---

[7]Recall that counterfactual analyses concerning what an agent could have done had she had a desire different from the one she actually had *are compatible with determinism, since they rely on the hypothesis that the agent's past is different from the actual one.* This means that libertarians following AP should insist that a free, responsible action is possible only if, *in the same circumstances and presupposing the same set of beliefs and desires,* the agent could do both x and y, and we have already seen that this can be possible only by postulating some form of ontic, non-epistemic *indeterminism.*

resolution, that generates some tiny stochastic (quantum) mechanism in the brain that may amplify through chaos, and may eventually terminate the conflict by making us decide to do x or y. AP would, thereby, be satisfied, since both actions are *ontically, i.e. non-epistemically*, possible given the same past. Moreover, given that before the choice we were undecided *by having good reasons to do x and to do y*, after the choice is made, whichever way we chose, we can still say we have wanted and chosen responsibly and rationally the outcome, whatever that was. Furthermore, since in the process of rational deliberation, it was our *effort to come to a decision* within our divided self that generated the random mechanism precipitating our choice, we can say with no contradiction that we were *in (partial) control* of the choice, and that *we have chosen* its outcome despite the fact the choice itself obeys AP (for further discussion see Kane (1996) and his contribution in this volume).

In order to begin our evaluation of this interesting proposal, notice first that the agent, who is torn between two conflicting desires cannot in principle have sufficient or overriding *a priori* reasons to do x *rather than y*. Otherwise, on the basis of Kane's empirical hypothesis, a deterministic account of the action would suffice: In fact, he argues that it is the intervention of the agent's reasons to do x that create "the indeterministic disturbance" for the y action, and conversely. I think that his hypothesis of a link between our having a sufficient reason for x and deterministic accounts of x is quite reasonable also from a conceptual viewpoint: True, an agent might have sufficient, overriding reasons to do x rather than y, and yet y might still be physically possible for her, thereby saving AP. However, in circumstances in which the agent knows what to do or needs no deliberation at all, *any* option other than the one she chooses is not really open for her: at least introspectively, *she would not and could not do otherwise. AP seems to "practically" fail when the agent is not torn between alternatives or even when there is only a negligibly small probability that the agent might do otherwise.* It is only when both options are open that the intervention of the indeterministic disturbance creates the sufficient reason to do x or y.

Granting this point to Kane, I now ask: If we knew that, after a long and rational deliberation, it is a random mechanism created in the brain by our own effort that decides and *"cuts the Gordian knot"*,[8] why should we not help ourselves by tossing a coin whenever we find ourselves in the same circumstances of a self-forming action? This would be a perfectly rational procedure: Is not coin tossing or any other random process to that extent as

_____

[8]The English verb "to decide" derives from Latin "caedere", "to cut".

good as the ontically indeterministic processes in our brain?[9] Of course, I am
not claiming that we should always adopt this procedure: If we know what
to do, we can leave our coins alone, but, for the reasons seen above, in these
cases *deterministic explanations of the action suffice*, since we do have from
the start overriding, sufficient reasons to do *x* rather than *y* and AP does not
apply. However, whenever we are still at a loss in making a decision after a
long deliberation and a prolonged effort to decide, and we know in advance
from Kane's hypothesis that in the end the decisive probabilistic, causal
move will be made by a purely random mechanism generated by our own
doubts, *then tossing a coin just before the action of the natural "epicurean
swerve" in the brain is about to take place would be just as rational as letting
our neural pathways "make a decision for us".* Coin tossing is as good a
system to decide as any other indeterministic system that evolution might
have invented.

Please note that by raising this point I am not thereby disagreeing with
Kane on the following conceptual claim: If we chose to toss a coin in order
to decide (instead of relying on the unconscious "neural swerve"), we could
still *claim responsibility* for the outcome, as much we do in the case of the
"neural swerve", and we could claim that the *choice is, to some extent, ours*,
even though realized *via* an *external, artificial* device like a coin. In other
words, if we decided to entrust the choice to a coin rather than provoking it
directly in the brain via the swerve, we would not need to change a word in
Kane's account of indeterministic choices as still being the agent's choices.
This somehow reinforces his point: The internal swerve is *caused* by the
self's effort to decide (exactly as the external toss is), and its outcome is
indeterministically caused by the self, exactly as the result of the toss is
probabilistically caused by the toss, if we accept, incorrectly but for the
sake of the argument in this context, that a tossed coin models an ontically
indeterministic process.[10]

Analogously, since it does not make too much sense to claim in the coin
case that we are *in control* of the outcome, by symmetry it does not make
sense to claim that we are in control of the outcome of the neural "swerve".
While Kane acknowledges this, I think that its consequences for our worth
and responsibility as moral agents are much more serious than he admits:

---

[9]Of course, coin tossing is a *deterministic* process, and its indeterminacy is purely
epistemic, but for the sake of the argument we can treat it as a model of an ontically
undetermined process.

[10]If one is still unsatisfied with a coin (see the previous note), think of deciding with the
help of photons going through a polarizer in the example illustrated below.

we have become the kind of person we are as a consequence of a series of random coin tosses on whose outcomes we had no control whatsoever!

Perhaps this consequence is unavoidable if one wants to stick with AP, but consider now a further problem: Being undecided about what to do, or having frequent moral conflicts, might in part be a matter of *character*. Perhaps it is part of *human nature* to undergo moral conflicts in crucial circumstances of our lives. The important conceptual connection between "becoming a particular kind of person" and deciding is of course given by our being "at crossroads" sometimes and having to make important decisions affecting our whole lives. However, should we then say of a person P that by character *always* knows what to do, or that always solves her moral conflicts by finding some overriding reasons to do one thing rather than another, *without "the help" of neural indeterminacies*, that she is not free or responsible? If we answer no to this question, and I do not know why we should not do so on the level of *conceptual analysis*, then the connection between free will on the one hand and the whole idea of our being in moral conflict as something generating indeterminism on the other seems lost. True enough, Kane's hypothesis is *empirical*, but the lack of *conceptual* support for the empirical proposal in this case is a drawback: Being very often torn in conflicts of conscience may reflect badly on the wholeheartedness and solidity of our moral values.

This last remark suggests another question: Is being free a *matter of degree*, depending on the *number* of moral conflicts we have had in our lives and on *how* we solved them? Perhaps, but then it is also plausible to suppose that finding an overriding reason to do x after some time (having a sufficient, deterministic cause to act, in circumstances in which I could not do y) is at least as rational a procedure as letting the indeterminacy at the neuronal level play some role, no matter how small, in reaching the crucial decision. At least some of us would prefer to know that our important decisions have been the product of efforts eventuated in an overriding reason to do x rather than y *via* deterministic processes, rather than knowing that some amount of indeterminism has played a role.

Since I will return to the rationality of choosing under an ontically construed AP, let me just repeat that I am not claiming that the agent does not choose in the indeterministic circumstances that Kane has considered. Rather, all I am claiming is that if the parallel between the neural swerve and coin tossing is appropriate (imagine that whenever the swerve is about to take place we stop thinking and toss a coin), having become the kind of person we are *thanks to the results of a series of coin tosses* does not seem to help our moral dignity more than accepting the necessity of deterministic choices, that at least can be fully (not just probabilistically) caused by the self's reasons.

Often, Kane seems to underline the advantage of the risky and future-oriented nature of indeterministic choices ("only time will tell"). However, what prevents the compatibilist from accepting risks in deciding, and then making her necessary choice, consequent to her necessary decision, *her own choice*, by claiming *full responsibility* for it as much as the "indeterminist" does? Is this not a way of identifying yourself (Frankfurt's notion), namely what you are, with what you have become after what you have chosen in virtue of your strongest, sufficient reason? Such an identification serves, of course, the purpose of reinforcing your decision if doubts were to arise after the choice has been made. Moreover, the libertarian must concede that also the determinist ignores the outcome of her decisions beforehand, even though a compatibilist must insist on purely *epistemic* limitations, dependent on the fact that the decision is deterministically caused by the deliberation process itself. I am not begging the question about the epistemic nature of the probabilities here, but just reminding us that even if we discovered that instability and chaos were predominant in the brain, as some empirical hypothesis nowadays seem to imply, the compatibilist would have her own *epistemic explanation* of the chaotic and unpredictable but deterministic nature of our decisions.

Just to mention another undesirable moral consequence of indeterministic choices, let me remark that the alleged stochastic or indeterministic mechanism of decision would not have any other effect than that of *separating* the action from (i) the desires of the agent or (ii) from her decision, depending on whether the mechanism itself intervenes *before* (i) or *after* (ii) the decision itself. As libertarians know too well, if the separation in question occurred *after* the decision has been taken, our desires and beliefs would end up (more or less often) in ineffective and frustrating actions, due to the intervention of (more or less radical) probabilistic processes. Our experience, however, refutes this hypothesis. Since the separation realized by a slight amount of chance must occur *before the decision or the agent's choice*, the agent's *values and interests*, which form an essential part of what we call "character" and which accumulated in the past existence of the person, can influence the decision only probabilistically.[11] It follows that, as the libertarian acknowl-

---

[11] One could pose the following evolutionary question: How is it possible that two mechanisms with opposite evolutionary features (deterministic and indeterministic) are welded together in a coherent way in the same organisms, so as to be separated only by a few instants (before and after the choice)? Furthermore, if our decisions were not always the expression of our desires we would not easily survive. Libertarians might, however, surmise

edges, the more random the probabilistic mechanism, the less faithful is the agent's action to her values and will and, in some sense, the less free she is.[12]

However, as indicated above, we can ask whether a very small amount of indeterminism or randomness in choosing x (a negligibly small probability that one can do otherwise) would really be sufficient to make the libertarian happy, *given that in this case the other option of choosing y is practically deterministic.* It is clear that AP in some sense demands real open possibilities of choice and, therefore, "no overriding reasons", but *this demand, in turn, creates tension with the important moral value of faithfulness to our past.* For instance, it is possible to demonstrate that if our decisions were governed by irreducibly stochastic processes, similar to those modelled by so-called Markov chains, later states would have no memory of earlier states, in the sense that they would not depend on them even in a probabilistic sense (they would be statistically independent of the remote past).[13] Analogous considerations, that can be generalized, show that moral values like "coherence with oneself", which presupposes an important amount of continuity, would be threatened by significant, non-negligible indeterministic processes in the sense specified above.[14]

It then seems that the libertarian faces a dilemma. *Either* the possibility of doing otherwise is trivially satisfied also in a deterministic world – and then it is referred to a possible world with a history that differs from the actual past – *or* it presupposes some sort of indeterministic processes, in the sense that in that very circumstance the agent could have done otherwise. However, by taking the latter horn of the dilemma, it is possible to argue that if such indeterminism did occur, it could not be invoked to preserve our dignity as moral agents, because, besides the problems already discussed, it would in addition make our actions utterly *unexplainable*, though probabilistically caused by the agent. How plausible is a view of our life in which its decisive moments, the "bifurcating" choices, cannot be literally *justified*? To the extent that the *rationality* of a decision requires our capacity to *justify* it, and the justification of an action in turn entails the possibility of *explaining*

---

that some indeterminism in the decision mechanism could help us to decide more quickly.

[12] For the idea of chance as a separating mechanism, I am indebted to Fine 1993, pp. 551–572.

[13] Roughly speaking, Markov chains are sequences of stochastic events in which the probability that a particular event gets realized depends only on the preceding event.

[14] Even if it were possible to choose one's character anew every day, or to choose a course of action expressing a different moral essence every day, such a way of living would still be the expression of a character, namely of a stable and to some extent predictable tendency to behave in a changeable way.

it, even a small amount of indeterminism introduces a small explanatory gap, and, therefore, by *modus tollens*, a small hole in the game of giving reason and, therefore, in the rationality of the choice.

As an example, consider a person that must decide whether to lie in front of a jury, in a situation in which she has some prudential and moral reasons not to do so. According to AP, such a person is considered to be free$_3$ if in those very circumstances she could also lie. Remember that the sense of "could" in question has *nothing* to do with her possessing the "ability to lie", in the sense in which most of us do not have the ability of running 100 meters under 10 seconds. We are talking here about an individual that has no psychological compulsion to tell the truth, but rather the ability to lie if necessary and advisable, but in this circumstance has some possibility to lie but also to tell the truth. Let us also suppose that relative to the same previous circumstance, *the two alternative actions* – to lie and to tell the truth – *can be assigned*, as libertarians want, *two distinct non-epistemic probabilities* greater than zero, in such a way that both actions cannot be regarded as lacking causes. Let us suppose, in other words, that the (unknown) probability of lying is smaller than 0.5, but still significantly greater than 0, just to avoid a case of a "practically deterministic alternative" mentioned above, in which AP would not apply.

It is instructive to compare the outcome of the choice of this person to the case of a vertically polarized photon either going or not going trough a polarizer inclined at more than 45 degrees. Since in the hypothesis that quantum mechanics is complete the individual process of being either absorbed or passing the polarizer by a single photon is ontically undetermined, *each photon is completely identical to any other, but still some of them go through and the rest of the photons do not*, according to the probability given by the ($\cos^2$) of the angle between the vertical direction and the orientation of the polarizer. Note that in this experimental situation, quantum mechanics in its standard interpretation tells us that *there is no reason or explanation whatsoever as to why one photon passes and another one does not*. Of course, by obeying the ($\cos^2$) probabilistic law, *we know that in a large number of trials*, behind the polarizer we will have counted the appropriate proportion of photons that have passed the test.

By analogy, now consider a great number of identical replicas of the person deciding whether to lie or not in front of the jury. Recall that probabilities are ontic, so that the past of each individual is identical to any other replica up to the moment of decision, and the rest of the world is identical, too. Only in a certain percentage of the worlds we are considering does the person lie, while in the others she tells the truth according to the probability we may have. It then follows that the set of *single individual* events and circumstances preceding the decision not to lie – in which we include all the desires, the beliefs, and the moral values of the person in question, and, therefore, anything that matters for her – *literally cannot fully explain the decision not to lie, given that they are compatible also with the opposite choice.*

This conclusion holds independently of one's interpretation of probability, and cannot be blocked by the typical libertarian move of refuting the identification of indeterminism with absence of cause. Here the probabilistic cause of the decision is the agent's past, together with her values and her evaluation of the situation in which she finds herself, while in the photon case the cause is the state of the photon before the impact, but the point is that such causes are not *sufficient* to give us an explanation of the *particular outcome*. Suppose in fact that the person tells the truth in this world: The very same set of events or circumstances should be taken into consideration also in order to explain the decision to lie in *another possible* world, which was an alternative possibility open to the agent. In other words, what can be invoked to explain the event in question is only a *probabilistic, objective, non-epistemic disposition* to tell the truth in particular circumstances, given the agent's past.

In this latter hypothesis, however, everything depends on how to read the vague term "objective disposition". Many compatibilists have argued that if by "objective disposition" we just mean chance or "absence of cause", and if there is literally nothing that causes the decision in question, *then certainly not even the self can do it.*[15] If by "disposition" we more charitably refer to an non-epistemic, probabilistic tendency of the individual agent (of the photons) to react in a particular circumstance in a particular way in a great number of trials (probabilistic cause), we are still at a loss to explain the single case, because "disposition" refers to the whole set of possible worlds that we may want to introduce to make sense of a probability assignment. Notice that in the case of the photons, the existence of a precise quantitative law ($\text{Intensity}_{out} = \text{Intensity}_{in} \times \cos^2 \psi$) always affords the opportunity to interpret any talk of propensity attributed to single photons as a roundabout way of talking about *the law* referring to many repetitions of single trials. On the contrary, the attribution to a person of a *quantitatively* precise propensity to tell the truth *in those same circumstances* according to a law is highly doubtful, given that experiments controlling all the circumstances

---

[15] Here I am replacing causing with explaining, thereby weakening Fine's argument (Fine 1993, p. 557).

of the action are practically impossible. And even if talking about dispositions or propensities of individuals does not require introducing precisely formulated quantitative laws but only qualitative possibilities or probabilities, the propensity interpretation of probability in this case suffers from many difficulties (e.g. the time-symmetric nature of probability contrasted by the time-asymmetric character of dispositions).

Being forced to grant that the evaluation of the probability of particular actions is essentially *qualitative* or *comparative*, the libertarian must also admit that even if *there were* irreducibly statistical laws of behavior, these laws would not serve to apply AP to individuals. Let us suppose the existence of hypothetical statistical laws affirming, for example, that a person born in a given suburb has a fixed probability of committing a crime. With respect to such laws, Grünbaum (1972, p. 614) writes: "An irreducibly statistical law enables us to say with respect to any individual *A* that commits a crime, that *A* might have been among those that do not commit crimes. But such a laws does not allow us to say that the individual that commits the crime could have done otherwise." The fact that a statistical law by definition does not give us any information on a specific individual turns the appeal of indeterminism into a completely useless strategy, at least from the perspective of using AP and, therefore, freedom$_3$ to explain the particular self-forming action. And if we cannot explain why we chose what we chose, except for mentioning our effort to decide as a probabilistic cause, how can we consider our choice to be justifiable and, therefore, rational?

In summary, an action in which ontic stochastic mechanisms are present so that AP is fulfilled would not *fully express the character of a person, but would only result in loosening the link with her moral values, diminishing her control of the outcome and its justifiability and, therefore, rationality*, the more so the closer the probability in question approaches mere chance. However, if the amount of indeterminism introduced is too small, it may be insufficient to open the possibilities to the agent as AP requires, since the agent would only have a negligible probability to do otherwise and overriding reasons not to do so.

7   Living With Second-Order, Deterministic Desires

In order to claim that we are ultimately responsible for what we are, have become, and will become, we must assume that we are capable of influencing or even partially shaping our character by making particular choices rather than others. The main question is, of course, whether in order to ground this capacity we must surrender to AP and to its related problems or whether determinism suffices, despite its limitations concerning our not being able to do otherwise (except counterfactually).

If we are compatibilists, for instance, we must argue that when we decide to act in a generous way in a given circumstance, we must have an overriding and sufficient reason to realize our desire to be generous, *arrived at without the help of any indeterministic process.* In particular, this means that our thinking of acting otherwise before the action just reflects our not having yet decided what to do. Though in that very circumstance we cannot do otherwise but act generously, a fact that may seem to jeopardize our responsibility, the desire to be generous that is so prevalent in that moment may of course have been absent in previous stages of our life and it can have begun to be more active at other stages, due to the causally deterministic influence of someone else, or due to our own experience of acute unhappiness following a selfish act, and of pleasure and self-esteem after a generous act.

This seems to justify the claim that the determinist has plenty of resources to explain a modification in the motivational structure of our moral intentions, and need not assume that the desires characterizing our moral life are unchanging. Following Frankfurt, let us baptize desires to be a particular kind of persons, or desires to have particular desires, *"second-order desires"*. It is plausible to suppose that our moral worth is constituted by the capacity of overcoming the biological and social lottery of our first-order desires by cultivating such second-order desires. Even if we may be lacking social impulses in the first part of our lives, we have the capacity for developing the desire to have generous desires, a capacity which is manifested by an increased control of our first-order desires, and by our progressive *"identification"* with such acquired second-order desires (see Frankfurt 1987).

What exactly is such an identification with a second-order desire? Essentially, as I see it, our capacity of identifying ourselves with a certain second-order desire is a dynamic *relation between our moral and personal identity* on the one hand, and the desires itself on the other, where the intentional content of the latter involves our wanting to be or to become a particular kind of person. For the self-perceived identity of some persons, it is *essential* (in the sense of being a defining feature of who they are) to *believe* that they belong or will belong more and more to the set of *courageous* people. For others – and these desires are not exclusive – it matters more to believe that they now belong or will belong ever more so to the learned, or pious, or generous, or feared, or respected or self-respecting or magnanimous, or *responsible* set of people, etc.

Of course, there is an epistemic and social component in this identification, coming into play in the *definition* of the criteria for instantiating a particular virtue, and in the way in which a person perceives herself. A person may be generous while perceiving herself as rottenly selfish or vice versa, but this problems of wrong self-evaluation need not concern us here, as long as we recognize that our moral *identity before* an important moral decision is given by the different weights we assign to some of the relevant second-order desires (or virtues) listed above.[16] And deciding means essentially finding out what these desires are and which one of them matters most to who we are and what we want to be. If among our second-order desires there is, as there ought to be, the desire to be a responsible kind of person, we will then assume responsibility for what we have decided to become, as the libertarian claims the agent does after her AP-abiding choice (see above).

We must not forget that the notion of responsibility is essentially *normative*, and need not be assessed solely from the perspective of the metaphysical problem of free will. If a person does not have the second- or first-order desire of being responsible (that is, of accepting the duties that her station and role assign her), the fact that her action obeyed AP rather than a deterministic process matters little for evaluating the morality of the person. A person acting deterministically may be much more responsible in this normative sense than a person deciding with the help of some indeterministic processes while not keeping her promise or not doing what she has to.

Let us now consider the already mentioned capacity of shaping our character from a deterministic perspective. We have seen that second-order desires can be considered a defining characteristic of our moral and personal *identity*, and that the latter is not *static* but essentially future-oriented, by involving what we want to become in the future. Suppose now that we presently lack generous desires, and do not perceive ourselves as generous at present, but want to become generous: How can we influence our present character in a deterministic fashion? Following Aristotle, we may believe that by acting generously we may *become* generous in the future and the desire to desire to act generously may change our overall motivational structure by inducing in us the first-order desire. Identification with a second-order desire then also implies the recognition that *if* there is a conflict between *two* second-order desires (say between justice and goodness), by having to choose between them we must give more weight to one rather than the other.

---

[16]Of course, who the "we" or self assigning these weights is and on what basis the assignments are made are among the most difficult questions to answer in theorizing about agency.

As a consequence, we *discover* upon deliberation that for our own identity the property of "being just" matters more than that of "being good" (or vice versa). There is a sense in which we discover the kind of person we are only after we reach a difficult decision *via* a deterministic but unpredictable process.

After expanding some on the notion of "identification with a second-order desire, I can now explain why it should rely on *deterministic* causation. Since second-order desires serve the purpose of evaluating how much weight first-order desires must be assigned to in order to become what we want to become, they function like a control mechanism. Now the question is: How can we guarantee to such higher-order desires any kind of efficacious and *reliable* control over the first-, lower-order ones, *without a deterministic causal influence?* The more random the control, the less successful we are in trying to accomplish our moral goals, given that we would fail at least some of the time. In other words, if the process leading to a choice and then to the corresponding action must express the moral character of the person, that is, it must realize the second-order desire that has the most important defining role in that moment of her life, the process itself must be deterministic. If there is no other way to become a generous person but acting according to the corresponding second-order desire, in order to ensure success the link between the desire in question – however we came to have it – and the action should be as deterministic as possible (recall the separation arguments in section 6). Of course, lacking the right education or external influence, some of us also might lack some important second-order desires, but this just shows how important these causal factors are in shaping our moral life, something we know from our everyday experience.

Furthermore, for the morality of a person what matters is, following Aristotle, that that person has developed the "right" character, that is, those dispositions to act morally in every circumstance of our life that the Greek ethic called virtues (cf. MacIntyre 1981). Since "one swallow does not make spring", such dispositions *must be rooted in very stable tendencies to interpret and act on the environment by way of emotional and cognitive reactions.* Such actions must be such that, in the same situation or in similar circumstances, they can manifest themselves in the same way or in similar ways.

Clearly, if in the moral evaluation of a person deciding to abstain from torturing a child during a military campaign, we claim that there is for him a particular probability, significantly greater than zero, to do otherwise, we are *projecting a sinister shadow on his morality.* A person less inclined than another to inflict tortures on innocents is morally (and socially) better than persons that have some tendency, probabilistically grounded, to "do otherwise". Some libertarians, of course, recognize this, but then why not grant that AP can be violated in all cases with no detriment to our moral life? The fact that in an individual the disposition to act morally is a determining, necessitating cause for doing the "right thing" seems less frightening than a person that has both a disposition to be good as well as to be violent, alternating between them depending on the outcomes of delicate indeterministic mechanisms over which control is limited. The stronger (that is, the more deterministic) the disposition to act morally, the stronger our admiration for the person enacting it. The very concept of "life-plan", which is so important in contemporary political philosophy (see Rawls 1971), requires persons with stable character traits, and, therefore, persons who are socially reliably because predictable. Such traits are incompatible with the capricious and unpredictable mechanisms associated with indeterminism that libertarians want to introduce.

8   The Pragmatic Component of the Debate

At this point I can bring forward the question separating hard determinists from compatibilists: Is freedom$_1$ sufficient to claim that we are free *tout court*? I have tried to give some positive arguments in answer to this question. The Kantian conviction that freedom$_1$ is the kind of freedom characterizing the chicken on the roasting-jack, however, cannot be easily dismissed by such arguments, as it depends on deep rooted emotional experiences leading us to believe that the other two kinds of freedom are necessary for our dignity. Such forms, however, in their postulating (i) an unconditioned Self or (ii) some indeterministic mechanisms of choice, appear to make it more difficult to give a coherent sense to our lives. In particular, I argued that the AP is neither necessary nor sufficient to guarantee a form of self-control by higher-order desires over lower-order ones. Such second-order desires are certainly causally determined by the social education and perhaps depend also on our biological make up, but become causally efficacious only thanks to a process of *identification* allowing us to define our identity in the way sketched above. The compatibilist must acknowledge that the remote causes of our actions are independent of our will (since they date back to events preceding our births), but the causes that are less remote, however, are not, since it is our identification with some of our desires that is causally efficacious in determining our actions.[17]

---

[17]In any case, in order to avoid misunderstandings of the conceptual consequences of compatibilism, it is important to distinguish carefully the determination of an action by

In conclusion, it is worth mentioning the existence of a sometimes neglected pragmatist dimension of the debate. For example, accepting the view that our actions are causally determined implies some emotional attitudes that, at least for some of us, are particularly adaptive, and that have already been well-illustrated by Spinoza in his *Ethics*. I am referring here not only to an identification with our biological nature suggested by Honderich or with the whole of nature suggested by Rolland's "oceanic feeling", but also to a softening of the pain originating in our experience of regret for a mistake committed in the past. Such a mistake must be framed in a conception of ourselves characterized by the recognition of the limits of our causal powers already preached by Stoic philosophers; analogously, the awareness that we could not have done otherwise limits an illusory and damaging sense of omnipotence of the Self, who may be convinced to be able to construe and destroy oneself every day. As Spinoza had already anticipated, the fact that we could not do otherwise in a given circumstance may have the beneficial effect of liberating us from obsessive and useless feelings of guilt on the one hand, and, on the other, can be regarded as compatible with a firm intention to act differently in the future. A future that the determinist can regard, unlike the fatalist, as being partially the deterministic fruit and consequence of our actions and our will, but that will not be anticipated by an anxious oscillation between fear and hope caused by an exaggeration of our causal powers.

This very oscillation may well be tormenting the libertarian, who feels condemned "to carry the weight of the world on her shoulders", and who may be brought by her position to feel much more responsible than a compatibilist for situations in her life that do not depend in any sense on her. It should also be clear why the compatibilist does not spare any person from the pain of choosing: Since it is the very decisional process that determines the outcome, the latter may be unpredictable and yet be completely determined by our past. However, it is one thing to know that we incline toward some action rather than another because our past values (plus the causal effects of the deliberation) are such as to have more "weight" than competing values and desires, and quite another to assume that the action is caused by the self also thanks to an indeterministic process.

Clearly, whoever is frightened by this view of the place occupied by human beings in the universe can defend the option sanctioned by freedom$_2$ and freedom$_3$ and *postulate*, like Kant, that we are free in other senses. The pain originated by the awareness of not being able to completely change oneself

---

events antecedent to it with the psychological notion of *compulsion*.

may induce some of us toward radical forms of libertarianism. Now, whoever lives a fuller life by believing, without any evidential reasons, in her capacity of radical self-determination (not just the process of identification accepted also by the compatibilist) *may have good practical reasons to continue believing it.* Until we know more about the precise mechanisms causing our actions, this attitude is rational. I hope, however, that the considerations mentioned above are sufficient to show that without such a pragmatic justification coming from the *utility* of believing in freedom$_2$ or freedom$_3$, beliefs in them would at the moment be either unjustified or affected by some serious conceptual difficulties. And we should remember that trying to convince ourselves of something that we know to be implausible is often unsuccessful (see Elster 1983).

Acknowledgment

I want to thank an anonymous referee for valuable criticism and suggestions forcing me to rethink some issues I introduced in a previous version of this paper.

References

Anscombe E. (1959): *Intention*, Blackwell, Oxford.

Chisholm R. (1982): Freedom and the self. In *Free Will*, ed. by G. Watson, Oxford University Press, Oxford, pp. 24–35.

Davidson D. (1984): *Inquiries into Truth and Interpretation*, Clarendon Press, Oxford, p. 261.

Earman J. (1986): *A Primer on Determinism*, Reidel, Dordrecht.

Elster J. (1983): *Sour Grapes*, Cambridge University Press, Cambridge.

Fine A. (1993): Indeterminism and freedom of the will. In *Philosophical Foundations of the Internal and the External Worlds. Essays in Honor of Adolf Grünbaum*, ed. by J. Earman, A. Janis, G. Massey, N. Rescher, University of Pittsburgh Press, Pittsburgh.

Frankfurt H. (1987): Identification and wholeheartedness. In *Responsibility, Character and the Emotions*, ed. by F. Shoeman, Cambridge University Press, Cambridge, pp. 27–45.

Grünbaum A. (1972): Free will and laws of human behavior. In *New Readings in Philosophical Analysis*, ed. by H. Feigl, W. Sellars, and K. Lehrer, Appleton-Century Crofts, New York, pp. 605–627.

Honderich T. (1993): *How Free Are You?* Oxford University Press, Oxford.

James W. (1956): The dilemma of determinism. In *The Will to Believe*, Dover, New York, p. 10.

Kane R. (1996): *The Significance of Free Will*, Oxford University Press, Oxford.

Kenny A. (1963): *Action, Emotion and Will*, Routledge and Kegan Paul, London.

MacIntyre A. (1981): *After Virtue*, University of Notre Dame Press, Notre Dame.

Nozick R. (1981): *Philosophical Explanations*, Harvard University Press, Cambridge MA.

Quine W. van O. (1981): *Theories and Things*, Cambridge University Press, Cambridge, p. 11.

Rawls J. (1971): *A Theory of Justice*, Harvard University Press, Cambridge MA.

Ryle G. (1949): *The Concept of Mind*, University of Chicago Press, Chicago.

Salmon W. (1990): *Forty Years of Scientific Explanation*, University of Minnesota Press, Minneapolis.

Free Will, Determinism, and Indeterminism

Robert Kane

1   Introduction

The traditional idea of free will was associated with a kind of ultimate responsibility that humans were supposed to have for their own wills and actions. The wills and actions of truly free and responsible agents must have their source in the agents themselves and not wholly in other things over which the agents have no control – such as fate or God's will, the laws of physics, heredity and environment, social conditioning, psychological compulsion or historical forces. It is owing to this requirement that the traditional notion of free will was thought to conflict with determinism in all its varieties – fatalistic, theological, physical, biological, psychological, social and historical. In order to be truly deserving of praise and blame, we – and not any of these other factors beyond our control – must be ultimately responsible (to some degree at least) for our being the sorts of persons we are – in other words, for having the kinds of wills, characters and motives that we do have.

In a number of writings over the past twenty years, and notably in my book *The Significance of Free Will* (Kane 1996), I have argued that this *is* the traditional idea of free will that has been in dispute for centuries. Moreover, it is the idea most ordinary people still have when they intuitively believe that there is some kind of conflict between free will and determinism (before they have been talked out of this belief by the clever arguments of philosophers). And I think this ordinary intuitive belief is ultimately right.

If this traditional idea of free will is correct, then the issues about determinism and indeterminism that are the focus of this volume have abiding significance for matters of everyday life. Esoteric as issues about determinism and indeterminism may often seem to be in the natural, psychological and social sciences, they are relevant to questions of everyday life that matter to us, such as whether we have free will or are morally responsible for our actions or are ultimately deserving of praise and blame, and many other related issues. Or so I believe and will argue in this paper.

Yet this traditional conception of free will just described, which seems to conflict with determinism, has been under sustained attack by philosophers and scientists in the modern era of Western thought ever since the seventeenth century; and these attacks have reached a crescendo in the twentieth century, when many philosophers and scientists have come to believe that the traditional idea of free will just described is outmoded and has no place in the modern scientific picture of the world. This modern attack on traditional free will has two parts.

Part 1. The first prong of the modern attack on traditional free will concerns *determinism*. The goal is to show that the alleged conflict between free will and determinism is not real by showing that all the kinds of freedoms we want and care about – freedoms from coercion, or compulsion, physical restaint, addictions, and political oppression – are really compatible with determinism. Even if the world should turn out to be deterministic, there would be a difference between being free from these impediments to freedom and free will (coercion, compulsion, addiction and oppression) and not being free from them, and we would prefer to be free from them rather than not, even in a determined world. So esoteric questions about whether determinism is true or not – in the physical or psychological sciences – are considered to be irrelevant to the freedoms we really care about in everyday life.

Part 2. The second prong of the modern attack against traditional free will concerns *indeterminism* rather than determinism. The charge here is that even if it should turn out that there is some indeterminism in the physical world – given modern quantum physics, for example – or in human affairs, this would not help believers in traditional free will. For indeterminism in human affairs would amount to chance; and one cannot have control over events that are undetermined or occur merely by chance. Even if indeterminism in the microphysical world should sometimes be amplified to have large-scale effects on the human brain or nervous system, this would be no help for free will, because undetermined events in the brain would be uncontrollable by the agents themselves, like the unanticipated emergence of a thought or the uncontrolled jerking of an arm – quite the opposite of what we take free and responsible actions to be like. Indeterminism in nature, if it did play a role in human affairs, would not enhance our freedom and control over events, but diminish freedom and control; and so it is considered to be irrelevant to free will at best, and an obstacle at worse.

This two-part modern attack on traditional free will is very powerful and seems to have convinced a majority of modern thinkers, scientists and philosophers as well as many ordinary persons. Its upshot is that we need not worry about esoteric questions in the sciences that are the concern of this volume about whether determinism or indeterminism is true in the physical world or in human affairs. Such questions do not really matter for mundane issues about whether we are free or have free wills, whether we are morally responsible for our actions, whether we are truly worthy of praise or blame, and so on. These questions do not matter because *determinism is no threat to free will after all* (Part 1 of the modern attack) and *indeterminism is no help to free will if it does exist* (Part 2).

I think both these parts of what I have called the modern attack on traditional free will are misguided and will try to show why I think so in this paper. I will argue that if determinism were in fact true in the physical sciences or psychology or the social and historical sciences, it would be a genuine threat to free will (cf. Primas, and Richardson and Bishop in this volume). And I shall argue that it is false to say that indeterminism would undermine rather than enhance free will and responsibility because indeterminism in human affairs would merely amount to chance (in contrast to Dorato in this volume). If my arguments are correct, then issues about determinism and indeterminism in physics and psychology and in other natural and human sciences that are the topic of this volume have great relevance to things that matter to us in everyday life concerning freedom, responsibility and human worth.

2 Modern Attack on Traditional Free Will

2.1 Is Free Will Compatible with Determinism?

In a number of writings over the past two decades, I have sought to answer four questions about free will: (i) Is it compatible (or incompatible) with determinism? (ii) Why do we want it? (iii) Can we make sense of a free will that is incompatible with determinism? (iv) Can such a free will be reconciled with modern images of human beings in the natural and social sciences?[1] On all four questions, I have tried to point current debates about free will in new directions. The first two questions – the Compatibility Question and the Significance Question, as I call them – are related to the Part 1 of the modern attack on free will. We shall consider them first (returning later to the second two questions, which are related to Part 2 of the modern attack).

---

[1]See especially my book (Kane 1996), which provides an overview of philosophical debates about all four questions over the past fifty years and further development of many of the ideas of this paper. Also, see earlier work (Kane 1985) and the articles cited in that book.

Of the four questions, question (i) – the Compatibility Question (Is free will compatible or incompatible with determinism?) – has received most of the recent attention in philosophical debates about free will. The first thing I think we learn from these debates is that if we formulate the Compatibility Question as in most textbook discussions of free will – "Is freedom compatible with determinism?" – the question is too simple and ill-formed. The reason is that there are many meanings of "freedom" and many of these kinds of freedom – from coercion, compulsion, covert control and political oppression – *are* compatible with determinism. Thus, I believe that those who defend a traditional free will, as I do, should grant this much to Part 1 of the modern attack against free will. *Many* everyday freedoms we value are compatible with determinism. What defenders of a traditional free will should insist upon instead is that *not all* the significant freedoms are compatible with determinism; and at least one kind of freedom worth wanting is not. This significant further freedom is "free *will*", which I define as "the power to be the *ultimate* originator and sustainer of one's own ends or purposes". To say this further freedom is significant is not to deny the importance of everyday compatibilist freedoms from coercion, compulsion, political oppression, and the like; it is only to say that human longings transcend them.

The compatibilist freedoms from coercion, compulsion and the like are associated with what Honderich has called *voluntariness* (see, e.g., Honderich 1988) – our ability to act in accordance with our own wills rather than against our wills under coercion or compulsion, control or oppression. (This idea of voluntariness is quite ancient and goes back at least as far as Aristotle.) I agree with Honderich that such voluntariness, and most of the freedoms associated with it, are compatible with determinism; and I agree that these compatibilist freedoms are important for human life. Unlike other believers in a traditional incompatibilist or anti-determinist conception of free will, I do not summarily dismiss the importance of compatibilist freedoms – and in this, Honderich and I are in agreement. But in also holding to the traditional idea of *free will* as ultimate creation of purposes, I also believe that there is an additional notion of freedom and responsibility that transcends mere voluntariness and is incompatible with determinism. It is this further notion of (traditional) "free will" that Honderich associates with *origination* and which he contrasts with *voluntariness*. Free will in this sense of origination, as I conceive it, presupposes voluntariness as a necessary condition, but transcends mere voluntariness, presupposing other things as well, including indeterminism. A free choice must be voluntary to be sure (which means among other things uncoerced and uncompelled), but it must be more than that to be truly originating.

Honderich also thinks origination (or free will in this deeper more, ultimate sense) would be important, if we could have it. But he does not think we can have it. He believes this because he believes macroscopic human behavior is for all intents and purposes determined, even if it should turn out that there is some quantum indeterminacy in the microphysical world. But Honderich is sceptical about ultimate origination for another and deeper reason as well. Like many other modern philosophers and scientists, he doubts that one can even make sense of an (ultimate) origination that requires indeterminism; and he and other modern philosophers and scientists believe this for the reasons given above in Part 2 of the modern attack on free will. That is to say, indeterminism in human affairs would amount to chance and would be of no help to free will, diminishing rather than enhancing our freedom and responsibility. In the second part of this paper (which deals with Part 2 of the modern attack on free will), I will try to show to the contrary how one might make sense of such origination and a free will involving indeterminism. For the moment we are still pressing the issue of whether there *is* a significant kind of freedom (free will) worth wanting that is incompatible with determinism.

So this is one shift in direction for the Compatibility Question ("Is free will compatible with determinism?") that I insist upon. We should grant to the first part of the modern attack on free will that many kinds of everyday freedoms worth wanting are compatible with determinism. What we should deny is that these are the only kinds of freedom worth wanting. There is another kind of freedom worth wanting – free will – that goes deeper than these other freedoms and is not compatible with determinism.

But there is another shift in direction for the Compatibility Question about free will and determinism that I insist upon of even more importance. Most recent and past philosophical debate about the incompatibility of free will and determinism has focused on the question of whether determinism is compatible with "the condition of alternative possibilities" (which I shall call AP) – the requirement that the free agent "could have done otherwise". The idea is that if every event were determined, no one ever could have acted otherwise; and so no one has free will. Most contemporary arguments for incompatibism focus on this supposed conflict between determinism and could-have-done-otherwise (AP). The most widely discussed of these current arguments is the so-called "Consequence Argument" of van Inwagen (1983); see also Wiggins (1973), and Ginet (1990).

This Consequence Argument adds a further twist: If determinism is true then all of our actions are determined by events occurring before we were born given the laws of nature. But we do not have the power to alter what happened before we were born nor the power to alter the laws of nature. Therefore we do not have the power to alter our present actions since the past and the laws necessitate them; and so we do not have alternative possibilities or the power to do otherwise and therefore lack free will. Critics of arguments like this for the incompatility of determinism and free will that depend on AP either deny that AP conflicts with determinism or deny that alternative possibilities are required for moral responsibility or free will in the first place. In my book (Kane 1996, chapters 3–5), I survey and critically evaluate current criticisms of the Consequence Argument and current debates in general about whether AP conflicts with determinism. I will not repeat that discussion here but will merely state its conclusions. As I view these current debates about whether free will requires AP or whether AP is incompatible with determinism, the debates inevitably tend to stalemate over differing interpretations of "can", "power", "ability" and "could have done otherwise". Some interpretations of these terms render them compatible with determinism, some do not. Moreover, I think there are good reasons for these stalemates having to do with the different meanings of freedom just mentioned. If some notions of freedom (from coercion, compulsion, etc.) are compatible with determinism, and some others are not, we would expect that some corresponding notions of could-have-done-otherwise would also be compatible with determinism and some would not. What is needed, therefore, are further grounds for deciding which senses of freedom and could-have-done-otherwise count for genuine free will and responsibility and which do not. And that problem takes us beyond considerations of AP alone to further criteria for free will. In short, the power to do otherwise (AP) by itself provides too thin a basis on which to rest the case for the incompatibility of free will and determinism: *the Compatibility Question cannot be resolved by focusing on alternative possibilities alone.*

Fortunately, there is another place to look for insight into the Compatibility Question. In the long history of free will debate, one can find another criterion fueling intuitions that determinism is incompatible with free will that is even more important than AP, though comparatively neglected. I call it the condition of ultimate responsibility or UR. The basic idea is this: to be ultimately responsible for an action, an agent must be responsible for anything that is a sufficient reason (condition, cause or motive) for the action's occurring.[2] If, for example, a choice issues from, and can be sufficiently explained by, an agent's character and motives (together with background conditions), then to be *ultimately* responsible for the choice, the agent must

---

[2]For a formal statement and defense of this condition, see Kane (1996, chapter 3).

be at least in part responsible by virtue of choices or actions voluntarily performed in the past for having the character and motives he or she now has. Compare Aristotle's claim that if a man is responsible for wicked acts that flow from his character, he must at some time in the past have been responsible for forming the wicked character from which these acts flow.

This UR condition accounts for the "ultimate" in the original definition of free will: "the power of agents to be the *ultimate* creators and sustainers of their own ends or purposes". Now UR does not require that we could have done otherwise (AP) for *every* act done of our own free wills – thus vindicating philosophers such as Frankfurt (1969), Fischer (1994), and Dennett (1984), who insist that we can be held morally responsible for many acts even when we could not have done otherwise. But the vindication is only partial. For UR *does* require that we could have done otherwise with respect to *some* acts in our past life histories by which we formed our present characters. I call these "self-forming actions", or SFAs. Consider Dennett's example of Martin Luther. When Luther finally broke with the Church at Rome, he said "Here I stand, I can do no other". Suppose, says Dennett, at that moment Luther was literally right. Given his character and motives, he could not then and there have done otherwise. Does this mean he was not morally responsible, not subject to praise or blame, for his act, or that he was not acting of his own free will? Dennett says "not at all". In saying "I can do no other", Luther was not disowning responsibility for his act, but taking full responsibility for acting of his own free will. So "could have done otherwise", or AP, says Dennett, is not required for moral responsibility or free will.

My response to Dennett is to grant that Luther could have been responsible for this act, even *ultimately* responsible in the sense of UR, though he could not have done otherwise then and there and even if his act was determined. But this would be so to the extent that he was responsible for his present motives and character by virtue of many earlier struggles and self-forming choices (SFAs) that brought him to this point where he could do no other. Those who know Luther's biography know the inner struggles and turmoil he endured getting to that point. Often we act from a will already formed, but it is "our own free will" by virtue of the fact that we formed it by other choices or actions in the past (SFAs) for which we could have done otherwise. If this were not so, there is nothing we could have *ever* done to make ourselves different than we are – a consequence, I believe, that is incompatible with our being (at least to some degree) ultimately responsible for what we are. So SFAs are only a subset of those acts in life for which we are ultimately responsible and which are done "of our own free will". But if none of our acts were self-forming in this way, we would not be *ultimately* responsible for anything we did.

If the case for incompatibility cannot be made on AP alone, it can be made if UR is added; and thus, I suggest, the too-often neglected UR should be moved to center stage in free will debates. If agents must be responsible to some degree for anything that is a sufficient cause or motive for their actions, an impossible infinite regress of past actions would be required unless some actions in the agent's life history (that is, self-forming actions or SFAs) did not have either sufficient causes or motives (and hence were undetermined). This, then, is my answer to the first part of the modern attack on traditional free will, which says that *determinism is no threat to free will after all* because determinism does not really conflict with free will. My answer is that if you think free will is significant because it is associated with our being ultimately responsible (UR) for our own wills, then free will is indeed incompatible with determinism. This, by the way, provides an answer to question (ii) above as well – the Significance Question (why do we want free will?). We want it because it matters to us that we are the ultimate sources of at least some aspects of our own wills – rather than that our wills be wholly the product of forces beyond our control, such as fate or God, the laws of physics, heredity or environment, social or psychological conditioning, and so on.[3]

2.2   Can One Make Sense of a Free Will Requiring Indeterminism?

But this new route to the incompatibility of free will and determinism raises a host of further questions which go beyond Part 1 of the modern attack on traditional free will to the second part of that attack. How is it possible that actions lacking both sufficient causes and motives could themselves be free and responsible actions? And how, if at all, could such actions exist as something other than mere chance occurrences in the natural and social world where we live and have our being? These are versions of questions (iii) and (iv) listed above, which I call the Intelligibility and Existence questions for free will, to which I now turn. They take us to Part 2 of the modern attack on traditional free will, which says that *indeterminism*, even if it existed in the natural world, would be of no help in accounting for free will

The Intelligibility Question (question (iii)) rests on an ancient dilemma: if free will is not compatible with determinism, it does not seem to be compatible with indeterminism either. It seems that one cannot make sense of

---

[3]For more discussion, see Kane (1996, chapter 6).

free will either way, whether determinism is true or not. The arguments for the second horn of this dilemma (free will is not compatible with indeterminism either) are familiar ones going back to ancient times. Indeterminism, it seems, would amount to chance. An undetermined or chance action would occur spontaneously and would not be controlled by anything, hence not controlled by the agent. How then could it be a free action for which the agent could be held responsible? If, for example, a choice occurred by virtue of a quantum jump or other undetermined event in one's brain it would seem a fluke or accident rather than a responsible choice.

Or look at the problem in a deeper way. If my choice is really undetermined, that means I could have made a different choice *given exactly the same past* right up to the moment when I did choose. That is what indeterminism and probability mean: exactly the same past, different possible outcomes (cf. Bishop, this volume). Imagine, for example, that I had been deliberating about spending my vacation in Hawaii or Colorado, and after much thought and deliberation had decided I prefered Hawaii and chose it. If the choice was undetermined, then exactly the same deliberation, the same thought processes, the same beliefs, desires and other motives – not a sliver of difference – that led up to my favoring and choosing Hawaii over Colorado, might by chance have issued in my choosing Colorado instead. This is very strange. If such a thing happened it would seem a fluke or accident, like that quantum jump in the brain just mentioned, not a rational choice. Since I had come to favor Hawaii and was about to choose it, when by chance I chose Colorado, I would wonder what went wrong and perhaps consult a neurologist. For reasons such as these, people have argued through the centuries that undetermined free choices would be "arbitrary", "capricious", "random", "irrational", "uncontrolled", "inexplicable", or "merely matters of luck or chance", not really free and responsible choices at all.

Defenders of an incompatibilist or libertarian free will have a dismal record of answering these familiar charges. Realizing that free will cannot merely be indeterminism or chance, they have appealed to various obscure or mysterious forms of agency or causation to make up the difference. Kant said we cannot explain free will in scientific and psychological terms, even though we require it for belief in morality (Kant 1956, part III). To account for free will we have to appeal to the agency of what he called a "noumenal self" outside space and time that could not be studied in scientific terms. Many other respectable thinkers continue to believe that only an appeal to some sort of substantial mind/body dualism of a Cartesian or other kind can make sense of free will (e.g. Eccles 1970, Eccles and Popper 1977, Swinburne 1986). Science might tell us there was indeterminacy or a place for causal gaps in the brain, but a non-material self, or what Eccles calls a "transempirical power center", would have to fill the causal gaps left by physical causes by intervening in the natural order (Eccles 1970). The most popular appeal among philosophers today is to a special kind of *agent- or immanent causation* that cannot be explained in terms of the ordinary modes of causation in terms of events familiar to the natural or behavioral sciences (Campbell 1967, Watson 1987, Clarke 1996, O'Connor 2000). Free and responsible actions are not determined by prior events, but neither do they occur merely by chance. Rather, such actions are caused by agents in a way that transcends and cannot be explained in terms of ordinary modes of causation by events involving the agents. (I will return to a discussion of this agent-causation view below.)

I call these familiar libertarian strategies for making sense of free will "extra factor" strategies. The idea behind them is that, since indeterminism leaves it open which way an agent will choose or act, some "extra" kind of causation or agency must be postulated over and above the natural flow of events to account for the agent's going one way or another. Early in my encounters with free will debates, I became disenchanted with all such extra factor strategies. I agree with other libertarian critics, such as van Inwagen and Ginet, that extra factor strategies – including agent-causal theories – do not solve the problems about indeterminism they are supposed to solve and create further mysteries of their own (e.g. van Inwagen 2000, Ginet 1990). If we are going to make progress on the Intelligibility and Existence questions about incompatibilist free will (and hence in answering Part 2 of the modern attack on free will), I think we have to strike out in new directions, avoiding appeals to extra factor strategies altogether, including special forms of agent-causation. To do this means rethinking issues about indeterminism, freedom and responsibility from the ground up, a task to which I now turn.

3   Indeterminism and Responsibility

First, note that indeterminism does not have to be involved in all acts done "of our own free wills" for which we are ultimately responsible, as argued earlier. Not all such acts have to be undetermined, but only those by which we made ourselves into the kinds of persons we are, which I called self-forming actions or SFAs. Now I believe these undetermined SFAs occur at those difficult times of life when we are torn between competing visions of what we should do or become. Perhaps we are torn between doing the moral thing or acting from ambition, or between powerful present desires and long term goals, or we are faced with a difficult tasks for which we have aversions. In all such cases, we are faced with competing motivations and have to make an effort to overcome temptation to do something else we also strongly want. There is tension and uncertainty in our minds about what to do at such times, I suggest, that is reflected in appropriate regions of our brains by movement away from thermodynamic equilibrium leading to a kind of "stirring up of chaos" in the brain that makes it sensitive to micro-indeterminacies at the neuronal level. The uncertainty and inner tension we feel at such soul-searching moments of self-formation is thus reflected in the indeterminacy of our neural processes themselves. What is experienced internally as uncertainty then corresponds physically to the opening of a window of opportunity that temporarily screens off complete determination by influences of the past in the sense that the combined effects of heredity and earlier conditioning prior to this moment no longer completely determine the outcome.[4] (By contrast, when we act from predominant motives or settled dispositions, the uncertainty or indeterminacy is muted. If it did play a role in such cases, it *would* be a mere nuisance or fluke, as critics of indeterminism contend.)

When we do decide under such conditions of uncertainty, the outcome is not determined because of the preceding indeterminacy – and yet it can be willed (and hence rational and voluntary) either way owing to the fact that in such self-formation, the agents' prior wills are divided by conflicting motives. Consider a businesswoman who faces such a conflict. She is on her way to an important meeting when she observes an assault taking place in an alley. An inner struggle ensues between her conscience, to stop and call for help, and her career ambitions, which tell her she cannot miss this meeting. She has to make an effort of will to overcome the temptation to go on. If she overcomes this temptation, it will be the result of her effort, but if she fails, it will be because she did not *allow* her effort to succeed. And this is due to the fact that, while she willed to overcome temptation, she also willed to fail, for quite different and incommensurable reasons. When we, like the woman, decide in such circumstances, and the indeterminate efforts we are making become determinate choices, we *make* one set of competing reasons or motives prevail over the others then and there *by deciding*.

Now let us add a further piece to the puzzle. Just as indeterminism need not undermine rationality and voluntariness, so indeterminism in and of itself

---

[4] "Screening off" is meant here in a sense suggested by Salmon (1984), according to which, to take a simple example, the original order in a newly opened deck of cards is "screened off" by subsequent shufflings of the deck so the initial order no longer determines what cards are selected from the deck. For further discussion see Berkovitz, this volume.

need not undermine control and responsibility. Suppose you are trying to think through a difficult problem, say a mathematical problem, and there is some indeterminacy in your neural processes complicating the task – a kind of chaotic background. It would be like trying to concentrate and solve the problem with background noise or distraction. Whether you are going to succeed in solving the problem is uncertain and undetermined because of the distracting neural noise. Yet, if you concentrate and solve the problem none the less, we have reason to say you did it and are responsible for it even though it was undetermined whether you would succeed. The indeterministic noise was an obstacle that you overcame by your effort.[5]

There are numerous examples of more familiar kinds supporting this point, where indeterminism may function as an obstacle to success in human action without precluding responsibility. Consider an assassin who is trying to shoot the prime minister, but might miss because of some undetermined events in his nervous system that may lead to a jerking or wavering of his arm. If the assassin does succeed in hitting his target, despite this indeterminism, can he be held responsible? The answer is clearly yes because he intentionally and voluntarily succeeded in doing what he was *trying* to do – kill the prime minister. Yet his action, killing the prime minister, was undetermined. Or, here is another example: a husband, while arguing with his wife, in a fit of rage swings his arm down on her favorite glass-top table top intending to break it. Again, we suppose that some indeterminism in his outgoing neural pathways makes the momentum of his arm indeterminate so that it is undetermined whether the table will break right up to the moment when it is struck. Although whether or not the husband breaks the table is undetermined, he is clearly responsible if he does break it. (It would be a poor excuse for him to say to his wife: "chance did it, not me". Even though indeterminism was involved, chance did not do it. He did.)

Now these examples – of the mathematical problem, the assassin and the husband – are not all we want since they do not amount to genuine exercises

---

[5]Of course, there are larger questions to be asked here about the status of the "you" who is doing the acting in such cases of mental action. But such questions as "who or what is this 'you' (this self) that is acting?" arise even if one assumes the mental activity of the brain is determined. Compatibilists and determinists about free will have to face such questions about the nature of the self or agent just as clearly as do incompatibilists. And my point here in the text is a conditional one: *if* one can make sense of selfhood and agency should the brain be determined (as determinists and compatibilists believe it is or may be), then one can as well make sense of it if some indeterminacy should be introduced into the functioning of the brain. (Conversely, if one cannot make sense of selfhood or agency even when the brain is determined, then determinists and compatibilists are in as much trouble as we incompatibilists and indeterminists. I will return to selfhood and agency later.)

of (self-forming) free will in SFAs, like the businesswoman's, where the will is divided between conflicting motives. The woman wants to help the victim, but she also wants to go on to her meeting. By contrast, the assassin's will is not equally divided. He wants to kill the prime minister, but does not also want to fail. (If he fails, therefore, it will be merely by chance.) Yet these examples of the assassin, the husband and the like, do provide some clues. To go further, we have to add some new twists.

In cases of inner conflict characteristic of SFAs, like the businesswoman's, the indeterministic noise which is providing an obstacle to her overcoming temptation is not coming from an external source, but is coming from her own will, since she also deeply desires to do the opposite. Imagine that two crossing (recurrent) neural networks are involved, each influencing the other, and representing her conflicting motivations. (These are complex networks of interconnected neurons in the brain circulating impulses in feedback loops that are generally involved in higher-level cognitive processing.[6]) The input of one of these neural networks consists in the woman's reasons for acting morally and stopping to help the victim; the input of the other, consists in her ambitious motives for going on to her meeting. The two networks are connected so that the indeterministic noise which is an obstacle to her making one of the choices is coming from her desire to make the other, and vice versa – the indeterminism thus arising from a tension-creating conflict in the will, as we supposed earlier. In these circumstances, when either of the pathways "wins" (i.e. reaches an activation threshold, which amounts to choice), it will be like your solving the mathematical problem by overcoming the background noise produced by the other. And just as when you solved the mathematical problem by overcoming the distracting noise, one can say you did it and are responsible for it, so one can say this as well, I argue, in the present case, *whichever one is chosen*. The pathway through which the woman succeeds in reaching a choice threshold will have overcome the obstacle in the form of indeterministic noise generated by the other.

Note that, under such conditions, the choices either way will not be "inadvertent", "accidental", "capricious", or "merely random", (as critics of indeterminism say) because they will be *willed* by the agents either way when they are made, and done for *reasons* either way – reasons that the agents then and there *endorse*. But these are the conditions usually required to say something is done "on purpose", rather than accidentally, capriciously or merely by chance. Moreover, these conditions taken together, I argue, rule

---

[6]Readable and accessible introductions to the role of neural networks (including recurrent networks) in cognitive processing include Churchland (1996) and Spitzer (1999).

out each of the reasons we have for saying that agents act, but do not have _control_ over their actions, (compulsion, coercion, constraint, inadvertence, accident, control by others, etc.).[7] Of course, for undetermined SFAs, agents do not control or determine which choice outcome will occur _before_ it occurs; but it does not follow, because one does not control or determine which of a set of outcomes is going to occur before it occurs, that one does not control or determine which of them occurs _when_ it occurs. When the above conditions for SFAs are satisfied, agents exercise control over their future lives _then and there_ by deciding. Indeed, they have what I call "plural voluntary control" over the options in the following sense: they are able to bring about _whichever_ of the options they will, _when_ they will to do so, for the reasons they will to do so, on purpose rather than accidentally or by mistake, without being coerced or compelled in doing so or willing to do so, or otherwise controlled in doing or willing to do so by any other agents or mechanisms. Each of these conditions can be satisfied for SFAs as conceived above (Kane 1996, chapter 8). The conditions can be summed up by saying, as we sometimes do, that the agents can choose either way, _at will._

Note also that this account of self-forming choices amounts to a kind of "doubling" of the mathematical problem. It is as if an agent faced with such a choice is _trying_ or making an effort to solve _two_ cognitive problems at once, or to complete two competing (deliberative) tasks at once – in our example, to make a moral choice and to make a conflicting self-interested choice (corresponding to the two competing neural networks involved). Each task is being thwarted by the indeterminism coming from the other, so it might fail. But if it succeeds, then the agents can be held responsible because, as in the case of solving the mathematical problem, they will have succeeded in doing what they were knowingly and willingly trying to do. Recall the assassin and the husband. Owing to indeterminacies in their neural pathways, the assassin might miss his target or the husband fail to break the table. But if they _succeed,_ despite the probability of failure, they are responsible, because they will have succeeded in doing what they were trying to do.

And so it is, I suggest, with self-forming choices, except that in the case of self-forming choices, _whichever way the agents choose_, they will have succeeded in doing what they were trying to do because they were simultane-

---

[7] We have to make further assumptions about the case to rule out some of these conditions. For example, we have to assume, no one is holding a gun to the woman's head forcing her to go back, or that she is not paralyzed, etc. But the point is that none of these conditions is inconsistent with the case of the woman as we have imagined it. If these other conditions are satisfied, and the businesswoman's case is otherwise as I have described it, we have an SFA. For the complete argument, see Kane (1996, chapter 8).

ously trying to make both choices, and one is going to succeed. Their failure to do one thing is not a *mere* failure, but a voluntary succeeding in doing the other. Does it make sense to talk about the agent's trying to do two competing things at once in this way, or to solve two cognitive problems at once? Well, we now have much evidence that the brain is a parallel processor; it can simultaneously process different kinds of information relevant to tasks such as perception or recognition through different neural pathways. Such a capacity, I believe, is essential to the exercise of free will. In cases of self-formation (SFAs), agents are simultaneously trying to resolve plural and competing cognitive tasks. They are, as we say, of two minds. Yet they are not two separate persons. They are not dissociated from either task. The businesswoman who wants to go back to help the victim is the same ambitious woman who wants to go to her meeting and make a sale. She is torn inside by different visions of who she is and what she wants to be, as we all are from time to time. But this is the kind of complexity needed for genuine self-formation and free will. And when she succeeds in doing one of the things she is trying to do, she will endorse that as *her* resolution of the conflict in her will, voluntarily and intentionally, not by accident or mistake.

4   Responsibility, Luck, and Chance

You may find all this interesting and yet still find it hard to shake the intuition that if choices are undetermined, they *must* happen merely by chance – and so must be "random", "capricious", "uncontrolled", "irrational", and all the other things usually charged. Such intuitions are deeply ingrained. But if we are ever going to understand free will, I think we will have to break old habits of thought that support such intuitions and learn to think in new ways. The first step in doing this is to question the intuitive connection in most people's minds between "indeterminism's being involved in something" and "its happening merely as a matter of chance or luck". "Chance" and "luck" are terms of ordinary language that carry the connotation of "its being out of my control". So using them already begs particular questions, whereas "indeterminism" is a technical term that merely precludes *deterministic* causation, though not causation altogether. Indeterminism is consistent with nondeterministic or probabilistic causation, where the outcome is not inevitable. It is therefore a mistake (alas, one of the most common in debates about free will) to assume that "undetermined" means "uncaused". Another way one may be unwittingly led to this mistake is by accounts of determinism defined as "every event is caused". On such accounts, everything is "deterministically caused" (trivially so), but one can easily overlook the qualification. Events may be caused (probabilistically caused) without being determined. Denying that free actions are determined is not to say they are uncaused.

Here is another source of misunderstanding. Since the outcome of the businesswoman's effort (the choice) is undetermined up to the last minute, we may have the image of her first making an effort to overcome the temptation to go on to her meeting and then at the last instant "chance takes over" and decides the issue for her. But this is misleading. On the view I proposed, one cannot separate the indeterminism and the effort of will, so that *first* the effort occurs *followed* by chance or luck (or vice versa). One must think of the effort and the indeterminism as fused; the effort *is* indeterminate and the indeterminism is a property of the effort, not something separate that occurs after or before the effort. The fact that the effort has this property of being indeterminate does not make it any less the woman's *effort*. The complex recurrent neural network that realizes the effort in the brain is circulating impulses in feedback loops and there is some indeterminacy in these circulating impulses. But the whole process is her effort of will and it persists right up to the moment when the choice is made. There is no point at which the effort stops and chance "takes over". She chooses as a result of the effort, even though she might have failed. Similarly, the husband breaks the table as a result of his effort, even though he might have failed because of the indeterminacy in the neural pathways of his arm. (That is why his excuse, "chance broke the table, not me" is so lame.)

Just as expressions like "she chose *by* chance" can mislead us in such contexts, so can expressions like "she got lucky". Recall that, with the assassin and husband, one might say "they got lucky" in killing the prime minister and breaking the table because their actions were undetermined. Yet they were responsible. So ask yourself this question: why does the inference "he got lucky, *so he was not responsible*?" fail in the cases of the husband and the assassin? The first part of an answer has to do with the point made earlier: "luck", like "chance", has question-begging implications in ordinary language that are not necessarily implications of "indeterminism" (which implies only the absence of deterministic causation). The core meaning of "he got lucky" in the assassin and husband cases, which *is* implied by indeterminism, I suggest, is that "he succeeded *despite the probability or chance of failure*"; and this core meaning implies no lack of responsibility, *if he succeeds*.

If "he got lucky" had other meanings in these cases, often associated with "luck" and "chance" in ordinary usage (e.g. the outcome was not his doing, or occurred by *mere* chance, or he was not responsible for it), the inference would not fail for the husband and assassin, as it clearly does. But the point is that these further meanings of "luck" and "chance" do not follow *from the mere presence of indeterminism*. The second reason why the inference "he got lucky, so he was not responsible" fails for the assassin and the husband is that *what* they succeeded in doing was what they were *trying* and wanting to do all along (kill the minister and break the table respectively). The third reason is that *when* they succeeded, their reaction was not "oh dear, that was a mistake, an accident – something that *happened* to me, not something I *did*". Rather they *endorsed* the outcomes as something they were trying and wanting to do all along, knowingly and purposefully, not by mistake or accident.

But these conditions are satisfied in the businesswoman's case as well, *either way* she chooses. If she succeeds in choosing to return to help the victim (or in choosing to go on to her meeting) (i) she will have "succeeded *despite the probability or chance of failure*", (ii) she will have succeeded in doing what she was *trying* and *wanting* to do all along (she wanted both outcomes very much, but for different reasons, and was trying to make those reasons prevail in both cases), and (iii) when she succeeded (in choosing to return to help) her reaction was not "oh dear, that was a mistake, an accident – something that happened to me, not something I did". Rather she *endorsed* the outcome as something she was trying and wanting to do all along; she recognized it as her resolution of the conflict in her will. And if she had chosen to go on to her meeting she would have endorsed that outcome, recognizing it as her resolution of the conflict in her will.

Perhaps the problem is that we are begging the question by assuming the outcomes of the woman's efforts are actually *choices*, if they are undetermined. One might argue this on the grounds that "if an event is undetermined, it must be something that merely *happens* and cannot be somebody's choice or action". But to see how question-begging such a claim would be, one has only to note what it implies: if something is a choice or action, it must be determined – that is, "all choices and actions are determined". Is this suppose to be true of necessity or by definition? If so, the free will issue would be solved by fiat. But beyond that, there is no reason to assume such a claim is true at all. Was the husband's breaking the table not something he *did* simply because the outcome was not determined? Recall that "undetermined" does not mean "uncaused". The breaking of the table was caused by the swing of his arm and, though the outcome was not inevitable, that was good enough for saying he did it and was responsible. Turning to choices, a choice is the formation of an intention or purpose to do something. It resolves uncertainty and indecision in the mind about what to do. Nothing in such a description implies that there could not be some indeterminism in the deliberation and neural processes of an agent preceding choice corresponding to the agent's prior uncertainty about what to do. Recall that the presence of indeterminism does not mean the outcome happened merely by chance and not by the agent's effort. Self-forming choices are undetermined, but not uncaused. They are caused by the agent's efforts.

Well, perhaps indeterminism does not undermine the idea that something is a *choice* simply, but rather that it is the *agent's* choice. But again, why must it do that? What makes the woman's choice her own is that it results from her efforts and deliberation which in turn are causally influenced by her reasons and her intentions (for example, her intention to resolve indecision in one way or another). And what makes these efforts, deliberation, reasons and intentions *hers* is that they are embedded in a larger motivational system of the person in terms of which she defines herself as a practical reasoner and actor. Current neuroscientific research would relate this motivational system, in terms of which the agent defines herself as practical reasoner and actor, to a complex system in the brain linking higher cortical regions with emotional regions of the limbic system and with perceptual and motor regions in other parts of the brain, tied together by the associational areas of the prefrontal cortex.[8] A choice is the agent's when it is produced intentionally by efforts, deliberation and reasons that are part of this self-defining motivational system and when, in addition, the agent *endorses* the new intention or purpose created by the choice so that it becomes an additional part of that motivational system and thereafter functions as a further purpose guiding *future* practical reasoning and action.

Well, then, perhaps the issue is not whether the undetermined SFA is a *choice*, or even whether it is the *agent's* choice, but, rather, how much

---

[8]See Damasio et al. (1996), Fuster (1989), Walter (2001). That some such larger motivational system is necessary to define personhood and agency has been persuasively argued by philosophers of otherwise widely different persuasions (e.g. about such issues as the relation of mind to body and free will). For example, the need for such a motivational system in terms of which persons define themselves as practical reasoners and actors has been emphasized by hermeneuticists like Gadamer and Taylor as well as by analytic philosophers such as Dretske, Flanagan, and Velleman. Agreement on this issue need not depend on any particular view of the mind/brain nexus (reduction, supervenience, emergentist, etc.) and may be shared by those who take different views on the mind-body problem. What the neuroscientific research cited above does suggest, however, is that there is a complex system in the brain that subserves this larger motivational system in terms of which agents define themselves as practical reasoners and agents, however one imagines this neurological system to be related to the mental. I call the complex system in the brain that plays this role the "self-network" (Kane 1996, pp. 137–142).

control she had over it. It may be true, as I argued earlier (regarding plural voluntary control), that the presence of indeterminism need not eliminate control altogether. But would not the presence of indeterminism at least *diminish* the control persons have over their choices and other actions? Is it not the case that the assassin's control over whether the prime minister is killed (his ability to realize his purposes or what he is trying to do) is lessened by the undetermined impulses in his arm – and so also for the husband and his breaking the table? And this limitation seems to be connected with another problem often noted by critics of libertarian freedom – the problem that indeterminism, wherever it occurs, seems to be a *hindrance* or *obstacle* to our realizing our purposes and hence an obstacle to (rather than an enhancement of) our freedom.

There is something to these claims, but I think what is true in them reveals something important about free will. We should concede that indeterminism, wherever it occurs, *does* diminish control over what we are trying to do and *is* a hindrance or obstacle to the realization of our purposes. But recall that in the case of the businesswoman (and SFAs generally), the indeterminism that is admittedly diminishing her control over one thing she is trying to do (the moral act of helping the victim) *is coming from her own will* – from her desire and effort to do the opposite (go to her business meeting). And the indeterminism that is diminishing her control over the other thing she is trying to do (act selfishly and go to her meeting) is coming from her desire and effort to do the opposite (to be a moral person and act on moral reasons). So, in each case, the indeterminism is functioning as a hindrance or obstacle to her realizing one of her purposes – a hindrance or obstacle in the form of resistance within her will which has to be overcome by effort.

If there were no such hindrance – no resistance in her will – she would indeed in a sense have "complete control" over one of her options. There would be no competing motives standing in the way of her choosing it. But then also she would not be free to rationally and voluntarily choose the other purpose because she would have no good competing reasons to do so. Thus, by *being* a hindrance to the realization of some of our purposes, indeterminism paradoxically opens up the genuine possibility of pursuing other purposes – of choosing or doing *otherwise* in accordance with, rather than against, our wills (voluntarily) and reasons (rationally). To be genuinely self-forming agents (creators of ourselves) – to have free will – there must at times in life be obstacles and hindrances in our wills of this sort that we must overcome.

Let me conclude with one final objection that is perhaps the most telling and has not yet been discussed. Even if one granted that persons, such as the businesswoman, could make genuine self-forming choices that were undetermined, is their not something to the charge that such choices would be *arbitrary*? A residual arbitrariness seems to remain in all self-forming choices since the agents cannot in principle have sufficient or overriding *prior* reasons for making one option and one set of reasons prevail over the other. There is some truth to this charge as well, but again I think it is a truth that tells us something important about free will. It tells us that every undetermined self-forming free choice is the initiation of what I have elsewhere called a "value experiment", whose justification lies in the future and is not fully explained by past reasons. In making such a choice we say, in effect, "Let's try this. It is not required by my past, but it is consistent with my past and is one branching pathway my life can now meaningfully take. Whether it is the right choice, only time will tell. Meanwhile, I am willing to take responsibility for it one way or the other" (Kane 1996, pp. 145–146).

It is worth noting that the term "arbitrary" comes from the Latin *arbitrium*, which means "judgment" – as in *liberum arbitrium voluntatis*, "free judgment of the will" (the medieval philosophers' term for free will). Imagine a writer in the middle of a novel. The novel's heroine faces a crisis and the writer has not yet developed her character in sufficient detail to say exactly how she will act. The author makes a "judgment" about this that is not determined by the heroine's already formed past which does not give unique direction. In this sense, the judgment (*arbitrium*) of how she will react is "arbitrary", but not entirely so. It had input from the heroine's fictional past and in turn gave input to her projected future. Similarly, agents exercising free will are both authors of and characters in their own stories all at once. By virtue of "self-forming" judgments of the will (*arbitria voluntatis*), they are "arbiters" of their own lives, "making themselves" out of a past that, if they are truly free, does not limit their future pathways to one.[9]

Suppose we were to say to such actors "But look, you didn't have sufficient or *conclusive* prior reasons for choosing as you did since you also had viable reasons for choosing the other way". They might reply. "True enough. But I did have *good* reasons for choosing as I did, which I'm willing to stand by *and take responsibility for*. If they were not sufficient or conclusive reasons, that's because, like the heroine of the novel, I was not a fully formed person before I chose (and still am not, for that matter). Like the author of the novel, I am in the process of writing an unfinished story and forming an unfinished character who, in my case, is myself".

---

[9]For a similar and instructive "narrative" conception of selfhood and self-formation, see Guignon's contribution to this volume. I believe that Guignon's account of narrative selfhood in this contribution and in other writings of his cited in his contribution is very much in line with what I want to say here about self-formation and agency.

5   Agent Causation

In discussing the Intelligibility Question in prior sections, I have avoided appealing to any "extra factors" to account for libertarian free agency, such as noumenal selves, transempirical power centers, or special forms of agent- or nonevent causation, to which libertarians have often appealed. According to those who appeal to agent- or nonevent (or nonoccurrent) causation to account for free will, the causation of free actions by agents (agent-causation hyphenated) is a *sui generis* kind of causation that cannot be fully spelled out in terms of events or states of affairs (either physical or psychological) involving the agent. Hence, it is a kind of causation by an agent that cannot be understood in terms of the usual kinds of causation of events or states of affairs by other events or states of affairs recognized in the physical and psychological sciences.

Normally when we say a substance or agent caused something (the rock broke the window; the cat caused the lamp to fall; the man opened the window), we spell out such causation by substances or agents in terms of events or states of affairs involving the substances or agents. We say, for example, that it was the rock's *striking* the window and *having* a particular mass or momentum that caused the window to break. Or it was the cat's *jumping* onto the table and *bumping* the lamp that caused it to fall, or the man opened the window because he *wanted* to call to his friend and he *believed* his friend was outside. In the case of free actions, however, believers in agent- or nonevent causation say that explanations of why agents acted as they did cannot be fully given like this in terms of events and states of affairs involving the agents (including their beliefs, desires and other psychological states) because free actions are not determined by antecedent events and states of affairs. To make up the difference we must suppose there is an additional *sui generis* causation of the action by the agent that is over and above the causal influences of its physical and psychological states. This is "agent"- or "nonevent" causation and we must add it to our picture of the world, they insist, to account for free will. Now this doctrine has often been criticized as mysterious or obscure or explanatorily empty (much like the vital forces of nineteenth century biology; see, e.g., Watson 1987). And I agree with such criticisms (see Kane 1996, chapters 7 and 10.) But I want to focus here on a different complaint – that appeals to nonevent or nonoccurrent forms of causation or agency are *not necessary* to account for incompatibilist or indeterminist free will. We can do without them.

Note, for example, that the preceding account of free will in this paper makes no such appeals to such special forms of nonevent or nonoccurrent causation or to any other "extra factors" to account for libertarian free agency. The account of free will in this paper does appeal to the fact that free choices and actions can be caused by efforts, deliberations, beliefs, desires, intentions and other reasons or motives of agents. But this is causation by events or states of affairs involving agents. It is not the special causation of agent-causal theories that cannot be spelled out in terms of events or states of affairs involving agents, either physical or psychological.[10] Moreover, causation by efforts, beliefs, desires, intentions and the like is something to which even non-libertarian theories of free will, including compatibilist theories, must appeal in their accounts of free actions and choices; and even compatibilists could hardly avoid appealing to causation by such mental states and processes if they wish to give accounts of free *agency*. The case is otherwise with such things as noumenal selves, transempirical power centers or nonevent causation, which are invoked specifically *to salvage libertarian intuitions* about free will and are not needed by compatibilists and other non-libertarians to account for free agency.

This is what I mean by not invoking "extra" factors. My account of free will postulates no additional ontological entities or relations not already needed by any other accounts of free agency, libertarian or non-libertarian, compatibilist or incompatibilist. The theory postulates efforts, deliberations, desires, intentions and the like, and causation of actions by these.[11] But compatibilists must postulate these also if they are going to talk about *free agency*. The only added assumption I have made to account for libertarian free agency is just what you would expect – that some of the mental events or processes involved must be *undetermined*, so that the causation by mental events may be nondeterministic or probabilistic as well as deterministic.

Of course, if any such theory is to succeed, there must be some indeterminism in the brain where undetermined efforts and choices occur. But such a requirement holds for any libertarian theory. If free choices are unde-

---

[10]The nature of mental causation (or causation by mental states such as beliefs and desires) is itself a matter of controversy among philosophers. But I am making only two simple points about it here. First, since mental causation must be assumed by compatibilist accounts of free agency as well as libertarian accounts such as my own, whatever problems attach to the idea are not simply problems for libertarian theories or theories like mine. Second, causation by desires, beliefs, etc. is causation by states or events and does not commit one to nonevent agent-causation. These are minimal defensible claims.

[11]Of course there are further questions to be asked here about *how* mental states and processes cause actions, whether their causation is merely efficient causation or also involves some kind of "intentional" or "formal" causation in Aristotle's sense. But these are issues that any theory of free will must face, whether libertarian or compatibilist. They are not special problems for my theory.

termined, as libertarians suppose, there must be some indeterminacy in the natural world to make room for them; and it is an empirical question whether the indeterminism is there.[12] This is true even if one postulates special kinds of agent-causes or a non-material self to intervene in the brain. The indeterminism must be there to begin with in the brain, if these special forms of agency are to have room to operate. As the ancient Epicurean philosophers said, the atoms must sometimes "swerve" in undetermined ways, if there is to be room in nature for free will.

My suggestion about how indeterminism might enter the picture, if it were available in the physical world, was that conflicts in the wills of agents associated with self-forming choices would "stir up chaos" in the brain sensitizing it to quantum indeterminacies at the neuronal level, which would then be magnified to effect neural networks as a whole. The brain would thus be stirred up by such conflict for the task of creative problem solving. This is speculative to be sure. Others have suggested different ways in which indeterminacy might be involved in the brain and free will (Prigogine and Stengers 1984, Hodgson 1991, Stapp 1993, Eccles 1994, Penrose 1994). But such speculations are not entirely idle either. There is growing evidence that chaos may play a role in human cognitive processing, as it does in many complex physical systems, providing some of the flexibility the nervous system needs to adapt creatively to an ever-changing environment.[13] Of course, it is often said that chaotic behavior, though unpredictable, is usually deterministic and does not of itself imply indeterminism.[14]

But even if this should be true, chaos does involve "sensitivity to initial conditions". Minute differences in the initial conditions of chaotic systems, including living things, may be magnified giving rise to large-scale undetermined effects. If the brain does "make chaos in order to understand the world" (as Skarda and Freeman 1987 put it), its sensitivity to initial conditions may magnify quantum indeterminacies in neural networks, whose outputs can depend on minute differences in the timing of firings of individual neurons. The general idea is that some combination of quantum physics and the new sciences of chaos and complexity in self-organizing systems may

---

[12]The empirical question of whether there is sufficient indeterminism in the physical world to make room for free will is complex. Two useful essays that discuss the latest research bearing on this question are Bishop (2002) and Hodgson (2002).

[13]Walter (2001) summarizes much of this recent research. See also Babloyantz and Destexhe (1985), Skarda and Freeman (1987) and Bishop (2002).

[14]Even this commonly made assumption must be qualified. Bishop and Kronz (1999) have argued that chaotic behavior may indeed imply indeterminism, depending on the nature of quantum mechanics involved.

provide sufficient indeterminacy in nature for free will.[15] What I emphasize is that only a small amount is needed in the precise timing of neuron firings. But this is only one idea among others. The question is ultimately an empirical one, to be decided by future research.

What I have tried to do in this paper is answer a different, but equally daunting, question: What could we *do* with the indeterminism to make sense of free will, supposing it were there in the brain? Would the indeterminism not just amount to chance? How could it amount to free will unless one added some "extra factor" in the form of a special kind of agent-causation or transempirical power center to account for agency? As a final test of the answer given to these questions in this paper, it will be instructive to conclude with the following question: What is missing in the account of free will presented in earlier sections that an extra postulate of a special form of nonevent *agent-causation* is supposed to provide? We could ask the same question for other extra factor strategies, but most of these have gone out of favor in recent philosophy, while theories of nonevent agent-causation are still the most commonly discussed and defended libertarian theories today. So I will concentrate on contrasting agent-causal theories with the kind of libertarian theory I defend, which is often called *causal indeterminism*.

Let it be clear first of all that the causal indeterminist theory presented in this paper *does* postulate *agent causation* (though not of the nonevent or nonoccurrent kind). Agents cause or bring about their undetermined self-forming choices (SFAs) on this theory by making efforts to do so, voluntarily and intentionally; and agents cause or bring about many other things as well by making efforts to do so, such as deaths of prime ministers, broken tables, messes, accidents, fires, pains and so on. Whether there is agent causation *in general* is not the issue here. What is at issue is agent-causation (hyphenated) – a *sui generis* form of causation postulated by agent-causal theorists. It is misleading to frame this debate in such a way that libertarians who are agent-cause theorists believe in agent causation, while non-agent-causal libertarians like myself do not – presumably because we only believe in event causation. The fact is that both sides believe in agent causation. The issue is how it is to be spelled out.

Just as agents can be said to cause their self-forming choices and many other things, on the theory I propose, so it can be said that agents *produce* or *bring about* their self-forming choices by making efforts to do so and *produce* many other things by their efforts and other actions. This point

---

[15] For a discussion of this strategy and other possible ways of relating indeterminacy in nature to free will, see Bishop (2002).

is worth making since defenders of agent-causation often claim that causal indeterminist theories like mine lack – and (nonevent) agent-causation supposedly provides – a conception of agents really *producing* or *bringing about* their undetermined free choices rather than those choices merely occurring by chance. But, as argued earlier, the mere presence of indeterminism does not imply that SFAs and other actions (such as the assassin's or husband's) occur *merely* by chance and not as a result of the agent's voluntary and intentional efforts. Of course, the causation or production in the case of SFAs is nondeterministic or probabilistic, since they are undetermined. But so it is also in the cases of the assassin and the husband who breaks his wife's table. And the burden of my argument was that such nondeterministic causation can support claims that agents really do *produce* what they cause by their voluntary efforts and can be held responsible for doing so.

So we are still looking for what the postulation of nonevent agent-causation is supposed to add to the picture that is still missing. O'Connor, a perceptive recent defender of agent-causation, provides some further clues about this matter worth considering. Speaking to the issue of what causal indeterminist theories like mine lack that nonevent agent-causation is supposed to provide, O'Connor says the following. For causal indeterminist theories, "the agent's internal states [including reasons, motives, etc.] have objective tendencies of some determinate measure to cause certain outcomes. While this provides an *opening* in which the agent might freely select one option from a plurality of real alternatives, it fails to introduce a causal capacity that fills it. And what better here than its being the agent himself that causes the particular action that is to be performed?" (O'Connor 2002, p. 345). The missing element suggested in this quote is the "causal capacity" to "freely select one option from a plurality of real alternatives" left open by the (causal) indeterminism of prior events.

Now such a causal capacity is surely important. But why do we have to suppose that agent-causation of a nonevent kind is needed to capture it? The fact is that, on the causal indeterminist view presented, the agent *does* have such a causal capacity. Not only does the businesswoman facing an SFA have a plurality of real alternatives from which to choose, she has the *capacity* to make either choice by making an effort to do so. The conflicting motives in her will and the consequent divisions within her motivational system make it possible for her to choose either way for reasons, voluntarily and intentionally. And this is clearly a causal capacity since it is the capacity to *cause* or *produce* either choice outcome (nondeterministically, of course) as a result of her effort against resistance in her will.

This is a remarkable capacity to be sure; and we may assume that it is possessed only by creatures who attain the status of *persons* capable of self-reflection and having the requisite conflicts within their wills. So O'Connor's calling it a form of *"personal causation"* is appropriate. But there is no reason to suppose we need to postulate a *nonevent* form of causation to account for it. The *capacity* itself (prior to its exercise) is a complex dispositional *state* of the agent; and its *exercise* is a sequence of *events* or *processes* involving efforts leading to choice and formation of intention, which intention then guides subsequent action (going back to help the victim or going on to a meeting.) This is a capacity *of* the agent, to be sure, but both the capacity and its exercise are described in terms of properties or states of the agent and in terms of states of affairs, events and processes involving the agent.

Is there a residual fear functioning here that the "agent" will somehow disappear from the scene if we describe its capacities and their exercise, including free will, in terms of states and events? Such a fear would be misguided at best. A continuing substance (such as an agent) does not absent the ontological stage because we describe its continuing existence – its *life*, if it is a living thing – including its capacities and their exercise, in terms of states of affairs, events and processes involving it. One needs more reason than this to think that there are no continuing things or substances, or no agents, but only events, or to think that agents do not cause things, only events cause things. For my part, I should confess that I am a substance ontologist and indeed something of an Aristotelian when it comes to thinking about the nature of living things and the relation of mind to body. Agents are continuing substances with both mental and physical properties. But there is nothing inconsistent in saying this and being a causal indeterminist about free will who thinks that the *lives* of agents, their capacities and the exercise of those capacities, including free will, must be spelled out in terms of states, processes and events involving them.

Similar remarks are in order about O'Connor's comments about "emergence" or "emergent properties" of agents (such as emergent causal capacities) in connection with free will. Issues about the existence of emergent properties (like issues about continuing substances) must also be distinguished from issues about nonevent causation. Indeed, I also believe that emergence of a particular kind (now recognized in self-organizing systems) is necessary for free will, even of the causal indeterminist kind that I defend. Once the brain reaches a particular level of complexity, so that there can be conflicts in the will of the kind required for SFAs, the larger motivational system of the brain stirs up chaos and indeterminacy in a part of itself which is the realization of a specific deliberation. In other words, the whole motivational system realized as a comprehensive "self-network" in the brain has the capacity to influence specific parts of itself (processes within it) in novel ways once a particular level of complexity of the whole is attained. This is a kind of emergence of new *capacities* and indeed even a kind of "downward causation" (novel causal influences of an emergent whole on its parts) such as are now recognized in a number of scientific contexts involving self-organizing and ecological systems (Küppers 1992, Kauffman 1995, Gilbert and Sarkar 2000).[16] But this kind of emergence characteristic of self-organizing systems does not, in and of itself, imply causation of a nonoccurrent or nonevent kind, since the wholes and parts involved are states and processes of the organism of various levels of complexity. Of course, O'Connor would like a stronger form of emergence, which would require nonoccurrent causation. But his argument – that some kind of emergence of capacities for holistic or downward causation of wholes on parts is required for free will – does not prove the need for a *nonevent* kind of causation. Such emergence, which I agree is important for free will, can be accommodated within a theory of the kind I have proposed.

O'Connor offers yet another argument when he says that what non-agent-causal theories lack and what agent-causation supplies is "the agent's directly controlling the outcome" of an undetermined choice. This is the issue of *control* about which I have said a great deal earlier in this contribution. What is it for an agent to have direct *control* at a given time over a set of choice options (e.g. to help the assault victim or go on to a meeting)? The answer given earlier is embodied in the idea of plural voluntary control. Stating it more precisely, agents have plural voluntary control over a set of options at a time when they have the (i) *ability* or *capacity* to (ii) *bring about* (iii) at that time (iv) *whichever* of the options they will or want, (v) for the reasons they will to do so, (vi) on purpose or intentionally rather than accidentally, by mistake or merely by chance, hence (vii) voluntarily (in accordance with their wills rather than against them), (viii) as a result of their efforts, if effort should be required, (ix) without being coerced or compelled or (x) otherwise controlled or forced to choose one way or the other by some other agent or mechanism. Agents *exercise* such control *directly* when they voluntarily and intentionally *produce* one of the options (a particular self-forming choice or SFA) *then and there* (at the time in question) under these conditions. I have argued here and in other writings that these conditions can be satisfied for SFAs without appealing to any kind of nonevent agent-causation (Kane

---

[16]It should be noted that the emergent complexity assumed here (and by the authors just cited) does not involve violations of fundamental physical laws. We do not want to require, nor need we require, that emergent phenomena would violate quantum level laws, even if they add higher level laws based on novel complex boundary conditions.

1996, chapter 8; Kane 1999a). Moreover, these conditions of plural voluntary control are the kinds we look for when deciding whether persons are or are not *responsible* for their choices or actions (e.g. when they produce something voluntarily and intentionally as a result of making an effort to do so).

Finally, I will consider an objection about control made to my theory by another agent-causal theorist. Clarke (1996) argues that causal indeterminist theories, like mine, provide "leeway" for choice, but no more control over actions *than compatibilists* offer; and more control than compatibilists offer is needed to account for the genuine libertarian free will and responsibility.[17] I agree that something more in the way of control than compatibilists offer is needed to account for libertarian free will. But I think the "more" control libertarians need is not more of the same *kind* of control compatibilists offer, but rather *another kind of control altogether*. Compatibilists concern themselves with what might be called "antecedent determining control" – the ability to guarantee or determine *beforehand* which of a number of options is going to occur. If free choices are undetermined, we cannot have antecedent determining control over them, for exercising such control would mean *pre*determining them – determining beforehand just which choice we

---

[17]Clarke and others have also posed questions about the (dual) "efforts of will" preceding self-forming choices or SFAs on my theory. The SFAs are nondeterministically caused by these preceding efforts, but are the efforts themselves determined by the agents prior reasons or motives? My answer is that the efforts agents make in SFA situations are *causally influenced* by their prior reasons or motives, but they are not strictly speaking determined by those reasons because the efforts themselves are indeterminate, meaning there is some indeterminism involved in the complex neural processes realizing them in the brain. Thus, the reasons do not determine that an exact amount of effort will be made. This means that indeterminism enters the picture in two stages, first, with the efforts, then with SFAs. One might say that, with the efforts, one opens a "window" of indeterminacy, whose upshot is that the choice outcome (the SFA) will not be determined. But the primary locus of indeterminism is in the moment of choice itself, the SFA. The latter is undetermined in a way that allows for robust alternative possibilities (making a moral choice or an ambitious choice). To prepare for this, a measure of indeterminacy enters the picture earlier, in the preceding indeterminate efforts. A related question: do the agents cause these efforts? No, not in the way they cause their SFAs, because the efforts are basic actions. Agents make the efforts, they do not cause them by doing something else. And what it means to say they make the efforts was spelled out earlier (section 4) in the account of what it means to say that the businesswoman's choice was hers. Finally, are the efforts freely made? I distinguish three senses of freedom, all of which I think are required for a complete account of free action and free will: (i) not being coerced, compelled, controlled etc. (ii) acting "of one's own free will" in the sense of a will of one's own making (i.e., satisfying UR) and (iii) being an undetermined self-forming action or SFA. Sense (i) is compatibilist (and I think it is necessary for free will, though not sufficient); senses (ii) and (iii) are incompatibilist. Efforts of will preceding SFAs are free in senses (i) and usually (ii) also; SFAs (the full flowering of free will) are true in all three senses.

are going to make. (Even nonevent agent-causation cannot give us that.) What libertarians must require for undetermined SFAs is another kind of control altogether (that compatibilists cannot get) – namely, *ultimate* control – the originative control exercised by agents when it is "up to them" which of a set of possible choices or actions will now occur, and up to no one and nothing else over which the agents themselves do not also have control. This is the kind of control required by ultimate responsibility and it is not something that can be captured by compatibilists, since it requires indeterminism. But neither does such ultimate control require nonevent causation, as I have been arguing. What it does require is the ability or capacity to cause or produce any one of a set of possible choices or actions each of which is undetermined (hence nondeterministic) and to do so "at will", that is, rationally (for reasons), voluntarily and intentionally.

Note also that there is a trade-off between this ultimate control and the antecedent determining control compatibilists want. Ultimate control over our destinies means giving up some antecedent determining control at crucial points in our lives.[18] We must accept a measure of uncertainty and genuine indeterminacy right up to the moment of decision. Indeterminism does not leave everything unchanged, for it implies "the probability or chance of failure" – though with genuine free will, every failing is also a succeeding, so we are responsible either way. If libertarians were after the same kind of control that compatibilists have to offer – only more of it – then I would agree with Clarke. But I think that what motivates the need for incompatibilism is an interest in a different kind of "control over our lives" altogether – a control having to do with our being to some degree the ultimate creators or originators of our own purposes or ends and, hence, ultimate "arbiters" of our own wills. We cannot have that in a determined world.[19]

---

[18]The exclusive desire for antecedent control is closely related to an instrumental view of action criticized by Richardson and Bishop (this volume). Antecedent control has a place in human life but it is not all we want when we desire "control over our lives". Similarly, as Richardson and Bishop correctly note, while instrumental reasoning and action have obvious places in human life, we unwarrantedly narrow the scope of human reasoning and activity if we think of them as exclusively instrumental.

[19]On the themes of the last few paragraphs and particularly on the importance of being arbiters of our own wills, see the contributions to this volume of Guignon, Primas, and Richardson and Bishop.

Appendix

Dorato's contribution to this volume contains (in section 7) some discussion and criticisms of the view put forward in this paper to which I would like to respond. Dorato's article is an insightful and exceptionally well-informed discussion of many issues currently being debated about free will and determinism; and I agree with a great deal of what he says throughout his article. But I will comment here only on disagreements (he defends a compatibilist position while I defend a libertarian one) and particularly on the objections he makes to my view in his section 7. (All subsequent quotes from his article are from this section.) I discern five distinct objections. Some of them (at least other versions of some of them) I have discussed at length in other writings; and I will refer to those other writings in what follows. But I want to expand on a few crucial objections which he makes.

First, Dorato says that if indeterminism is involved in the outcome of a free choice as my view contends, why would not tossing a coin to decide the outcome do as well and why does my view not amount to merely submitting the choice to a random procedure of this sort?

This is a common and important objection. The answer is that there is a significant difference between the role of indeterminism in my view and mere coin tossing. On my view, the choice (either way) is the direct result of the agent's effort of will. This means, as I emphasized, that for self-forming choices or SFAs there is no point prior to the choice at which the effort stops and "chance takes over" to decide the issue, as would be the case in a coin toss or the spinning of a wheel. In other words, it is not as if we first make an effort, then we stop at the last minute and hand over the decision to a random process in the brain to make the final decision for us. Indeterminism does not enter in that way. The indeterminism is not "external" to the effort as in a coin toss; it is "internal" to the effort. To explain what this means, consider that the neural process corresponding to the effort is a complex process of circulating impulses in recurrent (feedback) networks of the brain. There is some indeterminacy in the circulating impulses of these networks fed upward from the neuronal level which causes some indeterministic "static" or "noise" in their processing, but this static or neural noise is not enough to completely disrupt the networks' functioning or potential efficacy. In other words, despite the neural static or noise, the networks corresponding to the effort can still issue in the choice; but their doing so is rendered probable and less than certain because of the neural noise.

Compare the husband in my example who is trying to break his wife's glass table. Indeterminacies in the neural impulses of his arm make it uncertain whether he will succeed in breaking the table. But these indeterminacies do not entirely disrupt his arm swing nor undermine its potential efficacy. In short, he might still break the table; the indeterminacy merely makes it less than certain that he will do so. And so it is with agent's making SFAs. The agent's effort to choose is rendered less than certain by the indeterminacy provoked by conflicting desires and efforts, but not impossible. And if the agent does succeed in making the choice under these conditions, the effort will persist right through till the choice is made. The choice will causally result from the effort, just as the breaking of the glass table causally results from the swing of the husband's arm, even though whether the table breaks or whether the choice is made is undetermined in both cases because of indeterminacies in the nervous systems of the agents. The presence of the indeterminacies will, thus, mean that if the agents succeed in doing what they were trying to do (breaking the table or making the self-forming choice), the causation in both cases will be probabilistic, not deterministic. But it will be no less causation for all that. The agents' efforts will have produced or brought about the outcomes, though the efforts might have failed because of the neural noise. This is quite unlike stopping the effort at some point and handing over the choice to a coin toss or spin of the wheel, thus taking it entirely out of the agent's hands. The agents in SFAs keep trying until they either succeed or fail in producing the desired outcome. And given the "dual" efforts involved in SFAs, even when they fail to produce one of the desired outcomes, that failure is a succeeding in their effort to produce the other desired outcome. So they succeed by their efforts in producing a choice either way.

The key idea here is that indeterminism functions as a hindrance or obstacle to our realizing particular desires or goals, but a hindrance that can be overcome by our efforts. When the indeterministic noise is overcome, it is the effort that causes the choice by overcoming the indeterminism, just as it is the husband's swing of his arm that causes the table to break despite the hindering indeterminism in his arm. That is why the husband cannot excuse himself to his wife by saying "chance broke the table, not me" when the table breaks. It is true that in both cases (the husband and the self-forming chooser) indeterminism is a causal factor in the process, but it is an inhibiting causal factor. Such inhibiting causal factors in probabilistic causation are "causally relevant" to the effect, but they not its "causes". To show why this is so, consider that there is a 28% probability that persons who have syphilis will also develop a medical condition known as paresis. When this 28% who have syphilis do also contract paresis, we say that the syphilis was the cause of the paresis, though of course it was only a probabilistic cause;

it might have failed. Suppose now that some persons have a protective gene against paresis and in this subgroup, because of the protective gene, only 10% of persons who get syphilis contract paresis. When the 10% of this subgroup who get syphilis also contract paresis, we can again say that syphilis was the cause of the paresis, despite the protective gene. But we do not say in such a case that the presence of the protective gene was the cause of their getting paresis. For the protective gene was an inhibiting, not a promoting, causal factor; it lowered the probability that paresis would be contracted rather than raising the probability. Thus, the gene is causally relevant, but not the cause of the paresis. Similarly, the presence of indeterminism in the nervous systems of the husband and the self-forming chooser is causally relevant to the outcome, but it is an inhibiting causal factor. It lowers the probability that the effort will result in choice, rather than raising that probability. So when the effort does in fact result in choice, the indeterminism is not the "cause" of the choice, though it is of course "causally relevant" to the choice. The cause of the choice is the effort whose efficacy is hindered by the indeterminism, but not entirely undermined by the indeterminism, just as the cause of the table's breaking is the swing of the husband's arm, though the efficacy of that swing was hindered by the indeterminism in his arm, and just as the cause of the paresis was the syphilis though its efficacy as a cause was hindered by the protective gene.

It is now clear why I would reject statements such as Dorato's to the effect that on my view "we are the sorts of persons we are thanks to the results of a series of random coin tosses". Rather, we are the kinds of persons we are as a result of making efforts of will to overcome inhibiting factors (including indeterminism) generated by conflicting desires and tendencies in our wills. For similar reasons, I would reject claims that the choice is being made "by a purely random mechanism" or involves handing the decision over to an "external artificial device". The indeterminism is not external or artificial. It is an ingredient of the neural processing involved in the agent's deliberations and efforts, and is, hence, internal to the agent's will; and it arises quite naturally due to agitation caused by conflicts in the agent's will.

Another objection of Dorato's concerns the agents' "control" over choices given the presence of indeterminism. It is true that the presence of indeterminism diminishes the agents' control over any particular outcome, making it less than certain whether the agent will succeed in making a particular choice – just as the indeterminism in the husband's arm diminishes his control over whether the table will break. But such diminished control is not the same as no control at all, as would be the case in the toss of a coin or the spin of a wheel, where the agent relinquishes, or hands over, all control over what is chosen to the coin or the wheel. The self-forming chooser never does that; she continues to make an effort to make each choice until she succeeds in making one choice rather than the other. But what then is the advantage of indeterminism if it diminishes our control in this way over each outcome? Precisely this: It is the diminished control over each outcome that makes it possible to freely choose the other outcome without being determined to choose either one. Free will is thus a trade off, as I suggested, between "antecedent determining control" (being able to determine beforehand which one of the outcomes will be chosen) and "ultimate control" over our wills – being able to freely set our wills in one direction or another without being determined to do so by other agents or mechanisms.

Indeterminism is thus like the air in Kant's analogy of the bird. The bird, finding the resistance of the wind and the air an obstacle to its flight, imagines that it could fly better if there were no air. What a nuisance the air is! But of course without the resistance of the air the bird could not fly at all. And so without the resistance of indeterminism, though it is an obstacle and an inhibiting force, we could not have free will at all, in the sense that we would not be able to voluntarily make a contrary choice.

Another important objection made by Dorato is that if indeterminism is involved in deliberation and choice, as I suppose, it would "separate" or sever the causal connections between motives and desires and the agent's character, on the one hand, and the choice, on the other. So in a sense, the choice would not flow from the agent's motives and character, but would rather merely result from chance. This would undermine the "faithfulness" of the agent's choice to her past and would undermine the "justifiability" of the choice and hence its "rationality". I have responded more fully to objections of this sort elsewhere (Kane 1996, chapter 8) and will only make a brief comment here. The causal connections between character and motives, on the one hand, and choice, on the other, are not entirely severed by the indeterminism, as it functions in the way I have described. Rather the causal connection is rendered probabilistic rather than deterministic. That the businesswoman has strong moral motives for wanting to help the assault victim makes it probable but does not determine that she will return to help. And these motives will causally influence her decision if she does decide to return. If she had not had these motives, she would have done the opposite. The key point here is that when persons face SFAs, they are of two minds about what to do. Their characters and motives incline them in more than one direction and they must decide which of the directions they will go in the future. But each choice will be consistent with their past character and motives and will flow from some aspect of their past characters and motives; and each can thus be "faithful" in different ways to their past. It is just that in SFA-situations, past characters and motives are divided in their signals and give conflicting directions. The agents must decide which of these conflicting directions to take into the future. Yet each choice can be rational, given the agents' past character and motives, from a different internal point of view. The choices are incommensurable, but equally rational, given their pasts.

Dorato introduces one final and insightful line of criticism that I have also addressed at length in other writings. He considers a great number of identical replicas of a person having to make exactly the same choice in the same circumstances. Since these replicas would have the same backgrounds, motives and character prior to their choices and yet they might make different choices due to the indeterminism, it seems that we could not explain the difference in their choices in terms of their past characters and motives. And so it might seem that the different outcomes (whether for example they acted morally or immorally) would be a matter of mere chance or luck. This is an important objection, which I have elsewhere referred to as the "luck objection". It is far too complicated to consider here in any detail, but I have addressed it elsewhere (Kane 1999a, 1999b).

Finally, let me say that while I would like to think Dorato's objections could be answered, they are crucial objections, not easily answered, and I welcome the dialogue. I also agree with the main theme of Dorato's fine article. He argues that different points of view about free will reflect differences of fundamental evaluations. Compatibilists and libertarians, for example, want different things when they want free will and that is why they differ. Libertarians, like myself, want to believe that we are to some degree ultimately responsible for what we are and what we do; while compatibilists, of whom Dorato is one, think that such a notion is either unrealizable or unimportant or both. They might be right for all I know, but I hope not.

References

Babloyantz A. and Destexhe A. (1985): Strange Attractors in the Human Cortex. In *Temporal Disorder in Human Oscillatory Systems*, ed. by L. Rensing, U. an der Heiden, and M.C. Mackey, Springer, Berlin, pp. 48–56.

Berofsky B. (1987): *Freedom From Necessity*, Routledge and Kegan Paul, London.

Bishop R. (2002): Chaos, indeterminism and free will. In *The Oxford Handbook of Free Will*, ed. by R. Kane, Oxford University Press, Oxford, pp. 111–124.

Bishop R. and Kronz F. (1999): Is chaos indeterministic? In *Language, Quantum, Music: Selected Contributed Papers to the Tenth International Congress of Logic, Methodology and Philosophy of Science*, ed. by M.L. Dalla Chiara et al., Kluwer, London, pp. 129–141.

Campbell C.A. (1967): *In Defense of Free Self*, Allen and Unwin, London.

Chisholm R. (1982): Human freedom and the self. In *Free Will*, ed. by G. Watson, Oxford University Press, Oxford, pp. 24–35.

Churchland P.M. (1996): *The Engine of Reason, the Seat of the Soul*, MIT Press, Cambridge MA.

Clarke R. (1996): Agent causation and event causation in the production of free action. *Philosophical Topics* **24**, 19–48.

Damasio A. et al. (1996): *Neurobiology of Decision Making*, Springer, New York.

Dennett D. (1984): *Elbow Room*, MIT Press, Cambridge MA.

Eccles J. (1970): *Facing Reality*, Springer, New York.

Eccles J. (1994): *How the Self Controls the Brain*, Springer, New York.

Eccles J. and Popper K. (1977): *The Self and Its Brain*, Springer, New York.

Fischer J. (1994): *The Metaphysics of Free Will*, Blackwell, Oxford.

Frankfurt H. (1969): Alternative possibilities and moral responsibility. *Journal of Philosophy* **66**, 829–839.

Fuster J. (1989): *The Prefrontal Cortex*, Raven Press, New York.

Gilbert S. and Sarkar S. (2000): Embracing complexity: Organicism for the twenty-first century. *Developmental Dynamics* **219**, 1–9.

Ginet C. (1990): *On Action*, Cambridge University Press, Cambridge.

Ginet C. (2002): Freedom, responsibility and agency. *Journal of Ethics* **1.1**, 374–390. Reprinted in R. Kane (ed.) (2002), pp. 206–221.

Hodgson D. (1991): *The Mind Matters*, Clarendon Press, Oxford.

Hodgson D. (2002): Physics and free will. In *The Oxford Handbook of Free Will*, ed. by R. Kane, Oxford University Press, Oxford, pp. 85–100.

Honderich T. (1988): *A Theory of Determinism*, Clarendon Press, Oxford.

Kane R. (1985): *Free Will and Values*, SUNY Press, Albany.

Kane R. (1996): *The Significance of Free Will*, Oxford University Press, Oxford.

Kane R. (1999a): Responsibility, luck and chance: reflections on free will and indeterminism. *Journal of Philosophy* **96**, 217–240.

Kane R. (1999b): On free will, responsibility and indeterminism: responses to Clarke, Haji and Mele. *Philosophical Explorations* **2**, 105–121.

Kane R., ed. (2002): *Free Will*, Blackwell, Oxford.

Kant I. (1956): *The Critique of Practical Reason*, transl. by L. Beck, Bobbs-Merrill, Indianapolis.

Kaufman S. (1995): *At Home in the Universe*, Oxford University Press, Oxford.

Küppers B.-O. (1992): Understanding complexity. In *Emergence or Reduction? Essays on the Prospects of a Nonreductive Physicalism*, ed. by A. Beckermann, H. Flohr and J. Kim, Walter de Gruyter, Berlin, pp. 241–256.

O'Connor T. (2000): *Persons and Causes*, Oxford University Press, Oxford.

O'Connor T. (2002): Libertarian Theories: Agent-Causal and Dualist Theories. In *The Oxford Handbook of Free Will*, ed. by R. Kane, Oxford University Press, Oxford, pp. 337–355.

Penrose R. (1994): *Shadows of the Mind*, Oxford University Press, Oxford.

Prigogine I. and Stengers I. (1984): *Order Out of Chaos*, Bantam Books, New York.

Salmon W. (1984): *Scientific Explanation and the Causal Structure of the World*, Princeton University Press, Princeton.

Skarda C. and Freeman W. (1987): How the brain makes chaos in order to understand the world. *Behavioral and Brain Sciences* **10**, 161–195.

Spitzer M. (1999): *The Mind Within the Net*, MIT Press, Cambridge MA.

Stapp H. (1993): *Mind, Matter and Quantum Mechanics*, Springer, Berlin.

Swinburne R. (1986): *The Evolution of the Soul*, Clarendon Press, Oxford.

van Inwagen P. (1983): *An Essay on Free Will*, Oxford University Press, Oxford.

van Inwagen P. (2000): Free will remains a mystery. *Philosophical Perspectives* **14**, 1–19.

Walter H. (2001): *Neurophilosophy of Free Will*, MIT Press, Cambridge MA.

Watson G. (1987): Free action and free will. *Mind* **96**, 145–172.

Wiggins D. (1973): Towards a reasonable libertarianism. In *Essays on Freedom of Action*, ed. by T. Honderich, Routledge and Kegan Paul, London, pp. 31–61.

Agency and Soft Determinism in Psychology

Jack Martin and Jeff Sugarman

1 Agency, Compatibilism, and Psychology

Broadly speaking, *agency* is the capability of individual human beings to make their own choices and to act on these choices in ways that make a difference in their lives. Agency is assumed in most psychological practices that purport to help people solve problems, cope, make decisions, change, "make a difference", and "take control". Ironically, agency is mostly denied or devalued in psychological science, which seeks to explain human experience and action by reducing agency to behavioral contingencies, statistical regularities, neurophysiological states and processes, computational functions and models, or evolutionary biology (see, e.g., Gantt in this volume). Since psychological practice, especially in North America, is understood to be based on psychological science (witness the much vaunted "scientist-practitioner" model of educating psychologists advocated by the American Psychological Association) a clear difficulty presents itself. However, for the most part, this is a difficulty that is conveniently skirted by psychologists, whose practices benefit from an association with science, and psychological researchers, whose grants promise practical advances.

We argue that agency is an irreducible and defining aspect of what it is to be a person, and propose a soft deterministic conception and developmental theory of situated, deliberative agency that emerges from the embeddedness of biological individuals in pre-existing historical and sociocultural lifeworlds. We begin by positioning our account within the longstanding attempt within philosophy to reconcile a practical, everyday picture of persons as free choosers and actors, and a scientific picture of persons as determined by factors and events (biological, cultural, and situational). Our purpose is to outline an argument for and theoretical approach to agency that might be of use to psychologists interested in forging a more coherent nexus between their science and their practice. However, we forewarn that such yield is contingent on a willingness to accept a conception of agency as emergent and at least partially irreducible self-determination, within what is overall a deterministic framework.

2 Libertarianism, Hard Determinism, and Compatibilism

Two philosophical positions concerning agency are predicated on a strict contradiction between free choice and complete causal determinism, and are often referred to as being *incompatibilist*. *Hard determinists*, including eighteenth-century thinkers like d'Holbach, some twentieth-century behaviorists, and a few contemporary philosophers like Honderich, view free choice and action as illusory, submit that all behavior is fully determined by environmental and genetic factors, and consequently deny the existence of conventional moral responsibility. In direct opposition, *libertarians*, including eighteenth-century figures like Reid and twentieth-century philosophers like Chisholm, proclaim humans as both free and responsible, assert that past events and factors do not determine a unique future, and moreover claim that in human affairs such indeterminism reflects authentic agent choice, not merely random events. At the most basic level, libertarians argue from the premises (a) that free choice exists and (b) that, if this is so, by the principle of contradiction (with free choice and complete causal determinism being the direct opposites of each other) complete causal determinism is false, to the conclusion that complete causal determinism is false. Hard determinists argue from the premises (a) that complete causal determinism is true and (b) that if this is so, by the principle of contradiction (with free choice and complete causal determinism being the direct opposites of each other) free choice does not exist, to the conclusion that free choice does not exist. At least two things should be clear from these basic statements of extreme incompatibilist arguments. The premises in both arguments do not allow conclusions other than those stated. And, the resultant impasse asks us either to give up a crucial aspect of our everyday conception of ourselves, or to reject a scientific account of ourselves.

Given such difficulties, many ancient (e.g. the Stoics), enlightenment (e.g. Hobbes, Locke, Spinoza, Hume), and modern (e.g. Schopenhauer, Mill, Strawson) philosophers have employed dissolutionist strategies of various kinds to claim that the freedoms we embrace in everyday life are really not ruled out by hard determinism, and that complete freedom of the will is unintelligible. For example, Strawson (1959) argued that reactive attitudes, such as gratitude, that assume the possibility of morally praiseworthy freedom of action are so deeply embedded in our form of life that it would be impossible for us to abandon them even if determinism were true. Such dissolutionist strategems certainly qualify as compatibilist (in opposition to the incompatibilist positions just sketched). However, some more contemporary compatibilists (e.g. the philosopher Frankfurt 1971, and the psychologist Rychlak 1988) have not so much treated incompatibilism as a pseudo-problem that should be dissolved, but have attempted to provide alternative conceptions of freedom that do not deny, although they do "soften", determinism. Thus, Frankfurt talks about the uniquely human capacity to form "higher-order desires", and Rychlak speaks about a kind of "transpredication" rooted in the use of language that allows humans to respond antithetically to their determination.

Compatibilists typically proceed by denying the second premises in the basic libertarian and deterministic arguments. In the manner of Hobbes' (1962) famous seventeenth-century debate with Bishop Bramwell, traditional compatibilist arguments point out that our ordinary sense of freedom, as an absence of coercion or compulsion or constraint, is not at all incompatible with determinism. This is because we are free when we are self-determining, and we are self-determining when nothing prevents us from doing what we will. Consequently, we can be free in the sense of intending and doing what we will even if our intentions and actions are necessitated by antecedent circumstances. Moreover, Hobbes declared that determinism actually is required in order to make coherent sense of the idea of freedom as self-determination. For, in the absence of determination, resultant conditions of chaos hardly could be viewed as an adequate context for purposeful self-determination. He, therefore, concluded that any kind of mysterious freedom that might be incompatible with determinism was simply unintelligible, a point of view reiterated ever since by various compatibilists in response to a succession of allegedly mysterious libertarian conceptions such as noumenal selves, nonoccurrent causes, transempirical egos, and the like. Thus, for the traditional compatibilist, freedom of choice is not ruled out by virtue of a decision being causally determined. The law of contradiction is not seen to apply. And, for many compatibilists, freedom of choice is itself a kind of causally determined sequence of events.

Like Hobbes, many contemporary compatibilists also claim that a decision or choice can be causally determined by oneself (i.e. *self-determination*). But, as previously indicated, for this sort of contemporary compatibilist, self-determination occurs when the factors that cause a choice are aspects (e.g. desires, beliefs, reasons) of the person who makes it. Thus, Frankfurt (1971) asserts that not only must a choice be self-determined, but it must be in accord with, if not actually caused by, a person's higher-order desires. Higher-order desires take lower-order desires as their objects, and are uniquely human. Thus, my first-order desire for a cigarette is governed by my second-order desire not to give in to my first-order desire to smoke. A choice is free if the resulting action is in accord with the person's higher-order desires, and the choice was caused by the person's own deliberations. Deliberation is necessary because in most situations more than a single higher-order desire is involved, and relevant higher-order desires may compete with each other.

While some compatibilists and most libertarians hold that freedom of choice requires alternative possibilities of action, such that were an agent's deliberations to differ, the resulting action would also differ, Frankfurt disagrees, or at least restricts the range of application of this kind of thinking. Through a series of so-called Frankfurt-style cases, he argues that even in situations where alternative courses of action are somehow blocked or otherwise made unavailable, a choice is agentic and responsible so long as the resulting action accords with the person's higher-order desires and context-specific deliberations. So long as we choose in relation to our higher-order desires, even if unbeknownest to us we could not have done otherwise, we are agents. Frankfurt wants to convince us that it is our happiness in such cases, not our total freedom, that is critical and makes us both agents and responsible. Frankfurt's account goes beyond the traditional Hobbesean strategy of dissolutionism, in that it attempts to make intelligible a limited kind of agency that seems compatible with determinism, but which is recognizable as a kind of capability that is uniquely human and worth having. However, it still leaves intact a view of agency as mere voluntarism, without any significant aspect of origination.[1]

Rychlak's (1988, 1997) rigorous humanism offers a more psychological version of contemporary compatibilism. Rychlak's attempted compatibilism assumes a kind of self-determination that is not entirely determined by antecedent events, conditions, and factors. As such, it may be seen to probe the general kind of compatibilist possibility that we seek and attempt to develop herein. For Rychlak (1997), the agent is "an organism that behaves or believes in conformance with, in contradiction to, in addition to, or without regard for environmental or biological determinants" (p. 7). In this construal, agency is the capacity to influence one's behavior intentionally, and

---

[1]It should be noted that while Frankfurt himself avoids taking a position with respect to the compatibilist-incompatibilist debate, he most often has been interpreted as presenting a compatibilist argument and position.

such a capacity cannot be explained reductively in terms of material and efficient causation, but requires the admission of formal and telic causal processes appropriate to the study of human language, logic, and reason. The most important aspect of human language, reason, and logic is the process of predication that refers to the purposeful affirmation, denial, or qualification of patterns of meaning. To behave intentionally or agentically is to behave with the goal of affirming particular understandings rather than others. Free will is defined "as this capacity to frame the predication for the sake of which behavior will be intentionally carried out" (p. 61). "The very meaning of free will is to transpredicate, to reply to theses with antitheses, to negate and redirect the course of events according to purpose" (p. 279). An interesting and potentially important implication of Rychlak's construal of freedom as "transpredication" (which can be understood broadly as the framing of alternative possibilities) is that even if all of the contents of agentic deliberation are socioculturally and linguistically determined, the "attitude" taken toward such contents (as a consequence of the ever-present possibility of transpredication) still may be self-determined. And, of course, this "taking of an attitude" (given that it might involve contradiction or negation, amongst other possibilities) can make a great deal of difference with respect to what is decided and done.

Despite an extremely lively period of recent debate in which compatibilists have demonstrated considerable ingenuity in attempting to fend off various criticisms (including claims that they have ignored freedom of choice or the need for truly open alternatives), compatibilism still appears to face at least three daunting difficulties (cf. Brook and Stainton 2000, Kapitan 1999). Indeed, it is for precisely these reasons that many prominent incompatibilists, including both Kant and James, have regarded compatibilism as a quagmire of evasion and subterfuge. First, despite various dissolutionist arguments, compatibilism still runs counter to our ordinary sense that we cannot be free if all of our choices and actions, including our self-determinations, are determined by conditions and factors outside of our authentic desires and purposes. It is for this reason that, even if the direct opposite of "being determined" is considered to be "being random" rather than "being free", random actions can in no way be held to be "free" in any genuine sense of being "self determined". Second, compatibilists have not provided nonquestion-begging arguments for agency as self-determination, or at least have not provided arguments of this kind that have been widely accepted as such. Finally, compatibilists have not provided an adequate theory of agency, especially in relation to its possible development, that fits their purposes.

3   A Strategy for Defending Compatibilism as Soft Determinism

In response to the foregoing three problems, we want to: (1) attempt a nonquestion-begging argument for agency as self-determination, (2) sketch a theory of agency that fits our kind of compatibilism, and (3) indicate, on the basis of (1) and (2), how human agency can be both determined and free (in our compatibilist sense of self-determination).[2] First, we offer a more detailed definition of agency. For us, *human agency is the deliberative, reflective activity of a human being in framing, choosing, and executing his or her actions in a way that is not fully determined by factors and conditions other than his or her own understanding and reasoning.*[3]

Note several things about this definition of agency. First, agency need not be unaffected by factors and conditions other than an agent's own authentic, reflective understanding and reasoning. It only must not be determined fully by such other factors, a state of affairs we refer to as *underdetermination.* Second, even if a given motive or desire may initially have been established by factors such as social conditioning or genetics, the actor (following Frankfurt 1971) remains an agent so long as he or she has assimilated such motives or desires so as to make them objects of his or her own deliberation. Third, in saying that agency is underdetermined by "other factors", we do not mean that agency is necessarily undetermined, only that it must itself figure in its own determination. This is what we mean by self-determination.

We especially wish to emphasize the distinction we draw between *undetermined* and *underdetermined,* because in our view the traditional Hobbesian framing of compatibilism is inadequate precisely because it fails to make this distinction. In the absence of the possibility of underdetermination, only two choices present themselves, these being strict determinism or randomness, either of which may be argued effectively to rule out a coherent sense of self-determination. The problem we see with the traditional Hobbesian dissolutionist argument is that, as Bishop Bramwell and many others have sensed, it reduces self-determination too radically to nothing more than a link in a chain of antecedent events, factors, and conditions. It leaves no room for the deliberation (reflective understanding and reasoning) of an agent that

---

[2]Our compatibilism, it will become clear, is *not* a compatibilism of dissolutionism and/or voluntariness alone. Moreover, it issues in a kind of soft determinism that is not entailed by either of these more traditional compatibilisms.

[3]Such other factors and conditions include external constraints and coercions, as well as internal constraints over which the person has no conscious control.

is not entirely determined by other factors and conditions – in other words, it rules out even a limited origination. From this, it should be obvious that our position is not intended to be compatibilist in the traditional sense of dissolving agency to determinism. Rather, it is intended to be compatibilist in the more radical sense of demonstrating how an agentic capability in deliberation and action is compatible with a deterministic, nonmysterious, and non-reductive account of the development of human agency within biological/physical, historical, and sociocultural context.

Finally, by avoiding the word "cause", in our definition of agency, we do not restrict determination to efficient causation. Given well-known difficulties with the concept of cause (e.g. problems of infinite regress, the question of reasons as causes, the difficulty in selecting specific causes from other conditions and factors in open systems, the satisfactory formulation of conditions of necessity and sufficiency), we feel justified in avoiding its use. Nonetheless, our conception of determinism is broadly consistent with the folk psychological idea of antecedent events, factors, and conditions influencing subsequent events with varying degrees of completeness, such that when such influence is complete, full determinism results.

4 An Argument for the Underdetermination of Agency

4.1 Structure of the Argument

The only factors or conditions other than agency (understood as self-determination) that might determine human choice and action, aside from explicit coercion that does not always exist are: (a) physical/biological (e.g. neurophysiological) states and processes; (b) sociocultural rules and practices; (c) unconscious processes over which an agent has no control; or (d) random events.[4] Assuming that these options exhaust plausible possibilities for explaining human choice and action (other than the positing of human agency understood as self-determination in the manner we have specified in our definition of agency), elimination of each and all of these options as fully determinate of human choice and action will establish the underdetermination of human agency by factors and conditions other than agency (in our sense of self-determination) itself.

---

[4]We omit theological speculation because in our opinion invoking an omniscient being or beings removes any rationale for human argument with respect to agency.

4.2 Against Full Physical/Biological Determinism

Human actions are meaningful, and meaning requires a context. Meaning refers to the conventional, common, or standard sense of an expression, construction, or sentence in a given language, or of a non-linguistic signal, symbol, or practice in a particular sociocultural setting. Therefore, the meaningfulness of human actions requires sociocultural rules and practices, the most important of which are linguistic or language-related. Consequently, the only way in which human choice and action could be determined entirely by biological/neurophysiological states and processes is if the sociocultural rules, practices, and conventions are determined by or reducible to such states and processes. Such a full reduction of societies and cultures to physical biology seems highly implausible, given that we currently do not possess, nor we would argue, ever are likely to possess adequate physical descriptions of sociocultural, linguistic practices. Without such descriptions, attempting to explain agency in solely physical terms is rather like attempting to explain the activity of baseball players without reference to the rules and regulations of the game of baseball.[5]

Furthermore, the meanings found in sociocultural and linguistic practices constitute and are constituted by those very practices. These meanings provide a coherence for the human lifeworld that does not exist at the level of biology or neurophysiology. So even if some kind of biological/neurophysiological account of sociocultural and linguistic practices were put forward, such an account itself would only draw its meaning from that very sociocultural/linguistic level that it was attempting to explain.

4.3 Against Full Sociocultural Determinism

Socioculturally governed meanings change over historical time. Such change could not occur if past sociocultural rules, conventions, and practices were fully determining of meaning. Therefore, past sociocultural rules, conventions, and practices cannot be fully determinate of meaningful human action, but must be at least partially open-ended. Further, it seems highly likely that the partially open-ended nature of whatever conventional sociocultural meanings are operative at any given time allows for the development of personal understanding and possibilities for action that may contribute significantly to sociocultural change. However, allowance is not determination.

---

[5]Note that this argument against full physical/biological determinism does not rule out human biology and neurophysiology as requirements for human action. However, requirement alone is not determination.

4.4   Against Randomness and Unconscious Processes Alone

Despite ongoing sociocultural change, a good deal of order is discernible in sociocultural conventions, rules, and practices. Randomness cannot account for such meaningful order. At a purely physical level, random processes might contribute to the establishment of order or patterns in physical systems. However, this kind of order can only be one among many necessary conditions for meaning. Meaning is more than mere organization or patterns, but involves significance as well. Even the recognition of something as a pattern and the evaluation of its significance presupposes meaning. Therefore, the sociocultural meaning that is required for human action cannot be random.

Moreover, humans are, at least, partially, aware of many of their choices and actions in ways that converge and coordinate with the observations, accounts, and activities of others. Unconscious processes alone cannot account for such awareness and coordination of human choice and action. We accept that change in sociocultural practices, conventions, and rules that guide human choice and action may, and probably often does, reflect human activity that is nondeliberative in the sense of being tacit or inarticulate. However, we submit that our phenomenal experience of ourselves as intentional agents, in combination with our ability to coordinate our actions with those of others to achieve commonly-judged, orderly social ends, provides sufficient reason to forego a commitment to fully random or unconscious determination.

4.5   Agency as the Surviving, Plausible Option

Having eliminated full biological and cultural determination of human action, and argued against randomness and unconscious processes alone, we are left with the possibility that human choice and action, at least in part and sometimes, result from the irreducible understanding and reasoning of human agents. The underdetermination of human agency by these other conditions and factors does not mean that human agency is undetermined, only that it figures in its own determination. Such self-determination means that human agency is not reducible to physical, biological, sociocultural, and/or random/unconscious processes, even though (as we will suggest next) many of these may be required for, and/or help to constitute it.

Of course, it might be argued that some combination of physical/biological, sociocultural, random, and/or unconcious factors and conditions might provide a fully deterministic account that does not require self-determination. Indeed, this may be a logical possibility if one assumes some kind of generative, nonadditive interactivity among these various conditions and factors.

However, without an exacting theoretical description and empirical demonstration of precisely such a generative effect (preferably one displayed at the level of everyday events, not one based speculatively on psychologists' and/or philosophers' interpretations of chaos theory or quantum mechanics), such possibilities amount to little more than gestures of faith that assume a determinism that is complete without self-determination. Consequently, they seem to us to beg the question as long as they cannot be demonstrated.

At this point, we also should add that human agency, understood as self-determination, may not always be exercised. Just as we do not become unable to stand after we have been sitting, we do not become unable to exercise self-determination because there are occasions and circumstances in which our choices and actions reflect no deliberative self-determination. In other words, the fact that we may not always be self-determining, does not imply that we can not self-determine at other times and in other circumstances.

5   A Very Brief Sketch of a Developmental Theory of Situated, Emergent, and Deliberative Agency

In making our argument for agency, in the broadly compatibilist sense of self-determination, we do not mean to imply that agency arises mysteriously, in some manner other than through a comprehensible *emergence* within the physical, biological, and sociocultural world. Elsewhere (Martin and Sugarman 1999a, 1999b, 2001), we have articulated a developmental theory in which we propose that deliberative agency arises, as a kind of self-determination, in an intelligible manner within an inescapable and required physical and biological context, and within constitutive historical and sociocultural structures and practices. However, once emergent, agency cannot be reduced back to these required and constituitive factors and conditions, but always may play a part in its own subsequent development and exercise. It is this thesis of irreducible emergence that makes agency, in our sense of self-determination, more than a readily replaceable or less than significant link in a chain of other determinants.

This way of thinking developmentally and situationally about agency has much in common with some versions of social constructionist, discursive (Harré and Gillett 1994), symbolic interactionist (e.g. Blumer 1969), sociocultural (Vygotsky 1986), and especially hermeneutic (Richardson et al. 1999; Taylor 1985) theorizing. The conception of agency invoked is an always in-the-world agency exercised by embodied, developmentally emergent, historically and socioculturally situated persons. Such individuals have emerged within their basic existential condition, a condition that consists initially of complex human biological organisms born into the physical and sociocultural world. Acting in this world, these individuals enter into a developmental trajectory through which they come to take up and use sociocultural means and practices in a deliberative manner as reflective psychological agents capable of influencing both themselves and their societies.

Of course, this way of thinking is somewhat foreign to much mainstream psychology and analytic philosophy, both of which often have treated the human agent as somewhat detached from relevant context, as disembodied, and as without a developmental history.[6] It is entirely possible to discuss "brains in vats", computational "minds", and other such hypotheses and associated arguments about the relation between minds and brains, with little more than a passing nod to human history or culture. We suspect that this kind of talk, with its restricted conception of a mostly "world-less" human agent, has contributed much to the seeming intractability of debates such as that between libertarians and hard determinists, and to the failure to articulate viable alternatives (cf. Guignon, and Richardson and Bishop, this volume).

While a detailed presentation of our theory of the developmental emergence of situated, deliberative, self-determining agency is beyond the scope of this essay, part of that theory is especially important with respect to extending our compatibilist conception of agency as self-determination. As already indicated, it is our contention that agency (understood as the reflective, deliberative, partially self-determined activity of a person that is in accordance with his or her own desires and choices) arises developmentally from the prereflective activity of an individual born into a collective life world.

5.1   From Prereflective Activity to Self-Determining Agency

At the beginning of individual human life, the infant is equipped with nothing more than primitive, biologically-given capabilities of limited motion and sensation (e.g. nonreflective movements and sensations associated with feeding and physical discomfort), and the prereflective ability to remember, in a very limited physical manner, something of what is encountered and sensed. However, the human biological infant both matures and develops within its inescapable historical and sociocultural context. This sociocultural world

---

[6]See Kane (1996) and Mele (1995) for some notable exceptions. However, even in these instances, possibly relevant developmental theorizing is more suggested than elaborated.

of linguistic and other relational practices comes increasingly to constitute the emergent understanding of the developing infant. Within this life world, nested within the ever-present biological and physical world, caregivers and others interact with the infant in ways that furnish the developing infant with the various practices, forms, and means of personhood and identity extant within the particular society and culture within which the infant exists. Psychological development now proceeds as the internalization and appropriation of sociocultural practices as psychological tools – i.e. vehicles for language and thought, much in the manner envisioned by Vygotsky (1978, 1986) (also see Harré's 1998 neo-Vygotskian account). In this way, developing psychological persons come to talk and relate to themselves in much the same way as others have talked and related to them. In so doing, they become engaged in both the ongoing, always present sociocultural practices in which they are embedded, and those appropriated, internalized linguistic and relational practices they now employ as means for thinking and understanding.

With such appropriation and internalization, and the thinking and understanding it enables, the individual's mode of being is transformed from one of prereflective activity to one in which reflective, intentional agency is possible.[7] The psychological person is a biological individual who becomes capable of understanding some of what the life world (in its history, culture, and social relations and practices) and her being in it consists. Such understanding always involves an interpretation of available sociocultural meanings and practices, but as development unfolds, the never-ending process of interpretation and reinterpretation becomes increasingly available to conscious reflection and deliberation, should such reflection and associated deliberation be required. Open to the life world, the psychological person gradually becomes capable of increasingly sophisticated feats of recollection and imagination. Concomitant with these capabilities of projecting backward and forward in time is the gradual understanding of one's embodied being in the world as a center of experiencing, understanding, intending, and acting. In this way, "self" understanding emerges, and continues to develop, within the historical, sociocultural contexts into which humans are born as biological individuals, but come to exist as psychological persons.

Such psychological persons are capable of reflective, intentional thought

---

[7]In our developmental theory, vehicles for such appropriation and transformation include a wide variety of contingent processes that psychologists have labeled as reinforcement, observational learning, and so forth. However, our theoretical treatment of such "vehicles" differs sharply from that found in the more reductive accounts of behavioral and social-cognitive psychologists (see Degrandpre 2000).

and action directed outward and inward. The self now has emerged as a particular kind of interpreted, reflexive understanding of an embodied, "in-the-world" human being – an understanding that discloses and extends particular, individual existence. When this occurs, thought and action are no longer entirely determined by the sociocultural practices from which they initially were constituted, and within which they continue to unfold. Given the inevitably unique history of individual experience within a life world, and the capacity for self as reflexive, interpretive understanding of experience in that world, psychological persons are underdetermined by their constitutive, sociocultural and biological origins. This does not mean that psychological persons are undetermined, only that together with biological, cultural, and situational determinants, the "self" understanding and deliberations of such persons may, and frequently do, enter into their determination. Even as psychological persons continue to be formed by the relational and discursive practices in which they are embedded, they also come to contribute to those practices in innovative ways that reflect a self-interpreting agency. As Rychlak (1988, 1997) might say, as agents, we are capable of framing "transpredications" (alternative possibilities) that draw upon but purposefully transform what we have experienced and learned as participants in sociocultural and linguistic practices and forms of understanding.

For us, agency as self-determination equates to a kind of self-understanding that permits a deliberative, reflective activity in selecting and choosing, framing and executing actions. While there is some limited origination in this, it is important not to overstate it. Psychological persons never can stand outside of the influence of relevant physical, biological, and sociocultural (especially relational and linguistic) factors and conditions. Nonetheless, their self-understanding is underdetermined by such other factors and conditions, and capable of entering into the choosing, framing, and execution of actions, both experienced and mildly innovative.

5.2   A Brief Comparison

One way to understand the implications of our approach to agency as self-determination, in the manner just indicated, is to contrast it with a recently influential conceptualization of self-determination that has been advanced by the libertarian Kane (1996, p. 191):

> To say that persons self determine ... is to say that they perform ... acts and that they have plural voluntary control over their doing so and doing otherwise [right up to the very point of acting]. Agents have plural voluntary control when they are able to do what they will to do,

> when they will to do it, on purpose rather than by accident or mistake, without being coerced or compelled in doing, or willing to do, it, or otherwise controlled by other agents or mechanisms.

Kane, unlike many other contemporary libertarians, insists that such self-determination need not invoke a mysteriously unique kind of nonoccurrent agent causation (see, e.g., Kane in this volume for discussion). His tactic here is to take seriously the possibility that a kind of self network exists that somehow can be mapped onto neural occurrences, and that all of this (both the conscious experience of agency and the intervening self network) is somehow related to the quantum character of reality. Here, it is interesting to note just how closely Kane seems to come to the kind of functionalism currently favored by many hard determinists who employ computational, superveninent models in an attempt indirectly to link agentic kinds to an underlying physical level of strict causation (e.g. Kim 1996).

While sometimes seen as alternatives to contemporary hard determinist, materialist accounts of agency, functionalist accounts that employ supervenience seem to us mostly to beg the reductive question by proposing an intermediate level of rather mysterious "computational", "connectionist", or "schematic network" kinds that somehow are supposed to mediate between psychological, agentic and physical kinds. In our view, such efforts experience the same kinds of difficulty as earlier, more directly and obviously reductive, central state materialist and computational models in accounting for important features of our psychological states such as intentionality, rationality, normativity, and first-person perspective (cf. McDowell 1994, Searle 1992). Moreover, they frequently seem to conflate requirement with identity relations in apparently assuming that because human agents require biological bodies, they are nothing more than biological bodies, albeit "computerized" and/or "schematized" ones. In all such approaches, sociocultural meanings, rules, conventions, and practices, which for us play critically important background, contextual, and constituitive roles in the development of human self understanding and agency receive extremely short shrift.

In contrast to Kane's version of contemporary libertarianism, our own treatment of agentic self-determination is more modest in requiring only that self-determination be an irreducible part of the determination of a particular choice and action. Moreover, for us, such self-determination need not always be active. In addition, we understand self-determination as emerging developmentally, as a kind of reflective self-understanding linked to deliberate action, within the constraints and influences of both biology and culture, but not reducible to either. We thus attempt to avoid both a reduction of agency to neurophysiology and a speculative appeal to microparticulate theorizing that seems ultimately to substitute quantum uncertainty and "indeterminacy" for agentic reason, intention, and perspective. To us, such moves seem to sacrifice precisely what we hope to maintain and try to explain. Interestingly, Kane's contribution to this volume indicates to us that he recognizes a need to balance the neurophysiological aspect of his theorizing with a kind of emergence, perhaps not totally dissimilar to that discussed herein.

6 Conclusions

Traditional libertarian and hard determinist approaches to agency tend to ignore the historical, sociocultural constitution of agency (as do many compatibilist accounts, cf. Richardson and Bishop, this volume). In the case of libertarianism, this tendency manifests in assertions of radical freedom emanating from a metaphysically isolated agent somehow disconnected from the physical, biological, and sociocultural world. In the case of hard determinism, this tendency often manifests in implausible attempts to reduce agency to nothing more than physical kinds and causes. By bringing agency "into the world", we hope to have moved some small way toward addressing the three problems associated with compatibilist theories that we posed earlier. In particular, we have attempted a nonquestion-begging argument for agency as self-determination and indicated, through a brief elaboration of our theory of agentic development, how this conception of agency may be held coherently as being both determined and determining.

What we claim is that agency arises from the prereflective activity of biological humans embedded inextricably within a real physical and sociocultural world. It is this activity and its consequences that make available sociocultural practices, conventions, and meanings to the increasingly reflective understanding of human persons. That part of such understanding that reveals aspects of the particular being of a human individual is constitutive of the self of that person. With the onset of reflective, "self" understanding capable of memorial recollection, imaginative projection, and reason, a kind of situated, deliberative agency becomes possible. This is an agency of non-mysterious origin, being constituted by relevant physical, biological conditions and requirements, and sociocultural practices and meanings. Yet because of the reflective self understanding and reason upon which it rests, such agency also consists in a kind of self-determination that never acts outside of historical and sociocultural situatedness, but which can aspire beyond, and cannot be reduced to such situatedness alone, nor to its other biological and physical requirements. Moreover, the resultant agency is not only voluntary, but has an aspect of origination, not in any radically free sense, but in the capability of self-interpreting, self-determining agents to selectively take up, modify, and employ available sociocultural practices and conventions as bases for psychologically significant activity. It is in this sense that the situated, deliberative agency we argue for, and theorize about, is both determined and determining.

Our approach is compatibilist in the sense that it relies centrally on an idea of self-determination, but it is not dissolutionist, nor restricted to voluntariness alone. With respect to psychology, we are of the opinion that the kind of compatibilist theorizing we have attempted herein eventually may contribute to an understanding of psychology as a rigorous, but nonreductive study of the experiences and actions of human agents in historical, sociocultural, and developmental context. Such a psychology would carry implications for a form of psychological practice that approaches concerns of living within relevant traditions and practices, without forgetting, but also without elevating inappropriately, necessary physical and biological factors and considerations. It is this nesting of the psychological within the historical and sociocultural, which in turn are nested within biological and physical reality, that we regard as a proper "metaphysics" of the human condition. This is not a traditional metaphysics of transcendental or first principles, certainty, and essentials, but a "neo-metaphysics" consisting in historical, situational, and developmental contingencies that are inseparable from, the "acting-in-the-world" of embodied, biologically evolved human beings who seem uniquely "culture-capable".

Obviously, there is much of importance to learn about the physical, neurophysiological, and biological requirements, operations, and conditions that permit human agency, just as there is much still unanswered concerning the sociocultural constitution of agency, and the developmental contexts within which it emerges. The task of understanding human agency is large, and our advances to date small. However, the enormous complexity of the task should not be avoided in favor of overly simplified, reductive models and programs of research that, in our opinion, can be expected to reveal little of what we find significant in our lives.

At the same time, it is important explicitly to identify a likely consequence of our work herein for traditional scientific psychology. We have claimed that the underdetermination of human agency by factors and conditions other than the irreducible understanding and reasoning of human agents does not mean that human agency is undetermined, only that it figures into its own determination. As such, it might be concluded that the possibility of a deterministic science of psychology still exists, so long as the self-determination of individual agents can be accessed through methods of scientific inquiry. However, the practical difficulties of achieving veridical access to such self-determination should not be underestimated. It may prove to be the case that our underdetermination thesis with respect to human agency, if true, while not denying the possibility of a deterministic psychological science, may imply the practical impossibility of such a science. For, even if human agency is not undetermined, so long as self-determination is admitted, it may prove to be indeterminate in the sense of being outside the reach of the methods of psychological science.

Turning to the practice of psychology, we believe that psychological practitioners are right to insist on the self-determining agentic capability of human persons. However, such insistence should not be instrumentally and/or romantically exaggerated in aid of purely psychological, decontextualized administrations and interventions. Nor, should it lay claim to the kind of support common in more appropriately reductive branches of natural, physical science. In psychology, we should not reductively make human beings small as a means of doing large things with them.

References

Blumer H. (1969): *Symbolic Interactionism: Perspective and Method*, Prentice-Hall, Englewood Cliffs.

Brook A. and Stainton R.J. (2000): *Knowledge and Mind: A Philosophical Introduction*, MIT Press, Cambridge, MA.

Degrandpre R.J. (2000): A science of meaning: Can behaviorism bring meaning to psychological science? *American Psychologist* **55**, 721–739.

Frankfurt H.G. (1971): Freedom of the will and the concept of a person. *Journal of Philosophy* **68**, 5–20.

Harré, R. (1998): *The Singular Self: An Introduction to the Psychology of Personhood*, Sage, London.

Harré R. and Gillett G. (1994): *The Discursive Mind*, Sage, Thousand Oaks.

Hobbes T. (1962): *The English Works of Thomas Hobbes, Vol. 5*, ed. by W. Molesworth, Scientia Aalen, London.

Kane R. (1996): *The Significance of Free Will*, Oxford University Press, Oxford.

Kapitan T. (1999): Free will problem. In *The Cambridge Dictionary of Philosophy*, 2nd edition, ed. by R. Audi, Cambridge University Press, Cambridge, pp. 326–328.

Kim J. (1996): *Philosophy of Mind*, Westview Press, Boulder.

Martin J. and Sugarman J. (1999a): *The Psychology of Human Possibility and Constraint*, State University of New York Press, Albany.

Martin J. and Sugarman J. (1999b): Psychology's reality debate: A "levels of reality" approach. *Journal of Theoretical and Philosophical Psychology* **19**, 177–194.

Martin J. and Sugarman J. (2001): Is the self a kind of understanding? *Journal for the Theory of Social Behavior* **31**, 103–114.

McDowell J. (1994): *Mind and World*, Harvard University Press, Cambridge, MA.

Mele A. (1995): *Autonomous Agents: From Self-Control to Autonomy*, Oxford University Press, New York.

Richardson F.C., Fowers B.J., and Guignon C. (1999): *Re-Envisioning Psychology: Moral Dimensions of Theory and Practice*, Jossey-Bass, San Francisco.

Rychlak J.F. (1988): *The Psychology of Rigorous Humanism*, 2nd ed., Kriegar, Malabar.

Rychlak J.F. (1997): *In Defense of Human Consciousness*, American Psychological Association, Washington, DC.

Searle J.R. (1992): *The Rediscovery of the Mind*, MIT Press, Cambridge, MA.

Strawson, P. (1959): *Individuals*, Methuen, London.

Taylor C. (1985): *Human Agency and Language. Philosophical Papers Vol. 1*, Cambridge University Press, Cambridge.

Vygotsky L.S. (1978): *Mind in Society: The Development of Higher Psychological Processes*, Harvard University Press, Cambridge, MA.

Vygotsky L.S. (1986): *Thought and Language*, transl. by A. Kozulin, MIT Press, Cambridge, MA (Original work published 1934).

Rethinking Determinism
in Social Science

Frank Richardson and Robert Bishop

The danger of trying to explain evil is that we risk falling into the abyss of predestination: that given these life events, this social surround, and this personality type, the evil deed was inevitable. Explanation becomes exculpation, and volition gets eclipsed. To understand all should not be to forgive all.

"The Roots of Evil" – *Newsweek* 5/21/01

What can be controlled is never completely real; what is real can never be completely controlled.

Vladimir Nabokov

1 Introduction

Thoughtful social scientists, mental health professionals, and students in the social disciplines often confront a particular dilemma concerning determinism and freedom (Rychlak 1988; Slife and Williams 1995). On the one hand, they realize that much theory and research in psychology assumes a strong deterministic picture of human behavior. Investigators try to devise explanations consisting in context-free laws or models that identify the efficient causes of events in the human realm. Such accounts show how current attitudes and actions are largely the inevitable product of genetic make-up, cultural context, an individual's life history, current situational influences, or several of these. On the other hand, they realize that we deliberately seek to map the determinants of human activity in order to lay a basis for liberating individuals from unwanted influences so that they might live freer lives, or for actively fostering more fulfilling and creative forms of social living. However, these sincere purposes seem to be rendered illusory and to be undermined by a picture of the world in which human action is reduced to just another passive link in the causal chain of events (Williams 2001). In addition, this picture of things appears to clash rather harshly with the investigator's self-image as an ingenious and creative social scientist! Perhaps philosophical therapy will one day be available for this peculiar form of fractured self-image and divided will. In the meantime, however, this picture can drain one's sense of individual purpose and disciplinary integrity.[1]

Increasingly, a second concern, on the surface a very different one, also preoccupies many critics of modern psychology from both inside and outside the field. They are concerned less with a deflating determinism than an exaggerated sense of human autonomy or freedom (Cushman 1995, 1999; Fancher 1995; Richardson et al. 1999; Taylor 1989). For example, the cultural critic Bailie (1995) suggests that many current social pathologies from epidemics of violence to disarray in the institution of the family are fostered by a "dismantling of sturdy, stable, and lifelong loyalties in the interest of increasingly fragile and fickle forms of selfhood". Unfortunately, he adds, many of those "on whom this process takes its greatest toll turn for help and solace to a psychological establishment still wedded to the theoretical misconceptions that helped foster the crisis in the first place" (p. 4).

In this same vein, the historian of psychology Cushman (1990) argues that modern times has celebrated a "bounded, masterful self" that "is expected to function in a highly autonomous, isolated way" and "to be self-soothing, self-loving, and self-sufficient" (p. 604). Unfortunately, he suggests, there is evidence that such exaggerated pretensions to autonomy and uniqueness almost inevitably collapse into an "empty self", whose characteristics of fragility, sense of emptiness, and proneness to fluctuation between feelings of worthlessness and grandiosity are often said to be the hallmarks of neurotic psychopathology in our day (e.g. Kohut 1977). Cushman (1990, p. 604) defines emptiness as, "in part, an absence of communal forms and beliefs" that leaves individuals quite vulnerable to influence from cultural forms such as advertising and many types of psychology which emanate authority and certainty. So it is telling that the goals of psychotherapy are usually rendered quite narrowly in terms of more effective individual behavior or individual self-actualization (Bellah et al. 1985; Cushman 1995; Fancher 1995; Frank and Frank 1991; Rieff 1966). Little is said about ethical qualities of character

---

[1]A sense of direction and integrity in social science may also be undermined by what many take to be its remarkable failure, after at least a century of effort, to come up with anything resembling genuinely explanatory or predictive theory of the human realm (Bernstein 1976; Taylor 1985). There is no space to discuss this controversial matter in this paper. It does, however, raise the interesting possibility that both these putative failures and our attachment to a freedom-quashing determinism might derive in part from mistaken beliefs about the very nature of the human life-world and the proper form of knowledge or understanding in human science inquiry.

or commitment that many feel are essential to a worthwhile or fulfilled life, the absence of which may be a virtual recipe for emotional difficulties and social fragmentation.

To many of its critics, modern psychology is both hampered by the specter of determinism and permeated with questionable ethical and social ideals. In this paper, we argue that it may not be possible to untangle familiar paradoxes of freedom and determinism in psychology or the human sciences without rethinking some of their implicit ethical and social ideals, and vice versa. At the conference on determinism from which this book derives, Honderich provided those present with a splendid example of pondering difficult and puzzling features of our human condition and insisting that our best sense of them must be reflected in our accounts of the world, including determinism and free will. He told us he had arrived at the conclusion that the experience of looking back on one's life and deeply regretting things one had done or roads not taken was harder to square with the deterministic world picture than moral approval and blame, or life hopes, for which he thought he had previously made a satisfactory home in a world without free will. Thus some significant shift, presently unknown to him, in his account of determinism (not necessarily abandoning it) seemed to be called for. One could not ask for a finer example of blending moral insight and philosophical exactitude in the search for understanding.

Social science may need a lot of help from philosophy in dealing with questions concerning determinism in the human sphere. But Kane (1996, pp. 15-16) points out that there is a growing awareness on the part of many philosophers that "different views on free will reflect not only differences about factual and conceptual issues, but differences about *values* as well, about what is or is not important". According to Kane, "the traditional argument has been that free will is significant and worth having because it is a prerequisite for other goods that humans highly value", including such things as "autonomy, moral responsibility, desert, dignity ... [and] individuality". Nevertheless, he suggests, the "debate has usually stalemated over the meaning of these goods and whether they really require an incompatible free will".

In this paper, we suggest that there is important work to be done in both philosophy and the social sciences in clarifying, in Kane's words, the "meaning of these goods". Specifically, we contend that confusing, seemingly intractable dilemmas concerning the compatibility or incompatibility of determinism and freedom may be due in part to tacit, unexamined assumptions about the nature of human autonomy, both as a human reality and a moral ideal – assumptions that are shared, interestingly, by all sides in this debate. We merely hope to shed some new light on important questions about human freedom and dignity.

2 Autonomy

According to Christman (1989, pp. 3-23), most philosophers, dating at least back to Kant, consider "autonomy" as crucial to understanding free will.[2] At the core of most of these notions of autonomy is the idea of a person's capacity to exercise the power of self-government. Historically, the notion of an autonomous person was developed in analogy with the self-government of individual nations. But it has proved difficult to pin down the exact nature and conditions of self-government in the context of human agency. Here are two descriptions or definitions of autonomy by well-known 20th century philosophers. First, Berlin (1969, p. 131): "I wish my life and decisions to depend upon myself, not on external forces of whatever kind. I wish to be the instrument of my own, not other acts of will. I wish to be a subject, not an object ... I wish to be somebody, not nobody". Second, Dworkin (quoted in Christman 1989, p. 61): "A person is autonomous if he identifies with his desires, goals, and values, and such identification is not itself influenced in ways which make the process of identification in some way alien to the individual".[3]

Clearly, autonomy in this sense involves what we might call *external* conditions which are identified relatively easily, such as having the right or privilege to live our lives free of interference from the state or other people. But it also involves *internal* conditions, such as the psychological capacity for self-government just mentioned. Identifying some of these internal conditions, e.g., freedom from compulsions, seems to be a relatively straightforward matter. But others are quite controversial. For example, Kane (1996, this volume) argues that genuine freedom involves our being "ultimately responsible" for and the "ultimate cause" of at least some choices and actions. This means, following Aristotle, that if one is held responsible for immoral acts issuing from his or her character, then one "must at some time in the

---

[2]In the light of the ensuing argument, Christman's book has a telling title: *The Inner Citadel*.

[3]Anticipating the rest of this chapter, note how much these conceptions of autonomy reflect notions and ideals of individualism, self-containment, and a highly instrumental conception of human action. For Kant autonomy was assumed to be embedded in a serious moral and religious context. Disputants in the free will debates after Kant have paid much less attention to such contexts and the limitations these contexts might impose on conceptions and ideals of autonomy.

past have been responsible for forming this character" (p. 35). Some will find this kind of "ultimate responsibility" essential to meaningful free will; others will find it to be an otherworldly, unintelligible mystification. (Like Kane, we seek to clarify how such freedom and responsibility can be part of the warp and woof of an everyday, earthbound existence.) But most of the thinkers on either side of this argument embrace some conception of autonomy as self-determination, typically involving such things as the absence of internal and external constraints, the ability to make our own decisions and to chart our own course in life, an exercise of individual responsibility, and thus the possession of human dignity.

3   Compatibilism and Incompatibilism

A relatively small number of philosophers hold to a strict determinism, concluding that there is no free will and that human autonomy is an illusion. Some might feel that this position is rendered less plausible in the light of the indeterministic picture of the natural world emerging from contemporary physics. But, of course, nothing is ever settled that easily. Although we will not be able to address them directly, several stimulating defenses of strict determinism have been offered in recent years (e.g. Honderich 1988, 1993; Pereboom 1995).[4]

Most philosophers who are not strict determinists divide into incompatibilists and compatibilists. Incompatibilitists contend that freedom or autonomy is crucially incompatible with determinism reigning in the sphere of human thought and action (e.g. Kane, this volume). One of the core intuitions of incompatibilists is that we must have some form of ultimate responsibility for our purposes, decisions, and actions in order for notions like praise, blame, desert, creativity and individuality to make any sense. From this perspective, if there is no sense in which our purposes and ideals are up to us, then we cannot make any legitimate claims to dignity or moral responsibility. In favor of this view, one might also argue that it is not merely desirable that we be able to make such claims and judgements, but that we seem quite unable *not* to make them in earnest and thoughtful ways as we go about the ordinary business of living.

---

[4]From the point of view of this paper, strict determinism, defended as it is by capable and responsible thinkers, might be considered to be in part an understandable reaction of frustration to the enormous difficulties meshing freedom and determinism the way we usually approach the problem, including the stalemates encountered in the debate between incompatibilists and compatibilists.

In contrast, compatibilists see meaningful free will as compatible with determinism in the human realm. The key intuition for compatibilists is that all of the ordinary freedoms we desire and experience – freedom from coercion, compulsion, oppression, physical restraint, and the like – are not only compatible with determinism but actually require it. The sort of constraint that prevents us from doing what we want may be objectionable, but it is not the only category of causation or determination. In fact, compatibilists argue, there is a kind of determination without constraint – indeed, it is self-determination – that does not impede, but actualizes our will. As long as we are free to do as we want – that is to say, act in the absence of anybody or anything constraining, restraining, or coercing us – our will is not impeded and the source of our own values and purposes lies within us in as ultimate a sense as is possible in our world. We are somebody and not nobody, to use Berlin's phrase, because determination does not prevent our being the source of our deliberations or destroy our causal efficacy. Dennett (1984) and other compatibilist philosophers ask: What additional types of freedom over and above freedom from constraint, coercion and restraint could be worth having or desiring? These are the ordinary freedoms we want – to be free to do as we please – and they are compatible with determinism.

Incompatibilists reply that although freedom from constraint, coercion and restraint are important, these are insufficient to guarantee that an agent is the ultimate source of her values and purposes. Compatibilists find this worry bewildering and believe the search for any further freedoms over and above these "ordinary everyday freedoms" to be misguided or a form of mystification.

Most of this debate is framed in terms of physical determinism. But the concept of psychological determinism, which is directly related to the internal conditions for autonomy, also plays an important role. Psychological determinism is often understood as the determination of our decisions and actions by prior character and motives, which in turn are determined by a chain of events tracing back through our upbringing to our birth and, perhaps, beyond. Certainly such determinism appears to undercut autonomy. Compatibilists attempt to diffuse this threat by clarifying how agents can have a robust freedom from compulsion, constraint, and restraint in such a deterministic world. They attempt to articulate meaningful notions of responsibility, praiseworthiness and blameworthiness, and the like in terms of self-determination as they understand it. Unconvinced by these arguments, incompatibilists either try to show that human agents can contravene the influences of one's history and previously formed psychological make-up or that such determining factors are not so rigid after all.

Compatibilists criticize incompatibilist freedom as at best an impossible dream and at worst incoherent. Incompatibilists argue that compatibilist freedom is an illusion and does not capture the notion of freedom we most deeply desire. Common sense suggests that there might be important truths on both sides of this debate. On the one hand, there would seem to be no viable sense of freedom without some form of determination or ordered realm of causes and influences in which to act and make a difference. On the other hand, that freedom has to be real and meaningful and cannot just amount to simply another predictable effect of causes that play upon the human agent. Common sense notwithstanding, however, it has turned out to be maddeningly difficult to blend these insights in a coherent picture of the human situation.

4 Modern Ideals of Freedom and Autonomy

The novelist and philosopher Murdoch (1985, p. 26) describes what she takes to be the predicament of modern moral philosophy today in this way:

> Philosophy ... has been busy dismantling the old substantial picture of the "self", and ethics has not proved itself able to rethink this concept for moral purposes. The moral agent then is pictured as an isolated principle of will, or a burrowing principle of consciousness, inside, or beside, a lump of being which has been handed over to other disciplines. ... On the one hand a Luciferan philosophy of adventures of the will, and on the other natural science. Moral philosophy, and indeed morals, are thus undefended against an irresponsible and undirected self-assertion which easily goes hand in hand with some brand of pseudo-scientific determinism.

Murdoch suggests that our contemporary understanding of the "self" or human agency is deeply divided between the notion of an unbridled and unhindered will and that of a passive "lump of being" to be investigated by natural (and perhaps also social) science. And yet somehow, she suggests, they go "hand in hand". Her remarks suggest possible hidden sources of the freewill debates and fresh reasons for their tendency to stalemate.

In a scientific age, philosophers, social scientists, and the man in the street alike are heirs of a deep-seated view of ourselves as more or less products of the past and outside influences. Such a view can easily lead to the kind of determinism picturesquely described by James (1956, p. 150):

> [T]hose parts of the universe already laid down absolutely appoint and decree what the other parts shall be. The future has no ambiguous

> possibilities in its womb: the part we call the present is compatible
> with only one totality. Any other complement than the one fixed from
> eternity is impossible. The whole is in each and every part, and welds
> it with the rest into an absolute unity, an iron block ...

But Murdoch reminds us that such a deterministic picture of the world is but half of a two-sided coin. To imagine the natural and social worlds in these terms can inspire us in our efforts to bring them under our sway, to re-engineer them for the better. But this picture of things also works to defeat and discourage our confidence in these quintessential human capacities and possibilities, because we seem to be trapped within an "iron block" universe. It seems to encourage *both* a sense of potentially unlimited mastery *and* utter impotence – not the best recipe for sane or balanced living.

In the freewill debates, this tension between sharply contrasting images of our place and possibilities in the world, that nevertheless oddly go "hand in hand", shows up as a picture of ourselves *both* as able to rise above and freely manipulate the flow of efficient causes and their effects in the natural and social realms, *and* as brutely dominated by such a flow. We suggest that resolving this dilemma must include examining particular assumptions about freedom and autonomy that appear surreptitiously to shape the free will debates. These assumptions, it turns out, their differences notwithstanding, are typically shared by compatibilists and incompatibilists alike.

Recall Dworkin's definition of autonomy, namely that an agent is autonomous if she identifies with her goals, desires, and values, and if this process of identification is in no sense alien to her. Both sides of the free will debates articulate similar conceptions of autonomy, which appear to assume both self-determination and the availability of alternative possibilities. We believe this definition of autonomy is more blatant ideology than a careful description of a human phenomenon. It is heavily colored by the ideals of the modern moral outlook often termed philosophic liberalism or liberal individualism. Richardson et al. (1999) have suggested that this individualistic outlook, which suffuses the worlds of modern psychology and psychotherapy, usually takes one of three forms: The first is (1) *utilitarian* individualism, where agents are viewed as more or less efficient in procuring desired satisfactions and payoffs in living (Bellah et al. 1985, p. 32). The second is (2) *expressive* individualism, where unhindered expression or realization of an agent's "true self" or "real self" is the goal and social roles and commitments are valued largely because they enhance the well-being of this self (ibid., p. 47). The last is (3) *existential* individualism, where the self is viewed as exercising a radically free, unconstrained choice of its own meanings and values (Richardson et al. 1999, p. 106).

All three varieties of individualism have in common a highly instrumental conception of human agency and action. They assume that in acting freely agents manipulate the causal chain of events to suit their purposes. Expressive and existential individualism incorporate elements that go beyond an exclusively utilitarian account of human action – indeed, they are often thought to be opposed to and reactions against a coarse utilitarian outlook. The first advocates "getting in touch" with and expressing authentic inner impulses, while the second exhorts us to authentically choose one's own self-determined values and projects in living and carry through on them rather than shrink from that challenge. But after these inward moves take place, the individual still adopts a markedly instrumental stance toward the world, others, or the past in order to achieve ultimately inwardly determined rather than externally imposed or unexamined aims. These purposes ideally derive from the inbuilt inclinations or personal choices of the individual, not from some wider cultural, moral, or spiritual community to which the individual belongs or with which they identify. This conception of self-determination is premised on a sharp dichotomy between (1) autonomy or drawing our purposes out of our selves and (2) heteronomy or being unreflectively or oppressively subordinated to the purposes of others. So this notion of autonomy incorporates a profound aspiration to individuality and separateness distinctive of modern culture. It assumes what Taylor (1995, p. 7) calls the modern "punctual" view of the self, a self that is

> ideally disengaged, that is free and rational to the extent he has fully distinguished himself from the natural and social worlds ... ideally ready as free and rational to treat these worlds – and even some of the features of his own character – instrumentally, as subject to change and reorganizing in order to better secure the welfare of himself and others.

Much 20th century social science appears to have bought heavily into this modern view of a deep split between self and world, including the social world it inhabits, and a largely instrumental relationship between them. Social scientists have found a way, up to a point, to make their peace with determinism, or to maintain a more or less robustly humanistic sense of agency and individuality in the midst of deep commitments (of which they may not be fully aware) to determinism and efficient causation in the human realm merely (Richardson et al. 1999). For many, the flow of events as sequences of efficient causes and their effects seems to mesh well with the conception of human agency as mainly concerned with an individual's manipulation of those causes to produce desired results. The abstract problem of determinism and freedom seems resolved by a concrete and auspicious fit between the way the world appears to work and the conditions needed for successful instrumental action. In the end, however, the problem remains. Determinism seems bound to crowd out freedom and reduce it to just another passive link in the causal chain. And yet we require such determinism to be able to project a promising world for successful instrumental action. We can neither abandon freedom nor find a place for it in our picture of the world, as impasses in debate between compatibilists and incompatibilists suggest.

5   The Critique of Instrumental Reason

In our judgment, stalemated debates between compatibilists and incompatibilists stem, in part, from a tacit conception of autonomy that is closely linked to a questionable view of human action or agency as exclusively or primarily instrumental in nature. The critical theorists of the Frankfurt School (Held 1980) and Habermas (1973, 1991) – rarely if ever consulted by thinkers in the freewill debates – have propounded a famous "critique of instrumental reason" containing rich resources for helping to unravel familiar quandaries concerning freedom and determinism.

According to Habermas, modern society to a great extent is built upon a damaging confusion of *praxis* with *techne*, Greek words meaning roughly culturally meaningful activities and technical capacity, respectively. This kind of society tends to collapse the cultural and moral dimensions of life into merely technical and instrumental considerations. As a result, according to Habermas (1973, p. 254), we imagine applying theory to practice chiefly as a matter of applying principles uncovered by empirical science in a manipulative or instrumental manner to produce desired results. This heavy emphasis on technical or instrumental action reflects our acute focus in modern times on gaining control over natural and social processes. No doubt our stunning successes in this enterprise have often benefited us. But, in Habermas' view, one of the key shortcomings of this elevation of *techne* over *praxis* is that, even as we grow in instrumental prowess, we progressively lose our ability to evaluate the worth of ends on any basis other than the sheer fact that they are preferred or desired. As a result, too many spheres of life have become dominated by a calculating and instrumental viewpoint which discerns means-ends relationships, performs cost-benefit analyses, and seeks to maximize our control or mastery over events as a kind of end in itself. Thus we come to inhabit a largely "control or be controlled" social universe in which the exercise of human agency or influence tends to be a zero sum game.

The critical theorist Horkheimer (1974) explored the contradictions and deleterious consequences of this one-sided instrumental view of human action. He argued that the modern outlook glorifying instrumental reason actually turns into its opposite or an "eclipse of reason". Scientific "neutrality" dictates that we concentrate on discerning lawful means-ends connections among events, thought to be "objective", and regard cultural and moral values as merely "subjective" and irrelevant to scientific inquiry. But this seriously undermines our ability to reason together about the inherent quality of our way of life and about what ends we might best seek. As the means of control and influence grow, life gets more organized and complicated at the same time that we lose the ability to set priorities and impose needed limits.[5] In this way, critical theory tries to illumine the sources of our tendency to despoil the environment, our fascination with power and control to the neglect of other important values, and our stressful, overextended lifestyles.

Habermas attacks this problem at its ontological root by explicitly denying the view that human action or social life is fundamentally instrumental. Instead, he argues, what he calls "communicative action" or "interaction" is more basic (Habermas 1991, p. 294 ff.).[6] For Habermas there is "an ontological reality beyond the autonomous subject [which] is communicative action, with the community and life-world it creates" (Davis 1990, p. 170). Communicative action is not instrumental activity governed by technical rules but "symbolic interaction" that is "governed by consensual norms, which define reciprocal obligations about behavior" (Habermas 1970, p. 92). In other words, humans characteristically cooperate with, deliberate with, and argue or contend with one another concerning cultural and ethical matters. We pursue activities and meanings not so much for their instrumental value in gaining control over events as for what we take to be their inherent decency, worth, or goodness. Even when we subordinate praxis to techne in a damaging way, we do so in part because we believe it advances human welfare, procures for us the status of mature, liberated individuals, or enhances rather than effaces human dignity as we understand it. Thus in Habermas' view, some intrinsic values or cherished ends of this sort always direct our instrumental activity, whether we appreciate that fact or not. To conceive of human action as fundamentally instrumental tragically confuses quintessential and important human powers with narrow technical prowess.

_____

[5] Rather than finding the scope of our autonomy broadened as the range of choices opens up, we "may become volitionally debilitated by an increasing uncertainty both concerning how to make decisions and concerning what to choose" (Frankfurt 1993, p. 17).

[6] One does not have to agree with the exact details of Habermas' analysis to concur with the general direction of his thought on these matters.

6   Rethinking Cultural Ideals

The congruence between the instrumental view and our cultural ideals runs deeper than merely its affinity with our ingrained orientation toward mastery and control. The dominant epistemological outlook of modern times is a "representational" one according to which knowledge consists essentially in the correspondence of our beliefs to an external reality from which they must be sharply distinguished. Often this epistemological doctrine has seemed to support and be supported by the successes of natural science in modern times. That is no longer the case. Powerful critiques of positivism and new "postempiricist" views of this history and nature of scientific inquiry (such as Kuhn's or Polanyi's) now stress its hermeneutical dimensions. Observation is considered to be dependent to some degree on theory and the confirmation or rejection of theories is to some degree conventional and influenced by particular values (Bernstein 1983). Still, the representational view seems to have done little damage in the past to deter progress in the natural sciences. In other areas of cultural and moral life, however, its picture of the knowing subject as a rather bloodless observer of an independent and objective order of reality or fact is not so benign.

The main reason for the persistence of the instrumental conception of human activity may be because the profound aspiration to individuality and separateness entailed by this view of the knowing subject – the punctual self – is as much a moral as an epistemological or scientific ideal (Taylor 1995, p. 7). It reflects the intense liberationist or anti-authoritarian temper of the modern era. According to Taylor, the modern ideal of "freedom as self-autonomy" dictates that any overlap between self and world will compromise the individual's integrity and dignity. It has been suggested that this fact helps explain why mainstream social science typically advocates strictly value-neutral explanations or descriptions of human dynamics and has insisted on treating cultural and moral values as purely subjective (Richardson et al. 1998). In trying to adopt such a neutral stance, "we force ourselves to study human beings at a distance" (Slife and Williams 1995, p. 195). The motivation for this approach may be, in part, that important meanings and values "must be kept at a considerable distance or they will compromise our autonomy and integrity in a domineering manner" (Richardson et al. 1998, p. 499).

In other words, the instrumental conception of human action is deeply reinforced by and in turn reinforces, a powerful set of cultural and moral ideals tied directly to one or another of the forms of individualism mentioned above. One such ideal is that of a highly autonomous self that pursues a developmental trajectory psychologists term "separation and individuation", often without realizing that it is a culture-bound ideal and anything but a universally held conception of the good life. Another is a prizing of individual dignity and rights that makes people the responsible center of their own moral universe, but risks emotional isolation and debilitating alienation by significantly downplaying lasting social ties, a sense of tradition, or wider purposes beyond individual self-realization. In psychology, Fromm (1969, pp. 48–53) argued this point a half century ago. Fromm analyzed what he calls the "ambiguous" modern view of freedom as consisting in "freedom from" arbitrary authority or other irrational constraints but lacking a corresponding "freedom to" or "freedom for" that would provide needed purpose and direction in living. Fromm himself, deeply committed to modern ideals of political liberation and individual self-realization, nevertheless argued that this one-sided conception of freedom is a virtual recipe for individual and social fragmentation, "shaky self-esteem", a "constant need of confirmation by others", and feelings of "depersonalization, emptiness, and meaninglessness".

7   Beyond Compatibilism and Incompatibilism

Resolving the problem of determinism and freedom in both philosophy and psychology may have to go hand in glove with rethinking some cherished modern ideals. Conceiving human action as largely instrumental is crucial to the modern ideal of autonomy, which paradoxically requires the kind of determinism that ends up undermining that very ideal. Horkheimer (1974, p. 1997) graphically portrayed the disengaged, instrumental stance toward the world lying at the heart of this dilemma. We have

> on the one hand, the self, the abstract ego emptied of all substance except its attempt to transform everything in heaven and on earth into means for its preservation, and on the other hand an empty nature degraded to mere material, mere stuff to be dominated, without any other purpose than that of this very domination.

One consequence of this view is an ever-widening gulf between the self on the one hand and nature and society on the other. This gulf exists as a constant yet ignored feature of the freewill landscape. Perhaps few of these thinkers in the freewill debates hold to an exclusively instrumental view of human action (a notable exception is Dorato in this volume). But their concerns and approach seem at least to be significantly colored by individualism and instrumentalism.

Is there any credible alternative conception of how freedom and determinism might interweave in the human realm, so that freedom is neither quashed by its context nor deprived of one? In this paper, we can only hint at what such an alternative might look like. For example, Taylor (1975) advocates that we develop a notion of "situated freedom". He contends that the modern understanding of freedom as "negative liberty", as largely a matter of "freedom from" constraints, can lead to a destructive, "anything-goes" attitude of "doing whatever feels good". Instead, he recommends that we develop a conception of "positive liberty" or the freedom to do things deemed worthwhile by one's community and oneself. On this account of freedom, the agent is always situated in a cultural and historical context providing meaningful objectives and guidelines in terms of which people can deliberate meaningfully about possible courses of action. In his view, the modern individualism's precious values of respect for human rights and dignity can best and perhaps only be preserved if they are embedded in a more profound and affirmative conception of human freedom.

Contemporary hermeneutic philosophy (e.g. Gadamer 1981, 1989; Taylor 1989; Guignon 1991; Ricoeur 1992; see Gantt and Guignon in this volume) contains rich resources for elaborating such a notion of positive freedom. In the hermeneutic view, the enormous successes of the natural sciences in modern times depend heavily on the capacity to ignore or abstract away from "subject-related qualities" (Taylor 1980, p. 31; Bishop forthcoming). Such an objectifying stance seeks to "regard the world as it is independently of the meanings it might have for human subjects, or of how it figures in their experience" (Taylor 1980, p. 31).[7] But hermeneutic thinkers insist that it is

---

[7]The objectifying stance certainly reveals much and has its uses, in social as well as natural science. However, when applied to the subject matter of social life, experimental and correlational methods produce only limited information about the make-up and dynamics of human phenomena. Still, there is no reason to accept the claim of some humanists and phenomenologists that such methods should be confined to specialized areas of psychology such as physiological psychology or studies in perception, areas which are generally seen as under the purview of natural science. Surely these methods have a place in the kind of social inquiry that studies meaningful human action nonreductively in its various historical and cultural contexts. In these forms of inquiry, experimental and correlational methods can be employed to detect significant patterns and regularities that might otherwise be difficult or impossible to ascertain. But one might argue (Slife and Williams 1995, Taylor 1995) that such information only has meaning for us when it is integrated into a richer account of human dynamics, an account which brings to light the meanings and goals that shape and define people's actions in particular contexts as well as how they reinterpret and modify those contexts. Indeed, to cut the realm of meaning and freedom off from its embodiment in the natural world and profound embedding in history and culture sets one up for dilemmas that resemble, for the same reasons, the problems incurred by many

neither the only nor the most basic way of knowing (Heidegger 1962; Slife and Williams 1995, p. 83ff). In fact, this kind of detached, analytical thinking seems to presuppose a more fundamental and practical mode of engagement with a life-world that occupies most of our living. For such an "engaged agent" (Taylor 1993), understanding is more a matter of "knowing how" than "knowing that", for example, comforting a small child or distinguishing gestures of flattery from those of respect. Be it understanding history, the interpretation of works of art, ethical discernment, or full-blooded dialogue about these important matters, such understanding and dialogue takes place against an implicit, background sense of the way the world is, who we are in it, and what comprises the good life that can never be fully objectified. A denuded, objectified picture of the world is the *product* of disengagement and objectification. However, it deletes from this picture the kind of creative human agency that alone would be capable of such an intellectual achievement (in exactly the way as we see it, Primas, in his chapter in this volume, describes how the assumption of determinism in natural science, if taken as a basic truth about the world, obscures or excludes the free and creative activity of the natural scientist!).

Taylor (1999) argues that in both everyday life and much human science inquiry, understanding another person should be construed not on the model of the 'scientific' grasp of an object but in terms of "speech-partners who come to an understanding" (p. 1). This sort of coming-to-understanding relates only secondarily to mastery and control, and mainly concerns clarifying and advancing the kinds of meanings and goals that channel our living (p. 2). As a result, we always live in a considerable tension. On the one hand, we harbor self-defining beliefs and values concerning things we care about greatly, in which we have a "deep identity investment" (p. 3.) On the other hand, our ideals and images of others are always partial or distorted in some way, so that we not only need to compromise and get along with others, but also *learn from* others (as well as from the past and other cultures). However, in opening ourselves to the challenge of such learning we can incur a painful "identity cost" as we may have to give up or significantly modify some of our cherished beliefs and values (Taylor 1999, p. 12).

According to hermeneutics, human existence and understanding have a fundamentally dialogical character. The shape of our practices and quality of our experience result from the interplay and mutual influence between present and past, interpreters and events, readers and texts, oneself and

---

imcompatibilist views of freedom (Guignon, this volume).

others.[8] This process can be distorted by dishonesty, defensiveness, or force. But done poorly or well, it remains basic in an ontological sense.

This perspective, it seems to us fits very well with many ideas about free will as elaborated by Kane (1996). Kane argues that the best place to see human freedom at work is when and where we are torn between competing ideals or between ethically important visions of our selves or the course of our lives, as in his example of the woman who must decide between rushing on to a very important business meeting and stopping to help someone who has just been mugged. At these moments, we might say, the direction of the story of our lives is in important respects up for grabs. Kane defends the idea that the outcome of deliberation or the weighing of *reasons* for action, whatever form that takes, is underdetermined but still may produce a coherent and meaningful result. The stronger will wins, Kane says, but not because it was *antecedently* stronger.

Streams of efficient causes and their effects play a subordinate role in a holistic life-world. Law-governed processes in the natural world, including the human body and brain, clearly cannot be revoked or directly violated by an act of will. They impose unalterable constraints or limitations on human activity (Williams 2001). To some extent, we may, in a manner of speaking, cooperate with these processes and instrumentally manipulate states of affairs in some desired way. But the *purposes* that guide both that sort of *techne* as well as other culturally meaningful pursuits are hammered out through mutual influence and dialogue among the participants in an intersubjective life-world.

In this realm, "determinism" can be understood as referring to forms of influence and constraint that shape human personality and action in rather more profound and intimate ways than being the product of hard causal forces. One is "thrown" (Heidegger 1962) into a historical cultural that not only prescribes outward practices and institutions to which one must conform in order to survive and flourish, but shapes many of one's most inward beliefs and feelings, indeed one's very identity as a person. "Freedom" in this context can be understood in terms of an ongoing, creative reinterpretation of these practices and norms. The direction of this reinterpretation, including the changing shape or our norms and ethical convictions, is underdetermined by our past, partly because it occurs in response to unanticipated failures or challenges and partly because it must be carried out in close concert with

---

[8]Martin and Sugarman (1999, p. 3) describe this very helpfully as a "dynamic interactionism" between mostly "sociocultural origins and practices of human psychology, and individual psychological experience".

perspectives and values of others. One finds one needs these "others" to make adequate sense of one's predicament and options, even though their influence may transform one's self-defining aims in living, sometimes at their very core (e.g. Gantt, this volume). In this world, being "determined" or shaped by history and culture and being "free" or capable of individual creativity and responsibility do not exclude or deny one another.[9]

Historical and cultural embeddedness is a *condition* of this kind of creativity. And a high degree of creativity and responsibility are essential to maintaining a decent and vital cultural enterprise. Indeed, in the view toward which we are aiming, "autonomy" is de-emphasized while more demanding and perhaps also more fulfilling exercises of freedom and responsibility are brought to the fore.[10]

---

[9]Hence, like Kane, we affirm the importance of the everyday freedoms integral to the interests of compatibilist philosophers while simultaneously affirming incompatibilist intuitions that our human longings transcend these everyday freedoms. Both sets of insights are needed to make sense of the free will we live out in the face of uncertainty and social interactions.

[10]In our opinion, the thought of Bakhtin (1984), which has exerted a great deal of influence in many sectors of the academic world – although only sparsely in philosophy and psychology – has much to offer in terms of fleshing out a conception of situated freedom. It offers a "partly decentered" (Richardson et al. 1998) view of the self, as an alternative to *both* the disengaged, "punctual" modern self and the postmodern erasure of free and responsible human agency (or "freedom" and "determinism" as viewed from the disengaged, instrumental perspective). On this account, the self is most fundamentally *not* a center of monological consciousness but a locus of dialogue among diverse "voices" and values who clash and/or cooperate with one another in the search for genuine understanding and ethical insight, in an immensely practical way in everyday life first of all, but also in the kind of more theoretical conversation we are now pursuing. The rough, changing, unity of this "dialogical self" consists in an attitudinal or conversational stance toward diverse meanings and perspectives, not one single standpoint or another.

It is difficult to portray the relations between a centralized, monological self and others in a satisfactory manner. Most theories of personality or psychotherapy discuss how personality is formed through internalizing the perspective or evaluations of others as part of the self. Such theories then are faced with the problem of making sense of how a central "I" relates to these introjected elements. This central "I", however, seems to be modeled after the modern punctual self, which can only relate to the internalized representations or evaluations by either arbitrarily submitting to their influence or treating them merely instrumentally, at arms length. But the dialogical self never exists apart from the natural and cultural surroundings in the first place. One becomes a self at the outset or acquires an identity by gradually coming to occupy a place in the wider cultural conversation. The only "internalization" that takes place is not one of adopting this or that belief or value but of "internalizing the whole conversation" (Taylor1991) and becoming a part of it. This view opens up the possibility of an alternative to a rather stark dichotomy between dominating and being dominated in the affairs of the inner life. This radically culturally embedded self is profoundly "determined" by history and culture. But in Bakhtin's and Taylor's view,

So far as rethinking modern ideals is concerned, a hermeneutic ontology seems quite congruent with the efforts of current "communitarian" thinkers (e.g. Etzioni 1996, Sandel 1996, Selznick 1998) who seek to revive core ideals of the civic republican political theory, stemming from Aristotle, in a form consistent with modern pluralism and egalitarianism.[11] Etzioni (1996) argues that there can be "excessive liberty". Without limits on choice, provided first and foremost by some "shared moral convictions", neither a coherent sense of personal identity nor social peace are really possible, providing a further reason for holding in suspicion views emphasizing "autonomy". This approach seeks to nourish shared values that are "largely voluntary". For the most part, these shared values are enforced and sustained not by the imperatives of the state or market, but by conscience and a sense of obligations to others. And this approach envisions not one overall community but a "community of communities" in a modern democracy (p. 176). Thus, Etzioni recommends that in the "next historical phase" we find a way to "blend the virtues of tradition with the liberation of modernity" (p. xvii).

Communitarian thinkers present a distinctive view of freedom or liberty. Focusing on individual conduct, Etzioni (1996) suggests that the familiar "golden rule" which appears in different forms in many cultural traditions be broadened for contemporary purposes as: "Respect and uphold society's moral order as you would have society respect and uphold your autonomy" (p. xvii). Such a notion fully acknowledges our dependence on society and others at the same time that it encourages individuals to cultivate excellence and develop their unique powers to the fullest extent possible. The good life, in Beiner's (1992, p. 51) words, is not conceived of primarily in terms of the "maximization of autonomy" but as the "cultivation of ... a variety of excellences, intellectual and moral". If so, then felt moral ties and individual goals, a coherent sense of identity and openness to learning from others, or healthy limits and the expansion of human powers are not pitted against one another to the extent our modern individualist credo implies.

---

this fact does anything but dilute freedom and responsibility. Rather, one must exercise a more strenuous kind of freedom and responsibility for carrying on the conversation as it appears in the unique place one occupies in the natural world and a cultural universe. This is a more demanding exercise of creativity and duty than that of disengaging from the world to identify individual wants and preferences, and then returning to the world to instrumentally pursue these wants. In Bakhtin's words, there is no "alibi for being".

[11]We find this line of thought quite compelling, although we hasten to add that we feel, like most of these contemporary contemporary "communitarian" thinkers themselves, that finding a way to reconcile personal liberty with lasting social ties and commitments is an unfinished enterprise, and ought to be pursued with caution.

References

Bailie G. (1995): *Violence Unveiled*, Crossroad Publishing, New York.

Bakhtin M. (1984): *Problems of Dostoevsky's Poetics*, ed. and transl. by C. Emerson, University of Minnesota Press, Minneapolis.

Beiner R. (1992): *What's the Matter with Liberalism?*, University of California Press, Berkeley.

Bellah R., Madsen R., Sullivan W., Swindler A., and Tipton S. (1985): *Habits of the Heart*, University of California Press, Berkeley.

Berlin I. (1969): *Four Essays on Liberty*, Oxford University Press, Oxford.

Bernstein R. (1983): *Beyond Objectivism and Relativism*, University of Pennsylvania Press, Philadelphia.

Bishop R. (forthcoming): Crisis in the behavioral sciences.

Cushman P. (1990): Why the self is empty? *American Psychologist* **45**, 599–611.

Cushman P. (1995): *Constructing the Self, Constructing America*, Addison-Wesley, Menlo Park.

Cushman P. (1999): From emptiness to multiplicity: The self at the year 2000. *The Psychohistory Review*, **27**, 15–32.

Christman J., ed. (1989): *The Inner Citadel: Essays on Individual Autonomy*, Oxford University Press, Oxford.

Dennett D. (1984): *Elbow Room*, MIT Press, Cambridge MA.

Etzioni A. (1996): *The New Golden Rule: Community and Morality in a Democratic Society*, Basic Books, New York.

Fancher R. (1995): *Cultures of Healing: Correcting the Image of American Mental Health Care*, Freeman, New York.

Frank J.D. and Frank J.B. (1991): *Persuasion and Healing: A Comparative Study of Psychotherapy*, Johns Hopkins Press, Baltimore.

Fromm E. (1969): *Escape from Freedom*, Avon, New York (first published in 1941).

Gadamer H.-G. (1989): *Truth and Method*, second revised edition, transl. by J. Weinsheimer and D. Marshall, Crossroad, New York.

Habermas J. (1973): *Theory and Practice*, Beacon Press, Boston.

Habermas J. (1991): *The Philosophical Discourse of Modernity*, MIT Press, Cambridge MA.

Held D. (1980): *Introduction to Critical Theory: Horkheimer to Habermas*, University of California Press, Berkeley.

Horkheimer M. (1974): *Eclipse of Reason*, Continuum, New York (first published in 1947).

James W. (1956): The dilemma of determinism. In *The Will to Believe and Other Essays in Popular Philosophy*, Dover, New York.

Kane R. (1996): *The Significance of Free Will*, Oxford University Press, Oxford.

Martin J. and Sugarman J. (1999): *The Psychology of Human Possibility and Constraint*, State University of New York Press, Albany.

Murdoch I. (1985): *The Sovereignty of the Good*, Routledge Kegan and Paul, London.

Pereboom D. (1995): Determinism al dente. *Nous* **29**, 21–45.

Richardson F., Rogers A., and McCarroll J. (1998): Toward a dialogical self. *American Behavioral Scientist* **41**, 496–515.

Richardson F., Fowers B., and Guignon C. (1999): *Re-Envisioning Psychology: Moral Dimensions of Theory and Practice*, Jossey-Bass, San Francisco.

Rychlak J. (1988): *The Psychology of Rigorous Humanism*, New York University Press, New York (2nd edition).

Sandel M. (1996): *Democracy's Discontent: America in Search of a Public Philosophy*, Harvard University Press, Cambridge MA.

Selznick P. (1998): Foundations of communitarian liberalism. In *The Essential Communitarian Reader*, ed. by A. Etzioni, Rowman and Littlefield, Lanham, pp. 3–14.

Slife B. and Williams R. (1995): *What's behind the research? Discovering hidden assumptions in the behavioral sciences*, SAGE Publications, Thousand Oaks.

Taylor C. (1975): *Hegel*, Cambridge University Press, Cambridge.

Taylor C. (1989): *Sources of the Self: The Making of the Modern Identity*, Harvard University Press, Cambridge MA.

Taylor C. (1991): The dialogical self. In *The Interpretive Turn: Philosophy, Science, Culture*, ed. by D. Hiley, J. Bohman, and R. Schusterman, Cornell University Press, Cornell, pp. 304–314.

Taylor C. (1993): Engaged agency and background in Heidegger. In *The Cambridge Companion to Heidegger*, ed. by C. Guignon, Cambridge University Press, Cambridge, pp. 317–336.

Taylor C. (1995): *Philosophical Arguments*, Harvard University Press, Cambridge MA.

Taylor C. (1999): Gadamer and the human sciences. Unpublished manuscript.

Watson G. (1987): Free action and free will. *Mind* **96**, 145–172.

Williams R. (2001): The biologization of psychotherapy: Understanding the nature of influence. In *Critical Issues in Psychotherapy: Translating New Ideas into Practice*, ed. by B. Slife, R. Williams, and S. Barrows, SAGE Publications, Thousand Oaks, pp. 51–67.

Agency, Embodiment, and the Ethical: On Saving Psychology from Biology

Edwin E. Gantt

Abstract

Recent decades have witnessed an astounding increase in the amount of research and theorizing in the discipline of psychology that is conducted from within a primarily biological framework of explanation (e.g. Adams et al. 1996, Beatty 2001, Gazzaniga 1995, Silk 1998). Because the majority of biological explanations of human experience that one finds in contemporary psychology are fundamentally reductive in nature, they are also usually committed to some form of efficient causality or necessary determinism. Indeed, it is typically taken for granted that the only truly viable forms of scientific explanation in psychology are those firmly grounded in the language of biological function and necessary causality. However, one immediate consequence of this position is that human behavior comes to be seen as essentially devoid of genuine meaning, as simply the necessitated product of impersonal and mechanical processes operating in accordance with natural law. Likewise, insofar as human acts are taken to be the necessary products of fundamentally impersonal and mechanical biological causes, human behavior is also thought to lack any truly moral content. In response, this paper seeks to articulate a philosophically defensible alternative to biologically reductive explanations of human action that is nonetheless sensitive to both the fundamentally embodied nature of human experience and the inescapably social and moral nature of that experience. To these ends, this paper will examine the thinking of the French phenomenologists, Merleau-Ponty and Levinas.

1   Introduction

Recent decades have witnessed an astounding increase in the amount of research and theorizing in the discipline of psychology that is conducted from within a primarily biological framework of explanation (e.g. Adams et al. 1996, Beatty 2001, Gazzaniga 1995, Silk, 1998). Although biologically based forms of explanation have been present in the discipline from its very inception (see Leahey 2000), recent advances in biotechnology (e.g., magnetic resonance imaging, computerized tomography, positron-emission tomography, etc.) and psychopharmacology have lent increased weight to biological explanations of human psychological phenomena (Shorter 1997, Zachar 2000). Likewise, recent conceptual developments in evolutionary psychology have resulted in increased acceptance of genetic explanations for psychological and social phenomena (e.g. Buss 1999, Cartwright 2000, Fisher 1992, Janov 2000, Simpson and Kenrick 1997, Thornhill and Palmer 2000). Indeed, it has become an almost exceptionless practice among introductory psychology textbook authors to begin their examination of the discipline with a discussion of the evolutionary or biological bases of behavior (see, for example, Baron 2001, Bernstein and Nash 2002, Feldman 2000, Gleitman et al. 1999, Huffman et al. 2000).

In light of intellectual developments such as these, it has become increasingly acceptable in psychology and related disciplines to advance the notion that "social science *is* a branch of biology, even if [only] a special branch" (Plotkin 1998, p. 1). As Rosenzweig and Leiman (1989, p. 3) state in the opening paragraphs of one widely used textbook, "We [now] recognize that individual identity, personality, and talents are mainly functions of the brain; nevertheless, we also acknowledge the influences on the brain of other bodily systems, such as endocrine glands". Likewise, Guze (1992, p. 130) writes, "one's feelings and thoughts are as biological as one's blood pressure or gastric secretion: feelings and thoughts are manifestations of the brain's operations just as blood pressure reflects the operations of the cardiovascular system and gastric secretion the stomach's function". Given such assumptions, it should come as no surprise that students of psychology are frequently taught that (Edwards 1999, p. 58):

> We must always build on the fact that we are biological organisms of wonderful complexity. We construct, sense, and defend in multiple ways, all having roots in existing body mechanisms. We often focus on our unusually developed cerebral cortex, tending to underrate the reality that it administers and is served by complex mechanisms lower down in the brain and the body. It all works together, and we must constantly look to what physiological information is there as we try to understand [psychological] topics.

Perhaps most disturbingly, however, is the fact that it is increasingly the case that those who raise objections to the biologically reductive direction psychology is taking are characterized as hopelessly anachronistic, clinging to outdated and dangerously anti-scientific attitudes – if not patently magical and irrational beliefs. Indeed, as one ardent defender of the biogenetic paradigm in psychotherapy has said (Winokur 1981, p. 115): "Only a troglodyte would not recognize that pharmacotherapy is the preferred treatment of depression".

Clearly, this "trend toward biologization" (Williams 2001) has not been limited to the often abstract and technical discussions of highly specialized academic researchers and neuroscientists, but has become a pervasive feature of our everyday discourse and cultural self-understanding. This is particularly the case in the United States where we are just now coming out of what was officially designated by the Bush administration the "Decade of the Brain" (see Breggin 1991, p. 11). It has become ever more difficult to make it through the day without encountering a television report or reading a newspaper or magazine article discussing the most recent scientific research to finally identify the gene(s) responsible for some bit of our behavior, a given personality trait, emotional experience, or some particular sexual inclination. Recent cover stories in Newsweek magazine, for example, were devoted to examining the burgeoning new discipline of neurotheology, which seeks to uncover the biological origins of spirituality, and the evolutionary basis of evil and cruelty. It has become commonplace – at least in America – to hear idle speculation around the office water cooler or in the company lunchroom centered on the genes or brain chemicals that must surely be the source of our various individual anxieties, desires, foibles and griefs. The self-help and popular psychology sections at the local bookstore, once dominated by workbooks on self-affirmation and "soul-talk", now display an ever-expanding array of titles such as:

What Makes You Tick? The Brain in Plain English (Czerner 2001),
The Craving Brain (Ruden 2000),
Change Your Brain, Change Your Life: The Breakthrough Program for Conquering Anxiety, Depression, Obsessiveness, Anger, and Impulsiveness (Amen 2000),
How Brains Make Up Their Minds (Freeman 2000),
Brain Lock: Free Yourself from Obsessive-Compulsive Disorder: A Four-Step Self-Treatment Method to Change Your Brain Chemistry (Schwartz 1996),
A User's Guide to the Brain: Perception, Attention, and the Four Theaters of the Brain (Ratey 2001),
Super Brain Power: 28 Minutes to a Supercharged Brain (Spotts 1999).

Of course, whether we are really convinced that our lives, our thoughts and feelings, our fears and desires are really just the result of impersonal biological states and genetic conditions is an open question. Still, it is worth noting that whether or not we truly believe the biological accounts we so commonly give of ourselves, we are nonetheless giving such accounts, and assuming that doing so is acceptable and warranted.

2 Biological Reductionism and Necessary Determinism

Because the majority of biological explanations of human experience in contemporary psychology are fundamentally reductive in nature, they are also usually committed to one or another form of efficient causality or necessary determinism.[1] Indeed, as one textbook author states, in discussing the importance of reductionism to scientific psychology, "no attempt to understand the biological basis of behavior is satisfactory unless the neural determinants of that behavior can be specified" (Beatty 2001, p. 3). That is, accounts of complex and meaningful human behaviors are thought to be incomplete and inadequate (i.e., unscientific) until they have rendered the behaviors in question as the necessitated products of more primitive and impersonal biochemical antecedent conditions. Feelings of romantic attraction, for example, are frequently said to be the direct result of mechanical reactions by various peptide neurotransmitters, such as oxytocin and vasopressin, in the limbic system of the brain (cf. Fisher 1994). In fact, the commitment to this type of materialist reduction, and its attendant necessary determinism, is so strong in contemporary psychology that its status as a philosophical assumption about the nature of human beings is rarely, if ever, noted or questioned. It

---

[1]In this paper, I will address what I take to be some of the problematic implications of what has been called "necessary determinism" (see, for example, Slife and Williams 1995). This (somewhat cumbersome) term is meant to designate the notion that events (whether physical, psychological, social, etc.) are, in the final analysis, nothing more nor less than the necessitated outcomes of prior events. As such, it is impossible that these subsequent events could have occurred in any other way than they in fact did. It should not be assumed, however, that because I am rejecting the notion of necessary determinism, that I am rejecting all conceptions of determinism, or that I am arguing for a fundamental indeterminism. In fact, I am firmly convinced that some manner of determinism must be assumed operative in human events for any fruitful understanding of those events to be possible. After all, a fundamentally indeterministic theory, or what Taylor (1985) calls a "radical choice" theory, destroys meaning just as thoroughly as one advocating necessary determinism – absolute randomness is no more meaningful than absolute necessity (see also Williams 1992, 1994 for an excellent discussion of these issues). Unfortunately, space constraints prevent me from addressing in more detail an alternative conception of determinism that would not compromise possibility and agency. In this regard, see Guignon, and Richardson and Bishop, in this volume.

is, rather, typically taken as a matter of fact that the only truly viable forms of (scientific) explanation in psychology are those that are firmly grounded in biological function and which invoke some manner of necessary causality at the root of behavior. Indeed, as one noted author has observed, "determinism is a basic assumption of all science, so questioning it makes many psychologists uneasy" (Baron 2001, p. 468).[2]

This is not to say that reductive accounts are by their nature inescapably wedded to necessary determinism. There are many different types of reductionism, not all of which require efficient causal forms of explanation. Indeed, it may well be the case that some form of reductionism will always be necessary in psychology insofar as no single account we might offer will be able to include everything in it (for a more detailed treatment of this issue, see Slife and Williams 1995). Our accounts of human actions, no matter how specific in their details or how global in their intent, will of practical necessity be selective and, therefore, reductive. The problem here is not with reductionism, per se, but with the type of reductionism most typically employed in contemporary psychobiological explanations of human actions – a type of reductionism that clearly requires the assumption of efficient causality and necessary determinism.

3   Meaning, Morality, and Necessary Determinism

One of the immediate consequences of psychology's adoption of biological reductionism, and the necessary determinism that it entails, is that human behavior comes to be seen as essentially devoid of genuine meaning, as simply the necessitated product of certain impersonal and mechanical processes operating in accordance with natural law. As Slife and Williams (1995) have argued, however, meaning requires possibility – where there is no possibility, there can be no genuine meaning (see also Heidegger 1927/1962, James 1897/1956, Merleau-Ponty 1989, Rychlak 1994, Sartre 1956). If a given behavior is determined to be what it is by the activity of some biological process operating in accordance with natural law, then that behavior becomes "no more meaningful than a plant growing or a stone rolling down a hill.

---

[2]Of course, whether determinism is, indeed, a "basic assumption of science" is an issue that is still very much open to debate. Further, one wonders how it is that the questioning of assumptions – the sort of thing that would seem to be at the very heart of any genuinely scientific enterprise – has become for many so social scientists the sort of thing that makes them uneasy.

These things don't *mean* anything, they just happen" (Slife and Williams 1995, p. 145). Granted, we might attach some subjective significance to such things, but the "meaning would be subjectively created and very difficult to sustain when the true story of the behavioral laws and principles is known" (Slife and Williams 1995, pp. 145–146). If, for example, I find myself empathizing with the suffering of another person, but this empathy is in actuality nothing more than the necessitated result of a specifiable set of biogenetic conditions outside my awareness and beyond my active participation (see Buck and Ginsberg 1997 for an excellent example of just such an account of empathy), then my empathy is in itself a meaningless phenomenon. In so far as I could not have done *otherwise than* empathize with the suffering of this other person, it makes no difference that I did empathize with them. Indeed, from within a necessarily deterministic conceptual framework, the only way in which I could have felt otherwise than I did would be if the particular causal forces (i.e., the biogenetic conditions) underlying and producing my behavior had been altered in some way. But, even then, there would still be nothing in my behavior that was not in the first instance necessitated by some presumably more fundamental impersonal or mechanical process operating outside my active participation and awareness. Without genuine possibility, both my empathy and my indifference are without genuine meaning.[3] They just are as they are, and as they must be. Meaning simply cannot be manufactured *ex nihilo* within a causal system of biology and environmental influence.

It is not unusual at this point, of course, for defenders of biological reductionism to object to my claim that their project for psychology necessarily implies a commitment to determinism in explaining human behavior. Many advocates of a biological psychology argue that ascribing human behavior solely to biogenetic forces or conditions is far too simplistic and ignores the complex and crucial role that both culture and individuality play in guiding behavior (e.g. Fisher 1994). For example, in rebutting charges of genetic determinism in evolutionary explanations of psychological events, Buss (1999, p. 18) argues that, "evolutionary theory represents a truly interac-

---

[3] Again, this is not to say that such things are not or will not be *experienced* as meaningful or significant. The advocate of necessary determinism is correct to say that even if our actions are necessitated, we still experience them as having meaning. What is being argued here, however, is that if the deterministic thesis is true, then our very real experience of meaning and moral significance must be seen to be in a very real sense epiphenomenal, an illusory and purely subjective byproduct of fundamentally impersonal and non-meaningful processes or events. Thus, the question here is not whether we experience our lives as having meaning, but whether the explanatory accounts of a biological psychology committed to necessary determinism allow for those experienced meanings to be genuinely meaningful.

tionist framework. Human behavior cannot occur without two ingredients: (1) evolved adaptations and (2) environmental input that triggers the development and activation of these adaptations." Likewise, Fisher (1994, p. 61), following a detailed discussion of the "chemistry of attraction and attachment", assures us that "none of the above is meant to suggest that men and women are biologically *compelled* to fall in love, to attach or detach from one another. Cultural forces play a powerful role in directing behavior, as does one's idiosyncratic perspective – what philosophers have long called 'free will'."

From such declarations it would seem, then, that advocates of biological explanations of human behavior are not as guilty of the charges of necessary determinism as I and others make them out to be. However, when examined more closely it becomes apparent that while eschewing simple genetic determinism in their explanations of psychological phenomena, these theorists are nonetheless still committed to necessarily deterministic forms of explanation. Notice the language of "environmental input that triggers the development and activation" of naturally selected adaptations and cultural forces that "play a powerful role in directing behavior". Despite claiming to offer a "truly interactionist framework" that escapes determinism, Buss, Fisher, and their like-minded colleagues remain committed to understanding human behavior as the passive product of external natural forces rather than the active result of individual choice. The interaction that takes place within such a framework is not one that takes place between will and world, but one that occurs between genes and environment. As Thornhill and Palmer (2000, p. 25) assert in their controversial new book on the biological bases of sexual coercion, "an individual's cultural behavior is still a product of gene-environment interactions". Thus, even though such an "interactionist framework" seems at first glance to make room for the role that culture and individuality might play in the unfolding of human experience, it is clear that both culture and personal idiosyncracy are the products of genetic conditions and mechanical evolutionary processes. One wonders, then, how exactly culture and individual perspective can genuinely free human behavior from the grip of biogenetic determinism when those things are themselves the necessitated outcomes of natural genetic selection and complex neural functions.

Clearly, as many others have already argued (e.g. James 1897/1956, Kockelmans 1990, Kruks 1990, Taylor 1985, Williams 1992, 1994), the possibility of genuine meaning in human action is intimately bound up with the question of human agency and freedom (see also essays by Guignon, Kane, and Richardson and Bishop in this volume). So, too, is the possibility of morality in human action. For, where there is no meaningfulness at the foundation of human activity such activity can have no genuine moral content. If the world of human psychological and social activity is simply a causally necessitated one, as much of contemporary biological psychology would suggest, then it becomes conceptually indefensible to ascribe any differential moral worth to any human actions that happen to take place in that world. For example, as Slife and Williams (1995, p. 165) point out, "We might meaningfully say that it is bad *that* the act happened. However, to say it is bad *that* an act occurred is not the same thing as saying that *the act itself* is bad". Indeed, even to claim that it is bad that an event occurred requires some criterion for making such a judgment.

In short, then, if we assume, along with the majority of mainstream biological psychology, that human action is causally necessitated, it is difficult to imagine any legitimate criterion by which to make moral judgments about given human acts. If the course and outcome of a particular event is fundamentally determined in a biogenetic field of efficient causal variables, there would seem to be no viable grounds upon which to assert that it should have been otherwise than it was – and, thus, no viable grounds for asserting the moral worth of one behavioral occurrence over another. Granted, we might try to attach some moral significance to particular human acts, but the moral worth of such acts would (again) be "subjectively created and very difficult to sustain when the true story of the behavioral laws and principles is known" (Slife and Williams 1995, p. 145–146). As with meaning, morality, too, simply cannot be manufactured *ex nihilo* within a causal system of biology and environmental influence.

4   Exploring Alternatives

Ultimately, contemporary psychology's increasing preference for biologically reductive and necessarily deterministic explanations of human behavior would seem to require that we either (a) accept the epistemological and ontological claims of such a psychology and, thereby, reject as epiphenomenal the experiential reality of a deeply meaningful and moral rich world, or (b) begin to seriously explore alternative conceptions of the nature of human existence – conceptions that would rigorously avoid conceiving of human events in biologically reductive and necessarily deterministic ways. Fortunately, for those not yet ready to dismiss the meaning and morality of human existence as merely the byproducts of mechanical and impersonal biological forces, there are a number of intellectually defensible theoretical and philosophical alternatives available for re-conceptualizing and re-understanding human behavior.

For example, work in such philosophically diverse yet congenial traditions as social constructionism (Burr 1995, Gergen 1994), deconstructionism and poststructuralism (Kvale 1992, Rosenau 1992), existentialism (van Deurzen-Smith 1997, Schneider and May 1995, Yalom 1980), hermeneutics (Cushman 1995, Messer et al. 1988, Richardson et al. 1999), and phenomenology (Fuller 1990, Kunz 1998, Varela et al. 1991) suggest a wide variety of non-reductive, non-deterministic formulations of the psychological enterprise.

The remainder of this paper, however, will be limited to a brief exploration of two possible alternative approaches to psychology. In particular, I will examine a few of the ways in which the philosophical thought of the French phenomenologists Merleau-Ponty and Levinas might contribute to the development of a more fully human science of psychology. These two approaches have been chosen because they are not only sensitive to the fundamentally embodied and physical dimension of human existence, but also recognize the inescapably social, meaningful, and moral nature of that existence.

5 Merleau-Ponty

In sharp contrast to the reductive and deterministic accounts of human embodiment typically offered in natural science psychology, Parts I and II of Merleau-Ponty's *Phenomenology of Perception* (1989) are devoted to a careful phenomenological description of the constitutive relationships between: (1) consciousness and the body, (2) the embodied subject and the world, and (3) the self and others. Merleau-Ponty argues that each of these "dialectical relations" is fundamentally circular in nature, the terms interdependently constituted and mutually enformed and enforming. Additionally, each of these circular structures is taken up in the following one so as to create an even more elaborate and encompassing structure and, thus, more fully account for the inherent multidimensionality of human existence. As one of Merleau-Ponty's foremost commentators, Madison (1990, p. 22) points out:

> I am a subject only by means of the many unbreakable bonds which tie my consciousness and my body together; I am an embodied subject only by being in a direct mutual relation with the world; and I am in the world only through my co-existence with others who, themselves, are also so many beings in the world. Inversely, the other exists for me only because I am directly linked to the world by a body which is inseparable from my existence.

In other words, I am always already a *situated* being, situated simultaneously in a social, physical, temporal, and spatial field of various relationships and meanings (see also Guignon, this volume). I am immersed in what I perceive, and, as such, I am not wholly in control of the "field which *my* perception organizes around me" (Kruks 1990, p. 119). Rather, the field of my perception is as much a creation of those who share it with me as it is of my own embodied intentionality. The interrelation of human existence is not "created from a position of initial separation: it is part of what it is to be human" (Kruks 1990, p. 124). And although, for purposes of exposition, Merleau-Ponty often makes a distinction between the "natural" world (i.e., the physical world of perceptible things) and the social or "human" world, he continually insists that in actuality we never experience these worlds as separate or distinct. In fact, he maintains that there is always already a meaningful social and historical context that we bring to any perception. We are, at all times, situated both in the natural and the human worlds, not only perceiving but acting in various ways in and on these inseparable worlds.

As Kruks (1990, p. 124) points out, for Merleau-Ponty, "intersubjectivity exists insofar as I and the Other are both situated in, perceive and communicate about the same natural and social world". Granted, we do not (and cannot) share an identical perceptual experience, in that we are not the same beings, each of us occupying our own unique situation and perceptual position. There is, however, sufficient overlap or interplay between our perceptions that such an "interworld" of primordial communication and understanding is created between us. As Merleau-Ponty argues in a latter section of the *Phenomenology of Perception* (1989, p. 354):

> In the experience of dialogue, there is constituted between the other person and myself a common ground; my thought and his are interwoven into a single fabric, my words and those of my interlocutor are called forth by the state of the discussion, and they are inserted into a shared operation of which neither of us is the creator. We have here a dual being, where the other is for me no longer a mere bit of behavior in my transcendental field, nor I in his; we are collaborators for each other. ... Our perspectives merge into each other, and we co-exist through a common world.

Note also that the term "dialogue" here does not mean just verbal or written communications. For Merleau-Ponty, dialogue is any form of engagement or involvement we may have with others and the world. Thus, the thoughtful caress, the irritated frown, the distracted yawn, the tightly folded arms, and the face reddened with embarrassment are all forms of dialogue. Indeed, it is clear that for Merleau-Ponty much of the most significant dialogue in which we engage is that carried out in terms of our "body language". Thus, facial expressions and gestural movements are not simple manifestations or symptomatic presentations of deeper or hidden internal emotional states as often suggested in naturalistic accounts. Neither are they simply the means by which genes or limbic systems communicate with one another (Buck and Ginsberg 1997, Dawkins and Krebs 1978). Rather, they are the very way in which we most directly enter into and sustain dialogue with one another in the interworld of our emotional and social co-existence.

Merleau-Ponty further argues that biologically reductive explanations of the body fail to recognize that before it can be conceptualized and treated as merely one physiological thing among other such things, the body as "lived-body" (*Le corps propre*) is a fundamental expression of the temporal, spatial, and social dimensionality of our existence. Accordingly, our primary access to the body is not via objectifying or reflective knowledge. Rather, the body is in the first instance neither an object to be known nor a matter of intellectual reflection, but rather that with which we possess an intimate familiarity long before engaging in abstracting activities of scholarly reflection or empirical objectification. "Our own body", Merleau-Ponty (1989, p. 203) says, "is in the world as the heart is in the organism, it keeps the visible spectacle constantly alive, it breathes life into it and sustains it inwardly, and with it forms a system".

Prior to reflecting on one's embodiment, and thus prior to knowing about the body as an object, one *lives* the body and *lives-through* the body, developing its capacities for action by relating *pre-reflectively* to a world of meaningful objects, people, and events. Before being an object that we can "conceptualize or treat conceptually as a physiological thing, a mere material mass" (Madison 1981, p. 22), the body is a dimension of our existence. It is in the first instance a *lived body*, and we are always already a *body-subject*. Thus, the body is only secondarily, and at an abstracted remove from actual lived-experience, a passive object responding in mechanical and deterministic fashion to the autonomous stimulus configurations of an external world. Considered solely in physiological terms, the body is "a body in itself; it is a body which belongs to no one" (Madison 1981 p. 24). The lived body, however, is "for everyone his particular way of inhabiting the world ... a strange *mixture of being-in-itself and being-for-itself*" (Madison 1981, p. 24). The lived body is fundamentally the intentional site and source of our being-in-the-world as we engage and are engaged by the world in all of our projects. In other words, before the body can be reflectively conceptualized as a mechanical, anatomical object – and thus before one can begin to speculate on the possible role which a given component piece of that object (genes, neurons, hormones, etc.) might play in that object's functioning – the body is revealed as the necessary condition or grounds for the undertaking of any actions whatsoever (reflective or otherwise).

For Merleau-Ponty (1989, p. 137), then, consciousness, or the embodied subject, is "in the first place not a matter of 'I think that' but of 'I can'." For example, one builds up a "lived familiarity with the _hands as instruments of grasping and pointing_, before acquiring the knowledge that this is a hand or that the hand has a muscle called the 'palmar brevis' and a bone called the 'trapezium'" (Moss 1989, p. 66). Thus, our primordial engagement with the world and others takes place, not as one object "brushing up" against another object in some necessitated chain of causal events, but as an embodied intentionality which is fundamentally situated in spatially, temporally, and socially meaningful ways. The body is, as Merleau-Ponty (1964, p. 163) says, a self "that is caught up in things, that has a front and a back, a past and a future. ... Things are an annex or prolongation of itself; they are encrusted into its flesh, they are part of its full definition; the world is made of the same stuff as the body".

In other words, the embodied self, the world, and others are not a reflectively formed system abstractly posited at some secondary theoretical level, the final product of some underlying genetic design or impersonal neuronal activity. Rather they are an original unity in the dimensionality of lived-experience, an ontological unity out of which all other formulations and reflections take place and to which all such formulations must finally refer if they are to be held in any sense valid. Indeed, for Merleau-Ponty, it is only because we are both intensely situated in the world (socially, historically and physically) and also able to transcend the world that talk of freedom can make any sense at all. Freedom is, for Merleau-Ponty, always one aspect of a fundamental existential dialectic in which possibility and necessity both _deny_ and _sustain_ one another.

Ultimately, then, as we have seen above, because psychobiological explanations of human actions begin at the abstracted and objectified level of explanation (i.e. an inferred relationship between mental and neurological states), rather than at the more readily accessible and phenomenologically valid level of embodied experience, they are unable to provide a account of those actions that can preserve the their inherent meaningfulness. By choosing to concentrate almost exclusively on the mechanical operations of neurons and genes, psychobiological explanations of human actions render those actions meaningless and without genuine content. In contrast, Merleau-Ponty's analysis strongly suggests that only by returning to the readily accessible level of our embodied experience is it possible to articulate an understanding of human action in which meaning is preserved.

6   Levinas

Levinas, too, insists that lived-experience must be the principle starting point in any serious investigation of the meaning of human action. Both complementing and contrasting Merleau-Ponty, however, Levinas encourages us to concentrate on the nature and significance of language as the source and site of human sociality. Levinas seeks to avoid the sort of naive communalism and relativism which so often besets many other theories that likewise seek to ground our humanity solely in context, interpretation, and discourse (cf. Gantt 2001). His account of human existence is not, however, just an exercise in speculative metaphysics. Rather, its foundation is a careful phenomenology of our concrete lived experience as social and moral beings.

A hallmark of many modern psychological accounts of human nature has been the granting of ontological priority to the private, individual self, conceived of as mind, consciousness, or intellect. In such a scheme, each of us – an essentially private rationality – encounters others in a realm outside our own existence, as a peculiar sort of object of perception. Because of this, the being of other persons must be reconciled somehow with the immediacy of our own experience. The classical problem of "other minds" is the all but inescapable result of granting ontological priority to the private self (cf. Nagel 1995). This problem is usually solved by inferring that the other is essentially like me, in some sense, another instance of the self – literally, an alter ego. My esteem for the other, and my concern is an inference ultimately grounded in self-esteem and self-concern (cf. Oliner et al. 1992).

Levinas, however, reverses the ontological priority, grounding the existence of the self, and thus, in important ways, the very ontological status of the self, in the prior existence of the other. Simply put, without the otherness of the other – the other than self – preexisting the self, there are no reasons for the self to "be", and no grounds or context within which the self can appear at all (Levinas 1978). Indeed, as I have argued elsewhere, "one cannot even begin to recognize one's own consciousness sufficient to comprehend and name it for oneself except in contradistinction to the absolute priority of that which is other than one's self; the infinite surplus of the existence of an-other, in the face of whom I discover my own humanity" (Gantt 1996, p. 34).

For Levinas, the essence of the humanity discovered in the face of the other is an infinite ethical responsibility to not only have our own projects and wants be called into question by the Other, but to care for the Other. Our immediate relationship to the other is one of ethical obligation. The origin of this ethical obligation is, for Levinas, preeminently revealed in the existence and exercise of language, which, he argues, is "primordially composed in a plurality of interlocutors" (Levinas 1969, p. 73).

According to Levinas, when the other (of necessity, a person) who has a face appears, she resists our efforts to "totalize" – to make the other a part of the self – and does so in a way that other aspects of the world do not. The primordial experience of the other is not as an instrument of our own purposes. In this way, Levinas offers an alternative to hedonism as a primordial motivation – a concept frequently found in psychobiological explanations of human action. We do not derive our sociality from hedonistic concern. Rather, hedonistic concern is a response made possible by our innate sociality, by the perception, occasioned by the presence of the other, that one is in competition with others for scarce resources. Thus, in the other we do not see ourselves, but we receive the possibility for acting *as* selves, as *oneself-for-an-other* (cf. Levinas 1969). Ironically, it is in this process of being thus "called out" of ourselves that the self as agent emerges. The self – that part of us we experience as ourselves – is the product of an innately and profoundly social experience. Sociality predates individual identity and self-awareness both logically and chronologically. Sociality is, thus, not the product of fundamentally impersonal and mechanical chemical processes taking place in the nervous system.

Even as Levinas is describing the self as radically social in this way, however, he does not entirely dissolve the personal self. To do so would involve a radical diffusion of individual identity that would ultimately obviate the very possibility of identity he seeks to defend. Therefore, Levinas begins with and preserves interiority even in the midst of grounding our being in obligation to the other. This interiority does not, of course, reduce to the subjectivity of the isolated modern ego, thought to be the product of the isolated modern brain. Rather, it is metaphysically innocent. Interiority is that sense, incumbent in each person, that he or she is not simply the product of larger social or moral processes, but distinctly individual, and thus ethically – *because* socially – responsible. In fact, it is because our ethical obligations are so exquisitely particular that they are intensely ours and cannot be diminished by appeal to abstract principles of fairness and reciprocity, nor by shunting them off to others. It is, Levinas (1985, p. 101) says, knowing that "I am I in the sole measure that I am responsible, a non-interchangeable I". Such interiority and distinctiveness – our very individuality – requires other people. It requires sociality. One can only be an individual by virtue of occupying a unique situation – being called into relationships uniquely by others to whom one is uniquely confronted: I am who I am by virtue of my relatedness with others; I am the father of this child, the husband of this wife, the teacher of this student, the neighbor of this stranger, and so on. Each of these relationships calls me, and only me, to ethical response. My identity is my responsibility, and my responsibility is the fundamental feature of a shared, primordial sociality.

This radical alternative suggested by Levinas begins its analysis of human being not in the self-same – individual genetic make-up or neural functioning – but with the alterity of the other that grounds both identity and experience. Levinas suggests that our being, our identities as individuals, are emergent in the embodied, face-to-face relation with the Other. In other words, our life comes to have meaning and take on character only insofar as we first respond to the Other and our fundamental relatedness to him or her. Furthermore, this relationship is immediately, and primordially one of obligation. Life is a being-for-the-Other. It is the other to whom I must answer for my being, to whom I must render an accounting of my existence, as it is only because of the other that I have achieved an existence at all. And in that moment, the moment of awakening, of being brought forth in the call of the other in the face-to-face relation, I must respond to the ethical demands placed upon me by that call. Human subjectivity, then, is a continuous questioning and answering, and must to be understood as both congenitally moral and inherently meaningful, in that it can never take place outside of a sociality with others. It is "discourse and, more exactly, response or responsibility which is this authentic relationship" (Levinas 1985, p. 88).

What is more important, perhaps, is that Levinas does not ground this sense of obligation in some structure of neurochemical functioning or genetically selected socialization that would allow the person to "see" and "understand" or "internalize" such obligation. To do so would be to make the moral content of our lives secondary to the biological structures and functions responsible for producing such abilities, thereby destroying – or at least ameliorating – the moral intensity and reality of the obligation. Instead, Levinas places the obligation prior to such processes, locating it at the very beginning point of our being human. To be a human being at all is to be in obligation to the other. No sophisticated neurocognitive capacity nor developed interpersonal sensitivity are necessary to experience or recognize this obligation. Indeed, this is what makes Levinas most clearly a phenomenologist. He undertakes a phenomenological investigation into the experience of being human and finds, at the origin of that experience, the ethical obligation to the other.

In summary, then, for Levinas, isolated subjectivity – the inescapable product of subjectivity as the necessitated result of isolated neurological functions – is not the beginning point of human experience. Rather it is response to the presence of the other. In fact, as Levinas shows, both subjectivity and objectivity derive from the Other (cf. Levinas 1969, pp. 194–240). One important benefit of beginning in and preserving interiority is that it makes it clear whose obligation it is when one is confronted with and called into relationships of obligation. The obligation, for Levinas, cannot diffuse because the interiority, wherein we are distinct, is never compromised. We do not diffuse into the other and thus lose our sense of obligation. The other makes clear both the obligation, and the fact that it is mine.

Since the other occasions our speaking of the world at all, and thus occasions our being who we are, we are not, in that important sense – at all – without those others to whom we stand in obligation. For Levinas, the obligation is infinite and asymmetrical. Contemporary psychobiological thinking, when it does take up the problem of the other, generally, because it begins with an assumption of the primacy of the individual ego as a product of private neurological activity, must explain our sense of obligation in one of two ways. First, contemporary psychobiological theory can suggest that we feel such obligation to others because we recognize them as being "like us", as possessing a genetic similarity, and, therefore, our obligation is really self-interest. Or, alternatively, we assume that if we fulfill our obligations to them – treat them well – they will fulfill a similar reciprocal obligation to us, and thus our sense of obligation is, again, merely self-interest.

In contrast, Levinas proposes that we are who we are by virtue of our ethical relatedness to the other, and since that relation is not based on any assumptions of reciprocity, it is, in effect, an infinite obligation. It transcends those others with whom we may just happen to come into direct conflict, and extends beyond them, to yet others before whom any particular other might stand in relationships of obligation. We are fundamentally social beings, not by virtue of the genetically determined social structures in which we find ourselves, but by virtue of a fundamental and infinite obligation.

There is, for Levinas, always before us a choice regarding how to respond to the needs of the others with whom we are in relation. In that choice, we can either act consistently with the obligation we have toward these others, and thus live in a manner that is congruent with our ethical and moral sensibilities, or we can refuse and betray the gift of humanity with which we have been endowed by these others. In any given situation we may, as agents, choose to deploy ourselves in such a way as to fulfill the expectations of others and thus submit ourselves to their control. On the other hand, we may, in responding to the ethical obligation, deploy ourselves so as to attend solely to another's needs, acting without manipulation because there is simply no reason to do so. In yielding to this obligation our conduct is shaped in a way that lacks self-interest or manipulative stratagem. In refusing the ethical obligation, however, our conduct is stigmatized by anxiety, self-consciousness, militancy and defensiveness. How we choose to respond to the ethical obligation incumbent upon us as social beings gives life to the many possible ways in which we can be-in-the-world meaningfully, morally, and intimately with others. Because this obligation is the source of identity, and lies prior to conceptualization, sociality is genuinely fundamental. Grounded in this obligation, then, psychology might truly be a science of the social and the moral, and non-trivially so.

If sociality, meaning, and morality (manifest in ethical obligation) are connected in the way Levinas suggests they are, then a psychology grounded in such a conception of sociality would be a genuinely *ethical* discipline. It would be a psychology that would seek to articulate the fundamentally ethical character of our relations and social exchanges with one another, opening a discourse within which the parameters of ethical life would emerge as the primary subject matter. Since Levinas's understanding of our sociality begins in a pre-reflective ethical obligation, a psychology faithful to that understanding would not privilege the biological in accounting for the nature and meaning of our social responses and relationships. At the same time, this understanding would erase the barriers that have long insulated the individual ego from others. As has been argued elsewhere (Williams and Gantt 1998), the recognition of ethical obligation as the grounds for selfhood makes genuine human intimacy possible. A psychology thus grounded would not begin with the thesis that individuality must be overcome in order to establish intimacy, but that the false consciousness of biologism must be overcome so that intimacy, morality, and meaning might reveal themselves.

References

Adams R. L., Parsons O. A., Culbertson J. L, and Nixon S. J., eds. (1996): *Neuropsychology for Clinical Practice: Etiology, Assessment, and Treatment of Common Neurological Disorders*, American Psychological Association, Washington, DC.

Amen D. G. (2000): *Change Your Brain, Change Your Life: The Breakthrough Program for Conquering Anxiety, Depression, Obsessiveness, Anger, and Impulsiveness*, Times Book, New York.

Baron R.A. (2001): *Psychology*, 5th edition, Allyn and Bacon, Boston.

Beatty J. (2001): *The Human Brain: Essentials of Behavioral Neuroscience*, SAGE Publications, Thousand Oaks.

Bernstein D.A., and Nash P.W. (2002): *Essentials of Psychology*, 2nd edition, Houghton Mifflin, Boston.

Breggin P.R. (1991): *Toxic Psychiatry*, St. Martin's Press, New York.

Buck R. and Ginsberg B. (1997): Communicative genes and the evolution of empathy. In *Empathic Accuracy*, ed. by W. Ickes, Guilford Press, New York, pp. 17–43.

Burr V. (1995): *An Introduction to Social Construction*, Routledge, London.

Buss D.M. (1999): *Evolutionary Psychology: The New Science of the Mind*, Allyn and Bacon, Boston.

Cartwright J. (2000): *Evolution and Human Behavior*, MIT Press, Cambridge.

Cushman P. (1995): *Constructing the Self, Constructing America: A Cultural History of Psychotherapy*, Addison-Wesley, Reading.

Czerner T.B. (2001): *What Makes You Tick? The Brain in Plain English*, John Wiley and Sons, New York.

van Deurzen-Smith, E. (1997): *Everyday Mysteries: Existential Dimensions of Psychotherapy*, Routledge, London.

Edwards DC. (1999): *Motivation and Emotion: Evolutionary, Physiological, Cognitive, and Social Influences*, SAGE Publications, Thousand Oaks.

Feldman, RS. (2000): *Essentials of Understanding Psychology*, 4th edition, McGraw-Hill, Boston.

Fisher H.E. (1992): *Anatomy of Love*, Norton, New York.

Fisher H.E. (1994): The nature of romantic love. *The Journal of NIH Research* **6**(4), 59–64.

Freeman, WJ. (2000): *How Brains Make Up Their Minds*, Columbia University Press, New York.

Fuller A.R. (1990): *Insight into Value: An Exploration of the Premises of a Phenomenological Psychology*, State University of New York Press, Albany.

Gantt E.E. (1996): Social constructionism and the ethics of hedonism. *Journal of Theoretical and Philosophical Psychology* **16**(2), 123–140.

Gantt E.E. (2001): Rationality, irrationality, and the ethical: On saving psychology from nihilism. *Journal of Theoretical and Philosophical Psychology* **21**(1), 1–20.

Gazzaniga M.S., ed. (1995): *The Cognitive Neurosciences*, MIT Press, Cambridge.

Gergen K.J. (1994): *Realities and Relationships: Soundings in Social Construction*, Harvard University Press, Cambridge.

Gleitman H., Fridlund A.J., and Reisberg D. (1999): *Psychology*, 5th edition, Norton, New York.

Guze S. (1992): *Why Psychiatry Is a Branch of Medicine*, Oxford University Press, New York.

Heidegger M. (1962): *Being and Time*, transl. by J. Macquarrie and E.S. Robinson, Harper and Row, New York. (Original work published 1927.)

Huffman K., Vernoy, M., and Vernoy J. (2000): *Psychology in Action*, 5th edition, John Wiley and Sons, New York.

James W. (1956): The dilemma of determinism. In *The Will to Believe and Other Essays in Popular Philosophy*, Dover, New York, pp. 145–183. (Original work published 1897.)

Janov A. (2000): *The Biology of Love*, Prometheus Books, Amherst.

Kocklemans J.J. (1990): Some reflections on empirical psychology: Toward an interpretive psychology. In *Reconsidering Psychology: Perspectives from Continental Philosophy*, ed. by E. Faulconer and R.N. Williams, Duquesne University Press, Pittsburgh, pp. 75–91.

Kruks S. (1990): *Situation and Human Existence: Freedom, Subjectivity, and Society*, Unwin Hyman, London.

Kunz G. (1998): *The Paradox of Power and Weakness: Levinas and an Alternative Paradigm for Psychology*, State University of New York Press, Albany.

Kvale S. (Ed.) (1992): *Postmodernism and Psychology*, SAGE Publications, Thousand Oaks.

Leahey T.H. (2000): *A History of Psychology: Main Currents in Psychological Thought*, 5th edition, Prentice Hall, Upper Saddle River.

Levinas E. (1969): *Totality and Infinity*, transl. by A. Lingis, Duquesne University Press, Pittsburgh. (Original work published 1961.)

Levinas E. (1978): *Existence and Existents*, transl. by A. Lingis, Kluwer, London.

Levinas E. (1985): *Ethics and Infinity*, transl. by R.A. Cohen, Duquesne University Press, Pittsburgh.

Madison G.B. (1990): *The Phenomenology of Merleau-Ponty: A Search for the Limits of Consciousness*, Ohio University Press, Athens.

Merleau-Ponty M. (1964): Eye and mind. In *The Primacy of Perception*, ed. by J. Edie, Northwestern University Press, Evanston, pp. 159–190.

Merleau-Ponty M. (1989): *Phenomenology of Perception*, transl. by C. Smith, Routledge, London.

Messer S.B., Sass L.A., and Woolfolk R.L. (1988): *Hermeneutics and Psychological Theory: Interpretive Perspectives on Personality, Psychotherapy, and Psychopathology*, Rutgers University Press, New Brunswick.

Nagel T. (1995): *Other Minds: Critical Essays 1969-1994*, Oxford University Press, Oxford.

Oliner P.M., Oliner, S.P., Baron L., Blum L.A., Krebs D.I., and Smolenska M.Z., eds. (1992): *Embracing the Other: Philosophical, Psychological, and Historical Perspectives on Altruism*, New York University Press, New York.

Plotkin H. (1998): *Evolution in Mind: An Introduction to Evolutionary Psychology*, Harvard University Press, Cambridge.

Ratey J.J. (2001): *A User's Guide to the Brain: Perception, Attention, and the Four Theaters of the Brain*, Pantheon Books, New York.

Richardson F.C., Fowers B.J., and Guignon C.B. (1999): *Re-Envisioning Psychology: Moral Dimensions of Theory and Practice*, Jossey-Bass Publishers, San Francisco.

Rosenau P.M. (1992): *Post-Modernism and the Social Sciences: Insights, Inroads, and Intrusions*, Princeton University Press, Princeton.

Rosenzweig M.R., and Leiman A.L. (1989): *Physiological Psychology*, 2nd edition, Random House, New York.

Ruden R.A. (2000): *The Craving Brain*, 2nd edition, HarperCollins, New York.

Rychlak J.F. (1994): *Logical Learning Theory: A Human Teleology and Its Empirical Support*, Nebraska University Press, Lincoln.

Sartre J-P. (1956): *Being and Nothingness*, transl. by H. Barnes, Philosophical Library, New York.

Schneider K.J. and May R. (1995): *The Psychology of Existence: An Integrative, Clinical Perspective*, McGraw-Hill, New York.

Schwartz J.M. (1996): *Brain Lock: Free Yourself from Obsessive-Compulsive Behavior: A Four-Step Self-Treatment Method to Change Your Brain Chemistry*, Regan Books, New York.

Shorter E. (1997): *A History of Psychiatry: From the Era of the Asylum to the Age of Prozac*, John Wiley and Sons, New York.

Silk K.R., ed. (1998): *Biology of Personality Disorders*, American Psychological Association, Washington.

Simpson J.A., and Kenrick D.T. (1997): *Evolutionary Social Psychology*, Lawrence Erlbaum, Mahwah.

Slife B.D., and Williams R.N. (1995): *What's Behind the Research? Discovering Hidden Assumptions in the Behavioral Sciences*, SAGE Publications, Thousand Oaks.

Spotts D. (1999): *Super Brain Power: 28 Minutes to a Supercharged Brain*, LifeQuest, Seattle.

Taylor C. (1985): What is human agency? In *Human Agency and Language: Philosophical Papers I*, ed. by C. Taylor, Cambridge University Press, New York, pp. 15–44.

Thornhill R., and Palmer C.T. (2000): *A Natural History of Rape: Biological Bases of Sexual Coercion*, MIT Press, Cambridge.

Varela F.J., Thompson E., and Rosch E. (1991): *The Embodied Mind: Cognitive Science and Human Experience*, MIT Press, Cambridge.

Williams R.N. (1992): The human context of agency. *American Psychologist* **47**(6), 752–760.

Williams R.N. (1994): The modern, the post-modern, and the question of truth: Perspectives on the problem of agency. *Journal of Theoretical and Philosophical Psychology* **14**(1), 25–39.

Williams R.N. (2001): The biologization of psychotherapy: Understanding the nature of influence. In *Critical Issues in Psychotherapy: Translating New Ideas into Practice*, ed. by B.D. Slife, R.N. Williams, and S.H. Barlow, SAGE Publications, Thousand Oaks, pp. 51–67

Williams R.N. and Gantt E.E. (1998): Intimacy and heteronomy: On grounding psychology in the ethical. *Theory and Psychology* **8**(2), 255–270.

Winokur G. (1981): *Depression: The Facts*, Oxford University Press, Oxford.

Yalom I. (1980): *Existential Psychotherapy*, Basic Books, New York.

Zachar P. (2000): *Psychological Concepts and Biological Psychiatry*, John Benjamins, Philadelphia.

Time, Information, and Determinism in Psychology

Brent D. Slife

1 Introduction

Time has long played a vital role in physics and philosophy, as evidenced by many of the chapters of this volume (e.g. Guignon, Gustafson, Primas, this volume). However, psychologists have rarely acknowledged the important role of time in their own discipline. They have studied how people perceive and manage time, but they have rarely examined the assumptions of time in their own theories and practices (for exceptions see McGrath and Kelly 1986, Slife 1993, Slife 1995a). The purpose of this chapter is to explicate the overlooked role of time in psychologists' understandings of determinism.

Here, conceptions of time in physics and philosophy are helpful, because relatively unexamined beliefs will, as Burtt (1954) once put it, "share the ideas of [their] age (p. 229). In this case, Newton and his followers dominated the age with Absolute Time, leading psychologists to adopt a singularly atomistic conception of time. Unfortunately, this temporal atomism has fostered a dilemma of determinism and free will in psychology that has enfeebled and befuddled theoreticians and practitioners. Some psychologists assume these problems have been solved by the modern notions of information and the vaunted "information processor". However, it is argued here that this "solution" is a sham. Instead, a holistic conception of time is proposed that dissolves the determinism/free will dilemma and allows the notion of information to be truly meaningful.

2 Newton and Absolute Time

As many historians have noted, Newton's popularity cannot be underestimated. He was truly a legend in his own time (Cohen 1985, Koyre 1965, Slife 1995b, Thayer and Randall 1953). At the point of psychology's conception, his physics had enjoyed almost two centuries of relatively unchallenged status. It seemed only natural for psychologists to copy the successful methods of Newton. However, the popularity of Newton's physics was the Trojan horse of his metaphysics. As Burtt (1954) said it so eloquently, Newton made a "metaphysic out of his methods" (p. 229). Veneration for Newton's methods – thought to be without metaphysics, at Newton's own insistence – allowed an unrecognized metaphysic to be brought into psychology. My particular focus of this metaphysic today is Newton's conception of Absolute Time.

As Newton put it in his *Principia*, "absolute, true, and mathematical time, of itself, and from its own nature, flows equably without relation to anything external, and by another name is called duration" (Newton 1990, p. 8). Newton's time is absolute, because it is independent of other natural entities – "without relation to anything external", as he put it. Newton's time also "flows equably", as a continuum in which "all things are placed in time as to order of succession" (Newton 1990, p. 10). This is the reason that subsequent scholars and "underlaborers" of Newton, as Locke (1990, p. 89) characterized himself, likened his conception of time to a Euclidian line (Whitrow 1980). Time flows like a line or continuum, with the succession of its instants analogous to points on a line. The present point on the line, then, is the point separating the points of the past from the points of the future.

Consider Newton's view of time as described by Whitrow (1980, p. 35; first quotation) and Burtt (1954, p. 263; second quotation):

> Newton regarded the moments of absolute time as forming a continuous sequence like that of the real numbers and believed that the rate at which these moments succeed each other is a variable which is independent of all particular events and processes.

> Time is a succession of discrete parts, or moments, no two of which are present simultaneously, and hence nothing exists or is present except the moment *now*. But the moment now is constantly passing into the past, and a future moment is becoming now. Hence, from this point of view time simmers down till it is contracted into a mathematical limit between the past and the future.

From these descriptions, it is clear that Newton's conception of time was an extension of his atomistic or corpuscular understanding of the universe (Burtt 1954, Faulconer 1995, Williams 1995). The universe, for Newton, consisted of separable regions of time and space, each as independent corpuscles or atoms. Each region of space, at a particular time, was a self-contained cell, because each had its own qualities and characteristics inherent in it.

That is, each region derived none of its qualities from its simultaneous relation to other regions or atoms of time and space. This atomism meant that Newton's conception of time was itself separable into self-contained instants or points, each with its own properties and qualities, independent of other instants and moments. Even sets of instants, such as the past, present, or future, were absolutely separate from one another. Although these points and these moments together form the line and flow of time, they each have their own properties and qualities, separate from one another.[1]

Newton conceived of time in this atomistic manner to serve his view of motion, and thus change and causation. He regarded absolute time as the perfect measure of motion precisely because it was independent of all physical change (Adler 1990, p. 713). If time were *de*pendent on motion, then Newton would be left without any independent or objective means of gauging motion – his cherished focus in the natural world. This independence is another important aspect of his corpuscular understanding of the universe. Each corpuscle – in this case, motion and time – is independent and autonomous from every other corpuscle. Change, in this sense, takes place across the three parts of time – past, present, and future – without change itself being connected to these parts. Causation, too, is ordered in this same temporal sequence, with self-contained cause separate (in time) from self-contained effect, and both cause and effect independent from time itself. This means not only that change takes place across time but also that the self-contained past is sufficient to cause the self-contained present – Newton's primary conception of determinism.

Here, the issue of determinism is somewhat controversial. Newton's understanding of determinism is somewhat more complex than described thus far. Faulconer (1995), for example, contends that Newton did not *require* the determinism of science to have these efficient causal properties. Although many of Newton's own physical explanations were atomistic, as described (above), this does not mean his general conception of science necessitates this atomistic style of explanation. Important interpreters of Newton, such as Locke, may have "read", or rather misread, his conception too narrowly.

The Newtonian picture seems to be further complicated by the uses of "Newtonian" mechanics in contemporary physics. For example, the notion of a system's "state" is often considered to incorporate a memory of the

---

[1] Although there is some question about whether Newton believed in the indivisibility of temporal instants (Whitrow 1980), I wish to avoid this question and use atomism here to refer to the self-containment of these instants, no matter how divisible they might be. That is, their qualities are inherent in them and do not stem from their relation to other instants and points of time.

past, as if the past is inherent, in some sense, to the present (e.g. Packard et al. 1980). Nevertheless, this *modern* sense of "Newtonian" physics must be distinguished from the *historic* sense of Newton's *meta*physics. As the descriptions of Whitrow (1980) and Burtt (1954) clearly indicate, Newton's own view of time was ultimately atomistic. Most importantly, the past and present, *as parts of time*, were viewed as independent of one another. This is to say nothing about the ways in which Newton (or Newtonians) tied these parts together (e.g. causation).

However, as important as Newton's original understanding of time is, the main issue for this chapter is *psychology's* understanding of Newtonian metaphysics. Here, there seems to be little doubt that psychology – through Locke and other Newtonian "underlaborers" – understood Newton's metaphysics in this atomistic manner. The prestige of his science figured prominently in psychology's adopting atomistic conceptions of time and causality (McGrath and Kelly 1986, Slife 1993). The problem is, psychologists never looked back to the natural sciences after they had their own project going.

If psychologists *had* looked back, only a few decades later, they would have noticed many influential criticisms of Newton's atomistic legacy. Einstein, for example, directly disputed Newton's "habit of treating time as an independent continuum" (Adler 1990, p. 712). Time, for Einstein, was related to the inertial frame of reference of its observer, and thus was relational rather than absolute (Whitrow 1980). Many other prominent physicists – including Heisenberg, Bohr, and more recently Bohm – have disputed the independence of physical space-time regions in this Newtonian sense as well as the atomism of time and causality.

3   Atomistic Time and Determinism

Unfortunately, this atomism lives on in the social sciences, where not only the past, present, and future, but also cause and effect are thought to be sequentially ordered in self-contained and independent regions of time and space. This is "unfortunate" because the atomistic conception has fostered all manner of unacknowledged problems in the discipline of psychology (Slife 1993). Two important problems, for the purposes of this paper, are psychology's free will/determinism dilemma (Slife and Fisher 2000) and one of psychology's most popular "solutions" to this dilemma – the mind as information processor (Slife 1995b).

Let us begin with two implications of atomistic time in psychology. First, the sequential independence of moments of time implies that the past and present are themselves naturally separate. This implication is the common notion that the past is not in the present, and the present is not in the past. The second implication of this sequential atomism is the prevalent conception – culturally and psychologically – that the past is unchangeable. Because the past and present are separate from one another, the past is not reachable from the present. All living beings supposedly reside in the present, from this perspective, so none of these beings can reach *back* to change the past. The past is passed.

Whether the past constantly reaches *forward* in time is the main point of contention between the free willists and the determinists of psychology. By far the most popular position is the deterministic one. Here, many theoretical and practical psychologists have argued forcefully that the past is important to understanding the present, however independent it might actually be from the present. Freud, of course, is a notable supporter of this thesis, but one could also summon the support of most behaviorists, humanists, and cognitivists. The point is, most psychologists believe they need some means of bridging the temporal separation between the past and the present. What could this bridge be?

Efficient causation is clearly the most popular means of building this bridge. This form of causation is itself thought to be sequential – moving from the past to the present – where the cause (in the past) transfers its influence onto the effect (in the present). This causal bridge not only seems to make good conceptual sense, it also allows psychologists to discuss the predictability of human organisms and thus become real scientists. Practitioners, too, are often caught in this deterministic net, because they also sense the importance of the past. Understanding clients in therapy, for instance, seems to necessitate some contact with the past, and efficient causation seems the only, or at least the most scientific way to make this contact.

The difficulty is, the free willists of psychology believe they must resist this presumption of efficient causation (e.g. Rychlak 1994). Free willists note that when the cause (in the past) transfers its causal influence onto the effect (in the present), this is a hard determinism. Because the past is unchangeable, the past's influence on the present is itself unchangeable. Unless the present has unique influences – influences that are simultaneous with the present – then the present is *completely determined* by the unchangeable past. No mainstream theory in psychology postulates such simultaneous influences, so each theory assumes that the present is an extension of the past, thus rendering the present completely unchangeable.

The free willist knows too well the implications of this temporal and causal arrangement. Humans cannot be distinguished from any other natural object that is subject to this form of causal determinism. Whatever change is observed in the present is accounted for, and thus determined by, unchangeable causal laws acting from the past. Humans, in this sense, cannot be praised or blamed, experience any meaning, or participate in moral discourse – any more than a rock rolling down a mountain. If the rock rolls into a hiker, we cannot say "bad rock", because the rock has no responsibility for the direction of its roll. Presumably, natural forces, acting through efficient causation, are responsible for this direction. What would a psychology be, the free willists protest, without morality and meaning?

Again, many practitioners are sympathetic with these issues. They see the significance of meaning and responsibility in their practices. Indeed, many practitioners attempt to empower their clients and facilitate meaning. How would this be possible if the clients were completely determined by a separate, unchangeable past? This impossibility is the reason many free willists have questioned the presumption of causation (e.g. Rychlak 1994, Howard 1994). Efficient causation transfers the unchangeable past to the present – in effect, making the present unchangeable as well. The free willist solution, then, is to eliminate the bridge between the past and present – sequential causation – and focus on the present where the free will is presumably located. This elimination allows the present to be "free of" or independent of the past – as the word "free" would seem to imply. If choices were *de*pendent on the past, they reason, these choices would be determined and thus not be choices in any meaningful sense.

A major problem with this independence of the past is that the present makes little sense without the past. This is the reason psychotherapists have traditionally had difficulty taking a purely free will perspective; it is difficult to understand a client's will without the client's past as a context for that will (Williams 1992). Even the notion of "choice" cannot be understood without some sort of historic context in which to understand that a choice is required. Without the past, a choice would be arbitrary or random; it could not be based on infomation or consequences, because knowledge of these stems from past experiences.

Here, then, is the dilemma of modern psychology: Either we embrace the present only (for "free will" decisions) because the influence of the past must be denied, or we embrace the past only (for determinism) because the present must be an extension (via efficient causality) of the past (Slife and Fisher 2000). The first position leads psychologists to assume that free will is chaotic and contextless – as Dennett (1984) puts it, a free will not worth having. The second leads to the lack of possibility, and, thus, precludes agency, responsibility, and meaning. The upshot is, we lose meaning either way. Either meaning is lost through the contextlessness of a present that has no past, or it is lost through the determinism of a present that is the extension of an immutable past.

4 Atomistic Time and Information

Obviously, neither alternative is very appealing. However, psychologists have not questioned the atomistic conception of time that leads to this loss of meaning. They have questioned, instead, the need for meaning. Indeed, cognitive psychologists are progressively replacing the supposedly "old-fashioned" notion of meaning with another concept that seems to require neither possibility nor context – the concept of information. Part of the reason for the popularity of this replacement conception, as I have argued elsewhere (Slife 1995b), is that it fits so nicely within the atomistic assumption of time. Cognitive models consider data from the environment to be transmitted to the brain across time and space. In this sense, information is distributed across some span of time and space. This means that atoms of the information – information bits – occur at separate points of time and space, and the mind must process or store each bit as it is received. The human mind is, thus, an information processor, *not* a meaning processor.

Unfortunately, the problem of meaning does not go away that easily. The meaning of a particular message cannot be discerned from *any* combination of information bits. No cognitive scientist believes that the elements of information are simply "added up" to produce the meaning. The elements themselves have an organization that is crucial to the understanding of the overall meaning of the input. How does the receiver discern this organization when the bits of data are received independently of one another? Meaning is a particular relationship between two or more referents, and the independence of these data bits as separate carriers of information would seem to obviate their original relationship or organization. In other words, their *de*pendence before transmission cannot be reconstructed after their reception, when the parts are *in*dependent by their very nature.

The relations among parts can never be represented with independent parts. The core of the problem is that form and content cannot be realistically separated (Slife 1995b). Even *if* the "content" of a message can be coded into independent pieces, the original "form" of the content – as a *simultaneous* structure – cannot be coded into a *sequential* entity, such as the modern concept of information (Slife 1993, Slife 1995b). Oral and written communications may seem to occur sequentially, but in actuality they are experienced as nested meanings – simultaneous relationships among the words – rather than individual words, each with its own portion of the message (McClelland et al. 1988, Saussure 1966). To read a sequence of words without this simultaneous relationship is to experience meaningless gibberish. All that is available at the end of this informational stream is the cumulative record of independent elements – as each element is received in atomistic time – and not the qualities of the elements that are derived from their relationship to one another in the original structure.

This is where the issue of atomistic time most visibly reveals its fundamental role in conceptions of information. Because most scientific processes are thought to be distributed along the sequence of temporal atoms, these processes can literally never exist *as a whole* at any moment in time. That is, if a process begins at Time 1, proceeds through Time 2, and ultimately ends at Time 3, only a reduced portion of this process can be studied at any point in this sequence. Recording devices, such as a scientist's memory, permit each piece of the process to be "photographed" and compared to the next moment's piece until all the process is viewed *at the same time*. However, none of the pieces contain information about their original relationships, and so their original "meaning" is lost.

As applied to the sequence of information bits, we cannot understand their meaning (their relation to the whole) as we receive each data piece sequentially in time. Without the meaning of each piece, we cannot know the meaning of the whole, even if we "store" them for comparison. Once again, our atomistic conception of time is the crux of the problem. Just as it precluded meaningful conceptions of free will and determinism in psychology, it precludes meaningful conceptions of information. Information, in this sense, does not save us from the issues of meaning. If anything, it highlights these issues and clarifies the need for an alternate conception of time.

5   An Alternate Conception of Time

The temporal holism of several hermeneutic philosophers is particularly helpful in this regard (Bergson 1959, Fuller 1990, Heidegger 1962, Manning 1993). Indeed, the hermeneutic contributions to this volume (Guignon, Martin and Sugarman, Richardson and Bishop) implicitly, if not explicitly, assume this holistic approach to time. Temporal holism is not particularly well known, forsaking, as it does, the better known *a*temporal (timeless) and atomistic (corpuscular) conceptions.

Temporal holism postulates, instead, a dynamic interplay among the three dimensions of time – past, present, and future – that does not assume these dimensions are wholly separate from one another. Indeed, the interplay of the past, present, and future is considered to be simultaneous rather than sequential in nature. As Fuller (1990, p. 184) characterizes temporal holism, "our life's temporal moments – alreadiness [past], present, future – are in active communication with one another at any given moment, reciprocally determining one another". Heidegger (1972, p. 15) put it this way: "The unity of time's three dimensions consists in the interplay of each toward each". The point, for our purposes, is that the past, present, and future are thought to happen, as Manning (1993, p. 85) wrote, "as synchrony, not as diachrony".

This holistic synchrony may seem provocative. However, its provocative nature is not because it violates our experience, but rather because it violates a familiar intellectual abstraction – atomistic time. Just because many Western thinkers have been taught to organize time in this manner does not mean this organization is a person's *experience* of time. On the contrary, Heidegger (1962) and others (Bergson 1959, Bohm 1980, Lewin 1936) claim that time, as experienced, is at least as much simultaneous as sequential.[2] These temporal holists do not deny that we experience a sequentiality of sorts, with some events happening – as a narrative – before other events. Holists merely want to affirm the experience we have of the simultaneity of time's dimensions.

As already described, many people have a strong experiential sense that their past pervades their present. After all, memories and information from the past exist in the present. Some holists even claim we have an intuitive feeling for the presentness of our future. This future is not the unreachable future of the linear theorist. Goals and expectations are present images of the future. They do not exist except in the "now", affecting one's actions in the present and one's memory of the past. Indeed, neither the past nor the future can exist for us experientially, except in the present.

This holistic present is not the durationless instant of atomistic time. This present is a "lived now" – an experienced, practical present that requires the lived past and lived future as context.[3] That is, the present is always

---

[2]It is important to note here that no one, including scientists, gets outside his or her experiences. Our experience of the world – and hence our interpretation of it – is thus crucial for understanding how it is that we conduct and undergo investigations.

[3]Heidegger (1962) shifts the meaning of the present from that *in which* something occurs to the actual carrying out of an action. Ontologically conceived, the present is *making present* (Gelven 1989).

"coming from" and "going to" somewhere (Heidegger 1962). We are always in the midst of a story. Just as the understanding of any moment of a story requires knowing (in the present) what has happened before and anticipating (in the present) what is about to happen, so, too, any "now" of holistic time is considered to require both the synchronous past and co-occurring future. In this sense, then, the simultaneity of the three dimensions of time is not counterintuitive; it is *thoroughly* intuitive and experiential.

The "experiential" nature of temporal holism is itself a problem for many psychologists. Psychologists prefer, as Newton before them, a more "objective" conception of time than one based upon lived experience. However, holists note that atomistic time is not itself objective; it is not an object in any conventional sense and thus cannot be objectively observed. Clocks and watches may *measure* time, but they are not themselves the entity they presume to measure. The fact is there are no objective atoms of time. Atomistic time is a social or intellectual construction that has itself been abandoned by many natural scientists (Slife 1993). Unless scientists can somehow move outside their experience, experiential or temporal time is the only time we have (Slife and Williams 1995).

6   Determinism and Information

What implications does this holistic view of time have for the dilemmas related to determinism and information? First, the condition of simultaneity is crucial to any meaning. Meanings are parts of wholes, and wholes do not exist without the simultaneity of their parts. Holistic (and simultaneous) relationships must be recognized "first", at least logically, to endow the part with its partness, its meaning. As Heidegger (1962, p. 116) puts it, "the totality of involvements which is constitutive of the context of significance is 'earlier' than any single item". Modern advocates of information reverse this order, assuming that a message begins with parts or information bits. These advocates hope that the aggregate of independent and discrete elements will be organized into a whole that is similar to the whole of which they were originally part. Unfortunately, atomistic time precludes any access to the simultaneous whole, because the parts of a whole must be distributed across the succession of time.

Holistic time, on the other hand, allows the relationship among parts to be accessible from the start. Information is not spread across a continuum of time. Information is the meaning of the lived "now" with all its interrelatedness. Heidegger (1985, p. 187), for example, argues that "things constantly step back into the referential totality, or, more properly stated, in the immediacy of everyday occupation they never even first step out of it. ... Things recede into relations" (Heidegger 1985, p. 187). Similarly, Todes (1963, 1966) describes a field-structure of experience that is prior to the facts and implicitly determines their relevance and significance. For philosophers such as these, lived events are not experienced as isolated facts but as nested meanings within a simultaneity of contexts.

Crucial to this simultaneity is not only spatial context but also temporal context. No meaning is a meaning of the present only, such as an information bit. All meanings of the "now" necessarily involve meanings of the past and future. The past, for example, is not dead and gone, nor is this supposedly immutable entity stored for later retrieval. The past is a constant and dynamic presence *in* the present–in flux with respect to both our simultaneous spatial and simultaneous temporal contexts. Without this present past and present future, no meaning is possible. Indeed, the presentness of the past and future implies that the meaning of each dimension shifts in the light of our present reinterpretations, with these new past and future meanings affecting, in turn, our view of the present.

Perhaps surprisingly, recent empirical findings in psychology support this holistic understanding of time. Many researchers, for example, have concluded that memories are dynamic rather than static (Ashcraft 1989, pp. 306–320). That is, the past is not stored but is constantly being reconstructed in light of present situations and future objectives. In this sense, it is as correct to hold that the present "causes" the meanings of the past (which are themselves in the present) as it is to say that the past causes the meanings of the present.[4] A "childhood trauma", in this case, can be seen in retrospect (and in happier times) as a good lesson learned. The past in cognition is not a fixed and "dead" entity, as atomistic theorists have contended. The past is alive in the experiential present and is constantly intermingling with the other two temporal dimensions.

From this research, cognitive theorists have become aware of the past as a simultaneous context for the present. Unfortunately, their only option for bringing the past into the present, given their atomistic view of time, is atomistic causality. A self-contained cause (from the past) is thought to produce a self-contained effect (in the present). This popular notion of

---

[4]The use of "cause" here may seem problematic. From an atomistic perspective, causal processes are considered to be distributed across atomistic time, and thus causes are thought to have to precede effects. As others have shown, however, this notion of antecedence is not a formal property of causality (Bunge 1959, p. 63, and Bunge 1963, p. 189). Cause and effect work just fine as simultaneous events.

causality, however, destroys time in any meaningful sense (Slife 1993). The present is lost because it is at the mercy of the immediately preceding event. As a mere "effect" of this causal event, the present cannot make its own contribution to meaning. This, of course, is the objection of the free willist (as described above). However, mainstream cognitivists seem to welcome the determinism of past information in their explanations, because it seems so scientific (read Newtonian). The problem is, the past is also lost in this deterministic framework. The past as a totality – as a *simultaneous* whole – is *not* involved in determining the present with atomistic causality. What is involved in this determinism is the most recent, ending event of the past and not the past as a whole.

The upshot is that atomistic causality cannot bring temporal context to events of the present. The present – where all people supposedly reside in this framework – remains fundamentally contextless. Similar to the information bit, the present is a discrete event, independent from other present moments that have now passed away. The fundamental difficulty with this framework is that humans do not experience the world in this manner. Even if a person experiences a sequence of events (e.g. words on a page or sights on a trip), these events are not experienced as atoms of reality. We do not experience present moments only, divorced from related past memories and future anticipations. We experience wholes and meanings, full-blown and alive with possibility. The atomist's divorce of past and present, however, denies these meanings and thus creates the free will/determinism dilemma – the dilemma of how the divorced become connected.

With temporal holism, on the other hand, these meanings are affirmed and the free will/determinism dilemma of psychology falls away. The present is no longer contextless, nor is it merely an extension of the past, because the past and present are always and already connected. The concerns of the determinist are assuaged because the past influences the present (though not by mechanical necessity). The concerns of the free willist are assuaged because possibility is permitted. The past underdetermines the present, and the past itself is dynamic rather than immutable.

The issue of meaning is also readdressed for the notion of information. Currently, the mind and its environment are portrayed as residing in separate, Newtonian space-time regions (cf. Slife 1995b). The environment must traverse the space and time distance between these regions to reach the mind with its information. The radical contextuality of temporal holism challenges this information processing model. No informational flow is necessary because the mind and its environment communicate with one another by virtue of their relation as parts of a superordinate gestalt – Heidegger's *Dasein*.

When I see a new bloom on a Bavarian tree, for example, I am not merely receiving, and thus being determined by, stimuli or information from one space-time region which I then must represent mentally in another region of time and space.[5] If I am situated and embodied in the holist sense, I am part of the *same* region of time and space as the tree, the same life world as the tree. The new bloom I see has a direct and immediate impact on me, because the bloom and I are parts of the same *Dasein*, parts of the same whole. As with any whole, a change in a part (the bloom on the tree) can have a simultaneous impact on the gestalt of the whole (the world) and thus the qualities of all other parts (my perception of the tree).

7   Conclusion

Only the notions of atomistic time – with their sequencing of past, present, and future – can make this simultaneous change appear to occur in a sequence. Temporal holism, by contrast, not only prevents the tree and the mind from being distributed along the line of atomistic time, it also disallows atomistic causality, and, thus, a prevalent form of determinism, from assuming a privileged status. Indeed, it allows the mind and tree to exist in the same dynamic world, a world of context and possibilities. From this perspective, the free will/determinism dilemma dissolves and atomistic conceptions of information are no longer needed.

References

Adler M.J. (1990): *The Syntopicon: II.*, Encyclopedia Brittanica, Chicago.

Ashcraft M.H. (1989): *Human Memory and Cognition*, Scott Foresman, New York.

Bergson H. (1959): *Essai sur les Donnees Immediates de la Conscience*, Presses Univ. de France, Paris.

Bohm D. (1980): *Wholeness and the Implicate Order*, Routledge and Kegan Paul, London.

Bunge M. (1959): *Causality*, Harvard University Press, Cambridge MA.

Bunge M. (1963): *The Myth of Simplicity*, Prentice-Hall, Englewood Cliffs.

---

[5]Dennett (1991, p. 253) seems to have a similar concern when he criticizes the "Cartesian Theatre" of many cognitive models. His remedy to this concern, however, is quite different from the one offered here.

Burtt E.A. (1954): *The Metaphysical Foundations of Modern Physical Science*, Doubleday, Garden City.

Cohen I.B. (1985): *Revolutions in Science*, Balknap Press, Cambridge MA.

Dennett D. (1984): *Elbow Room*, MIT Press, Cambridge MA.

Dennett D. (1991): *Consciousness Explained*, Little Brown, Boston.

Faulconer J. (1995): Nature, science, and causation. *Journal of Mind and Behavior* **16**, 77–86.

Fuller A. (1990): *Insight into Value: An Exploration of the Premises of Phenomenological Psychology*, SUNY Press, Albany.

Gelven M. (1989): *A Commentary on Heidegger's Being and Time*, Northern Illinois University Press, Dekalb, Ill.

Heidegger M. (1962): *Being and Time*, Harper Collins, San Francisco. Original work published 1926.

Heidegger M. (1972): *On Time and Being*, transl. by J. Stambaugh, Harper and Row, New York.

Heidegger M. (1985): *History of the Concept of Time*, Indiana University Press, Bloomington.

Howard G.S. (1994): Some varieties of free will worth practicing. *Journal of Theoretical and Philosophical Psychology* **14**(1), 50–61.

Koyré A. (1965): *Newtonian Studies*, Harvard University Press, Cambridge MA.

Lewin K. (1936): *Principles of Topological Psychology*, McGraw-Hill, New York.

Locke J. (1990): *An Essay Concerning Human Understanding*, University of Chicago Press, Chicago. Originally published 1690.

Manning R.J.S. (1993): *Interpreting Otherwise Than Heidegger*, Duquesne University Press, Pittsburgh.

McClelland J., Rumelhart D., and Hinton G. (1988): The appeal of parallel distributed processing. In *Parallel Distributed Processing*, ed. by J. McClelland and J. Rumelhart, MIT Press, Cambridge MA.

McGrath J.E. and Kelly J.R. (1986): *Time and Human Interaction: Toward a Social Psychology of Time*, Guilford, New York.

Newton I. (1990): *Mathematical Principles of Natural Philosophy*, transl. by A. Motte, University of Chicago Press, Chicago. Original work published 1678.

Packard N., Crutchfield J., Farmer J., and Shaw R. (1980): Geometry from a time series. *Physical Review Letters* **45**, 712–716.

Ricoeur P. (1983): *Time and Narrative*, transl. by K. McLaughlin and D. Pellauer, University of Chicago Press, Chicago.

Rychlak J.F. (1994): *Logical Learning Theory: A Human Teleology and Its Empirical Support*, University of Nebraska Press, Lincoln.

Saussure F. (1966): *Course in General Linguistics*, ed. by C. Ball and A. Sechehaye, transl. by W. Baskin, McGraw-Hill, New York. Original work published 1907.

Slife B.D. (1993): *Time and Psychological Explanation*, SUNY Press, Albany.

Slife B.D. (1995a): Information and time. *Theory and Psychology* **5**(3), 533–550.

Slife B.D. (1995): Introduction to "Newton's Legacy for Psychology". *Journal of Mind and Behavior* **16**(1), 1–7.

Slife B.D. and Fisher A. (2000): Modern and postmodern approaches to the free will/determinism dilemma in psychology. *Journal of Humanistic Psychology* **40**(1), 80–108.

Slife B.D., and Williams R.N. (1995): *What's Behind the Research? Discovering Hidden Assumptions in the Behavioral Sciences*, Sage Publications, Thousand Oaks.

Thayer H.S. and Randall J.H. (1953): *Newton's Philosophy and Nature: Selections from His Writings*, Hafner, New York.

Todes S.J. (1963): *The Human Body as the Material Subject of the World*, Doctoral Dissertation, Harvard University.

Todes S.J. (1966): Comparative phenomenology of perception and imagination, Part I: Perception. *Journal of Existentialism* **6**, 253–268.

Whitrow G.J. (1980): *The Natural Philosophy of Time*, 2nd edition, Oxford University Press, Oxford.

Williams R.N. (1992): The human context of agency. *American Psychologist* **47**(6), 752–760.

Williams R.N. (1995): Temporality and psychological action at a distance. *Journal of Mind and Behavior* **16**, 63–76.

Eastern Determinism Reconsidered From a Scientific Point of View

Takehisa Abe and Fusako Kobayashi

1 Introduction

It is difficult to define exactly what "determinism" means as it has so many meanings depending on the context. When talking about determinism and indeterminism, we are not directly concerned with the Western tradition. The theological and philosophical questions of free will and responsibility for one's own behavior have generated heated discussions in the West from ancient times right up to the present day. We are more concerned with the wider implications of the Eastern view, the concrete metaphysical questions of free will and behavior. The Yi-King of China, and especially the Buddhism of China and Japan are concerned with these issues. In this presentation we want to concentrate on the two viewpoints of Buddhism and the Yi-King, and discuss them from a scientific point of view.

To summarize: the two Eastern systems of Yi-King and Buddhism can be compared with, and correspond to, the European concepts of determinism and indeterminism, respectively. Using a different definition of "determinism", however, both systems can also be regarded as deterministic. The Yi-King involves specific methods of divination. Since there is a degree of uncertainty in these methods, it can be described as a probabilistic-statistical determinism. Buddhism is similar to scientific determinism in that it describes progress toward an ultimate goal as part of its doctrine. It can, therefore, be described as a "quasi-scientific" determinism.

Both the Yi-King and Buddhism have been well received up to the present day. The Yi-King is appealing because of its fortune telling, and Buddhism because of the universal relevance of its doctrine. In today's uncertain times, fortune telling has become increasingly popular in modern Japan, which has led to criticism from the Buddhist point of view. This is something worth attention. Since the Yi-King is deterministic and Buddhism is indeterministic from a Western point of view, such criticism could be construed as criticism from the indeterministic side against determinism.

Underlying this trend is the Western distinction of determinism and indeterminism. This is well known (Mackay 1988, Omura 1973, Inoue 1973), but we will summarize some of its crucial aspects here for background.

Determinism is often viewed as incompatible with human free will and responsibility for our actions. This can be seen in several of the presentations in this volume (e.g. Guignon, Kane, Primas, and Richardson and Bishop). A particularly illustrative example of this incompatibility can be found in Spinoza's *Ethics*, where everything – including what we consider to be human free will and responsibility – exists necessarily as an attribute of God. In a more philosophical framework, everything that exists is an inevitable part of the attributes of God. Therefore, human will depends on this existence (Spinoza).

Indeterminism is often associated with free will, either of God or of humans. The free will of God, for instance, was used as an argument against the intellectualism of Thomas Aquinas. For God, will takes precedence over reason. The eternal truths of reason were formed by the free will of God (Duns Scotus, Ockham, Descartes, Schelling). Human free will was emphasized by Luther and others. It stands in contrast to the predetermined will of God (e.g. Erasmus). The existence of human free will is also contrasted with the inevitable laws of nature. For example, while acknowledging the inevitable cause and effect properties of natural laws, Kant believed the human will could transcend the field of experience and be expressed in the realm of sense (transcendental freedom). More recently, Boutroux and Bergson considered free will as part of a basic uncertainty in natural law.

In Sect. 2 an overview of the concepts of the Yi-King and Buddhism will be given, finishing with a comparison between these two concepts and Western determinism. Section 3 is the focal point of the presentation. We propose a detailed definition of determinism and discuss what this means from a scientific standpoint. Using such a definition, we will demonstrate how the two Eastern thought systems involve a new type of determinism in addition to those of the Western tradition. Section 4 deals with fortune telling as it is currently practiced in Yi-King and Buddhism. We will specifically attempt to interpret the reaction from Buddhists to the Yi-King in a classical deterministic framework.

2   The Yi-King and Buddhism

2.1   The Yi-King

There is an extensive amount of literature on the Yi-King. For the topics to be discussed here, we recommend Honda (1973a,b,c) and Kou (1973).

2.1.1   Establishment and Development

The Yi-King was originally founded as the "Chou divination" during the Chou dynasty (1700BC–800BC). After adopting one of the five classics of Confucianism as its scripture during the Warring states period (500BC–200BC), the movement expanded during the Han dynasty (200BC–AD220, consisting of the Earlier and Later Han), and changed its name to the Yi-King.

The Yi-King is based on the theories of Yin and Yang and the Five Natural Elements. It is a philosophy grounded on methods of telling the future, and interpreting the results gained from these methods. It started as a political theory based on predictions of political events and their interpretation, and then expanded to include the idea of universal phenomena and rules of life, which predict individual destiny.

Such expansion of the Yi-King led to free interpretation because of the ambiguity of the outcome of predictions by the divination. The Yi-King was used by the Chinese, who adapted its interpretation to their national characteristics. And it developed with various accompanying contents complying with the demands of the ages.

2.1.2   The Fundamental Principles of the Yi-King: Yin and Yang and the Five Natural Elements

The principles of the Yi-King were formed within the worldview of an agricultural people in ancient China, particularly in the period of the Warring States and the Han dynasty, when Chou divination was incorporated into its philosophy. These theories contain ideas which played a fundamental role for Chinese and Japanese thought systems before Western philosophy gained influence. The Yi-King's presence was especially felt in Japan during the Edo period, where it influenced Confucianism.

The theories of Yin and Yang and the Five Natural Elements as basic principles of the Yi-King are as follows:

1. The dualistic Yin and Yang theory proposes to explain universal phenomena in terms of Yin and Yang, on the basis of co-ordinate concepts

of light and darkness as natural phenomena. The Yin and Yang theory is the basis of explanation for ideals, politics, literature, astronomy, geography, medicine, religion, life, etc.

2. The Five Natural Elements are wood, fire, earth, metal and water. They are regarded as natural elemental forces controlling the universe. All phenomena are believed to come about because of the vicissitudes of these elements. As a consequence, human history is also conceived as being governed by these elements in a deterministic fashion.

These two theories have been used since the early Han dynasty to make predictions about politics, religion, as well as every other aspect of human life. As a result, both theories were blended together as parts of the fundamental founding principle of the Yi-King. They became an integral part of the life of ancient Chinese people and strongly influenced subsequent developments in philosophy.

All existing phenomena come about through the perpetual motion of Yin and Yang, symbolizing different facets of the Yi-King. The Yi-King has 8 elementary facets – sky, swamp, thunder, wind and mountains, in addition three of the Five Elements, fire, water and earth. The Yi-King teaches that combinations of 2 facets (64 permutations) will provide predictive knowledge of all phenomena. We should then act according to appropriate interpretations of these predictions.

2.1.3   Foreknowledge in the Yi-King: Divination

Before the Yin dynasty, the *bu* method of divination used the bones of animals or the shells of turtles. These were burned, and the patterns of the cracks gave predictions of fortune. In the *shi* method, predictions were based on the arrangement and combination of composite plants. In the *shu* dynasty, the *bu* and *shi* methods were used in combination. After the Warring States period, the *bu* method was discontinued because it was too complex. The *shi* method has continued to be used up to the present day.

The *shi* method is an arithmetic operation on 50 composite plants' stalks or divining sticks providing (or being fated to provide) 3 *yao*. Each *yao* is either called a Yin-*yao* or a Yang-*yao*. That is, the total number of permutations is $2 \times 2 \times 2 = 8$. The result of the first operation is called the lower *gua*, and the result from any other operation is called an upper *gua*. Combining the upper *gua* with the lower *gua* gives a permutation of 6 *yao* and a total number of $8 \times 8 = 64$ *gua*. These permutations of 6 *yao* are supposed to give the answer for which the diviner asks. This answer is interpreted according to the words attached to the *gua* and *yao*. The effectiveness of the interpretation depends on the diviners skill and inspiration. (For more details on the divining procedure see Sect. 3.2.1.)

2.2 Buddhism

Our discussion of Buddhism is mainly based on Tamura et al. (1973), Furuta and Kondou (1973), Sahashi (1973), Yamaori (1978), Fukushima (2001), and Streng (1967).

2.2.1 Formation and Development

It is believed that the Indus civilization (3000BC–2000BC) existed before the Aryans invaded India, and that Hindu thought appeared after the Aryan invasion. There was some variation and change in thinking during the first to third periods (1500BC–500BC) but, by and large, Indian philosophy was dominated by the Veda and Brahman systems of thinking. Buddhism evolved during the fourth period (500BC–300BC). The third period was one of philosophical scepticism, centered around the Ganges river, and spearheaded by the philosophy of the Upanishad. The result was a number of new ways of thinking, affirming the metaphysics of the Brahmans system, which were not questioned that strongly. During this period, Gautama Siddharta (463BC–383BC) achieved enlightenment through the law of truth (*dharma*, or *hou* in Japanese), became the Buddha, and preached his new doctrine throughout India until entering Nirvana. His teachings became the basis of Buddhism as we know it today.

Buddhism spread southward to Ceylon (Sri Lanka), later reaching Southeast Asian countries, and northward to Sinkiang, Tibet, China, Korea and Japan. The religion developed from a proto-Buddhism into denominational and Mahayana Buddhism during the past 2500 years. At the same time, the Buddhist scriptures evolved, leading to different interpretations and a multitude of inconsistent denominations. Such a wide level of disagreement within groups all claiming to be part of Buddhism has not been seen in other religions. The current status of Buddhism will be addressed in Section 4.

2.2.2 The Fundamental Doctrines of Buddhism: *Dharma* and *Kuu* (Inner Emptiness)

Buddhism can be called Buddha *sasan*, Buddha *dharma*, or Buddha *marga*. The focus of Buddhism is on reality. It takes a critical stance on the reality of human existence, points to our inconsistencies and deficiencies, and advocates a practical way leading to a wholeness of our existence. How can one achieve this goal? The first principle is to observe existing truth as it stands. What all Buddhist orders and denominations have in common is that they value the spiritual awakening which Buddha obtained as the absolute truth. This includes *dharma* (the law) and *kuu* (emptiness of self, also known as *mu*) which are regarded as the basis for this belief.

> **Dharma**, the concept of origins: The universe was neither created by God nor governed by God. It was formed through an interdependent relationship between human beings, matter, phenomena, and everything else, living or dying according to *karma*. According to *dharma*, present human life is transitory and full of *ku* (affliction) and *muga* (nothingness). Kuu, explained as follows can overcome *ku* and *muga*.

> **Kuu**, the transcendence of duality: The realms of spiritual awakening are realized by overcoming the duality of transitoriness versus permanence, pleasure versus affliction (*ku*), and awareness versus nothingness (*muga*).

A number of conclusions follow from these concepts. For example, the law of *karma* (cause and effect) can be derived from *dharma*, and *kuu* can lead to the view of "supreme enlightenment".

It is believed that these two concepts provide powerful solutions to all the problems we are likely to face. In Eastern countries, Buddhism's influence on politics, economics, society and culture in general, regardless of individual groups and nations, is significant. Buddhism not only has played an important role in the past, but even now the need for the vision it provides is becoming increasingly apparent in modern society. Accordingly, *dharma* and *kuu* have become an inexhaustible source of religious wisdom.

2.2.3 Buddhism for *Satori* and its Discipline: The *Zen* Sect and *Zen*

The first goal of Buddhism is to obtain *satori* (spiritual awakening). Among methods for obtaining *satori*, the most widely known is Zen, especially exercised by the Zen sect *Zazen*. This literally means "sitting down Zen", and comprises the Rinzai, Soutou, and Oubaku sects.

The Buddha himself introduced *Zazen* as a means of discipline. Zen was, therefore, first formulated in India, and the first members of the Zen sect were Indian. Bodhi-Dharma, the 28th descendent of Buddha, introduced Zen into China in the 6th century, and this was the start of *Daijou Zen*. After the *dharma*, *Daijou Zen* split into two sects, the northern sect (gradually awakening Zen), and the southern sect (suddenly awakening Zen), during the 7th to the 9th century. Both sects were active in this period, but eventually only the southern sect developed. Although there were many talented priests and high priests who formed various sects and denominations, by the time of the *shu* dynasty (900–1300) through to the *shi* dynasty (1600–1900), the Rinzai sect was the dominant one.

In Korea and Japan, the Zen sect was introduced during the Shilla (356–935) and Kamakura (1192–1333) periods, respectively. Many prominent people have contributed to the development of the Zen sect. Especially in Japan, Eihei Dougen (1200–1253) as the founder of Soutou sect, Ingen Ryuki (1592–1673) as the founder of the Oubaku sect, and Hakuin Keikaku (1685–1768) as the founder of the Rinzai sect deserve special mention.

The basis of Zen teaching is to attain the *satori* of Buddha, to find a solution to life's problems, and to contribute to society. This can be summarized as follows.

1. Zen teaches *mu* (forgetting of self, *kuu*). The state of *mu* is attained as an experience of transcending the self and reaching a self-awareness of *muga* (the same meaning as *mu* or *kuu*, not the meaning of "nothingness").

2. Zen teaches freedom. It liberates our selves from the state of inner emptiness (*mu*) to the state of freedom. In other words, it shows that the self of *mu* acts voluntarily and freely.

3. Zen is a religion of salvation. This is a realization of the world around us, and an appreciation of love and mercy.

A great deal of popular, everyday words and concepts are derived from Zen thought and spirituality. Also, similar to Christianity, Buddhism emphasizes a state of *muga* (*mu*). These two religions are, therefore, thought to be keys to world peace and human salvation.

Zen discipline is a means of achieving spiritual awakening, and is mostly found in *Zazen*. Zen discipline follows a sequence:

1. *mon*: listening to the reverend's teaching;

2. *shi*: believing in the teaching through introspection;

3. *shu*: emptying our selves *(mushin)* through an application of (1) and (2), and the realization of *kuu*.

After attaining the third step, one has to learn to apply Zen spirituality to real-life situations. One must not place reliance on *satori*, but go beyond it, to the state of *satori* after *satori*. To achieve this requires the discipline of working for others in the real world. It has been said that the Buddha and the *dharma* are still undergoing exercise.

2.3 The Yi-King and Buddhism as Types of Determinism and Indeterminism

The Yi-King and Buddhism are neither inherited nor developed from Western determinism or indeterminism, nor were they influenced by these concepts. They cannot, therefore, easily be given a place within the Western framework or evaluated with reference to it. It is possible, however, to compare and contrast the Eastern concepts and their Western counterparts. With this in mind, we have come to understand that the Yi-King and Buddhism can be considered as categories of Eastern determinism and Western indeterminism, respectively. At the same time, they can both be considered within Eastern determinism.

2.3.1 The Yi-King

As stated earlier, the foundations of the Yi-King are the theories of Yin and Yang and the Five Natural Elements. The Yin and Yang are the opposing forces of light and darkness; they govern all natural phenomena and all human affairs. The Five Natural Elements are natural forces which not only have a profound influence on cosmic evolution, but also control human history. A basic part of this belief is that all actions and phenomena, including human will and behavior, are subject to forecasts gained through divination. Therefore we can base our actions on them.

In much of the Western philosophical tradition of determinism, human will and action are subject to the absolute will of God. In the Yi-King philosophy, the Five Natural Elements take the place of the Western concept of God. In this sense, the Yi-King can be characterized as Eastern philosophical determinism.

Nevertheless, the sovereignty of the Yin and Yang and the Five Natural Elements only extends as far as the forecast from a *gua* of 6 *yao*. Because of the diversity and uncertainty of judgements and actions according to the instructions of the forecast, the very nature of the Yi-King does not exclude the possibility of human freedom of will and behavior. Such freedom, however, is limited in scope by the forecasts, so it is still (deterministically) governed by Yin and Yang and the Five Natural Elements. Therefore, the Yi-King can be viewed as a type of Eastern determinism.

2.3.2   Buddhism

According to the first part of the Buddhist *dharma*, the universe is neither created by God nor ruled by God. This contrasts with a key idea of Western determinism, the sovereignty of God. The second part of the Buddhist *dharma* claims that all natural and human phenomena come about through mutual dependence, and that life and death are a result of *karma*. The universe is not a natural manifestation of God's absolute will, but exists through mutual dependence and is governed by the law of cause and effect. The universe as defined here points to the realm of reality, and since human affairs are part of this realm, they are also governed by those laws. The second part of the *dharma* therefore also contrasts with determinism in its Western theological sense.

Buddhist theory is thus critical of Western theological determinism, and sets itself up as an opposing view. This could imply that Buddhism may be regarded as an alternative deterministic view, though from the Western viewpoint it is often (mis)understood as being a strongly indeterministic religion.

As stated earlier, Buddhism was born out of criticism of Brahmanism. Buddhists denied the presence of the sun god (Mithra, also known as the chief god), the wind and thunder god Indra, and the creator Brahma, as described in the four volumes of the Sutras. As a result, Buddhism opposed the caste system, and supported the concept of human equality. Buddhism can also be seen as an Eastern denial of Western theological determinism since it denies that everything is ruled by the absolute will of God and God's sovereignty over humanity. Instead, it interprets the unfolding of history from the viewpoint of a realm subject to the *dharma*.

Let us finally compare the Buddhist view of the inevitability of cause and effect with the Western concept of human free will. The former principle is part of the *dharma*. It tells us that, while we may have an impression that human will and behavior are free, this impression of freedom may be an illusion when we consider the full extent of the law of cause and effect. The *dharma* does not, however, refer to the existence of free will as an abstract concept. The connection between the spiritual freedom obtained after achieving *satori* in Eastern thought and the Western concept of free will requires further consideration.

3 Reconsidering Buddhism and the Yi-King as Eastern Determinism

Briefly speaking, classical determinism is the position that human will and behavior are all predetermined by some causal factor. In Western deterministic and indeterministic theories, the causal factor is God or natural laws. Compared to its Western counterpart, the Yi-King as Eastern determinism is easy to understand. This may be due to its historical context: The Yi-King was formulated in order to solve issues connected with humans and society in general. Buddhism is different from classical determinism. Insofar as Buddhism is a religious system, it offers universal and timeless application.

In this section we will not restrict ourselves to the proposition of determinism in its relation to human will and actions, but address the latter in terms of a general concept related to a scientific approach. We will attempt to formulate a concept of determinism consistent with natural science, social science, and the humanities. We will also try to construct a paradigm of cognition and its meaning, together with methods of gaining knowledge and understanding. Our purpose is to look at the Yi-King and Buddhism as Eastern deterministic theories from a scientific point of view, to ascertain whether this may highlight any special features and, if so, to re-evaluate them. In so doing, philosophical and religious concepts of determinism will be addressed using the scientific method.

3.1 Scientific Determinism

3.1.1 General Remarks

A crucial issue of classical deterministic theory in the Western tradition is the issue of free will and action. Both determinism and indeterminism relate to the possibility of free will and action. With respect to this possibility, they can both be understood as ways in which human decisions and acts become determined. As such, the human will may still be determined by a causal factor outside of it (see Kane in this volume). For this reason it is desirable to break free from the classical meaning of the word "determinism", and to broaden our interpretation.

Scientific determinism more correctly recognizes and defines the essence of the true nature of all existence, including humans, substance, societies, special phenomena, and concepts, as well as the interconnections and relationships among all these. Such a notion of determinism is not necessarily a final principle, nor does it aim at perfection. The belief in the permanent renewal of knowledge and understanding is observed in the social sciences and the humanities. Even in mathematics and logic, as well as in the natural sciences, we are often urged to alter and improve our knowledge and understanding.

In every area of science, many cases of resurgence of determinism have occurred. Deterministic theories have been constantly tried, modified and tried again. After a finite number of modifications it should be possible to find a way to apply them (more or less) universally. This may be expressed in a schematic way such as the following.

For an initial deterministic theory P_0, related to an object domain 0, and an $(i + 1)$st deterministic theory, where $i = 0, 1, 2, ..., n - 1$, the tendency toward a universal theory of determinism can be represented as:

$$P_o \Rightarrow P_1 \Rightarrow P_2 \Rightarrow ... \Rightarrow P_n \tag{1}$$

where the symbol $\Rightarrow$ denotes implication. $A \Rightarrow B$ means that, if A holds, then B holds.

3.1.2 Step-by-Step Developmental Stages of Understanding: Improvement and Heterogeneous Development

Let us examine the sequence (1) in more detail. For any value of i, P_i is a more universal application of determinism than P_{i-1}, and P_n is the most universal form of determinism for $n \to \infty$. This means that a final theory can only be reached in an asymptotic limit, and in our search for a universal theory, we will go on modifying existing systems of propositions indefinitely. Nevertheless, the sequence (1) shows the step-wise progression toward a universally applicable principle, the final form, indicating a gradual development in understanding.

The development of a deterministic theory requires switching conceptions, creative ideas, or even paradigm shifts in our thought processes. What is important in this discussion is not the creative process as such, but the gradual development of determinism as understanding gets refined in the course of time. There are two ways in which such a step-wise development of understanding can come about.

Improvement: Gradual Type Development

A deterministic theory is improved each time it is refined. This gradual type of development is characterized by the fact that any two deterministic theories adjacent to each other in the sequence (1) are related by:

$$P_i \Rightarrow P_{i+1} \quad (i = 0, 1, 2, ..., n - 1) \tag{2}$$

Relation (2) expresses improvement of a deterministic theory as a gradual type of its development. The improvement can stop after a finite number of iterations or can extend to infinity. The renewal P_{i+1} in (2) is more or less divided into local and global improvements of P_i. For local improvement, the renewal is obtained through improvements accompanied by local modifications of conditions imposed upon the subject matter under consideration. For global improvement, the renewal is obtained by altering the level of understanding, e.g., by a leap to another level of understanding. This can achieved by complete or global modifications, such as generalization procedures, imposed upon the subject matter under consideration.

Both types of improvement are often observed in the fields of mathematics, applied mathematics and natural science, but also in social sciences such as economics and psychology. Global improvement is obviously more involved than local improvement. However, if it happens, it can produce revolutionary renewals P_{i+1} of determinism.

Heterogeneous Development: Three Stage Type Development

The Three Stage type of development is primarily based on a dialectical method, using naturalistic principles similar to the dialectical materialism of Marx and Engels. It indicates a gradual development of determinism grounded on natural dialectics.

The main features of this development are basically comprised of three stages, called the phenomena stage S_1, the entities stage S_2, and the essence stage S_3. Every stage is assumed to be reached by dialectical sublation, i.e. synthesizing two apparently contradictory propositions. The detailed meaning of each stage is described by Taketani (1947) and Sakata (1963).

The Three Stage theory was advocated by Taketani (1911–2000) in the 1940s, who together with Sakata (1911–1972) and his team made a major contribution in elementary particle theory. The Three Stage theory has gained international recognition as a way of achieving awareness in the natural sciences and other disciplines. In the development model corresponding to the Three Stage theory each stage consists of a finite number of deterministic theories. On the whole each stage type is considered as a compound stage type. This can also be expressed schematically in a way extending sequence (1) to the notion of heterogeneous development. For $i < j < k$, we have

$$
\begin{aligned}
& (P_0 \Rightarrow \ldots \Rightarrow P_{i-1} \Rightarrow) \quad P_i \\
\nearrow_1^2 \ & (P_{i+1} \Rightarrow \ldots \Rightarrow P_{j-1} \Rightarrow) \quad P_j \\
\nearrow_2^3 \ & (P_{j+1} \Rightarrow \ldots \Rightarrow P_{k-1} \Rightarrow) \quad P_k
\end{aligned}
\tag{3}
$$

where the first term refers to S_1 (phenomena stage) the second term refers to S_2 (entities stage), and the third term refers to S_3 (essence stage), and $P_\alpha (\alpha = i, j, k)$ is the final deterministic theory in each stage. The sloped arrows indicate (qualitative) transitions from S_1 to S_2 and from S_2 to S_3, respectively.

The three stage type is a developmental form of determinism partially including the gradual type. But it is not a simple generalization of the gradual type. This derives from the fact that the three stage type emphasizes aspects of the qualitative development in our understanding of deterministic theories. Sequence (3) represents three phases of qualitative development in understanding of our deterministic theories.

The development of determinism following the three stage theory is considered not only to contribute to the solution of issues in which the subject in question is a real existing matter, e.g., in the case of physical entities, but also to provide guidelines for obtaining new insights. The underlying background of determinism as stated here is also based on the process of conceptual formation in the natural sciences and mathematics as well (see, e.g., Abe 1977, Mittelstraß 1978). In addition, it is a basis for our understanding of economics and sociology.

So far the discussion has been centered on establishing the concepts of determinism, its general structure, and a particular type of this structure in the gradual development toward universally applicable understanding of deterministic theories. We have also discussed the developmental formation obtained by focusing on qualitative phases of deterministic theories, and provided a kind of schematic formulation of developmental formation. This may not be sufficient. Further progress remains necessary.

3.1.3 The Purpose and Practice of Determinism: Basic Science, Applied Science, Practical Sciences

So far we have outlined the developmental formation of understanding in determinism dealing with science, especially basic science or pure science. In this section we will fill in some of the details for basic science, applied science, and practical science. Insofar as deterministic theories consider basic science as the basis of an applied science, the developmental formation of understanding is similar to basic science, but it may be more complicated depending on the application. In the case of determinism with respect to practical science, such a dependence is required on the practical level of the subject matter. As a result, it is difficult to define the developmental formation of determinism in general.

The purpose of determinism in basic science in most cases is pursuing understanding, namely achieving a universal application concerning the subject matter in a narrow sense. Needless to say, this refers not only to pure mathematics and the natural sciences, but also to philosophy, linguistics, literature, culture, history, sociology, political science, law, and economics. Deterministic theories of basic sciences should be realized by means of the practical sciences (such as engineering, medicine, agriculture, commerce and so on) and the applied sciences, in order to solve issues of practicality at which they are originally not aiming. Moreover, the objective of deterministic theories experienced in the applied sciences and practical sciences should be subject to social practical benefits.

3.2   A Critical Evaluation of the Yi-King and Buddhism

Here we would like to point out the synthetic views of the Yi-King and Buddhism, which we have already characterized roughly as Eastern determinism, by re-examining how they fit into the framework of scientific determinism.

First, we have to discuss where these two thought systems should be placed in the developmental process in modern deterministic theory. This implies the analysis of the developmental process of understanding. In other words, the discussion focuses on the extent to which the two systems of thought can be completed in the developmental process of understanding.

Second, we will characterize the two systems by examining the methods used to realize the purpose in both deterministic theories. Such an evaluation benefits from reflection upon the content of each type of deterministic theory and understanding their characteristics.

3.2.1   The Yi-King

The Yi-King is based on the principles of Yin and Yang and the Five Natural Elements, claiming that these principles govern the process of all existing matter in nature including the destiny of life, societies and nations. It has been developed not only for providing answers to life questions of common people, but also for producing strategies for monarchs and politicians. In this sense, it can be regarded as a philosophical approach.

As mentioned earlier, a primitive form of divination was practiced before the Yin period in ancient China. The interpretation for the ancient people was dominated by the existence of sun, moon, water, fire, wind, earth etc. as the elements of the natural phenomena and other factors relevant to the everyday lives of people, whose experience was agriculturally based. From the Chou Dynasty to the time of the Warring States, sun and moon, which were understood as the forces behind divination, became generalized to Yin and Yang. Natural phenomena coalesced into five main elements (later eight elements). As a result, the central idea of a deterministic theory of the entire universe was established with rules based on Yin and Yang and the Five Natural Elements.

The view that the theories of Yin and Yang and the Five Natural Elements govern the entire universe as elementary existential objects in the natural world, is derived from experience and speculation. In our contemporary world, we cannot ignore natural disasters, earthquakes, famines, etc., and their influences on people, politics, etc. Nevertheless, explaining the phenomena of complex modern societies requires more than causes consisting in parts of the natural world.

From the developmental viewpoint, the present age is in the entities stage after having gone through the final understanding at the level of the phenomena stage, where assumptions for observing phenomena of the entire universe were developed. Since the phenomena stage does not provide the detailed function and mutual operation of entities, we have not yet achieved an understanding of how these entities interact with each other to influence all the events in the cosmos. The present stage is still a long way from the highest level of awareness, the (third) essence stage. The Yi-King could, therefore, be viewed as an incomplete deterministic theory, if it remains in the elementary phase of the (second) entities stage. In fact, from our present standpoint we can recognize errors made at the (first) phenomena stage; for instance, the governing forces and their influence (cause and effect) were not thoroughly observed. This had the result that subsequent scientific development was stunted. Nevertheless, the Yi-King has evolved from a folk philosophy, born out of a visceral response to the everyday world, into a mature thought system with divination as its philosophical foundation (see section 4.2).

A deterministic system based on the Yin and Yang and the Five Natural Elements provides a simple basis for explaining events, but cannot be used directly to predict the future. Divination plays the role of a catalyst, combining the theories of the Yi-King and models of the future. The essential purpose of the Yi-King is to predict future events before they occur, and divination is a means to achieve this. The forecasts must be based on correct interpretations of the influence of determinism. Two sources of vagueness need to be kept in mind for the operation of the Yi-King.

The first source of vagueness lies in the method of divination. The diviner takes 50 divining sticks, pulls one out and leaves it aside, then opens the remaining 49 sticks like a fan. The diviner then divides the set of sticks in two subsets while concentrating hard on the problem to be solved. Next the diviner transfers one stick from the right hand to the left. A bundle of eight sticks is then removed from the left hand containing the extra stick. The number of remaining sticks will then range from 1 to 8. This number represents the *gua*, which can be sky (1), swamp (2), fire (3), thunder (4), wind (5), water (6), mountain (7), or earth (8) (see Sec. 2.1). If, for example, three sticks remain, the result is "fire". The symbol for fire is then displayed as a divining block and placed on a table.

The entire operation is then repeated a second time. If two sticks remain, the result is "swamp". The corresponding symbol is displayed as a divining block as before. The first symbol is a lower *gua*, and the second symbol (the upper *gua*) is placed on top of it. The resulting symbol (a *gua* of six *yao*), will be interpreted by the diviner.

The procedure of dividing the 49 sticks into two subsets provides the variation in the number of sticks between 1 and 8. Because there are two casts, the number of variations is multiplied, giving rise to a total of $8 \times 8 = 64$ possible permutations. After each divination the result could be one of 64 possibilities. The probability of each one of these 64 possibilities is thus 1 in 64.

The second point of vagueness is implied by the nature of the interpretation. The interpretation of the results of divinations is basically achieved by the deterministic theory of the Yi-King, i.e. by the Yin and Yang and the Five Natural Elements. Interpretation of the forecast is a symbolic answer. It attempts to predict future events by extrapolating an appropriate answer to the asked question, provided by the divining procedure. Whether an answer can be given or whether there are a number of possible answers, depends on the diviner's skill. This uncertainty, on top of the uncertainty in the results themselves, indicates the vague nature of the Yi-King.

The forecasting operation as such is entirely rational. There are always 8 upper and 8 lower *gua* and two casts. The answer to the question (the future prediction) is determined rationally by the mentioned operations. The received wisdom, based on the accumulated experience of the ages, is that the Yi-King can forecast everything through the interaction of 2 *gua*, a view which is pretty hard to swallow for us, living in the 21st century.

Divination is a method through which future events are extrapolated. Although it may appear that there is no reason for the manipulations of the 2 *gua*, getting a correct result from the 1 in 64 chance of a single forecast, and then correctly interpreting this forecast, is not an easy matter. Only an exceptional diviner with a sense for the future can have any hope of a practical result, and it is said that such people can even affect the fortunes of others (Kou 1973). Whether this kind of sense even exists is another issue. Because divination does not give a single unique answer, it has to be described as an inexact science.

Conclusions: The Yi-King is a deterministic theory grounded on simple experience. It has not progressed to the final step of the phenomena stage, but progresses as far into the elemental level of the entities stage as its imperfections allow. It does not present a coherent rational explanation for the law of cause and effect. Divination thus does not obey the laws of cause and effect, and so there is an inherent vagueness in its operation. If we stress this aspect of the Yi-King, it can be described as a probabilistic theory of determination (compare Dowe in this volume). The cause is known, but not the outcome.

3.2.2 Buddhism

Gautama Siddhartha, later to become the Buddha, was born and brought up in a noble family in India. As an adult he became occupied with the sufferings of humanity, and advocated his way of discipline. According to the Buddha, all problems are a result of misperceiving the existing world. If we wish to find solutions we, therefore, need to discern the true nature of this world and everything in it, and then we will be able to detect the underlying pattern. By continually observing the many events that occur day by day, we can come to understand their cause and effect relationship. Through this understanding we become aware that we can control all problems, including those of human suffering. These insights were revealed to the Buddha after spending ten years undergoing rigorous discipline and contemplation.

Similar to other religions, Buddhism intends to liberate human beings from the emptiness of the soul through the grace of an all-powerful Deity upon which we can base our trust. At the same time, Buddhism explains the necessity of its significance to people. The doctrine of Buddhism takes the existence of the real world as a basic axiom. Needless to say, Buddhism is a religion, but the determinism described previously is a pivotal part of its doctrine, derived from *dharma* (*hou*) and *kuu*. *Hou* is the way of truth; *kuu*, which is based on *hou*, emphasizes the nature of the world of *satori*. *Hou* is a deterministic theory, which explains all existence in dispassionate terms. The determinism of *kuu* is based on sublation, the synthesis of two opposing concepts. It is revealed through *satori* by experiencing the truth. The determinism of *dharma*, recall, is based on the laws of cause and effect.

The essence of *hou* is a thorough examination of all existence and the factors causing it. It strives for a true understanding of everything that exists. If there is no God, or any other supernatural cause, then we must necessarily come to the conclusion that there must exist some truth which brings this existence into being, and which links all existing phenomena together through mutual dependence. On a broad macroscopic level, *hou* asserts that all natural events – including the human realm – obey the law of cause and effect. When the Buddha thought of human suffering, including birth, ageing, sickness and death, he came to the rather bleak conclusion that such suffering is unavoidable. Thus, *hou* describes a world of transitoriness, affliction, doubt and *muga* (*mu* or *kuu*); a world where birth and death follow each other cyclically, connected by cause and effect.

If we take this view, and apply the law of cause and effect to scientific phenomena, we can see that it is nothing other than a deterministic theory for the human realm. The development of this theory will end up with the final essence stage after achieving the phenomena and entities stages. This deterministic theory, which states the causes of all phenomena in reality, is valued as a universally applicable framework allowing us to improve our awareness through inductive logical steps. Propositions about the human realm can follow deductively from more general propositions.

Such a viewpoint is possible only if *dharma* is considered as distinct from the determinism of the natural sciences. If this were not the case, it would be a nihilistic theory of despair, without salvation for humankind. Even at the time of the Buddha, many non-Buddhists criticized Buddhism on just these grounds. This is recorded in the 22nd scripture of the middle part of the Sutras, which was written by the Buddha himself for the benefit of his disciples. The Buddha claimed that he never taught such a doctrine of despair, but rather provided the opportunity to understand the meanings of affliction and its eradication.

Kuu is a deterministic theory obtained through experience, after rigorous training. It cannot be simply derived from everyday living or contemplation. The understanding of *kuu*, therefore, requires us to consider experienced understanding as a phenomenal object, and to analyze to it. The underlying idea of *kuu* is an awareness of *hou*; knowing that there is no way to escape from the transitory, uncaring world of suffering and *muga*. Considered from the Three Stage point of view, this circumstantial awareness corresponds to the initial stage in the recognition of *kuu*, the phenomena stage. However, it is not very pleasant to remain in this stage, as the Buddha also came to realize.

For most people the basic factors of their lives are intransitoriness, joy, and selfness in contrast to transitoriness, suffering and *muga* as existential forces. Understanding this antithesis invites the development of experiential understanding corresponding to the entities stage. Direct experience in this second stage combines dualistic elements such as transitoriness and intransitoriness, affliction and joy, and *muga* and *ga* (selfness). At this stage, people spend days without knowing any periods of peace because of fury and anguish in the state of illusory *maya*, resulting from the permanent complexities of life.

The final purpose of *kuu* is to liberate us from this situation. It is known as *Vimukti*, the emancipation from the souls of the misguided. It is the final understanding of experienced determinism, a stage of understanding grounded in rigorously disciplined experience leading to the essence stage. All dualities reach unity through a process of dialectical sublation. The resulting mental state transcends dualism and achieves the concrete stage of *satori*. At this stage there is no more conflict between any two dualistic elements.

To achieve this transcendental state, to obtain *satori*, we must not avoid the conquest of the dualistic realm. And a logical interpretation of the attainment of *satori* requires an explanation of the theory of dualism. This is a standard step in dialectical method. An example from physics which demonstrates the above thought processes is the interpretation of wave and particle properties of micro-physical entities in terms of dialectical logic (Taketani and Nagasaki 1993). As this example shows, although Buddhism and natural science are very much different from each other, their ways of finding truth have much in common.

Let us now proceed to a more detailed exposition of the way *satori* is achieved, as taught by the Zen sect. We have already described the series of steps through which adherents of Zen can reach *satori* in Sect. 2.2.3. To recapitulate, these are the stages of *mon* (listening to the reverend's teaching), *shi* (gaining belief through introspection), and *shu* (a realization of *mon* and *shi*). *Mon* is the primary stage, *shi* is the second stage, and *shu* is the advanced stage in which *satori* is achieved through the exercise of discipline.

The significance ascribed to the final stage differs more or less among different Buddhist sects. Among the variants of *Zen*, the Rinzai sect practices particularly strict discipline. The disciples are spurred on by *koan* (questions given by the reverend to priests during training for *Za-Zen*), which prepare them for a full experiential understanding. They then achieve *satori* through realizing the self in *Vimukti*.

Buddhism analyzes every occurence in life deeply, and deals with it based on its grounding in past, present and future. *Hou* is the deterministic theory described from a very wide perspective, but the Buddha did not use it to investigate natural events, believing they had no relation to the problems of everyday life. For instance, there are four questions, to which even the natural sciences of today have no answers:

1. Is the universe eternal or not?

2. Is the universe finite or infinite?

3. Are the body and spirit the same or are they separate?

4. Can the *tathagata* (a honorific term for the Buddha, *nyorai* in Japanese) exist after death?

Conclusion: Buddhism is a religion indicating a universal way to recognize truth for life and related issues. Its deterministic base is highly relevant and universally applicable. It can be compared in many ways with fields outside its scope, particularly those of the natural science. In these fields the subjects of investigation are different, but the way of achieving logical solutions is similar. In this sense, the doctrine of Buddhism is quasi-scientific.

4   Comments on the Current Status of the Yi-King and Buddhism

If classical determinism were reconsidered from a scientific point of view, there would be no difference between Eastern and Western deterministic theories. Both of them involve a way of developing toward a complete understanding of truth, and a method to achieve this goal. Both of them aim for the universal applicability of understanding using rational methods within a deterministic stance. In particular, both the Yi-King and Buddhism refer to areas of practical science. In this final section we wish to examine some current trends with respect to determinism in the systems of Yi-King, Confucianism, and Buddhism.

In addition to the Shi-King (the book of songs), the Shao-King (the scripture of documents), the book of the Chou's system of etiquette, and the chronicles of Lu, the Yi-King is one of the five classics of Confucianism. Confucianism is a system of thought introduced by Kon-zi (Confucius, 552BC–479BC), who is regarded as a spiritual authority for the Chinese people. The thoughts of Confucius represent the Chinese way of thinking and influenced politics and education. The teachings of Kon-zi were developed further by Meng-zi (Mencius, 372BC–289BC) among others.

These teachings continued to govern the lives of the Chinese people up to the time of the Xin-hai revolution (1911) in the Ching dynasty, when the last emperor fell. At that time, the Yi-King was deeply rooted in the lives of the people. From the fall of the last emperor to the present day, the Yi-King was both restored and criticized for political reasons. To some extent, Confucianism was used by tyrants as a tool of suppression and a means to command allegiance and maintain feudalism. Although Confucianism was brought into Japan in the Kamakura era, it did not make much headway against existing Buddhist beliefs. During the Edo period (1603-1876), various Confucianist schools were founded, and Confucianism became a government-sponsored philosophy, used to support and maintain the feudal system.

After the Second World War, Confucianism was certainly not a strong force in China and had almost no influence in Japan and Korea. Today it is somewhat influential among the older generation in all three countries. Confucianism, like Buddhism, has contributed many everyday words to their languages, mainly due to the appeal of the "Analects of Confucius", one of the four Chinese classics. The others are the "Doctrine of Morality", the "Doctrine of the Mean" (the middle path), and the "Doctrine of Mencius".

Divination according to the Yi-King and the Analects of Confucius are among the most popular variants of Confucianism up to the present age. We have not discussed the Analects in detail here, but just wish to say that there are hidden gems in the teachings of Confucius (see, e.g., Morohashi 1989).

Buddhism has permeated the entire East in the 2500 years since the appearance of the Buddha. During this time it has strongly influenced thoughts, beliefs, customs and culture. Buddhism has also become part of the cultural heritage in Japan. Nevertheless, it changed since the persecution of Christians in the Edo area. This historical event resulted in the establishment of a series of Buddhist temple parishioners, whose philosophy separated from the original teachings of its founder. Many temples were also burned during the anti-Buddhist riots in the Meiji era (1868–1911). Some Buddhist priests tried to recover from this disaster, but in general the influence of Buddhism in society waned considerably and became restricted to funeral ceremonies and Buddhist services supported by the system of temples.

In recent years, many priests have attempted to revive Buddhism by various activities. In parallel to these attempts, Buddhist scholarship has become modernized, and the study and interpretation of the original scriptures have become more widespread. On the other hand there is some concern that the study of Buddhism will become too specialized, and that this will weaken the living power of the faith. There has been a resurgence of Buddhist scholarship in the West, and this has led to translations of the Indian, Chinese and

Japanese Buddhist texts. Courses on Buddhism have been set up in modern universities, with modern methods of research and teaching.

Philosophers, thinkers and the general public are increasingly turning to Buddhism as a way of getting through blockages in Western culture. Since 1950, the World Buddhist Convention has been held every other year, in a different country each time. This opens opportunities for the people involved to get to know each other more intimately and to have lively discussions and interactions. For Buddhism, this is a new development. There has been active interchange between Buddhism, Christianity and other religions, which allows for mutual understanding and enrichment in religious experiences. The expansion of Buddhism throughout the world might contribute to unity and peace among humankind.

We would like to believe that Buddhism in Japan is poised to take off and lead us into a new age. This could be achieved through social progress by the religious denominations, public lectures by Buddhist priests, and improvements and renovations of the temples. The spirit of Buddhism can be disseminated to the general public by developing creativity through the practice of Zen and through introducing Buddhist thought and its application by private sectors such as enterprise, educational institutions, hospitals, and community organizations.

4.1   The Attraction and the Hidden Art of the Yi-King

In spite of the vagueness of the Yi-King in terms of science, it has been of immense value to Eastern people since ancient times. The Yi-King had applications not only in recreation, but also in serious life affairs, and its appeal was not limited to single groups of individuals or nations. Today its popularity is expanding. Diviners can be seen in every city: on the streets, in hotels, in the alcoves of department stores. Shops display several types of fortune telling almanacs around the start of a new year (see, e.g., Hirakiba 2000, Taguchi and Gakkai 2000).

Many Japanese people rely on unscientific methods of divination, not only out of curiosity, but because of apprehensions about the future. It may be truly impossible for people to predict the future based on a purely logical extrapolation of circumstances through the past to the present. For us the future is always uncertain, but divination can mitigate our anxiety about the future to some extent. In general, people do not appear to be concerned about the failure of a prediction unless the matter is crucial. The act of divination itself gives us comfort and releases us from anxiety so it has a valuable function in our everyday lives. There are various reasons why people look for divination. Some supposed knowledge of future events allows us to make strategic plans, to prepare for them, and to cope with the present circumstance. In addition, prediction can provide hope for the future.

Why is divination so attractive to many? For the professional diviners it was the Yi-King itself with all its associated teachings, but this cannot be assumed for ordinary people. The general public does not ultimately understand the Yi-King or the 64 *gua*, and the Yi-King is too abstract to provide any concrete answers. The divination is also too difficult for ordinary people to perform. Hence, the source of appeal in divination are the diviners themselves.

What makes a good diviner? Two basic skills are common sense and good general knowledge. Such knowledge must not be merely superficial, but too much specialized knowledge produces the risk of bias. Common sense is therefore desirable. It must be combined with a profound understanding of the interpretation of the Yi-King, which is the basic doctrine for diviners. Interpretation of a forecast can only be made on the basis of the raw material presented to the diviner. For this reason both doctrine and common sense are required. The diviner needs to be able to draw the correct conclusion by choosing the proper *gua* from the 64 possible outcomes.

However, the real mission of the diviners is to use their ability to predict and evaluate future issues, which are (from an objective point of view) unresolved at present. It is believed that predictive ability is inherent in every human being, and that it improves through long experience. The best diviners are said to be those whose skill is deeply rooted in this instinctive ability. There are no diviners who achieve full accuracy with their predictions, though some of them have remarkable success.

Divination is not accurate in the scientific sense, but people are attracted to it because of the sophisticated forecasting ability shown by the diviner. If it were not for this, divination would have lost its popularity long ago. It may appear surprising that the popularity of the Yi-King is based on an instinctive ability to forecast the future. The ancients based their belief in the Yi-King on experience and intuition, and the possibility of such an ability should not be easily dismissed.

From our present standpoint, the Yi-King can be seen as an incomplete form of determinism, but from the above discussion, it should be apparent that there is more to it. If the predictive ability of the diviner is real, one wonders whether this might become the last reliable resort of the Yi-King. Investigations on whether such a sense actually exists could be a topic for future research.

4.2   Controversy and Transfiguration in Buddhism

Buddhism has changed and developed through the centuries since the Buddha, while maintaining its underlying basic thoughts. But it has never been free of controversy in all its long history (e.g. Sugawara 1999, 2000). Recent criticism was raised concerning the relation of the Yi-King to Buddhism by one of the Buddhist factions (Sugawara 2000). Should this be regarded as part of the development process? We will briefly explore this idea from the standpoint of determinism.

Buddhism denies the presence of a God or any other Absolute. It therefore does not fit into the framework of most religions, which believe that humans are governed by one or more gods and should be obedient to them. In addition, Buddhists claim that life's occurrences should be viewed not just at a superficial level. For a deeper way to deal with them we need to understand them in relation to past, present and future. Since Buddhism is neither a code of ethics nor a social philosophy, it is critical of Confucianism with its narrow focus on morality and discipline. Conversely, Confucianists criticized Buddhist thought on the basis that it would cause the breakdown of social morality.

Early disputes between Buddhism and Christianity were observed in China. In Japan, Buddhist priests came into conflict with Christian missionaries in the period of Azuchi-Momoyama (1573–1602; cf. Sugawara 2000). The Christians criticized the Buddhist denial of a Creator, the doctrine of the immortality of the soul, and the notion of *kuu*. The Buddhists responded by pointing out inconsistencies in Christianity, such as a God who created an unfulfilled world full of injustice. They also attacked the notion of a God who chose to create human beings with a tendency to sin, and then ruthlessly judges those human beings for breaking His laws.

When Buddhism spread into other countries, it maintained its underlying doctrine while still adapting itself to the belief systems in those countries. The width and flexibility of Buddhism facilitated such complex developments. Although Christianity and Buddhism are fundamentally different in their structure, it is encouraging to note that mutual understanding between the two religions is now being promoted internationally.

Buddhists have been criticized by both Christians and materialists. While Christians denounce Buddhism as being anti-religious, materialists criticize it as being a religion. On the other hand, it is interesting that Christians ally themselves with Buddhists when arguing against materialism. When materialists attack religions such as Christianity they often exclude Buddhism from their attack, and even speak quite favourably toward it. However, both Christians and materialists change their position when they criticize Buddhism. We assume that this outside view on Buddhism also shows an essential characteristic feature of Buddhism.

Finally we wish to address a conflict within Buddhism which recently developed in Japan (Sugawara 2000). The Jodo sect sell a calendar called the *Jodo houreki* which shows various forecasts based on divinatory methods such as ancient Chinese astrology (e.g. Smith 1991). In a regular assembly of the Jodo sect, a member announced that "we should not be selling calendars full of such superstitious mumbo-jumbo". The background is that Hounen (1133–1212), the founder of the sect, denounced such vulgar beliefs in his teachings. He also pointed out that the people praying to *Amitabha* should not be snared by such superstitions. The order (conveniently leaving out commercial considerations) responded that "we do not necessarily believe in fortune telling ourselves. Nevertheless, it may be a means by which believers can come to the true faith". The issue remained unresolved, and the assembly made a decision without reaching general consensus. Through this event, other denominations, including the Zen sect, and other religions, including Shinto (a belief from ancient Japan incorporating elements from both Shamanism and the festival of the Sun God *Amaterasu Oumikami*) have joined in the debate.

Many prominent Buddhist sects have started to reconsider whether they should run events such as fortune telling. Some denominations run fortune telling on the condition that its nature as a superstition is clearly indicated. Others use it as a means of prayer. Still others such as the Jodo-Shinshu sect deny it completely. Shinto and some other religions use it for teaching or because it is commercially profitable. Some denominations do not use fortune telling because others reject it. What all religions and denominations have in common is that they do not recognize the validity of fortune telling. It seems apparent that most Japanese religions regard divination, astrology or similar kinds of fortune telling as superstition and not part of their religion. Nevertheless, they use it for commercial profit, and to gain as many believers as they can.

The meanings of the Yi-King and Buddhism at present are quite different. The Yi-King is appealing, but its reliability is in doubt. It is useful in the private domain insofar as consulting a fortuneteller may solve personal problems, but it is not recognized by any official body. Except for devoted Buddhists, the main use of Buddhism for the general public is in funeral ceremonies or memorial services for the dead. But Buddhism is profitable for those who have a purpose for believing in it, regardless of who they are. The influence of Buddhism is increasing more than ever before. Buddhism is an international religion, spreading through the world, and its universal applicability and tolerant nature can help to contribute toward global unification and world peace.

Acknowledgments

We deeply express our gratitude to Dr. H. Atmanspacher and Dr. R. Bishop for the opportunity to participate in the workshop on determinism. In particular, Dr. H. Atmanspacher did not only invite the first author to talk about Eastern determinism, but also helped to revise and edit our original manuscript. Also, Prof. K. Gustafson encouraged the first author to work on this topic, and offered his valuable information on determinism to us. We are sincerely grateful to him. Finally, we would like to heartily thank our familiar friend Prof. M. Morris. He read our original manuscript and helped to translate it into English.

References

Abe T. (1977): A note on the rigor in mathematics. *Research Reports of Shibaura Institute of Technology – Natural Sciences and Engineering* **11**, 72–78.

Fukushima K. (2001): Zen and Today. *J. of Daihourin* (Japanese) **67**, 54–59.

Furuta S. and Kondou F. (1973): The Zen Sect and 'Za-Zen'. In *World Encyclopedias Vol. 18* (Japanese), ed. by K. Shimonaka, Heibon-Sha, Tokyo.

Hirakiba Y. (2000): *Heisei 13 nen Fortune-Prediction Almanac* (Japanese), Jinguukan Inc., Tokyo.

Honda M. (1973a): The Yi-King. In *World Encyclopedias Vol. 3* (Japanese), ed. by K. Shimonaka, Heibon-Sha, Tokyo.

Honda M. (1973b): The Chou Divination. In *World Encyclopedias Vol. 3* (Japanese), ed. by K. Shimonaka, Heibon-Sha, Tokyo.

Honda M. (1973c): The Eight 'Gua'. In *World Encyclopedias Vol. 24* (Japanese), ed. by K. Shimonaka, Heibon-Sha, Tokyo.

Inoue S. (1973): Indeterminism. In *World Encyclopedias Vol. 25* (Japanese), ed. by K. Shimonaka, Heibon-Sha, Tokyo.

Kou S. (1973): *Introduction to the Chinese Fortune Book* (Japanese), Koubun-Sha, Tokyo.

Mackay D.M. (1988): Determinism. In *New Dictionary of Theology*, ed. by S.B. Ferguson and D.F. Wright, Inter-Versity Press, Leicester, England.

Mittelstraß J. (1978): Philosophie oder Wissenschaftstheorie? In *Wozu Philosophie? Stellungnahmen eines Arbeitskreises*, ed. by H.v. Lubbe, Springer, Berlin.

Morohashi T. (1989): *Lectures on the Analects of Confucius* (Japanese), Taishuukan Shoten, Tokyo.

Omura H. (1973): Determinism. In *World Encyclopedias Vol. 9* (Japanese), ed. by K. Shimonaka, Heibon-Sha, Tokyo.

Sahashi H. (1973): *Zen* (Japanese), Kadokawas's Selected Series No. 6, Kadokawa Shoten, Tokyo.

Sakata S. (1963): *Physics and its Method* (Japanese), Riron Sha, Tokyo.

Smith R.J. (1991): *Fortune-Tellers and Philosophers: Divination in Traditional Chinese Society*, Westview Press Inc., Oxford.

Streng F.J. (1967): *Emptiness, A Study in Religious Meaning*, Abingdon Press, Nashville.

Sugawara N. (1999): The Period of F. Xavier – Religious Controversy (Japanese). A series of articles in the *Asahi evening paper*, June 1999.

Sugawara N. (2000): Report on the controversy in the Jodo Sect. Newsstory in the *Asahi evening paper*, October 30, 2000.

Taguchi N. and Gakkai J.U. (2000): *Heisei 13 nen Fortune-Prediction Almanac* (Japanese), Nagaoka Shoten, Tokyo.

Tamura Y., Watanabe T., Furuta S., and Nakamura H. (1973): Buddhism and Its Development, in *World Encyclopedias Vol. 26* (Japanese), ed. by K. Shimonaka, Heibon-Sha, Tokyo.

Taketani M. (1947): *Many Problems in Dialectics I & II* (Japanese), Keisou Shobou, Tokyo.

Taketani M. and Nagasaki M. (1993): *Formation and Logic of Quantum Mechanics* (Japanese), Keisou Shobou, Tokyo.

Yamaori T. (1978): *Dougen and his Thought* (Japanese), Century Books, Shimizu Shoin, Tokyo.

Contributors

Takehisa Abe
Faculty of Systems Engineering
Shibaura Institute of Technology
307 Fukasaku, Saitama City
Saitama 330–8570
Japan

Harald Atmanspacher
Institut für Grenzgebiete der
Psychologie und Psychohygiene
Wilhelmstr. 3a
D–79098 Freiburg
Germany

Joseph Berkovitz
Philosophy Department
University of Maryland
Baltimore County
1000 Hilltop Circle
Baltimore, MD 21250
USA

Robert Bishop
Institut für Grenzgebiete der
Psychologie und Psychohygiene
Wilhelmstr. 3a
D–79098 Freiburg
Germany

Theodor Christidis
Department of Primary Education
University of Thessaly
Argonafton–Philellinon
GR–38221 Volos
Greece

Dennis Dieks
Institute for the History
and Foundations of Mathematics
University of Utrecht
PO Box 80.000
NL–3508 TA Utrecht
Netherlands

Mauro Dorato
Philosophy Department
University of Rome 3
Via Ostiense 234
I–00146 Rome
Italy

Phil Dowe
Department of Philosophy
University of Tasmania
Sandy Bay Campus
Hobart 7001
Tasmania

Ed Gantt
Department of Psychology
Brigham Young University
1086 SWKT
Provo, UT 84602
USA

Jochen Gemmer
Institute for Theoretical Physics
Universität Stuttgart
Pfaffenwaldring 57
D–70550 Stuttgart
Germany

Daniel Greenberger
Department of Physics
City University of New York
New York, NY 10031
USA

Charles Guignon
Department of Philosophy
University of South Florida
4202 E. Fowler – FAO–226
Tampa, FL 33620
USA

Karl Gustafson
Department of Mathematics
University of Colorado
Boulder, CO 80309–0395
USA

Robert Kane
Department of Philosophy
University of Texas
Austin, TX 78712-1180
USA

Fusako Kobayashi
Department of Philosophy
Victoria University
57 Cornford St.
Karori, Wellington
New Zealand

Frederick Kronz
Department of Philosophy
University of Texas
Austin, TX 78712
USA

Olimpia Lombardi
Facultad de Filosofia y Letras
Universidad Nacional
de Buenos Aires
Pun 480,1406
Ciudad de Buenos Aires
Argentina

Günter Mahler
Institute for Theoretical Physics
Universität Stuttgart
Pfaffenwaldring 57
D–70550 Stuttgart
Germany

Jack Martin
Faculty of Education
Simon Fraser University
Burnaby, British Columbia V5A 1S6
Canada

Amy McLaughlin
Department of Philosophy
University of Texas
Austin, TX 78712
USA

Baidyanath Misra
International Solvay Institutes
Campus Plaine, ULB
Boulevard du Triomphe
B–1050 Bruxelles
Belgium

Gregor Nickel
Mathematisches Institut
Universität Tübingen
Auf der Morgenstelle 10
D–72076 Tübingen
Germany

Alexander Otte
Institute for Theoretical Physics
Universität Stuttgart
Pfaffenwaldring 57
D–70550 Stuttgart
Germany

Hans Primas
Kusenstr. 21
CH–8700 Kuesnacht
Switzerland

Frank Richardson
Department of Educational
Psychology
504 Sanchez Building
University of Texas
Austin, TX 78712
USA

Brent Slife
Department of Psychology
Brigham Young University
1134 SWKT
Provo, UT 84602
USA

Jeff Sugarman
Faculty of Education
Simon Fraser University
Burnaby, British Columbia V5A 1S6
Canada

Karl Svozil
Institut für Theoretische Physik
Technische Universität
Wiedener Hauptstr. 8–10/136
A–1040 Wien
Austria

Index